PHILIP'S

ESSENTIAL
WORLD
ATLAS

PHILIP'S

ESSENTIAL
WORLD
ATLAS

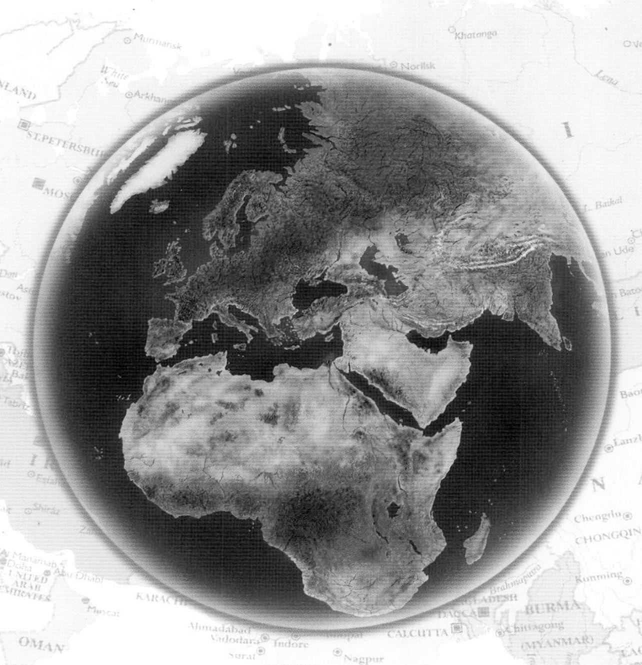

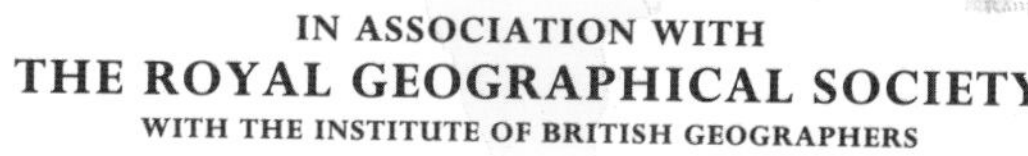

IN ASSOCIATION WITH
THE ROYAL GEOGRAPHICAL SOCIETY
WITH THE INSTITUTE OF BRITISH GEOGRAPHERS

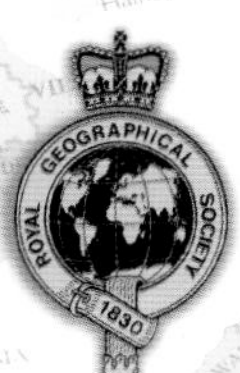

Contents

World Statistics

vi–ix	Countries
x–xi	Cities
xii–xv	Physical
xvi	Climate

The Earth in Focus

2–3	The Universe & Solar System
4–5	The Changing Earth
6–7	Earthquakes & Volcanoes
8–9	Water & Ice
10–11	Weather & Climate
12–13	Landforms & Vegetation
14–15	Population
16–17	Languages & Religions
18–19	Agriculture & Industry
20–21	Trade & Commerce
22–23	Transport & Travel
24–27	International Organizations
28–29	Regions in the News
30–32	World Flags

Cartography by Philip's

Text
Keith Lye

Picture Acknowledgements
Robert Harding Picture Library /Photri 1
Image Bank /Lionel Brown 10
Rex Features /Sipa 6, 24
Still Pictures 26, /Anne Piantanida 8,
/Chris Caldicott 16, /Mark Edwards 18, 20,
/Hartmut Schwarzbach 14, 22, /Luke White 4
Tony Stone Images /Kevin Kelley 2, /Art Wolfe 12

First published in Great Britain in 1996
under the title Philip's Desk Reference Atlas

This new edition first published in 1998
by George Philip Limited,
an imprint of Reed Consumer Books Limited,
Michelin House, 81 Fulham Road,
London SW3 6RB, and Auckland and Melbourne

© 1998 George Philip Limited

A CIP catalogue record for this book is available
from the British Library.

ISBN 0–540–07621–X

Printed in China

World Maps

1	General Reference
2–3	Northern Hemisphere
4–5	Southern Hemisphere
6–7	Europe
8–9	Scandinavia
10–11	British Isles
12–13	France
14–15	Germany & Benelux
16–17	Central Europe
18–19	Spain & Portugal
20–21	Italy & the Adriatic
22–23	Greece & the Balkans
24–25	Eastern Europe
26–27	Asia
28–29	Western Russia & Central Asia
30–31	Eastern Siberia
32–33	Japan
34–35	China
36–37	South-east Asia
38–39	Philippines & Eastern Indonesia
40–41	Eastern India, Bangladesh & Burma
42–43	Western India & Pakistan
44–45	Iran, the Gulf & Afghanistan
46–47	The Middle East & Turkey
48–49	Arabia & the Horn of Africa
50–51	Africa
52–53	North-east Africa
54–55	North-west Africa
56–57	Central Africa
58–59	Southern Africa
60–61	Australia
62–63	South-east Australia
64–65	New Zealand, Central & South-west Pacific
66–67	North America
68–69	Eastern Canada
70–71	Western Canada
72–73	North-east USA
74–75	South-east USA
76–77	North-central USA
78–79	Southern USA
80–81	North-west USA
82–83	South-west USA
84–85	Mexico
86–87	Caribbean & Central America
88–89	South America
90–91	South America – North-west
92–93	South America – North-east
94–95	South America – South
96	Antarctica
97–160	**Index to World Maps**

World Statistics – Countries

Listed below are all the countries of the world; the more important territories are also included. If a territory is not completely independent, then the country it is associated with is named. The area figures give the total area of land, inland water and ice. Annual income is the GNP per capita. The figures are the latest available: 1995–97.

Country / Territory	Area (1,000 sq km)	Area (1,000 sq mls)	Population (1,000s)	Capital City	Annual Income US$
Afghanistan	652	252	23,000	Kabul	300
Albania	28.8	11.1	3,600	Tirana	670
Algeria	2,382	920	29,300	Algiers	1,600
Andorra	0.45	0.17	75	Andorra la Vella	14,000
Angola	1,247	481	11,200	Luanda	410
Argentina	2,767	1,068	35,400	Buenos Aires	8,030
Armenia	29.8	11.5	3,800	Yerevan	730
Australia	7,687	2,968	18,400	Canberra	18,720
Austria	83.9	32.4	8,200	Vienna	26,890
Azerbaijan	86.6	33.4	7,700	Baku	480
Azores (Portugal)	2.2	0.87	238	Ponta Delgada	4,466
Bahamas	13.9	5.4	300	Nassau	11,940
Bahrain	0.68	0.26	605	Manama	7,840
Bangladesh	144	56	124,000	Dhaka	240
Barbados	0.43	0.17	300	Bridgetown	6,560
Belarus	207.6	80.1	10 500	Minsk	2,070
Belgium	30.5	11.8	10,200	Brussels	24,710
Belize	23	8.9	228	Belmopan	2,630
Benin	113	43	5,800	Porto-Novo	370
Bhutan	47	18.1	1,790	Thimphu	420
Bolivia	1,099	424	7,700	La Paz/Sucre	800
Bosnia-Herzegovina	51	20	3,600	Sarajevo	2,600
Botswana	582	225	1,500	Gaborone	3,020
Brazil	8,512	3,286	159,500	Brasília	3,640
Brunei	5.8	2.2	300	Bandar Seri Begawan	14,500
Bulgaria	111	43	8,600	Sofia	1,330
Burkina Faso	274	106	10,900	Ouagadougou	230
Burma (= Myanmar)	677	261	47,500	Rangoon	1,000
Burundi	27.8	10.7	6,300	Bujumbura	160
Cambodia	181	70	10,500	Phnom Penh	270
Cameroon	475	184	13,800	Yaoundé	650
Canada	9,976	3,852	30,200	Ottawa	19,380
Canary Is. (Spain)	7.3	2.8	1,494	Las Palmas/Santa Cruz	7,905
Cape Verde Is.	4	1.6	410	Praia	960
Central African Republic	623	241	3,400	Bangui	340
Chad	1,284	496	6,800	Ndjaména	180
Chile	757	292	14,700	Santiago	4,160
China	9,597	3,705	1,210,000	Beijing	620
Colombia	1,139	440	35,900	Bogotá	1,910
Comoros	2.2	0.86	630	Moroni	470
Congo	342	132	2,700	Brazzaville	680
Congo (= Zaïre)	2,345	905	47,200	Kinshasa	120
Costa Rica	51.1	19.7	3,500	San José	2,610
Croatia	56.5	21.8	4,900	Zagreb	3,250
Cuba	111	43	11,300	Havana	1,250

Country / Territory	Area (1,000 sq km)	Area (1,000 sq mls)	Population (1,000s)	Capital City	Annual Income US$
Cyprus	9.3	3.6	800	Nicosia	11,500
Czech Republic	78.9	30.4	10,500	Prague	3,870
Denmark	43.1	16.6	5,400	Copenhagen	29,890
Djibouti	23.2	9	650	Djibouti	1,000
Dominica	0.75	0.29	78	Roseau	2,990
Dominican Republic	48.7	18.8	8,200	Santo Domingo	1,460
Ecuador	284	109	11,800	Quito	1,390
Egypt	1,001	387	63,000	Cairo	790
El Salvador	21	8.1	6,000	San Salvador	1,610
Equatorial Guinea	28.1	10.8	420	Malabo	380
Eritrea	94	36	3,500	Asmara	500
Estonia	44.7	17.3	1,500	Tallinn	2,860
Ethiopia	1,128	436	58,500	Addis Ababa	100
Fiji	18.3	7.1	800	Suva	2,440
Finland	338	131	5,200	Helsinki	20,580
France	552	213	58,800	Paris	24,990
French Guiana (France)	90	34.7	155	Cayenne	6,500
French Polynesia (France)	4	1.5	226	Papeete	7,500
Gabon	268	103	1,200	Libreville	3,490
Gambia, The	11.3	4.4	1,200	Banjul	320
Georgia	69.7	26.9	5,500	Tbilisi	440
Germany	357	138	82,300	Berlin/Bonn	27,510
Ghana	239	92	18,100	Accra	390
Greece	132	51	10,600	Athens	8,210
Grenada	0.34	0.13	99	St George's	2,980
Guadeloupe (France)	1.7	0.66	440	Basse-Terre	9,500
Guatemala	109	42	11,300	Guatemala City	1,340
Guinea	246	95	7,500	Conakry	550
Guinea-Bissau	36.1	13.9	1,200	Bissau	250
Guyana	215	83	800	Georgetown	590
Haiti	27.8	10.7	7,400	Port-au-Prince	250
Honduras	112	43	6,300	Tegucigalpa	600
Hong Kong (China)	1.1	0.40	6,500	–	22,990
Hungary	93	35.9	10,200	Budapest	4,120
Iceland	103	40	300	Reykjavik	24,950
India	3,288	1,269	980,000	New Delhi	340
Indonesia	1,905	735	203,500	Jakarta	980
Iran	1,648	636	69,500	Tehran	4,800
Iraq	438	169	22,500	Baghdad	1,800
Ireland	70.3	27.1	3,600	Dublin	14,710
Israel	27	10.3	5,900	Jerusalem	15,920
Italy	301	116	57,800	Rome	19,020
Ivory Coast	322	125	15,100	Yamoussoukro	660
Jamaica	11	4.2	2,600	Kingston	1,510
Japan	378	146	125,900	Tokyo	39,640
Jordan	89.2	34.4	5,600	Amman	1,510
Kazakstan	2,717	1,049	17,000	Aqmola	1,330
Kenya	580	224	31,900	Nairobi	280
Korea, North	121	47	24,500	Pyongyang	1,000
Korea, South	99	38.2	46,100	Seoul	9,700

Country / Territory	Area (1,000 sq km)	Area (1,000 sq mls)	Population (1,000s)	Capital City	Annual Income US$
Kuwait	17.8	6.9	2,050	Kuwait City	17,390
Kyrgyzstan	198.5	76.6	4,700	Bishkek	700
Laos	237	91	5,200	Vientiane	350
Latvia	65	25	2,500	Riga	2,270
Lebanon	10.4	4	3,200	Beirut	2,660
Lesotho	30.4	11.7	2,100	Maseru	770
Liberia	111	43	3,000	Monrovia	850
Libya	1,760	679	5,500	Tripoli	7,000
Lithuania	65.2	25.2	3,700	Vilnius	1,900
Luxembourg	2.6	1	400	Luxembourg	41,210
Macau (Portugal)	0.02	0.006	450	Macau	7,500
Macedonia	25.7	9.9	2,200	Skopje	860
Madagascar	587	227	15,500	Antananarivo	230
Madeira (Portugal)	0.81	0.31	253	Funchal	4,500
Malawi	118	46	10,300	Lilongwe	170
Malaysia	330	127	20,900	Kuala Lumpur	3,890
Maldives	0.30	0.12	275	Malé	990
Mali	1,240	479	11,000	Bamako	250
Malta	0.32	0.12	400	Valletta	11,000
Martinique (France)	1.1	0.42	405	Fort-de-France	10,000
Mauritania	1,031	398	2,400	Nouakchott	460
Mauritius	2.0	0.72	1,200	Port Louis	3,380
Mexico	1,958	756	97,400	Mexico City	3,320
Micronesia, Fed. States of	0.70	0.27	127	Palikir	1,560
Moldova	33.7	13	4,500	Kishinev	920
Mongolia	1,567	605	2,500	Ulan Bator	310
Morocco	447	172	28,100	Rabat	1,110
Mozambique	802	309	19,100	Maputo	80
Namibia	825	318	1,700	Windhoek	2,000
Nepal	141	54	22,100	Katmandu	200
Netherlands	41.5	16	15,900	Amsterdam/The Hague	24,000
Netherlands Antilles (Neths)	0.99	0.38	210	Willemstad	10,500
New Caledonia (France)	18.6	7.2	192	Nouméa	16,000
New Zealand	269	104	3,700	Wellington	14,340
Nicaragua	130	50	4,600	Managua	380
Niger	1,267	489	9,700	Niamey	220
Nigeria	924	357	118,000	Abuja	260
Norway	324	125	4,400	Oslo	31,250
Oman	212	82	2,400	Muscat	4,820
Pakistan	796	307	136,000	Islamabad	460
Panama	77.1	29.8	2,700	Panama City	2,750
Papua New Guinea	463	179	4,400	Port Moresby	1,160
Paraguay	407	157	5,200	Asunción	1,690
Peru	1,285	496	24,500	Lima	2,310
Philippines	300	116	73,500	Manila	1,050
Poland	313	121	38,800	Warsaw	2,790
Portugal	92.4	35.7	10,100	Lisbon	9,740
Puerto Rico (US)	9	3.5	3,800	San Juan	7,500
Qatar	11	4.2	620	Doha	11,600
Réunion (France)	2.5	0.97	680	Saint-Denis	4,500

Country / Territory	Area (1,000 sq km)	Area (1,000 sq mls)	Population (1,000s)	Capital City	Annual Income US$
Romania	238	92	22,600	Bucharest	1,480
Russia	17,075	6,592	147,800	Moscow	2,240
Rwanda	26.3	10.2	7,000	Kigali	180
St Lucia	0.62	0.24	150	Castries	3,370
St Vincent & Grenadines	0.39	0.15	114	Kingstown	2,280
São Tomé & Príncipe	0.96	0.37	135	São Tomé	350
Saudi Arabia	2,150	830	19,100	Riyadh	7,040
Senegal	197	76	8,900	Dakar	600
Sierra Leone	71.7	27.7	4,600	Freetown	180
Singapore	0.62	0.24	3,200	Singapore	26,730
Slovak Republic	49	18.9	5,400	Bratislava	2,950
Slovenia	20.3	7.8	2,000	Ljubljana	8,200
Solomon Is.	28.9	11.2	410	Honiara	910
Somalia	638	246	9,900	Mogadishu	500
South Africa	1,220	471	42,300	Pretoria/Cape Town/ Bloemfontein	3,160
Spain	505	195	39,300	Madrid	13,580
Sri Lanka	65.6	25.3	18,700	Colombo	700
Sudan	2,506	967	31,000	Khartoum	750
Surinam	163	63	500	Paramaribo	880
Swaziland	17.4	6.7	1,000	Mbabane	1,170
Sweden	450	174	8,900	Stockholm	23,750
Switzerland	41.3	15.9	7,100	Bern	40,630
Syria	185	71	15,300	Damascus	1,120
Taiwan	36	13.9	21,700	Taipei	12,000
Tajikistan	143.1	55.2	6,000	Dushanbe	340
Tanzania	945	365	31,200	Dodoma	120
Thailand	513	198	60,800	Bangkok	2,740
Togo	56.8	21.9	4,500	Lomé	310
Trinidad & Tobago	5.1	2	1,300	Port of Spain	3,770
Tunisia	164	63	9,200	Tunis	1,820
Turkey	779	301	63,500	Ankara	2,780
Turkmenistan	488.1	188.5	4,800	Ashkhabad	920
Uganda	236	91	20,800	Kampala	240
Ukraine	603.7	233.1	51,500	Kiev	1,630
United Arab Emirates	83.6	32.3	2,400	Abu Dhabi	17,400
United Kingdom	243.3	94	58,600	London	18,700
United States of America	9,373	3,619	268,000	Washington, DC	26,980
Uruguay	177	68	3,300	Montevideo	5,170
Uzbekistan	447.4	172.7	23,800	Tashkent	970
Vanuatu	12.2	4.7	175	Port-Vila	1,200
Venezuela	912	352	22,500	Caracas	3,020
Vietnam	332	127	77,100	Hanoi	240
Virgin Is. (US)	0.34	0.13	105	Charlotte Amalie	12,000
Western Sahara	266	103	280	El Aaiún	980
Western Samoa	2.8	1.1	175	Apia	1,120
Yemen	528	204	16,500	Sana	260
Yugoslavia	102.3	39.5	10,500	Belgrade	1,400
Zambia	753	291	9,500	Lusaka	400
Zimbabwe	391	151	12,100	Harare	540

World Statistics – Cities

Listed below are all the cities with more than 600,000 inhabitants (only cities with more than 1 million inhabitants are included for China, Brazil and India). The figures are taken from the most recent censuses and surveys, and are in thousands. As far as possible the figures are for the metropolitan area, e.g. greater New York or Mexico City.

	Population (1,000s)
Afghanistan	
Kābul	1,565
Algeria	
Algiers	1,722
Oran	664
Angola	
Luanda	2,250
Argentina	
Buenos Aires	10,990
Córdoba	1,198
La Plata	640
Mendoza	775
Rosario	1,096
San Miguel de Tucumán	622
Armenia	
Yerevan	1,226
Australia	
Adelaide	1,071
Brisbane	1,422
Melbourne	3,189
Perth	1,221
Sydney	3,713
Austria	
Vienna	1,560
Azerbaijan	
Baku	1,081
Bangladesh	
Chittagong	2,041
Dhaka	7,832
Khulna	877
Belarus	
Minsk	1,700
Belgium	
Brussels	952
Bolivia	
La Paz	1,126
Santa Cruz	767
Brazil	
Belém	1,246
Belo Horizonte	2,049
Brasília	1,596
Curitiba	1,290
Fortaleza	1,758
Manaus	1,011
Nova Iguaçu	1,286
Pôrto Alegre	1,263
Recife	1,290
Rio de Janeiro	9,888
Salvador	2,056
São Paulo	16,417
Bulgaria	
Sofia	1,117
Burkina Faso	
Ouagadougou	690
Burma (Myanmar)	
Rangoon (Yangon)	2,513
Cambodia	
Phnom Penh	920
Cameroon	
Douala	884
Yaoundé	750
Canada	
Calgary	822
Edmonton	863
Hamilton	624

	Population (1,000s)
Montréal	3,327
Ottawa–Hull	1,010
Québec	672
Toronto	4,264
Vancouver	1,832
Winnipeg	667
Chile	
Santiago	5,077
China	
Anshan	1,252
Baotou	1,033
Beijing	12,362
Changchun	1,810
Changsha	1,198
Chengdu	1,933
Chongqing	3,870
Dalian	1,855
Fushun	1,246
Fuzhou	1,380
Guangzhou	3,114
Guiyang	1,131
Hangzhou	1,185
Harbin	2,505
Hefei	1,110
Hong Kong (SAR*)	6,205
Jilin	1,118
Jinan	1,660
Kunming	1,242
Lanzhou	1,296
Macheng	1,010
Nanchang	1,169
Nanjing	2,211
Qingdao	1,584
Qiqihar	1,104
Shanghai	15,082
Shenyang	3,762
Shijiazhuang	1,159
Taiyuan	1,642
Tangshan	1,110
Tianjin	10,687
Ürümqi	1,130
Wuhan	3,520
Xi'an	2,115
Zhengzhou	1,324
Zibo	1,346
Colombia	
Barranquilla	1,064
Bogotá	5,026
Cali	1,719
Cartagena	746
Medellin	1,621
Congo	
Brazzaville	938
Congo (Zaïre)	
Kinshasa	3,804
Lubumbashi	739
Mbuji-Mayi	613
Costa Rica	
San José	1,186
Croatia	
Zagreb	931
Cuba	
Havana	2,143
Czech Republic	
Prague	1,217

	Population (1,000s)
Denmark	
Copenhagen	1,353
Dominican Republic	
Santiago	691
Santo Domingo	2,135
Ecuador	
Guayaquil	1,925
Quito	1,444
Egypt	
Alexandria	3,380
Cairo	9,656
El Gîza	2,144
Shubra el Kheima	834
El Salvador	
San Salvador	1,522
Ethiopia	
Addis Ababa	2,316
France	
Bordeaux	696
Lille	959
Lyons	1,262
Marseilles	1,087
Paris	9,469
Toulouse	650
Georgia	
Tbilisi	1,279
Germany	
Berlin	3,472
Cologne	964
Dortmund	601
Essen	618
Frankfurt	652
Hamburg	1,706
Munich	1,245
Ghana	
Accra	1,781
Greece	
Athens	3,097
Guatemala	
Guatemala	1,814
Guinea	
Conakry	1,508
Haiti	
Port-au-Prince	1,402
Honduras	
Tegucigalpa	739
Hungary	
Budapest	1,909
India	
Ahmadabad	3,298
Bangalore	4,087
Bhopal	1,064
Bombay (Mumbai)	15,093
Calcutta	11,673
Coimbatore	1,136
Delhi	9,882
Hyderabad	4,280
Indore	1,104
Jaipur	1,514
Kanpur	2,111
Lucknow	1,642
Ludhiana	1,012
Madras (Chennai)	5,361
Madurai	1,094
Nagpur	1,661

	Population (1,000s)
Patna	1,099
Pune	2,485
Surat	1,517
Vadodara	1,115
Varanasi	1,026
Vishakhapatnam	1,052
Indonesia	
Bandar Lampung	832
Bandung	2,368
Jakarta	11,500
Malang	763
Medan	1,910
Palembang	1,352
Semarang	1,366
Surabaya	2,701
Ujung Pandang	1,092
Iran	
Ahvaz	828
Bakhtaran	666
Esfahan	1,221
Mashhad	1,964
Qom	780
Shiraz	1,043
Tabriz	1,166
Tehran	6,750
Iraq	
Al Mawsil	664
Arbil	770
As Sulaymaniyah	952
Baghdad	3,841
Diyala	961
Ireland	
Dublin	1,024
Israel	
Tel Aviv	1,880
Italy	
Genoa	660
Milan	1,334
Naples	1,062
Palermo	695
Rome	2,688
Turin	946
Ivory Coast	
Abidjan	2,500
Jamaica	
Kingston	644
Japan	
Chiba	851
Fukuoka	1,269
Hiroshima	1,102
Kawasaki	1,200
Kitakyushu	1,020
Kobe	1,509
Kumamoto	640
Kyoto	1,452
Nagoya	2,159
Okayama	605
Osaka	10,601
Sakai	806
Sapporo	1,732
Sendai	951
Tokyo–Yokohama	26,836
Jordan	
Amman	1,300
Az-Zarqa	609

	Population (1,000s)
Kazakstan	
Almaty	1,151
Qaraghandy	613
Kenya	
Nairobi	2,000
Mombasa	600
Korea, North	
Chinnampo	691
Chongjin	754
Hamhung	775
Pyongyang	2,639
Korea, South	
Inchon	2,308
Kwangju	1,258
Puchon	779
Pusan	3,814
Seoul	11,641
Suwon	756
Taegu	2,449
Taejon	1,272
Ulsan	967
Kyrgyzstan	
Bishkek	584
Latvia	
Riga	840
Lebanon	
Beirut	1,500
Libya	
Tripoli	960
Madagascar	
Antananarivo	1,053
Malaysia	
Kuala Lumpur	1,145
Mali	
Bamako	746
Mauritania	
Nouakchott	600
Mexico	
Ciudad Juárez	798
Culiacán Rosales	602
Guadalajara	2,847
León	872
Mexicali	602
Mexico City	15,643
Monterrey	2,522
Puebla	1,055
Tijuana	743
Moldova	
Chişinău	700
Mongolia	
Ulan Bator	619
Morocco	
Casablanca	2,943
Fès	564
Marrakesh	602
Rabat–Salé	1,220
Mozambique	
Maputo	2,000
Netherlands	
Amsterdam	1,100
Rotterdam	1,074
The Hague	695
New Zealand	
Auckland	929
Nicaragua	
Managua	974
Nigeria	
Ibadan	1,365
Kano	657
Lagos	10,287
Ogbomosho	712
Norway	
Oslo	714
Pakistan	
Faisalabad	1,875
Gujranwala	1,663
Hyderabad	1,107
Karachi	9,863
Lahore	5,085
Multan	1,257
Peshawar	1,676
Rawalpindi	1,290
Paraguay	
Asunción	945
Peru	
Arequipa	620
Lima–Callao	6,601
Philippines	
Caloocan	643
Cebu	688
Davao	961
Manila	9,280
Quezon City	1,677
Poland	
Kraków	745
Lódz	826
Warsaw	1,638
Wroclaw	643
Portugal	
Lisbon	2,561
Oporto	1,174
Puerto Rico	
San Juan	1,816
Romania	
Bucharest	2,061
Russia	
Chelyabinsk	1,125
Irkutsk	632
Izhevsk	653
Kazan	1,092
Khabarovsk	609
Krasnodar	638
Krasnoyarsk	914
Moscow	9,233
Nizhniy Novgorod	1,425
Novosibirsk	1,418
Omsk	1,161
Perm	1,086
Rostov	1,023
St Petersburg	4,883
Samara	1,223
Saratov	899
Simbirsk	670
Togliatti	689
Ufa	1,092
Vladivostok	637
Volgograd	1,000
Voronezh	905
Yaroslavl	631
Yekaterinburg	1,347
Saudi Arabia	
Jedda	1,400
Mecca	618
Riyadh	2,000
Senegal	
Dakar	1,729
Singapore	
Singapore	2,874
Somalia	
Mogadishu	1,000
South Africa	
Cape Town	2,350
Durban	1,137
East Rand	1,379
Johannesburg	1,196
Port Elizabeth	853
Pretoria	1,080
Vanderbijlpark–Vereeniging	774
West Rand	870
Spain	
Barcelona	1,631
Madrid	3,041
Sevilla	714
Valencia	764
Zaragoza	607
Sri Lanka	
Colombo	1,863
Sweden	
Göteburg	788
Stockholm	1,553
Switzerland	
Zürich	915
Syria	
Aleppo	1,640
Damascus	2,230
Homs	644
Taiwan	
Kaohsiung	1,405
T'aichung	817
T'ainan	700
T'aipei	2,653
Tajikistan	
Dushanbe	602
Tanzania	
Dar-es-Salaam	1,361
Thailand	
Bangkok	5,876
Tunisia	
Tunis	1,827
Turkey	
Adana	1,472
Ankara	3,028
Antalya	734
Bursa	1,317
Diyarbakir	677
Gaziantep	930
Icel	908
Istanbul	7,490
Izmir	2,333
Kayseri	648
Kocaeli	669
Konya	1,040
Manisa	641
Urfa	649
Uganda	
Kampala	773
Ukraine	
Dnipropetrovsk	1,147
Donetsk	1,088
Kharkiv	1,555
Kiev (Kyyiv)	2,630
Kryvyy Rih	720
Lviv	802
Odesa	1,046
Zaporizhye	887
United Kingdom	
Birmingham	1,400
Glasgow	730
Liverpool	1,060
London	6,378
Manchester	1,669
Newcastle	617
United States	
Atlanta	3,331
Baltimore	2,458
Boston	3,240
Buffalo	1,189
Charlotte	1,260
Chicago	7,668
Cincinnati	1,581
Cleveland	2,222
Columbus	1,423
Dallas	2,898
Denver	1,796
Detroit	4,307
Hartford	1,151
Houston	3,653
Indianapolis	1,462
Jacksonville	665
Kansas City	1,647
Los Angeles	12,410
Memphis	614
Miami	2,025
Milwaukee	1,456
Minneapolis–St Paul	2,688
New Orleans	1,309
New York	16,329
Norfolk	1,529
Oklahoma	1,007
Omaha	663
Philadelphia	4,949
Phoenix	2,473
Pittsburgh	2,402
Portland	1,676
St Louis	2,536
Sacramento	1,441
Salt Lake City	1,178
San Antonio	1,437
San Diego	2,632
San Francisco	2,182
San Jose	1,557
Seattle	2,180
Tampa	2,157
Washington, DC	4,466
Uruguay	
Montevideo	1,326
Uzbekistan	
Tashkent	2,106
Venezuela	
Barquisimento	745
Caracas	2,784
Maracaibo	1,364
Maracay	800
Valencia	1,032
Vietnam	
Haiphong	783
Hanoi	3,056
Ho Chi Minh City	4,322
Yemen	
Sana	972
Yugoslavia (Serbia and Montenegro)	
Belgrade	1,137
Zambia	
Lusaka	982
Zimbabwe	
Bulawayo	622
Harare	1,189

* Special Administrative Region

World Statistics – Physical

Under each subject heading, the statistics are listed by continent. The figures are in size order beginning with the largest, longest or deepest, and are rounded as appropriate. Both metric and imperial measurements are given. The lists are complete down to the > mark; below this mark they are selective.

Land and Water

	km²	miles²	%
The World	509,450,000	196,672,000	–
Land	149,450,000	57,688,000	29.3
Water	360,000,000	138,984,000	70.7
Asia	44,500,000	17,177,000	29.8
Africa	30,302,000	11,697,000	20.3
North America	24,241,000	9,357,000	16.2
South America	17,793,000	6,868,000	11.9
Antarctica	14,100,000	5,443,000	9.4
Europe	9,957,000	3,843,000	6.7
Australia & Oceania	8,557,000	3,303,000	5.7
Pacific Ocean	179,679,000	69,356,000	49.9
Atlantic Ocean	92,373,000	35,657,000	25.7
Indian Ocean	73,917,000	28,532,000	20.5
Arctic Ocean	14,090,000	5,439,000	3.9

Seas

Pacific Ocean	km²	miles²
South China Sea	2,974,600	1,148,500
Bering Sea	2,268,000	875,000
Sea of Okhotsk	1,528,000	590,000
East China & Yellow	1,249,000	482,000
Sea of Japan	1,008,000	389,000
Gulf of California	162,000	62,500
Bass Strait	75,000	29,000

Atlantic Ocean	km²	miles²
Caribbean Sea	2,766,000	1,068,000
Mediterranean Sea	2,516,000	971,000
Gulf of Mexico	1,543,000	596,000
Hudson Bay	1,232,000	476,000
North Sea	575,000	223,000
Black Sea	462,000	178,000
Baltic Sea	422,170	163,000
Gulf of St Lawrence	238,000	92,000

Indian Ocean	km²	miles²
Red Sea	438,000	169,000
The Gulf	239,000	92,000

Mountains

Europe		m	ft
Mont Blanc	France/Italy	4,807	15,771
Monte Rosa	Italy/Switzerland	4,634	15,203
Dom	Switzerland	4,545	14,911
Liskamm	Switzerland	4,527	14,852
Weisshorn	Switzerland	4,505	14,780
Taschorn	Switzerland	4,490	14,730
Matterhorn/Cervino	Italy/Switzerland	4,478	14,691
Mont Maudit	France/Italy	4,465	14,649
Dent Blanche	Switzerland	4,356	14,291
Nadelhorn	Switzerland	4,327	14,196
> Grandes Jorasses	France/Italy	4,208	13,806
Jungfrau	Switzerland	4,158	13,642
Barre des Ecrins	France	4,103	13,461
Gran Paradiso	Italy	4,061	13,323
Piz Bernina	Italy/Switzerland	4,049	13,284
Eiger	Switzerland	3,970	13,025

Europe (cont.)		m	ft
Monte Viso	Italy	3,841	12,602
Grossglockner	Austria	3,797	12,457
Wildspitze	Austria	3,772	12,382
Monte Disgrazia	Italy	3,678	12,066
Mulhacén	Spain	3,478	11,411
Pico de Aneto	Spain	3,404	11,168
Marmolada	Italy	3,342	10,964
Etna	Italy	3,340	10,958
Zugspitze	Germany	2,962	9,718
Musala	Bulgaria	2,925	9,596
Olympus	Greece	2,917	9,570
Triglav	Slovenia	2,863	9,393
Monte Cinto	France (Corsica)	2,710	8,891
Gerlachovka	Slovak Republic	2,655	8,711
Torre de Cerrado	Spain	2,648	8,688
Galdhöpiggen	Norway	2,468	8,100
Hvannadalshnúkur	Iceland	2,119	6,952
Kebnekaise	Sweden	2,117	6,946
Ben Nevis	UK	1,343	4,406

Asia		m	ft
Everest	China/Nepal	8,848	29,029
K2 (Godwin Austen)	China/Kashmir	8,611	28,251
Kanchenjunga	India/Nepal	8,598	28,208
Lhotse	China/Nepal	8,516	27,939
Makalu	China/Nepal	8,481	27,824
Cho Oyu	China/Nepal	8,201	26,906
Dhaulagiri	Nepal	8,172	26,811
Manaslu	Nepal	8,156	26,758
Nanga Parbat	Kashmir	8,126	26,660
Annapurna	Nepal	8,078	26,502
Gasherbrum	China/Kashmir	8,068	26,469
Broad Peak	China/Kashmir	8,051	26,414
Xixabangma	China	8,012	26,286
Kangbachen	India/Nepal	7,902	25,925
Jannu	India/Nepal	7,902	25,925
Gayachung Kang	Nepal	7,897	25,909
Himalchuli	Nepal	7,893	25,896
Disteghil Sar	Kashmir	7,885	25,869
Nuptse	Nepal	7,879	25,849
Khunyang Chhish	Kashmir	7,852	25,761
Masherbrum	Kashmir	7,821	25,659
Nanda Devi	India	7,817	25,646
Rakaposhi	Kashmir	7,788	25,551
Batura	Kashmir	7,785	25,541
Namche Barwa	China	7,756	25,446
Kamet	India	7,756	25,446
Soltoro Kangri	Kashmir	7,742	25,400
Gurla Mandhata	China	7,728	25,354
Trivor	Pakistan	7,720	25,328
Kongur Shan	China	7,719	25,324
> Tirich Mir	Pakistan	7,690	25,229
K'ula Shan	Bhutan/China	7,543	24,747
Pik Kommunizma	Tajikistan	7,495	24,590
Elbrus	Russia	5,642	18,510
Demavend	Iran	5,604	18,386
Ararat	Turkey	5,165	16,945
Gunong Kinabalu	Malaysia (Borneo)	4,101	13,455
Yu Shan	Taiwan	3,997	13,113
Fuji-San	Japan	3,776	12,388

Africa		m	ft
Kilimanjaro	Tanzania	5,895	19,340
Mt Kenya	Kenya	5,199	17,057
Ruwenzori	Uganda/Congo (Zaire)	5,109	16,762
Ras Dashan	Ethiopia	4,620	15,157

Africa (cont.)		m	ft
Meru	Tanzania	4,565	14,977
Karisimbi	Rwanda/Congo (Zaïre)	4,507	14,787
Mt Elgon	Kenya/Uganda	4,321	14,176
Batu	Ethiopia	4,307	14,130
Guna	Ethiopia	4,231	13,882
Toubkal	Morocco	4,165	13,665
Irhil Mgoun	Morocco	4,071	13,356
Mt Cameroon	Cameroon	4,070	13,353
Amba Ferit	Ethiopia	3,875	13,042
Pico del Teide	Spain (Tenerife)	3,718	12,198
Thabana Ntlenyana	Lesotho	3,482	11,424
Emi Koussi	Chad	3,415	11,204
Mt aux Sources	Lesotho/South Africa	3,282	10,768
Mt Piton	Réunion	3,069	10,069

Oceania		m	ft
Puncak Jaya	Indonesia	5,029	16,499
Puncak Trikora	Indonesia	4,750	15,584
Puncak Mandala	Indonesia	4,702	15,427
Mt Wilhelm	Papua New Guinea	4,508	14,790
Mauna Kea	USA (Hawaii)	4,205	13,796
Mauna Loa	USA (Hawaii)	4,170	13,681
Mt Cook (Aoraki)	New Zealand	3,753	12,313
Mt Balbi	Solomon Is.	2,439	8,002
Orohena	Tahiti	2,241	7,352
Mt Kosciuszko	Australia	2,237	7,339

North America		m	ft
Mt McKinley (Denali)	USA (Alaska)	6,194	20,321
Mt Logan	Canada	5,959	19,551
Citlaltepetl	Mexico	5,700	18,701
Mt St Elias	USA/Canada	5,489	18,008
Popocatepetl	Mexico	5,452	17,887
Mt Foraker	USA (Alaska)	5,304	17,401
Ixtaccihuatl	Mexico	5,286	17,342
Lucania	Canada	5,227	17,149
Mt Steele	Canada	5,073	16,644
Mt Bona	USA (Alaska)	5,005	16,420
Mt Blackburn	USA (Alaska)	4,996	16,391
Mt Sanford	USA (Alaska)	4,940	16,207
Mt Wood	Canada	4,848	15,905
Nevado de Toluca	Mexico	4,670	15,321
Mt Fairweather	USA (Alaska)	4,663	15,298
Mt Hunter	USA (Alaska)	4,442	15,573
Mt Whitney	USA	4,418	14,495
Mt Elbert	USA	4,399	14,432
Mt Harvard	USA	4,395	14,419
Mt Rainier	USA	4,392	14,409
Blanca Peak	USA	4,372	14,344
Longs Peak	USA	4,345	14,255
Tajumulco	Guatemala	4,220	13,845
Grand Teton	USA	4,197	13,770
Mt Waddington	Canada	3,994	13,104
Mt Robson	Canada	3,954	12,972
Chirripó Grande	Costa Rica	3,837	12,589
Mt Assiniboine	Canada	3,619	11,873
Pico Duarte	Dominican Rep.	3,175	10,417

South America		m	ft
Aconcagua	Argentina	6,960	22,834
Bonete	Argentina	6,872	22,546
Ojos del Salado	Argentina/Chile	6,863	22,516
Pissis	Argentina	6,779	22,241
Mercedario	Argentina/Chile	6,770	22,211
Huascaran	Peru	6,768	22,204
Llullaillaco	Argentina/Chile	6,723	22,057
Nudo de Cachi	Argentina	6,720	22,047
Yerupaja	Peru	6,632	21,758
N. de Tres Cruces	Argentina/Chile	6,620	21,719
Incahuasi	Argentina/Chile	6,601	21,654
Cerro Galan	Argentina	6,600	21,654
Tupungato	Argentina/Chile	6,570	21,555

South America (cont.)		m	ft
Sajama	Bolivia	6,542	21,463
Illimani	Bolivia	6,485	21,276
Coropuna	Peru	6,425	21,079
Ausangate	Peru	6,384	20,945
Cerro del Toro	Argentina	6,380	20,932
Siula Grande	Peru	6,356	20,853
Chimborazo	Ecuador	6,267	20,561
Cotapaxi	Ecuador	5,896	19,344
Pico Colon	Colombia	5,800	19,029
Pico Bolivar	Venezuela	5,007	16,427

Antarctica		m	ft
Vinson Massif		4,897	16,066
Mt Kirkpatrick		4,528	14,855
Mt Markham		4,349	14,268

Ocean Depths

Atlantic Ocean	m	ft
Mt Kirkpatrick	4,528	14,855
Puerto Rico (Milwaukee) Deep	9,220	30,249
Cayman Trench	7,680	25,197
Gulf of Mexico	5,203	17,070
Mediterranean Sea	5,121	16,801
Black Sea	2,211	7,254
North Sea	660	2,165
Baltic Sea	463	1,519

Indian Ocean	m	ft
Java Trench	7,450	24,442
Red Sea	2,635	8,454
Persian Gulf	73	239

Pacific Ocean	m	ft
Mariana Trench	11,022	36,161
Tonga Trench	10,882	35,702
Japan Trench	10,554	34,626
Kuril Trench	10,542	34,587
Mindanao Trench	10,497	34,439
Kermadec Trench	10,047	32,962
New Guinea Trench	9,140	19,987
Peru–Chile Trench	8,050	26,410

Antarctica	m	ft
Molloy Deep	5,608	18,399

Land Lows

		m	ft
Caspian Sea	Europe	−28	−92
Dead Sea	Asia	−403	−1,322
Lake Assal	Africa	−156	−512
Lake Eyre North	Oceania	−16	−52
Death Valley	North America	−86	−282
Valdés Peninsula	South America	−40	−131

Rivers

Europe		km	miles
Volga	Caspian Sea	3,700	2,300
Danube	Black Sea	2,850	1,770
Ural	Caspian Sea	2,535	1,575
Dnepr (Dnipro)	Black Sea	2,285	1,420
Kama	Volga	2,030	1,260
Don	Black Sea	1,990	1,240
Petchora	Arctic Ocean	1,790	1,110
Oka	Volga	1,480	920

Europe (cont.)		km	miles
Belaya	Kama	1,420	880
Dnister (Dniester)	Black Sea	1,400	870
Vyatka	Kama	1,370	850
Rhine	North Sea	1,320	820
North Dvina	Arctic Ocean	1,290	800
Desna	Dnepr (Dnipro)	1,190	740
Elbe	North Sea	1,145	710
>Wisla	Baltic Sea	1,090	675
Loire	Atlantic Ocean	1,020	635
West Dvina	Baltic Sea	1,019	633

Asia		km	miles
Yangtze	Pacific Ocean	6,380	3,960
Yenisey–Angara	Arctic Ocean	5,550	3,445
Huang He	Pacific Ocean	5,464	3,395
Ob–Irtysh	Arctic Ocean	5,410	3,360
Mekong	Pacific Ocean	4,500	2,795
Amur	Pacific Ocean	4,400	2,730
Lena	Arctic Ocean	4,400	2,730
Irtysh	Ob	4,250	2,640
Yenisey	Arctic Ocean	4,090	2,540
Ob	Arctic Ocean	3,680	2,285
Indus	Indian Ocean	3,100	1,925
Brahmaputra	Indian Ocean	2,900	1,800
Syrdarya	Aral Sea	2,860	1,775
Salween	Indian Ocean	2,800	1,740
Euphrates	Indian Ocean	2,700	1,675
Vilyuy	Lena	2,650	1,645
Kolyma	Arctic Ocean	2,600	1,615
Amudarya	Aral Sea	2,540	1,575
Ural	Caspian Sea	2,535	1,575
>Ganges	Indian Ocean	2,510	1,560
Si Kiang	Pacific Ocean	2,100	1,305
Irrawaddy	Indian Ocean	2,010	1,250
Tarim–Yarkand	Lop Nor	2,000	1,240
Tigris	Indian Ocean	1,900	1,180
Angara	Yenisey	1,830	1,135
Godavari	Indian Ocean	1,470	915
Sutlej	Indian Ocean	1,450	900

Africa		km	miles
Nile	Mediterranean	6,670	4,140
Congo	Atlantic Ocean	4,670	2,900
Niger	Atlantic Ocean	4,180	2,595
Zambezi	Indian Ocean	3,540	2,200
Oubangi/Uele	Congo (Zaïre)	2,250	1,400
Kasai	Congo (Zaïre)	1,950	1,210
Shaballe	Indian Ocean	1,930	1,200
Orange	Atlantic Ocean	1,860	1,155
Cubango	Okavango Swamps	1,800	1,120
>Limpopo	Indian Ocean	1,600	995
Senegal	Atlantic Ocean	1,600	995
Volta	Atlantic Ocean	1,500	930
Benue	Niger	1,350	840

Australia		km	miles
Murray–Darling	Indian Ocean	3,750	2,330
Darling	Murray	3,070	1,905
Murray	Indian Ocean	2,575	1,600
Murrumbidgee	Murray	1,690	1,050

North America		km	miles
Mississippi–Missouri	Gulf of Mexico	6,020	3,740
Mackenzie	Arctic Ocean	4,240	2,630
Mississippi	Gulf of Mexico	3,780	2,350
Missouri	Mississippi	3,780	2,350
Yukon	Pacific Ocean	3,185	1,980
Rio Grande	Gulf of Mexico	3,030	1,880
Arkansas	Mississippi	2,340	1,450
Colorado	Pacific Ocean	2,330	1,445
Red	Mississippi	2,040	1,270

North America (cont.)		km	miles
Columbia	Pacific Ocean	1,950	1,210
Saskatchewan	Lake Winnipeg	1,940	1,205
Snake	Columbia	1,670	1,040
Churchill	Hudson Bay	1,600	990
Ohio	Mississippi	1,580	980
Brazos	Gulf of Mexico	1,400	870
>St Lawrence	Atlantic Ocean	1,170	730

South America		km	miles
Amazon	Atlantic Ocean	6,450	4,010
Paraná–Plate	Atlantic Ocean	4,500	2,800
Purus	Amazon	3,350	2,080
Madeira	Amazon	3,200	1,990
São Francisco	Atlantic Ocean	2,900	1,800
Paraná	Plate	2,800	1,740
Tocantins	Atlantic Ocean	2,750	1,710
Paraguay	Paraná	2,550	1,580
Orinoco	Atlantic Ocean	2,500	1,550
Pilcomayo	Paraná	2,500	1,550
Araguaia	Tocantins	2,250	1,400
Juruá	Amazon	2,000	1,240
Xingu	Amazon	1,980	1,230
Ucayali	Amazon	1,900	1,180
>Marañón	Amazon	1,600	990
Uruguay	Plate	1,600	990
Magdalena	Caribbean Sea	1,540	960

Lakes

Europe		km²	miles²
Lake Ladoga	Russia	17,700	6,800
Lake Onega	Russia	9,700	3,700
Saimaa system	Finland	8,000	3,100
Vänern	Sweden	5,500	2,100
Rybinskoye Reservoir	Russia	4,700	1,800

Asia		km²	miles²
Caspian Sea	Asia	371,800	143,550
Aral Sea	Kazak./Uzbek.	33,640	13,000
Lake Baykal	Russia	30,500	11,780
Tonlé Sap	Cambodia	20,000	7,700
>Lake Balqash	Kazakstan	18,500	7,100
Lake Dongting	China	12,000	4,600
Lake Ysyk	Kyrgyzstan	6,200	2,400
Lake Orumiyeh	Iran	5,900	2,300
Lake Koko	China	5,700	2,200
Lake Poyang	China	5,000	1,900
Lake Khanka	China/Russia	4,400	1,700
Lake Van	Turkey	3,500	1,400
Lake Ubsa	China	3,400	1,300

Africa		km²	miles²
Lake Victoria	East Africa	68,000	26,000
Lake Tanganyika	Central Africa	33,000	13,000
Lake Malawi/Nyasa	East Africa	29,600	11,430
Lake Chad	Central Africa	25,000	9,700
Lake Turkana	Ethiopia/Kenya	8,500	3,300
Lake Volta	Ghana	8,500	3,300
Lake Bangweulu	Zambia	8,000	3,100
Lake Rukwa	Tanzania	7,000	2,700
Lake Mai-Ndombe	Congo (Zaïre)	6,500	2,500
>Lake Kariba	Zambia/Zimbabwe	5,300	2,000
Lake Mobutu	Uganda/Congo (Zaïre)	5,300	2,000
Lake Nasser	Egypt/Sudan	5,200	2,000
Lake Mweru	Zambia/Congo (Zaïre)	4,900	1,900
Lake Cabora Bassa	Mozambique	4,500	1,700
Lake Kyoga	Uganda	4,400	1,700
Lake Tana	Ethiopia	3,630	1,400
Lake Kivu	Rwanda/Congo (Zaïre)	2,650	1,000
Lake Edward	Uganda/Congo (Zaïre)	2,200	850

Australia		km²	miles²
Lake Eyre	Australia	8,900	3,400
Lake Torrens	Australia	5,800	2,200
Lake Gairdner	Australia	4,800	1,900

North America		km²	miles²
Lake Superior	Canada/USA	82,350	31,800
Lake Huron	Canada/USA	59,600	23,010
Lake Michigan	USA	58,000	22,400
Great Bear Lake	Canada	31,800	12,280
Great Slave Lake	Canada	28,500	11,000
Lake Erie	Canada/USA	25,700	9,900
Lake Winnipeg	Canada	24,400	9,400
Lake Ontario	Canada/USA	19,500	7,500
Lake Nicaragua	Nicaragua	8,200	3,200
Lake Athabasca	Canada	8,100	3,100
Smallwood Reservoir	Canada	6,530	2,520
Reindeer Lake	Canada	6,400	2,500
Lake Winnipegosis	Canada	5,400	2,100
Nettilling Lake	Canada	5,500	2,100
Lake Nipigon	Canada	4,850	1,900
Lake Manitoba	Canada	4,700	1,800

South America		km²	miles²
Lake Titicaca	Bolivia/Peru	8,300	3,200
Lake Poopo	Peru	2,800	1,100

Islands

Europe		km²	miles²
Great Britain	UK	229,880	88,700
Iceland	Atlantic Ocean	103,000	39,800
Ireland	Ireland/UK	84,400	32,600
Novaya Zemlya (North)	Russia	48,200	18,600
West Spitzbergen	Norway	39,000	15,100
Novaya Zemlya (South)	Russia	33,200	12,800
Sicily	Italy	25,500	9,800
Sardinia	Italy	24,000	9,300
North-east Spitzbergen	Norway	15,000	5,600
Corsica	France	8,700	3,400
Crete	Greece	8,350	3,200
Zealand	Denmark	6,850	2,600

Asia		km²	miles²
Borneo	Southeast Asia	744,360	287,400
Sumatra	Indonesia	473,600	182,860
Honshu	Japan	230,500	88,980
Sulawesi (Celebes)	Indonesia	189,000	73,000
Java	Indonesia	126,700	48,900
Luzon	Philippines	104,700	40,400
Mindanao	Philippines	101,500	39,200
Hokkaido	Japan	78,400	30,300
Sakhalin	Russia	74,060	28,600
Sri Lanka	Indian Ocean	65,600	25,300
Taiwan	Pacific Ocean	36,000	13,900
Kyushu	Japan	35,700	13,800
Hainan	China	34,000	13,100
Timor	Indonesia	33,600	13,000
Shikoku	Japan	18,800	7,300
Halmahera	Indonesia	18,000	6,900
Ceram	Indonesia	17,150	6,600
Sumbawa	Indonesia	15,450	6,000
Flores	Indonesia	15,200	5,900
Samar	Philippines	13,100	5,100
Negros	Philippines	12,700	4,900
Bangka	Indonesia	12,000	4,600
Palawan	Philippines	12,000	4,600
Panay	Philippines	11,500	4,400
Sumba	Indonesia	11,100	4,300
Mindoro	Philippines	9,750	3,800
Buru	Indonesia	9,500	3,700

Asia (cont.)		km²	miles²
Bali	Indonesia	5,600	2,200
Cyprus	Mediterranean	3,570	1,400

Africa		km²	miles²
Madagascar	Indian Ocean	587,040	226,660
Socotra	Indian Ocean	3,600	1,400
Réunion	Indian Ocean	2,500	965
Tenerife	Atlantic Ocean	2,350	900
Mauritius	Indian Ocean	1,865	720

Oceania		km²	miles²
New Guinea	Indon./Papua NG	821,030	317,000
New Zealand (South)	New Zealand	150,500	58,100
New Zealand (North)	New Zealand	114,700	44,300
Tasmania	Australia	67,800	26,200
New Britain	Papua NG	37,800	14,600
New Caledonia	Pacific Ocean	19,100	7,400
Viti Levu	Fiji	10,500	4,100
Hawaii	Pacific Ocean	10,450	4,000
Bougainville	Papua NG	9,600	3,700
Guadalcanal	Solomon Is.	6,500	2,500
Vanua Levu	Fiji	5,550	2,100
New Ireland	Papua NG	3,200	1,200

North America		km²	miles²
Greenland	Greenland	2,175,600	839,800
Baffin Is.	Canada	508,000	196,100
Victoria Is.	Canada	212,200	81,900
Ellesmere Is.	Canada	212,200	81,800
Cuba	Cuba	110,860	42,800
Newfoundland	Canada	110,680	42,700
Hispaniola	Atlantic Ocean	76,200	29,400
Banks Is.	Canada	67,000	25,900
Devon Is.	Canada	54,500	21,000
Melville Is.	Canada	42,400	16,400
Vancouver Is.	Canada	32,150	12,400
Somerset Is.	Canada	24,300	9,400
Jamaica	Caribbean Sea	11,400	4,400
Puerto Rico	Atlantic Ocean	8,900	3,400
Cape Breton Is.	Canada	4,000	1,500

South America		km²	miles²
Tierra del Fuego	Argentina/Chile	47,000	18,100
Falkland Is. (East)	Atlantic Ocean	6,800	2,600
South Georgia	Atlantic Ocean	4,200	1,600
Galapagos (Isabela)	Pacific Ocean	2,250	870

World Statistics – Climate

For each city, the top row of figures shows total rainfall in millimetres; the bottom row shows the average temperature in ° Celsius or centigrade. The total annual rainfall and average annual temperature are given at the end of the rows.

	Jan.	Feb.	Mar.	Apr.	May	June	July	Aug.	Sept.	Oct.	Nov.	Dec.	Total
Europe													
Berlin, Germany	46	40	33	42	49	65	73	69	68	49	46	43	603
Altitude 55 metres	1	0	4	9	14	17	19	18	15	9	5	1	9
London, UK	54	40	37	37	46	45	57	59	49	57	64	48	593
5 m	4	5	7	9	12	16	18	17	15	11	8	5	11
Málaga, Spain	61	51	62	46	26	5	1	3	29	64	64	62	474
33 m	12	13	16	17	19	29	25	26	23	20	16	13	18
Moscow, Russia	39	38	36	37	53	58	88	71	58	45	47	54	624
156 m	13	-10	-4	6	13	16	18	17	12	6	-1	-7	4
Paris, France	56	46	35	42	57	54	59	64	55	50	51	50	619
75 m	3	4	8	11	15	18	20	19	17	12	7	4	12
Rome, Italy	71	62	57	51	46	37	15	21	63	99	129	93	744
17 m	8	9	11	14	18	22	25	25	22	17	13	10	16
Asia													
Bangkok, Thailand	8	20	36	58	198	160	160	175	305	206	66	5	1,397
2 m	26	28	29	30	29	29	28	28	28	28	26	25	28
Bombay (Mumbai), India	3	3	3	<3	18	485	617	340	264	64	13	3	1,809
11 m	24	24	26	28	30	29	27	27	27	28	27	26	27
Ho Chi Minh, Vietnam	15	3	13	43	221	330	315	269	335	269	114	56	1,984
9 m	26	27	29	30	29	28	28	28	27	27	27	26	28
Hong Kong, China	33	46	74	137	292	394	381	361	257	114	43	31	2,162
33 m	16	15	18	22	26	28	28	28	27	25	21	18	23
Tokyo, Japan	48	74	107	135	147	165	142	152	234	208	97	56	1,565
6 m	3	4	7	13	17	21	25	26	23	17	11	6	14
Africa													
Cairo, Egypt	5	5	5	3	3	<3	0	0	<3	<3	3	5	28
116 m	13	15	18	21	25	28	28	28	26	24	20	15	22
Cape Town, South Africa	15	8	18	48	79	84	89	66	43	31	18	10	508
17 m	21	21	20	17	14	13	12	13	14	16	18	19	17
Lagos, Nigeria	28	46	102	150	269	460	279	64	140	206	69	25	1,836
3 m	27	28	29	28	28	26	26	25	26	26	28	28	27
Nairobi, Kenya	38	64	125	211	158	46	15	23	31	53	109	86	958
1,820 m	19	19	19	19	18	16	16	16	18	19	18	18	18
Australia, New Zealand & Antarctica													
Christchurch, New Zealand	56	43	48	48	66	66	69	48	46	43	48	56	638
10 m	16	16	14	12	9	6	6	7	9	12	14	16	11
Darwin, Australia	386	312	254	97	15	3	<3	3	13	51	119	239	1,491
30 m	29	29	29	29	28	26	25	26	28	29	30	29	28
Mawson, Antarctica	11	30	20	10	44	180	4	40	3	20	0	0	362
14 m	0	-5	-10	-14	-15	-16	-18	-18	-19	-13	-5	-1	-11
Sydney, Australia	89	102	127	135	127	117	117	76	73	71	73	73	1,181
42 m	22	22	21	18	15	13	12	13	15	18	19	21	17
North America													
Anchorage, Alaska, USA	20	18	15	10	13	18	41	66	66	56	25	23	371
40 m	-11	-8	-5	2	7	12	14	13	9	2	-5	-11	2
Kingston, Jamaica	23	15	23	31	102	89	38	91	99	180	74	36	800
34 m	25	25	25	26	26	28	28	28	27	27	26	26	26
Los Angeles, USA	79	76	71	25	10	3	<3	<3	5	15	31	66	381
95 m	13	14	14	16	17	19	21	22	21	18	16	14	17
Mexico City, Mexico	13	5	10	20	53	119	170	152	130	51	18	8	747
2,309 m	12	13	16	18	19	19	17	18	18	16	14	13	16
New York, USA	94	97	91	81	81	84	107	109	86	89	76	91	1,092
96 m	-1	-1	3	10	16	20	23	23	21	15	7	2	11
Vancouver, Canada	154	115	101	60	52	45	32	41	67	114	150	182	1,113
14 m	3	5	6	9	12	15	17	17	14	10	6	4	10
South America													
Antofagasta, Chile	0	0	0	<3	<3	3	5	3	<3	3	<3	0	13
94 m	21	21	20	18	16	15	14	14	15	16	18	19	17
Buenos Aires, Argentina	79	71	109	89	76	61	56	61	79	86	84	99	950
27 m	23	23	21	17	13	9	10	11	13	15	19	22	16
Lima, Peru	3	<3	<3	<3	5	5	8	8	8	3	3	<3	41
120 m	23	24	24	22	19	17	16	17	18	19	21	20	
Rio de Janeiro, Brazil	125	122	130	107	79	53	41	43	66	79	104	137	1,082
61 m	26	26	25	24	22	21	21	21	21	22	23	25	23

The Earth in Focus

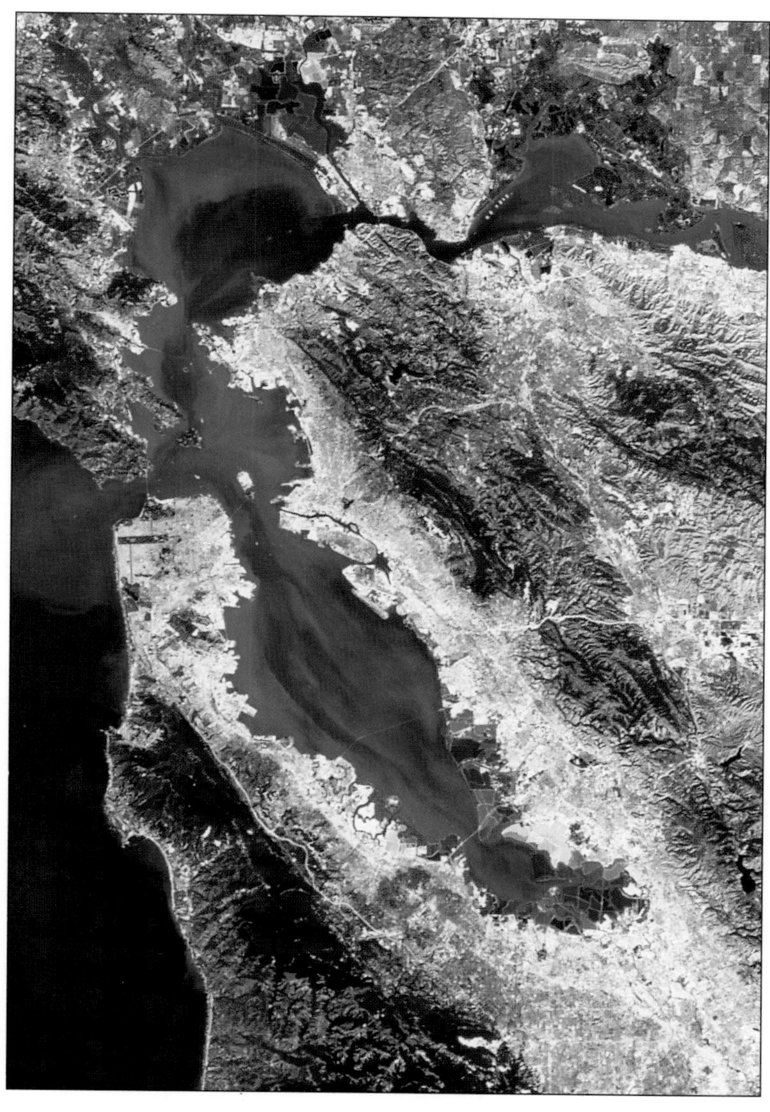

> Landsat image of the San Francisco Bay area. The narrow entrance to the bay (crossed by the Golden Gate Bridge) provides an excellent natural harbour. The San Andreas Fault runs parallel to the coastline.

The Universe & Solar System

BETWEEN 10 AND 20 billion (or 10,000 to 20,000 million) years ago, the Universe was created in a huge explosion known as the 'Big Bang'. In the first 10^{-24} of a second the Universe expanded rapidly and the basic forces of nature, radiation and subatomic particles, came into being. The Universe has been expanding ever since. Traces of the original 'fireball' of radiation can still be detected, and most scientists accept the Big Bang theory of the origin of the Universe.

The Nearest Stars ▾	
The 20 nearest stars, excluding the Sun, with their distance from Earth in light-years.*	
Proxima Centauri	4.25
Alpha Centauri A	4.3
Alpha Centauri B	4.3
Barnard's Star	6.0
Wolf 359	7.8
Lalande 21185	8.3
Sirius A	8.7
Sirius B	8.7
UV Ceti A	8.7
UV Ceti B	8.7
Ross 154	9.4
Ross 248	10.3
Epsilon Eridani	10.7
Ross 128	10.9
61 Cygni A	11.1
61 Cygni B	11.1
Epsilon Indi	11.2
Groombridge 34 A	11.2
Groombridge 34 B	11.2
L789-6	11.2

A light-year equals approximately 9,500 billion km [5,900 billion miles].

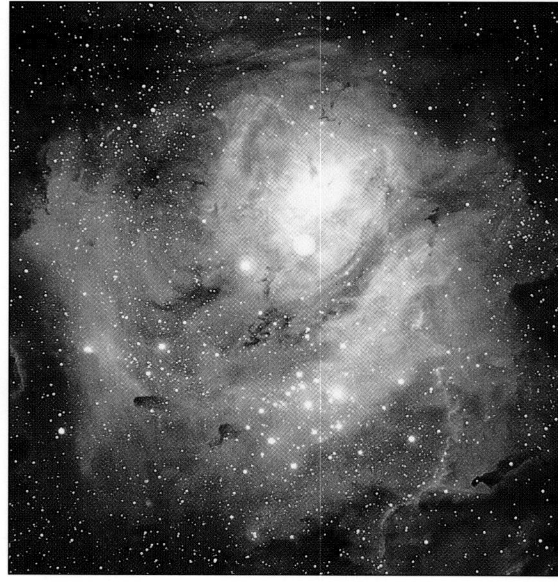

> The Lagoon Nebula is a huge cloud of dust and gas. Hot stars inside the nebula make the gas glow red.

GALAXIES

Almost a million years passed before the Universe cooled sufficiently for atoms to form. When a billion years had passed, the atoms had begun to form proto-galaxies, which are masses of gas separated by empty space. Stars began to form within the protogalaxies, as particles were drawn together, producing the high temperatures necessary to bring about nuclear fusion. The formation of the first stars brought about the evolution of the protogalaxies into galaxies proper, each containing billions of stars.

Our Sun is a medium-sized star. It is

Mercury •   Venus 🌑   Earth 🌍   Mars •   Jupiter

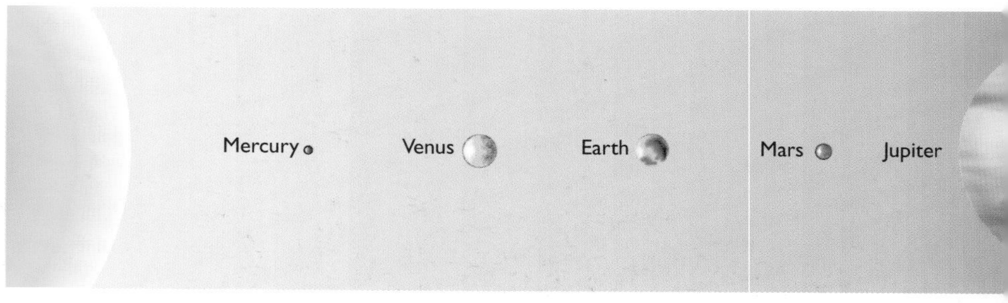

PLANETARY DATA

	Mean distance from Sun (million km)	Mass (Earth = 1)	Period of orbit (Earth years)	Period of rotation (Earth days)	Equatorial diameter (km)	Escape velocity (km/sec)	Number of known satellites
Sun	–	332,946	–	25.38	1,392,000	617.5	–
Mercury	58.3	0.06	0.241	58.67	4,878	4.27	0
Venus	107.7	0.8	0.615	243.0	12,104	10.36	0
Earth	149.6	1.0	1.00	0.99	12,756	11.18	1
Mars	227.3	0.1	1.88	1.02	6,787	5.03	2
Jupiter	777.9	317.8	11.86	0.41	142,800	59.60	16
Saturn	1,427.1	95.2	29.46	0.42	120,000	35.50	20
Uranus	2,872.3	14.5	84.01	0.45	51,118	21.30	15
Neptune	4,502.7	17.2	164.79	0.67	49,528	23.3	8
Pluto	5,894.2	0.002	248.54	6.38	2,300	1.1	1

one of the billions of stars that make up the Milky Way galaxy, which is one of the millions of galaxies in the Universe.

THE SOLAR SYSTEM

The Solar System lies towards the edge of the Milky Way galaxy. It consists of the Sun and other bodies, including planets (together with their moons), asteroids, meteoroids, comets, dust and gas, which revolve around it.

The Earth moves through space in three distinct ways. First, with the rest of the Solar System, it moves around the centre of the Milky Way galaxy in an orbit that takes 200 million years.

As the Earth revolves around the Sun once every year, its axis is tilted by about 23.5 degrees. As a result, first the northern and then the southern hemisphere lean towards the Sun at different times of the year, causing the seasons experienced in the mid-latitudes.

The Earth also rotates on its axis every 24 hours, causing day and night. The movements of the Earth in the Solar System determine the calendar. The length of a year – one complete orbit of the Earth around the Sun – is 365 days, 5 hours, 48 minutes and 46 seconds. Leap years prevent the calendar from becoming out of step with the solar year.

> The diagram below shows the planets around the Sun. The sizes of the planets are relative but the distances to the Sun are not to scale. Closest to the Sun are dense rocky bodies, known as the terrestrial planets. They are Mercury, Venus, Earth and Mars. Jupiter, Saturn, Uranus and Neptune are huge balls of gas. Pluto is a small, icy body.

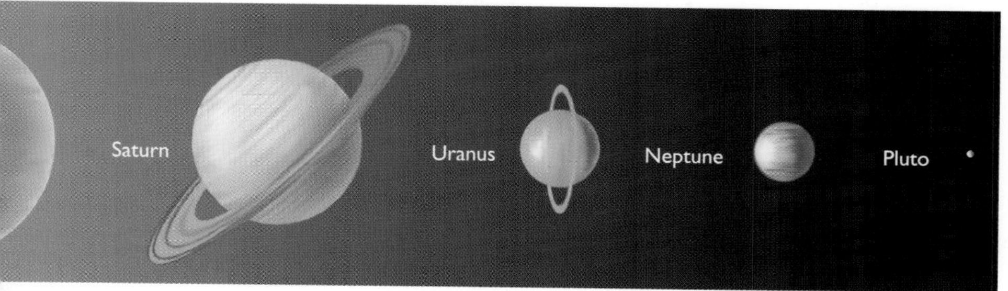

Saturn   Uranus   Neptune   Pluto

The Changing Earth

THE SOLAR SYSTEM was formed around 4.7 billion years ago, when the Sun, a glowing ball of gases, was created from a rotating disk of dust and gas. The planets were then formed from material left over after the creation of the Sun.

After the Earth formed, around 4.6 billion years ago, lighter elements rose to the hot surface, where they finally cooled to form a hard shell, or crust. Denser elements sank, forming the partly liquid mantle, the liquid outer core, and the solid inner core.

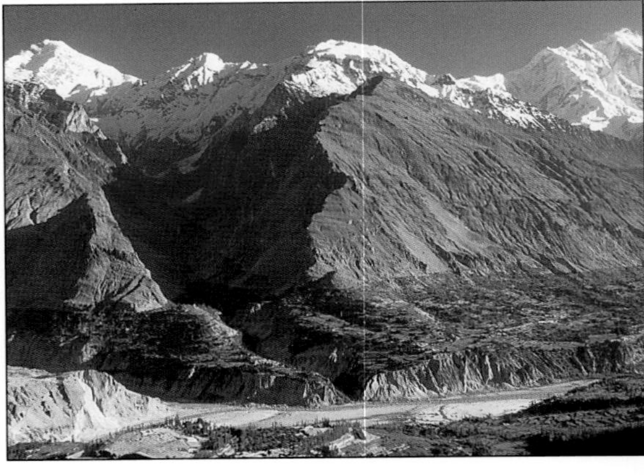

EARTH HISTORY

The oldest known rocks on Earth are around 4 billion years old. Natural processes have destroyed older rocks. Simple life forms first appeared on Earth around 3.5 billion years ago, though rocks formed in the first 4 billion years of Earth history contain little evidence of life. But

> Fold mountains, such as the Himalayan ranges which are shown above, were formed when two plates collided and the rock layers between them were squeezed upwards into loops or folds.

rocks formed since the start of the Cambrian period (the first period in the Paleozoic era), about 590 million years ago, are rich in fossils. The study of fossils has enabled scientists to gradually piece together the long and complex story of life on Earth.

THE PLANET EARTH

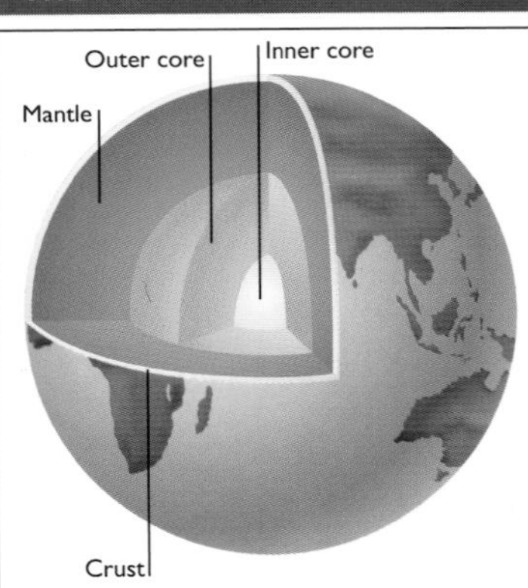

Outer core | Inner core
Mantle
Crust

CRUST The continental crust has an average thickness of 35–40 km [22–25 miles]; the oceanic crust averages 6 km [4 miles].

MANTLE 2,900 km [1,800 miles] thick. The top layer is solid, resting on a partly molten layer called the asthenosphere.

OUTER CORE 2,100 km [1,300 miles] thick. It consists mainly of molten iron and nickel.

INNER CORE (DIAMETER) 1,350 km [840 miles]. It is mainly solid iron and nickel.

ELEMENTS

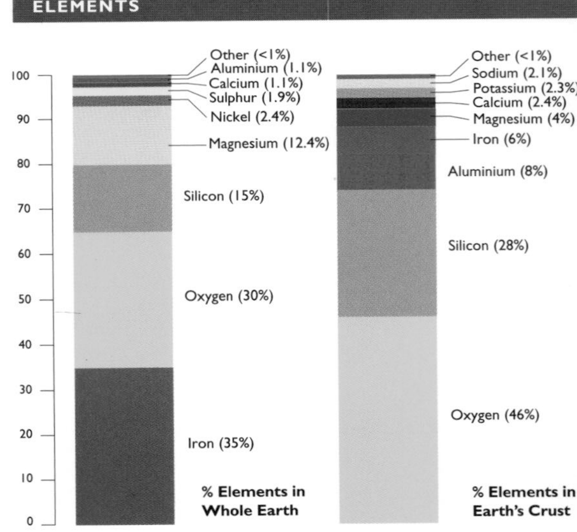

Other (<1%)
Aluminium (1.1%)
Calcium (1.1%)
Sulphur (1.9%)
Nickel (2.4%)
Magnesium (12.4%)
Silicon (15%)
Oxygen (30%)
Iron (35%)

% Elements in Whole Earth

Other (<1%)
Sodium (2.1%)
Potassium (2.3%)
Calcium (2.4%)
Magnesium (4%)
Iron (6%)
Aluminium (8%)
Silicon (28%)
Oxygen (46%)

% Elements in Earth's Crust

> The Earth contains about 100 elements, but eight of them account for 99% of the planet's mass. Iron makes up 35% of the Earth's mass, but most of it is in the core. The most common elements in the crust – oxygen and silicon – are often combined with one or more of the other common crustal elements, to form a group of minerals called silicates. The mineral quartz, which consists only of silicon and oxygen, occurs widely in such rocks as granites and sandstones.

PLATE BOUNDARIES

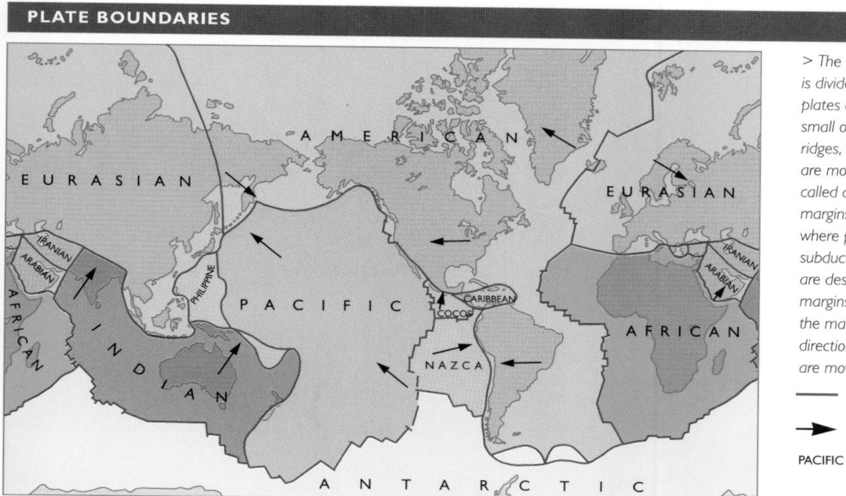

> The Earth's lithosphere is divided into six huge plates and several small ones. Ocean ridges, where plates are moving apart, are called constructive plate margins. Ocean trenches, where plates collide, are subduction zones. These are destructive plate margins. The map shows the main plates and the directions in which they are moving.

——— Plate boundaries

➤ Direction of plate movements

PACIFIC Major plates

THE DYNAMIC EARTH

The Earth's surface is always changing because of a process called plate tectonics. Plates are blocks of the solid lithosphere (the crust and outer mantle), which are moved around by currents in the partly liquid mantle. Around 250 million years ago, the Earth contained one super-continent called Pangaea. Around 180 million years ago, Pangaea split into a northern part, Laurasia, and a southern part, Gondwanaland. Later, these huge continents, in turn, also split apart and the continents drifted to their present positions. Ancient seas disappeared and mountain ranges, such as the Himalayas and Alps, were pushed upwards.

PLATE TECTONICS

In the early 1900s, two scientists suggested that the Americas were once joined to Europe and Africa. Together they proposed the theory of continental drift to explain the similarities between rock structures on both sides of the Atlantic. But no one could offer an explanation as to how the continents moved.

Evidence from the ocean floor in the 1950s and 1960s led to the theory of plate tectonics, which suggested that the lithosphere is divided into large blocks, or plates. The plates are solid, but they rest on the partly molten asthenosphere, within the mantle. Long ridges on

the ocean floor were found to be the edges of plates which were moving apart, carried by currents in the asthenosphere. As the plates moved, molten material welled up from the mantle to fill the gaps. But at the ocean trenches, one plate is descending beneath another along what is called a subduction zone. The descending plate is melted and destroyed. This crustal destruction at subduction zones balances the creation of new crust along the ridges. Transform faults, where two plates are moving alongside each other, form another kind of plate edge.

GEOLOGICAL TIME SCALE

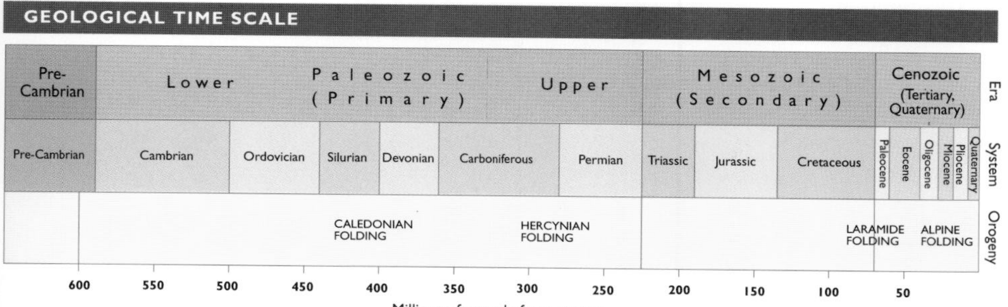

Pre-Cambrian	Lower Paleozoic (Primary)					Upper	Mesozoic (Secondary)			Cenozoic (Tertiary, Quaternary)		Era
Pre-Cambrian	Cambrian	Ordovician	Silurian	Devonian	Carboniferous	Permian	Triassic	Jurassic	Cretaceous	Paleocene / Eocene / Oligocene	Miocene / Pliocene / Quaternary	System
			CALEDONIAN FOLDING		HERCYNIAN FOLDING					LARAMIDE FOLDING	ALPINE FOLDING	Orogeny

600   550   500   450   400   350   300   250   200   150   100   50

Millions of years before present

Earthquakes & Volcanoes

PLATE TECTONICS HELP us to understand such phenomena as earthquakes, volcanic eruptions, and mountain building.

EARTHQUAKES

Earthquakes can occur anywhere, but they are most common near the edges of plates. They occur when intense pressure breaks the rocks along plate edges, making the plates lurch forward in a sudden movement.

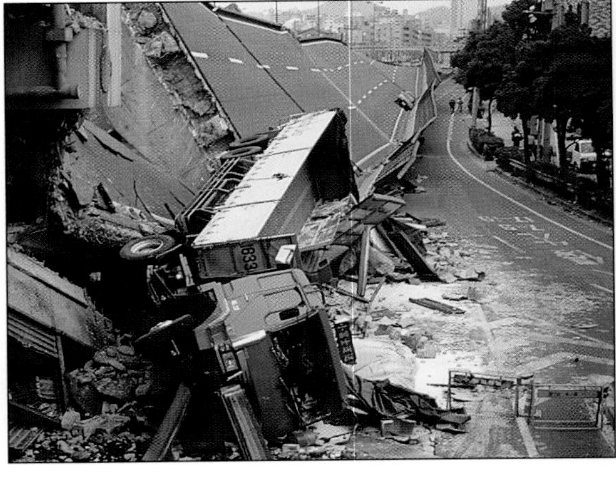

Major Earthquakes since 1900 ▼			
Year	Location	Mag.	Deaths
1906	San Francisco, USA	8.3	503
1906	Valparaiso, Chile	8.6	22,000
1908	Messina, Italy	7.5	83,000
1915	Avezzano, Italy	7.5	30,000
1920	Gansu, China	8.6	180,000
1923	Yokohama, Japan	8.3	143,000
1927	Nan Shan, China	8.3	200,000
1932	Gansu, China	7.6	70,000
1934	Bihar, India/Nepal	8.4	10,700
1935	Quetta, Pakistan	7.5	60,000
1939	Chillan, Chile	8.3	28,000
1939	Erzincan, Turkey	7.9	30,000
1960	Agadir, Morocco	5.8	12,000
1964	Anchorage, Alaska	8.4	131
1968	North-east Iran	7.4	12,000
1970	North Peru	7.7	66,794
1976	Guatemala	7.5	22,778
1976	Tangshan, China	8.2	255,000
1978	Tabas, Iran	7.7	25,000
1980	El Asnam, Algeria	7.3	20,000
1980	South Italy	7.2	4,800
1985	Mexico City, Mexico	8.1	4,200
1988	North-west Armenia	6.8	55,000
1990	North Iran	7.7	36,000
1993	Maharashtra, India	6.4	30,000
1995	Kobe, Japan	7.2	5,000
1997	North-east Iran	7.1	2,400
1998	Takhar, Afghanistan	6.1	4,200

> The earthquake that struck Kobe in January 1995 was the worst one experienced in Japan since 1923. Japan lies alongside subduction zones.

> The section between the Pacific and Indian oceans shows a subduction zone under the American plate, with spreading ocean ridges in the Atlantic and Indian oceans. East Africa may one day split away from the rest of Africa as plate movements pull the Rift Valley apart.

Earthquakes are common along the mid-ocean ridges, but they are a long way from land and cause little damage. Other earthquakes occur near land in subduction zones, such as those that encircle much of the Pacific Ocean. These earthquakes often trigger off powerful sea waves, called tsunamis. Other earthquakes occur along transform faults, such as the San Andreas fault in California, a boundary between the North American and Pacific plates. Movements along this fault cause periodic disasters, such as the earthquakes in San Francisco (1906) and Los Angeles (1994).

VOLCANOES & MOUNTAINS

Volcanoes are fuelled by magma (molten rock) from the mantle. Some volcanoes, such as in Hawaii, lie above 'hot spots' (sources of heat in the mantle). But most volcanoes occur either along the ocean ridges or above subduction zones, where

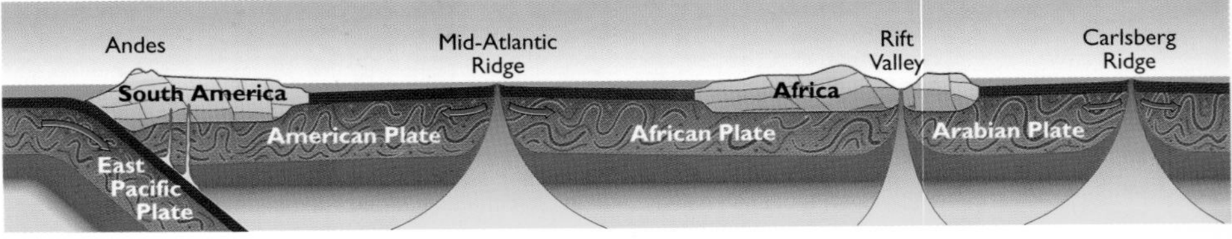

EARTHQUAKES

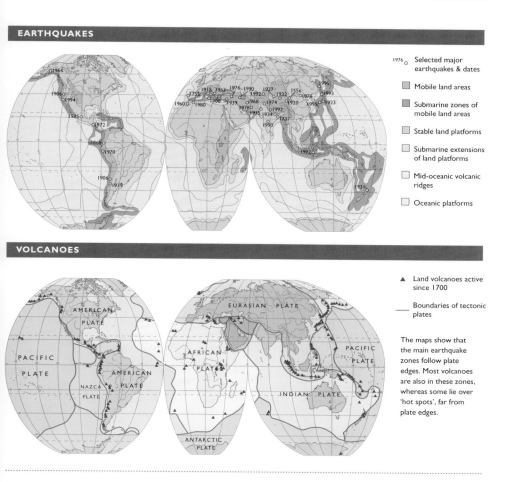

1976 ○	Selected major earthquakes & dates
▦	Mobile land areas
▦	Submarine zones of mobile land areas
▢	Stable land platforms
▢	Submarine extensions of land platforms
▢	Mid-oceanic volcanic ridges
▢	Oceanic platforms

VOLCANOES

▲ Land volcanoes active since 1700

―― Boundaries of tectonic plates

The maps show that the main earthquake zones follow plate edges. Most volcanoes are also in these zones, whereas some lie over 'hot spots', far from plate edges.

magma is produced when the descending plate is melted.

Volcanic mountains are built up gradually by runny lava flows or by exploded volcanic ash. Fold mountains occur when two plates bearing land areas collide and the plate edges are buckled upwards into fold mountain ranges. Plate movements also fracture rocks and block mountains are formed when areas of land are pushed upwards along faults or between parallel faults. Blocks of land sometimes sink down between faults, creating deep, steep-sided rift valleys.

> Volcanoes occur when molten magma reaches the surface under pressure through long vents. 'Quiet' volcanoes emit runny lava (called pahoehoe). Explosive eruptions occur when the magma is sticky. Explosive gases shatter the magma into ash, which is hurled upwards into the air.

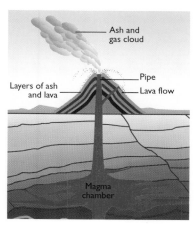

Ash and gas cloud

Pipe

Layers of ash and lava

Lava flow

Magma chamber

Water & Ice

A VISITOR FROM outer space might be forgiven for naming our planet 'Water' rather than 'Earth', because water covers more than 70% of its surface. Without water, our planet would be as lifeless as the Moon. Through the water cycle, fresh water is regularly supplied from the sea to the land. Most geographers divide the world's water into four main oceans: the Pacific, the Atlantic, the Indian and the Arctic. Together the oceans contain 97.2% of the world's water.

The water in the oceans is constantly on the move, even, albeit extremely slowly, in the deepest ocean trenches. The greatest movements of ocean water occur in the form of ocean currents. These are marked, mainly wind-blown

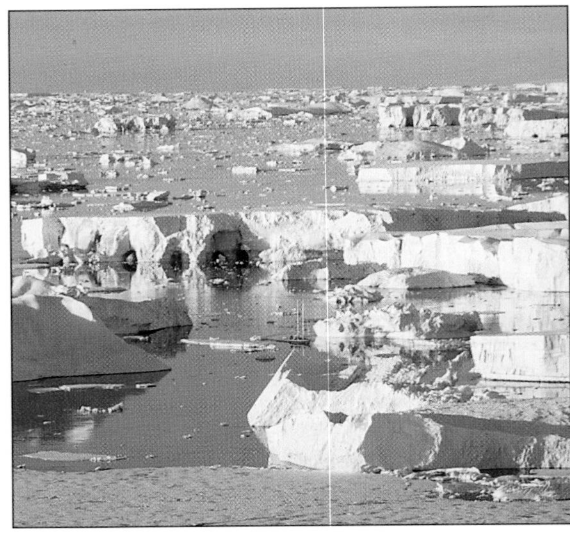

> Ice breaks away from the ice sheet of Antarctica, forming flat-topped icebergs. The biggest iceberg ever recorded came from Antarctica. It covered an area larger than Belgium.

EXPLANATION OF TERMS

GLACIER A body of ice that flows down valleys in mountain areas. It is usually narrow and hence smaller than ice caps or ice sheets.

ICE AGE A period of Earth history when ice sheets spread over large areas. The most recent Ice Age began about 1.8 million years ago and ended 10,000 years ago.

ICEBERG A floating body of ice in the sea. About eight-ninths of the ice is hidden beneath the surface of the water.

ICE SHEET A large body of ice. During the last Ice Age, ice sheets covered large parts of the northern hemisphere.

OCEAN The four main oceans are the Pacific, the Atlantic, the Indian and the Arctic. Some

people classify a fifth southern ocean, but others regard these waters as extensions of the Pacific, Atlantic and Indian oceans.

OCEAN CURRENTS Distinct currents of water in the oceans. Winds are the main causes of surface currents.

SEA An expanse of water, but smaller than an ocean.

JANUARY TEMPERATURE AND OCEAN CURRENTS

(Northern Hemisphere – Winter)

ACTUAL SURFACE TEMPERATURE

°C
30
20
10
0
−10
−20
−30
−40

OCEAN CURRENTS
Cold Warm Speed (knots)
Less than 0.5
0.5 – 1.0
Over 1.0

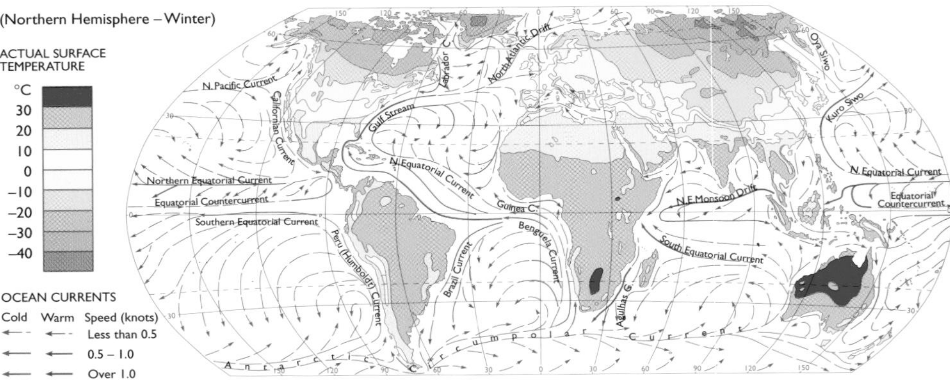

CROSS-SECTION OF ANTARCTICA

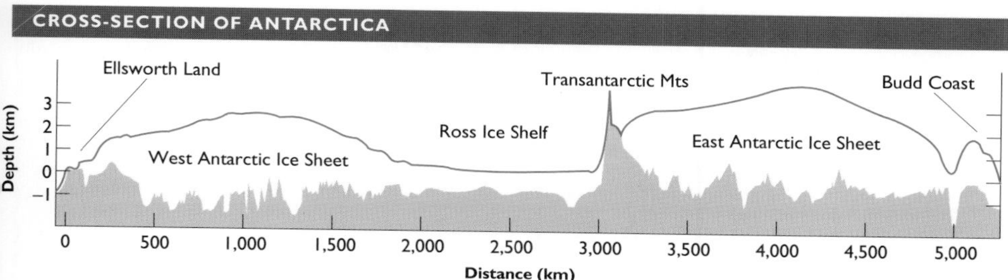

movements of water on or near the surface. Other dense, cold currents creep slowly across the ocean floor. Warm and cold ocean currents help to regulate the world's climate by transferring heat between the tropics and the poles.

ICE

About 2.15% of the world's water is locked in two large ice sheets, several smaller ice caps and glaciers. The world's largest ice sheet covers most of Antarctica. The ice is up to 4,800 m [15,750 ft] thick and it represents 70% of the world's fresh water. The volume of ice is about nine times greater than that contained in the world's other ice sheet in Greenland. Besides these two ice sheets, there are some smaller ice caps in northern Canada, Iceland, Norway and Spitzbergen, and

many valley glaciers in high mountain regions throughout the world.

If global warming was to melt the world's ice, the sea level could rise by as much as 100 m [330 ft], flooding low-lying coastal regions. Many of the world's largest cities and most fertile plains would vanish beneath the waves.

> This section across Antarctica shows the concealed land areas in brown, with the top of the ice in blue. The section is divided into the West and East Antarctic Ice Sheets. The vertical scale has been exaggerated.

Composition of Seawater ▼

The principal components of seawater, by percentage, excluding the elements of water itself:

Chloride (Cl)	55.04%	Potassium (K)	1.10%
Sodium (Na)	30.61%	Bicarbonate (HCO₃)	0.41%
Sulphate (SO₄)	7.69%	Bromide (Br)	0.19%
Magnesium (Mg)	3.69%	Strontium (Sr)	0.04%
Calcium (Ca)	1.16%	Fluorine (F)	0.003%

The oceans contain virtually every other element, the more important ones being lithium, rubidium, phosphorus, iodine and barium.

JULY TEMPERATURE AND OCEAN CURRENTS

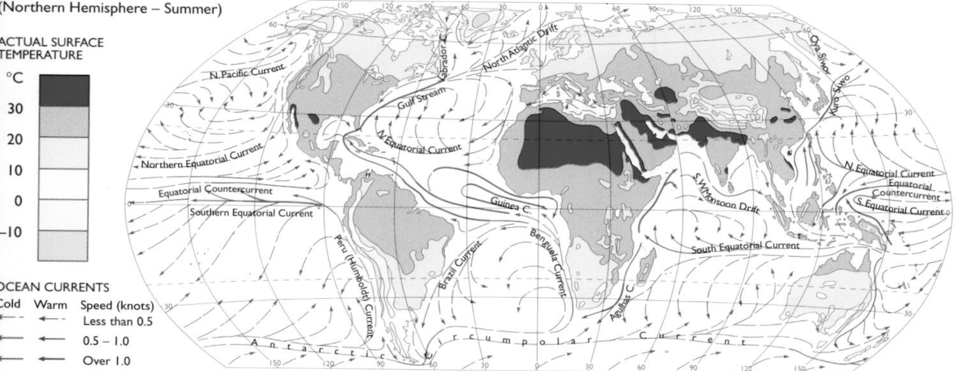

Weather & Climate

WEATHER IS A description of the day-to-day state of the atmosphere. Climate, on the other hand, is weather in the long term: the seasonal pattern of temperature and precipitation averaged over time.

In some areas, the weather is so stable and predictable that a description of the weather is much the same as a statement of the climate. But in parts of the mid-latitudes, the weather changes from hour to hour. Changeable weather is caused mainly by low air pressure systems, called cyclones or depressions, which form along the polar front where warm subtropical air meets cold polar air.

The main elements of weather and climate are temperature and rainfall. Temperatures vary because the Sun heats the Earth unequally, with the most intense heating around the Equator. Unequal heating is responsible for the general circulation of the atmosphere and the main wind belts.

Rainfall occurs when warm air containing invisible water vapour rises. As the rising air cools, the capacity of the air to hold water vapour decreases and so the water vapour condenses into droplets of water or ice crystals, which collect together to form raindrops or snowflakes.

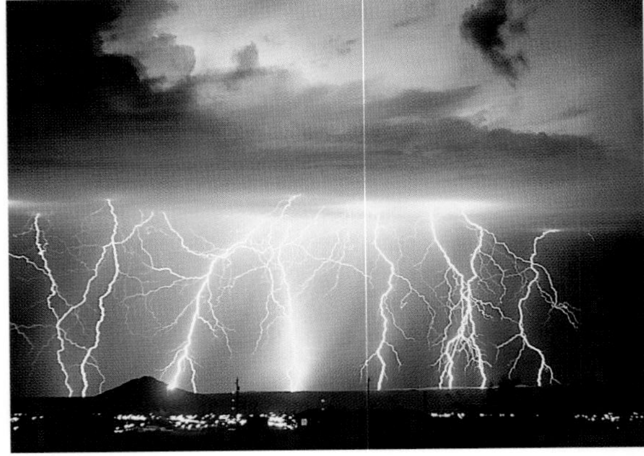

> Lightning occurs in clouds and also between the base of clouds and the ground. Lightning that strikes the ground can kill people or start forest fires.

> The rainfall map shows areas affected by tropical storms, which are variously called hurricanes, tropical cyclones, willy willies and typhoons. Strong polar winds bring blizzards in winter.

LIGHTNING

Lightning is a flash of light in the sky caused by a discharge of electricity in the atmosphere. Lightning occurs within cumulonimbus clouds during thunderstorms. Positive charges build up at the top of the cloud, while negative charges build up at the base. The charges are finally discharged as an electrical spark. Sheet lightning occurs inside clouds, while cloud to ground lightning is usually forked. Thunder occurs when molecules along the lightning channel expand and collide with cool molecules.

ANNUAL RAINFALL

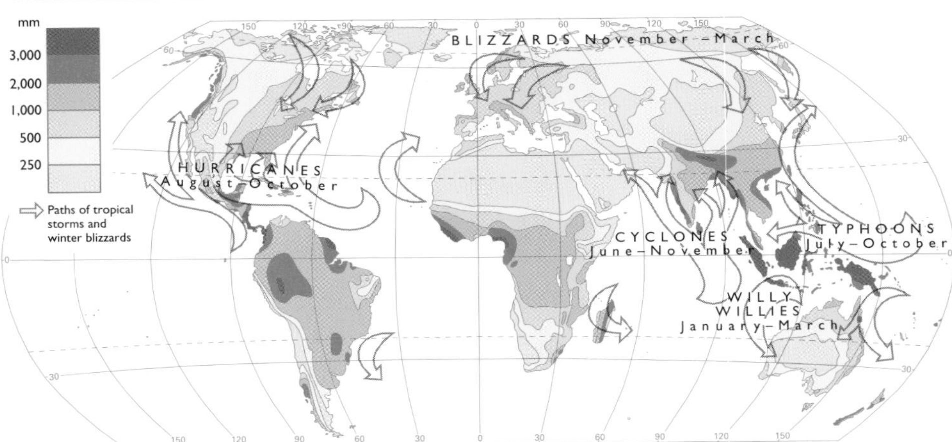

mm
3,000
2,000
1,000
500
250

Paths of tropical storms and winter blizzards

BLIZZARDS November–March

HURRICANES August–October

CYCLONES June–November

TYPHOONS July–October

WILLY WILLIES January–March

GLOBAL WARMING

The Earth's climates have changed many times during its history. Around 11,000 years ago, much of the northern hemisphere was buried by ice. Some scientists believe that the last Ice Age may not be over and that ice sheets may one day return. Other scientists are concerned that air

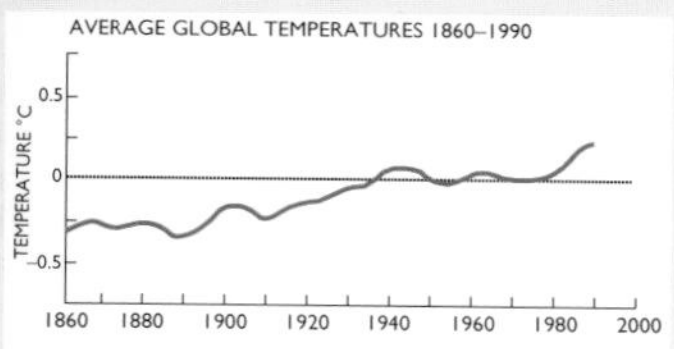

AVERAGE GLOBAL TEMPERATURES 1860–1990

pollution may be producing an opposite effect – a warming of the atmosphere. Since 1900, average world temperatures have risen by about 0.5°C [0.9°F] and increases are likely to continue. Global warming is the result of an increase in the amount of carbon dioxide in the atmosphere, caused by the burning of coal, oil and natural gas, together with deforestation. Short-wave radiation from the Sun passes easily through the atmosphere. But, as the carbon dioxide content rises, more of the long-wave radiation that returns from the Earth's surface is absorbed and trapped by the carbon dioxide. This creates a 'greenhouse effect', which will change the world's climates with, perhaps, disastrous environmental consequences.

CLIMATE

The world contains six main climatic types: hot and wet tropical climates; dry climates; warm temperate climates; cold temperate climates; polar climates; and mountain climates. These regions are further divided according to the character and amount of precipitation and special features of the temperature, notably seasonal variations. Regions with temperate climates include Mediterranean areas with hot, dry summers and mild, moist winters. The British Isles have a different type of temperate climate, with warm, rather than hot, summers and rain throughout the year.

CLIMATIC REGIONS

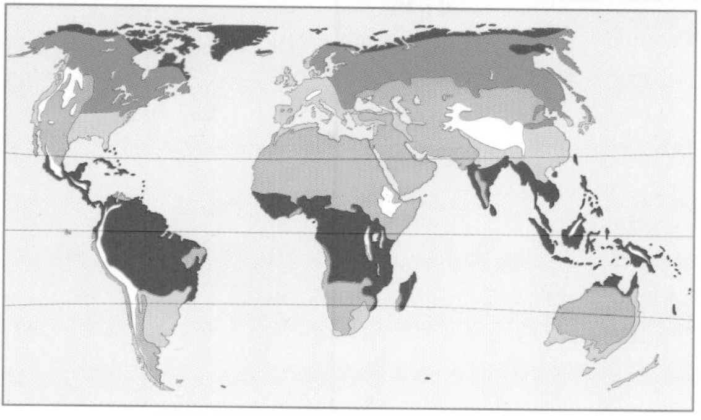

■ Tropical Climate (hot & wet)
■ Dry Climate (desert & steppe)
□ Temperate Climate (warm & wet)
■ Continental Climate (cold & wet)
■ Polar Climate (very cold & wet)
□ Mountainous Areas (where altitude affects climate types)

WORLD CLIMATIC RECORDS

Highest Recorded Temperature
Al Aziziyah, Libya: 58°C [136.4°F] on 13 September 1922

Highest Mean Annual Temperature
Dallol, Ethiopia: 34.4°C [94°F] from 1960–66

Lowest Mean Annual Temperature
Polus, Nedostupnosti, Pole of Cold, Antarctica: –57.8°C [–72°F]

Lowest Recorded Temperature (outside poles)
Verkhoyansk, Siberia, Russia: –68°C [–90°F] on 6 February 1933

Windiest Place
Commonwealth Bay, Antarctica: gales often exceed 320 km/h [200 mph]

Longest Heatwave
Marble Bar, Western Australia: 162 days over 38°C [94°F], 23 October 1923 to 7 April 1924

Driest Place
Calama, northern Chile: no recorded rainfall in 400 years to 1971

Wettest Place (average)
Tututendo, Colombia: mean annual rainfall 11,770 mm [463 in]

Wettest Place (24 hours)
Cilaos, Réunion, Indian Ocean: 1,870 mm [73.6 in] from 15–16 March 1952

Wettest Place (12 months)
Cherrapunji, Meghalaya, north-east India: 26,470 mm [1,040 in], August 1860 to1861. Cherrapunji also holds the record for rainfall in one month: 2,930 mm [115 in] in July 1861

Heaviest Hailstones
Gopalganj, central Bangladesh: up to 1.02 kg [2.25 lbs] in April 1986, which killed 92 people

Heaviest Snowfall (continuous)
Bessans, Savoie, France: 1,730 mm [68 in] in 19 hours over the period 5–6 April 1969

Heaviest Snowfall (season/year)
Paradise Ranger Station, Mt Rainier, Washington, USA: 31,102 mm [1,224 in] fell from 19 February 1971 to 18 February 1972

Landforms & Vegetation

THE CLIMATE LARGELY determines the nature of soils and vegetation types throughout the world. The studies of climate and plant and animal communities are closely linked. For example, tropical climates are divided into tropical forest and tropical grassland climates. The tropical forest climate, which is hot and rainy throughout the year, is ideal for the growth of forests that contain more than half of the world's known plant and animal species. But tropical grassland, or savanna, climates have a marked dry season. As a result, the forest gives way to grassland, with scattered trees.

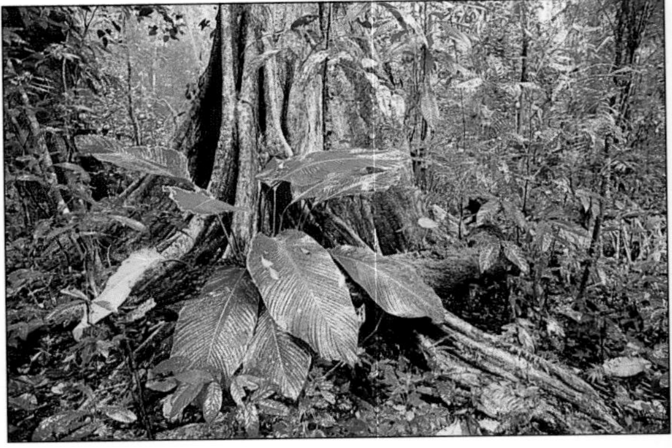

> The tropical broadleaf forests are rich in plant and animal species. The extinction of many species because of deforestation is one of the great natural disasters of our time.

CLIMATE & SCENERY

The climate also helps to shape the land. Frost action in cold areas splits boulders apart, while rapid temperature changes in hot deserts make rock surfaces peel away like the layers of an onion. These are examples of mechanical weathering.

Chemical weathering usually results from the action of water on rocks. For example, rainwater containing dissolved carbon dioxide is a weak acid, which reacts with limestone. This chemical process is responsible for the erosion of the world's most spectacular caves.

Running water and glaciers play a major part in creating scenery, while in

NATURAL VEGETATION

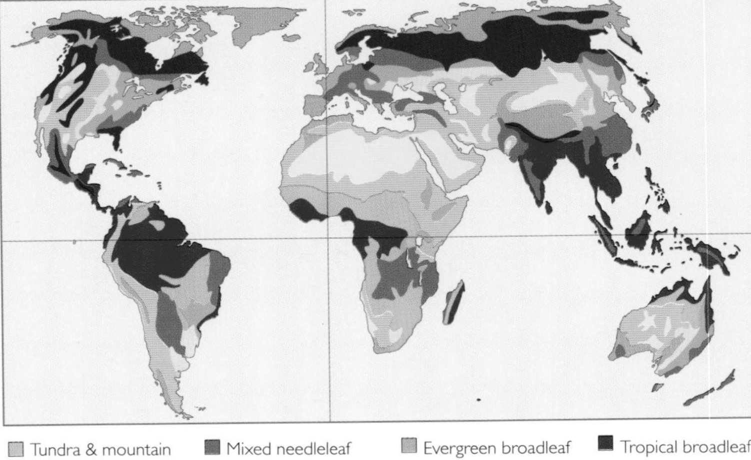

> Human activities, especially agriculture, have greatly modified plant and animal communities throughout the world. As a result, world vegetation maps show the natural 'climax vegetation' of regions – that is, the kind of vegetation that would grow in a particular climatic area, had that area not been affected by human activities. For example, the climax vegetation of western Europe is broadleaf, deciduous forest, but most of the original forest, together with the animals which lived in it, was destroyed long ago.

- Tundra & mountain vegetation
- Needleleaf evergreen forest
- Broadleaf deciduous forest
- Mixed needleleaf evergreen & broadleaf deciduous trees
- Mid-latitude grassland
- Semi-desert scrub land
- Evergreen broadleaf & deciduous trees & scrub
- Desert
- Tropical grassland (savanna)
- Tropical broadleaf & monsoon rainforest
- Subtropical broadleaf & needleleaf forest

DESERTIFICATION AND DEFORESTATION

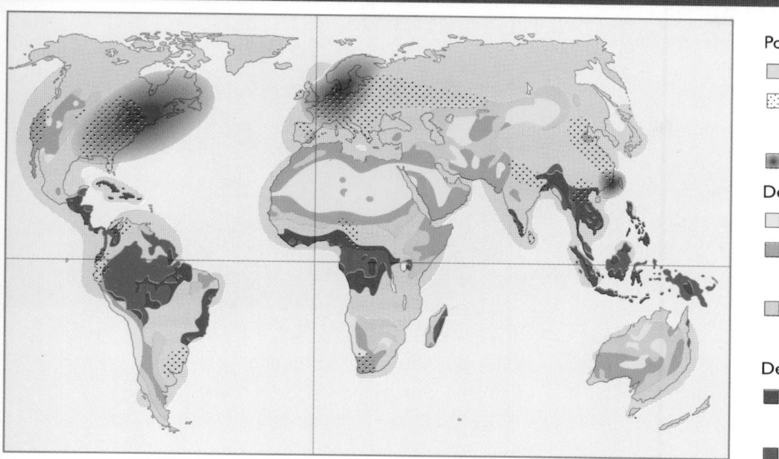

Pollution

☐ Polluted seas

▨ Main areas of sulphur & nitrogen emissions

■ Areas of acid rain

Desertification

☐ Existing deserts

■ Areas with a high risk of desertification

☐ Areas with a moderate risk of desertification

Deforestation

■ Former areas of rainforest

■ Existing rainforest

---

dry areas, wind–blown sand is a powerful agent of erosion. Most landforms seem to alter little in one person's lifetime. But geologists estimate that natural forces remove an average of 3.5 cm [1.4 in] from land areas every 1,000 years. Over millions of years, these forces reduce mountains to flat plains.

HUMAN INTERFERENCE

Climate also affects people, though air conditioning and central heating now make it possible for us live in comfort almost anywhere in the world.

However, human activities are damaging our planet. Pollution is poisoning rivers and seas, while acid rain, caused by air pollution, is killing trees and acidifying lakes. The land is also harmed by such things as nuclear accidents and the dumping of toxic wastes.

Some regions have been overgrazed or so intensively farmed that once fertile areas have been turned into barren deserts. The clearance of tropical forests means that some plant and animal species are disappearing before scientists have had a chance to study them.

MOULDING THE LAND

Powerful forces inside the Earth buckle rock layers to form fold mountain ranges. But even as they rise, the forces of erosion wear them away. On mountain slopes, water freezes in cracks in rocks. Because ice occupies more space than the equivalent amount of water, this 'frost action' shatters rocks, and the fragments tumble downhill. Some end up on or inside moving glaciers. Other rocks are carried away by running water. The glaciers and streams not only trans- port rock fragments, but they also wear out valleys and so add to their load. The eroded material breaks down into fragments of sand, silt and mud, much of which reaches the sea, where it piles up on the sea floor in layers. These layers eventually become compacted into sedimentary rocks, such as sandstones and shales. These rocks may eventually be squeezed up again by a plate collision to form new fold mountains, so completing a natural cycle of mountain building and destruction.

MAJOR FACTORS AFFECTING WEATHERING

	WEATHERING RATE		
	←— SLOW		FAST —→
Mineral solubility	low (e.g. quartz)	moderate (e.g. feldspar)	high (e.g. calcite)
Rainfall	low	moderate	heavy
Temperature	cold	temperate	hot
Vegetation	sparse	moderate	lush
Soil cover	bare rock	thin to moderate soil	thick soil

Weathering is the breakdown and decay of rocks in situ. It may be mechanical (physical), chemical or biological.

Population

THE ADVENT OF agriculture around 10,000 years ago had a great impact on human society. People abandoned their nomadic way of life and settled in farming villages. With plenty of food, some people were able to pursue jobs unconnected with farming. These developments eventually led to rapid social changes, including the growth of early cities and the emergence of civilization.

THE POPULATION EXPLOSION

The social changes had a major effect on the world's population, which rose from around 8 million in 8000 BC, to about 300 million by AD 1000. The rate of population increase then began to accelerate further, passing the 1 billion mark in the 19th century, the 2 billion mark in the 1920s, and the 4 billion mark in the 1970s.

Today the world has a population of about 5.8 billion and experts forecast that it will reach around 11 billion by 2075. However, they then predict that it will stabilize or even decline a little towards 2100. Most of the expected increase will occur in developing countries in Africa, Asia and Latin America.

> Many cities in India, such as Bombay (also known as Mumbai), have grown so quickly that they lack sufficient jobs and homes for their populations. As a result, slums now cover large areas.

POPULATION PYRAMIDS

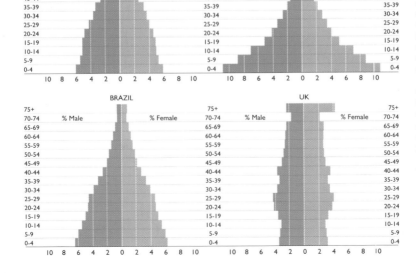

> The population pyramids compare the average age structures for the world with those of three countries at varying stages of development. Kenya, a developing country, had, until recently, one of the world's highest annual rates of population increase. As a result, a high proportion of Kenyans are aged under 15. Brazil has a much more balanced economy than Kenya's, and a lower rate of population increase. This is reflected in a higher proportion of people aged over 40. The UK is a developed country with a low rate of population growth, 0.3% per year between 1985–95, much lower than the world average of 1.6%. The UK has a far higher proportion of people over 60 years old.

The World's Largest Cities ▾

By early next century, for the first time ever, the majority of the world's population will live in cities. Below is a list of the 20 largest cities (in thousands) based on 1996 figures.

1	Tokyo, *Japan*	26,836
2	São Paulo, *Brazil*	16,417
3	New York, *USA*	16,329
4	Mexico City, *Mexico*	15,643
5	Bombay (Mumbai), *India*	15,093
6	Shanghai, *China*	15,082
7	Los Angeles, *USA*	12,410
8	Beijing, *China*	12,362
9	Calcutta, *India*	11,673
10	Seoul, *South Korea*	11,641
11	Jakarta, *Indonesia*	11,500
12	Buenos Aires, *Argentina*	10,990
13	Tianjin, *China*	10,687
14	Osaka, *Japan*	10,601
15	Lagos, *Nigeria*	10,287
16	Rio de Janeiro, *Brazil*	9,888
17	Delhi, *India*	9,882
18	Karachi, *Pakistan*	9,863
19	Cairo, *Egypt*	9,656
20	Paris, *France*	9,469

This population explosion has been caused partly by better medical care, which has reduced child mortality and increased the average life expectancy at birth throughout the world. But it has also created problems. In some developing countries, nearly half of the people are children. They make no contribution to the economy, but they require costly education and health services. In richer countries, the high proportion of retired people is also a strain on the economy.

By the late 20th century, for the first time in 10,000 years, the majority of people are no longer forced to rely on farming for their livelihood. Instead, nearly half of them live in cities where many of them enjoy a high standard of living. But rapid urbanization also creates problems, especially in the developing world, with the growth of slums and an increase in homelessness and crime.

POPULATION BY CONTINENT

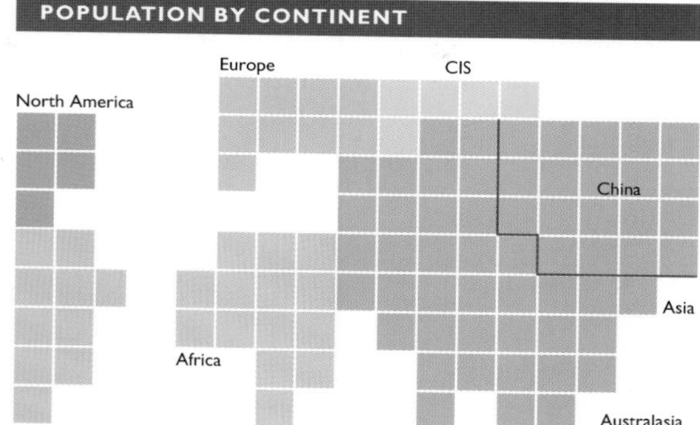

> The cartogram shows the populations of the continents in a diagrammatic way, with each square representing 1% of the world's population. For example, North America is represented by five squares, which means that it contains about 5% of the world's population, while Asia, the most populous continent even excluding the Asian part of the former USSR, is represented by 56 squares (China accounting for 19 of these). By contrast, Australasia is represented by less than half of a square because it contains only 0.45% of the world's population.

WORLD DEMOGRAPHIC EXTREMES

Fastest growing population; average annual % growth (1992–2000)		Slowest growing population; average annual % growth (1992–2000)	
1	Nigeria 5.09	1	Kuwait .... -1.39
2	Afghanistan 4.21	2	Ireland .... -0.24
3	Ivory Coast 3.54	3	St Kitts & Nevis ...... -0.22
4	Oman 3.52	4	Bulgaria .... -0.13
5	Syria 3.51	5	Latvia .... -0.10

Youngest populations; % aged under 15 years (1995)		Oldest populations; % aged over 60 years (1995)	
1	Togo 49.8	1	Sweden 22.1
2	Niger 48.7	2	Norway 21.1
3	Syria 48.5	=	Italy 21.1
4	Benin 48.3	=	United Kingdom 21.1
=	Burkina Faso 48.3	5	Germany 20.8

Highest urban populations; % of population in urban areas (1995)		Lowest urban populations; % of population in urban areas (1995)	
1	Singapore 100.0	1	Bhutan 6.0
=	Bermuda 100.0	=	Rwanda 6.0
3	Macau 99.0	3	Burundi 8.0
4	Kuwait 97.0	4	Ethiopia 13.0
5	Hong Kong 95.0	=	Uganda 13.0

Most male populations; number of men per 100 women		Most female populations; number of women per 100 men	
1	United Arab Emirates 206.7	1	Russia 110.0
2	Qatar 167.2	2	Austria 108.8
3	Bahrain 145.3	=	Somalia 108.8
4	Kuwait 128.3	4	Germany 108.0
5	Saudi Arabia 119.1	5	Barbados 107.9

Languages & Religions

ALL PEOPLE BELONG to one species, *Homo sapiens*, but within that species is a great diversity of cultures. Two of the main factors that give people an identity and sense of kinship with their neighbours are language and religion.

Definitions of languages vary and as a result estimates of the total number of languages in existence range from about 3,000 to 6,000. Many languages are spoken only by a small number of people. Papua New Guinea, for example, has only 4.2 million people but 869 languages.

The world's languages are grouped into families, of which the Indo-European is the largest. Indo-European languages are spoken in a zone stretching from

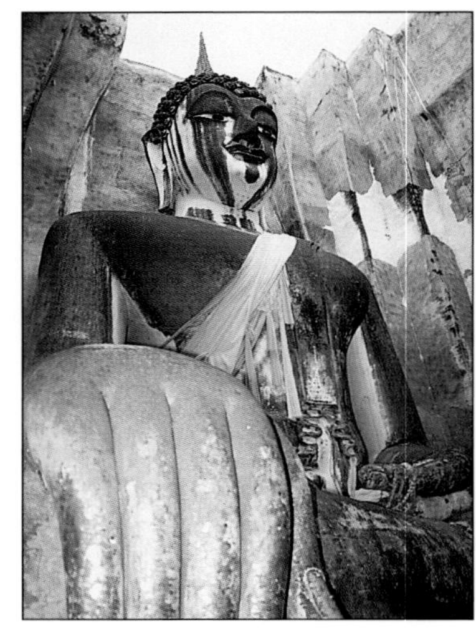

> Religion is a major force in South-east Asia. About 94% of the people in Thailand are Buddhists, and more than 40% of men over the age of 20 spend some time, if only a few weeks, serving as Buddhist monks. Confucianism, Islam, Hinduism, and Christianity are also practised in Thailand.

THE WORLD'S LANGUAGES

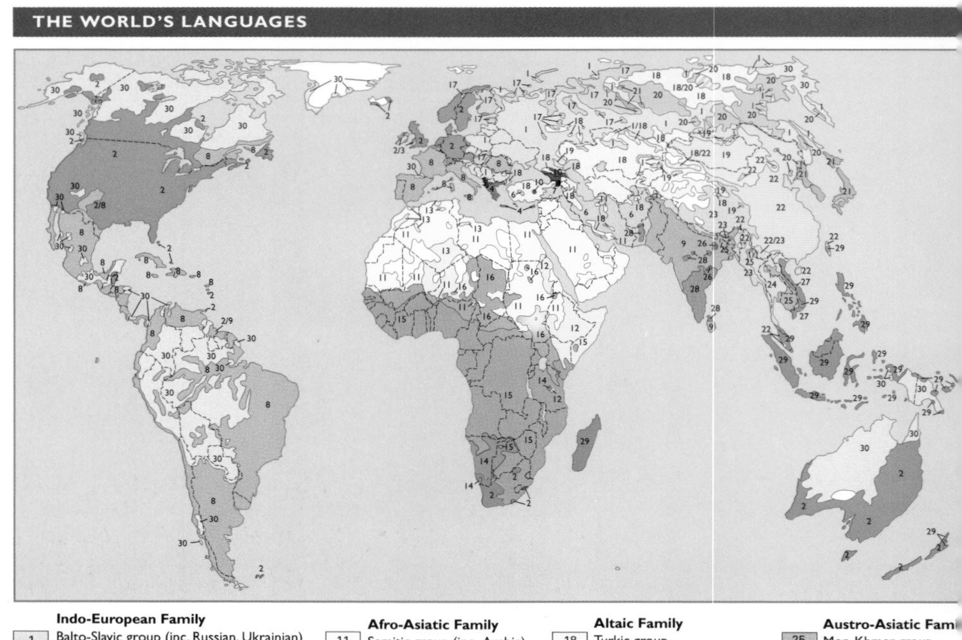

Indo-European Family
1. Balto-Slavic group (inc. Russian, Ukrainian)
2. Germanic group (inc. English, German)
3. Celtic group
4. Greek
5. Albanian
6. Iranian group
7. Armenian
8. Romance group (inc. Spanish, Portuguese, French, Italian)
9. Indo-Aryan group (inc. Hindi, Bengali, Urdu, Punjabi, Marathi)
10. **Caucasian Family**

Afro-Asiatic Family
11. Semitic group (inc. Arabic)
12. Kushitic group
13. Berber group

14. **Khoisan Family**

15. **Niger-Congo Family**

16. **Nilo-Saharan Family**

17. **Uralic Family**

Altaic Family
18. Turkic group
19. Mongolian group
20. Tungus-Manchu group
21. Japanese & Korean

Sino-Tibetan Family
22. Sinitic (Chinese) languages
23. Tibetic-Burmic languages

24. **Tai Family**

Austro-Asiatic Family
25. Mon-Khmer group
26. Munda group
27. Vietnamese

28. **Dravidian Family** (inc. Telugu, Tamil)

29. **Austronesian Family** (inc. Malay-Indonesian)

30. **Other Languages**

NATIVE SPEAKERS

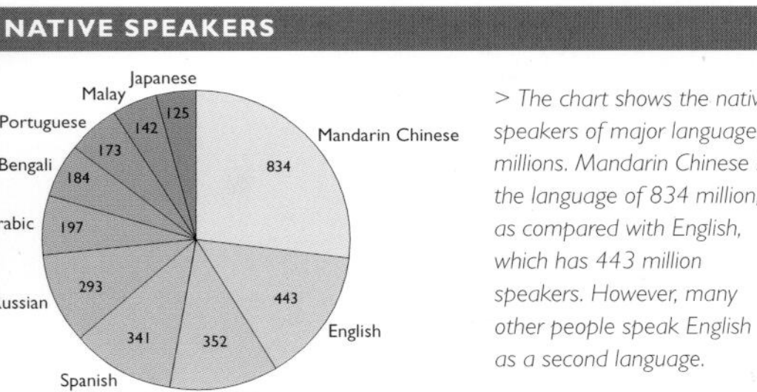

> The chart shows the native speakers of major languages in millions. Mandarin Chinese is the language of 834 million, as compared with English, which has 443 million speakers. However, many other people speak English as a second language.

Religious Adherents ▼	
The world's major religions, with the number of adherents in millions (latest available year)	
Christian	1,669
Roman Catholic	952
Protestant	337
Orthodox	162
Anglican	70
Other Christian	148
Muslim	945
Sunni	841
Shia	104
Hindu	663
Buddhist	312
Chinese folk	172
Ethnic/local	92
Jewish	18
Sikh	17

Europe, through south-western Asia into the Indian subcontinent. In addition, during the period of European colonization, they spread throughout North and South America and also to Australia and New Zealand. Today about two-fifths of the world's people speak an Indo-European language, as compared with one-fifth who speak a language belonging to the Sino-Tibetan language.

The Sino-Tibetan language family includes Chinese, which is spoken as a first language by more people than any other. English is the second most important first language, but it is more important than Chinese in international affairs and business, because so many people speak it as a second language.

RELIGIONS

Christianity is the religion of about a third of the world's population. Other major religions include Buddhism, Islam, Hinduism, Judaism, Chinese folk religions and traditional tribal religions.

Religion is a powerful force in human society, establishing the ethics by which people live. It has inspired great music, painting, architecture and literature, yet at the same time religion and language have contributed to conflict between people throughout history. Even today, the cause of many of the conflicts around the world are partly the result of linguistic and religious differences.

> Most languages have alphabetic systems of writing. The Greek alphabet uses some letters from the Roman alphabet, such as the A and B. Russians use the cyrillic alphabet, which is based partly on Roman and partly on Greek letters. The Cyrillic alphabet is also used for Bulgarian and some central Asian languages. Serbs use either the Cyrillic or the Roman alphabet to write Serbo-Croat.

ALPHABETS

The Greek Alphabet

Α	Β	Γ	Δ	Ε	Ζ	Η	Θ	Ι	Κ	Λ	Μ	Ν	Ξ	Ο	Π	Ρ	Σ	Τ	Υ	Φ	Χ	Ψ	Ω
A	V/B	G	D	E	Z	E	TH	I	K	L	M	N	X	O	P	R	S	T	Y	F	CH	PS	O

The Cyrillic Alphabet

А	Б	В	Г	Д	Е	Ё	Ж	З	И	Й	К	Л	М	Н	О	П	Р	С	Т	У	Ф	Х	Ц	Ч	Ш	Щ	Ю	Я
A	B	V	G	D	E	YO	ZH	Z	I	Y	K	L	M	N	O	P	R	S	T	U	F	KH	TS	CH	SH	SHCH	YU	YA

Agriculture & Industry

BECAUSE IT SUPPLIES so many basic human needs, agriculture is the world's leading economic activity. But its relative importance varies from place to place. In most developing countries, agriculture employs more people than any other activity. For example, the diagram at the bottom of this page shows that more than 90% of the people of Nepal are employed in farming.

Many farmers in developing countries live at subsistence level, producing barely enough to supply the basic needs of their families. Alongside the subsistence sector, some developing countries produce one or two cash crops that they export. Dependence on cash crops is precarious: when world commodity prices fall, the country is plunged into financial crisis.

In developed countries, by contrast, the proportion of people engaged in agriculture has declined over the last 200

> The cultivation of rice, one of the world's most important foods, is still carried out by hand in many areas. But the introduction of new strains of rice has greatly increased yields.

years. Yet, by using farm machinery and scientific methods, notably the selective breeding of crops and animals, the production of food has soared. For example, although agriculture employs only 3% of its workers, the United States is one of the world's top food producers.

INDUSTRIALIZATION

The Industrial Revolution began in Britain in the late 18th century and soon spread to mainland Europe and other parts of the world. Industries first arose in areas with supplies of coal, iron ore and cheap water power. But later, after oil and gas came into use as industrial fuels, factories could be set up almost anywhere.

The growth of manufacturing led to an increase in the number of industrial cities. The flight from the land was accompanied by an increase in efficiency in agriculture. As a result, manufacturing replaced agriculture as the chief source of

EMPLOYMENT

The number of workers employed in manufacturing for every 100 workers engaged in agriculture (latest available year)

- Under 10
- 10 – 50
- 50 – 100
- 100 – 200
- 200 – 500
- Over 500

DIVISION OF EMPLOYMENT

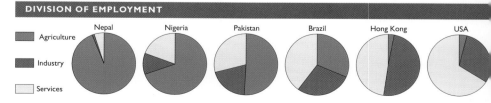

- Agriculture
- Industry
- Services

Nepal Nigeria Pakistan Brazil Hong Kong USA

PATTERNS OF PRODUCTION

The table shows how the economy breaks down (in terms of the Gross Domestic Product for 1995) in a selection of industrialized countries. Agriculture remains important in some countries, though its percentage share has steadily declined since the start of the Industrial Revolution. Industry, especially manufacturing, accounts for a higher proportion, but service industries account for the greatest percentage of the GDP in most developed nations. The figures for Manufacturing are shown separately from Industry because of their importance in the economy.

Country	Agriculture	Industry (excl. manufacturing)	Manufacturing	Services
Australia	3%	13%	15%	68%
Austria	2%	9%	26%	62%
Brazil	10%	12%	25%	53%
Denmark	4%	7%	20%	69%
Finland	5%	3%	28%	64%
France	3%	7%	22%	69%
Germany	1%	11%	27%	61%
Greece	18%	12%	20%	50%
Hungary	6%	9%	19%	66%
Ireland	8%	7%	3%	82%
Italy	3%	7%	25%	65%
Japan	2%	17%	24%	57%
Kuwait	0%	46%	9%	45%
Mexico	8%	8%	20%	63%
Netherlands	4%	9%	19%	68%
Norway	3%	21%	14%	62%
Singapore	0%	9%	28%	63%
Sweden	2%	5%	26%	67%
UK	2%	8%	25%	65%
USA	2%	9%	22%	67%

income and employment in industrialized countries and rapidly widened the wealth gap between them and the poorer non-industrialized countries whose economies continued to rely on agriculture.

SERVICE INDUSTRIES

Eventually, the manufacturing sector became so efficient that it could supply most of the things that people wanted to buy. Trade between industrialized countries also increased, so widening the choice for consumers in the developed world. These factors led to a further change in the economies of developed countries, namely a reduction in the relative importance of manufacturing and the growth of the service sector.

Service industries include such activities as government, transport, insurance, finance, and even the writing of computer software. In the United States, service industries now account for about two-thirds of the Gross National Product (GNP), while in Japan they account for more than half. But the wealth of both countries still rests on their massive industrial production.

AGRICULTURE

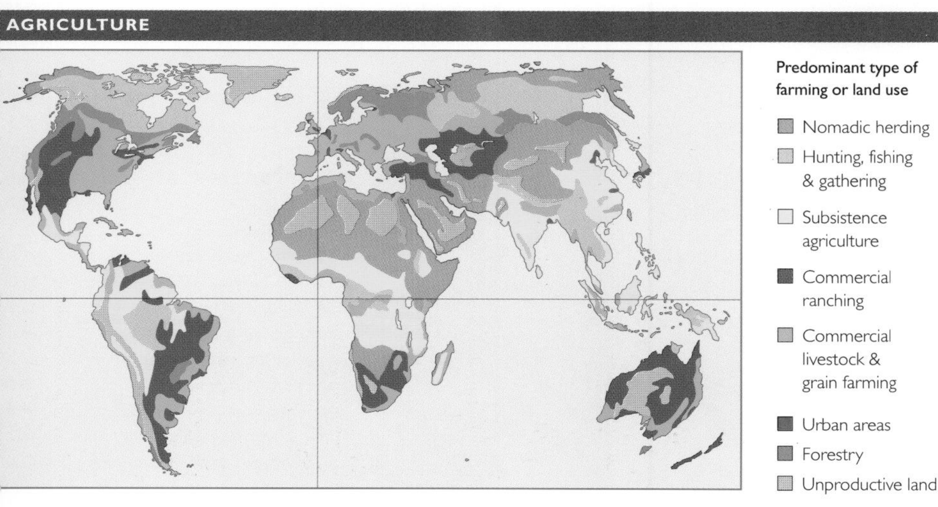

Predominant type of farming or land use

- Nomadic herding
- Hunting, fishing & gathering
- Subsistence agriculture
- Commercial ranching
- Commercial livestock & grain farming
- Urban areas
- Forestry
- Unproductive land

Trade & Commerce

TRADE HAS ALWAYS been an important human activity. It has widened the choice of goods available in any country, lowered prices and generally raised living standards. People regard any growth of world trade as a sign that the world economy is healthy, whereas a decline indicates a world recession.

Exports and imports are of two main kinds. Visible imports and exports include primary products, such as food and manufactures. Invisible imports and exports include services, such as banking, insurance, interest on loans, and money spent by tourists.

World trade, both visible and invisible, is dominated by the 29 members of the OECD (Organization for Economic Development), which includes the world's top trading nations, namely the United States, Japan, Germany, France, Italy and the United Kingdom, as well as Australia, New Zealand, Canada and Mexico. Hungary, Poland and South Korea joined in 1996.

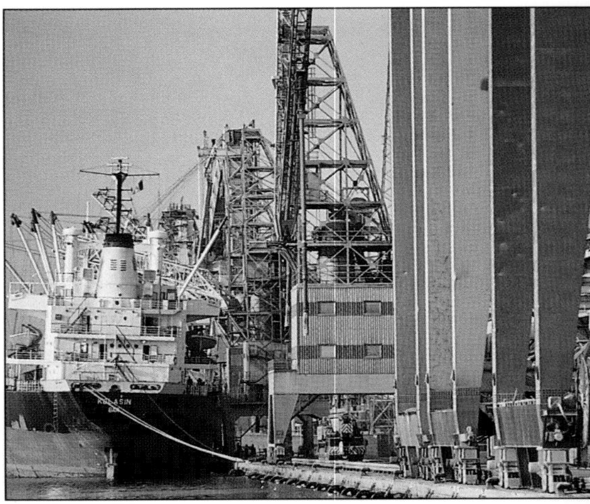

> The new port of the historic Italian city of Ravenna is linked to the Adriatic Sea by a canal. The port has large oil refining and petrochemical industries.

CHANGING EXPORTS

From the late 19th century to the 1950s primary products, including farm products, minerals, natural fibres, timber and, in the latter part of this period, oi

The World's Largest Businesses ▾

The world's largest businesses in 1996 by market capitalization, in billions of US$. Market capitalization is the number of shares the company has, multiplied by the market price of those shares.

1	General Electric, *USA*	150.3
2	Royal Dutch Shell, *Neths/UK*	135.3
3	Coca-Cola, *USA*	126.9
4	Nippon Telegraph & Tel., *Japan*	119.6
5	Exxon, *USA*	103.4
6	Bank of Tokyo-Mitsubishi, *Japan*	102.7
7	Toyota Motor Corporation, *Japan*	97.9
8	Merck, *USA*	85.1
9	AT & T, *USA*	84.1
10	Intel, *USA*	78.7
11	Microsoft, *USA*	78.5
12	Philip Morris, *USA*	73.6
13	Roche Holding, *Switzerland*	72.0
14	Johnson & Johnson, *USA*	68.3
15	Procter & Gamble, *USA*	66.8
16	Intl Business Machines, *USA*	65.7
17	Wal-Mart Stores, *USA*	60.5
18	Sumitomo Bank, *Japan*	58.9
19	British Petroleum, *UK*	58.2
20	Industrial Bank of Japan, *Japan*	57.6

DEBT AND AID

International debtors and the development aid they receive (latest available year)

The provision of aid by rich countries to developing countries is part of international politics. But the grants made to developing countries are often dwarfed by the burden of debt which the countries are expected to repay. In 1990, the debts of Mozambique, one of the world's poorest countries, were estimated to be 75 times its entire earnings from exports.

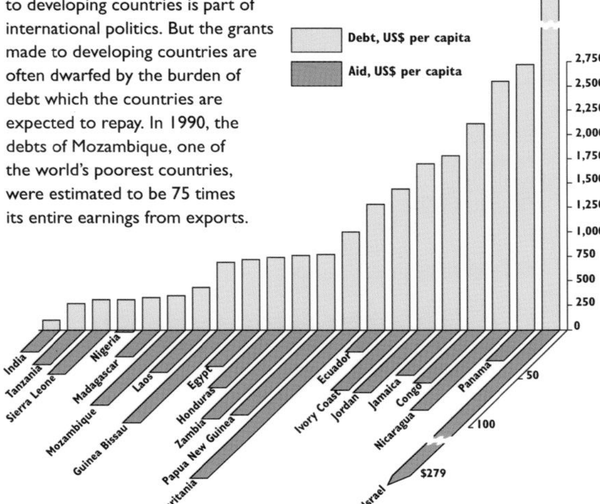

$4,853

Debt, US$ per capita
Aid, US$ per capita

2,750
2,500
2,250
2,000
1,750
1,500
1,250
1,000
750
500
250
0

India, Tanzania, Sierra Leone, Nigeria, Madagascar, Mozambique, Guinea Bissau, Laos, Honduras, Egypt, Zambia, Papua New Guinea, Mauritania, Jordan, Ivory Coast, Ecuador, Nicaragua, Jamaica, Congo, Panama, Israel

$279
50
100

TRADED PRODUCTS

The character of world trade has greatly changed in the last 50 years. While primary products were once the leading commodities, world trade is now dominated by manufactured products. Cars are the single most valuable traded product, followed by vehicle parts and engines. The next most valuable goods are high-tech products such as data processing (computer) equipment, telecommunications equipment, and transistors. Other items include aircraft, paper and board, trucks, measuring and control instruments, and electrical machinery. Trade in most manufactured products is dominated by the OECD countries. For example, the leading vehicle exporter is Japan, which became the world's leading car manufacturer in the 1980s. The United States, Germany, the United Kingdom, France and Japan lead in the production of data processing equipment.

and natural gas, dominated world trade.

Many developing countries still remain dependent on exporting mineral ores, fossil fuels, or farm products such as cocoa or coffee whose prices fluctuate according to demand. But today, manufactured goods are the most important commodities in world trade. The OECD nations lead the world in exporting manufactured goods, though they are being challenged by a group of 'tiger economies' in eastern Asia, notably Singapore, Hong Kong and Taiwan. Other rapidly industrializing countries in Asia include Thailand, Malaysia and the Philippines. The generally cheap labour costs of these countries have enabled them to produce manufactured goods for export at prices lower than those charged for goods made in Western countries.

Private companies carry on most of the world's trade. The small proportion handled by governments decreased recently with the collapse of Communist regimes in eastern Europe and the former Soviet Union.

SHARE OF WORLD TRADE

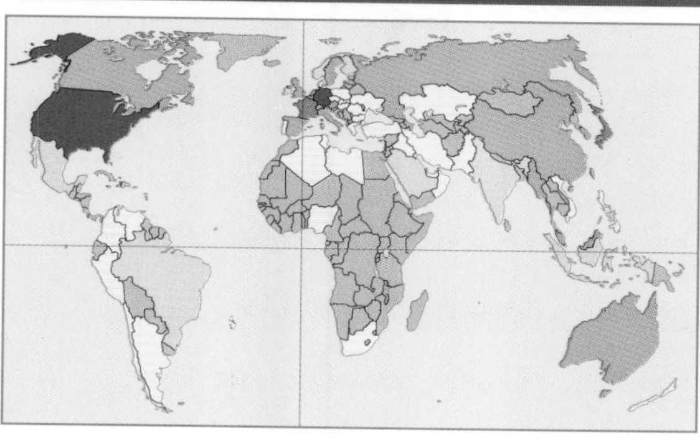

Percentage share of total world exports by value (1995)

- ■ Over 10%
- ■ 1 – 5%
- □ 0.1 – 0.5%
- ■ 5 – 10%
- □ 0.5 – 1%
- ■ Under 0.1%

DEPENDENCE ON TRADE

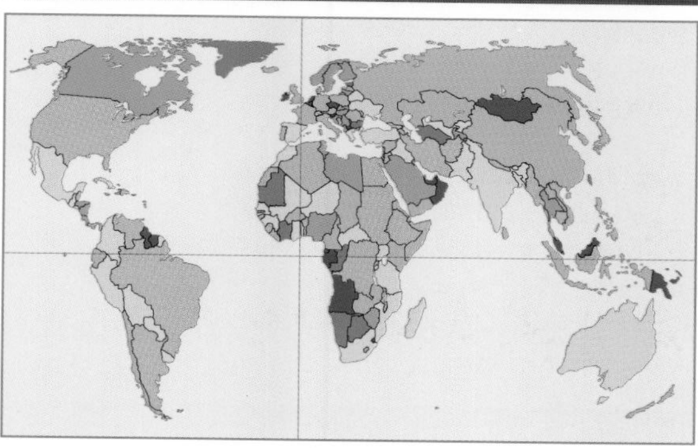

Value of exports as a percentage of Gross National Product (1995)

- ■ Over 50% GNP
- ■ 30 – 40% GNP
- □ 10 – 20% GNP
- ■ 40 – 50% GNP
- ■ 20 – 30% GNP
- ■ Under 10% GNP

Trade in Oil ▾

Major world trade in oil in millions of tonnes (1995)

Middle East to Asia (not Japan)	250	Mexico to USA	53
Middle East to Japan	204	W. Africa to W. Europe	42
Middle East to W. Europe	175	Western Europe to USA	37
S. and C. America to USA	111	Middle East to Africa	34
N. Africa to W. Europe	98	Middle East to South and Central America	33
CIS to Western Europe	79		
Middle East to USA	79	CIS to Central Europe	27
Canada to USA	65	Western Europe to Canada	17
West Africa to USA	63	*Total world trade*	1,815

Transport & Travel

ABOUT 200 YEARS ago, most people never travelled far from their birthplace. But adventurous travellers can now reach almost any part of the world.

Transport is concerned with moving goods and people around by land, water and air. Land transport was once laborious, and was dependent on pack animals or animal-drawn vehicles. But during the Industrial Revolution, railways played a vital role in moving bulky materials and equipment required by factories. They were also important in the opening up and development of remote areas around the world in North and South America, Africa, Asia and Australia.

Today, however, motor vehicles have taken over many of the functions once served by railways. Unlike railways, motor vehicles provide a door-to-door service and, through the invention of heavy trucks, they can also carry large loads. In the mid-1990s, about 90% of inland freight in Britain was carried by road, while car and van travel accounted for 86% of passenger travel, as compared with 6% by buses and coaches, 5% by rail and less than 1% by air.

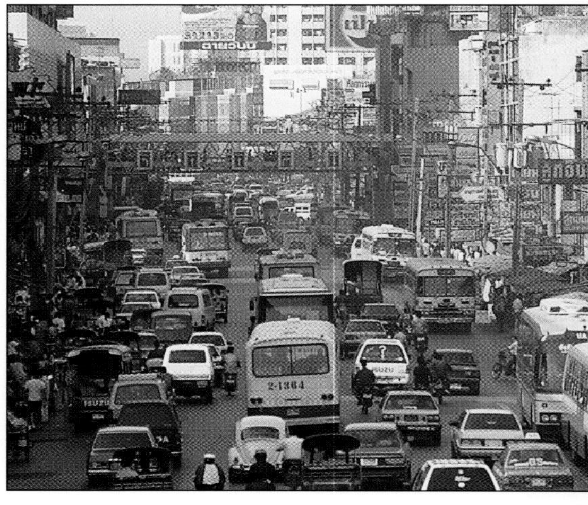

> Traffic jams and vehicle pollution have affected cities throughout the world. Many of Bangkok's beautiful old canals have been filled in to provide extra roads to cope with the enormous volume of traffic in the city.

TRAVEL & TOURISM

Sea transport, which now employs huge bulk grain carriers, oil tankers and container ships, still carries most of the world's trade. But since the late 1950s fewer passengers have travelled overseas by sea, because air travel is so much faster, though many former ocean liners now operate successfully as cruise ships.

Air travel has played a major part in the rapid growth of the tourist industry.

AIR TRAVEL

Number of passenger kilometres flown, in millions (1994). Passenger kilometres are the number of passengers (both international and domestic) multiplied by the distance flown by each passenger from airport of origin.

- ■ Over 100,000
- ▨ 10,000 – 50,000
- ☐ 500 – 1,000
- ▨ 50,000 – 100,000
- ☐ 1,000 – 10,000
- ☐ Under 500

The World's Busiest Airports ▾		
Total number of passengers, in thousands (1997)		
1	O'Hare Intl., *Chicago*	70,295
2	Hartsfield Atlanta Int., *Atlanta*	68,206
3	Dallas/Fort Worth Int., *Dallas*	60,489
4	Los Angeles Intl., *Los Angeles*	60,143
5	Heathrow, *London*	57,975
6	Haneda, *Tokyo*	49,302
7	San Francisco Intl., *San Francisco*	40,500
8	Frankfurt/Main, *Frankfurt*	40,263
9	Kimpo Intl., *Seoul*	36,757
10	Charles de Gaulle, *Paris*	35,294
11	Denver Intl., *Denver*	34,973
12	Miami Intl., *Miami*	34,533
13	Schiphol, *Amsterdam*	31,570
14	Metro Wayne County, *Detroit*	31,521
15	John F. Kennedy Intl., *New York*	31,229

The Longest Rail Networks ▾

Extent of rail network, in thousands of kilometres (1995)

1	USA	235.7
2	Russia	87.4
3	India	62.7
4	China	54.6
5	Germany	41.7
6	Australia	35.8
7	Argentina	34.2
8	France	31.9
9	Mexico	26.5
10	South Africa	26.3

which accounted for 7.5% of world trade by the mid-1990s. Travel and tourism have greatly increased people's understanding and knowledge of the world, especially in the OECD countries, which account for about 8% of world tourism.

Some developing countries have large tourist industries which have provided employment and led to improvements in roads and other facilities. In some cases, tourism plays a vital role in the economy. For example, in Kenya, tourism provides more income than any other activity apart from the production and sale of coffee. However, too many tourists can damage fragile environments, such as the wildlife and scenery in national parks. Tourism can also harm local cultures.

THE IMPORTANCE OF TOURISM

Nations receiving the most from tourism, millions of US$ (1996)			Fastest growing tourist destinations, % change in receipts (1994–95)		
1	USA	64,400	1	South Korea	49%
2	Spain	28,400	2	Czech Republic	27%
3	France	28,200	3	India	21%
4	Italy	27,300	4	Russia	19%
5	UK	20,400	5	Philippines	18%
6	Austria	15,100	6	Turkey	17%
7	Germany	13,200	7	Thailand	15%
8	Hong Kong	11,200	8	Poland	13%
9	China	10,500	9	China	12%
10	Switzerland	9,900	10	Israel	12%

Number of tourist arrivals, millions (1995)			Overseas travellers to the USA, thousands (1997)		
1	France	60,584	1	Canada	13,900
2	Spain	45,125	2	Mexico	12,370
3	USA	44,730	3	Japan	4,640
4	Italy	29,184	4	UK	3,350
5	China	23,368	5	Germany	1,990
6	UK	22,700	6	France	1,030
7	Hungary	22,087	7	Taiwan	885
8	Mexico	19,870	8	Venezuela	860
9	Poland	19,225	9	South Korea	800
10	Austria	17,750	10	Brazil	785

THE WORLD'S VEHICLES

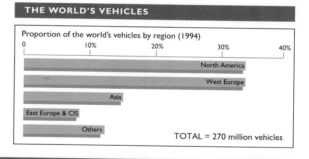

Proportion of the world's vehicles by region (1994)

North America
West Europe
Asia
East Europe & CIS
Others

TOTAL = 270 million vehicles

CAR OWNERSHIP

Number of people per car (1994)

- ■ Over 1,000
- ■ 500 – 1,000
- ▨ 100 – 500
- □ 25 – 100
- □ 5 – 25
- ▨ Under 5

Two-thirds of the world's vehicles are found in the developed countries of Europe and North America. Car ownership is also high in Australia and New Zealand, as well as in Japan, the world's leading car exporter. Car transport is the most convenient form of passenger travel, but air pollution caused by exhaust fumes is a serious problem in many large cities.

International Organizations

In the late 1980s, people rejoiced at the collapse of Communist regimes in eastern Europe and the former Soviet Union, because this brought to an end the Cold War, a long period of hostility between East and West. But hope of a new era of peace was shattered when ethnic and religious rivalries led to civil war in Yugoslavia and in parts of the former Soviet Union.

In order to help maintain peace, many governments have formed international organizations to increase co-operation. Some, such as NATO (North Atlantic

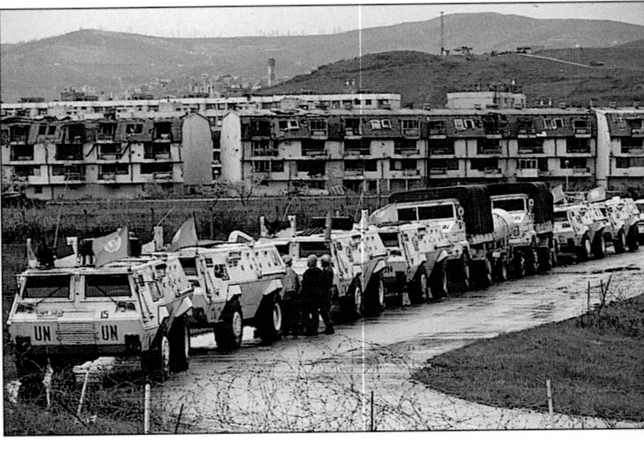

> In the early 1990s, the United Nations peacekeeping mission worked to end the civil war in Bosnia-Herzegovina and also to bring aid to civilians affected by the fighting.

Treaty Organization), are defence alliances, while others aim to encourage economic and social co-operation. Some organizations such as the Red Cross are non-governmental organizations, or NGOs.

UNITED NATIONS

The United Nations, the chief international organization, was formed in October 1945 and now has 185 member countries. The only independent nations that are not members are Kiribati, Nauru, Switzerland, Taiwan, Tonga, Tuvalu and the Vatican City.

UN Contributions ▾

In 1996–97, the top ten contributing countries to the UN budget, which was US$2.6 billion, were as follows:

1	USA	25.0%
2	Japan	15.4%
3	Germany	9.0%
4	France	6.4%
5	UK	5.3%
6	Italy	5.2%
7	Russia	4.5%
8	Canada	3.1%
9	Spain	2.4%
10	Brazil	1.6%

THE UNITED NATIONS

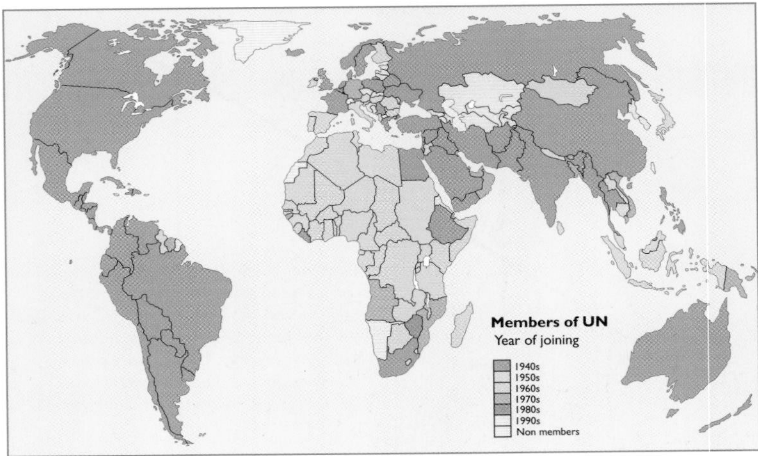

Members of UN
Year of joining

1940s
1950s
1960s
1970s
1980s
1990s
Non members

> The membership of the UN had risen from 51 in 1945 to 185 by the end of 1996. The first big period of expansion came in the 1960s when many former colonies achieved their independence. The membership again expanded rapidly in the 1990s when new countries were formed from the former Soviet Union and Yugoslavia. The most recent addition, Palau, is a former US trust territory in the Pacific Ocean and joined in 1994.

The United Nations was formed at the end of World War II to promote peace, international co-operation and security, and to help solve economic, social, cultural and humanitarian problems. It promotes human rights and freedom and is a forum for negotiations between nations.

The main organs of the UN are the General Assembly, the Security Council, the Economic and Social Council, the Trusteeship Council, the International Court of Justice and the Secretariat.

The UN also operates 14 specialized agencies concerned with particular issues, such as agriculture, education, working conditions, communications and health. For example, UNICEF (the United Nations International Children's Fund), established in 1946 to deliver post-war relief to children, now aims to provide basic health care to children and mothers worldwide. The ILO (International Labour Organization) seeks to improve working conditions, while the FAO (Food and Agricultural Organization) aims at improving the production and distribution of food. The WTO (World Trade Organization) was set up as recently as January 1995 to succeed GATT (General Agreements on Tariffs and Trade).

THE UNITED NATIONS

THE GENERAL ASSEMBLY is the meeting of all member nations every September under a newly-elected president to discuss issues affecting development, peace and security.

THE SECURITY COUNCIL has 15 members, of which five are permanent. It is responsible for maintaining international peace.

THE SECRETARIAT consists of the staff and employees of the UN, including the Secretary-General (appointed for a five-year term), who is the UN's chief administrator.

THE ECONOMIC & SOCIAL COUNCIL works with the specialized agencies to implement UN policies on improving living standards, health, cultural and educational co-operation.

THE TRUSTEESHIP COUNCIL was designed to bring several dependencies to independence. This work is now complete.

THE INTERNATIONAL COURT OF JUSTICE, or World Court, deals with legal problems and helps to settle disputes. Its headquarters are at The Hague, in the Netherlands.

UN DEPARTMENTS

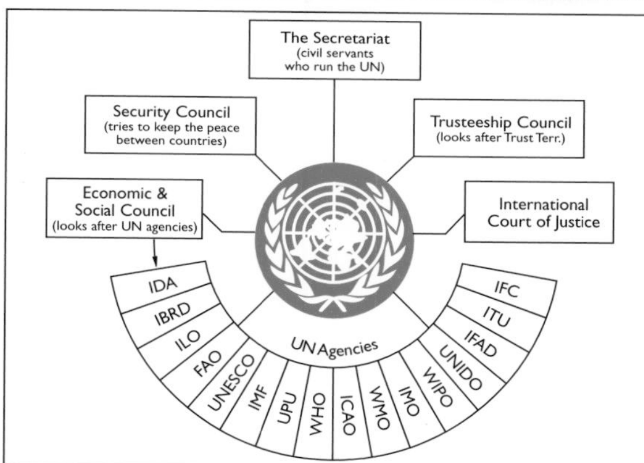

UN PEACEKEEPING MISSIONS

The United Nations tries to resolve international disputes in several ways. It sends unarmed observer missions to monitor cease-fires or supervise troop withdrawals, and the Security Council members also send peacekeeping forces.

This first of these forces was sent in 1948 to supervise the cease-fire between Arabs and Jews in disputed parts of Palestine and, since then, it has undertaken more than 30 other missions. The 'Blue Berets', as the 25,650 UN troops are called, must be impartial in any dispute

and they can fire only in self-defence. Hence, they can operate only with the support of both sides, which leaves them open to criticism when they are unable to prevent violence by intervening.

By the mid-1990s, the UN was involved in 15 world conflicts, was policing the boundary in partitioned Cyprus, and was seeking to enforce a peace agreement in Angola after 20 years of civil war. Other UN missions were in Tajikistan, Georgia, the Israeli-occupied Golan Heights, Haiti, Kuwait, southern Lebanon, the India–

Pakistan border, Liberia, Mozambique, Western Sahara and the former Yugoslavia. A force known as UNPROFOR (UN Protection Force) had been operating in Bosnia-Herzegovina and, by 1995, it accounted for 60% of the total UN peacekeeping budget. In February 1996, the Secretary-General of the UN approved the setting up of a new force, the United Nations Mission in Bosnia-Herzegovina (UNMIBH). Its main objective was to help create the right climate for the elections held in September 1996.

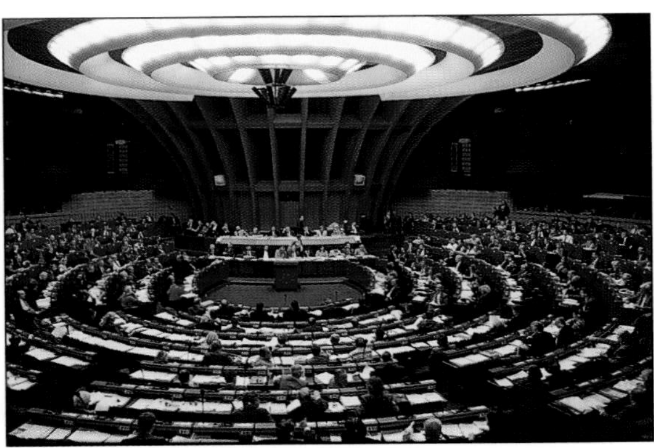

cludes the countries of East and South-east Asia, as well as North America, plus Australia, New Zealand and Chile. APEC aims to create a free trade zone by 2020.

Together the United States, Canada and Mexico form NAFTA (North American Free Trade Agreement), which aims at eliminating trade barriers within 15 years of its foundation on 1 January 1994. Other economic groupings link the countries of Latin America.

Another economic group with more limited aims is OPEC (Organization of Petroleum Exporting Countries). It works to unify policies concerned with the sale of petroleum on world markets.

The central aim of the Colombo Plan is to provide economic development assistance for South and South-east Asia.

ECONOMIC ORGANIZATIONS

> *The European Parliament, one of the branches of the EU, consists of 626 members. The number of members for each country is based mainly on population.*

Over the last 40 years, many countries have joined common markets aimed at eliminating trade barriers and encouraging the free movement of workers and capital.

The best known of these is the European Union. Other organizations include ASEAN (the Association of South-east Asian Nations), which aims at reducing trade barriers between its nine members: Brunei, Burma, Indonesia, Laos, Malaysia, the Philippines, Singapore, Thailand and Vietnam.

APEC (the Asia-Pacific Co-operation Group) was founded in 1989 and in-

OTHER ORGANIZATIONS

Some organizations exist for consultation on matters of common interest. The Commonwealth of Nations grew out of the links created by the British Empire, while the OAS (Organization of American States) works to increase understanding throughout the Western hemisphere. The OAU (Organization of

THE EUROPEAN UNION

At the end of World War II (1939–45), many Europeans wanted to end the ancient enmities that had caused such destruction and rebuild the shattered continent. It was in this mood that Belgium, France, West Germany, Italy, Luxembourg and the Netherlands signed the Treaty of Paris in 1951. This set up the European Coal and Steel Community (ECSC), the forerunner of the European Union.

In 1957, through the Treaty of Rome, the same six countries created the European Economic Community (EEC) and the European Atomic Community (EURATOM). In 1967, the ECSC, the EEC and EURATOM merged to form the single European Community (EC).

Another economic group, the European Free Trade Association (EFTA), was set up in 1960 by seven countries: Austria, Denmark, Norway, Portugal, Sweden, Switzerland, and the United Kingdom. However, Denmark, Ireland and the UK left to become members of the EC in 1973, followed by Greece in 1981, Spain and Portugal in 1986, and Austria, Finland and Sweden in 1995. The expansion of the EC to 15 members left EFTA with just four members: Iceland, Liechtenstein, Norway and Switzerland.

In 1993, following the signing of the Maastricht Treaty, the EC was reconstituted as the European Union (EU). The aims of the EU include economic and monetary union, a single currency for all 15 countries, and closer co-operation on foreign and security policies and also on home affairs. This step has led to a debate. Some people would like the EU to develop into a federal Europe, but others fear that this would lead to a loss of national identity. Another matter of importance is the future enlargement of the EU. By 1995, formal applications for membership had been received from Turkey, Malta, Cyprus, Poland, Hungary, Slovakia and Romania. Other possible members include the Czech Republic, Estonia, Latvia and Lithuania.

AUSTRALIA'S NEW ROLE

Most of the people who settled in Australia between 1788 and the mid-20th century came from the British Isles. However, the strong ties between Australia and Britain were weakened after Britain joined the European Community in 1973. Since 1973, many Australians have argued that their world position has changed and that they are part of a Pacific community of nations, rather than an extension of Europe. Some want closer integration with ASEAN, the increasingly powerful economic group formed by seven South-east Asian nations. But in 1995, the prime minister of Malaysia, Dr Mahathir Mohamad, argued that Australia could not be regarded as Asian until at least 70% of its people were of ethnic Asian origin.

African Unity) has a similar role in Africa, while the Arab League is made up of Arabic-speaking North African and Middle Eastern states. The recently formed CIS (Commonwealth of Independent States) aims at maintaining links between 12 of the 15 republics which made up the Soviet Union.

NORTH–SOUTH DIVIDE

The deepest division in the world today is the divide between rich and poor nations. In international terms, this is called the North–South divide, because the North contains most of the world's developed countries, while the developing countries lie mainly in the South. The European Union recognizes this division and gives special trading terms to more than 60 former European dependencies, which form the ACP (African, Caribbean and Pacific) states. One organization containing a majority of developing countries is the Non-Aligned Movement. This Movement was created in 1961 during the Cold War as a political bloc allied neither to the East nor to the West. However, the aims of the 113 members who attended the movement's 11th gathering in 1995 were concerned mainly with economic matters. The 113 countries between them produce only about 7% of the world's gross output and they can speak for the poorer South.

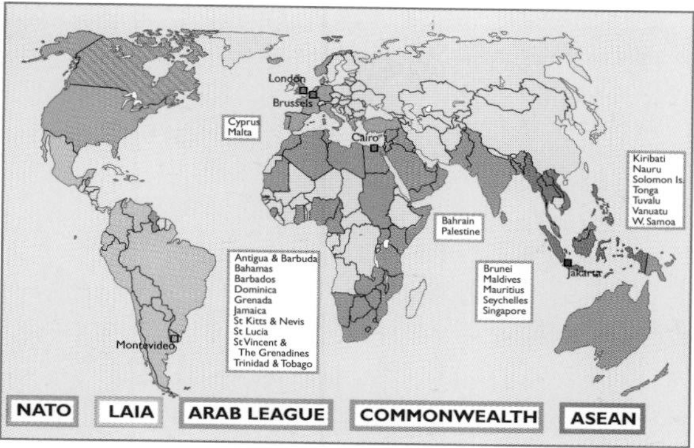

NATO   LAIA   ARAB LEAGUE   COMMONWEALTH   ASEAN

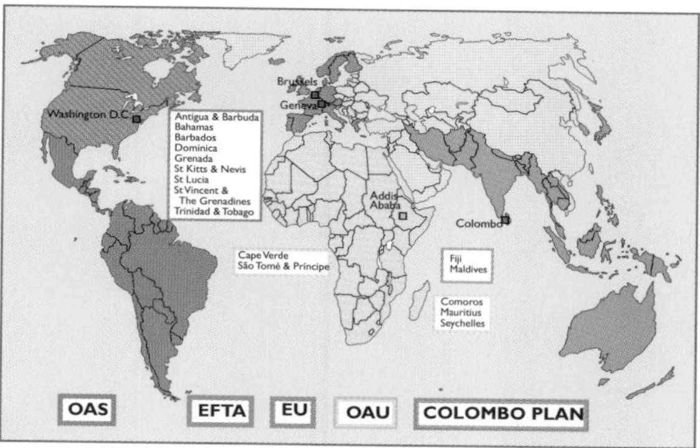

OAS   EFTA   EU   OAU   COLOMBO PLAN

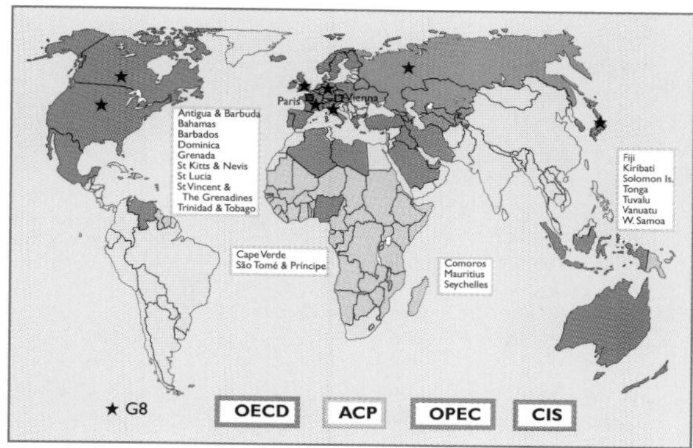

★ G8   OECD   ACP   OPEC   CIS

> The maps above show the membership of major international organizations. One important grouping shown on the bottom map is the Group of Eight (often called 'G8'). This group of eight leading industrial nations (comprising Canada, France, Germany, Italy, Japan, Russia, the United Kingdom and the United States) holds periodic meetings to discuss major problems, such as world recessions.

Regions in the News

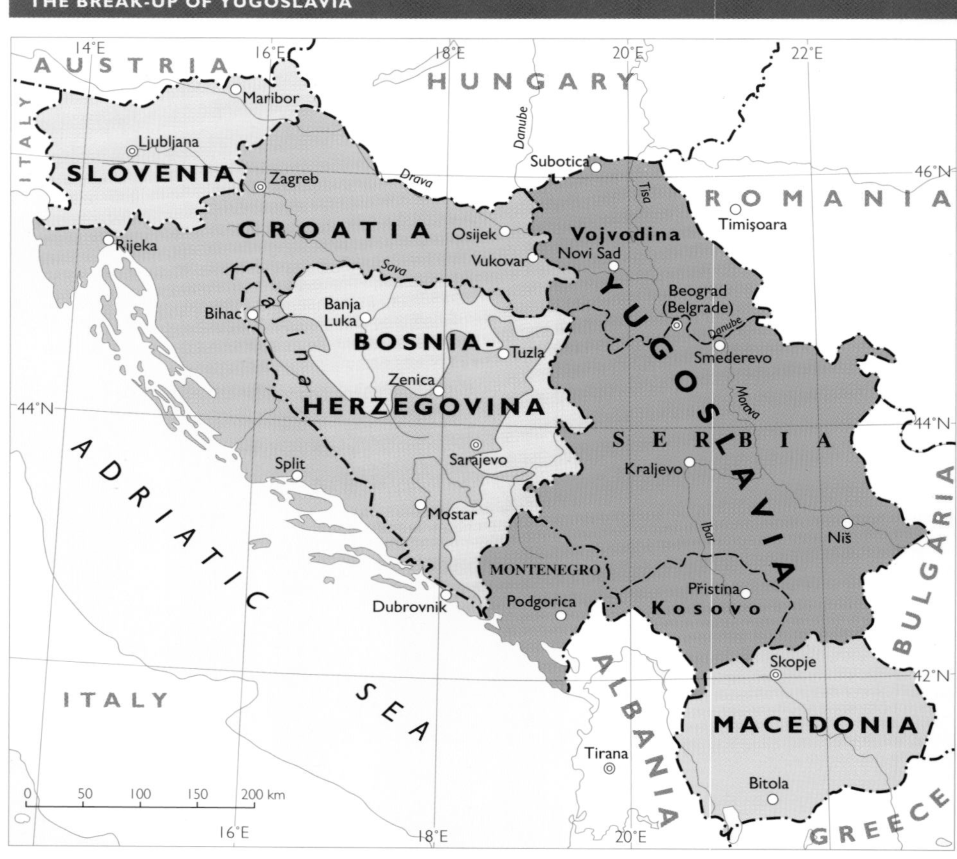

> The hoped-for era of peace following the end of the Cold War in Europe in the early 1990s was not to be. Former Yugoslavia, a federation of six republics ruled by a Communist government since 1946, split apart in 1991. First, Croatia, Slovenia and Macedonia declared themselves independent nations, followed by Bosnia-Herzegovina in 1992. This left two states, Serbia and Montenegro, to continue as Yugoslavia. The presence in Croatia and Bosnia-Herzegovina of Orthodox Christian Serbs, Roman Catholic Croats and Muslims proved an explosive mixture. Fighting broke out first in Croatia and then in Bosnia-Herzegovina. Following a bitter civil war, the signing of the Dayton Peace Accord in 1995 affirmed Bosnia-Herzegovina as a single state with its capital at Sarajevo. But the new country is partitioned into a Muslim–Croat Federation and a Serbian Republic. The fragility and ethnic diversity of the region was again highlighted in 1998, when the majority Albanian population in the Serbian province of Kosovo fought for self-determination.

Population Breakdown ▾

Population totals and the proportion of ethnic groups (1995)

Yugoslavia **10,881,000**
  Serb 63%, Albanian 17%, Montenegrin 5%,
  Hungarian 3%, Muslim 3%
Serbia 6,017,200
  Kosovo 2,045,600
  Vojvodina 2,121,800
Montenegro 696,400

Bosnia-Herzegovina **4,400,000**
  Muslim 49%, Serb 31%, Croat 17%

Croatia **4,900,000**
  Croat 78%, Serb 12%

Slovenia **2,000,000**
  Slovene 88%, Croat 3%, Serb 2%

Macedonia (F.Y.R.O.M.) **2,173,000**
  Macedonian 64%, Albanian 22%, Turkish 5%,
  Romanian 3%, Serb 2%

Legend:
- –·–·– International borders
- –··–··– Republic boundaries
- – – – – Province boundaries
- ——— Line of the Dayton Peace Accord
- Muslim–Croat Federation
- Serbian Republic

> Since its establishment in 1948, the State of Israel has seldom been out of the news. During wars with its Arab neighbours in 1948–49, 1956, 1967 and 1973, it occupied several areas. The largest of the occupied territories, the Sinai peninsula, was returned to Egypt in 1979 following the signing of an Egyptian–Israeli peace treaty. This left three Israeli-occupied territories: the Gaza Strip, the West Bank bordering Jordan, and the Golan Heights, a militarily strategic area overlooking south-western Syria.

Despite the peace agreement with Egypt, conflict continued in Israel with the PLO (Palestine Liberation Organization), which claimed to represent Arabs in Israel and Palestinians living in exile. Finally, on 13 September 1993 Israel officially recognized the PLO, and Yasser Arafat, leader of the PLO, renounced terrorism and recognized the State of Israel. This led to an agreement signed by both sides in Washington, DC. In May 1994, limited Palestinian self-rule was established in the Gaza Strip and in parts of the occupied West Bank. A Palestinian National Authority (PNA) was created and took over from the Israeli military administration when Israeli troops withdrew from the Gaza Strip and the city of Jericho. On 1 July 1994 the Palestinian leader, Yasser Arafat, stepped on to Palestinian land for the first time in 25 years.

Many people hoped that these developments would eventually lead to the creation of a Palestinian state, which would co-exist in peace with its neighbour Israel. But groups on both sides sought to undermine the peace process. In November 1995, a right-wing Jewish student assassinated the Israeli prime minister, Yitzhak Rabin, who was succeeded by Símon Peres.

In 1996, a right-wing coalition led by Binyamin Netanyahu was returned to power in a general election. The peace talks with the PLO were temporarily halted, but an agreement was reached in early 1997 over the withdrawal of Israeli troops from the town of Al Khalil (Hebron), on the West Bank. One-fifth of this town remained in the hands of about 400 Israeli settlers. Negotiations with Syria, however, over the Golan Heights were halted in 1996.

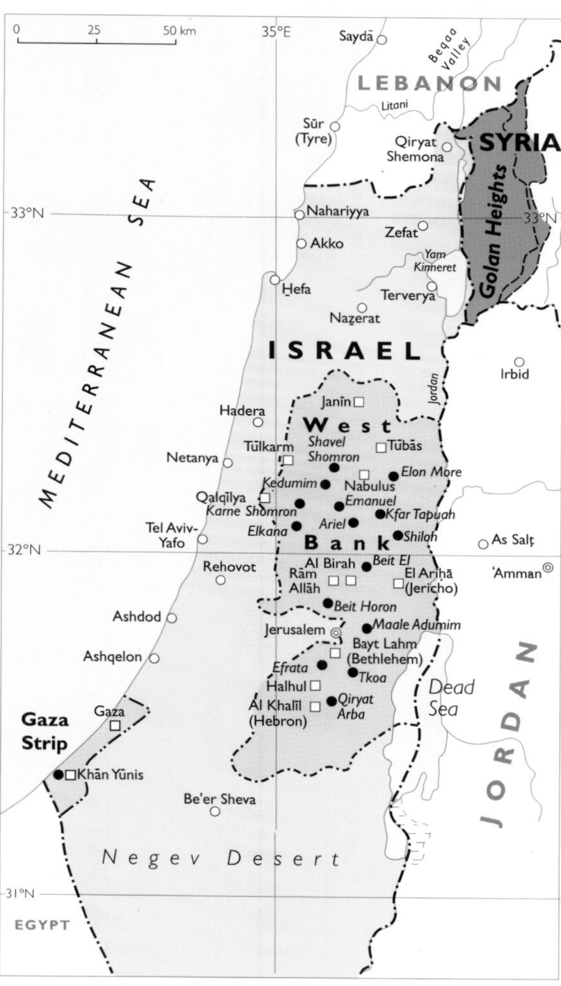

THE NEAR EAST

Population Breakdown ▾

Population totals and the proportion of ethnic groups (1995)

Israel **5,696,000**
    Jewish 82%, Arab Muslim 14%, Arab Christian 3%, Druse 2%
West Bank 973,500
    Palestinian Arab 97% (Arab Muslim 85%, Christian 8%, Jewish 7%)
Gaza Strip 658,200
    Arab Muslim 98%

Jordan **5,547,000**
    Arab 99% (Palestinian Arab 50%)

Syria **14,614,000**
    Arab 89%, Kurdish 6%

— · — · — 1949 Armistice Line

— — — — — 1974 Cease-fire Lines (Golan Heights)

Efrata Main Jewish settlements in the West Bank and Gaza Strip
●

Halhul Main Palestinian Arab towns in the West Bank and Gaza Strip
☐ – under Palestinian control since May 1994 (Gaza and Jericho) and 28 September 1995 (West Bank)

World Flags

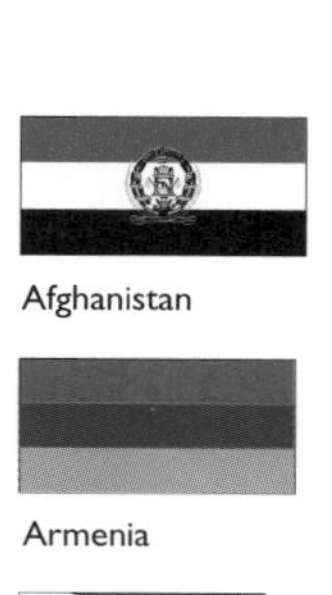

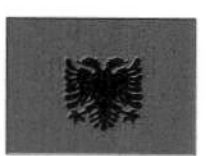

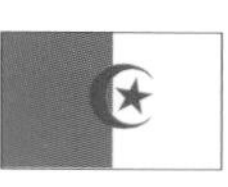

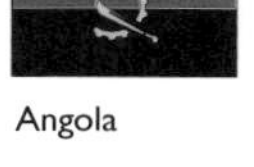

Afghanistan

Albania

Algeria

Angola

Argentina

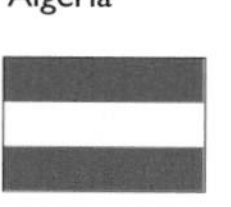

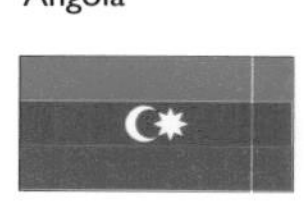

Armenia

Australia

Austria

Azerbaijan

Bahamas

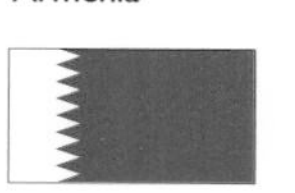

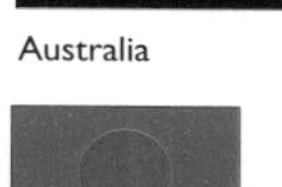

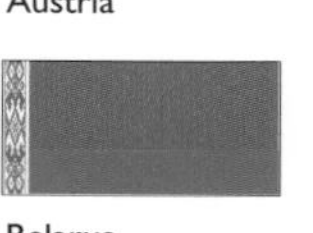

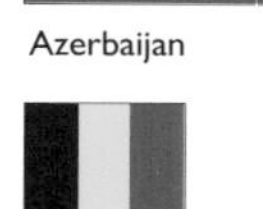

Bahrain

Bangladesh

Belarus

Belgium

Benin

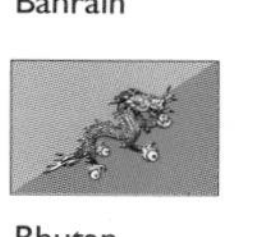

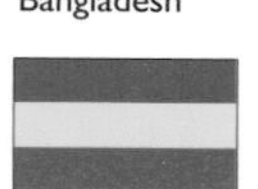

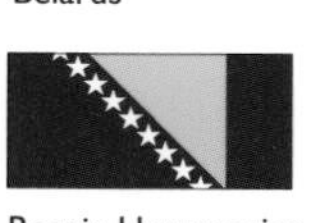

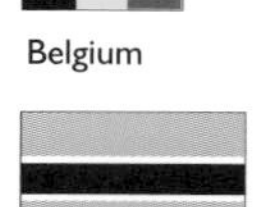

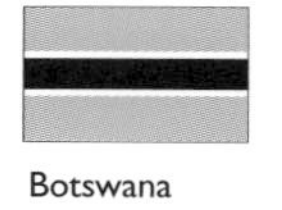

Bhutan

Bolivia

Bosnia-Herzegovina

Botswana

Brazil

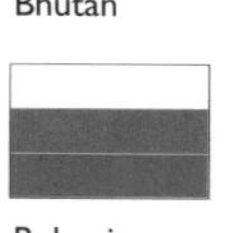

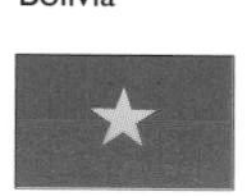

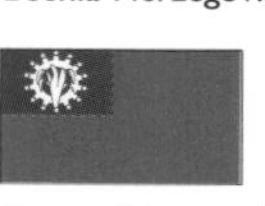

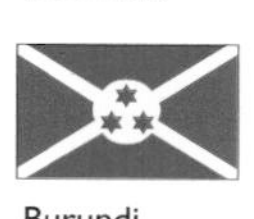

Bulgaria

Burkina Faso

Burma (Myanmar)

Burundi

Cambodia

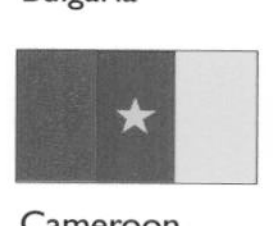

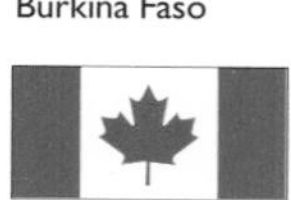

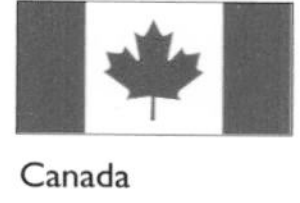

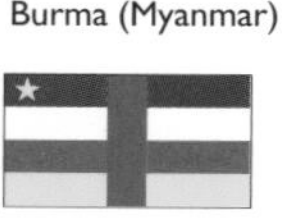

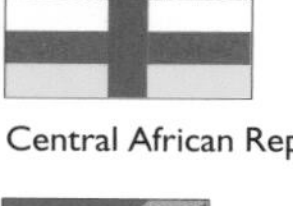

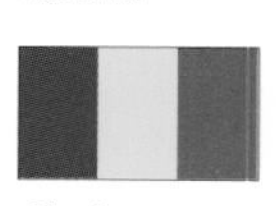

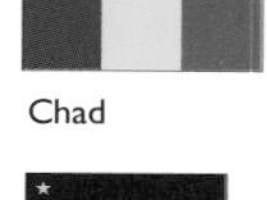

Cameroon

Canada

Central African Rep.

Chad

Chile

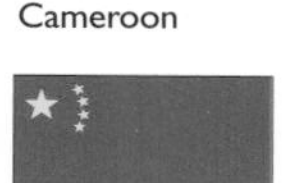

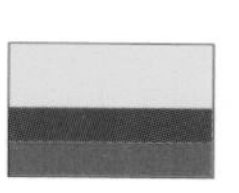

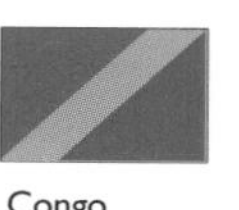

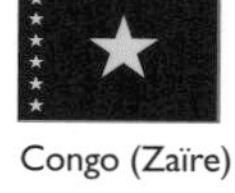

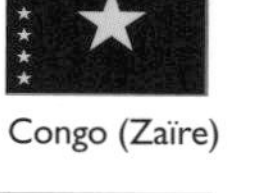

China

Colombia

Congo

Congo (Zaïre)

Costa Rica

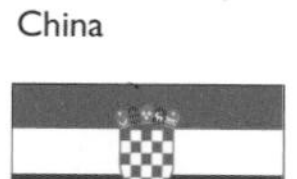

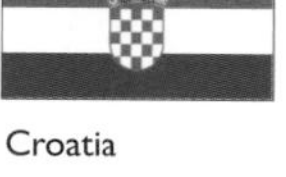

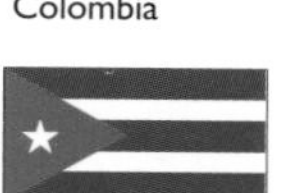

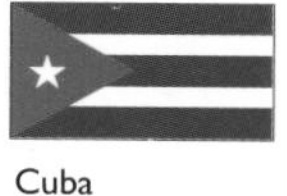

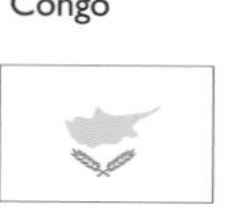

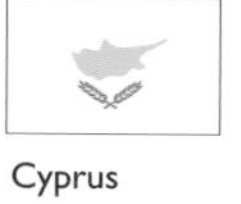

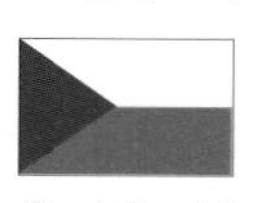

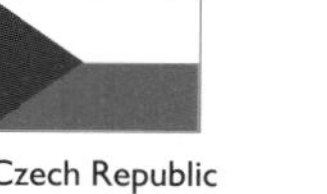

Croatia

Cuba

Cyprus

Czech Republic

Denmark

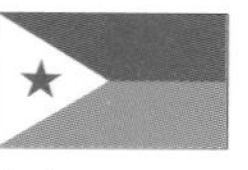

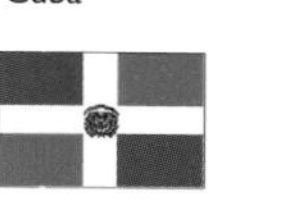

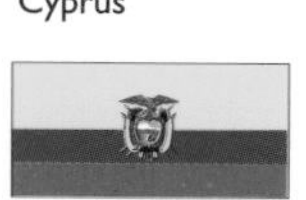

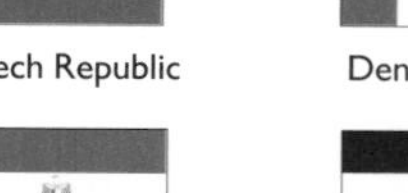

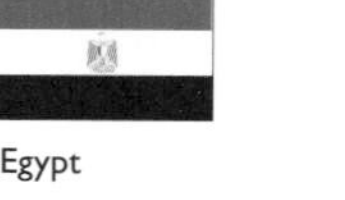

Djibouti

Dominican Republic

Ecuador

Egypt

El Salvador

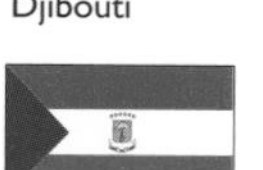

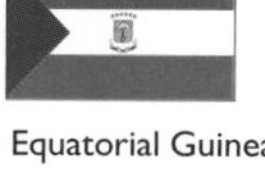

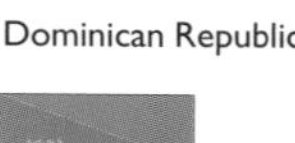

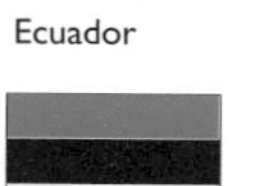

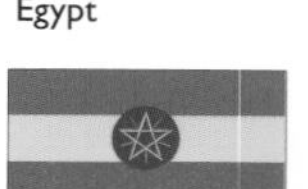

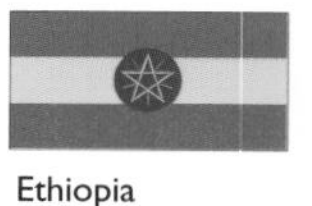

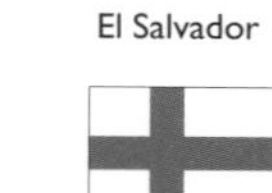

Equatorial Guinea

Eritrea

Estonia

Ethiopia

Finland

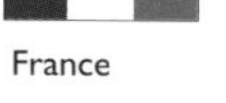

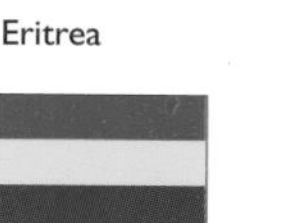

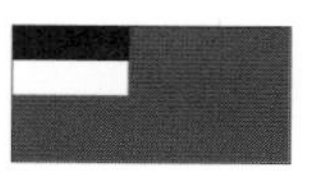

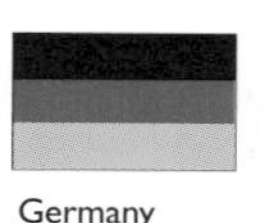

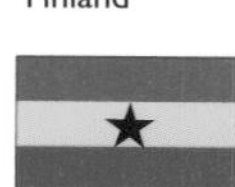

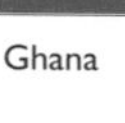

France

Gabon

Georgia

Germany

Ghana

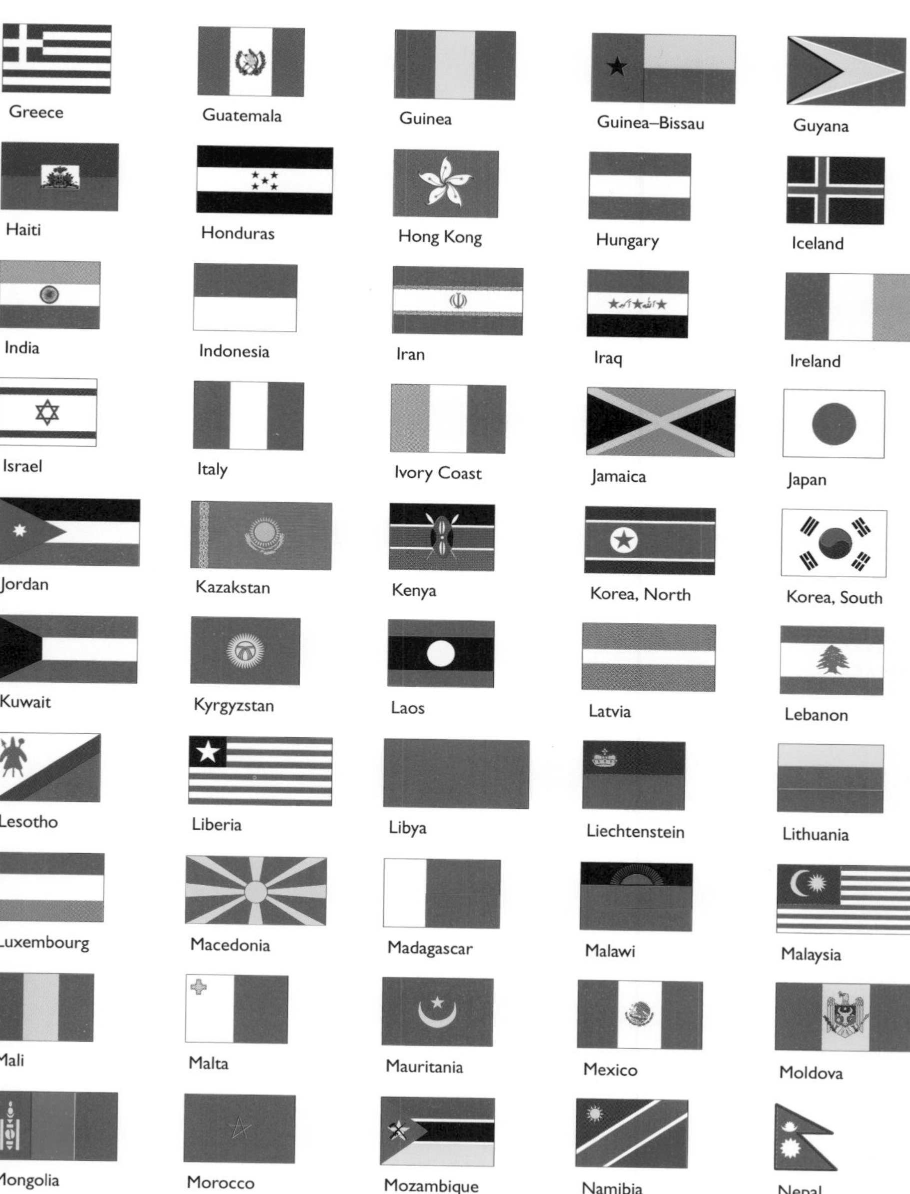

Greece

Guatemala

Guinea

Guinea–Bissau

Guyana

Haiti

Honduras

Hong Kong

Hungary

Iceland

India

Indonesia

Iran

Iraq

Ireland

Israel

Italy

Ivory Coast

Jamaica

Japan

Jordan

Kazakstan

Kenya

Korea, North

Korea, South

Kuwait

Kyrgyzstan

Laos

Latvia

Lebanon

Lesotho

Liberia

Libya

Liechtenstein

Lithuania

Luxembourg

Macedonia

Madagascar

Malawi

Malaysia

Mali

Malta

Mauritania

Mexico

Moldova

Mongolia

Morocco

Mozambique

Namibia

Nepal

Netherlands

New Zealand

Nicaragua

Niger

Nigeria

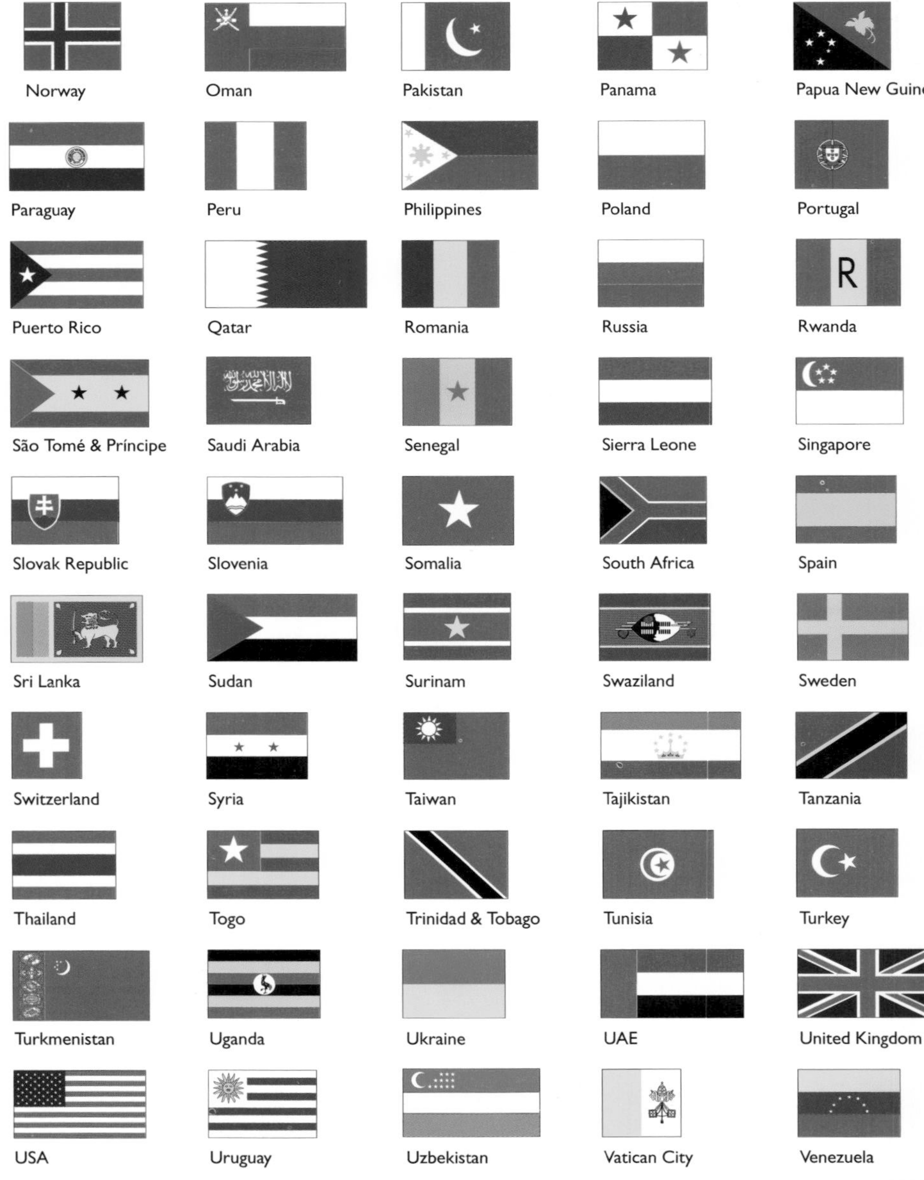

Norway	Oman	Pakistan	Panama	Papua New Guinea
Paraguay	Peru	Philippines	Poland	Portugal
Puerto Rico	Qatar	Romania	Russia	Rwanda
São Tomé & Príncipe	Saudi Arabia	Senegal	Sierra Leone	Singapore
Slovak Republic	Slovenia	Somalia	South Africa	Spain
Sri Lanka	Sudan	Surinam	Swaziland	Sweden
Switzerland	Syria	Taiwan	Tajikistan	Tanzania
Thailand	Togo	Trinidad & Tobago	Tunisia	Turkey
Turkmenistan	Uganda	Ukraine	UAE	United Kingdom
USA	Uruguay	Uzbekistan	Vatican City	Venezuela
Vietnam	Yemen	Yugoslavia	Zambia	Zimbabwe

World Maps — GENERAL REFERENCE

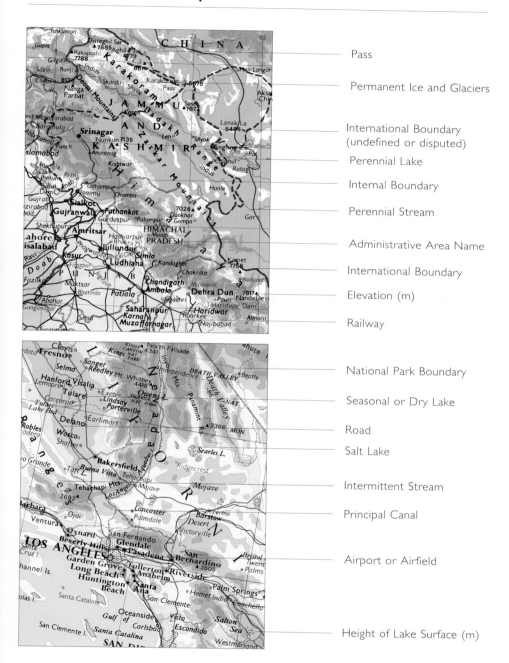

Pass

Permanent Ice and Glaciers

International Boundary (undefined or disputed)

Perennial Lake

Internal Boundary

Perennial Stream

Administrative Area Name

International Boundary

Elevation (m)

Railway

National Park Boundary

Seasonal or Dry Lake

Road

Salt Lake

Intermittent Stream

Principal Canal

Airport or Airfield

Height of Lake Surface (m)

Settlements

Settlement symbols and type styles vary according to the scale of each map and indicate the importance of towns rather than specific population figures.

All distances measured through the centre
of the map are correct for scale

PROJECTION CENTRED ON LONDON

• Capital cities

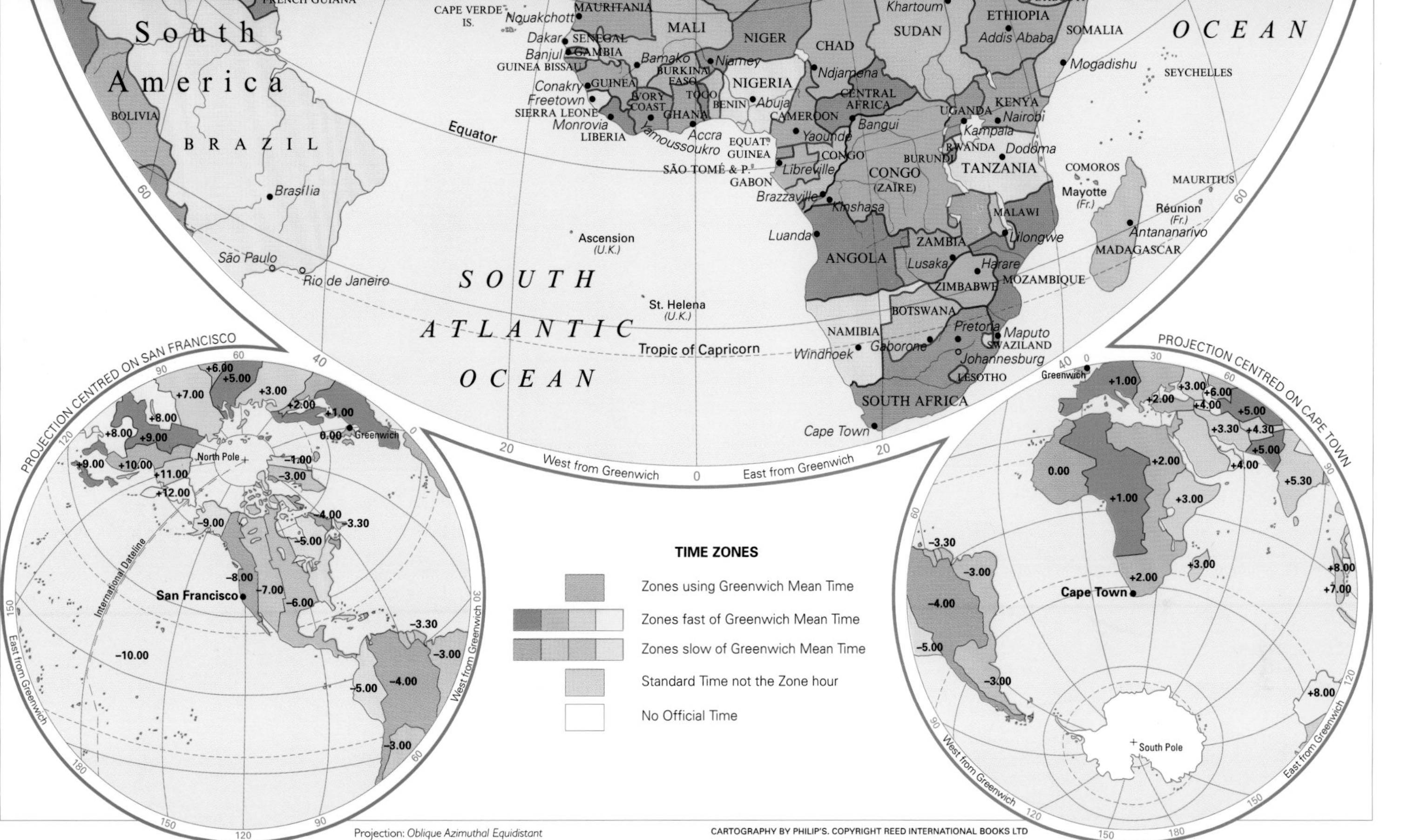

TIME ZONES

Zones using Greenwich Mean Time

Zones fast of Greenwich Mean Time

Zones slow of Greenwich Mean Time

Standard Time not the Zone hour

No Official Time

PROJECTION CENTRED ON CAPE TOWN

PROJECTION CENTRED ON SAN FRANCISCO

Projection: Oblique Azimuthal Equidistant

CARTOGRAPHY BY PHILIP'S. COPYRIGHT REED INTERNATIONAL BOOKS LTD

4 SOUTHERN HEMISPHERE

• Capital cities
East from Greenwich
180
West from Greenwich
160
140
120
100
PROJECTION CENTRED ON THE ANTIPODES OF LONDON
International Dateline
Midway I. (U.S.A.)
Tropic of Cancer
Hawaiian Is. (U.S.A.)
Bonin Is. (Japan)
Wake I. (U.S.A.)
Northern Marianas (U.S.A.)
Guam (U.S.A.)
MARSHALL IS.
PACIFIC
FED. STATES OF MICRONESIA
KIRIBATI
Equator
PHILIPPINES
Manila
PALAU
Oceania
TUVALU
PAPUA NEW GUINEA
Port Moresby
SOLOMON IS.
WESTERN SAMOA
OCEAN
VIETNAM
BRUNEI
Ho Chi Minh City
Borneo
MALAYSIA
SINGAPORE
Kuala Lumpur
INDONESIA
Jakarta
Ujung Pandang
VANUATU
FIJI
TONGA
New Caledonia (Fr.)
Marquesas Is. (Fr.)
Cook Is. (N.Z.)
Tahiti (Fr.)
FRENCH POLYNESIA
Tuamotu Arch. (Fr.)
Brisbane
Kermadec Is. (N.Z.)
Tropic of Capricorn
AUSTRALIA
Sydney
Canberra
Adelaide
Auckland
NEW ZEALAND
Wellington
Chatham Is. (N.Z.)
Pitcairn I. (U.K.)
Tasmania
Perth
Auckland Is. (N.Z.)
Antipodes Is. (N.Z.)
Macquarie Is. (Austral.)
Easter I. (Chile)
Galapagos Is. (Ecuador)
Cocos Is. (Austral.)
INDIAN
Antarctic Cir

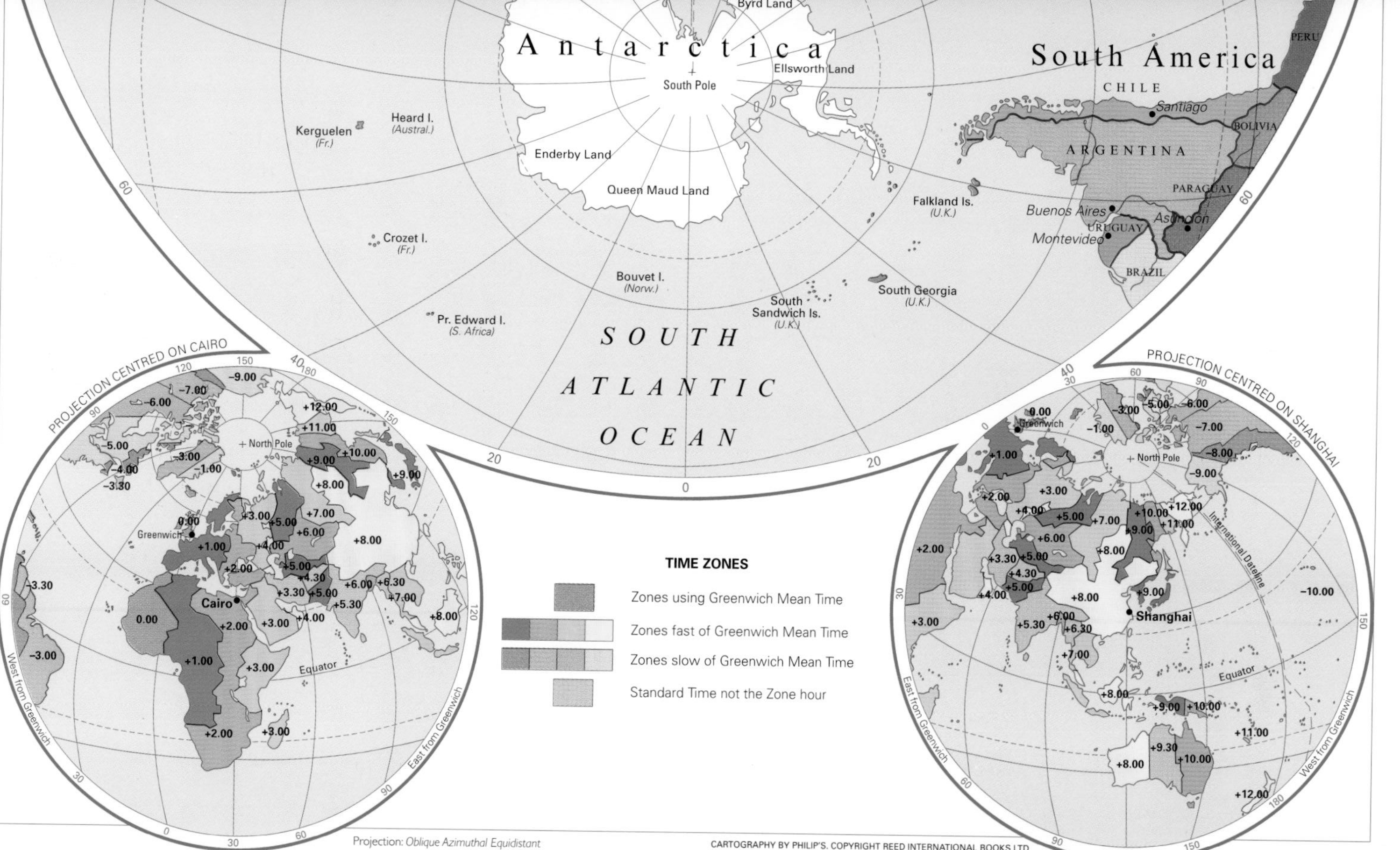

TIME ZONES

Zones using Greenwich Mean Time

Zones fast of Greenwich Mean Time

Zones slow of Greenwich Mean Time

Standard Time not the Zone hour

CARTOGRAPHY BY PHILIP'S. COPYRIGHT REED INTERNATIONAL BOOKS LTD

Projection: Oblique Azimuthal Equidistant

PROJECTION CENTRED ON SHANGHAI

PROJECTION CENTRED ON CAIRO

South America

Antarctica

SOUTH ATLANTIC OCEAN

South Pole

Byrd Land

Ellsworth Land

Enderby Land

Queen Maud Land

Bouvet I. (Norw.)

Pr. Edward I. (S. Africa)

Crozet I. (Fr.)

Kerguelen (Fr.)

Heard I. (Austral.)

South Sandwich Is. (U.K.)

South Georgia (U.K.)

Falkland Is. (U.K.)

CHILE

ARGENTINA

PARAGUAY

BOLIVIA

PERU

BRAZIL

URUGUAY

Santiago

Buenos Aires

Montevideo

Asunción

Shanghai

Cairo

Greenwich

International Dateline

Equator

North Pole

Projection: *Bonne*   West from Greenwich   0   East from Greenwich   5   10   15   ■ LONDON Capital Cities

1: 20 000 000

100   0   100   200   300   400   500 miles
100   0   200   400   600   800 km

11   **12**   **13**   **14**   **15**   **16**   **17**   **18**   **19**

C

Murmansk

White Sea

Arkhangelsk

60

D

N. Dvina

Nizhniy Tagil

FINLAND

Kotlas

Perm

L. Onega

Kirov

Yekaterinburg

Vyborg L. Ladoga

Chelyabinsk

55

Turku

Vologda

R U S S I A

Ufa

Helsinki

ST. PETERBURG

Rybinsk Res.

Kostroma

Magnitogorsk

Tallinn

Yaroslavl

Ivanovo

Nizhniy Novgorod

Kazan

E

ESTONIA

L. Chudskoye

ATVIA

Riga

MOSCOW

Simbirsk

Samara

Orenburg

W. Dvina

Smolensk

Tula

Penza

Volga

Ural

Uralsk

THUANIA

Vitebsk

50

Kaunas

K A Z A K S T A N

Vilnius

Orel

Tambov

Saratov

ngrad

Minsk

Mogilev

Atyraū

D

BELARUS

Gomel

Kursk

Voronezh

F

stok

Brest

Pripet

Chernigov

Volgograd

rsaw

Zhitomir Kiev

Dnieper

Kharkov

Don

Astrakhan

45

Lublin

Lvov

U K R A I N E

Dnepropetrovsk

Donetsk

Caspian Sea

rarsaw

Dniester

Krivoy Rog

Zaporozhye

Taganrog

Rostov

G

CP

Nikolayev

Kherson

Stavropol

Makhachkala

Debrecen

MOLDOVA

Kishinev Odessa

Cluj-Napoca

Krasnodar

ROMANIA

Brasov

Galati

Crimea

Sevastopol

Black Sea

GEORGIA

Tbilisi

AZERBAIJAN Baku

40

imisoara

Ploiesti

Constanta

ARMENIA

VIA

Bucharest

Varna

Yerevan

Araks

Sofia

Danube

Samsun

Erzurum

Tabriz

H

BULGARIA

Bosporus

T U R K E Y

a

Skopje

Plovdiv

ISTANBUL

Diyarbakır

IRAN

DONIA

Thessaloniki

Bursa

Ankara

i

35

EECE

İzmir

Konya

Kayseri

A

s

Aegean Sea

Adana

Euphrates

IRAQ

Pátrai

Athens

Antalya

Aleppo

Tigris

J

SYRIA

Baghdad

Rhodes

CYPRUS

Nicosia

10   **Crete**   **11**   30   **12**   35   **13**   **14**   **15**

CARTOGRAPHY BY PHILIPS. COPYRIGHT REED INTERNATIONAL BOOKS LTD.

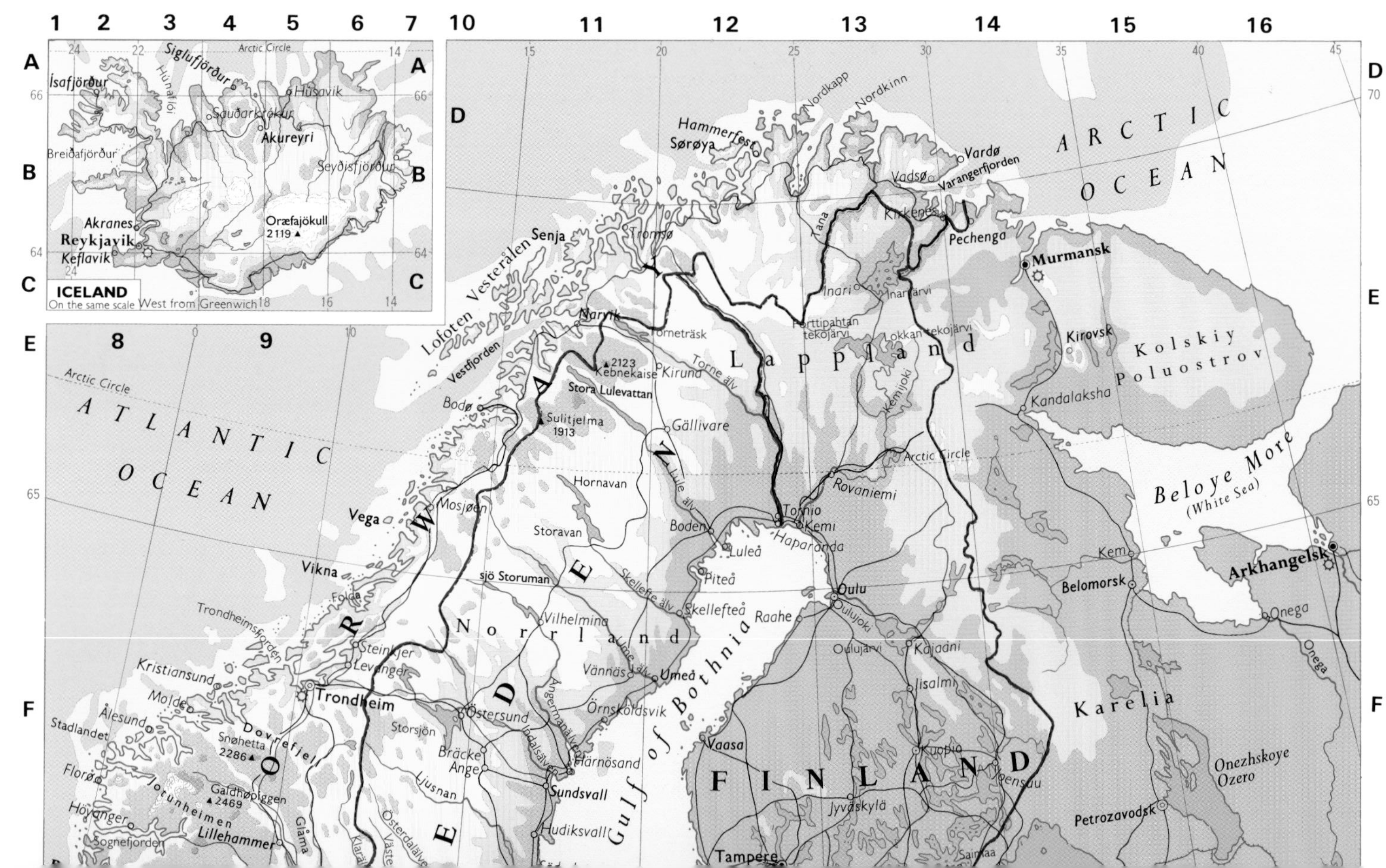
ARCTIC OCEAN
ATLANTIC OCEAN
Beloye More
(White Sea)
Kolskiy Poluostrov
Gulf of Bothnia
Lappland
Norrland
SWEDEN
NORWAY
FINLAND
Karelia
Onezhskoye Ozero
Arkhangelsk
Onega
Murmansk
Kirovsk
Kandalaksha
Kem
Belomorsk
Petrozavodsk
Pechenga
Vardø
Varangerfjorden
Vadsø
Kirkenes
Inarijärvi
Inari
Nordkinn
Nordkapp
Hammerfest
Sørøya
Tana
Lokkan tekojärvi
Kemijoki
Porttipahtan tekojärvi
Rovaniemi
Arctic Circle
Oulu
Oulujoki
Oulujärvi
Kajaani
Iisalmi
Kuopio
Joensuu
Jyväskylä
Tampere
Vaasa
Raahe
Tornio
Kemi
Haparanda
Luleå
Piteå
Boden
Skellefteå
Skellefte älv
Lule älv
Torne älv
Torneträsk
Gällivare
Kiruna
Kebnekaise
2123
Stora Lulevattan
Sulitjelma
1913
Narvik
Tromsø
Senja
Vesterålen
Lofoten
Vestfjorden
Bodø
Mosjøen
Vega
Vikna
Folda
Hornavan
Storavan
sjö Storuman
Vilhelmina
Vännäs
Umeå
Ume älv
Örnsköldsvik
Härnösand
Ångermanälven
Indalsälven
Sundsvall
Hudiksvall
Östersund
Bräcke
Ange
Ljusnan
Storsjön
Österdalälven
Klarälven
Steinkjer
Levanger
Trondheim
Trondheimsfjorden
Dovrefjell
Snøhetta
2286
Galdhøpiggen
2469
Jotunheimen
Lillehammer
Glåma
Kristiansund
Molde
Ålesund
Stadlandet
Florø
Høyanger
Sognefjorden
ICELAND
On the same scale
West from Greenwich
Ísafjörður
Siglufjörður
Húnaflói
Sauðárkrókur
Akureyri
Húsavík
Seyðisfjörður
Öræfajökull
2119
Breiðafjörður
Akranes
Reykjavík
Keflavík

1:10 000 000

50 0 50 100 150 200 250 miles
50 0 50 100 150 200 250 300 350 400 km

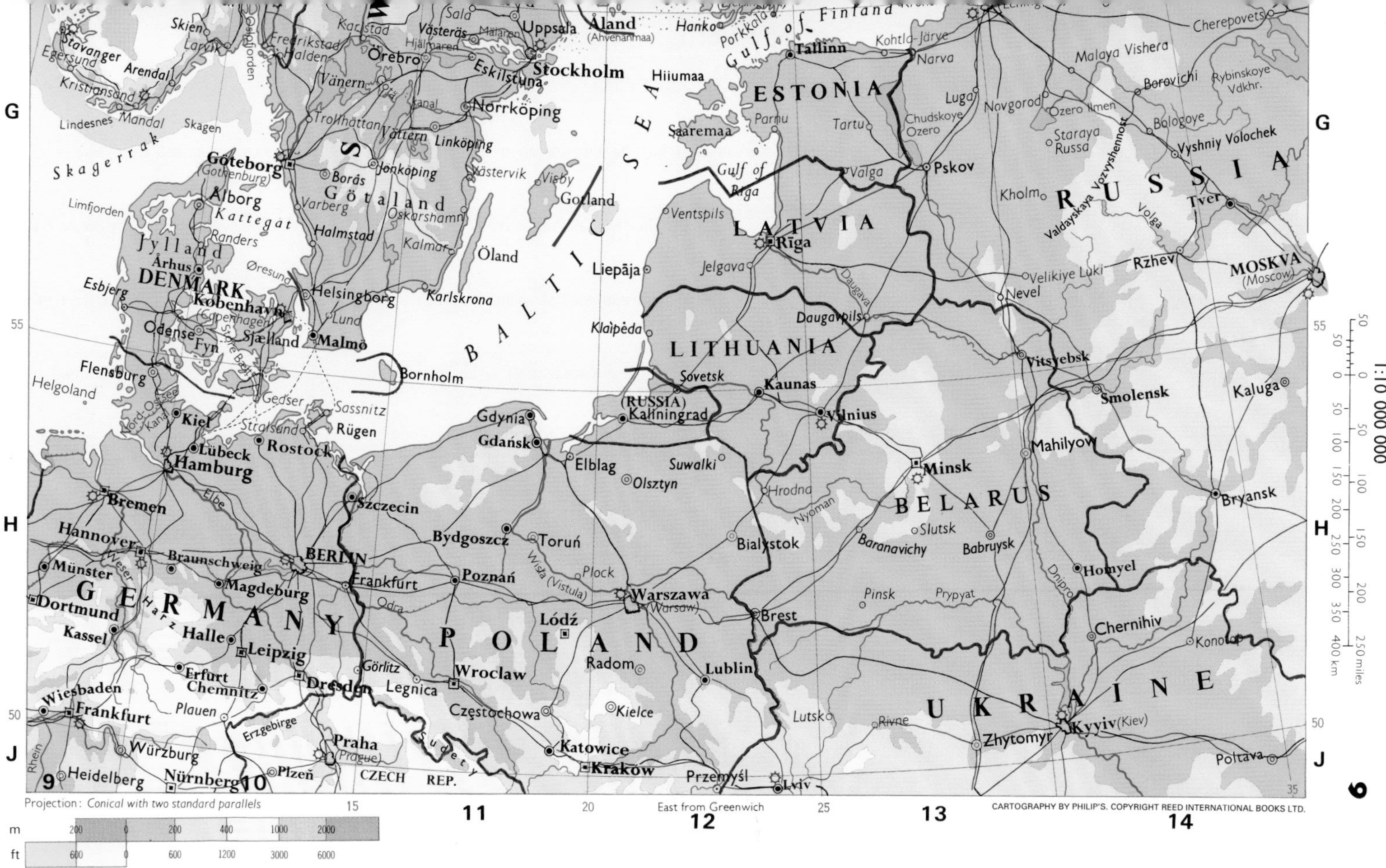

Projection: *Conical with two standard parallels*

15 11 20 East from Greenwich 12 25 13 14 35

m	200	0	200	400	1000	2000
ft	600	0	600	1200	3000	6000

10

NORWAY

Ask&y Bergen Osøyro Storð Bømlo Letvik Haugesund Kopervik Åkrahamn Bokn Stavanger Sandnes Bryne Nærbø

NORTH SEA

Shetland Is.
Unst
Fetlar
Yell
Mainland
Lerwick
Foula
Fair Isle

Orkney Is.
Westray
Sanday
Stronsay
Mainland
Kirkwall
Hoy
South Ronaldsay

Pentland Firth
Thurso
Wick
Helmsdale
C. Wrath
Golspie
Lairg
Tain
Dingwall
Invergordon
Ullapool
Aviemore
Inverness
L. Ness
Nairn
Elgin
Buckie
Banff
Fraserburgh
Peterhead
Huntly
Inverurie
Aberdeen
Stonehaven
Montrose
Arbroath
Dee
Ballater
Don
Spey

SCOTLAND

Moray Firth

Grampian Mts.
1311
Forfar
Dundee
St. Andrews
Perth
Glenrothes
Kirkcaldy
Dunbar
Stirling
Dunfermline
Tay
1214
L. Lomond
Glasgow
Edinburgh
Berwick-upon-Tweed
Galashiels
Greenock
Clyde
Paisley
Hamilton
East Kilbride
Irvine
Southern
Uplands
973

North West Highlands
Ben Nevis
1182
1344
Fort William
Mallaig
Tobermory
Oban
Mull

Inner Hebrides
Portree
Skye
Rhum
Eigg
Coll
Tiree
Colonsay
Jura
Islay
Arran

North Minch
Stornoway
789
Lewis
Harris

Outer Hebrides
North Uist
Benbecula
South Uist
Barra
St. Kilda

ATLANTIC OCEAN

238
1224
316

N O R T H   S E A

A T L A N T I C

m ft
2000 6000
1000 3000
500 1500
200 600
100 300
50 150
0 0
0 0
50 150
200 600
500 1500
1000 3000

1: 5 000 000
50 0 50 100 miles
50 0 50 100 150 km
UNITED KINGDOM
NORTHERN IRELAND
IRELAND
ENGLAND
WALES
NETHERLANDS
BELGIUM
FRANCE
IRISH SEA
CELTIC SEA
English Channel
St. George's Channel
Bristol Channel
Cardigan Bay
Galway B.
Str. of Dover
The Wash
Cambrian Mts.
Wicklow Mts.
Cumbrian Mts.
Cotswold Hills
Exmoor
Dartmoor
Connemara
Ulster
Munster
Leinster
Connacht
Pennines
Flandre
Artois
Picardie
Pays de Caux
Cotentin
Channel Is. (U.K.)
Guernsey
Jersey
Alderney
Sark
St. Peter Port
St. Helier
Isle of Wight
I. of Man
Douglas
Anglesey
Isles of Scilly
Land's End
C. Clear
Aran Is.
Achill I.
Valencia I.
Lough Neagh
Lower L. Erne
L. Conn
Lough Mask
Lough Corrib
Lough Ree
Lough Derg
Shannon
Liffey
Boyne
Blackwater
Severn
Thames
Trent
Humber
Great Ouse
Somme
Seine
Macgillycuddy's Reeks
Carrauntoohill 1041
Snowdon 1085
Dingle 953
926
886
893
978
636
618
99
16
36
33
Belfast
Dublin
Dun Laoghaire
Cork
Limerick
Galway
Waterford
Londonderry
Omagh
Antrim
Bangor
Larne
Lisburn
Lurgan
Portadown
Armagh
Newry
Enniskillen
Clones
Castleblaney
Dundalk
Drogheda
Ceanannus Mor
Cavan
Leitrim
Sligo
Donegal
Bundoran
Ballina
Castlebar
Westport
Roscommon
Longford
Mullingar
Athlone
Ballinasloe
Tullamore
Birr
Port Laoise
Athy
Bray
Arklow
Wexford
Rosslare
Carlow
Kilkenny
Thurles
Nenagh
Ennis
Kilrush
Listowel
Tralee
Killarney
Mallow
Tipperary
Clonmel
Carrick-on-Suir
Dungarvan
Youghal
Cobh
Bandon
Kinsale
Bantry
LONDON
BIRMINGHAM
Manchester
Liverpool
Leeds
Sheffield
Bradford
Kingston upon Hull
Newcastle
Carlisle
Durham
Hartlepool
Redcar
Middlesbrough
Stockton-on-Tees
Darlington
Scarborough
Bridlington
Beverley
York
Harrogate
Keighley
Lancaster
Barrow-in-Furness
Workington
Whitehaven
Stranraer
Mull of Galloway
Blackpool
Preston
Blackburn
Burnley
Halifax
Huddersfield
Bolton
Oldham
Barnsley
Doncaster
Rotherham
Scunthorpe
Grimsby
Louth
Lincoln
Skegness
Boston
Warrington
Stockport
Chesterfield
Mansfield
Nottingham
Derby
Stoke on Trent
Crewe
Chester
Colwyn Bay
Bangor
Holyhead
Wrexham
Pwllheli
Aberystwyth
Welshpool
Shrewsbury
Telford
Stafford
Wolverhampton
Grantham
Leicester
Nuneaton
Coventry
Redditch
Worcester
Hereford
Royal Leamington Spa
Rugby
Corby
Peterborough
King's Lynn
Cromer
Norwich
Great Yarmouth
Lowestoft
Thetford
Ely
Bury St. Edmunds
Cambridge
Ipswich
Felixstowe
Harwich
Colchester
Chelmsford
Northampton
Bedford
Milton Keynes
Stevenage
Luton
Harlow
Hemel Hempstead
Watford
Basildon
Southend-on-Sea
Margate
Chatham
Canterbury
Maidstone
Dover
Folkestone
Ashford
Reigate
Crawley
Hastings
Eastbourne
Brighton
Worthing
Portsmouth
Havant
Fareham
Southampton
Winchester
Guildford
Reading
Slough
High Wycombe
Oxford
Cheltenham
Gloucester
Swindon
Newbury
Basingstoke
Bristol
Bath
Salisbury
Bournemouth
Poole
Weymouth
Newport
Yeovil
Taunton
Weston-super-Mare
Cardiff
Newport
Cwmbran
Rhondda
Barry
Merthyr Tydfil
Brecon
Neath
Swansea
Port Talbot
Llanelli
Carmarthen
Haverfordwest
Milford Haven
Pembroke
Fishguard
Barnstaple
Bude
Exeter
Exmouth
Torbay
Plymouth
St. Austell
Truro
Newquay
Falmouth
Penzance
Texel
Den Helder
Alkmaar
Haarlem
's-Gravenhage (Den Haag)
Hoek van Holland
ROTTERDAM
Dordrecht
Vlissingen
Zeebrugge
Oostende
Brugge
Gent
Antwerpen
Mechelen
BRUSSEL (Bruxelles)
Tournai
Dunkerque
Calais
C. Gris-Nez
Boulogne-sur-Mer
Le Touquet-Paris-Plage
St.-Omer
Béthune
Bruay-en-Artois
Lille
Tourcoing
Villeneuve-d'Ascq
Lens
Valenciennes
Cambrai
St.-Quentin
Amiens
Abbeville
Le Tréport
Dieppe
Fécamp
Le Havre
Bolbec
Rouen
Elbeuf
Lisieux
Caen
Trouville-sur-Mer
Bayeux
Valognes
Cherbourg
Pte. de Barfleur
C. de la Hague
East from Greenwich
West from Greenwich
Projection: Conical with two standard parallels
E
F
G
2
3
4
5
6
7

12 FRANCE

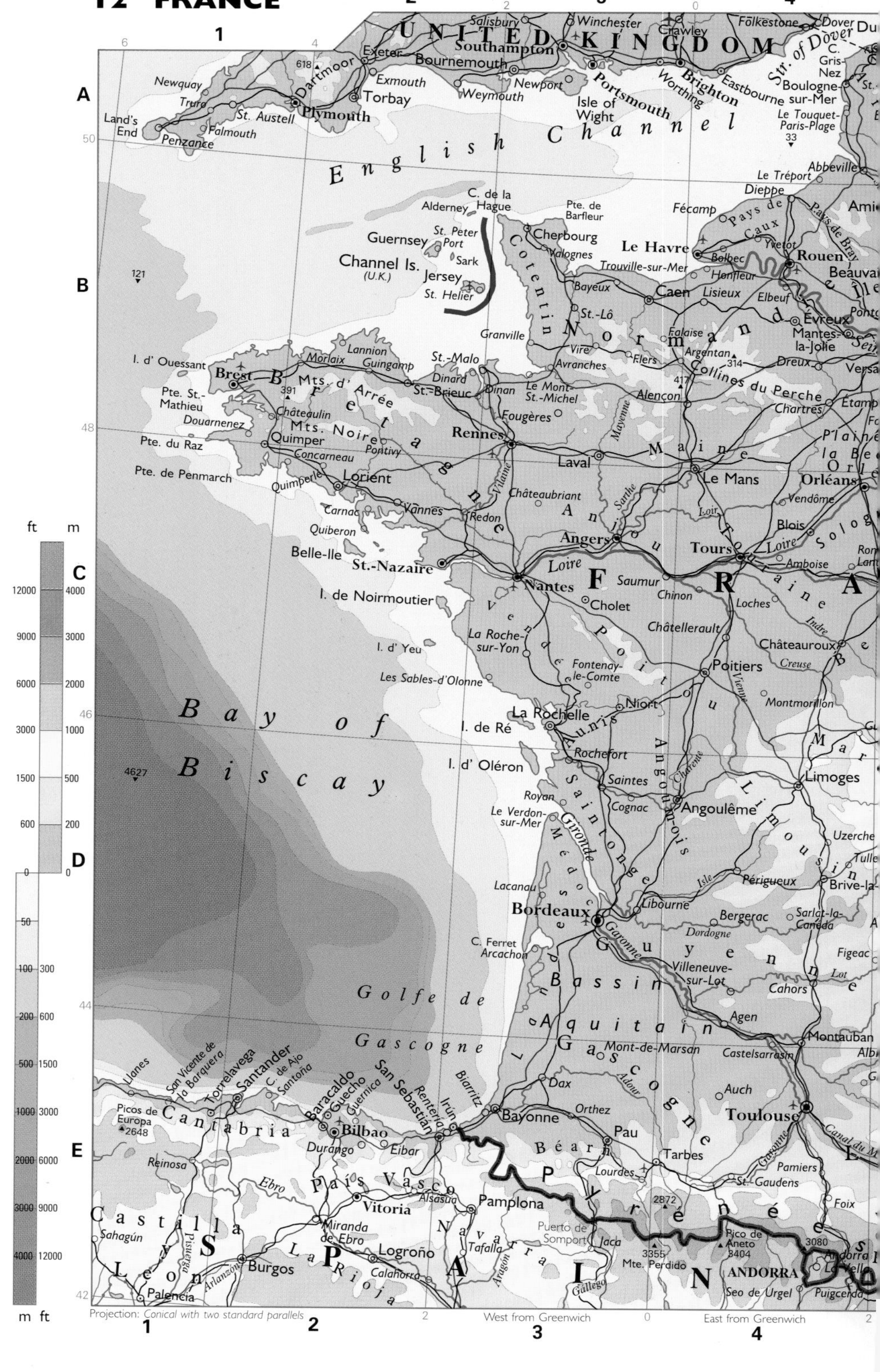

UNITED KINGDOM
English Channel
Str. of Dover
Land's End
Penzance
Newquay
Truro
Falmouth
St. Austell
Plymouth
Dartmoor
Exeter
Exmouth
Torbay
Bournemouth
Weymouth
Southampton
Salisbury
Winchester
Portsmouth
Newport
Isle of Wight
Crawley
Brighton
Worthing
Eastbourne
Folkestone
Dover
C. Gris-Nez
Boulogne-sur-Mer
Le Touquet-Paris-Plage
Abbeville
Le Tréport
Dieppe
Fécamp
Pays de Caux
Pays de Bray
Yvetot
Le Havre
Bolbec
Rouen
Honfleur
Trouville-sur-Mer
Elbeuf
Évreux
Mantes-la-Jolie
Alderney
C. de la Hague
Pte. de Barfleur
Cherbourg
Valognes
Cotentin
Guernsey
St. Peter Port
Sark
Channel Is. (U.K.)
Jersey
St. Helier
Bayeux
Caen
Lisieux
St.-Lô
Normandy
Granville
Falaise
Argentan
Vire
Flers
Avranches
Le Mont-St.-Michel
Collines du Perche
Alençon
Chartres
Dreux
I. d' Ouessant
Brest
Morlaix
Lannion
Guingamp
Mts. d' Arrée
St.-Malo
Dinard
Dinan
St.-Brieuc
Bretagne
Pte. St.-Mathieu
Châteaulin
Douarnenez
Mts. Noires
Pte. du Raz
Quimper
Concarneau
Pontivy
Pte. de Penmarch
Quimperlé
Lorient
Rennes
Fougères
Mayenne
Laval
Maine
Le Mans
Orléans
Vilaine
Châteaubriant
Sarthe
Loir
Vendôme
Carnac
Vannes
Redon
Quiberon
Anjou
Angers
Tours
Blois
Touraine
Sologne
Amboise
Belle-Ile
St.-Nazaire
Nantes
Loire
Saumur
Chinon
FRANCE
I. de Noirmoutier
Cholet
Loches
Vendée
La Roche-sur-Yon
Poitou
Châtellerault
Châteauroux
Indre
I. d' Yeu
Fontenay-le-Comte
Poitiers
Creuse
Les Sables-d'Olonne
Vienne
Montmorillon
Niort
La Rochelle
Aunis
I. de Ré
Bay of Biscay
Rochefort
I. d' Oléron
Saintes
Charente
Angoumois
Marche
Limoges
Royan
Cognac
Angoulême
Limousin
Le Verdon-sur-Mer
Saintonge
Gironde
Médoc
Uzerche
Lacanau
Isle
Périgueux
Brive-la-
Bordeaux
Libourne
Bergerac
Sarlat-la-Canéda
Dordogne
C. Ferret
Arcachon
Garonne
Guyenne
Villeneuve-sur-Lot
Figeac
Lot
Cahors
Golfe de Gascogne
Bassin d'Aquitaine
Landes
Agen
Mont-de-Marsan
Montauban
Castelsarrasin
Gascogne
Adour
Dax
Auch
Biarritz
Bayonne
Orthez
Toulouse
Pau
Béarn
Tarbes
Lourdes
Pamiers
St.-Gaudens
Foix
Pyrénées
2872
Puerto de Somport
3355
Mte. Perdido
Pico de Aneto 3404
3080
ANDORRA
Andorra la Vella
Seo de Urgel
Puigcerdà
Llanes
San Vicente de la Barquera
Torrelavega
Santander
C. de Ajo
Santoña
Baracaldo
Guecho
Guernica
San Sebastián
Rentería
Irún
Picos de Europa 2648
Cantabria
Bilbao
Durango
Eibar
Reinosa
Ebro
País Vasco
Vitoria
Alsasua
Pamplona
Navarra
Castilla y León
Sahagún
Pisuerga
Miranda de Ebro
Logroño
Tafalla
Jaca
Gállego
Aragón
Burgos
Arlanzón
La Rioja
Calahorra
SPAIN
Palencia
Projection: Conical with two standard parallels
West from Greenwich
East from Greenwich

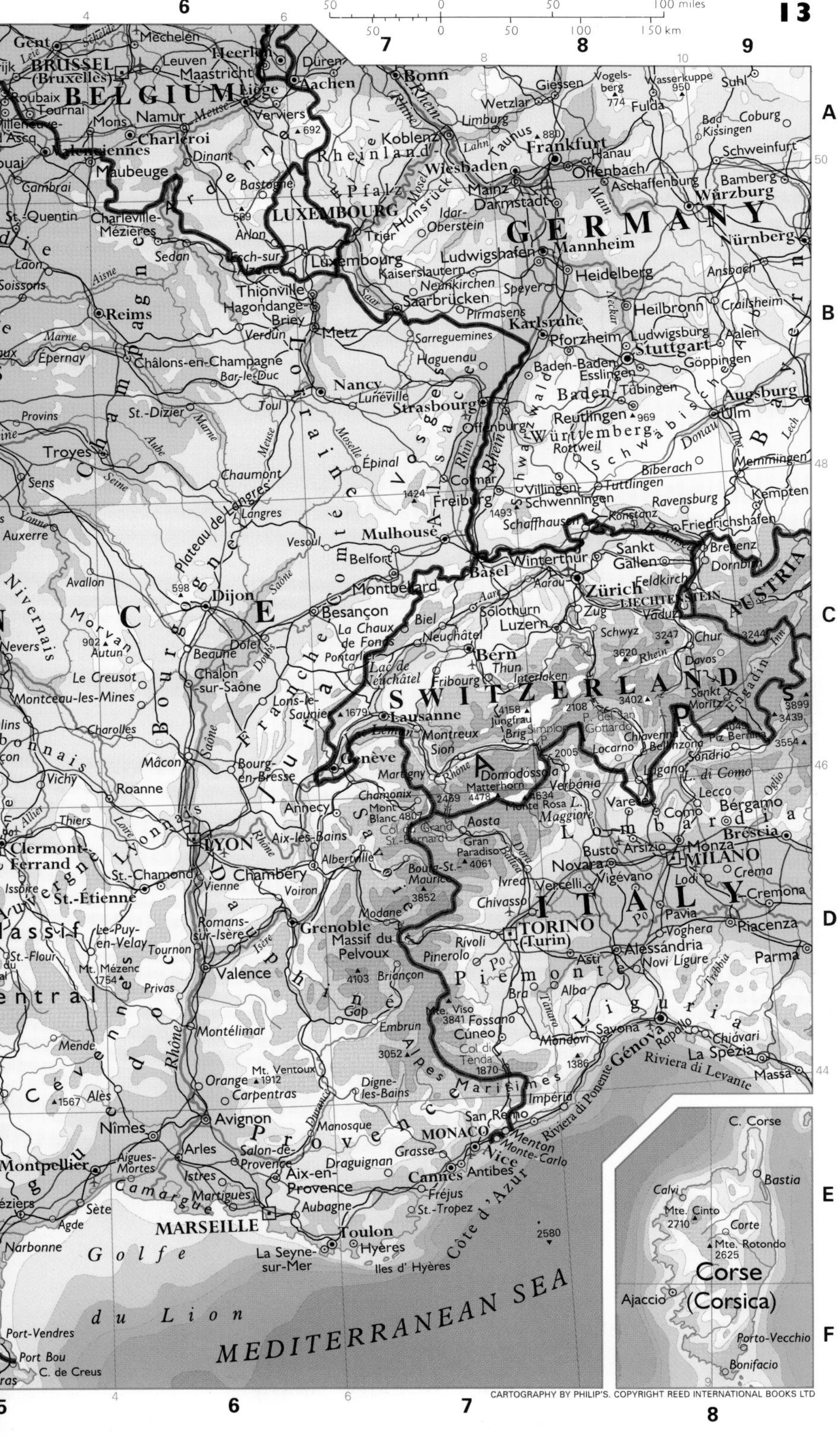

1: 5 000 000

50   0   50   100 miles
50   0   50   100   150 km

BELGIUM
BRUSSEL
(Bruxelles)
GERMANY
LUXEMBOURG
FRANCE
SWITZERLAND
AUSTRIA
ITALY
LIECHTENSTEIN

MEDITERRANEAN SEA

Corse
(Corsica)

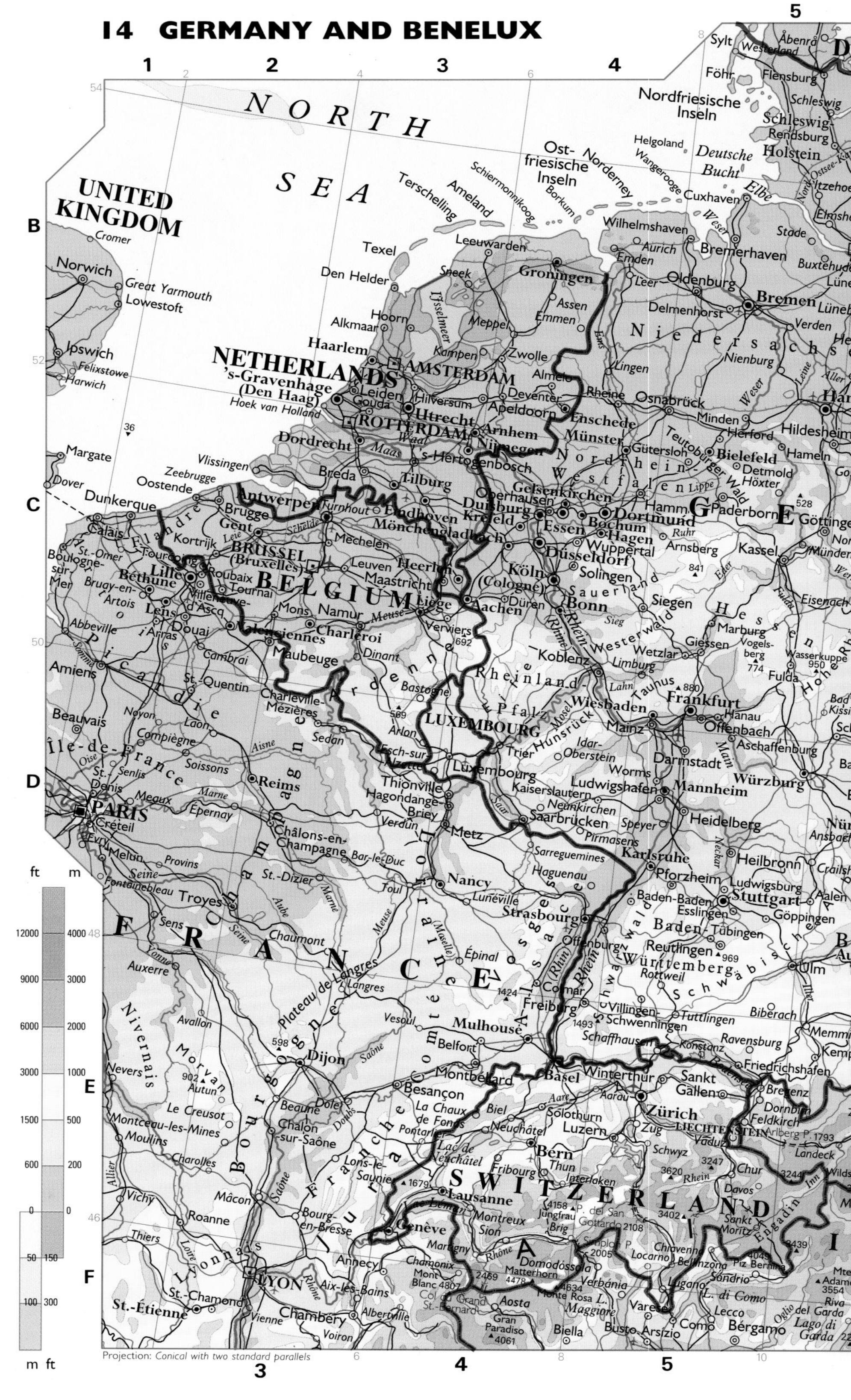

NORTH SEA
UNITED KINGDOM
NETHERLANDS
BELGIUM
LUXEMBOURG
FRANCE
SWITZERLAND
LIECHTENSTEIN
AMSTERDAM
's-Gravenhage (Den Haag)
ROTTERDAM
BRUSSEL (Bruxelles)
PARIS
Nordfriesische Inseln
Ostfriesische Inseln
Deutsche Bucht
Niedersachsen
Nordrhein-Westfalen
Hessen
Rheinland-Pfalz
Baden-Württemberg
Schwäbische Alb
Schwarzwald
Schleswig-Holstein
Ardennes
Sauerland
Westerwald
Taunus
Hunsrück
Picardie
Île-de-France
Champagne
Lorraine
Alsace
Bourgogne
Franche-Comté
Jura
Morvan
Nivernais
Lyonnais
Flandre
Artois
Plateau de Langres
Teutoburger Wald
Texel
Terschelling
Ameland
Schiermonnikoog
Borkum
Norderney
Wangerooge
Helgoland
Sylt
Föhr
Groningen
Leeuwarden
Haarlem
Leiden
Utrecht
Arnhem
Nijmegen
Eindhoven
Tilburg
Breda
Antwerpen
Gent
Brugge
Liège
Namur
Charleroi
Lille
Calais
Dunkerque
Amiens
Reims
Metz
Nancy
Strasbourg
Mulhouse
Dijon
Besançon
Lyon
Genève
Lausanne
Bern
Basel
Zürich
Luzern
Luxembourg
Köln (Cologne)
Bonn
Aachen
Düsseldorf
Essen
Dortmund
Duisburg
Münster
Osnabrück
Bielefeld
Bremen
Bremerhaven
Oldenburg
Cuxhaven
Wilhelmshaven
Emden
Flensburg
Kassel
Koblenz
Wiesbaden
Mainz
Frankfurt
Darmstadt
Mannheim
Heidelberg
Karlsruhe
Stuttgart
Würzburg
Saarbrücken
Freiburg
Ulm
Friedrichshafen
Konstanz
Sankt Gallen
Chur
Davos
Lugano
Como
Varese
Bergamo
Aosta
Mont Blanc 4807
Matterhorn 4478
Monte Rosa 4634
Jungfrau 4158
Projection: Conical with two standard parallels

1: 5 000 000
50 0 50 100 miles
50 0 50 100 150 km
7 8 9 10
A B C D E
BALTIC SEA
Zatoka Gdańska
Zalew Wiślany
Næstved
Møn
Nakskov
Lolland
Falster
Nykøbing
Rødbyhavn
Gedser
Fehmarn Bælt
Fehmarn
Mecklenburger Bucht
Rügen
Sassnitz
Stralsund
Greifswald
Rostock
Wismar
Usedom
Wolin
Świnoujście
Güstrow
Mecklenburg
Stettiner Haff
Schwerin
Parchim
Neubrandenburg
Müritz-see
Neustrelitz
Elde
Brandenburg
Wittenberge
Neuruppin
Havel
Salzwedel
Stendal
Oranienburg
Rathenow
Eberswalde-Finow
Schwedt
BERLIN
Fürstenwalde
Brandenburg
Potsdam
Spree
Magdeburg
Luckenwalde
Sachsen-Anhalt
Dessau
Wittenberg
Bernburg
Saale
Halle
Torgau
Cottbus
Lauchhammer
Leipzig
Merseburg
Riesa
Hoyerswerda
Naumburg
Mulde
Zeitz
Bautzen
Meissen
Elbe
Weimar
Gera
Dresden
Görlitz
Zgorzelec
Sachsen
Chemnitz
Zwickau
Děčín
Greiz
Reichenbach
Plauen
Erzgebirge
Teplice
Ústí nad Labem
Most
Chomutov
Ohre
Litoměřice
Hof
Karlovy Vary
Kladno
Cheb
Bayreuth
PRAHA (Prague)
Beroun
Plzeň
Weiden
Naab
Amberg
Böhmerwald
Klatovy
Příbram
Vltava
Písek
Tábor
Regensburg
Grosser Arber
České Budějovice
Straubing
Deggendorf
Plöckenstein
Isar
Landshut
Passau
Freising
MÜNCHEN (Munich)
Braunau
Ried
Wels
Linz
(Donau)
Inn
Freistadt
Zwettl
Gmünd
Horn
Krems
Stockerau
Melk
Sankt Pölten
WIEN (Vienna)
Steyr
Amstetten
Enns
Baden
Salzburg
Gmunden
Chiemsee
Bad Ischl
Kufstein
Wiener Neustadt
Neusiedler See
Bruck an der Leitha
Semmering P.
Mürzzuschlag
Eisenerz
Kapfenberg
Bruck an der Mur
Leoben
Salzach
Tauern
Badgastein
Gross Glockner
Lienz
Steiermark
Graz
Wolfsberg
Kärnten
Karnische Alpen
Villach
Klagenfurt
Drava
Maribor
Mur
Triglav
Karawanken
Kobarid
Kranj
Celje
Sava
Ljubljana
SLOVENIA
Kalce
Tagliamento
Udine
Gorizia
Pordenone
Vittório Véneto
Conegliano
Belluno
ITALY
Koszalin
Kołobrzeg
Darłowo
Słupsk
Lębork
Wejherowo
Rumia
Gdynia
Sopot
Gdańsk
Bytów
Tczew
Elbląg
Malbork
Białogard
Pojezierze Pomorski
Starogard Gdański
Kwidzyn
Iława
Wisła
Police
Goleniów
Szczecin
Szczecinek
Chojnice
Świecie
Grudziądz
Stargard Szczeciński
Wałcz
Chełmno
Brodnica
Piła
Bydgoszcz
Toruń
Rypin
Choszczno
Noteć
Gorzów Wielkopolski
(Vistula)
Inowrocław
POLAND
Warta
Międzychód
Gniezno
Włocławek
Płock
Oder
(Odra)
Poznań
Września
Nowy Tomyśl
Frankfurt
Kutno
Koło
Świebodzin
Śrem
Konin
Łęczyca
Zielona Góra
Kościan
Prosna
Turek
Leszno
Nowa Sól
Kalisz
Zduńska Wola
Łódź
Żagań
Krotoszyn
Sieradz
Pabianice
Żary
Bóbr
Głogów
Ostrów Wielkopolski
Lubin
Nysa
(Neisse)
Bolesławiec
Piotrków Trybunalski
Legnica
Oleśnica
Wieluń
Radomsko
Wrocław
Śląsk
Kluczbork
Częstochowa
Oława
Jelenia Góra
Liberec
Wałbrzych
Świdnica
Opole
Myszków
Jablonec
Sněžka
Dzierżoniów
Tarnowskie Góry
Zawiercie
Mladá Boleslav
Trutnov
Sudety
Kłodzko
Zabrze
Bytom
Gliwice
Katowice
Sosnowiec
Hradec Králové
Racibórz
Tychy
Oświęcim
(Labe)
Pardubice
Kolín
Šumperk
Opava
Karviná
Havířov
Bielsko-Biała
Ostrava
Sázava
Olomouc
Frýdek-Místek
Cieszyn
Żywiec
CZECH REP.
Českomoravská Vrchovina
Havlíčkův Brod
Přerov
Prostějov
Jihlava
Vyškov
Zlín
Povážská Bystrica
Žilina
Třebíč
Jindrichuv Hradec
Brno
Martin
Bielé Karpaty
Trenčín
Prievidza
Banská Bystrica
Znojmo
Hodonín
SLOVAK REP
Malé Karpaty
Váh
Topoľčany
Zvolen
Morava
Trnava
Nitra
Bratislava
Levice
Hron
Nové Zámky
(Dunaj)
Komárno
Mosonmagyaróvár
Győr
Esztergom
Dunakeszi
Sopron
Tatabánya
Vác
Rába
BUDAPEST
Pápa
Bakony Hegység
Szombathely
Székesfehérvár
Ajka
Veszprém
Dunaújváros
Balaton
Siófok
Zalaegerszeg
HUNGARY
Kalocsa
Nagykanizsa
Kaposvár
Szekszárd
(Duna)
Pécs
Baja
Mohács
Varaždin
Koprivnica
Virovitica
Drava
Zagreb
Bjelovar
East from Greenwich
12 14 16 18
54 52 50 48 46

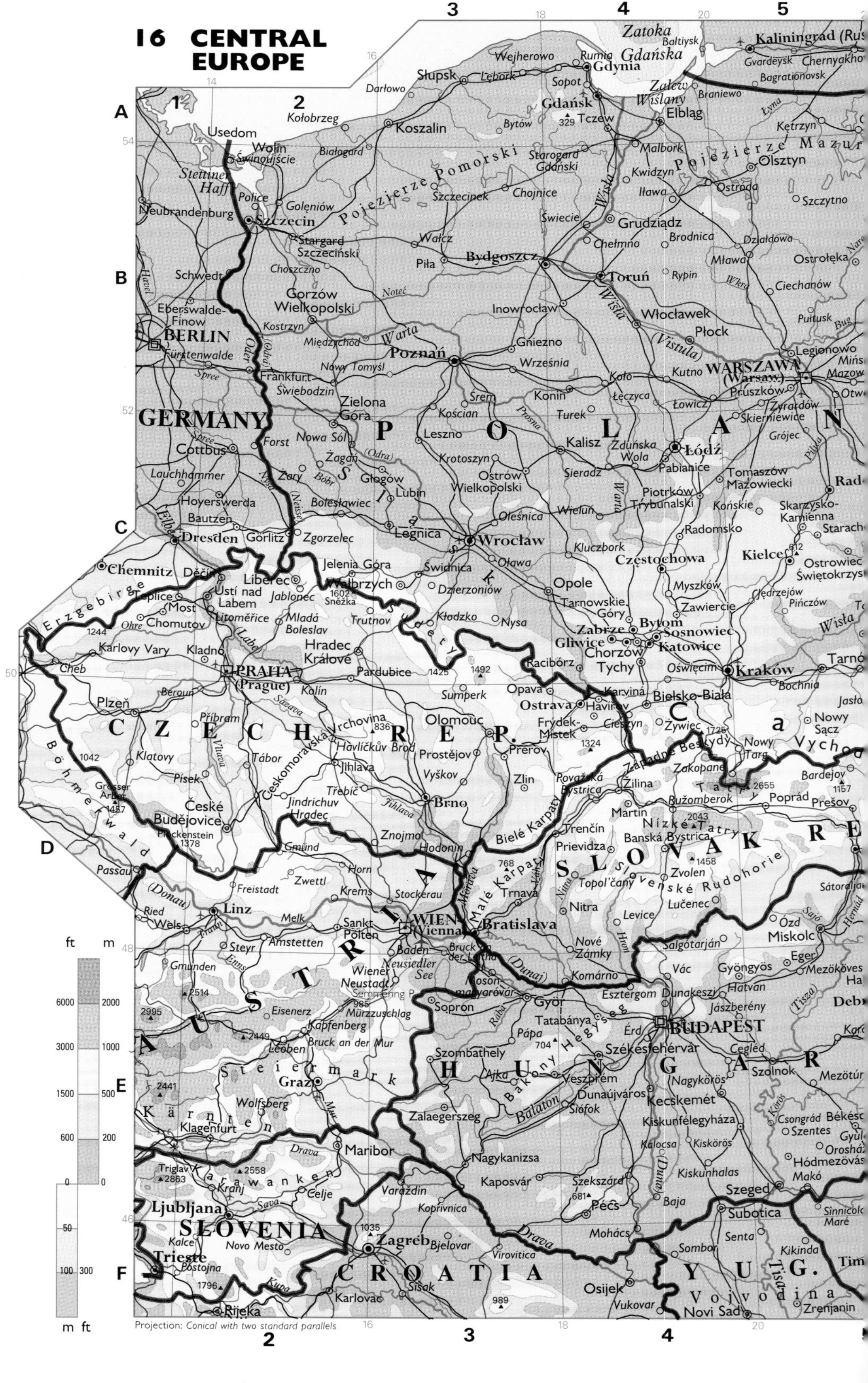

1: 5 000 000

50   0   50   100 miles
50   0   50   100   150 km

jampolė
Alytus
Druskininkai
ów
ski
Isk
Białystok
Hajnówka
Biała Podlaska
Międzyrzec Podlaski
Włodawa
Chełm
Wola
Novovolynsk
Zamość
Rava-Ruska
Nesterov
Sambir
Drohobych
Boryslav
Truskavets
Skole
Bolekhiv
Izhhorod
Mukacheve
Berehove
háza
Satu Mare
Carei
dea
Zalău
Cluj-Napoca
Turda
Munții Bihor
Abrud
Brad
Alba-Iulia
Deva
Hunedoara
goj
Vulcan
Petroșani

7   **8**   **9**   **10**

BELARUS
MINSK
346
Hrodna
Lida
Navahrudak
323
Dzyatlava
Dzyarzhynsk
Hrodzyanka
Stowbtsy
Nyasvizh
Masty
Vawkavysk
Slonim
Baranavichy
Klyetsk
Slutsk
Babruysk
Lyakhavichy
Hantsavichy
Salihorsk
Glusk
Svislach
Katsevichy
Tsyelyakhany
Pruzhany
Bereza
Luninyets
Kobryn
Dragichyn
Ivanava
Pinsk
Stolin
Davyd Haradok
Brest
Malaryta
Kamin-Kashyrskyy
Dubrovytsya

Asipovichy
Aktsyabrski
Svyetlahorsk
Pyetrykaw
Mazyr
Yelsk
Ovruch
Belokorovichi
Olevsk
Korosten
Novohrad-Volynskyy
Radomyshl
Malyn

Bykhaw
Slawharad
Rahachow
Zhlobin
Homyel
Rechytsa
Vasilevichi
Kalinkavichy
Khoyniki
Loyew
Chornobyl
Oster
Dymer
Irpin
KYYIV (Kiev)
Vasylkiv
Fastiv

Byelaviezhskaya

B

52

C

Kyyivske Vdskh.

316

Pripet Marsh
Yaselda
Pripyats (Pripet)
Haryn
Sluch
Uzh
Teteriv
Pripyat'

Lyuboml
Kovel
Staryy Chartoriysk
Kostopil
Rozhyshche
Kivertsy
Volodymyr-Volynskyy
Lutsk
Rivne
Zdolbuniv
Korets
Slavuta
Zhytomyr
Pershotravensk
Korostyshev
Horokhiv
Dubno
341
Ostroh
Shepetivka
Polonne
Berdychiv
Kozyatyn
Skvyra
Tarashcha
Berestechko
Kremenets
Izyaslav
Bila Tserkva
Tetiyev
Lipovets
Zhashkiv
Radekhiv
Kamyanka-Buzka
Brody
Starokonstyantyniv
Khemelnik
Yavoriv
Mostyska
Zolochiv
Zbarazh
Khmelnytskyy
Vinnytsya
nys
Horodok
Lviv (Lvov)
Ternopil
Skalat
384
Zhmerynka
327
Uman
270
Horodok
Haysyn
Radekhiv
Khodoriv
Berezhany
Hrymayliv
Bar
Haysyn
Drohobych
Rogatyn
Terebovlya
Kopychyntsi
Horodok
Tulchyn
Vapnyarka
Bershad
Balta
Kalush
Buchach
Chortkiv
Skala-Podilska
Mohyliv-Podilskyy
346
Horodenka
Zalishchyky
Kamyanets-Podilskyy
Ivano-Frankivsk
Nadvirna
Kolomyya
Khotyn
Ocnița
Yampil
1881
Pechenizhyn
Snyatyn
Novoselytsya
Lipcani
Drochia
Soroca
Ananyiv
Kotovsk
Volovets
Yaremcha
Chernivtsi
Hlyboka
Edineta
Ribnița
Yasinya
Storozhynets
Dorohoi
Bălți
Dubăsari
Khust
Rakhiv
Rădăuți
Fălești
Dubăsari Vdkhr.
Tyachiv
Cornești
Berehove
Sighetu-Marmatiei
1565
Botoșani
Orhei
1783
Baia Mare
Borșa
Suceava
Fălticeni
Ungheni
Chișinău
Tiraspol
Pietrosul
2303
Pașcani
Iași
Tighina
Vatra-Dornei
2100
Roman
418
Leova
Cimișlia
Basarabeasca
Bistrița
Pietrosul
1804
Huși
Comrat
Artsyz
Bârlad
Ceadâr-Lunga
Reghin
Mureș
Vaslui
Cahul
Tatarbunary
Tîrgu Mureș
1777
Piatra Neamț
Bîrlad
Bolhrad
Kiliya
Iud
Odorheiu Secuiesc
Bacău
Vulcanești
Vylkove
Tîrnăveni
Sighișoara
Onești
Tecuci
Reni
Izmayil
Sulina
Medias
Sfîntu Gheorghe
Focșani
Galați
Ozero Sasyk
Sibiu
Făgăraș
Brașov
Rîmnicu Sărat
Brăila
Tulcea
Carpați Meridionali
Săcele
Buzău
Dunărea (Danube)
Babadag
1380
Simeria
2543
Moldoveana
2507
Vf. Omul
Cîmpulung
P. Turnu Roșu
Buzău
Curtea de Argeș
445

D

E

50

48

46

F

Dnister (Nistru)
Dunărea (Danube)
Bilhorod-Dnistrovskyy

MOLDOVA

U K R A I N E

East from Greenwich
6   **7**   **8**   **9**

24   26

CARTOGRAPHY BY PHILIP'S. COPYRIGHT REED INTERNATIONAL BOOKS LTD.

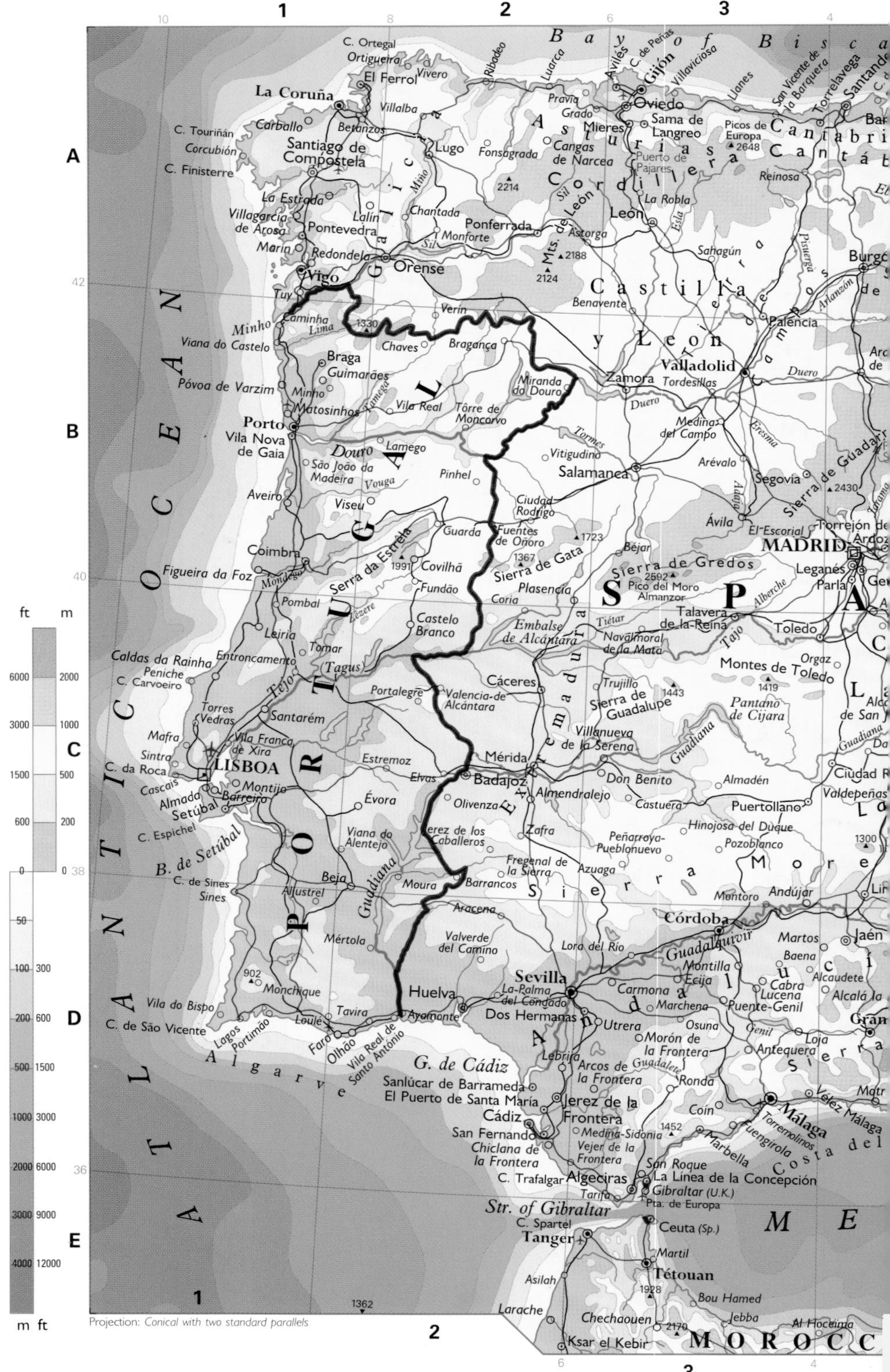

Projection: Conical with two standard parallels

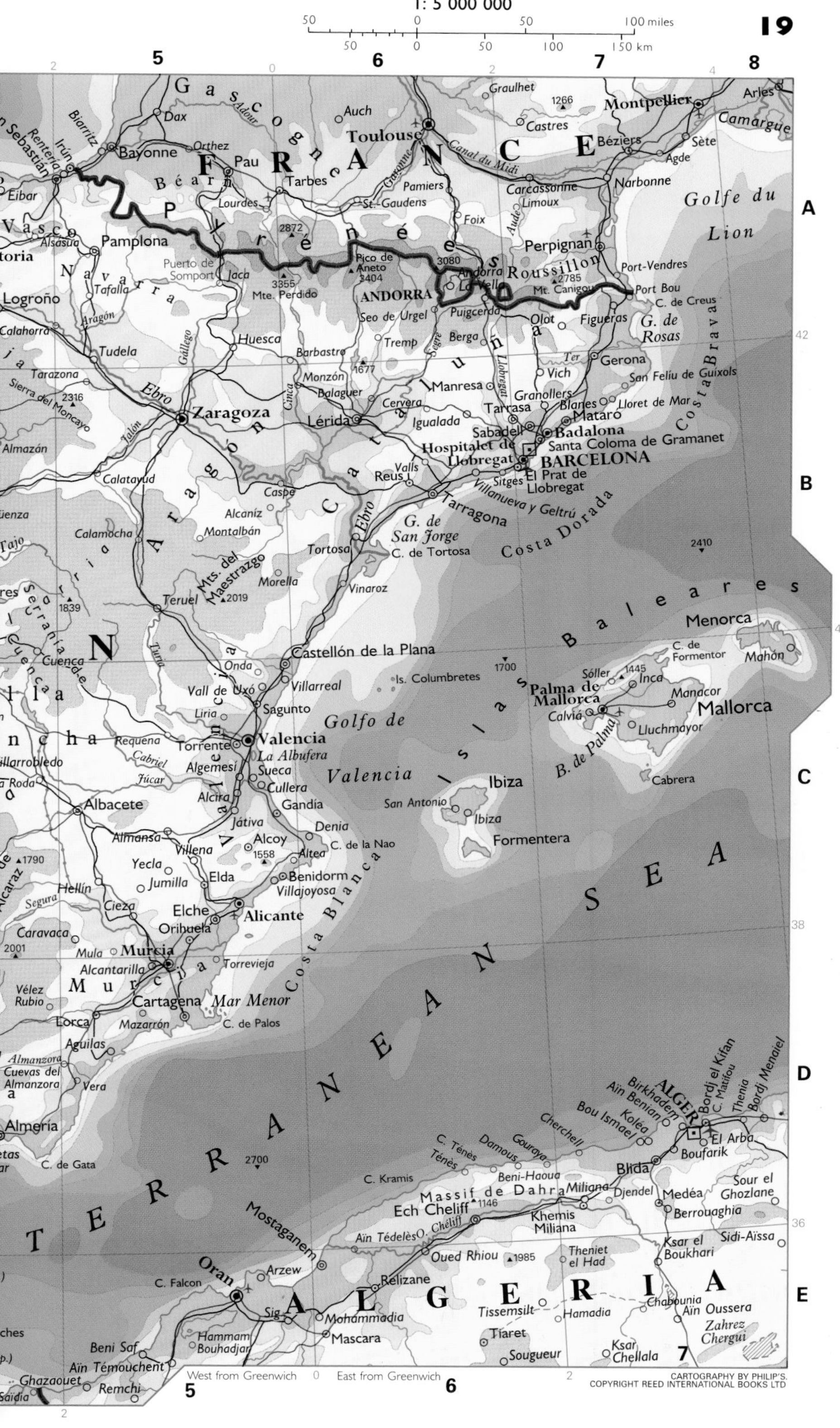

1 : 5 000 000

50   0   50   100 miles
50 0 50 100 150 km

A

B

C

D

E

Golfe du Lion

FRANCE

Gascogne

Pyrénées

Roussillon

Costa Brava

Costa Dorada

Islas Baleares

Menorca

Mallorca

Ibiza

Formentera

MEDITERRANEAN SEA

ANDORRA

Zaragoza

BARCELONA

Valencia

Golfo de Valencia

Palma de Mallorca

Murcia

Alicante

Almería

ALGERIA

ALGER

Oran

42

40

38

36

CARTOGRAPHY BY PHILIP'S.
COPYRIGHT REED INTERNATIONAL BOOKS LTD

West from Greenwich   0   East from Greenwich

AUSTRIA
SWITZERLAND
FRANCE
HUNGARY
SLOVENIA
CROATIA
BOSNIA-
HERZEGOVINA
MONACO
SAN MARINO
VATICAN CITY
I T A L Y
A D R I A T I C   S E A
L I G U R I A N   S E A
Golfo di Génova
Golfo di Venézia
Corse
Milano
Torino (Turin)
Génova
Venézia (Venice)
Firenze (Florence)
Bologna
Roma
Ljubljana
Zagreb
Sarajevo
Trieste
Rijeka
Split
Dubrovnik
Graz
Klagenfurt
Maribor
Verona
Pádova
Parma
Modena
Ravenna
Ancona
Pescara
Pisa
Livorno
Perúgia
Elba
Bastia
Ajaccio
Nice
Cannes
Grenoble
Lombárdia
Piemonte
Liguria
Toscana
Lazio
Dolomiti
Dalmacija
Velebit Planina
Dinara Planina
Alpes Maritimes
Po
Adige
Drava
Sava
1
2
3
4
5
6
7
A
B
C
D

1: 5 000 000

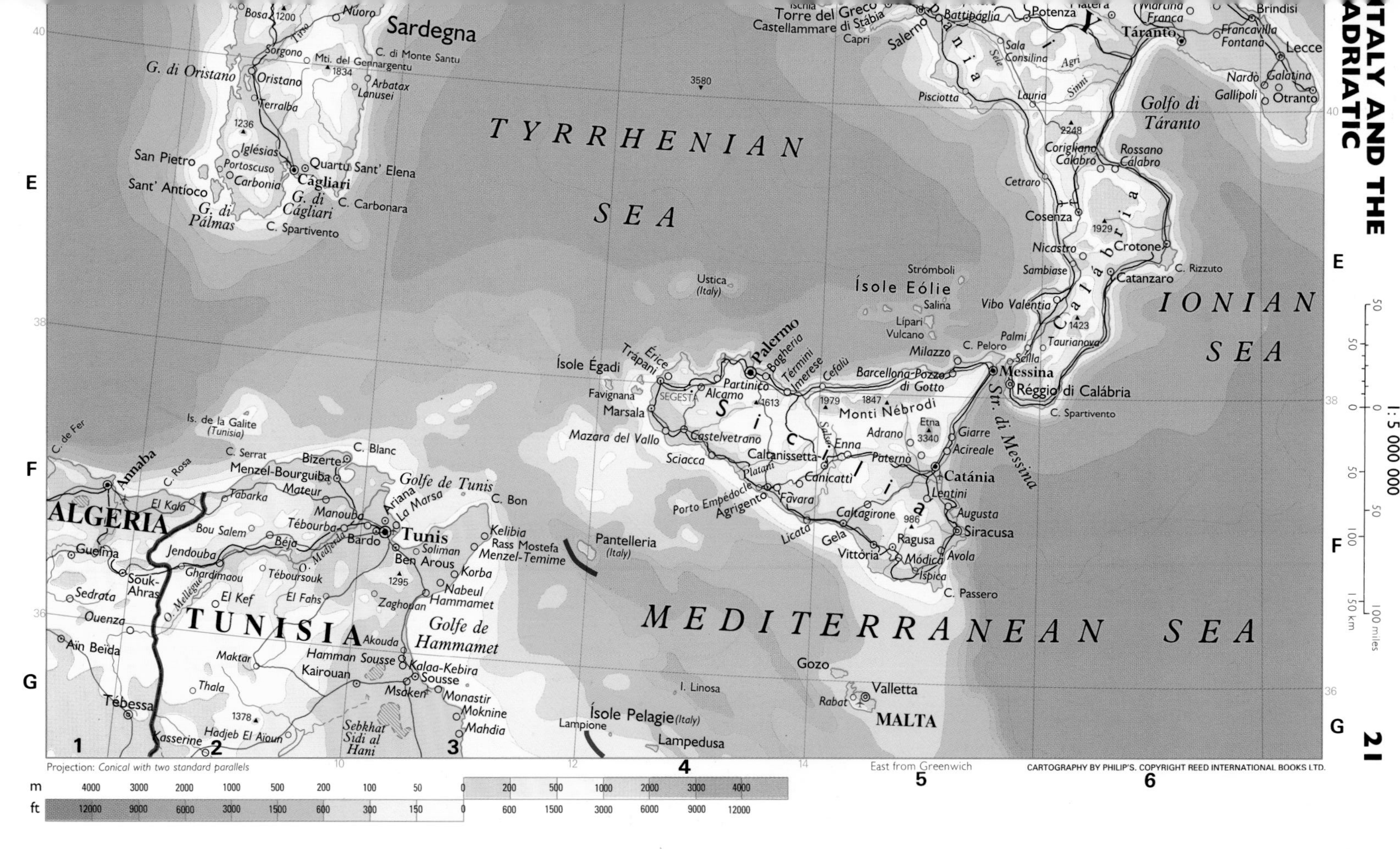
TYRRHENIAN SEA
IONIAN SEA
MEDITERRANEAN SEA
Sardegna
Sicilia
Calabria
TUNISIA
ALGERIA
MALTA
Palermo
Messina
Catánia
Siracusa
Réggio di Calábria
Cágliari
Tunis
Táranto
Lecce
Brindisi
Cosenza
Catanzaro
Crotone
Trápani
Marsala
Agrigento
Caltanissetta
Ragusa
Gela
Valletta
Gozo
Pantelleria (Italy)
Lampedusa
Ísole Pelagie (Italy)
Ísole Égadi
Ísole Eólie
Ustica (Italy)
Str. di Messina
Golfo di Táranto
Golfe de Tunis
Golfe de Hammamet
Bizerte
Sousse
Kairouan
Annaba
Tébessa
Oristano
Nuoro
Iglésias
Monti Nébrodi
Etna 3340
Salerno
Potenza
Capri
Projection: Conical with two standard parallels
East from Greenwich
CARTOGRAPHY BY PHILIP'S. COPYRIGHT REED INTERNATIONAL BOOKS LTD.

22 GREECE AND THE BALKANS

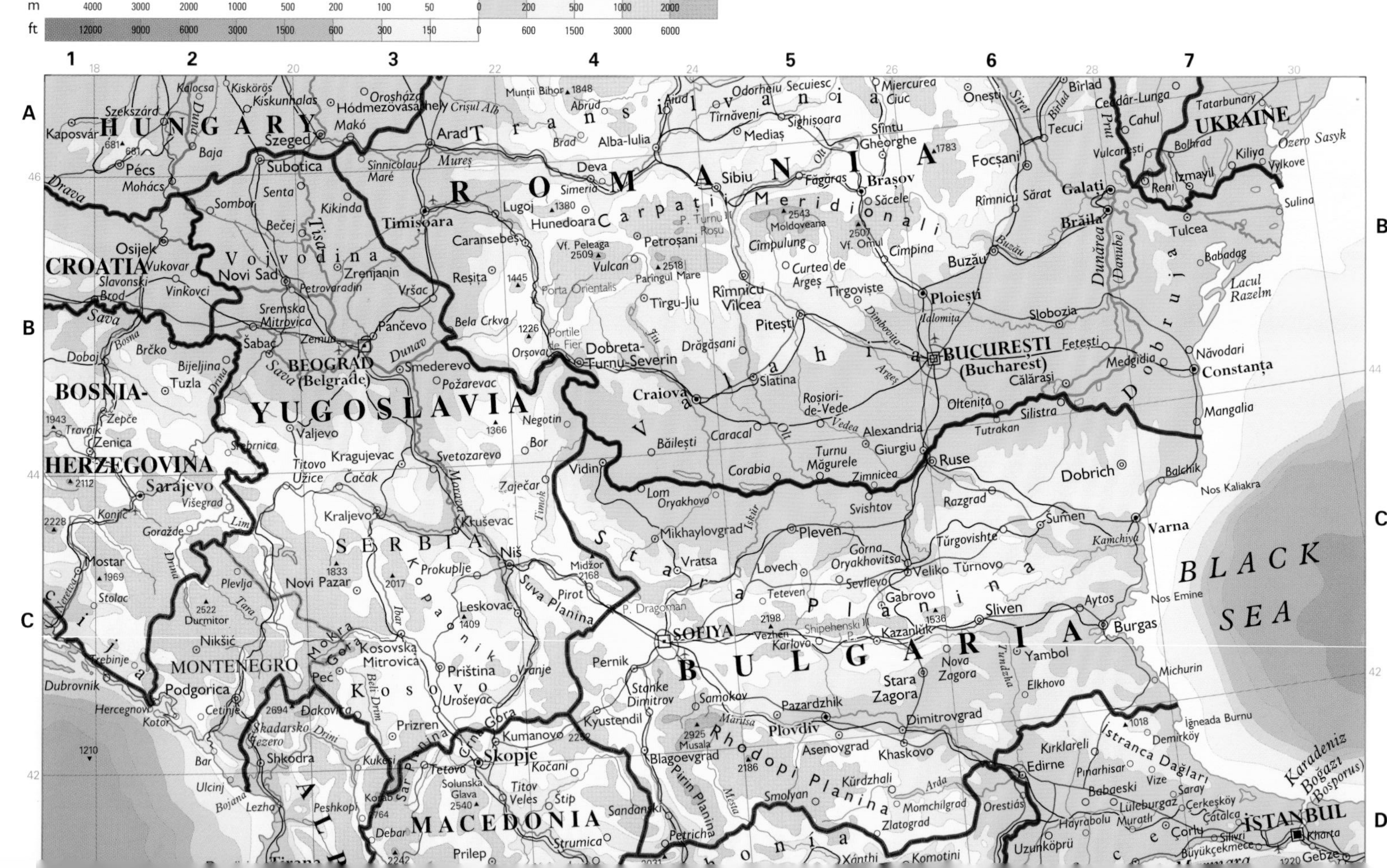

m
4000
3000
2000
1000
500
200
100
50
0
200
500
1000
2000
ft
12000
9000
6000
3000
1500
600
300
150
0
600
1500
3000
6000
HUNGARY
ROMANIA
UKRAINE
CROATIA
BOSNIA-HERZEGOVINA
YUGOSLAVIA
SERBIA
MONTENEGRO
KOSOVO
MACEDONIA
BULGARIA
BLACK SEA
Transilvania
Carpaţii Meridionali
Vojvodina
Stara Planina
Rhodopi Planina
Dobruja
BUCUREŞTI (Bucharest)
BEOGRAD (Belgrade)
SOFIYA
İSTANBUL
Sarajevo
Skopje
Podgorica
Constanţa
Varna
Burgas
Ruse
Plovdiv
Craiova
Ploieşti
Braşov
Galaţi
Brăila
Timişoara
Novi Sad
Niš
Szeged
Pécs
Dunărea (Danube)
Tisa
Sava
Drina
Morava
Prut
Siret
Olt
Mureş
Edirne
Tuzla
Mostar
Osijek
Subotica
Sibiu
Piteşti
Dobreta-Turnu-Severin
Pleven
Šumen
Dobrich
Sliven
Yambol
Stara Zagora
Haskovo
Blagoevgrad
Pernik
Vidin
Lom
Tulcea
Focşani
Buzău
Deva
Arad
Kragujevac
Kraljevo
Priština
Prizren
Shkodra
Dubrovnik
Karadeniz Boğazi (Bosporus)
İstranca Dağlari

1 : 5 000 000

50   0   50   100 miles

50   0   50   100   150 km

23

East from Greenwich

Projection: Conical with two standard parallels

CARTOGRAPHY BY PHILIP'S.
COPYRIGHT REED INTERNATIONAL BOOKS LTD

24 EASTERN EUROPE

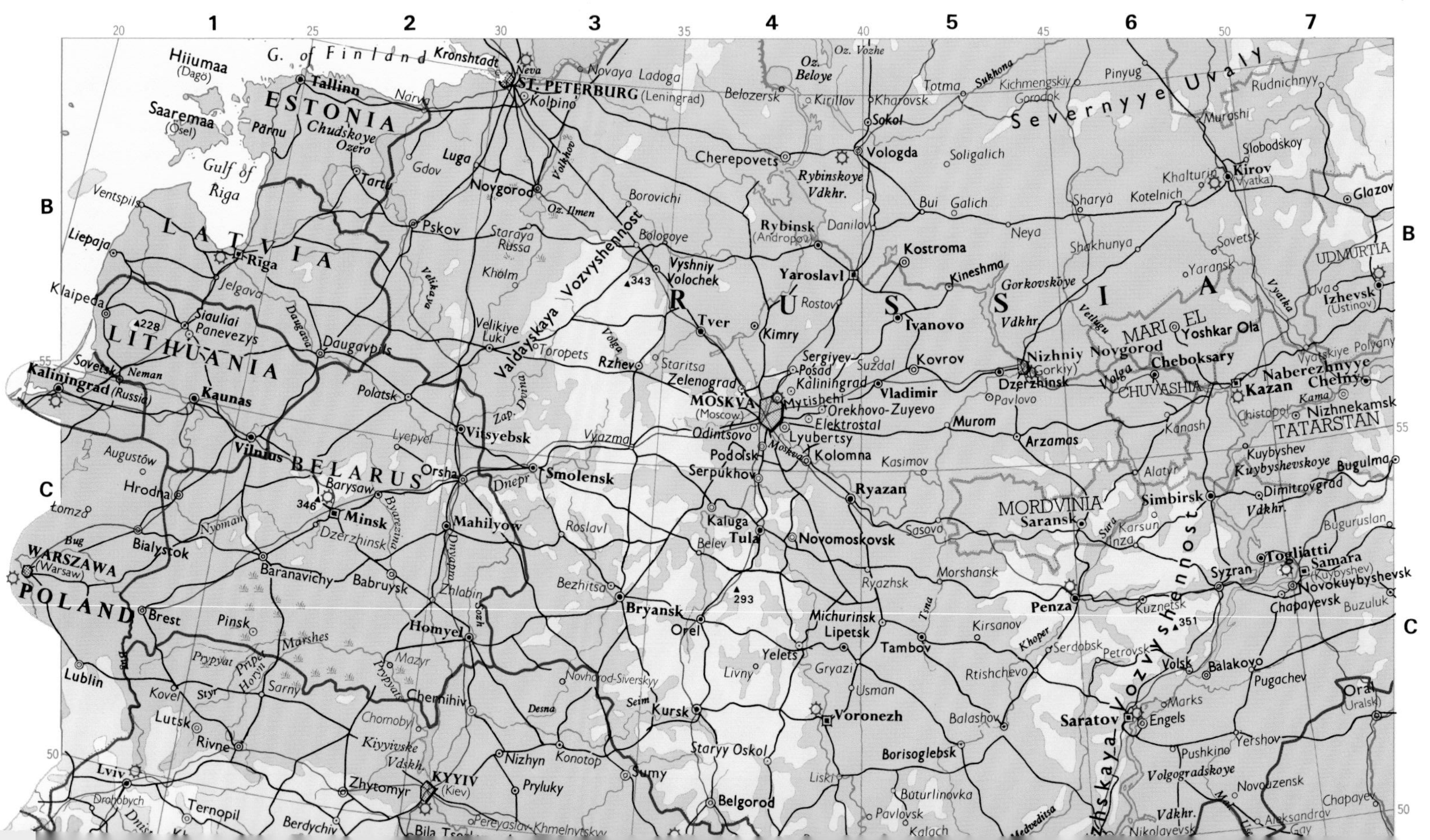

G. of Finland
Gulf of Riga
Hiiumaa (Dagö)
Saaremaa (Ösel)
ESTONIA
Tallinn
Pärnu
Chudskoye Ozero
Tartu
Narva
Kronshtadt
Neva
ST. PETERBURG (Leningrad)
Kolpino
Novaya Ladoga
Luga
Gdov
Pskov
Novgorod
Oz. Ilmen
Volkhov
Staraya Russa
Kholm
Velikiye Luki
Velikaya
LATVIA
Riga
Jelgava
Ventspils
Liepaja
Daugavpils
Daugava
LITHUANIA
Klaipeda
Siauliai
Panevezys
Kaunas
Vilnius
Neman
Sovetsk
Kaliningrad (Russia)
BELARUS
Polatsk
Vitsyebsk
Zap. Dvina
Orsha
Lyepyel
Barysaw
Minsk
Dzerzhinsk
Byarezina
Mahilyow
Dnyapro
Babruysk
Baranavichy
Hrodna
Nyoman
Augustów
Łomża
Bialystok
Pinsk
Brest
Homyel
Zhlobin
Sozh
Mazyr
Prypyat
Pripet
Horyn
Marshes
Sarny
Styr
POLAND
WARSZAWA (Warsaw)
Bug
Lublin
Lviv
Drohobych
Lutsk
Rivne
Kovel
Ternopil
Zhytomyr
Berdychiv
Chornobyl
Kiyyivske Vdskh.
KYYIV (Kiev)
Chernihiv
Nizhyn
Pryluky
Konotop
Desna
Novhorod-Siverskyy
Seim
Sumy
Pereyaslav-Khmelnytskyy
Valdayskaya Vozvyshennost
Vyshniy Volochek
Bologoye
Borovichi
Toropets
Rzhev
Volga
Staritsa
Tver
Zelenograd
MOSKVA (Moscow)
Odintsovo
Podolsk
Serpukhov
Kaluga
Tula
Belev
Vyazma
Dnepr
Smolensk
Roslavl
Bryansk
Bezhitsa
Orel
Kursk
Belgorod
Staryy Oskol
Livny
Yelets
Lipetsk
Gryazi
Voronezh
Liski
Usman
Michurinsk
Ryazhsk
Novomoskovsk
Ryazan
Kolomna
Moskva
Lyubertsy
Elektrostal
Orekhovo-Zuyevo
Mytishchi
Kaliningrad
Sergiyev Posad
Vladimir
Suzdal
Kovrov
Ivanovo
Kineshma
Kostroma
Yaroslavl
Rostov
Rybinsk (Andropov)
Rybinskoye Vdkhr.
Kimry
Cherepovets
Belozersk
Kirillov
Oz. Beloye
Oz. Vozhe
Vologda
Sokol
Kharovsk
Totma
Sukhona
Soligalich
Galich
Bui
Danilov
Neya
Sharya
Shakhunya
Kotelnich
Khalturin
Kirov (Vyatka)
Slobodskoy
Murashi
Rudnichnyy
Pinyug
Kichmengskiy Gorodok
Severnyye Uvaly
Sovetsk
Yaransk
Vyatka
Vetluga
Gorkovskoye Vdkhr.
Nizhniy Novgorod (Gorkiy)
Dzerzhinsk
Pavlovo
Murom
Arzamas
Kasimov
Sasovo
Morshansk
Tambov
Tsna
Kirsanov
Rtishchevo
Balashov
Borisoglebsk
Buturlinovka
Pavlovsk
Kalach
MORDVINIA
Saransk
Penza
Khoper
Serdobsk
Petrovsk
Kuznetsk
Simbirsk
Karsun
Alatyr
Sura
Inza
CHUVASHIA
Cheboksary
MARI EL
Yoshkar Ola
Kanash
Kazan
Chistopol
TATARSTAN
Nizhnekamsk
Naberezhnyye Chelny
Kama
UDMURTIA
Izhevsk (Ustinov)
Uva
Glazov
Vyatskiye Polyany
Kuybyshev
Kuybyshevskoye Vdkhr.
Dimitrovgrad
Bugulma
Buguruslan
Togliatti
Samara (Kuybyshev)
Novokuybyshevsk
Chapayevsk
Syzran
Buzuluk
Oral (Uralsk)
Privolzhskaya Vozvyshennost
Balakovo
Pugachev
Volsk
Marks
Engels
Saratov
Volgogradskoye Vdkhr.
Pushkino
Yershov
Novouzensk
Aleksandrov Gay
Nikolayevsk
Chapayev
Medveditsa
343
293
228
346
351
20
25
30
35
40
45
50
55
B
C
1
2
3
4
5
6
7

1 : 10 000 000

CARTOGRAPHY BY PHILIP'S. COPYRIGHT REED INTERNATIONAL BOOKS LTD.

1. Karachey-Cherkessia
2. Kabardino-Balkaria
3. North Ossetia
4. Ingushetia

Projection: Conical with two standard parallels 30

35 East from Greenwich

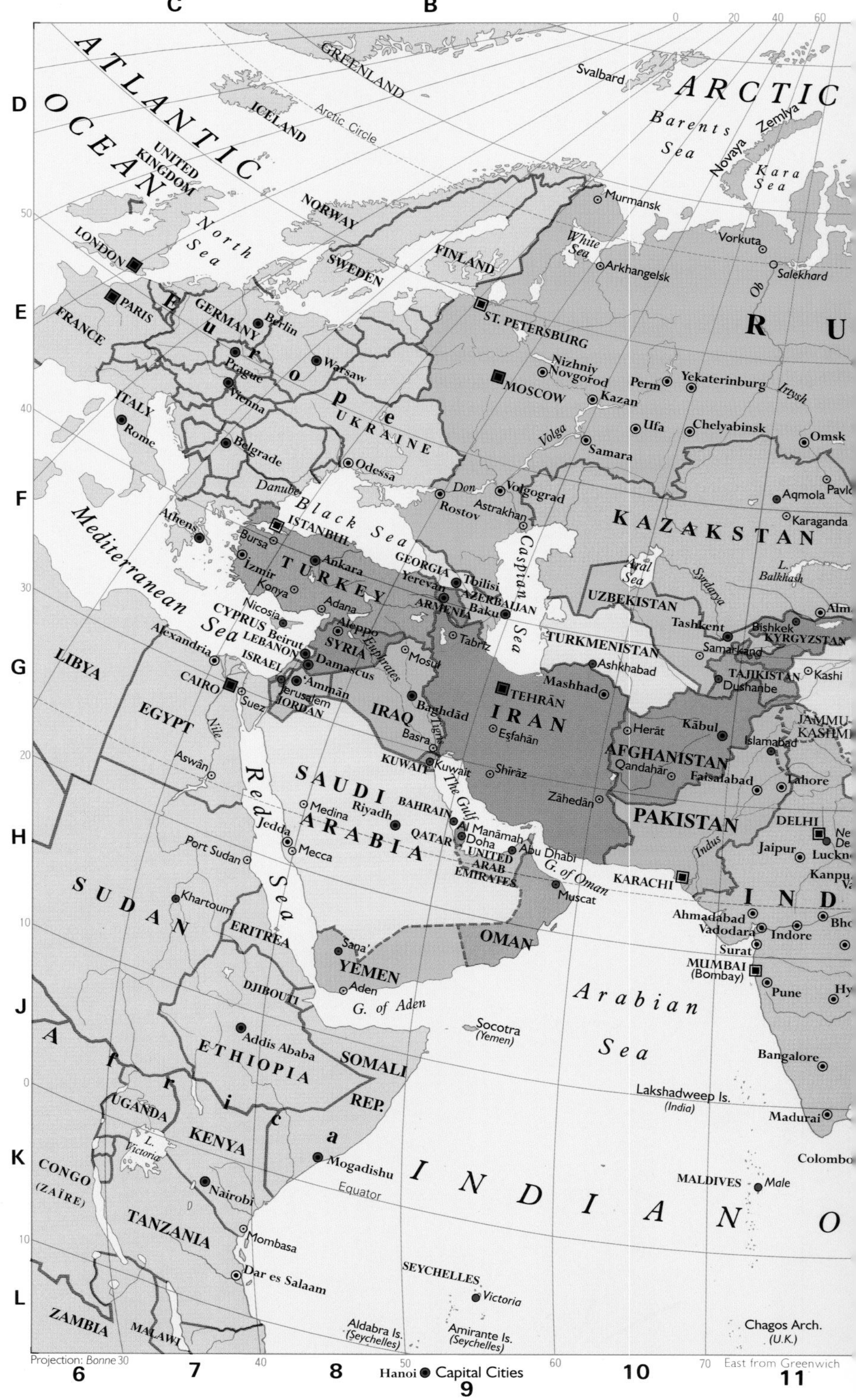

ATLANTIC OCEAN

GREENLAND
ICELAND
Arctic Circle
Svalbard
ARCTIC
Barents Sea
Novaya Zemlya
Kara Sea
Murmansk
Vorkuta
Ob
Salekhard

UNITED KINGDOM
LONDON
PARIS
FRANCE
North Sea
NORWAY
SWEDEN
FINLAND
White Sea
Arkhangelsk
St. PETERSBURG
R U

GERMANY
Berlin
Warsaw
Prague
Vienna
Europe
UKRAINE
MOSCOW
Nizhniy Novgorod
Perm
Yekaterinburg
Irtysh
Omsk
ITALY
Rome
Belgrade
Odessa
Danube
Don
Volga
Kazan
Ufa
Chelyabinsk
Samara
Astrakhan
Rostov
Volgograd
Aqmola
Pavl
KAZAKSTAN
Karaganda

Athens
Black Sea
ISTANBUL
Bursa
Izmir
Konya
TURKEY
Ankara
Adana
GEORGIA
Yerevan
ARMENIA
Tbilisi
AZERBAIJAN
Baku
Caspian Sea
Aral Sea
Syrdarya
L. Balkhash
UZBEKISTAN
Tashkent
Samarkand
Alm
Bishkek
KYRGYZSTAN
Kashi

Mediterranean Sea
LIBYA
Nicosia
CYPRUS
Beirut
LEBANON
ISRAEL
Alexandria
CAIRO
Jerusalem
Amman
JORDAN
Aleppo
SYRIA
Damascus
Euphrates
Mosul
Tabriz
IRAQ
Baghdad
Basra
Tigris
Mashhad
Ashkhabad
TURKMENISTAN
TEHRAN
IRAN
Esfahan
Herat
Kabul
Islamabad
TAJIKISTAN
Dushanbe
JAMMU KASHM
AFGHANISTAN
Qandahar
Faisalabad
Lahore

EGYPT
Aswan
Nile
Suez
Red Sea
SAUDI ARABIA
Medina
Jedda
Mecca
Riyadh
KUWAIT
Kuwait
Shiraz
The Gulf
BAHRAIN
QATAR
Al Manamah
Doha
Abu Dhabi
UNITED ARAB EMIRATES
Zahedan
PAKISTAN
DELHI
Ne De
Jaipur
Luckn
KARACHI
I N D
Kanpu
V
Ahmadabad
Vadodara
Indore
Bho
Surat
MUMBAI (Bombay)
Pune
Hy

SUDAN
Port Sudan
Khartoum
ERITREA
DJIBOUTI
ETHIOPIA
Addis Ababa
Muscat
G. of Oman
OMAN
YEMEN
Sana'
Aden
G. of Aden
Arabian Sea
Socotra (Yemen)
Lakshadweep Is. (India)
Madurai
Colombo

Af
UGANDA
L. Victoria
KENYA
SOMALI REP.
Nairobi
Mogadishu
Equator
i c a
INDIAN O
MALDIVES
Male

CONGO (ZAIRE)
TANZANIA
Mombasa
Dar es Salaam
SEYCHELLES
Victoria

ZAMBIA
MALAWI
Aldabra Is. (Seychelles)
Amirante Is. (Seychelles)
Chagos Arch. (U.K.)

Projection: Bonne 30
Hanoi ● Capital Cities
East from Greenwich

I: 67 000 000

200 0 200 400 600 800 1000 1200 miles
200 0 400 800 1200 1600 2000 km

B · C · D

OCEAN

Laptev Sea
New Siberian Is.
Wrangel I.
ALASKA (U.S.A.)

Bering Sea

Aleutian Is. (U.S.A.)

Khatanga
Verkhoyansk
Gizhiga
Okhotsk Magadan
Sea of Okhotsk
Petropavlovsk-Kamchatskiy

Lena
Yakutsk
Komsomolsk
Sakhalin

A S I A

Angara
Krasnoyarsk Bratsk
L. Baikal
Chita
Ulan Ude
Irkutsk
Blagoveshchensk
Khabarovsk
Yuzhno-Sakhalinsk
Hokkaidō
Sapporo

Kuril Is.

rsk
okuznetsk

Hailar
Qiqihar
Harbin
Changchun
Jilin
Vladivostok

Honshū

Ulan Bator

M O N G O L I A

SHENYANG
Jinzhou Anshan
NORTH KOREA
P'yongyang
Sea of Japan

TŌKYŌ
Yokohama
JAPAN

Irümqi
Hami

Baotou
BEIJING TIANJIN
SEOUL
SOUTH KOREA
Pusan
Kyoto
Nagoya
Osaka

Yumen
Taiyuan
Jinan
Hiroshima
Kitakyūshū

Lanzhou
Hwang-ho
Yellow Sea

Bonin Is. (Japan)

C H I N A

Xi'an
Nanjing
SHANGHAI
East China Sea

Volcano Is. (Japan)
Tropic of Cancer

Lhasa
Chengdu
Wuhan HANGZHOU
Nanchang
Fuzhou
Ryukyu Is.

P A C I F I C   O C E A N

Thimphu
BHUTAN
Kunming
CHONGQING Yangtze
Changsha
Taipei
TAIWAN

GUAM (U.S.A.)

BANGLADESH
DACCA
Si Kiang
GUANGZHOU
HONG KONG

BURMA
(MYANMAR)
Chittagong
Hanoi Haiphong
Macau (Port)
Hainan
Luzon
MANILA
PHILIPPINES
Cebu

FED. STATES OF MICRONESIA
PALAU

Bay of Bengal
LAOS
Vientiane
VIETNAM
Mekong
Rangoon
THAILAND
BANGKOK
CAMBODIA
Phnom Penh
Ho Chi Minh City
South China Sea
Palawan
Mindanao
Davao

Andaman Is. (India)
G. of Thailand
Sulu Sea
Zamboanga

Nicobar Is. (India)
Manado
Halmahera
IRIAN JAYA

BRUNEI SABAH
Bandar Seri Begawan
Celebes Sea
Ceram

Str. of Malacca
PEN. MALAYSIA
Kuala Lumpur
SARAWAK
MALAYSIA
Borneo
Celebes
Ambon
Banda Sea
Arafura Sea

Medan
SINGAPORE
Ujung Pandang

Sumatra
Banjarmasin
I N D O N E S I A

Palembang
Java Sea
Flores
Timor
Timor Sea

JAKARTA
Semarang
Surabaya
Sumba
AUSTRALIA
Bandung Java

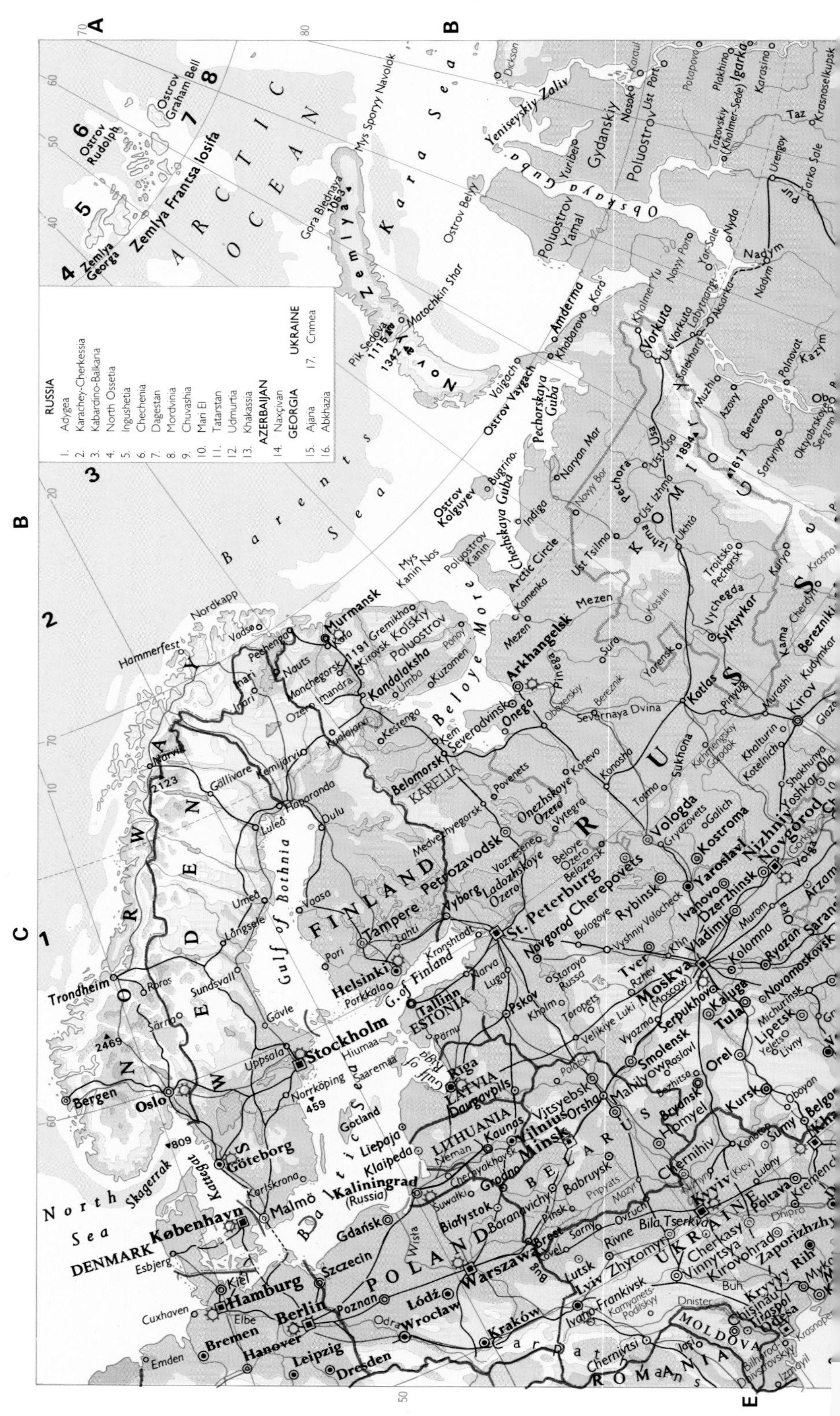

RUSSIA
1. Adygea
2. Karachey-Cherkessia
3. Kabardino-Balkara
4. North Ossetia
5. Ingushetia
6. Chechenia
7. Dagestan
8. Mordvinia
9. Chuvashia
10. Mari El
11. Tatarstan
12. Udmurtia
13. Khakassia
AZERBAIJAN
14. Naxçıvan
GEORGIA
15. Ajaria
16. Abkhazia
UKRAINE
17. Crimea

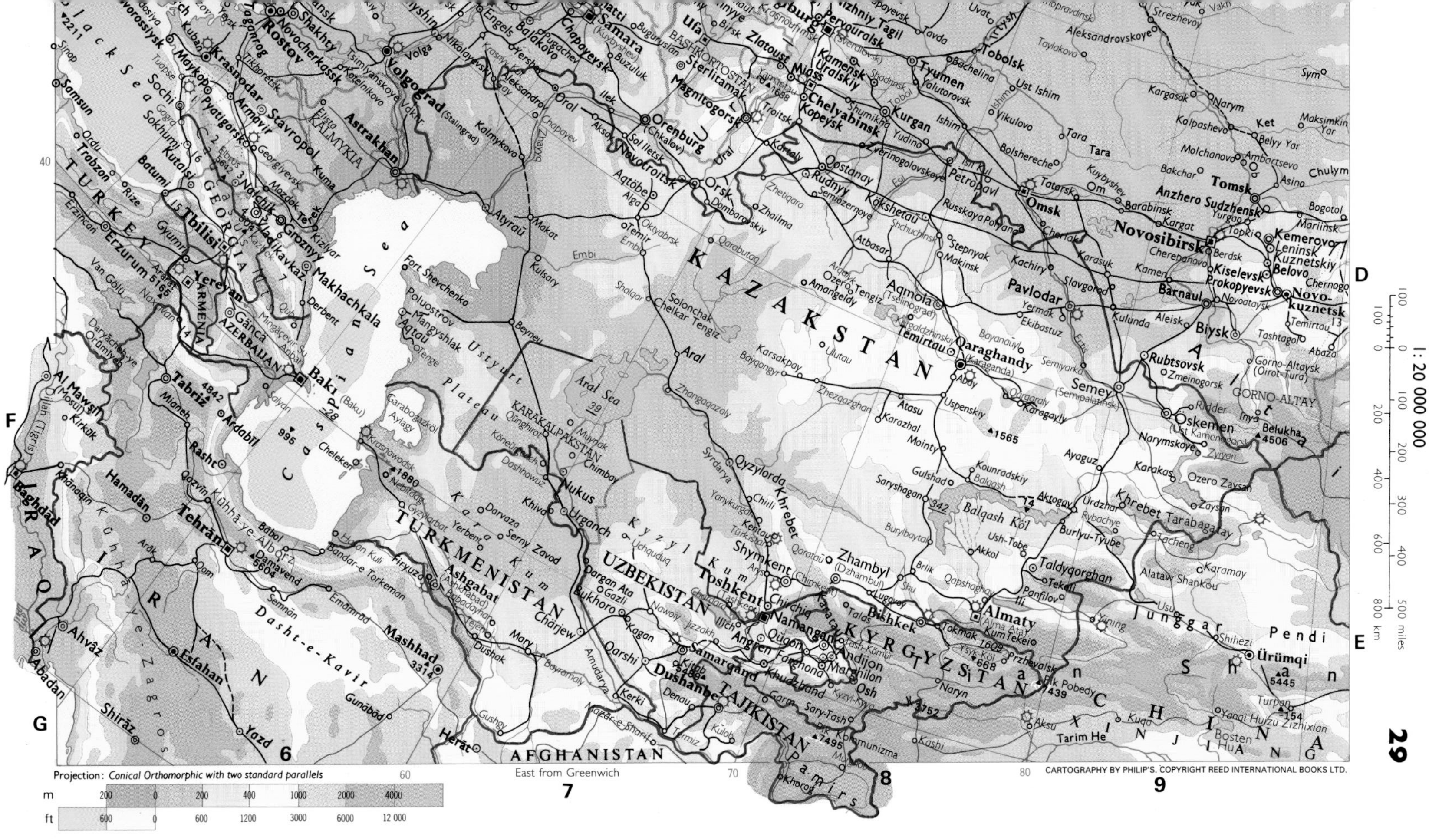

1 : 20 000 000

100   0   100   200   300   400   500 miles
100   0   200   400   600   800 km

CARTOGRAPHY BY PHILIP'S. COPYRIGHT REED INTERNATIONAL BOOKS LTD.

East from Greenwich

Projection: Conical Orthomorphic with two standard parallels

KAZAKSTAN

RUSSIA

UZBEKISTAN

TURKMENISTAN

TAJIKISTAN

KYRGYZSTAN

AFGHANISTAN

IRAN

IRAQ

TURKEY

GEORGIA

ARMENIA

AZERBAIJAN

XINJIANG

CHINA

Novosibirsk, Omsk, Tomsk, Barnaul, Almaty, Bishkek, Tashkent, Samarqand, Ashgabat, Tehran, Baghdad, Tbilisi, Baki, Volgograd, Astrakhan, Rostov

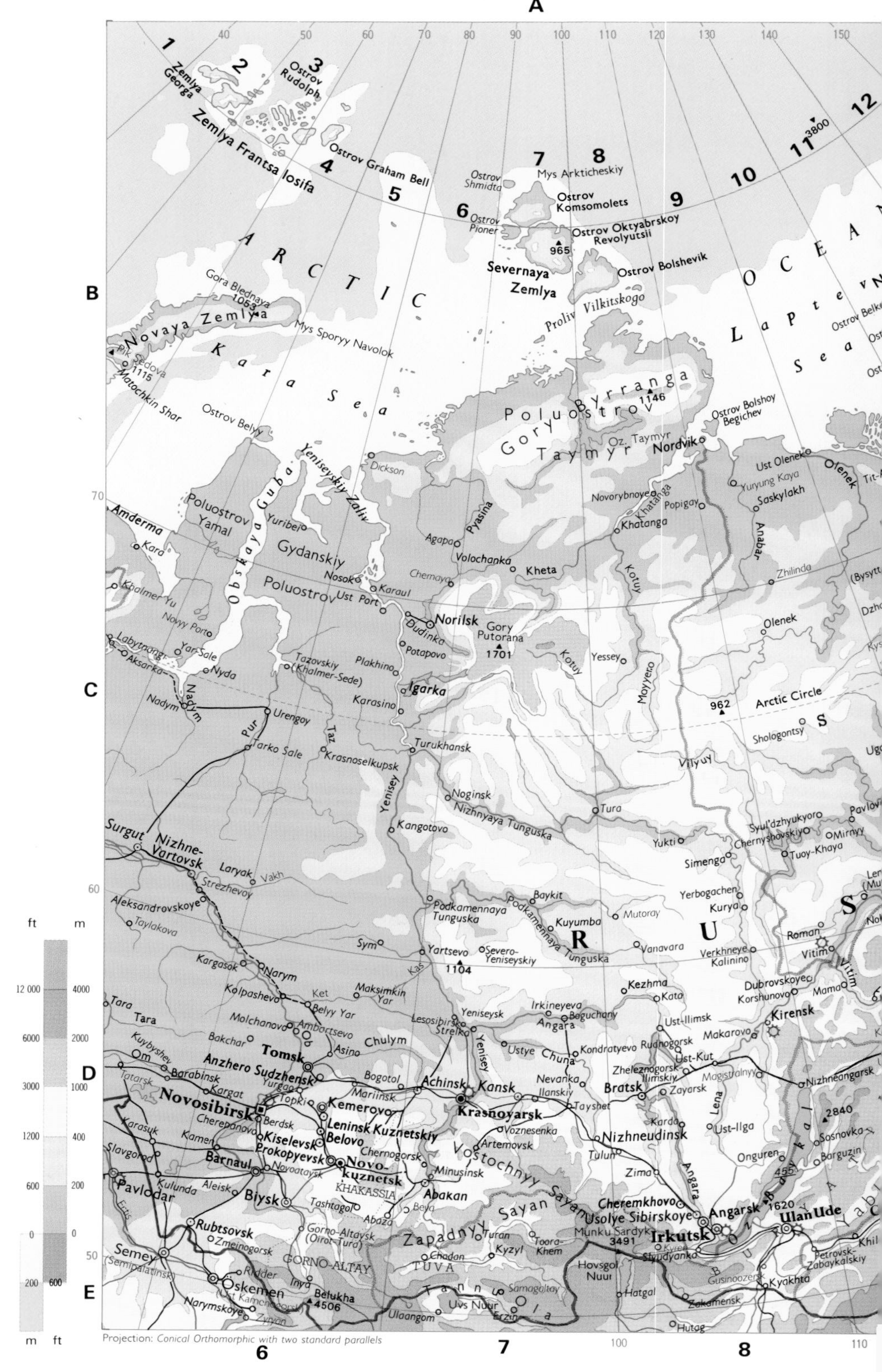

Projection: Conical Orthomorphic with two standard parallels

1:20 000 000

100   0   100   200   300   400   500 miles
100   0   200   400   600   800 km

CARTOGRAPHY BY PHILIP'S.
COPYRIGHT REED INTERNATIONAL BOOKS LTD.

from Greenwich   120   130

SOUTHERN HONSHU, KYUSHU AND SHIKOKU

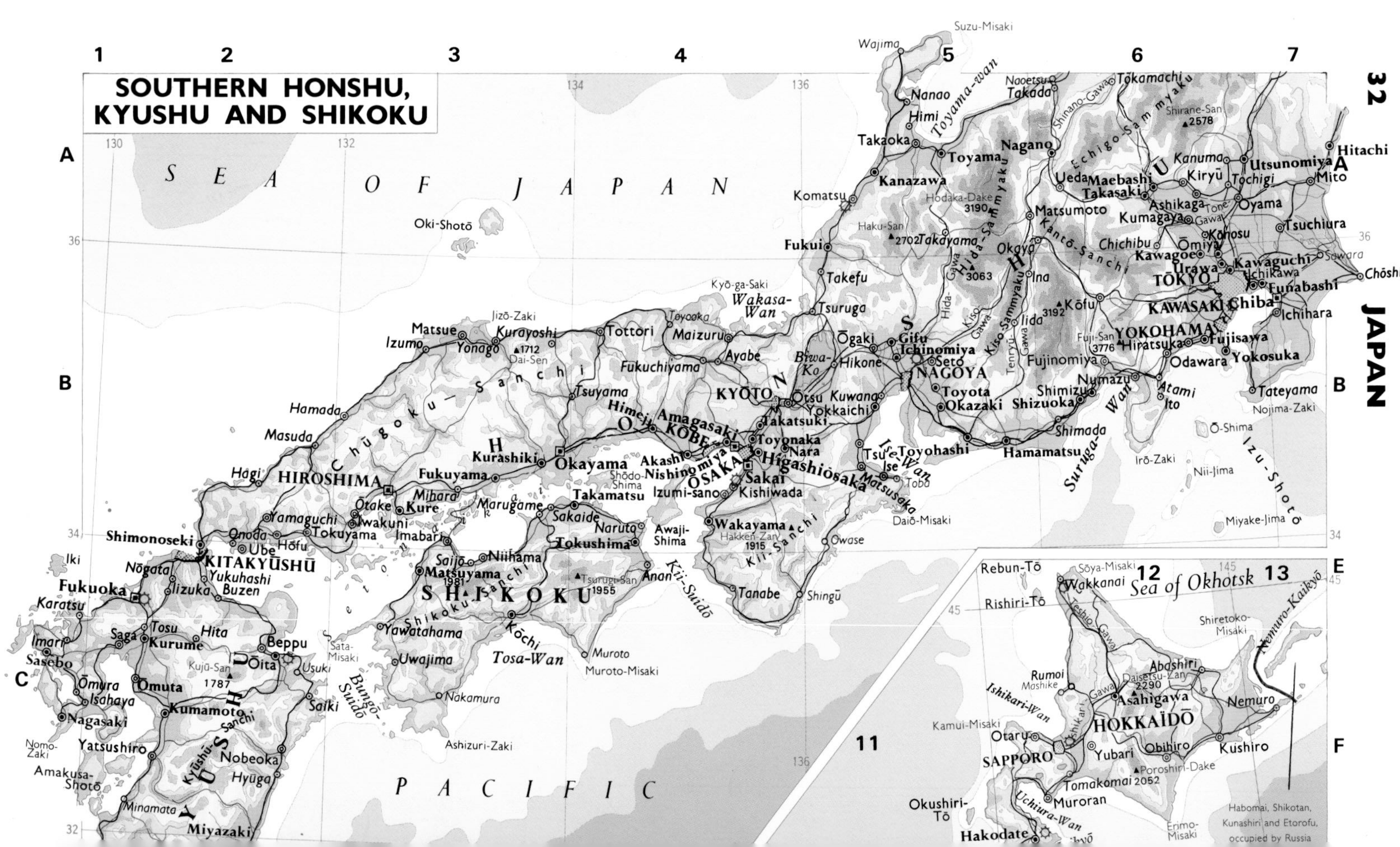

SEA OF JAPAN
PACIFIC
Sea of Okhotsk
Oki-Shotō
Suzu-Misaki
Wajima
Nanao
Himi
Toyama-wan
Takaoka
Toyama
Kanazawa
Komatsu
Fukui
Takefu
Tsuruga
Wakasa-Wan
Kyō-ga-Saki
Hodaka-Dake 3190
Haku-San 2702
Takayama
Hida-Sammyaku
3063
Naoetsu
Takada
Nagano
Shinano-Gawa
Tōkamachi
Echigo-Sammyaku
Shirane-San 2578
Ueda
Maebashi
Takasaki
Kanuma
Kiryū
Tochigi
Utsunomiya
Hitachi
Mito
Ashikaga
Tone-Gawa
Oyama
Matsumoto
Kumagaya
Konosu
Tsuchiura
Kantō-Sanchi
Chichibu
Ōmiya
Kawagoe
Urawa
Kawaguchi
Sawara
Chōshi
Okaya
Ina
TŌKYŌ
Ichikawa
Funabashi
Kōfu 3192
KAWASAKI
Chiba
Ichihara
Iida
Kiso-Sammyaku
Tenryū-Gawa
Kiso-Gawa
Hida-Gawa
Fuji-San 3776
YOKOHAMA
Hiratsuka
Fujisawa
Yokosuka
Fujinomiya
Odawara
Numazu
Atami
Itō
Tateyama
Nojima-Zaki
Shimizu
Shizuoka
Suruga-Wan
Shimada
Hamamatsu
Ō-Shima
Irō-Zaki
Nii-Jima
Izu-Shotō
Miyake-Jima
Ōgaki
Gifu
Ichinomiya
Seto
NAGOYA
Toyota
Okazaki
Toyohashi
Biwa-Ko
Hikone
Kuwana
Yokkaichi
Tsu
Ise-Wan
Ise
Toba
Matsusaka
Daiō-Misaki
KYŌTO
Ōtsu
Takatsuki
Toyonaka
Nara
Higashiōsaka
Sakai
Kishiwada
ŌSAKA
Amagasaki
KŌBE
Nishinomiya
Akashi
Himeji
Izumi-sano
Awaji-Shima
Wakayama
Hakken-Zan 1915
Kii-Sanchi
Owase
Tanabe
Shingū
Kii-Suidō
Maizuru
Ayabe
Toyooka
Fukuchiyama
Tottori
Tsuyama
Jizō-Zaki
Matsue
Izumo
Yonago
Kurayoshi
Dai-Sen 1712
Chūgoku-Sanchi
Hamada
Masuda
Hagi
HIROSHIMA
Okayama
Kurashiki
Fukuyama
Mihara
Kure
Ōtake
Iwakuni
Yamaguchi
Tokuyama
Hōfu
Onoda
Ube
Shimonoseki
Shōdo-Shima
Takamatsu
Marugame
Sakaide
Naruto
Tokushima
Anan
Imabari
Saijō
Niihama
Matsuyama
1981
SHIKOKU
Shikoku-Sanchi
Tsurugi-San 1955
Kōchi
Tosa-Wan
Muroto
Muroto-Misaki
Yawatahama
Uwajima
Nakamura
Ashizuri-Zaki
Sata-Misaki
Bungo-Suidō
Iki
KITAKYŪSHŪ
Nōgata
Yukuhashi
Buzen
Iizuka
Fukuoka
Karatsu
Tosu
Hita
Saga
Kurume
Beppu
Ōita
Imari
Sasebo
Kujū-San 1787
Usuki
Ōmura
Ōmuta
Isahaya
Saiki
Nagasaki
Kumamoto
Kyūshū-Sanchi
Nomo-Zaki
Yatsushiro
Nobeoka
Amakusa-Shotō
Hyūga
Minamata
Miyazaki
KYUSHU
Rebun-Tō
Sōya-Misaki
Wakkanai
Rishiri-Tō
Teshio-Gawa
Shiretoko-Misaki
Nemuro-Kaikyō
Rumoi
Mashike
Abashiri
Daisetsu-Zan 2290
Ishikari-Gawa
Asahigawa
Nemuro
Ishikari-Wan
Kamui-Misaki
HOKKAIDŌ
Otaru
SAPPORO
Yubari
Obihiro
Kushiro
Poroshiri-Dake 2052
Tomakomai
Muroran
Uchiura-Wan
Okushiri-Tō
Hakodate
Erimo-Misaki
Habomai, Shikotan, Kunashiri and Etorofu, occupied by Russia

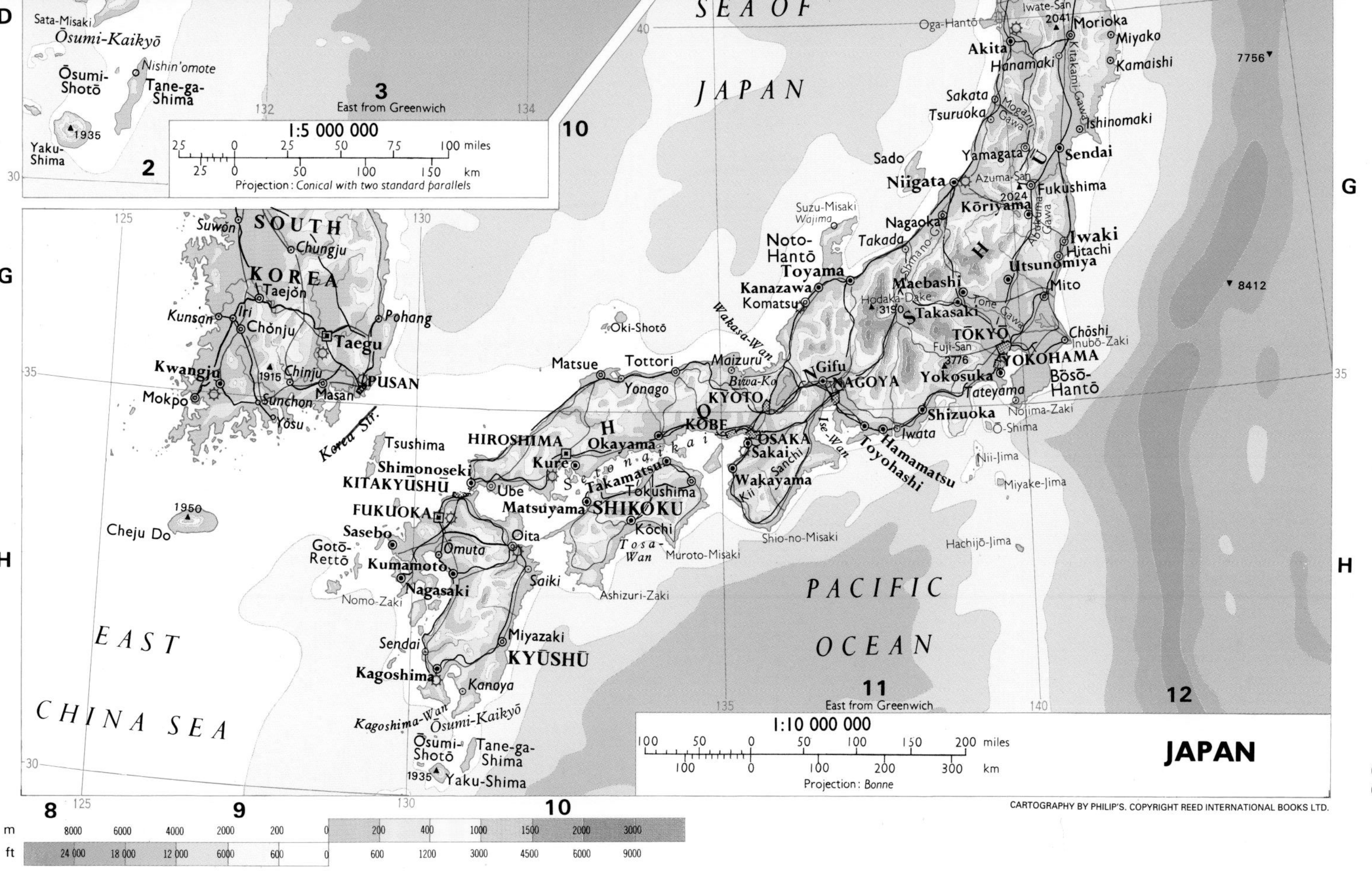

JAPAN

SEA OF

JAPAN

PACIFIC

OCEAN

EAST

CHINA SEA

SOUTH

KOREA

KYUSHU

SHIKOKU

TŌKYŌ

YOKOHAMA

NAGOYA

ŌSAKA

KYŌTO

KŌBE

HIROSHIMA

FUKUOKA

KITAKYŪSHŪ

PUSAN

Taegu

Kwangju

Mokpo

Sendai

Akita

Morioka

Niigata

Toyama

Kanazawa

Sado

Matsue

Tottori

Okayama

Takamatsu

Kōchi

Matsuyama

Ōita

Miyazaki

Kagoshima

Kumamoto

Nagasaki

Sasebo

Ōmuta

Sendai

Kanoya

Tane-ga-Shima

Yaku-Shima

1:10 000 000

East from Greenwich

Projection : Bonne

0   50   100   150   200 miles

0   100   200   300   km

1:5 000 000

East from Greenwich

Projection : Conical with two standard parallels

0   25   50   75   100 miles

0   25   50   75   100   150   km

CARTOGRAPHY BY PHILIP'S. COPYRIGHT REED INTERNATIONAL BOOKS LTD.

m   ft
8000 24 000
6000 18 000
4000 12 000
2000 6000
1000 3000
600   2000
400   1200
200   600
0   0
200   600
2000 6000
4000 12 000
6000 18 000
9000

7756

8412

2041

2024

2776

1935

1915

1960

34 CHINA

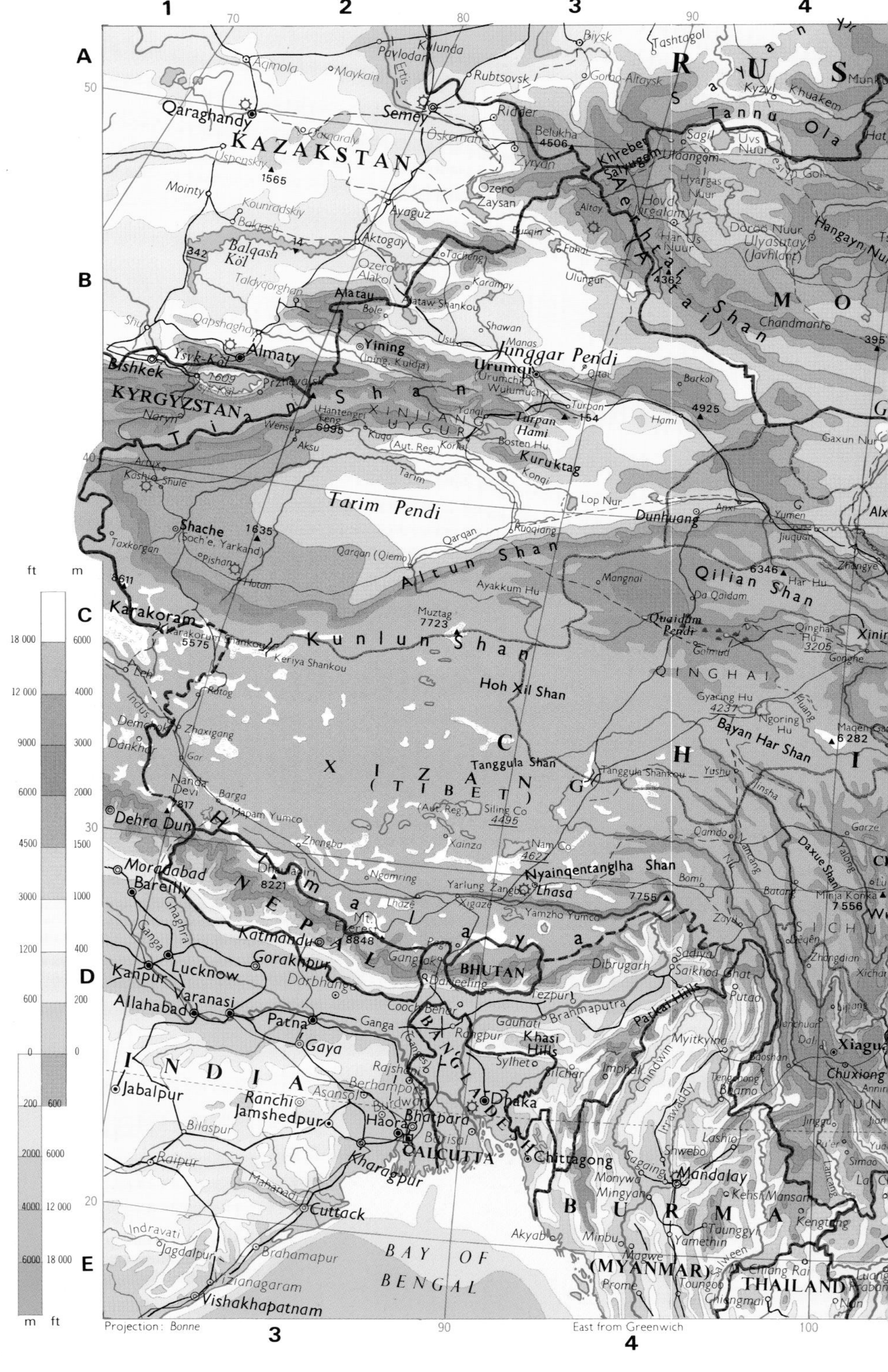

1
2
3
4
A
B
C
D
E
ft
m
18 000
12 000
9000
6000
4500
3000
1200
600
0
200
2000
4000
6000
6000
4000
3000
2000
1500
1000
400
200
0
600
6000
12 000
18 000
m
ft
RUSSIA
KAZAKSTAN
KYRGYZSTAN
Qaraghandy
Aqmola
Pavlodar
Kulunda
Maykain
Rubtsovsk
Biysk
Gorno-Altaysk
Tashtagol
Semey
Öskemen
Ridder
Zyryan
Belukha
4506
Qarqaraly
Uspenskiy
1565
Mointy
Kounradskiy
Balqash
Balqash Köl
342
Aktogay
Ayaguz
Ozero Zaysan
Ozero Alakol
Taldyqorghan
Alatau
Alataw Shankou
Bole
Tacheng
Karamay
Shawan
Manas
Qapshaghay
Almaty
Bishkek
Ysyk-Köl
1609
Przhevalsk
Naryn
Yining (Ining, Kuldja)
Junggar Pendi
Urumqi (Urumchi, Wulumuchi)
Qitai
Turpan
Turpan Hami
-154
Hantengri Feng
6995
Tian Shan
XINJIANG UYGUR (Aut. Reg.)
Wensu
Aksu
Kuqa
Korla
Bosten Hu
Kuruktag
Kongi
Tarim
Tarim Pendi
Artux
Kashi
Shule
Shache (Soch'e, Yarkand)
1635
Taxkorgan
Pishan
Hotan
Qarqan (Qiemo)
Qarqan
Ruoqiang
Lop Nur
Altun Shan
Ayakkum Hu
Mangnai
8611
Karakoram
Karakoram Shankou
5575
Kunlun Shan
Muztag
7723
Keriya Shankou
Hoh Xil Shan
Leh
Indus
Zhaxigang
Gar
Nanda Devi
7817
Barga
Mapam Yumco
Dehra Dun
XIZANG (TIBET) (Aut. Reg.)
CHINA
Tanggula Shan
Tanggula Shankou
Siling Co
4495
Nam Co
4627
Xainza
Zhongba
Nyainqentanglha Shan
Lhasa
Yarlung Zangbo
Xigaze
Yamzho Yumco
Ngamring
Lhaze
Dhaulagiri
8221
Mt. Everest
8848
Himalaya
NEPAL
Katmandu
Gangtok
Darjeeling
BHUTAN
7755
Dibrugarh
Sadiya
Saikhoa Ghat
Tezpur
Brahmaputra
Gauhati
Khasi Hills
Patkai Hills
Moradabad
Bareilly
Ghaghra
Ganga
Lucknow
Kanpur
Gorakhpur
Darbhanga
Allahabad
Varanasi
Patna
Gaya
Cooch Behar
Rangpur
Sylhet
Silchar
Imphal
INDIA
Jabalpur
Ranchi
Jamshedpur
Asansol
Berhampore
Burdwan
Rajshahi
BANGLADESH
Dhaka
Bhatpara
Haora
CALCUTTA
Barisal
Bilaspur
Raipur
Kharagpur
Mahanadi
Cuttack
Chittagong
Indravati
Jagdalpur
Brahamapur
Vizianagaram
Vishakhapatnam
BAY OF BENGAL
Akyab
BURMA (MYANMAR)
Chindwin
Irrawaddy
Myitkyina
Bhamo
Lashio
Shwebo
Sagaing
Mandalay
Monywa
Mingyan
Minbu
Magwe
Meiktila
Taunggyi
Yamethin
Prome
Toungoo
Salween
Chiang Rai
Chiangmai
THAILAND
Kengtung
MONGOLIA
Sayan
Kyzyl
Khuakem
Tannu Ola
Sagil
Uvs Nuur
Ulaangom
Khrebet Sailyugem
Hyargas Nuur
Hovd (Jargalant)
Har Us Nuur
Altay
Aerhtai Shan (Altai)
Burqin
Fuhai
Ulungur
4362
Doroo Nuur
Ulyasutay (Javhlant)
Hangayn Nuruu
Chandmani
3957
Barkol
4925
Hami
Gaxun Nur
Dunhuang
Anxi
Yumen
Jiuquan
Zhangye
6346
Har Hu
Qilian Shan
Da Qaidam
Qaidam Pendi
Golmud
Qinghai Hu
3205
Gonghe
Xining
QINGHAI
Gyaring Hu
4237
Ngoring Hu
Huang
Bayan Har Shan
Maqen Gangri
6 282
Yushu
Jinsha
Qamdo
Lancang
Nu
Bomi
Zayu
Batang
Daxue Shan
Minya Konka
7 556
Garze
Yalong
Deqen
Zhongdian
SICHUAN
Dali
Xiaguan
Chuxiong
YUNNAN
Baoshan
Tengchong
Putao
Kehsi Mansam
Projection: Bonne
East from Greenwich
70
80
90
100
50
40
30
20

1 : 20 000 000

100   0   100   200   300   400   500 miles
100   0   200   400   600   800 km

5   6   7   8

A

MONGOLIA

Ozero Baykal Bukachacha
heremkhovo 620
Angarsk
sk   455   Ulan Ude   Khilok   Chita   Sretensk   Yilehuli Shan   Shimanovsk
Babushkin   Zabaykalsk   Nerchinsk   Svobodnyy   Chegdomyn   2640
Kyakhta   Olovyannaya   Borzya   Argun   Aihui   Blagoveshchensk   Ozero
Sukhbaatar   Altanbulag   Nenjiang   Poyan   Furao   Obluchye   Birobidzhan   Boton
Orhon   Hentiyn   Onon   Hulun Nur   Hailar   Butha Qi   Bei'an   Nikhinsk   Khabarovsk
Nuruu   Buir   HEILONGJIANG   Hegang   Jiamusi
Ulaanbaatar   Choybalsan   Arxan   Qiqihar   Halun   Shuangyashan
(Urga)   Öndörhaan   Matad   Angangxi   Songhua   Yilan   Dalnerechensk
Dzuunmod   Kerulen   Da   Horqin Youyi Qianqi   HARBIN   Mishan
Saynshand   Boichang   Da'an   Acheng   Khanka   Ussuriysk
Dzamin Üüd   Erenhot   Linxi   Tao'an   Changchun   Mudanjiang   Vladivostok   Artem
Hongor   Hüld   Duolun   Siping   Jilin   Yanji   2744
Bolandzadgad   Sonid Youqi   Liaoyuan   Hailong   NORTH   Najin   Chongjin
Boyan Obo   Mumingqan   Fuxin   Fushun   KOREA   40
Hohhot   Jining   Chengde   SHENYANG   Benxi   P'yongyang   Hungnam
BAOTOU   Zhangjiakou   Xuanhua   Jinzhou   Liaoyang   Anshan   Dandong   Sinuiju   Wonsan
3015   Datong   Tong Xian   Qinhuangdao   Liaodong   KOREA BAY   Munch'on
Mu Us Shamo   BEIJING   Tangshan   Wan   Chinnampo   SOUTH   Kangnung
2894   (Peking)   TIANJIN   DALIAN   Inch'on   KOREA   Taegu
Shijiazhuang   Baoding   (Tientsin)   Bo Hai   Ye Xian   Taejon   Pusan
TAIYUAN   Yangquan   Bozhen   Yantai   Kunsan   Chonju   Masan
Wuzhong   Fenyang   Yuci   Jinan   Zibo   Weifang   Weihai   Kwangju   Fukuoka
Changzhi   Xingtai   Handan   Boshan   Mokpo   Tsushima   Sasebo
Xinxiang   Anyang   Jining   Qingdao   Cheju   Cheju   Nagasaki
Yongji   Liaozuo   SHANDONG   YELLOW   Do   1950   Kore
Baoji   Kaifeng   Shangqiu   Lianyungang   SEA
XI'AN   Zhengzhou   Xuzhou   Hai'an   JAPAN
Xuchang   HENAN   Shangshui   JIANGSU   Changzhou
Hanzhong   Nanyang   Huainan   Bengbu   Zhenjiang   30
Ankang   Zhumadian   NANJING   Suzhou   SHANGHAI
Xiangfan   Xinyang   Hefei   Wuxi   Jiaxing
Daba Shan   Ma'anshan   ANHUI   Wuhu   Shaoxing
Fengjie   Yichang   WUHAN   Anqing   Hangzhou   Ningbo
Nanchong   Shashi   Huangshi   ZHEJIANG   EAST
Wanxian   Jiujiang   Tunxi   Jingdezhen   Qu Xian   CHINA
CHONGQING   Changde   Nanchang   Shangrao   Linhai   SEA
Luzhou   Yiyang   Changsha   Yington   Wenzhou   Okinawa   7507
Xiangtan   HUNAN   Zhuzhou   FUJIAN   Ninde   Tropic of Cancer
Zunyi   Zhenyuan   Shaoyang   Nanping   Fuzhou
GUIZHOU   Hengyang   Nuyi Shan   Min   Taibei   Jilong   D
Anshun   Duyun   Guoyang   Quanzhou   Xinzhu   Miaoli   Taizhong
Guilin   Ganzhou   Xinzhu   Jiayi   TAIWAN   20
Liuzhou   Mei Xian   Xiameh   Zhanghua   3950
GUANGXI   Shaoguan   Chao'an   Taidong
Wuzhou   GUANGDONG   Shantou   Tainan   Pingdong
Nanning   GUANGZHOU   Gaoxiong
Foshan   (Canton)   Bashi Channel   Batan Is.
HANOI   Zhanjiang   Macau   Kowloon   E
Haiphong   Hainan Dao   HONG KONG
Tonkin   SOUTH CHINA   SEA
Haikou   PHILIPPINES
HAINAN   Luzon

CARTOGRAPHY BY PHILIP'S. COPYRIGHT REED INTERNATIONAL BOOKS LTD.

A
B
C
1
2
3
4
5
BURMA (MYANMAR)
THAILAND
LAOS
CAMBODIA
VIETNAM
PHILIPPINES
MALAYSIA
SABAH
SOUTH CHINA SEA
ANDAMAN SEA
Gulf of Thailand
G. of Martaban
Strait of Malacca
Balabac Strait
Rangoon
Bangkok
Vientiane
Phnom Penh
Phanh Bho Ho Chi Minh (Saigon)
Da Nang
Hue
Dong Hoi
Qui Nhon
Nha Trang
Phan Rang
Da Lat
Vung Tau
Can Tho
Ca Mau
Phu Quoc
Kampot
Kompong Som
Battambang
Siem Reap
Tonle Sap
Mekong
Udon Thani
Nong Khai
Khon Kaen
Nakhon Ratchasima (Khorat)
Ubon Ratchathani
Savannakhet
Thakhek
Pakse
Attopeu
Saravane
Chanthaburi
Chon Buri
Phitsanulok
Uttaradit
Tak
Moulmein
Tavoy
Mergui
Ranong
Chumphon
Surat Thani
Ko Samui
Nakhon Si Thammarat
Songkhla (Singora)
Pattani
Phuket
Kota Baharu
Kuala Terengganu
George Town
Kota Kinabalu
Sandakan
Palawan
Spratly I.
Amboyna I.
Hsisha
Chuntao
Con Son
Sabang
Banda Aceh (Kutaraja)

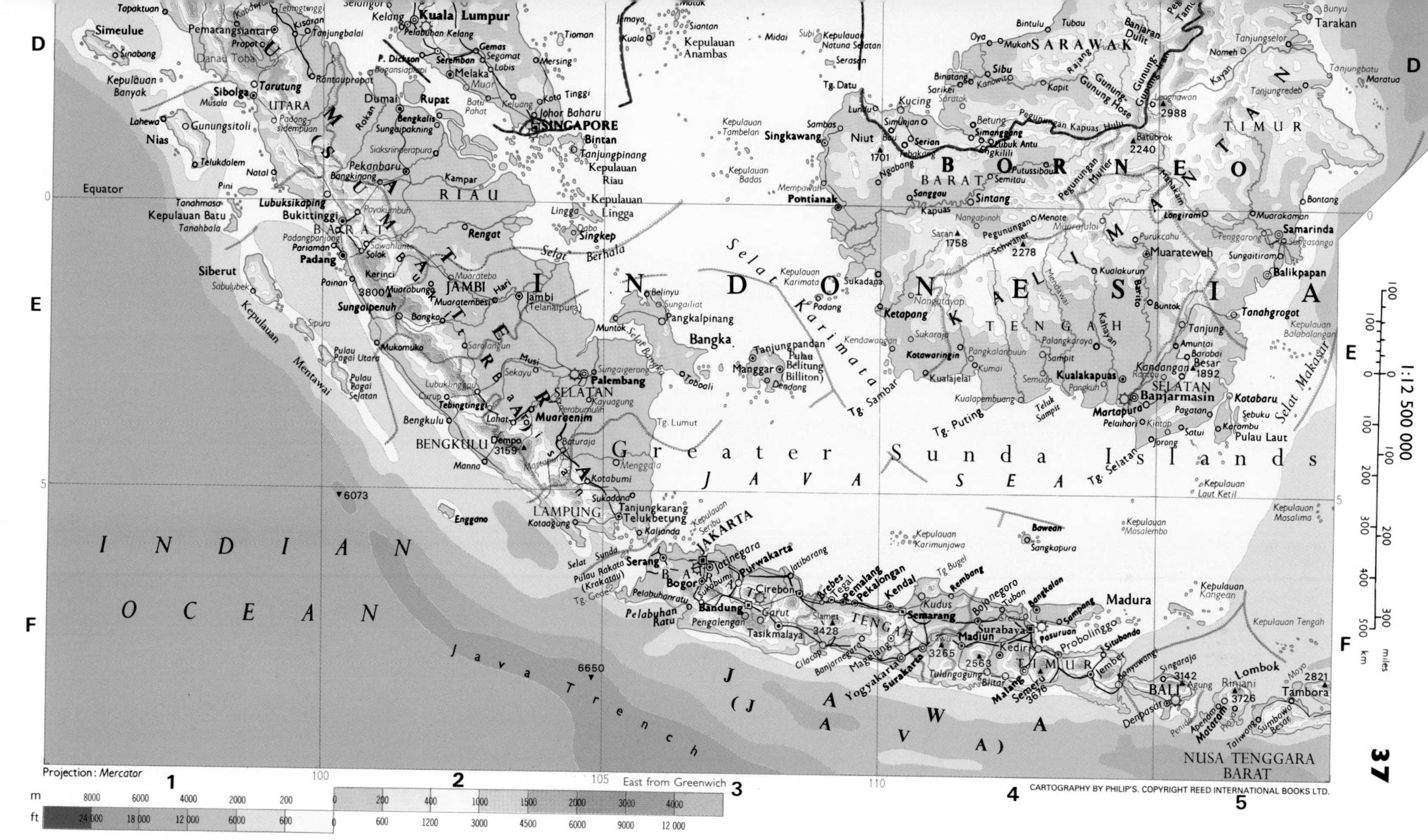

1:12 500 000
100 0 100 200 300 miles
100 0 100 200 300 400 500 km
INDIAN OCEAN
Java Trench
Greater Sunda Islands
JAVA SEA
Selat Karimata
Selat Makasar
Selat Sunda
Selat Berhala
Selat Bangka
I N D O N E S I A
SUMATERA
BORNEO
KALIMANTAN
SARAWAK
JAWA (JAVA)
UTARA
BARAT
RIAU
JAMBI
SELATAN
BENGKULU
LAMPUNG
TENGAH
TIMUR
NUSA TENGGARA BARAT
BALI
Lombok
Madura
Bangka
Pulau Belitung (Billiton)
Kepulauan Riau
Kepulauan Lingga
Kepulauan Anambas
Kepulauan Natuna Selatan
Kepulauan Mentawai
Kepulauan Batu
Kepulauan Banyak
Kepulauan Karimunjawa
Kepulauan Karimata
Kepulauan Tambelan
Kepulauan Badas
Kepulauan Masalembo
Kepulauan Kangean
Kepulauan Laut Ketil
Kepulauan Masalima
Kepulauan Tengah
Kepulauan Balabalangan
Nias
Siberut
Simeulue
Enggano
Pulau Laut
Bawean
Danau Toba
Kuala Lumpur
SINGAPORE
JAKARTA
Bandung
Semarang
Surabaya
Palembang
Padang
Pontianak
Banjarmasin
Balikpapan
Samarinda
Kuching
Pekanbaru
Jambi
Bengkulu
Tanjungkarang Telukbetung
Mataram
Sibu
Tarakan
Malang
Surakarta
Yogyakarta
Cirebon
Bogor
Serang
Pangkalpinang
Madiun
Kediri
Kudus
Pekalongan
Tegal
Equator
Projection: Mercator
East from Greenwich
m 8000 6000 4000 2000 200 0 200 400 1000 1500 2000 3000 4000
ft 24 000 18 000 12 000 6000 600 0 600 1200 3000 4500 6000 9000 12 000
D E F
1 2 3 4 5
100 105 110
CARTOGRAPHY BY PHILIP'S. COPYRIGHT REED INTERNATIONAL BOOKS LTD.

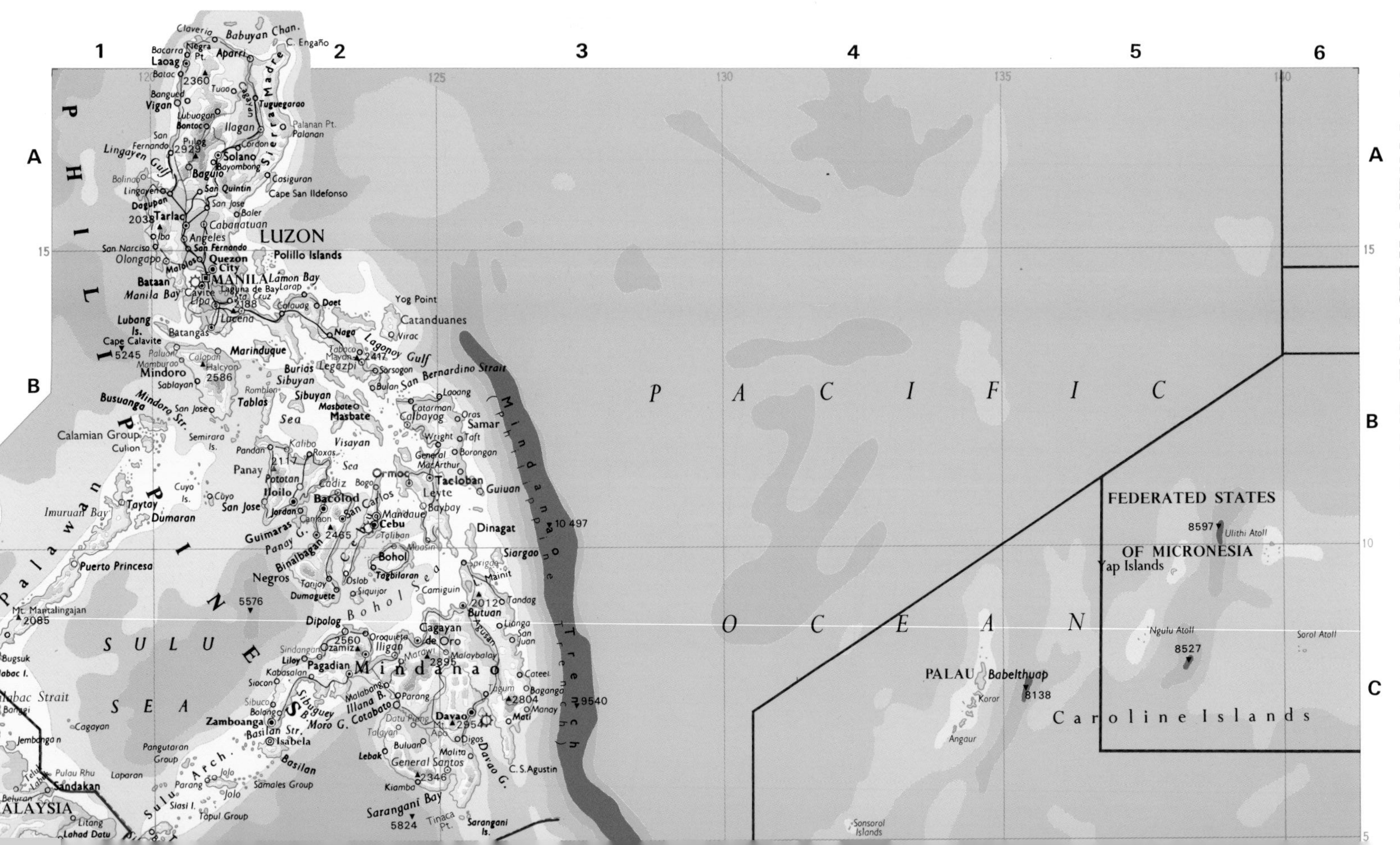
P A C I F I C
O C E A N
FEDERATED STATES
OF MICRONESIA
Yap Islands
Ulithi Atoll
Ngulu Atoll
Sorol Atoll
Caroline Islands
PALAU
Babelthuap
Koror
Angaur
Sonsorol Islands
PHILIPPINES
LUZON
MANILA
Quezon City
Polillo Islands
Lamon Bay
Manila Bay
Bataan
Lingayen Gulf
Babuyan Chan.
C. Engaño
Sierra Madre
Cape San Ildefonso
Catanduanes
Lagonoy Gulf
San Bernardino Strait
Samar
Leyte
Tacloban
Guiuan
Dinagat
Siargao
Bohol
Cebu
Negros
Panay
Iloilo
Bacolod
Mindoro
Mindoro Str.
Marinduque
Sibuyan Sea
Visayan Sea
Bohol Sea
Masbate
Tablas
Burias
Calamian Group
Culion
Busuanga
Palawan
Puerto Princesa
Imuruan Bay
Mindanao
Mindanao Trench
Philippine Trench
Cagayan de Oro
Butuan
Dipolog
Pagadian
Iligan
Zamboanga
Davao
Davao G.
General Santos
Sarangani Bay
Moro G.
Illana B.
Sibuguey B.
Basilan Str.
Basilan
Sulu Arch.
Jolo
Tapul Group
SULU SEA
Balabac Strait
Balabac I.
Sandakan
MALAYSIA
Mt. Mantalingajan
2085
2929
2360
5245
2586
2465
2954
2804
5576
5824
10 497
9540
8597
8527
8138

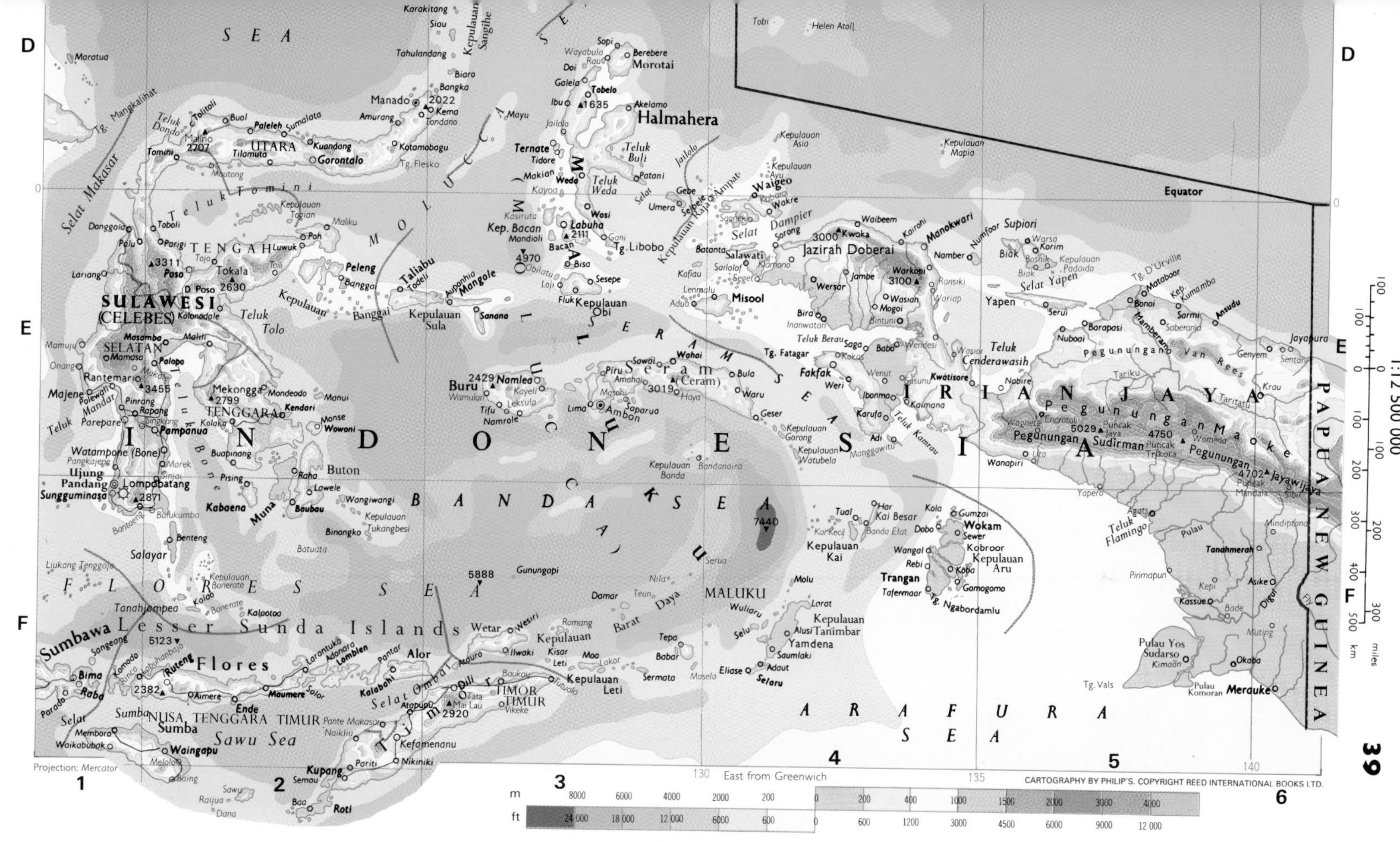

1:12 500 000

Projection: Mercator

East from Greenwich

PAPUA NEW GUINEA

IRIAN JAYA

Pegunungan Maoke

Puncak Sudirman 5029▲

A R A F U R A   S E A

M A L U K U

B A N D A   S E A

Halmahera

M O L U C C A

C E R A M

Misool

Buru

SULAWESI (CELEBES)

F L O R E S   S E A

M O L U C C A   S E A

SULAWESI TENGAH

SULAWESI UTARA

SULAWESI SELATAN

SULAWESI TENGGARA

Buton

Flores

Sumba

Sumbawa

Lesser Sunda Islands

NUSA TENGGARA TIMUR

TIMOR TIMUR

TIMOR

Kupang

Roti

Sawu Sea

Selat Makassar

Equator

S   S E A

EASTERN INDIA, BANGLADESH AND BURMA

1 2 3 4 5 6

78 80 82 84 86 88

A

Chamba
7026
Dankhar Gompa
Palampur
Kulu
Mandi
HIMACHAL PRADESH
Hoshiarpur
Bhakra Dam
Nganglong Kangri 7315
Gar
Shiquan He
Nganglong Kangri
Kangtog
XIZANG
Ombu
Tangra Yumco
Gyaring Co
Gangdisê Shan
(Sutlej)
Coqên

32

B

Ludhiana
Simla
Kandaghat
Chakrata
Kamet 7756
Badrinath
La'nga Co
Mapam Yumco
(TIBET)
Chandigarh
Ambala
Mussoorie
Patiala
Dehra Dun
7817
Nanda Devi
Pauri
Jagadhri
Haridwar Dam
Mayum La
Namse Shankou
4944
Simikot
Mugu
7059
Zhongba
Nyainqentanglha

30

Saharanpur
Karnal
Haridwar
Roorkee
Muzaffarnagar
Najibabad
Almora
Baitadi
Dandeldhura
Silgarhi Doti
Jumla
Mustang
Haldwani
Karnali
Bijnor
Hansi
HARYANA
Sonipat
Meerut
Amroha
Moradabad
Rampur
Saga
Maquan He
Gyala Shankou 5602
Muktinath
Dhaulagiri 8221
Dhangarhi
Xixabangma Feng 8013

C

Rohtak
New Delhi
DELHI
Bhiwani
Hapur
Ghaziabad
Faridabad
Rewari
Bulandshahr
Sambhal
Pilibhit
Bareilly
Shahjahanpur
Sarda
Nepalganj
Siwalik Range
Nuwakot
Gurkha
Nawakot
Nyalam
Mt. Everest 8848
Kanchenjunga
Katmandu
Lalitpur
Bhaktapur
Aligarh
Lakhimpur
Jarwa
Ramechhap
Sun Kosi

28

Alwar
Hathras
UTTAR PRADESH
Mathura
Bharatpur
Fatehgarh
Hardoi
Mainpuri
Kannauj
Sitapur
Bahraich
Balrampur
Gonda
Nautanwa
Thori
Birganj
Chisapani Garhi
NEPAL
Bettiah
Udaipur Garhi
Dhankuta

D

Agra
Firozabad
Lucknow
Basti
Gorakhpur
Motihari
Jaynagar
Daulpur
Etawah
Faizabad
Deoria
Gandak
Ghaghara
Chambal
Bhind
Kanpur
Unnao
Rae Bareli
Sultanpur
Azamgarh
Darbhanga
Nirmali
Kishanganj
Muzaffarpur
Supaul
Siwan
Gwalior
Sawai Madhopur
Ganga (Ganges)
Orai
Chhapra
Konch
Hamirpur
Fatehpur
Bela
Jaunpur
Ghazipur
Sheopur Kalan
Datia
Yamuna (Jumna)
Patna
Bankipore
Beharigani

26

Shivpuri
Mau Ranipur
Banda
Allahabad
Varanasi (Banaras)
Benares
Ara
Bihar
Munger
Bhagalpur
Jhansi
Jahanabad
Jamalpur
Baran
521
Chhatarpur
Manikpur
Mirzapur
Sasaram
Gaya

E

Guna
Lalitpur
Tikamgarh
Panna
Satna
Maugani
Aurangabad
Deoghar
Jhalawar
INDIA
Rewa
690
Dudhi
BIHAR
Rajgarh
Sironj
Bina Etawa
Banda
Vindhya Range
Hazaribag
Giridih
Rampur Hat
1366
Dhanbad
Gomoh

24

Sagar
Damoh
Murwara
Bharatpu
Vidisha
Umaria
Lohardaga
Ramgarh
Asansol
Shajapur
Bhanrer Range
Shahdol
Chirmiri
1225
Ambikapur
Ranchi
Puruliya
WEST BENGAL
Bankura
Bhopal
Jabalpur
Sehore
Narmada
Anuppur
Jamshedpur

F

Dewas
Narsinghpur
1127
Hoshangabad
Gadarwara
Chakradharpur
Chaibasa
Medinipur
Kannod
Mandla
Birmitrapur
MADHYA PRADESH
Raurkela
Kharagpur
Nainpur
Satpura Range
1353
Maikala Range
Bilaspur
Sundergarh
Gua
Badampahar
Makrai

22

Khandwa
Kawardha
Raigarh
Jharsaguda
Chhindwara
Balaghat
Betul
Tirodi
Katangi
Keonjhargarh
Baleshwar
Burhanpur
Satpura
Ramtek
Gondia
Khairagarh
Sarangarh
Hirakud Dam
Sambalpur
Gawilgarh Hills
1187
Achalpur
Nagpur
Raipur
Bhadrakh

G

Amravati
Rajnandgaon
Durg
Talcher
Brahmani
Jalgaon
Bhandara
Mahanadi
Sonepur
Bramhapuri
Dhenkanal
Kendrapara
Akola
Wardha
Dhamtari
Bolangir
Cuttack
Mahanadi
Paradip
Wainganga
Hinganghat
Darwha
Yavatmal
Kanker
1001
Titlagarh
ORISSA
Bhubaneshwar
Washim
Wardha

20

Penganga
Wani
Chandrapur
Ghugus
Bhawanipatna
Russellkonda
Hingoli
Puri
Adilabad
Chilka Lake
Satmala Hills
Ahiri
Bhamragarh
Bastar
Rayagada
Brahamapur
Chatrapur
Parbhani
Asifabad
665
Indravati
Nanded
Pranhita
1501
Ichchapuram

H

Palam
Nirmal
Jeypore
Bijapur
Jagdalpur
Parvatipuram
BAY OF BENGAL
Godavari
Jagtial
Bodhan
Bobbili
Tekkali
Nizamabad
Manthani
1240
Latur
Udgir
Karimnagar
Salur
Srikakulam
Venkatapuram
1680
ANDHRA PRADESH
Manjra
Eastern Ghats
Vizianagaram

18

Godavari
Siddipet
Warangal
Konta
Bidar
Kottagudem
Vishakhapatnam
Northern Circars
Anakapalle
Secunderabad
Gulbarga
Hyderabad
Rajahmundry
Pithapuram

J

Godavari Point
Nalgonda
Suriapet
Kakinada (Cocanada)
Yadgir
Narayanpet
Eluru (Ellore)
Bhima
Mahbubnagar
Krishna
Vijayawada
Bhimvaram
Krishna
Gudivada
Narasapur
Raichur
Gadwal
Guntur
Machilipatnam (Bandar)
917
Tenali

16

Bapatla
Tungabhadra
Kurnool
Adoni
Erramala Hills
Nallamalai Hills
Cumbum
Chirala
Ongole

K

Hospet
INDIAN OCEAN
1100
Bellary
Nandyal
Velikonda Range
Guntakal
Swamihalli
Deccan

ft m

18 000 — 6000
12 000 — 4000
9000 — 3000
6000 — 2000
4500 — 1500
3000 — 1000
1200 — 400
600 — 200
0 — 0
200 — 600
m ft

Projection: *Conical with two standard parallels* 80 82 East from Greenwich 84 86

1 2 3 4 5 6

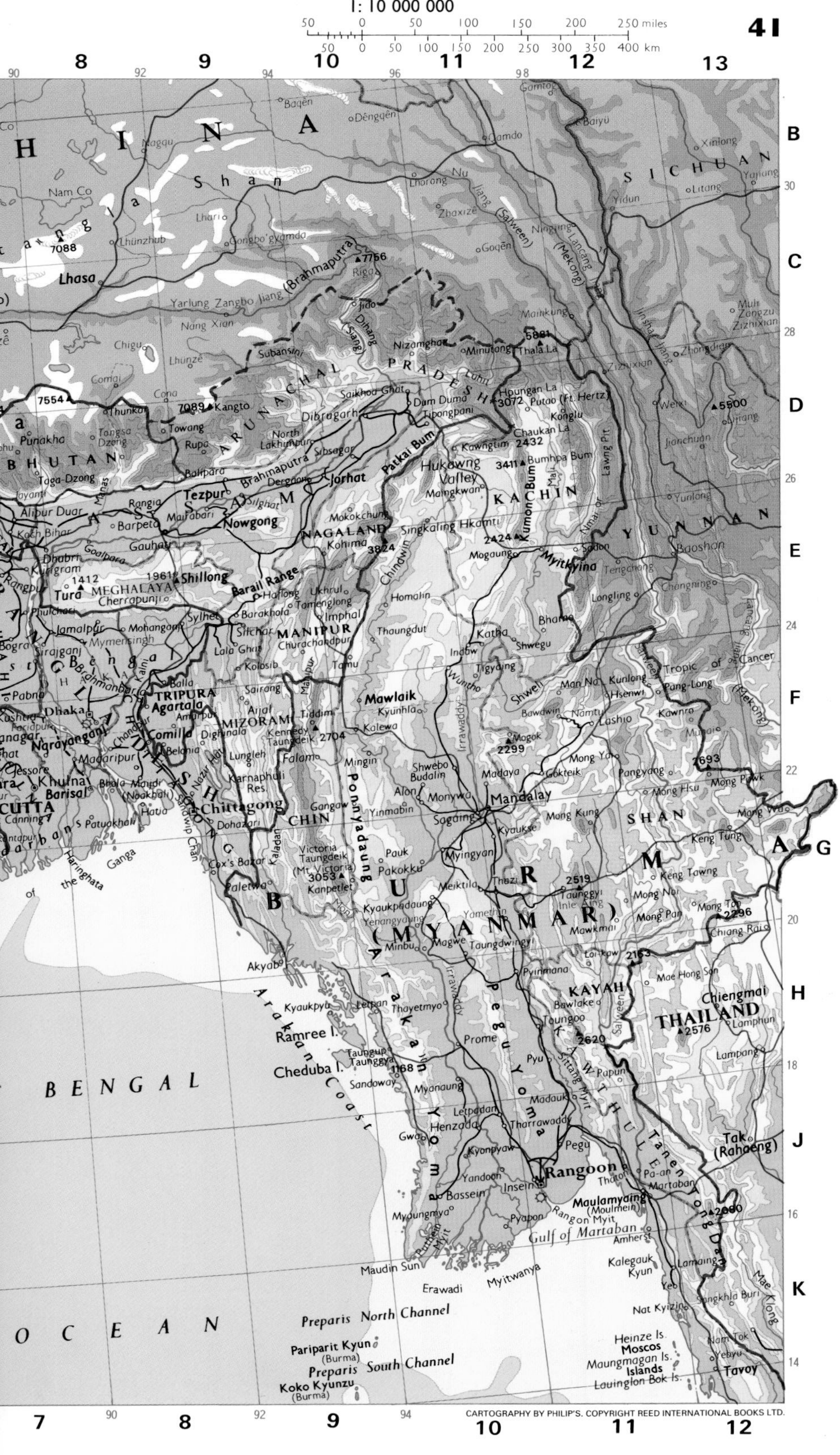

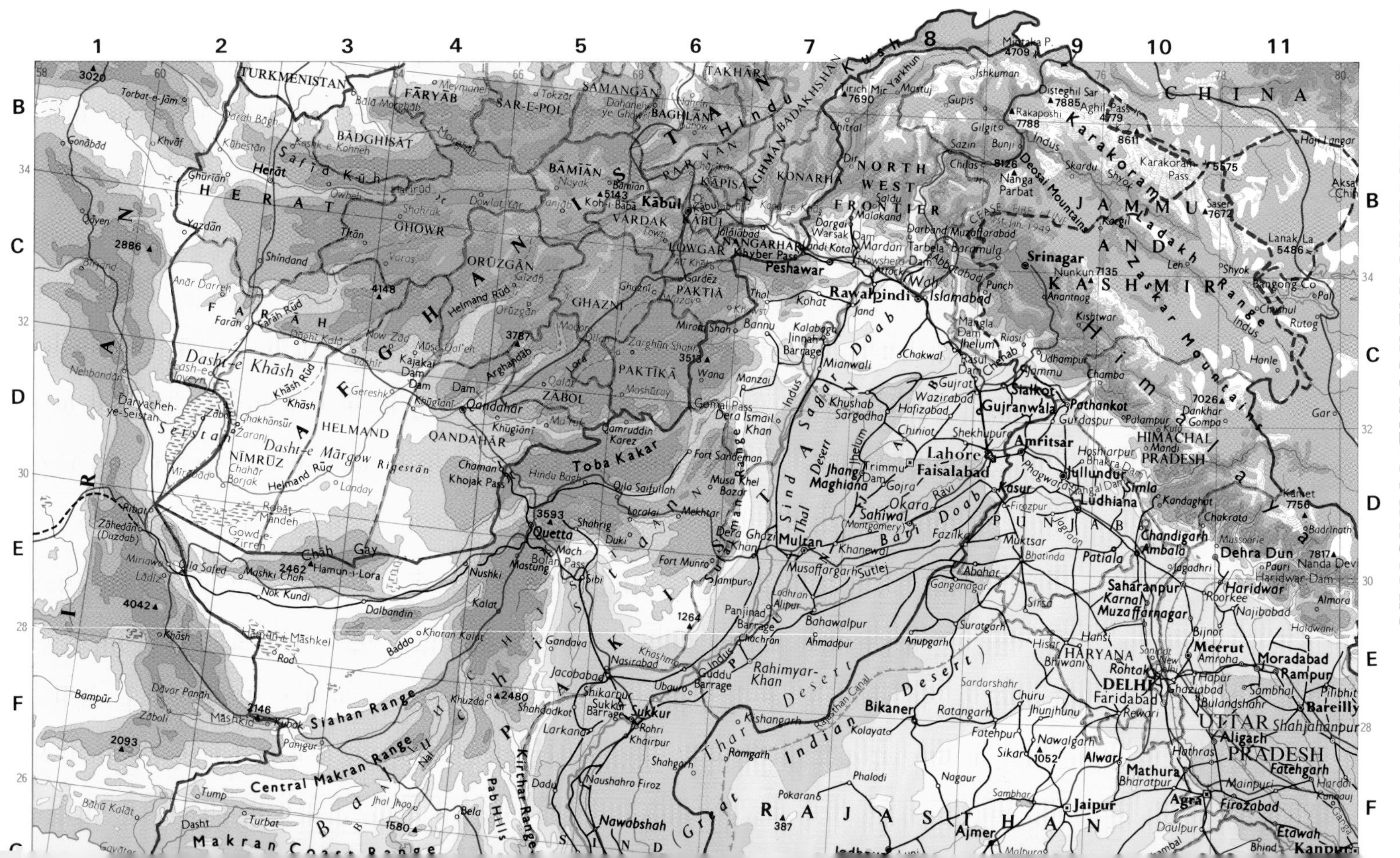

CHINA
IRAN
AFGHANISTAN
PAKISTAN
TURKMENISTAN
Hindu Kush
Karakoram
JAMMU AND KASHMIR
Ladakh Range
Zaskar Mountains
Himalaya
NORTH WEST FRONTIER
HIMACHAL PRADESH
PUNJAB
HARYANA
UTTAR PRADESH
DELHI
RAJASTHAN
Great Indian Desert
Thar Desert
Sind Sagar Doab
Thal Desert
Bari Doab
Srinagar
Islamabad
Rawalpindi
Peshawar
Lahore
Faisalabad
Amritsar
Gujranwala
Sialkot
Multan
Bahawalpur
Kabul
Qandahar
Herat
Quetta
Toba Kakar
Sukkur
Nawabshah
Bikaner
Jaipur
Ajmer
Agra
Aligarh
Meerut
Moradabad
Bareilly
Dehra Dun
Chandigarh
Ludhiana
Jullundur
Simla
Patiala
Kirthar Range
Pab Hills
Siahan Range
Central Makran Range
Makran Coast Range
Safid Kuh
HELMAND
Dasht-e Margow
Dasht-e Khash
Seistan
Khyber Pass
Bolan Pass
Khojak Pass
Gomal Pass

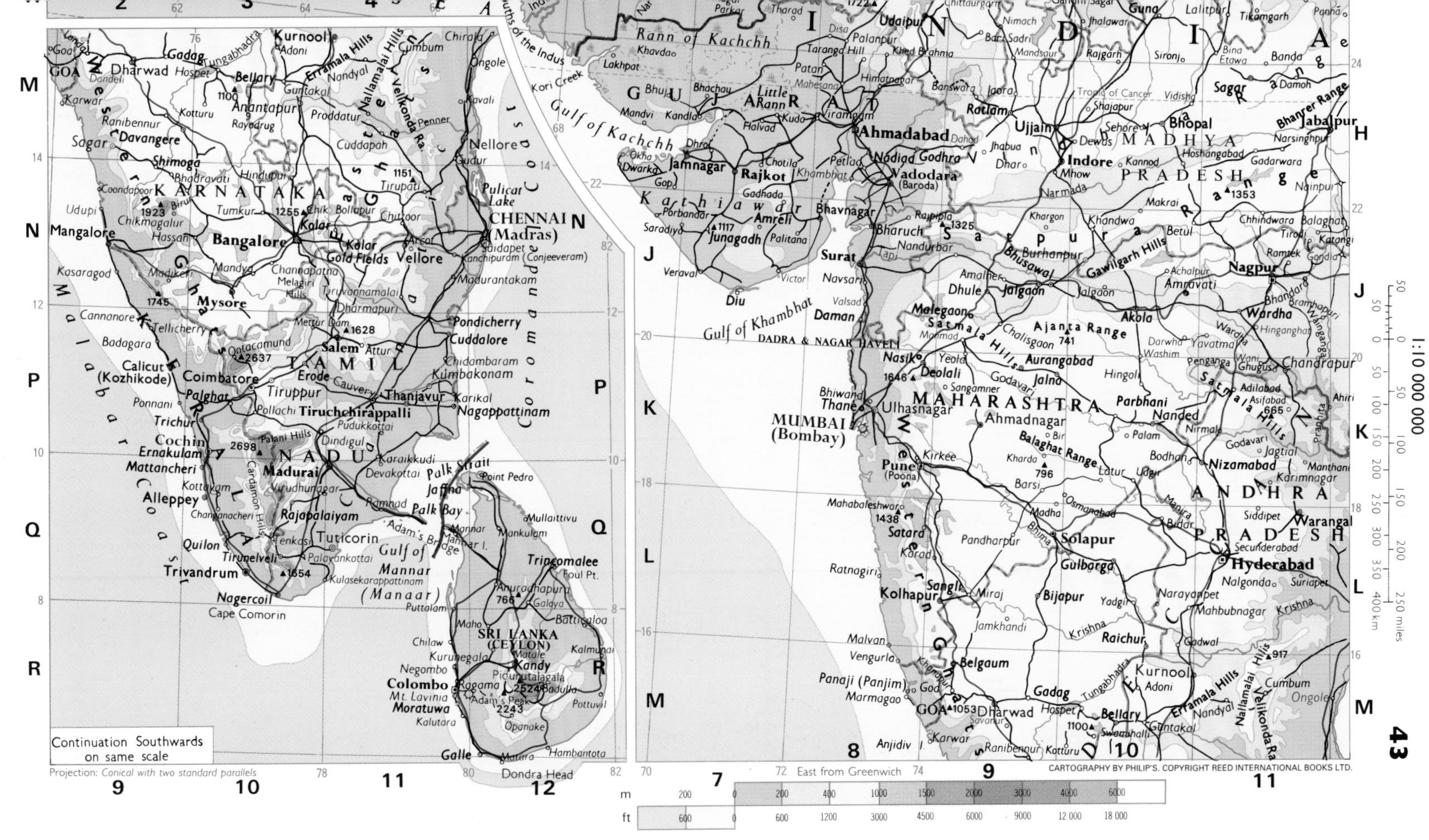
1:10 000 000
50 0 50 100 150 200 250 miles
50 0 50 100 150 200 250 300 350 400 km
CARTOGRAPHY BY PHILIP'S. COPYRIGHT REED INTERNATIONAL BOOKS LTD.
Continuation Southwards on same scale
Projection: Conical with two standard parallels
East from Greenwich
MADHYA PRADESH
MAHARASHTRA
ANDHRA PRADESH
KARNATAKA
TAMIL NADU
KERALA
SRI LANKA (CEYLON)
GUJARAT
MUMBAI (Bombay)
CHENNAI (Madras)
Hyderabad
Bangalore
Ahmadabad
Nagpur
Pune (Poona)
Colombo
Gulf of Khambhat
Gulf of Kachchh
Rann of Kachchh
Gulf of Mannar (Manaar)
Palk Strait
Palk Bay
Adam's Bridge
Malabar Coast
Coromandel Coast
Western Ghats
Eastern Ghats
Cape Comorin
Dondra Head
DADRA & NAGAR HAVELI
GOA
Trivandrum
Madurai
Mysore
Mangalore
Pondicherry
Vadodara (Baroda)
Surat
Indore
Bhopal
Jabalpur
Solapur
Kandy
Trincomalee
Jaffna
Galle

44 IRAN, THE GULF AND AFGHANISTAN

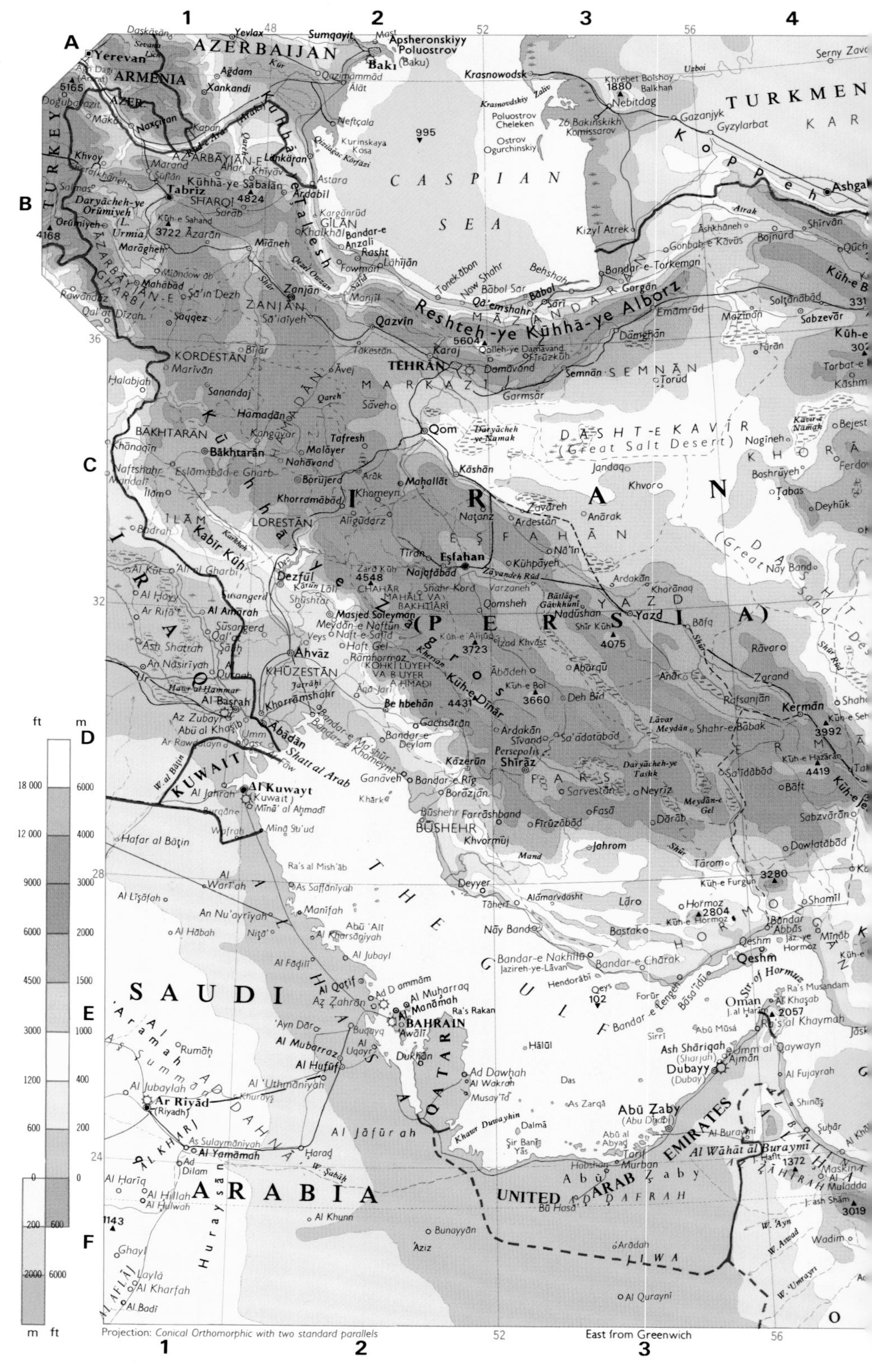

1
2
3
4
A
B
C
D
E
F
48
52
56
36
32
28
24
AZERBAIJAN
ARMENIA
Yerevan
TURKEY
AZER.
Yevlax
Sumqayit
Apsheronskiyy Poluostrov
Bakı (Baku)
Krasnowodsk
Nebitdag
TURKMEN
Gazanjyk
Gyzylarbat
Koppeh
Ashgabat
CASPIAN SEA
995
Kızyl Atrek
Ağdam
Xankandi
Naxçıvan
Lənkəran
Astara
Ardabil
Tabriz
Kūhhā-ye Sabalān
4824
AZARBĀYJĀN-E SHARQĪ
Daryācheh-ye Orūmīyeh (L. Urmia)
Orūmīyeh
4168
5165
Kūh-e Sahand
3722
Marāgheh
Mahābād
Saqqez
AZARBĀYJĀN-E GHARBĪ
Mīāneh
GĪLĀN
Bandar-e Anzalī
Rasht
Lāhījān
Zanjān
ZANJĀN
Qazvīn
Manjīl
Reshteh-ye Kūhhā-ye Alborz
5604
Qolleh-ye Damāvand
MĀZANDARĀN
Bābol Sar
Bābol
Sārī
Gorgān
Bandar-e Torkeman
Gonbad-e Kāvūs
Bojnūrd
Shīrvān
Emāmrūd
Dāmghān
Semnān
SEMNĀN
TEHRĀN
Karaj
Damāvand
MARKAZĪ
KORDESTĀN
Sanandaj
Hamadān
BĀKHTARĀN
Bākhtarān
Qom
Sāveh
Arāk
Kāshān
Daryācheh-ye Namak
DASHT-E KAVĪR (Great Salt Desert)
Jandaq
Khvoro
Nāgineh
Tabas
Boshrūyeh
KHORĀSĀN
Sabzevār
Torbat-e
Kūh-e
IRAN (PERSIA)
Borūjerd
Khorramābād
LORESTĀN
ĪLĀM
Ilām
Kabīr Kūh
Dezfūl
Shūshtar
Ahvāz
KHŪZESTĀN
Masjed Soleymān
Esfahān
EŞFAHĀN
Najafābād
Zard Kūh
4548
CHAHĀR MAHĀLL VA BAKHTIĀRĪ
Shahr-e Kord
Qomsheh
Nā'īn
Ardestān
Anārak
Yazd
YAZD
Ardakān
Shīr Kūh
4075
Bāfq
Rāvar
Zarand
Kermān
KERMĀN
Rafsanjān
3992
4419
Kūh-e Hazārān
Bāft
Sabzvārān
Dowlatābād
3723
Ābādeh
Kūh-e Bol
3660
Deh Bīd
Abarqū
Kūh-e Dīnār
4431
Zāgros
KOHKĪLŪYEH VA BŪYER AHMADĪ
Behbahān
Gachsārān
Shīrāz
Persepolis
FĀRS
Sarvestān
Neyrīz
Fasā
Dārāb
Fīrūzābād
Jahrom
Kāzerūn
BŪSHEHR
Būshehr
Bandar-e Rīg
Borāzjān
Khārk
Ganāveh
Bandar-e Deylam
Bandar-e Khomeynī
Bandar-e Ma'shūr
Ābādān
Khorramshahr
Shatt al Arab
IRAQ
Al Başrah
Al 'Amārah
An Nāşirīyah
Hawr al Hammār
Az Zubayr
Umm Qaşr
KUWAIT
Al Kuwayt (Kuwait)
Al Jahrah
Mīnā' al Ahmadī
Hafar al Bāţin
Ra's al Mish'āb
Al Wari'ah
As Saffānīyah
Manīfah
Al Khafjī
Abū 'Alī
Al Jubayl
Al Qaţīf
Ad Dammām
Az Zahrān
Al Muharraq
Al Manāmah
BAHRAIN
Awālī
Dukhān
QATAR
Ad Dawhah
Al Wakrah
Musay'īd
Ra's Rakan
Al Mubarraz
Al Hufūf
Al 'Uqayr
SAUDI ARABIA
Ar Riyāḑ (Riyadh)
Al Kharj
Al Yamāmah
Ad Dilam
Ad Dahnā
As Summān
Al 'Aramah
Rumāḥ
Al Jubaylah
Al Hillah
Al Hulwah
Al Harīq
1143
Ghayl
Laylā
Al Kharfah
Al Badi'
Al Aflāj
Al Khunn
Bunayyān
'Azīz
Al Jāfūrah
Harad
THE GULF
Tārom
Kūh-e Furgun
3280
Lāro
Hormoz
2804
Bastak
Bandar-e 'Abbās
Qeshm
Mīnāb
Bandar-e Chārak
Bandar-e Lengeh
Jazīreh-ye Lāvān
Qeys
102
Sirrī
Abū Mūsā
Str. of Hormuz
Ra's Musandam
Oman
Al Khaşab
2057
Ra's al Khaymah
Umm al Qaywayn
'Ajmān
Ash Shāriqah (Sharjah)
Dubayy (Dubai)
Al Fujayrah
Abū Zaby (Abu Dhabi)
UNITED ARAB EMIRATES
Abū Zaby
Al Wāhāt al Buraymī
Al Buraymī
Dalmā
Şīr Banī Yās
Halūl
Das
As Zarqā
Murban
Tarīf
Abū al Abyad
AD DAFRAH
LIWA
Arādah
Al Qurayni
1372
3019
Wadīm
Nāy Band
Bandar-e Nakhīlū
Deyyer
Tāherī
Khvormūj
Mand
Projection: Conical Orthomorphic with two standard parallels
East from Greenwich
ft
m
18 000
12 000
9000
6000
4500
3000
1200
600
0
200
2000
6000
4000
3000
2000
1500
1000
400
200
0
600
6000
m ft

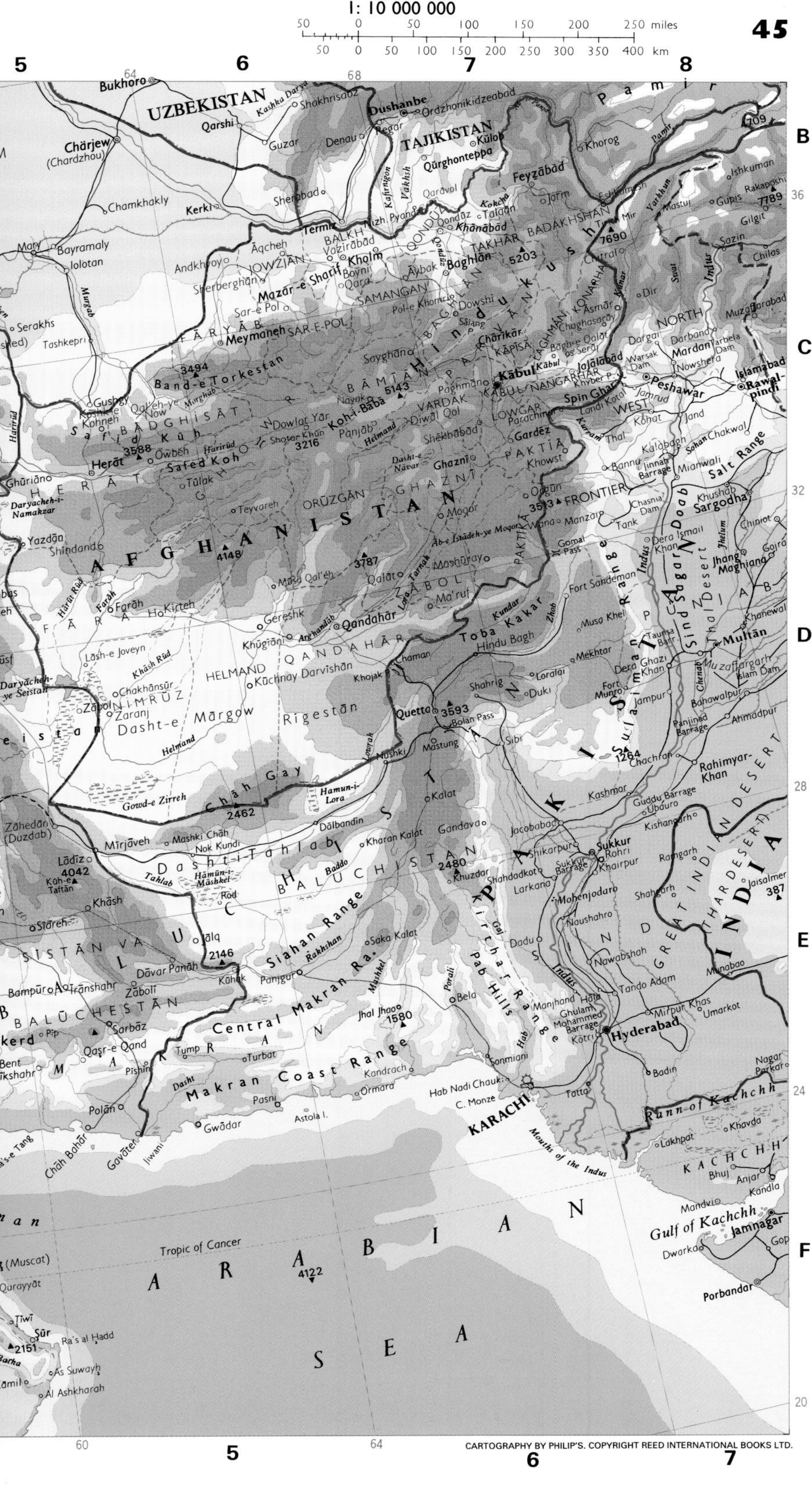

50   0   50   100   150   200   250 miles
50 0 50 100 150 200 250 300 350 400 km

5   **6**   **7**   **8**

Bukhoro
UZBEKISTAN
64   68   Pamir   **B**
Kaukha Darya Shakhrisabz
Chärjew   Qarshi   Denau   **Dushanbe** Ordzhonikidzeabad
(Chardzhou)   Guzar   **TAJIKISTAN**   Khorog 709
Qarshi   Kafirnigan Vakhsh Kūlob   Ishkuman
Chamkhakly   Sherabad   Qūrghonteppa   Gupis Rakaposhi
Kerki   Termiz   Qarovil Kokcha   Mir   Mastuj   7789   36
Mory   Bayramaly   Āqcheh   Izh Pyandzh Khānābād BADAKHSHĀN   Gilgit
Iolotan   Andkhvoy Sherberghān   Kholm   Dowshi   TAKHĀR 7690   Chilas
Serakhs Tashkepri FĀRYĀB   Mazār-e Sharīf Aybak 5203 CHITRAL   Chitral   Sazin
(shed)   JOWZJĀN   Sar-e Pol   SAMANGĀN Polle Khomri   NORTH Muzaffarabad
Meymaneh SAR-E POL Soyghान Dowshi   Dir   Darkot Darband Tarbela
Hariru   Sayghan   GHŌR   Charikar KĀPISA Asmār Dargai Mardan Nowshera Islamabad Rawal-
3494 Band-e Torkestān   Nayak 5143 Paghmān   NANGARHAR Warsak Peshawar Pindi
BĀDGHĪSĀT   Koh-i Baba VARDAK **Kabul** Kābul Jalālābād Dam Jamrud Kōhat   **C**
3588 Dowlat Yār   Panjāb Helmand Gardēz LOWGAR   Spin Ghar Khyber P. Thal
Herāt Qaleh-ye 3216   Shekhābād Diwāl Qol   PAKTIĀ   Parachinar Banu Kalābāgh
Safed Koh   Shōtōr Khūn   Dasht-i   Khowst   Thal Bannu Jinnah Barrage Sargodha
Tūlak   G   ŌRŪZGAN GHAZNĪ Nāwar Ghaznī   3593   Ōrgūn   Chasnia Dam Jhelum 32
Teyvareh   Mōqor PAKTIKĀ Gomal Fort Sandeman Tank Dera Ismail Chiniot
4148   3787   Āb-e Istādeh-ye Moqor   Khan   Jhang Maghiang
Farāh Hokirteh   Qalāto ZĀBOL Dāshōraray   Muso Khel Mekhtar Dera Ghazi Khanewal
Gereshk Arghandāb   Ma'rūf Kundar Toba Kakar   Fort Munro   Multan   **D**
Khūgiāni QANDAHĀR Khojak Pass Hindu Bagh   Duki Loralai Muzaffargarh
Khāsh Rūd Kūchnay Darvīshān Chaman Shahrig   Takht Banawalpur
Lāsh-e Joveyn Rīgestān   Quetta 3593   Bolan Pass Mastung   Ahmadpur
Dasht-e Mārgow   Kalat   1264   Kashmor Guddu Barrage Rahimyar-Khan   28
Goud-e Zirreh Chāh Gay 2462 Dālbandīn   Khuzdar Jacobabad Sukkur Rohri Kashmor
Zāhedān Mīrjāveh Mashki Chāh Nok Kundi Hamun-i Lora 2480 Gandava Shikarpur Khairpur Rohri Jaisalmer
(Duzdab)   Dasht-i Tahlab Baddo   Kharan Kalat Larkana Shahdadkot 387
Lādīz Kāhak Rōd   Kalat Mohenjodaro Khairpur GREAT INDIAN DESERT **E**
4042 Khāsh Baluchistan   Siahan Range Dadu Naushahro Tando Adam Minabao
Koh-i Tattān Jālq 2146 Sako Kalat Nawabshoh   **INDIA**
SISTĀN VA Dāvar Panāh   Makran Ra. Bela Manjhand Mirpur Khas Umarkot
Bampūr Īrānshahr Zāboli Panjgūr   Pab Hills Ghulam Nagar
BALŪCHESTĀN Sarbāz Central Makran Range Jhal Jhao 1580   Mohammed Barrage Parkar
Bent Qasr-e Qand Tump R Turbat Kandrach   Sonmiani Hyderabad Badin
Pishin   Makran Coast Range Pasni Hab Nadi Chauki C. Monze Tatta Runn of Kachchh   24
Polān Gwādar Astola I. Ormara   **KARACHI** Lakhpat Khavda
Chāh Bahar Gavātar Jiwani   Mouths of the Indus Bhuj Anjar Kandla
Tang   Mandvi   K A C H C H H
(Muscat) Tropic of Cancer   Gulf of Kachchh Jamnagar   **F**
Quryyāt A R A B I A N 4122   Dwarka Porbandar
2151 Şūr Ra's al Hadd
Al Ashkharah S E A   20

5   **6**   **7**

60   64

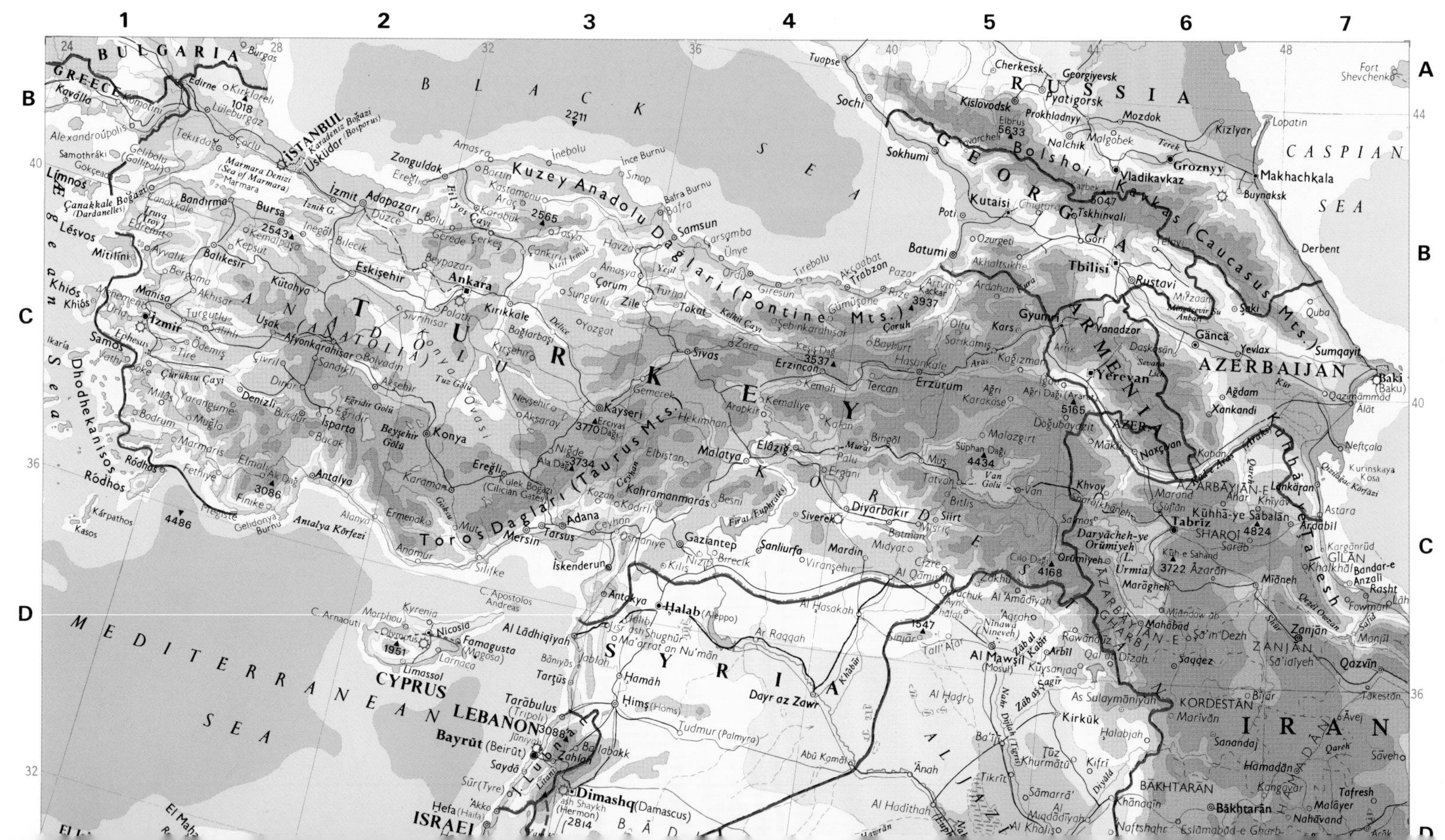

1
2
3
4
5
6
7
A
B
C
D
BLACK SEA
CASPIAN SEA
MEDITERRANEAN SEA
RUSSIA
GEORGIA
ARMENIA
AZERBAIJAN
TURKEY
SYRIA
IRAN
CYPRUS
LEBANON
ISRAEL
BULGARIA
GREECE
ANATOLIA
Bolshoi Kavkaz (Caucasus Mts.)
Kuzey Anadolu Dağlari (Pontine Mts.)
Toros Dağlari (Taurus Mts.)
Dhodhekanisos
Makhachkala
Groznyy
Vladikavkaz
Derbent
Sumqayit
Baki (Baku)
Tbilisi
Kutaisi
Batumi
Sokhumi
Sochi
Tuapse
Yerevan
Gyumri
Gäncä
Tabriz
Rasht
Zanjān
Qazvīn
Bākhtarān
Ardabīl
Orūmīyeh
Mahābād
Kirkūk
Arbīl
Al Mawşil (Mosul)
Dayr az Zawr
Halab (Aleppo)
Hamāh
Ḥimş (Homs)
Dimashq (Damascus)
Bayrūt (Beirūt)
Tarābulus (Tripoli)
Nicosia
Famagusta
Limassol
İSTANBUL
İzmit
Bursa
Ankara
Eskişehir
Kütahya
İzmir
Manisa
Balıkesir
Denizli
Isparta
Antalya
Konya
Kayseri
Sivas
Samsun
Trabzon
Erzurum
Erzincan
Malatya
Elâzığ
Diyarbakır
Mardin
Gaziantep
Adana
Tarsus
Mersin
İskenderun
Antakya
Van
Kars
Zonguldak
Adapazarı
Edirne
Rodhos
Lésvos
Límnos
Samos
Khíos
5633
5047
5165
4824
3937
3734
4434
4168
3722
3537
2565
2543
3086
1951
4486
2211

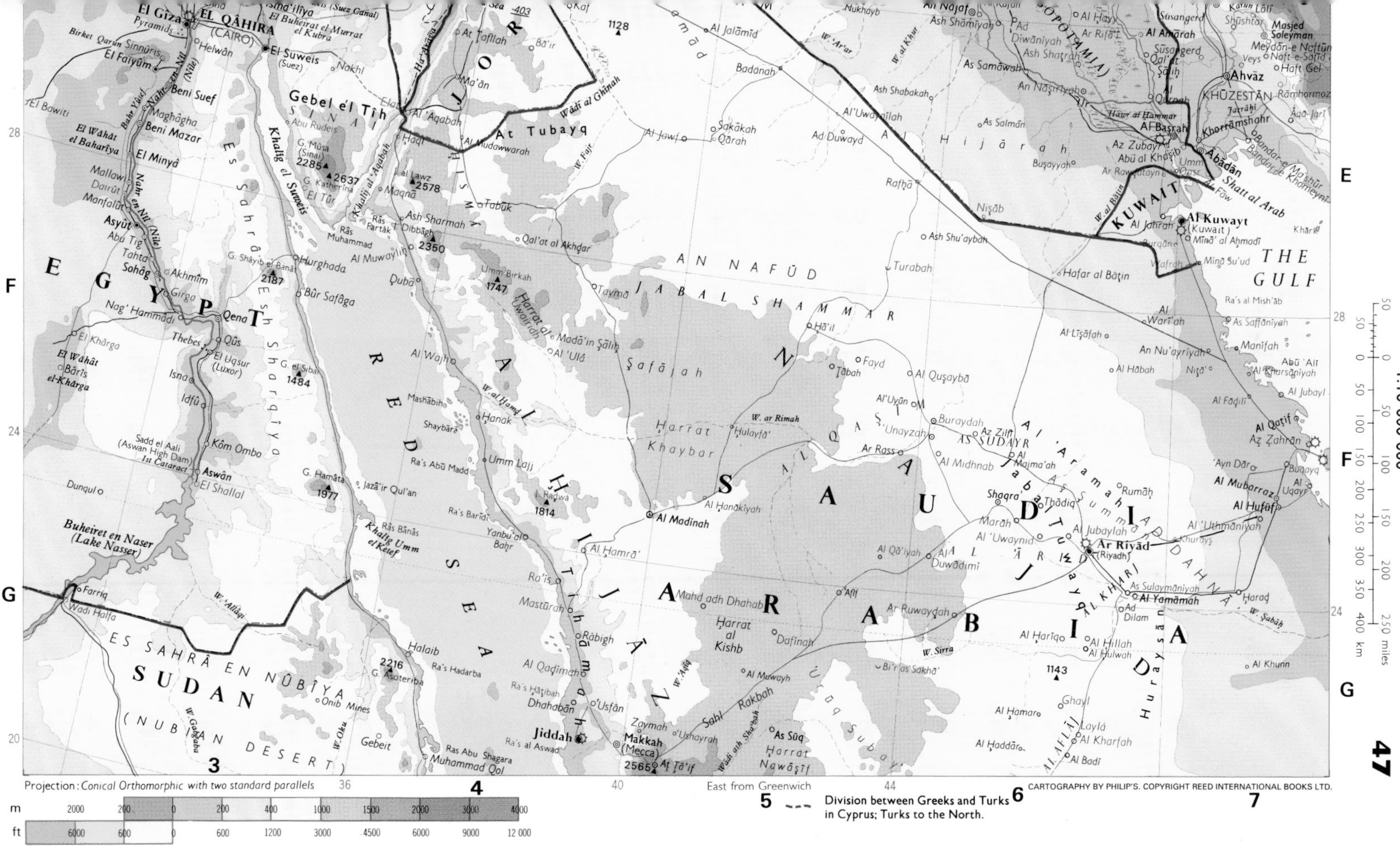

1:10 000 000

Division between Greeks and Turks
in Cyprus; Turks to the North.

East from Greenwich

CARTOGRAPHY BY PHILIP'S. COPYRIGHT REED INTERNATIONAL BOOKS LTD.

Projection: Conical Orthomorphic with two standard parallels

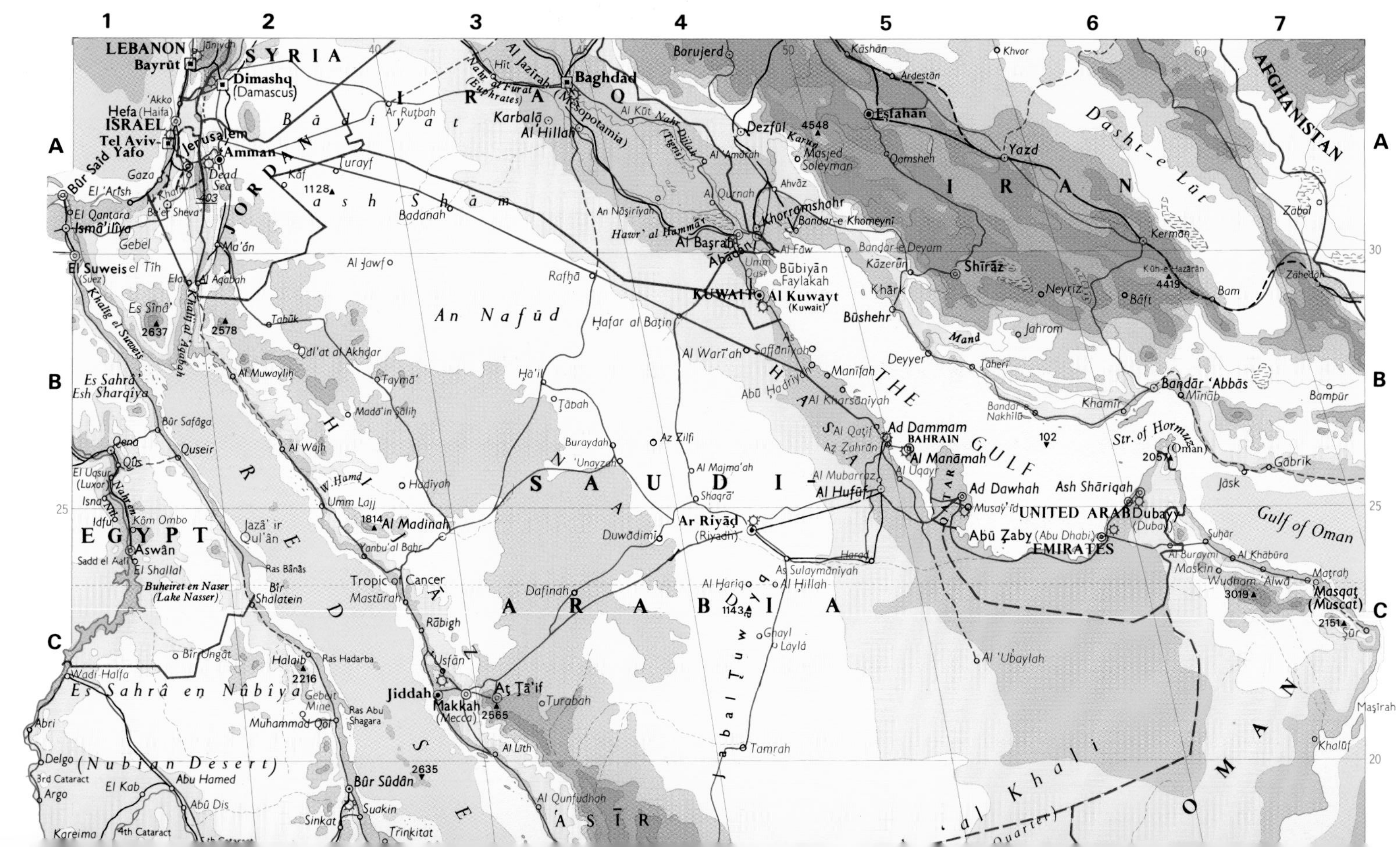

AFGHANISTAN
Dasht-e Lūt
IRAN
IRAQ
SYRIA
LEBANON
ISRAEL
JORDAN
KUWAIT
BAHRAIN
QATAR
UNITED ARAB EMIRATES
SAUDI ARABIA
EGYPT
OMAN
THE GULF
Gulf of Oman
Str. of Hormuz
RED SEA
Bādiyat ash Shām
An Nafūd
Jabal Tuwayq
HIJAZ
'ASĪR
Es Sahrâ en Nûbîya
(Nubian Desert)
Es Sahrâ Esh Sharqîya
Es Sînâ'
Mesopotamia
Baghdad
Borujerd
Kāshān
Eşfahān
Yazd
Kermān
Bam
Shīrāz
Būshehr
Bandār 'Abbās
Dezfūl
Abadan
Al Başrah
Al Kuwayt (Kuwait)
Ad Dammam
Al Manāmah
Ad Dawhah
Abū Zaby (Abu Dhabi)
Dubayy (Dubai)
Ash Shāriqah
Masqaţ (Muscat)
Ar Riyāḍ (Riyadh)
Al Hufūf
Al Madīnah
Makkah (Mecca)
Jiddah
Aţ Ţā'if
Ḩā'il
Buraydah
Tabūk
Dimashq (Damascus)
Bayrūt
Amman
Jerusalem
Tel Aviv-Yafo
Hefa (Haifa)
Dead Sea
Khalīj al 'Aqabah
Khalîg el Suweis
El Suweis (Suez)
Bûr Saîd
Ismâ'ilîya
Aswân
Buheiret en Naser (Lake Nasser)
Nahr en Nîl
Bûr Sûdân
Suakin
Tropic of Cancer
Karbalā'
Al Hillah
Nahr al Furāt (Euphrates)
Nahr Dijlah (Tigris)

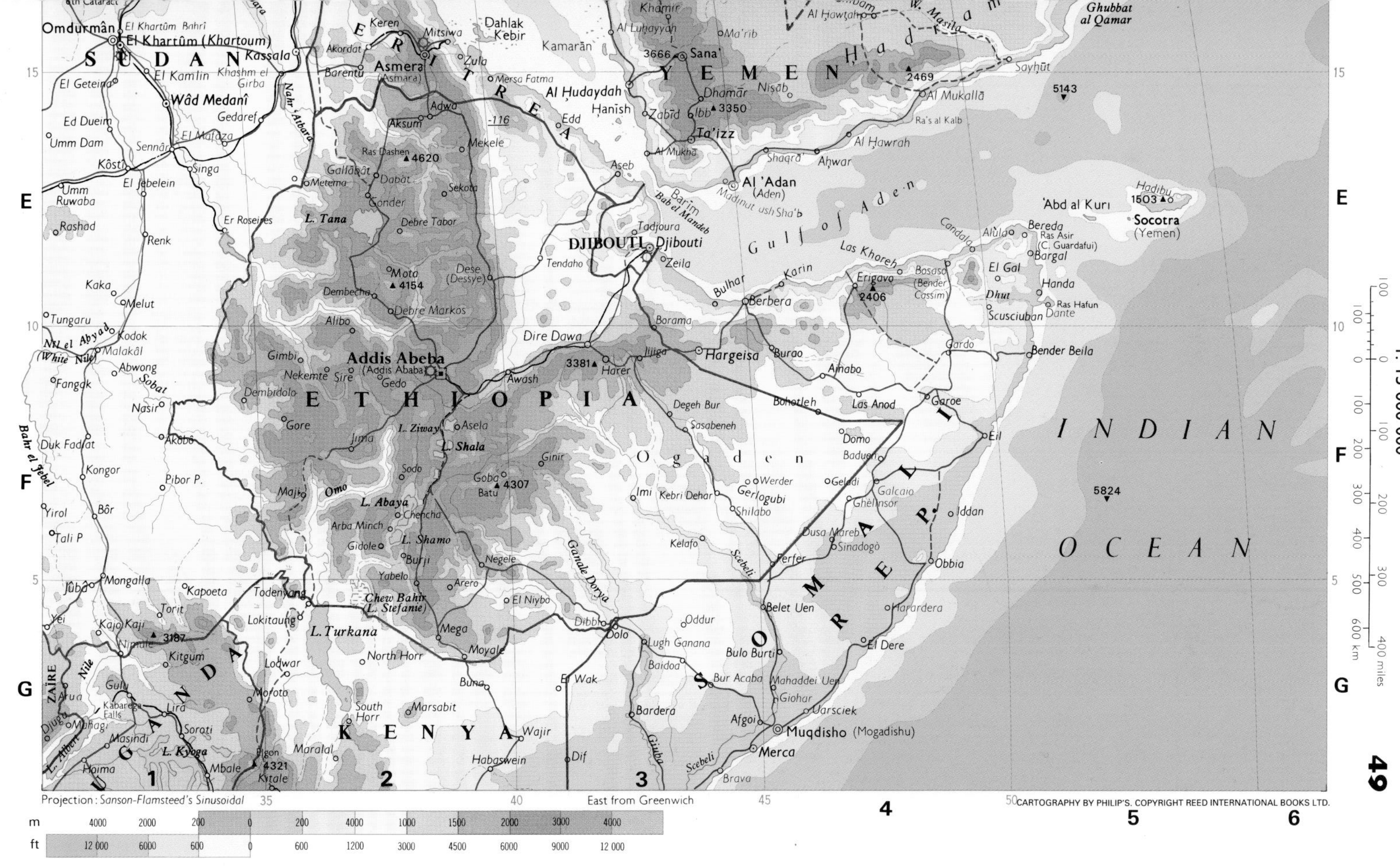

1: 15 000 000

100 0 100 200 300 400 miles
100 0 100 200 300 400 500 600 km

Projection: Sanson-Flamsteed's Sinusoidal

CARTOGRAPHY BY PHILIP'S. COPYRIGHT REED INTERNATIONAL BOOKS LTD.

East from Greenwich

m   4000   2000   0   600   1200   3000   4500   6000   9000 12 000
ft   12 000 6000   0   600   2000   4000   ...   12 000

NORTH ATLANTIC OCEAN
B. of Biscay
Azores (Port.)
Madeira (Port.)
Canary Is. (Sp.)
CAPE VERDE IS.
Praia
UNITED KINGDOM
LONDON
NETH.
BELG.
PARIS
FRANCE
GERMANY
POLAND
Warsaw
CZECH REP.
Prague
SLOVAK REP.
HUNGARY
AUSTRIA
Vienna
SWITZ.
CROATIA
BOS.-HERZ.
YUG.
MAC.
ALB.
ROMANIA
BULGARIA
GREECE
Athens
ITALY
Rome
Adriatic Sea
Corsica
Sardinia
Sicily
MALTA
Crete
CYPRUS
SPAIN
Madrid
PORTUGAL
Lisbon
RUSSIA
Volgograd
UKRAINE
Kiev
Odessa
KAZAKSTAN
Aral Sea
TURKMEN.
Caspian Sea
Black Sea
GEORGIA
ARM.
AZER.
Baku
TURKEY
Ankara
SYRIA
Aleppo
Damascus
LEB.
Tel Aviv-Jaffa
Jerusalem
ISRAEL
JORDAN
IRAQ
Mosul
Baghdād
Basra
Tigris
Euphrates
Syrian Desert
IRAN
TEHRĀN
Eşfahān
KUWAIT
BAHRAIN
QATAR
The Gulf
SAUDI ARABIA
Riyadh
Medina
Jedda
Mecca
YEMEN
G. of Aden
Socotra (Yemen)
Ras Asir
DJIBOUTI
Djibouti
ERITREA
Asmera
Mesewa
L. Tana
Red Sea
Mediterranean Sea
MOROCCO
Rabat
Casablanca
Marrakesh
Fès
Tétouan
ALGERIA
Algiers
Annaba
Constantine
Chott Djerid
In Salah
TUNISIA
Tunis
Sfax
LIBYA
Tripoli
Misrātah
Benghazi
Marzūq
Al Jawf
EGYPT
CAIRO
Alexandria
Port Said
Suez
El Faiyûm
Asyût
Aswân
Nile
SUDAN
Wadi Halfa
Port Sudan
Atbara
'Atbara
Khartoum
Omdurmân
Wâd Medanî
El Obeid
El Fâsher
Blue Nile
White Nile
CHAD
Abéché
Ndjamena
L. Chad
NIGER
Agadès
Niamey
Niger
Maiduguri
Kano
Sahara
Tropic of Cancer
WESTERN SAHARA
El Aaiún
Dakhla
MAURITANIA
Nouakchott
Fdérik
Ras Nouâdhibou
Senegal
SENEGAL
St-Louis
C. Vert
Dakar
GAMBIA
Banjul
GUINEA-BISSAU
Bissau
MALI
Bamako
Tombouctou
BURKINA FASO
Ouagadougou
Bobo-

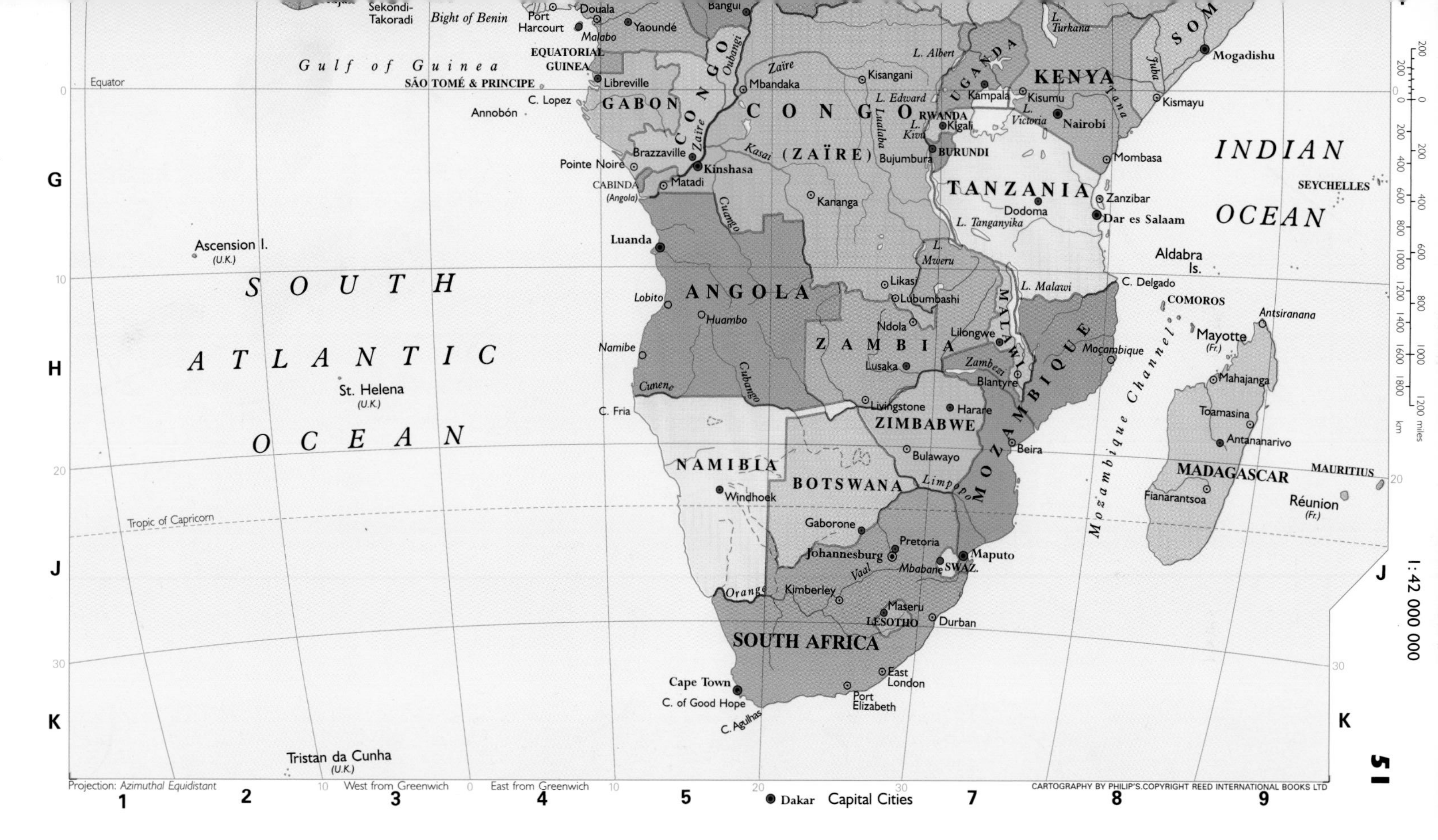

1:42 000 000

200   0   200   400   600   800   1000   1200 miles
200   0   200   400   600   800   1000   1200   1400   1600   1800   km

INDIAN OCEAN

SEYCHELLES

MAURITIUS
Réunion (Fr.)

MADAGASCAR

Antsiranana
Mahajanga
Toamasina
Antananarivo
Fianarantsoa

COMOROS
Mayotte (Fr.)

Aldabra Is.

C. Delgado

Mogadishu

Kismayu

WOS

Juba

KENYA
Nairobi
Mombasa
Zanzibar
Dar es Salaam

Mozambique Channel

Tana
L. Turkana

Kisumu
L. Victoria
Kampala
UGANDA
Kigali
RWANDA
BURUNDI
Bujumbura
L. Kivu
L. Edward
L. Albert

TANZANIA
Dodoma
L. Tanganyika
L. Malawi

MALAWI
Lilongwe
Blantyre

MOZAMBIQUE

Beira
Harare

ZIMBABWE
Bulawayo
Limpopo

Maputo
SWAZ.
Mbabane

Pretoria
Johannesburg
Maseru
LESOTHO

Durban

East London
Port Elizabeth

CONGO (ZAÏRE)

Kisangani
L. Mweru
L. Lualaba
Lualaba

Likasi
Lubumbashi
Ndola
Lusaka
Livingstone

ZAMBIA
Kananga

Zambezi

Kasai

Mbandaka
Zaïre

CONGO
Brazzaville
Kinshasa
Matadi

GABON
Libreville
Pointe Noire
C. Lopez
CABINDA (Angola)

Luanda

ANGOLA
Lobito
Huambo
Namibe
Cunene
C. Fria
Cubango

BOTSWANA
Gaborone
Cuando

NAMIBIA
Windhoek

SOUTH AFRICA
Kimberley
Orange
Cape Town
C. of Good Hope
C. Agulhas

EQUATORIAL GUINEA
Malabo

Douala
Yaoundé
Port Harcourt
Annobón
SÃO TOMÉ & PRINCIPE

Bangui

Ouango
Ubangi

Sekondi-Takoradi

Gulf of Guinea

Bight of Benin

SOUTH ATLANTIC OCEAN

Ascension I. (U.K.)

St. Helena (U.K.)

Tristan da Cunha (U.K.)

Tropic of Capricorn

Equator

Projection: Azimuthal Equidistant

West from Greenwich   East from Greenwich

● Dakar   Capital Cities

CARTOGRAPHY BY PHILIP'S. COPYRIGHT REED INTERNATIONAL BOOKS LTD

J   K   9   8   7   6   5   4   3   2   1

G   H   J   K

20   30

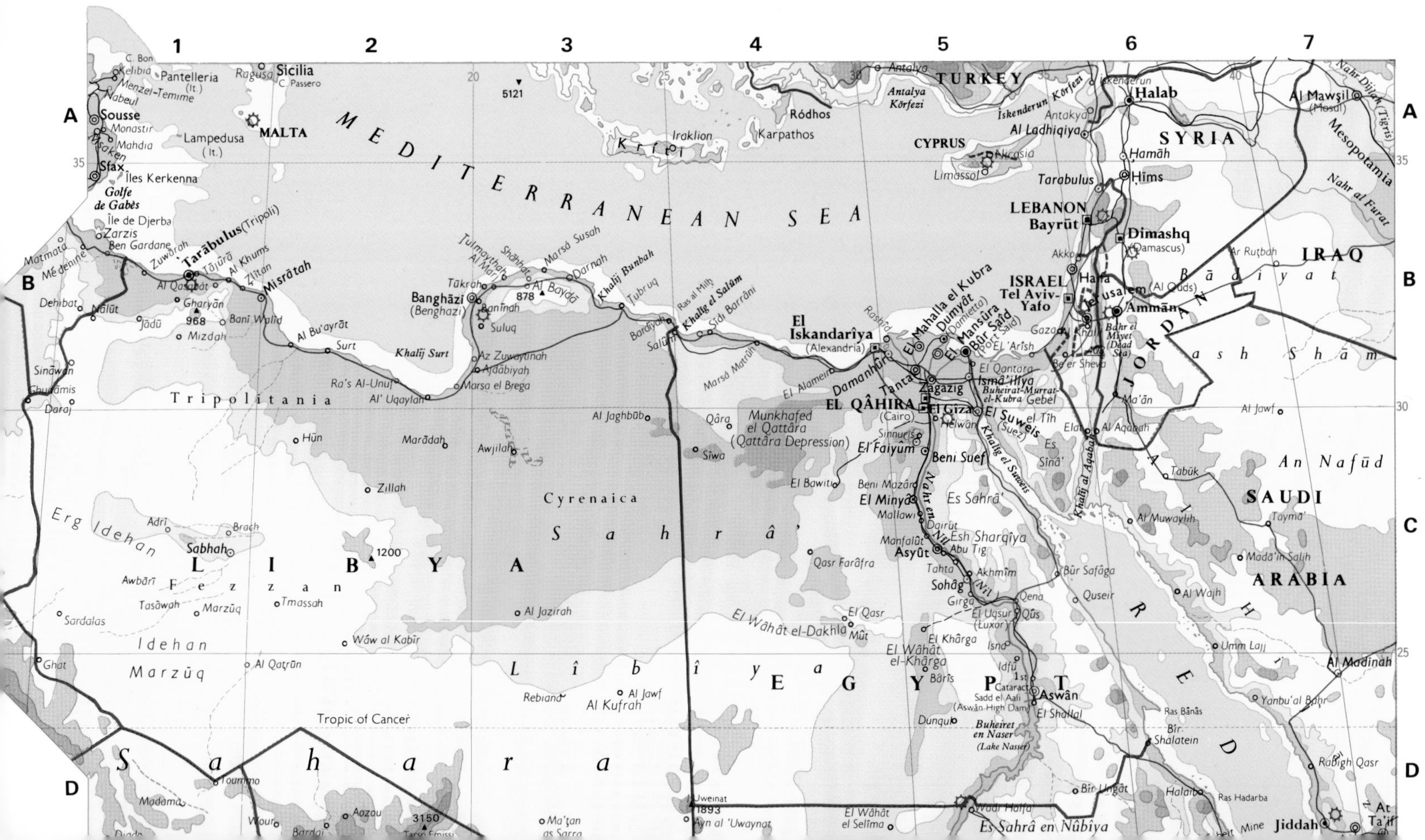

MEDITERRANEAN SEA
TURKEY
SYRIA
IRAQ
JORDAN
LEBANON
ISRAEL
CYPRUS
SAUDI ARABIA
MALTA
EGYPT
LIBYA
RED SEA
Sahara
Mesopotamia
Nahr Dijlah (Tigris)
Nahr al Furat
Al Mawşil (Mosul)
Halab
Hamāh
Hims
Dimashq (Damascus)
Ammān
Bayrūt
Tarabulus
Al Ladhiqiya
Antakya
Iskenderun Körfezi
Antalya
Antalya Körfezi
Rodhos
Karpathos
Kriti
Iraklion
Limassol
Nicosia
Tel Aviv-Yafo
Haifa
Akko
Gaza
Be'er Sheva
Bahr el Miyet (Dead Sea)
Ma'ān
Al 'Aqabah
Khalij al Aqaba
Ar Rutbah
Bādiyat ash Shām
Tabūk
Al Jawf
An Nafūd
Taymā'
Madā'in Salih
Al Muwaylih
Al Wajh
Umm Lajj
Yanbu'al Bahr
Al Madinah
Rābigh
Jiddah
Ras Bânâs
Bir Shalatein
Halaib
Ras Hadarba
El Iskandarîya (Alexandria)
EL QÂHIRA (Cairo)
El Giza
Bûr Sa'îd (Port Said)
El Mansûra
Dumyât (Damietta)
El Mahalla el Kubra
Rashîd
Tanta
Damanhûr
Zagazig
Ismâ'iliya
El Qantara
El 'Arîsh
El Suweis (Suez)
Khalig el Suweis
Gebel el Tîh
Es Sînâ'
Helwân
Beni Suef
El Faiyûm
Beni Mazâr
El Minya
Mallawi
Dairût
Manfalût
Asyût
Abu Tig
Esh Sharqîya
Tahta
Sohâg
Akhmîm
Girga
Qena
Qûs
El Uqsur (Luxor)
Isna
Idfû
1st Cataract
Aswân
Sadd el Aali (Aswân High Dam)
El Shallal
Buheiret en Naser (Lake Nasser)
Nahr en Nil
Es Sahrâ'
Bûr Safâga
Quseir
Bir Ungât
Wadi Halfa
Es Sahrâ en Nûbîya
El Wâhât el-Khârga
El Khârga
Bârîs
Dunqul
El Wâhât el-Dakhla
El Qasr
Mût
Qasr Farâfra
El Bawiti
Munkhafed el Qattâra (Qattâra Depression)
Sîwa
Qâra
El Alamein
Marsá Matrûh
Sîdi Barrâni
Khalig el Salûm
Salûm
Ras al Milh
Bardiyah
Tubruq
Khalij Bunbah
Darnah
Marsá Susah
Shahhat
Al Bayda
878
Tulmaythah
Al Marj
Tūkrah
Banghāzi (Benghazi)
Baninah
Suluq
Az Zuwaytinah
Ajdābiyah
Marsa el Brega
Khalij Surt
Al' Uqaylah
Ra's Al-Unuf
Surt
Al Bu'ayrat
Misrātah
Zlītan
Al Khums
Tājūrā
Tarābulus (Tripoli)
Zuwārah
Al Qasabat
Gharyān
968
Bani Walid
Mizdah
Jādū
Nālūt
Dehibat
Tripolitania
Cyrenaica
Al Jaghbūb
Awjilah
Marādah
Zillah
Hūn
Sahrâ'
Lîbîya
Al Jawf
Al Kufrah
Rebiana
Al Jazirah
'Uweinat
1893
'Ayn al 'Uwaynat
El Wâhât el Selîma
Ma'tan as Sarra
Wāw al Kabir
Tmassah
Sabhah
Brach
Adri
1200
Fezzan
Marzūq
Tasāwah
Awbārī
Idehan Marzūq
Erg Idehan
Al Qatrūn
Sardalas
Ghat
Tummo
Madama
Aozou
3150
Tropic of Cancer
Sousse
Sfax
Monastir
Mahdia
Msaken
Nabeul
Kelibia
C. Bon
Menzel-Temime
Golfe de Gabès
Zarzis
Île de Djerba
Îles Kerkenna
Ben Gardane
Médenine
Matmata
Ghudāmis
Sināwan
Daraj
Pantelleria (It.)
Lampedusa (It.)
Sicilia
Ragusa
C. Passero
5121

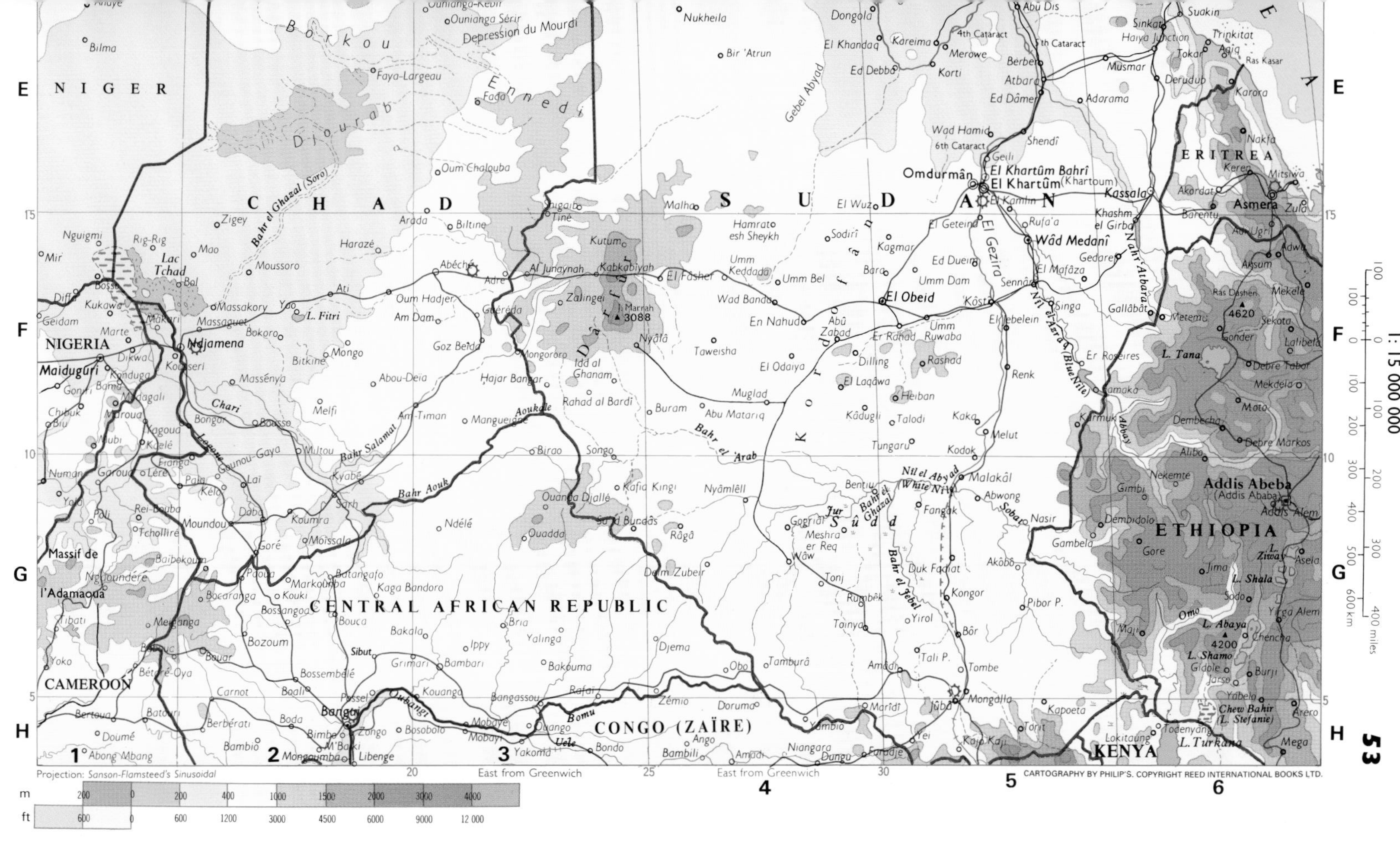

1: 15 000 000

100   0   100   200   300   400 miles

100   0   100   200   300   400   500   600 km

ERITREA
Ras Kasar
Karora
Nakfa
Mitsiwa
Asmera
Zula

Suakin
Tokar
Trinkitat
Aqiq
Haiya Junction
Musmar
Deraheib
Adarama
Sinkat

Abu Dis
1st Cataract
Berber
Atbara
Ed Dāme
Khashm
el Girba
Kassala
Gedaref
Nahr 'Atbara
Galabat
4th Cataract
Merowe
Korti
6th Cataract
Wad Hamid
Shendi
Ed Dueim
Nil el Azraq (Blue Nile)
Sennar
Ras Dashen
4620
Amba
Gonder
L. Tana
Aksum
Meqele
Lalibela
Debre Markos
Dembidollo
ETHIOPIA
Addis Abeba
Addis Alem
Nazret
Debre Zeyit
4200
L. Abaya
L. Shamo
Chew Bahir
L. Stefanie

SUDAN
El Khartūm Bahri
Omdurmân
El Khartūm (Khartum)
El Gezira
Wâd Medanî

Dongola
El Khandaq
Ed Debba
Karima

Nukheila
Bir Atrun

Gebel Abyad

El Wuda
Sodiri
Kagmar
Bâra
El Obeid
Er Rahad
Dilling
Kadugli
Talodi
Tungaro
Heiban
El Odaiya
Umm Bel
En Nahud
Abū Zabad

Hamrato esh Sheykh
Umm Keddada
Wad Banda

Toweisha
Muglad
Abu Matariq
Buram
Nyala
3088 Marrah
Kutum
Kabkabiyah
El Fasher
Zalingei
Edd al Fursan
Rahad al Bardi
Tine
Geneina
Al Junaynah

Malha
Radom
Kafia Kingi

Nil el Abyad
Malakal
Bahr el Jebel
Renk
Kodok
Melut
Kaka
Abwong
Fangak
Nasir
Akobo
Kongor
Bôr
Juba
Mongalla
Tombe
Tali P.
Bahr el Arab
Nyamlell
Rag̈a
Deim Zubeir
Wau
Meshra er Req
Tonj
Tonyu
Rumbek
Amadi
Maridi
Yambio
Tambura
Obo
Yei

KENYA
L. Turkana

CENTRAL AFRICAN REPUBLIC
Obo
Bondo
CONGO (ZAÏRE)
Niangara
Dungu
Doruma
Bambili
Ango
Zémio
Djema
Bangassou
Ouango
Bria
Ippy
Bambari
Kouango
Bangui
Mobaye
Sibut

Birao
Ouanda Djallé
Ndélé
Kaga Bandoro
Batangafo
Bossangoa
Bozoum
Bossembélé
Boda
Mbaïki
Libenge

Am Dam
Oum Hadjer
Abou-Deia
Ati
Mongo
Melfi
Bitkine
Mangueigne
Goz Beïda
Ab Timan
Sarh
Moïssala
Doba
Gore
Bébédja
Bédiondo
Kyabé
Bôkoro

CHAD
Arada
Biltine
Abéché
Haraze

Faya-Largeau
Fada
Ounianga-Kebir
Oum Chalouba
Zigey

BORKOU
Djourab
ENNEDI
Depression du Mourdi

NIGER
Bilma
Nguigmi

Maiduguri
Geidam
NIGERIA
Dikwa
Potiskum

Lac Tchad
Rig-Rig
N'Djamena
Massaguet
Mao
Moussoro
Bol
Chari
Logone

CAMEROON
Ngaoundéré
Massif de l'Adamaoua
Garoua
Maroua

East from Greenwich

m   ft
4400   12 000
3000   9000
2000   6000
1500   4500
1000   3000
600   1500
400   1200
200   600
0   0
600   600

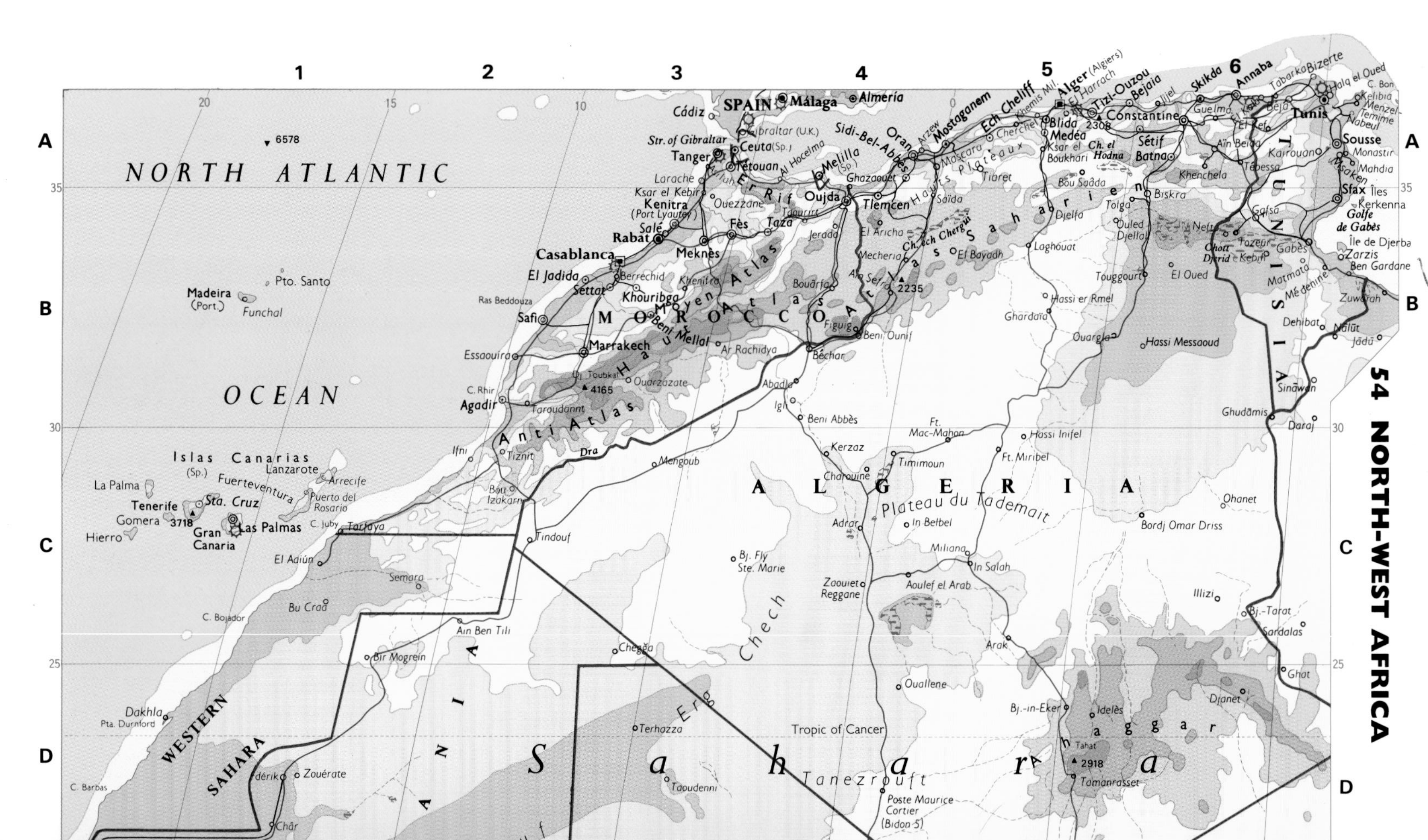

TUNISIA

C. Bon
Menzel Bourguiba
Bizerte
C. Serrat
Medjerda
Tabarka
Tunis
Karouan
Skikda
Annaba
Constantine
Sétif
Batna
Ch. el Hodna
Biskra
El Oued

ALGERIA

Ghudāmis
Ghanet
Ohanet
Bordj Omar Driss
Illizi
Ghat
Bardaïas
Djanet
Ahaggar
Idelès
Tamanrasset
Bj.-in-Eker
Tahat ▲2918
In Salah
Arak
Poste Maurice
Cortier
(Bidon 5)
Reggane
Tropic of Cancer
Plateau du Tademaït
Timimoun
Ft. Miribel
Hassi Inifel
Ft. MacMahon
Hassi er Mel
Ouargla
Hassi Messaoud
Touggourt
Ghardaïa
Laghouat
Djelfa
Bou Saâda
Boukhari
Médéa
Blida
Algiers (Alger)
Tizi-Ouzou
Oued
El Boyadh
Saïda
Tiaret
Mostaganem
Oran
Sidi-Bel-Abbès
Tlemcen
Beni Abbès
Béchar
Adrar
Reggane
Zaouiet
In Belbel
Aulef el Arab
Ouallene
Check
Tanezrouft
Erg Chech

MOROCCO

Oujda
Melilla
Nador
Taza
Fès
Meknès
Rabat
Salé
Casablanca
El Jadida
Safi
Essaouira
Marrakech
Agadir
Ifni
Tiznit
Ouarzazate
Er Rachidia
Boudnib
Figuig
Dra

SPAIN

Málaga
Almería
Str. of Gibraltar
Gibraltar (U.K.)
Ceuta (Sp.)
Tanger
Tetouan
Cádiz
Larache
Ksar el Kebir
Kenitra (Port Lyautey)

WESTERN SAHARA

El Aaiún
Dakhla
C. Bojador
C. Barbas
Pta Durnford
Semara
Bir Mogrein
Bu Craâ
Tah
Tarfaya
C. Juby

MALI

Tessalit
Taoudenni
Chegga
Terhazza

NORTH ATLANTIC OCEAN

▲6578
Madeira (Port.)
Funchal
Pto. Santo

Islas Canarias (Sp.)
Lanzarote
Arrecife
Fuerteventura
Puerto del Rosario
La Palma
Tenerife
Sta. Cruz
Gomera
Hierro
Gran Canaria
Las Palmas
▲3718

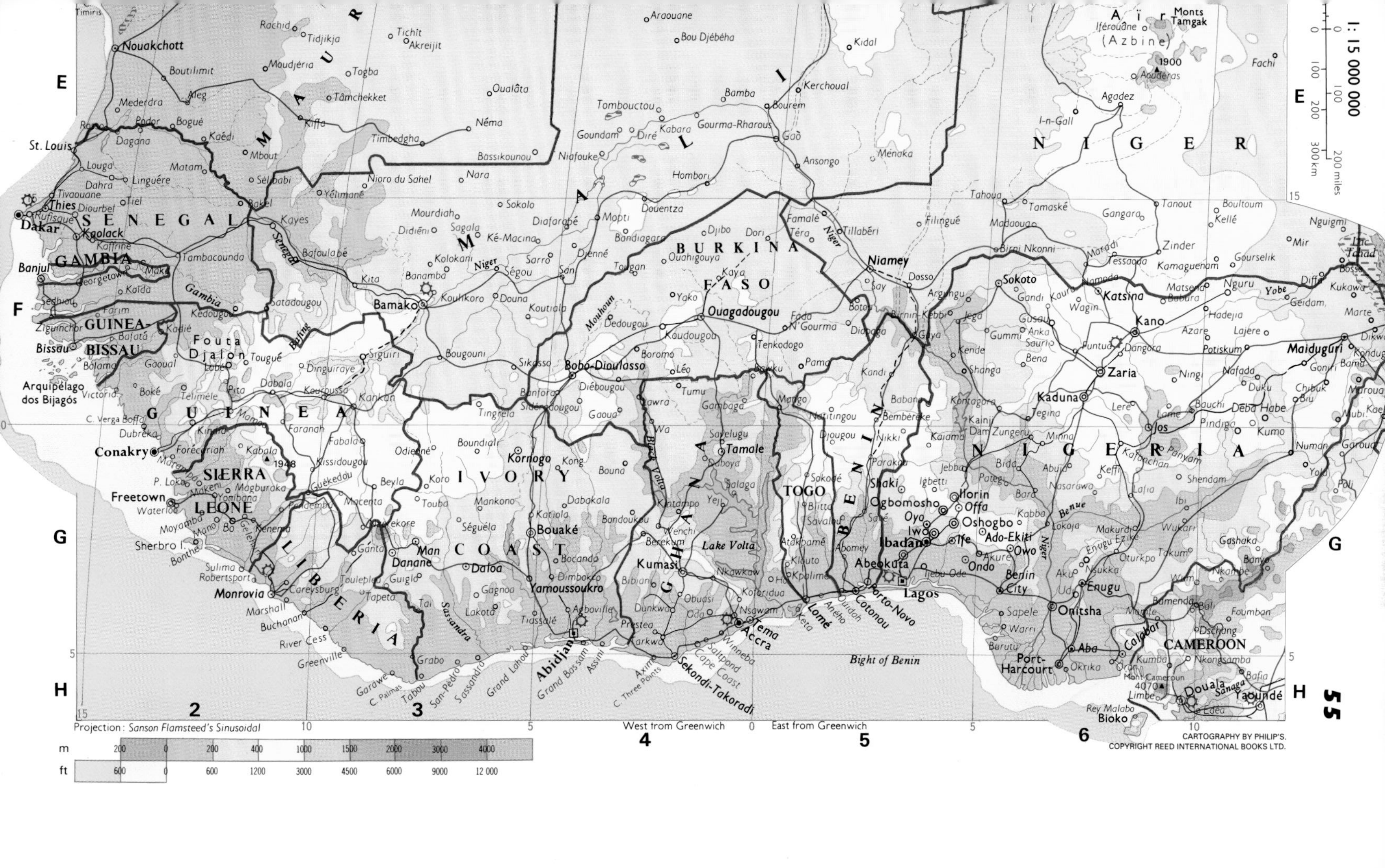
1: 15 000 000
0 100 200 miles
0 100 200 300 km
MAURITANIA
MALI
NIGER
SENEGAL
GAMBIA
GUINEA-BISSAU
GUINEA
SIERRA LEONE
LIBERIA
IVORY COAST
BURKINA FASO
GHANA
TOGO
BENIN
NIGERIA
CAMEROON
Aïr (Azbine)
Monts Tamgak
Fouta Djalon
Arquipélago dos Bijagós
Nouakchott
St. Louis
Dakar
Thies
Kaolack
Banjul
Bissau
Conakry
Freetown
Monrovia
Bamako
Tombouctou
Gao
Mopti
Ségou
Niamey
Agadez
Zinder
Ouagadougou
Bobo-Dioulasso
Yamoussoukro
Abidjan
Bouaké
Kumasi
Tamale
Accra
Tema
Sekondi-Takoradi
Lomé
Cotonou
Porto-Novo
Lagos
Ibadan
Abeokuta
Ogbomosho
Oshogbo
Ilorin
Benin City
Onitsha
Enugu
Aba
Port-Harcourt
Kaduna
Zaria
Kano
Katsina
Sokoto
Maiduguri
Jos
Douala
Yaoundé
Bioko
Niger
Gambia
Senegal
Black Volta
Lake Volta
Benue
Sanaga
Bight of Benin
Lac Tchad
Projection: Sanson Flamsteed's Sinusoidal
West from Greenwich
East from Greenwich
m 200 0 200 400 1000 1500 2000 3000 4000
ft 600 0 600 1200 3000 4500 6000 9000 12 000
CARTOGRAPHY BY PHILIP'S.
COPYRIGHT REED INTERNATIONAL BOOKS LTD.

N I G E R

Tanout Boultoum Nguigmi Rig-Rig Mao Zigey Bahr el Ghazal (Soro) Arada Biltine Tigabo Tiné

Gangara Kellé Mir Lac Tchad Moussoro Harazé Abéché Al Junaynah

Zinder Gourselik Bosso Bol Ati Oum Hadjer Am Dam Adré Zal

Tessaoua Kamaguenam Diffa Kukawa Massaguet C H A D Goz Beida Am Guereda

Matsena Nguru Yobe Geidam Marte Massakory L. Fitri Mongo Abou-Deïa Hajar Banzar Rahad

B Kano Hadejia Dikwa Koussen Ndjamena Bokoro Bitkine Mongororo

Azare Lajere Kanduga Boma (F-Lamy) Massenya Am-Timan Mangueigne

Dangora Potiskum Ganni Madagali Maroua Yagoua Chari Melfi Birao

Ningi Nafada Chibuk Mubi Kaélé Bongor Bousso Miltou Bahr Salamat Ouanda

Duku Biu Deba Habe Kumo Numan Garoua Lere Palg Lai Kyabe Sarh Bahr Aouk Ouadda

Lere Lame Bauchi Pindiga Figuil Rei Bouba Moundou Gore Koumra Ndélé

Jos Bogoro Panyam Shendam Pala Doba Kaga Bandoro Bria

Kafanchan Tchollire Baibokoum Marcounda Batangafo Ippy Yalinga

C Wukari Gashaka Massif de Bocaranga Kouki Bouca Bakala

Makurdi Takum Ngaoundere l'Adamaoua Bozoum Bossangoa Grimari Bambari Bakoum

Oturkpo Wum Nkambe Banyo Tibati Meiganga CENTRAL AFRICAN

Bali Bamenda Foumban Yoko Bouar Sibut REPUBLIC

Mamfe Dschang Bétaré-Oya Bossembélé Kouango Bangassou Bor

Calabar C A M E R O O N Carnot Boali Grimari Mobaye Ouango Yakoma

Kumba Nkongsamba Nanga Eboko Bertoua Baturi Bangui Zongo Bosobolo Mobayi

Oron Mont Cameroun Bafia Batouri Boda Bimbo M'Baiki Libenge Busingo

4070 Limbe Edéa Doumé Berbérati Bambio Manfoumbi Gemena Yahuma

Bioko Douala Yaoundé Abong-Mbang Nola Budjala Monveda Aketi

(Fernando Póo) M'Balmayo Yokadouma Bomboma Lisala Bumba

B. of Bonny Campo Sangmelima Lomié Dongou Busu-Djanoa Zaire

D EQUATORIAL Ambam Ebolowa Djoum Moloundou Impfondo Bongandanga Basankusa Yahuma

GUINEA Bitam Souanké Ouessa Bomongo Lulonga Djolu

Mbini Minvoul Oyem Bolomba Befale Boende

Cabo San Juan Evinayong Mvadi C O N G O Oubangi Mbandaka Bokungu

Cocobeach Ousye Belinga Makoua Irebu Ingende Boende Monkoto C O N G O

Libreville Mitzic Makokou Owanda Rukp Z A I R E

Owendo Kango Ndjolé Kelle Ewo Lac Tumba Bokote Lomela

C. Lopez Ogooué Lastoursville Okondja Okoyo Mossaka Lukolela Kiri Loto

E Port-Gentil G A B O N Fougamou Moula Mouanda Franceville Lokolama Inongo Dekese Kole

Iguéla Moabi Ndende Djambala L. Mai-Ndombe Kutu Oshwe Lubue

Omboué Tchibanga Zanaga Bolobo Mushie Lukenie Bandundu Ilebo Mweka Lusambo

Setté Cama Nyanga Kibangou Komono Kwamouth Tolo Dibaya Sankuru

Mayumba Sibiti Mindouli Brazzaville Kasai Lubue Basongo

Koulamoutou Loubomo Madingou Kinshasa Kenge Kikwit Idiofa Charlesville Lueba Demba

Pointe Noire Tsiela Luozi Kasangulu Masi-Manimba Gungu Makumbi Kananga

CABINDA Cacongo Mbanza Ngungu Madimba Popokabaka Feshi Kuzumba

Cabinda Boma Maquela Kasongo Lunda Tshikapa Luiza Kapanga

Soyo Nqui Camba do-Zombo Kahemba Luachimo Saurimo Sandoa

Mbanza Congo Damba Sanza Pombo Luremo Luiza Dilolo

F A T L A N T I C Nzeto Uige N'Gage Caungula Camissombo Lucapa

Ambriz Caxito Camabatela Lubalo Capaio Chiluage

O C E A N Luanda Quibaxe Malanje Quela Sando

Pta. das Palmeirinhas Ndalatando Cacolo Cambundi Cacolo Luau

Muxima Dondo Calulo Catembo Mucanda

Gunza Gabela A N G O L A Andulo Luacano

Sumbe

Projection: Sanson Flamsteed's Sinusoidal

ft m
12 000 4000
9000 3000
6000 2000
4500 1500
3000 1000
1200 400
600 200
0 0
200 600
m ft

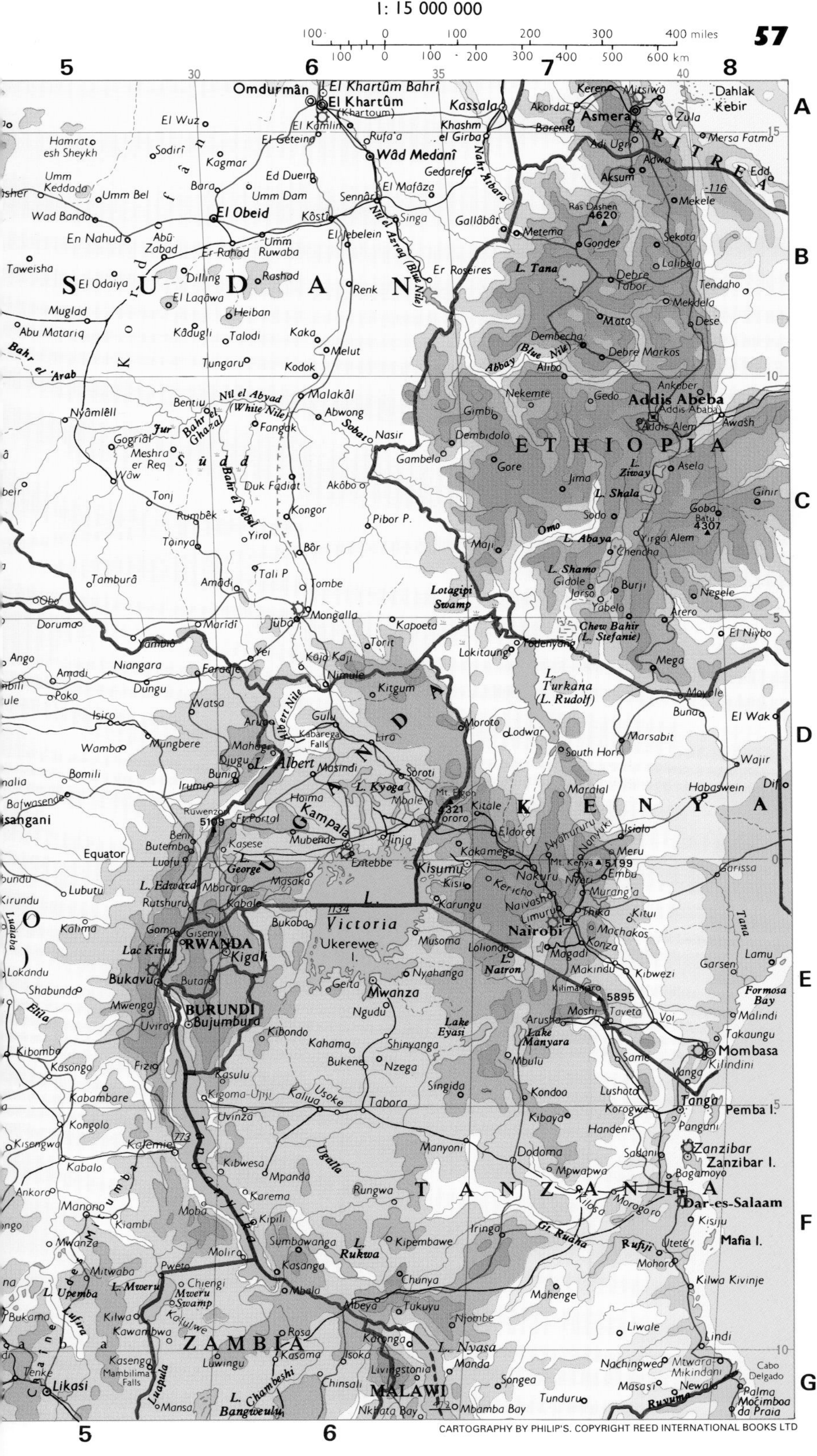

1: 15 000 000

100   0   100   200   300   400 miles
100   0   100 200   300 400   500 600 km

5   **6**   **7**   **8**

30   35   40

A

Omdurmân   El Khartûm Bahri   Keren Mitsiwa   Dahlak
El Khartûm (Khartoum)   Akordat   Zula   Kebir
El Wuz   El Kâmlin   Asmera ERITREA Mersa Fatma
Hamrat   El Geteina Kassala Adi Ugri   Edd
esh Sheykh Rufa'a   Khashm   Barentu Aksum −116
Sodiri Kagmar Wâd Medanî el Girba Adwa
Umm   Bara   Ed Dueim Gedaref Mekele
Keddada Umm Bel   Ras Dashen
Wad Banda Umm Dam Sennâr Gallâbât 4620 Sekota **B**
El Obeid Kôsti Singa Metema Gonder Lalibela
En Nahud Abû El Jebelein Er Roseires L. Tana Debre Tendaho
Taweisha Zabad Er Rahad Renk   Tabor Mekdela
Muglad El Odaiya Dilling Rashad Mota Dese
Abu Matariq El Laqawa Heiban Debre Markos
Bahr el 'Arab Kâdugli Talodi Kaka Dembecha Alibo
Nyâmlêll Tungaru Kodok Melut (Blue Nile) Debre Markos
Gogrial Bentiu Nil el Abyad Malakâl Nekemte Gedo Ankober **C**
Meshra (White Nile) Abwong Gimbi Addis Abeba
er Req Wâw Fangak Sobat Dembidolo Addis Alem Awash
Tonj Nasir Gore ETHIOPIA
Duk Fadiat Gambela Jima L. Ziway
Rumbek Kongor Pibor P. Sodo Asela
Toinya Yirol Bôr Omo L. Shala Goba
Tamburâ Amadi Tali P. Maji L. Abaya Yirga Alem 4307
Doruma Marîdi Tombe L. Shamo Chencha
Jûba Kapoeta Gidole Burji Negele
Mongalla Lotagipi Jarso Tabela
Yambio Yei Swamp Chew Bahir Arero **D**
Niangara Faradje Nimule Lakitaung (L. Stefanie) El Niybo
Dungu Watsa Kitgum Todenyang Mega
Isiro Gulu Moroto L. Moyale El Wak
Wamba Mungbere Lira Turkana Buna
Bomili Irumu Masindi Lodwar (L. Rudolf) Wajir
Bafwasende Bunia L. Kyoga Mt Elgon South Horr Habaswein Dif
Mahagi 4321 Kitale Maralal Marsabit
Beni Hoima Mbale Eldoret Meru
Butembo Fort Portal Soroti Nyahururu Isiolo **E**
Equator Kasese Mubende Jinja Kakamega Mt Kenya ▲5199 Embu Garissa
Lubutu L. Edward Kampala Kisumu Kericho Nakuru Nyeri Garsen
Kalima Rutshuru Masaka Kisii Naivasha Murang'a Kitui Lamu
Kabale Entebbe Karungu Limuru Machakos Formosa
Gisenyi Bukoba Musoma Nairobi Bay
RWANDA Ukerewe Nyahanga Magadi Makindu Malindi
Bukavu Kigali I. Geita L. Kibwezi
Butare Mwanza Natron Kilimanjaro Mombasa
BURUNDI Ngudu 5895 Moshi Kilindini
Bujumbura Kibondo Shinyanga Arusha Taveta Vanga
Uvira Kahama Lake Lake Same Pemba I. **F**
Fizi Bukene Eyasi Manyara Korogwe Tanga
Kasulu Nzega Mbulu Handeni Panguni
Kigoma-Ujiji Usoke Tabora Kondoa Kibaya Sabani
Uvinza Singida Dodoma Zanzibar
Kibwesa Mpanda Manyoni Mpwapwa Morogoro Bagamoyo Zanzibar I.
Karema TANZANIA Dar-es-Salaam
Kipili Rungwa Iringa Gt. Ruaha Kisiju
Sumbawanga Kipembawe Mafia I.
Molira L. Chunya Mahenge Rufiji Utete Mohoro
Pweto Rukwa Njombe Kilwa Kivinje
Chiengi Mbeya Tukuyu Liwale Lindi
L. Mweru Mwero Mbala Mahenge
Mambilima Swamp L. Nyasa Songea Nachingwe Mtwara
Falls Kasama Manda Masasi Mikindani
ZAMBIA Isoka Livingstonia Tunduru Newala Cabo
Kasenga Chinsali Ruvuma Delgado
Likasi Luwingu MALAWI Nkhata Bay Palma Moçimboa
L. Upemba L. Mweru L. Mbamba Bay da Praia **G**
Mansa Bangweulu

5   **6**

CARTOGRAPHY BY PHILIP'S. COPYRIGHT REED INTERNATIONAL BOOKS LTD

ATLANTIC

OCEAN

Tropic of Capricorn

ANGOLA

Lobito
Benguela
Bailundo
Planalto
Camacupa
Munhango
Luena
Cazombo
Zambezi
2619
Caála
Huambo
Kuito
Luvuei
Chavu
Lucira
Cuimbé
N·dé
Bié
Chitembo
Cuando
Lumai
Zam·Sezi
Quilengues
Caconda
Galangue
Lumbala
N'guimbo
Liuwa
Plain
Bibala
Lubango
Kipungo
Cubango
Kalabo
Mo
Namibe
Chibia
Cuchi
Menongue
Mavinga
Kwando
Ke
Tombua
Chianje
Chibemba
Mupa
Caiundo
Kavango
Kc
Oricocua
Xangongo
Ondjiva
Cuito
Luiana
Dirico
Andara
Chitado
Ondangua
Rundu
Caprivi
C. Fria

Ovamboland
Etosha Pan
Namutoni
Okavan
Swamp
Sesfontein
Okaukuejo
Tsumeb
Tsau
Toteng
Mo
Otavi
Grootfontein
Sehitwa
Ngam
Depres
Outjo
Otjiwarongo

Kaokoveld
Omuramba Omatako
Damaraland
Epukiro
Ghanzi
Omaruru
Okahandja
Gobabis
Tshwane
BOTSW
Usakos
Karibib
Windhoek
Swakopmund
2483
Walvisbaai
NAMIBIA
Rehoboth
Kalaha
Tsumis
Tshane
Kalkrand
Aranos
Namib
Desert
Mariental
Khakhea
Hardap Dam
Maltahöhe
Gibeon
Gochas
Werda
Namaland
Koes
Tshabong
Bethanie
Keetmanshoop
Lüderitz
Aus
Seeheim
Aroab
Molop
Fish
Kanus
Rietfontein
Vr
Karasburg
Nakop
Kuruman
Wo
Oranjemund
Alexander Bay
Warmbad
Kakamas
Upington
Kimb
Orange
Kaap
Port Nolloth
Pofadder
Okiep
Kenhardt
Prieska
Hopeto
Springbok
Brandvlei
Britstown
Hondeklipbaai
Carnarvon
Bitterfontein
Sakrivier
Victoria W.
No
Calvinia
5283
Vanrhynsdorp
Klawer
SOUTH
A
Clanwilliam
Nuweveldberge
Graaff-Rei
St. Helena B.
Piketberg
Beaufort West
Vredenburg
Ceres
Willowmore
Saldanha
Worcester
Oudtshoorn
Uit
Tafelbaai
Robertson
George
Cape Town
Stellenbosch
Swellendam
(Kaapstad)
Strand
Table Mt.
Caledon
Mosselbaai
Kaap die Goeie Hoop
False B.
Riversdale
(C. of Good Hope)
Danger Pt.
Bredasdorp
C. Agulhas

Projection : Sanson Flamsteed's Sinusoidal

East from Greenwich

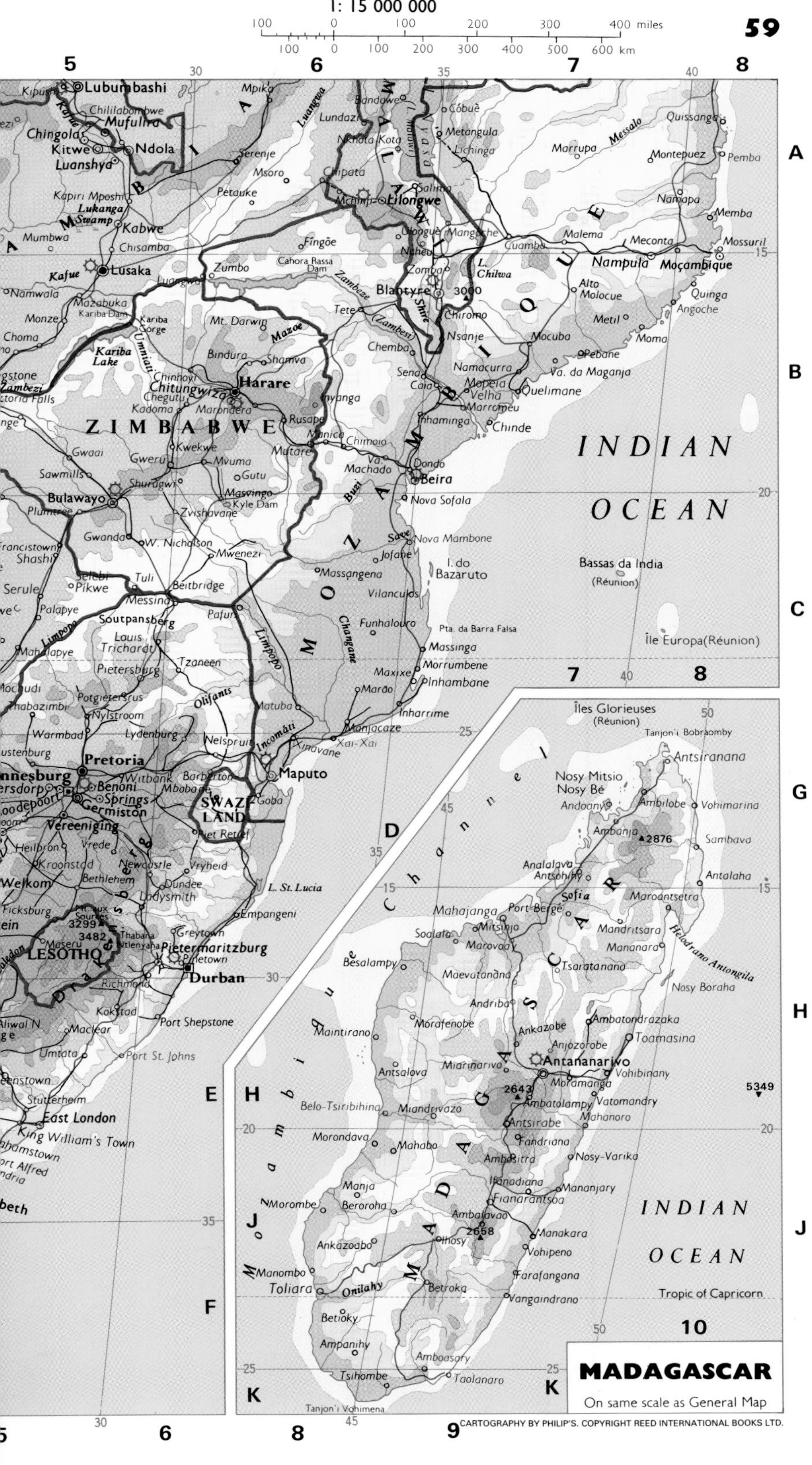

1: 15 000 000

100   0   100   200   300   400 miles

100 0 100 200 300 400 500 600 km

5   30   6   35   7   40   8

INDIAN

OCEAN

MADAGASCAR

On same scale as General Map

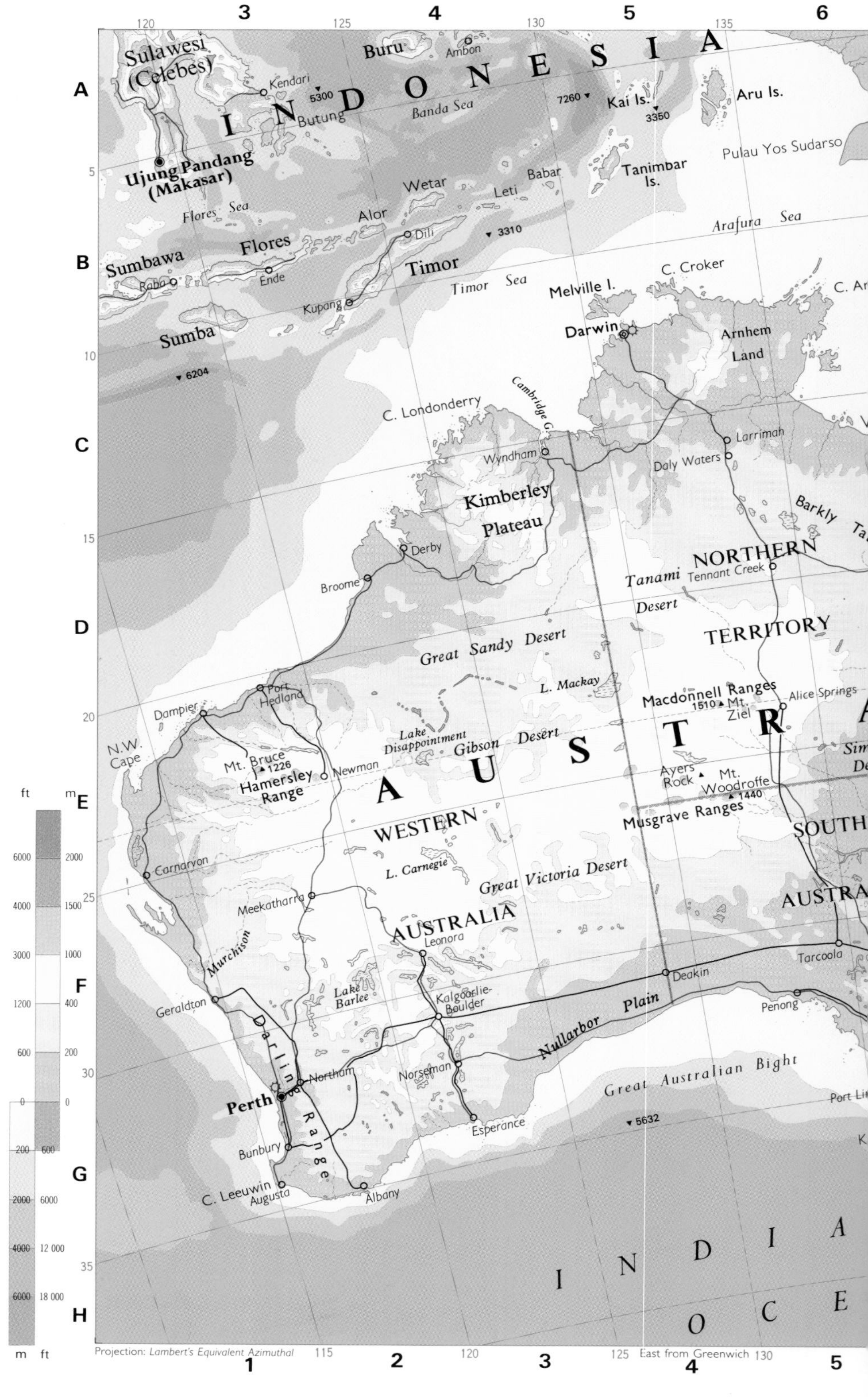

INDONESIA

Sulawesi (Celebes)

Buru

Ambon

Kendari

5300

Butung

Banda Sea

7260

Kai Is.

3350

Aru Is.

Pulau Yos Sudarso

Ujung Pandang (Makasar)

Wetar

Leti

Babar

Tanimbar Is.

Arafura Sea

Flores Sea

Alor

Dili

3310

Sumbawa

Flores

Timor

C. Croker

C. Ar

Raba

Ende

Timor Sea

Melville I.

C. Ar

Kupang

Darwin

Arnhem Land

Sumba

6204

C. Londonderry

Cambridge G.

Larrimah

Wyndham

Daly Waters

NORTHERN

Kimberley Plateau

Barkly Ta

Derby

Tanami

Tennant Creek

Broome

Desert

TERRITORY

Great Sandy Desert

L. Mackay

Macdonnell Ranges

Port Hedland

1510 Mt. Ziel

Alice Springs

Dampier

N.W. Cape

Mt. Bruce 1226

Newman

Lake Disappointment

Gibson Desert

AUSTRA

Simi De

Ayers Rock

Mt. Woodroffe 1440

Hamersley Range

WESTERN

Musgrave Ranges

SOUTH

Carnarvon

L. Carnegie

Great Victoria Desert

AUSTRA

Meekatharra

AUSTRALIA

Leonora

Tarcoola

Murchison

Lake Barlee

Deakin

Geraldton

Kalgoorlie-Boulder

Nullarbor Plain

Penong

Darling Range

Northam

Norseman

Great Australian Bight

Port Li

Perth

Bunbury

Esperance

5632

K.

C. Leeuwin

Albany

Augusta

INDIA

OCE

ft   m

6000   2000

4000   1500

3000   1000

1200   400

600   200

0   0

200   600

2000   6000

4000   12 000

6000   18 000

m   ft

1:20 000 000

100   0   100   200   300   400   500 miles
100   0   200   400   600   800 km

7   145   8   150   9   155   10   160   11

PAPUA NEW GUINEA

Mount Hagen   4508 ▲ Mt.
Wilhelm   ◉ Lae
Fly
Gulf of
Papua
Owen Stanley Range
Port ◉◉
Moresby

New Britain   ▼ Mt.
Balbi   9140

Solomon
Sea

D'Entrecasteaux Arch.

Louisiade
Archipelago

Bougainville   **SOLOMON**
Choiseul   **ISLANDS**

New
Georgia   Santa Isabel

Honiara ◉ ▲   Malaita
▲ 2331
Guadalcanal
San Cristobal

Rennell

B

10

C

C o r a l   S e a

Cape
York   ◉ Cape
York
Peninsula

Cooktown ◉

Mitchell
Cairns ◉
1611 ▲
Bartle Frere

Normanton ◉
Forsayth ◉

Coral

Sea

Islands

Territory

Chesterfield Is.

P A C I F I C

O C E A N

D

15

Townsville ◉
Charters Towers ◉
Hughenden ◉

t Isa

Winton ◉

QUEENSLAND
Longreach ◉

Yaraka ◉

Mackay ◉

Rockhampton ◉
Gladstone ◉

Bundaberg ◉

Maryborough ◉
Gympie ◉

Tropic of Capricorn

E

20

25

Charleville ◉   Roma ◉

Quilpie ◉
Cunnamulla ◉
Thargomindah ◉   Dirrabandi ◉

Grey Range

Creek

Walgett ◉

Bourke ◉

BRISBANE
Toowoomba ◉   ◉ Ipswich
Gold
Coast
Lismore ◉

1615 ▲
Round
Mt.

Lord Howe
(Austr.)
▼ 734

F

G

30

NEW SOUTH
Cobar ◉
Broken Hill ◉
Pirie ◉

WALES
Orange ◉

Dubbo ◉
Bathurst ◉

Tamworth ◉

Taree ◉

Newcastle
SYDNEY
Wollongong
Shellharbour ◉

35

Murray   Mildura ◉
Adelaide
Shepparton ◉
Horsham ◉
VICTORIA
Ballarat ◉   Bendigo ◉
Geelong
Gambier ◉   Warrnambool ◉

Wagga Wagga ◉
Murray   Mt.
Albury ◉   Kosciusko
2237 ▲   Australian Alps
Bombala ◉
C. Howe

Goulburn ◉
◉ Canberra
CAPITAL TERRITORY

T a s m a n   S e a

A u s t r a l i a n

H

40

King I.

Bass Strait
Furneaux Group

▼ 5267

J

Burnie ◉
Launceston ◉
1617 ▲
Mt. Ossa
TASMANIA
S.E. Cape

Hobart

140   7   150   8   145

9   10   11
CARTOGRAPHY BY PHILIP'S. COPYRIGHT REED INTERNATIONAL BOOKS LTD.

62 SOUTH-EAST AUSTRALIA

1 · 135 · **2** · 140

Tieyon · Abminga · L. Thomas · L. Cooninie · L. Yamma Yamma

Chandler · The Stevenson · Alton Downs · Arrabury · Cooper Cr.

Pedirka · The Hamilton · Peera Peera Poolanna L. · Andrewilla · Durham Downs

Marla · The Alberga · Oodnadatta · Clifton Hills · Goyder Lagoon · Coongie · Nappa Merrie · Nockatul

Welbourn Hill · The Macumba · Cowarie · L. Howitt · Innamincka · Naryilco · Bullo

Arckaringa Cr. · The Neales · L. Eyre (North) · Kittakittaooloo · Cooper Creek · L. Hope or Pando · Bulloo L.

A Cadney Park · Arckaringa · Peake Cr. · Warrina · Etadunna

Coober Pedy · Stuart Range · L. Cadibarrawirracanna Cr. · William Creek · L. Florence · L. Gregory · L. Hope

McDouall Peak · Coward Springs · Bopeechee · Marree · The Frome · Moolawatana · Milparinka

Mulgathing · Bulgunnia · Mt. Eba · Farina · Quinyambie · Cobham

SOUTH AUSTRALIA

Wynbring · L. Labyrinth · Lyndhurst · Benbonyathe Hill 1058 · The Frome

Malbooma · Tarcoola · Kingoonya · Leigh Creek South · Lake Frome · Kayrunnera

L. Younghusband · Beltana · Corona · Grassmere

Koonibba · L. Harris · L. Hanson · Woomera Pimba · Parachilna · Frome Downs · Benagerie · Little

Cedunca · L. Everard · Island Lagoon · Pernatty Lagoon · St. Mary Pk. 1165 · Hawker · Stephens Creek · Broken Hill

Denial B. · Puntabie · L. Acraman · Woocalla · Cradock · Cockburn · Menindee L.

B Nuyts Arch. · Wirrulla · Yardea P.O. · L. Macfarlane · Carrieton · Yunta · Mannahill · Cawndilla L.

Pt. Brown · Smoky Bay · Nukey Bluff 472 · Hawker · Oakbank · Tandou L.

C. Bauer · Streaky B. · Poochera · L. Gilles · Port Augusta · Wilmington · Paratoo · Quondong · L. Popita · Gum Willabc

Pt. Westall · Streaky Bay · Buckleboo · Iron Knob · Orroroo · Nackara · Traveller's L.

C. Blanche · Minnipa · Mt. Remarkable · Peterborough · Pooncc

C. Radstock · Port Kenny · Kimba · Iron Baron · 969 · Terowie · Burtundy

Anxious Bay · Kopi · Kyancutta · Whyalla · Jamestown · Braemar · Darling And Branch

C. Finniss · Elliston · Lock · Darke Peak · Port Pirie · Hallett · Victoria · Victoria

Flinders I. · Rudall · Cowell · Crystal Brook · Mt. Bryan 934 · Wentworth · Mildura

Investigator Group · Cummins · Arno Bay · Gladstone · Brinkworth · Farrell Flat · Berri · Merbein

Mt. Hope · Yeelanna · Wallaroo · Spalding · Clare · Robertstown · Renmark · Yamba · Wymple

Drummond Pt. · Tumby Bay · Moonta · Bowman · Burra · Kadina · Morgan · Murray · Loxton · Red Cliffs

Coffin B. · Wangary · Spencer · Maitland · Riverton · Kapunda · Barmera · Meringur · Werrimull · Euston

Coffin Bay Pen. · Port Lincoln · Gulf · Yorke Pen. · Ardrossan · Gawler · Angaston · Sedan · Wanbi · Hattah · Robii

C. Donington · Corny Pt. · Salisbury · Elizabeth · Mannum · Alawoona · Annuello · Ouyen · Kulwin

Sleaford B. · West Pt. · Edithburgh · ADELAIDE · Glenelg · Murray Bridge · Underbool · Tyrrell

Thistle I. · Str. G. St. Vincent · Brighton · Strathalbyn · Karoonda · Feebinga · Cowangie · Patchewollock · Swan

C. Carnot · Kingscote · Cape Willunga · Milang · Lameroo · Pinnaroo · Hopetoun

C. Borda · Investigator Str. · Jervis · Meningie · L. Albacutya · Birchi

C Kangaroo I. · Victor Harbor · Encounter Bay · L. Alexandrina · Salt Creek · Tintinara · Keith · L. Hindmarsh · Yaapel · Jeparit · Wychep

C. du Couedic · D'Estree B. · Younghusband Peninsula · Bordertown · Nhill · Warracknabeal · Donald

Kingston South East · Wolseley · Kaniva · Dimboola · Horsham · St. Arnaud

Lacepede Bay · Frances · Moree · Natimuk · Naracoorte · Edenhope · Maryborc

C. Jaffa · L. George · Balmoral · Casterton · Cavendish · Stawell

Beachport · Rivoli B. · Penola · Coleraine · Hamilton · Ararat · Ball

Millicent · Mount Gambier · Branxholme · Penshurst · Skipton · Alvic

C. Northumberland · Discovery Bay · McDonnell · Heywood · Keroit · Camperdown · Forre

C. Bridgewater · Portland · Port Fairy · Timboon

Warrnambool · C. Wick

King Islar · Curr

2 · 140 · **3** East from Greenwich

Scale (inset, left)
ft	m
4500	1500
3000	1000
1200	400
600	200
0	0
	200
2000	6000
4000	12 000

m · ft

Projection: Bonne

Tasmania inset
1 · King Island · **2**

Stokes Pt. · Palana · Flinders Island

C. Keraudren · Three Hummock I. · Prime Seal I. · Whitemark · Furneaux Group

Hunter I. · Robbins I. · Stanley · Cape Barren I.

Marrawah · Smithton · Wynyard · Burnie · Penguin · Ulverstone · Devonport · George Town · Banks Strait

Temma · Arthur · Somerset · Latrobe · Bridport · Herrick · Eddystone Pt.

Sandy C. · Waratah · Corinna · Railton · Mole Creek · Deloraine · Cottslove · St. Helens

Rosebery · Mt. Ossa 1617 · Westbury · Longford · Evandale · Launceston · St. Marys

D Zeehan · Strahan · Bronte Pk. · Ross · Ben Lomond · Conara Junc. · Freycinet Pen.

Queenstown · Wayatinah · Bothwell · Campbell Town · Cranbrook · Schouten I.

TASMANIA · Macquarie Harb. · Maydena · Ouse · Colebrook · Parattah · Oatlands · Triabunna · Maria I.

Hibbs Bay · New Norfolk · Glenorchy · Forestier Pen.

Port Davey · L. Pedder · Huonville · Hobart · Tasman Pen. · Port Arthur

Bathurst Harb. · Cygnet · Dover · Storm Bay · Bruny I.

S.W. Cape · S.E. Cape

3 · 145 · **4**

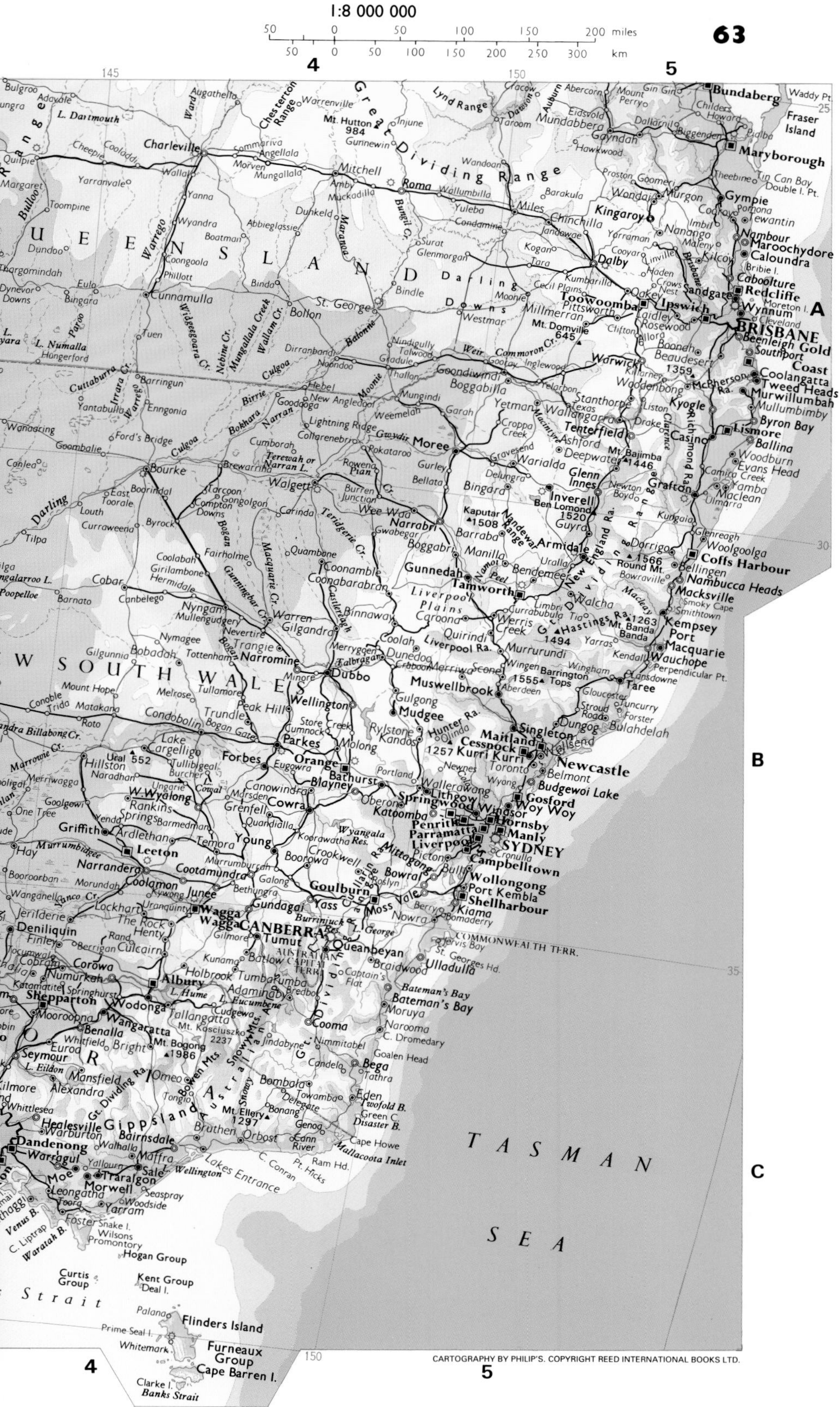

1:8 000 000

50   0   50   100   150   200 miles
50 0 50 100 150 200 250 300 km

4   **5**

A

B

C

TASMAN

SEA

QUEENSLAND

NEW SOUTH WALES

Great Dividing Range

Darling Downs

Liverpool Plains

Bundaberg
Fraser Island
Maryborough
Gympie
Nambour
Maroochydore
Caloundra
Caboolture
Redcliffe
BRISBANE
Ipswich
Southport
Coolangatta
Gold Coast
Tweed Heads
Murwillumbah
Mullumbimby
Byron Bay
Lismore
Ballina
Casino
Kyogle
Grafton
Coffs Harbour
Bellingen
Nambucca Heads
Macksville
Kempsey
Port Macquarie
Taree
Newcastle
Maitland
Gosford
SYDNEY
Wollongong
Port Kembla
Shellharbour
Kiama
Nowra

Charleville
Roma
Dalby
Toowoomba
Warwick
Stanthorpe
Tenterfield
Deepwater
Glen Innes
Inverell
Armidale
Tamworth
Gunnedah
Narrabri
Moree
Walgett
Bourke
Cunnamulla
St. George
Goondiwindi
Dubbo
Wellington
Mudgee
Muswellbrook
Singleton
Cessnock
Kurri Kurri
Orange
Bathurst
Parkes
Forbes
Canberra
Queanbeyan
Cooma
Albury
Wagga Wagga
Wodonga

COMMONWEALTH TERR.

Flinders Island
Furneaux Group
Cape Barren I.

4   **5**

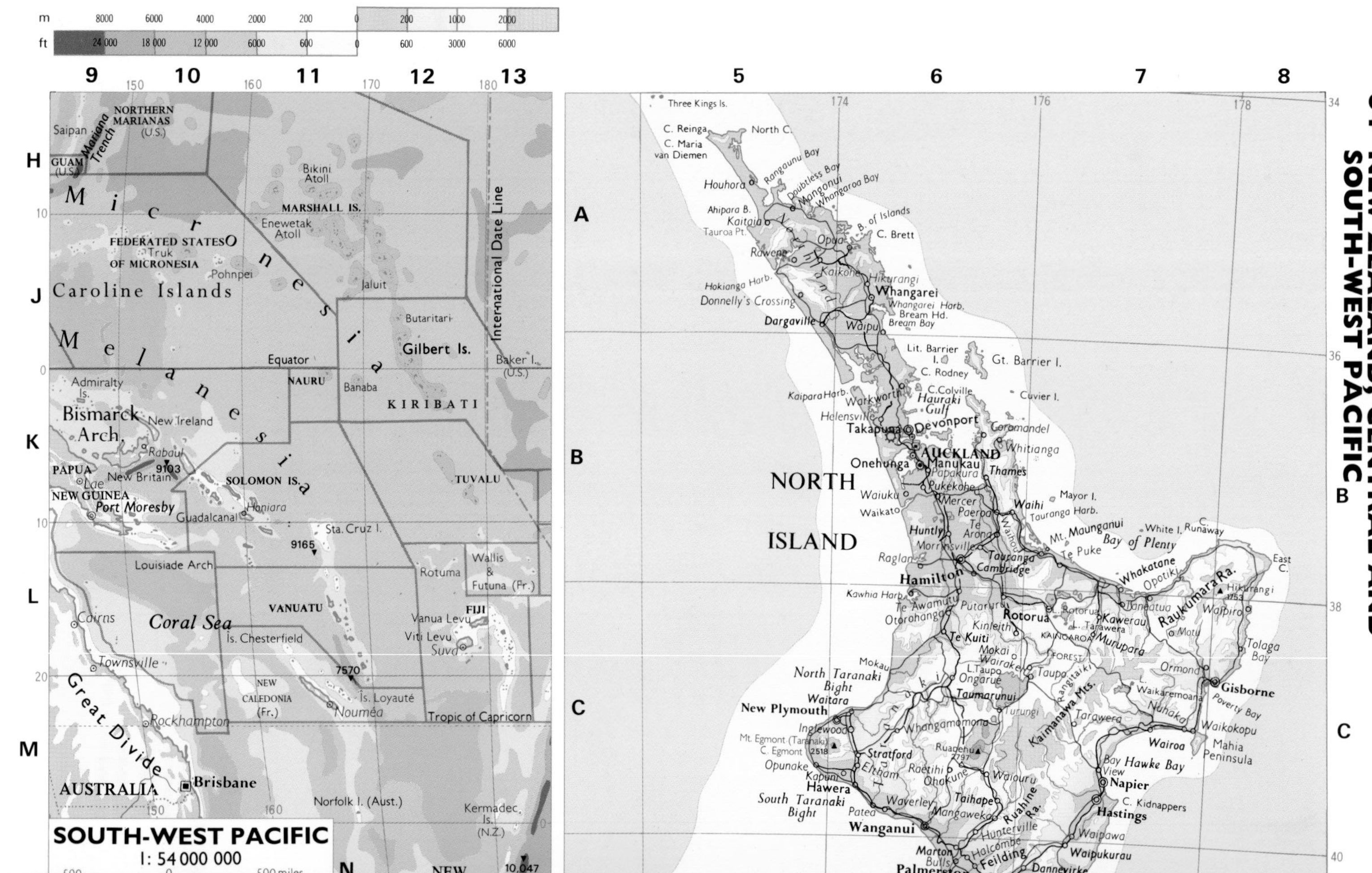

SOUTH-WEST PACIFIC
1: 54 000 000
NORTH ISLAND
Three Kings Is.
C. Reinga
North C.
Houhora
Kaitaia
Whangarei
Dargaville
Hauraki Gulf
Gt. Barrier I.
Coromandel
Thames
AUCKLAND
Devonport
Takapuna
Onehunga
Manukau
Hamilton
Cambridge
Tauranga
Rotorua
Whakatane
Bay of Plenty
Raukumara Ra.
East C.
Gisborne
Poverty Bay
Mahia Peninsula
Hawke Bay
Napier
Hastings
C. Kidnappers
Te Kuiti
Taumarunui
L. Taupo
North Taranaki Bight
New Plymouth
Mt. Egmont (Taranaki) 2518
Stratford
Hawera
South Taranaki Bight
Wanganui
Palmerston
Feilding
Dannevirke
Kaimanawa Mts.
Ruahine Ra.
Micronesia
Melanesia
NORTHERN MARIANAS (U.S.)
Mariana Trench
GUAM (U.S.)
FEDERATED STATES OF MICRONESIA
Caroline Islands
MARSHALL IS.
Bikini Atoll
Enewetak Atoll
Gilbert Is.
KIRIBATI
NAURU
Equator
TUVALU
Bismarck Arch.
New Ireland
New Britain
PAPUA NEW GUINEA
Port Moresby
SOLOMON IS.
Guadalcanal
Honiara
VANUATU
Coral Sea
NEW CALEDONIA (Fr.)
Nouméa
FIJI
Vanua Levu
Viti Levu
Suva
Wallis & Futuna (Fr.)
Tropic of Capricorn
International Date Line
Norfolk I. (Aust.)
Kermadec Is. (N.Z.)
AUSTRALIA
Great Divide
Brisbane
Rockhampton
Townsville
Cairns

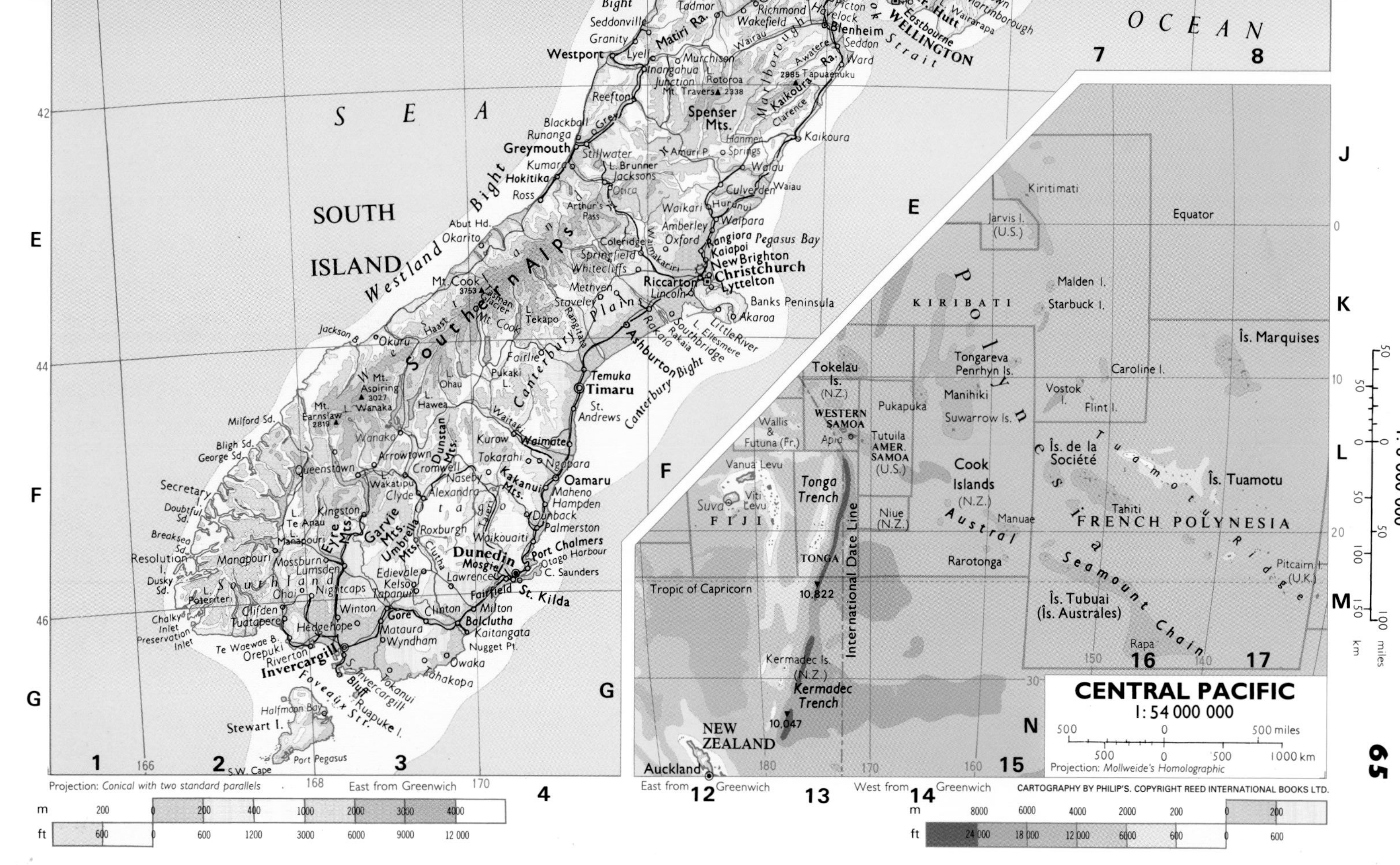

1: 6 000 000

50   0   50   100   miles
50   0   50   100   km

CENTRAL PACIFIC
1: 54 000 000

500   0   500   1000 km
500   0   500   miles

Projection: Mollweide's Homolographic

CARTOGRAPHY BY PHILIP'S. COPYRIGHT REED INTERNATIONAL BOOKS LTD.

ft   24 000   18 000   12 000   6000   2000   600   200   600
m   8000   6000   4000   2000   1000   200   200   600

West from Greenwich

FRENCH POLYNESIA

Is. Marquises

Equator

Caroline I.

Malden I.
Starbuck I.

Vostok I.
Flint I.

Jarvis I.
(U.S.)

Kiritimati

K I R I B A T I

P o l y n e s i a

Tongareva Penrhyn Is.
Manihiki
Suwarrow Is.

Pukapuka
Tokelau Is.
(N.Z.)

WESTERN SAMOA
Apia

Tutuila AMER. SAMOA
(U.S.)

Niue (N.Z.)

Wallis
Futuna (Fr.)

Is. de la Société
Tahiti

Is. Tuamotu

Pitcairn I.
(U.K.)

Rapa

Is. Tubuai
(Is. Australes)

Austral Ridge

Seamount Chain

Cook Islands
(N.Z.)

Rarotonga

Manuae

International Date Line

Tonga Trench

10,822

Kermadec Trench

10,047

Kermadec Is.
(N.Z.)

Vanua Levu
Viti Levu
Suva Lau Gp.

F I J I

Tropic of Capricorn

NEW ZEALAND

Auckland

East from Greenwich

O C E A N

S E A

SOUTH ISLAND

West Land

Southern Alps

Canterbury Plain

WELLINGTON
Hutt
Eastbourne
Petone

Cook Strait

Blenheim
Picton
Havelock
Nelson
Richmond
Wakefield

Marlborough
Ward
Seddon

Kaikoura

Spenser Mts.

Reefton
Greymouth
Hokitika
Ross

Westport
Granity
Seddonville
Lyell

Buller
Blackball
Runanga

Mt. Cook 3763
Mt. Tasman

Christchurch
New Brighton
Lyttelton
Riccarton
Akaroa
Banks Peninsula

Rangiora
Kaiapoi
Amberley
Oxford
Darfield
Rakaia
Ashburton

Timaru
Temuka
St. Andrews

Oamaru
Moeraki
Hampden
Palmerston
Port Chalmers
Dunedin
Mosgiel

Waimate
Kurow
Duntroon

L. Tekapo
L. Pukaki
L. Ohau

Mt. Aspiring 3027
L. Hawea
L. Wanaka
Wanaka

Queenstown
L. Wakatipu
Arrowtown
Kingston

Te Anau
L. Te Anau
L. Manapouri

Invercargill
Bluff
Riverton
Orepuki

Gore
Mataura
Edendale
Wyndham

Balclutha
Milton
Kaitangata
Owaka
Nugget Pt.

Lawrence
Roxburgh
Clyde
Alexandra
Cromwell

Milford Sd.
George Sd.
Bligh Sd.
Doubtful Sd.
Dusky Sd.
Breaksea Sd.
Chalky Inlet
Preservation Inlet

Stewart I.
S.W. Cape
Foveaux Str.

Projection: Conical with two standard parallels

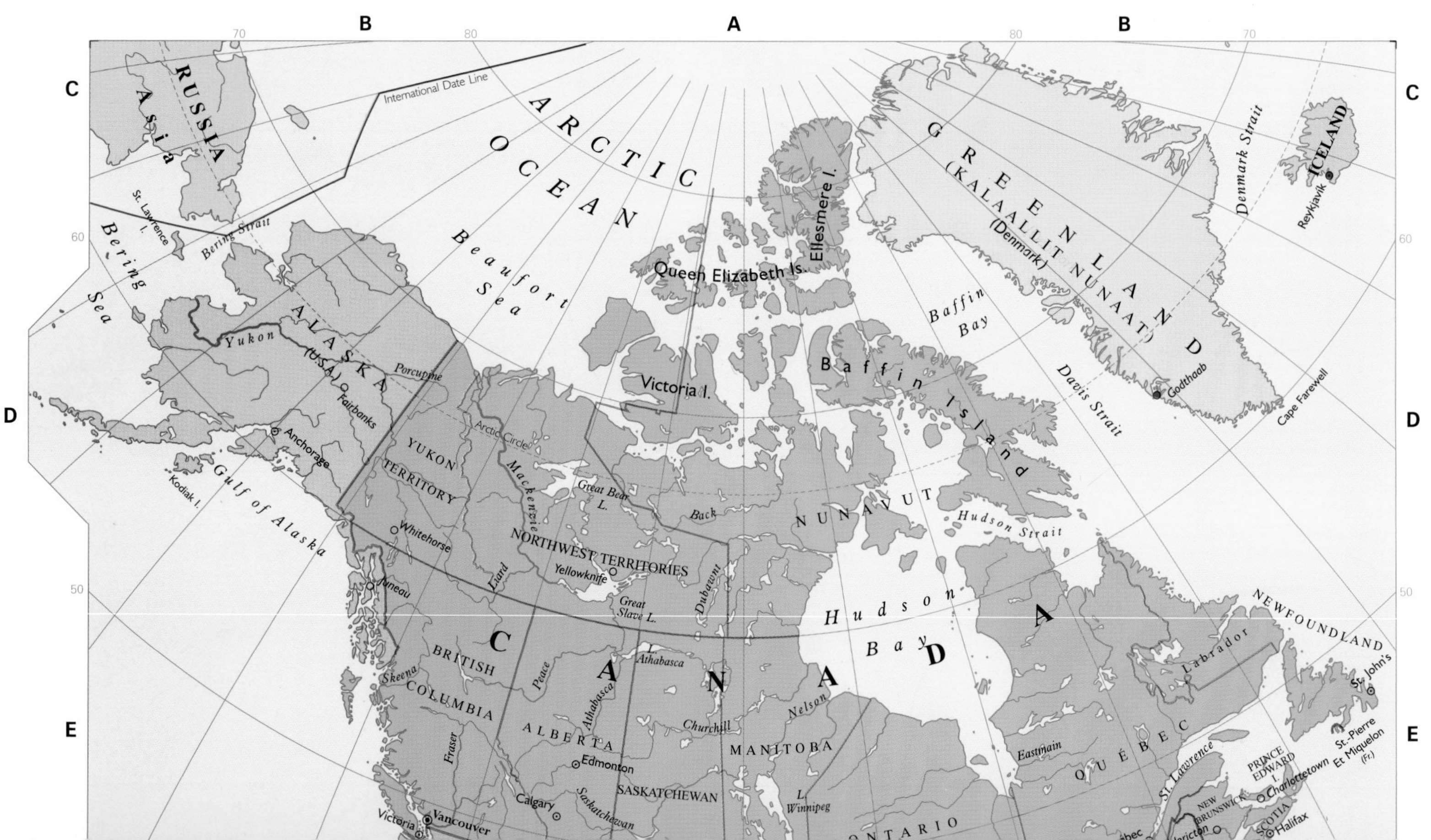
ARCTIC
OCEAN
RUSSIA
Asia
International Date Line
St. Lawrence I.
Bering Strait
Bering Sea
Beaufort Sea
Queen Elizabeth Is.
Ellesmere I.
GREENLAND
(KALAALLIT NUNAAT)
(Denmark)
Denmark Strait
ICELAND
Reykjavik
Baffin Bay
Davis Strait
Godthaab
Cape Farewell
Baffin Island
Victoria I.
ALASKA
(U.S.A.)
Yukon
Porcupine
Fairbanks
Anchorage
Kodiak I.
Gulf of Alaska
Arctic Circle
YUKON
TERRITORY
Whitehorse
Juneau
Mackenzie
Great Bear L.
Back
NUNAVUT
Hudson Strait
NORTHWEST TERRITORIES
Yellowknife
Liard
Great Slave L.
Dubawnt
Hudson Bay
CANADA
NEWFOUNDLAND
Labrador
St. John's
BRITISH
COLUMBIA
Skeena
Fraser
Peace
L. Athabasca
Athabasca
ALBERTA
Edmonton
Calgary
Churchill
Nelson
MANITOBA
SASKATCHEWAN
Saskatchewan
L. Winnipeg
Eastmain
QUÉBEC
St. Lawrence
NEW BRUNSWICK
PRINCE EDWARD I.
Charlottetown
NOVA SCOTIA
Halifax
St.-Pierre Et Miquelon (Fr.)
ONTARIO
Vancouver
Victoria
A
B
C
D
E
50
60
70
80

1: 35 000 000
0 200 400 600 800 miles
0 400 800 1200 km
UNITED STATES
MEXICO
PACIFIC OCEAN
NORTH ATLANTIC OCEAN
Gulf of Mexico
Caribbean Sea
South America
Tropic of Cancer
WYOMING
SOUTH DAKOTA
NEBRASKA
IOWA
WISCONSIN
MICHIGAN
ILLINOIS
INDIANA
OHIO
NEW YORK
PA.
N.J.
DE.
MD.
W.V.
VIRGINIA
KENTUCKY
NORTH CAROLINA
SOUTH CAROLINA
TENNESSEE
GEORGIA
ALABAMA
MISSISSIPPI
LOUISIANA
ARKANSAS
MISSOURI
KANSAS
OKLAHOMA
TEXAS
COLORADO
NEW MEXICO
ARIZONA
UTAH
NEVADA
CALIFORNIA
FLORIDA
Boise
Snake
Salt Lake City
Cheyenne
Denver
Lincoln
Kansas City
Topeka
Santa Fe
Albuquerque
Oklahoma City
Little Rock
Dallas
El Paso
Austin
Houston
Baton Rouge
New Orleans
Mississippi
Rio Grande
Colorado
Madison
Milwaukee
CHICAGO
L. Michigan
Lansing
Toledo
Detroit
Cleveland
Pittsburgh
Hartford
NEW YORK
PHILADELPHIA
Baltimore
Washington D.C.
Richmond
Raleigh
Charlotte
Columbia
Charleston
Atlanta
Columbus
Indianapolis
Cincinnati
Springfield
St. Louis
Nashville
Memphis
Birmingham
Montgomery
Jackson
Tallahassee
Jacksonville
Tampa
Miami
Sacramento
SAN FRANCISCO
San Jose
Carson City
Las Vegas
LOS ANGELES
San Diego
Phoenix
Tucson
Guadalupe (Mex.)
Hermosillo
Culiacan
Monterrey
Guadalajara
MÉXICO
Puebla
Acapulco
Revilla Gigedo Is. (Mex.)
Mérida
Belmopan
BELIZE
GUATEMALA
Guatemala
HONDURAS
Tegucigalpa
San Salvador
EL SALVADOR
NICARAGUA
L. Nicaragua
Managua
COSTA RICA
San José
PANAMA
Panamá
COLOMBIA
Medellín
Barranquilla
Maracaibo
VENEZUELA
Bermuda (U.K.)
Florida Str.
Nassau
BAHAMAS
Turks & Caicos Is. (U.K.)
Havana
CUBA
Cayman Is. (U.K.)
JAMAICA
Kingston
HAITI
Port-au-Prince
DOMINICAN REP.
Santo Domingo
PUERTO RICO (U.S.A.)
San Juan
30
20
10
120
110
100
90
80
70
West from Greenwich
F
G
H
J
7
8
9
10
11
12
Projection: Bonne
MÉXICO Capital Cities

1
2
3
4
5
6
7
A
B
C
GREENLAND
(KALAALLIT NUNAAT)
(Den.)
Angmagssalik
Kong Frederik VI's Kyst
2850
Christianshåb
Disko B.
Disko
Svartenhuk Halvø
Søndre Strømfjord
Holsteinsborg
Sukkertoppen
Godthåb (Nuuk)
Fiskenæsset
Frederikshåb
Ivigtut
Julianehåb
Sydprøven
Nanortalik
Kap Farvel
2136
Baffin Bay
Davis Strait
ATLANTIC OCEAN
3809
Prince of Wales Island
Somerset Island
Franklin Str.
Devon Island
Lancaster Sound
Brodeur Peninsula
Arctic Bay
Bylot I.
1890
Pond Inlet
Milne Inlet
Scott I.
Clyde
C. Hewett
Baffin Island
Gulf of Boothia
Boothia Peninsula
573
Spence Bay
King William I.
Gjoa Haven
Adelaide Pen.
Chantrey Inlet
Pelly Bay
Committee B.
Fury & Hecla Str.
Igloolik Island
Sanirajak
Melville Peninsula
Home B.
2591
Broughton Island
Padloping Island
C. Dyer
Cape Dyer
Cumberland Peninsula
Pangnirtung
Hoare B.
C. Mercy
Cumberland Sd.
Prince Charles I.
Foxe Basin
NUNAVUT
Nettilling L.
Rae Isthmus
Repulse Bay
Arctic Circle
Foxe Channel
C. Dorchester
Wager Bay
Wager B.
Roes Welcome Sd.
Foxe Penin.
Amadjuak L.
Amadjuak
Cape Dorset
Iqaluit
Frobisher Bay
Lake Harbour
Resolution I.
Baker L.
Baker Lake
Chesterfield Inlet
Southampton I.
Sallia
Bell Pen.
Hudson Strait
Digges Is.
Salluit
Ivujivik
C. Chidley
Quaqtaq
Akpatok I.
Igluligaarjuk
Rankin Inlet
Whale Cove
Coats I.
Mansel I.
Kangiqsujuaq
Ungava Peninsula
Arnaud
Kangirsuk
Ungava Bay
1676
Kangiqsualujjuaq
Hebron
Nutak
Arviat
Hudson
Ottawa Is.
257
Portland Promontory
Feuilles
Koksoak
Kuujjuaq
George
Nain
C. Harrison

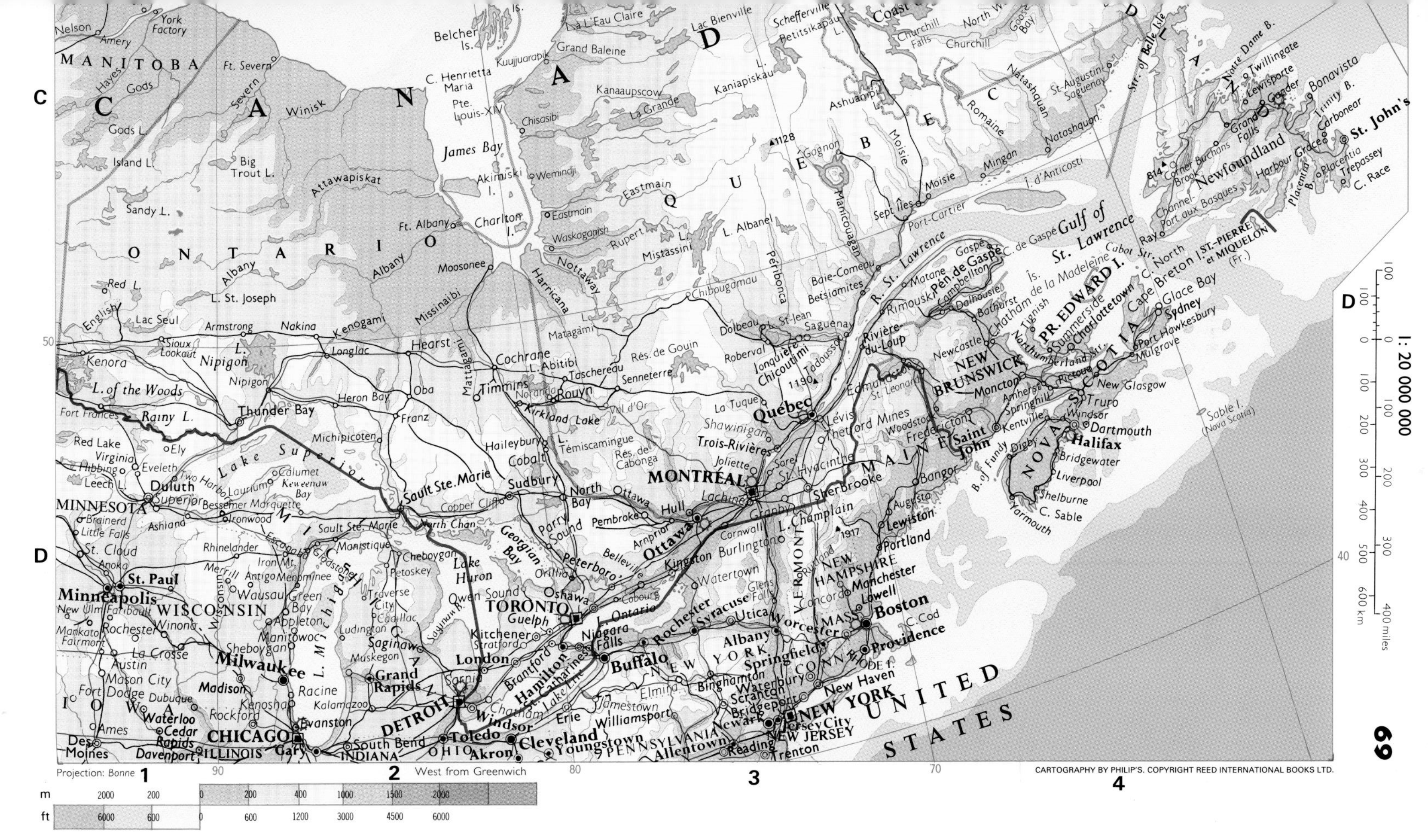

1: 20 000 000
100 0 100 200 300 400 miles
100 0 100 200 300 400 500 600 km
C A N A D A
O N T A R I O
Q U É B E C
MANITOBA
NEW BRUNSWICK
NOVA SCOTIA
PR. EDWARD I.
Newfoundland
ST.-PIERRE et MIQUELON (Fr.)
U N I T E D S T A T E S
MINNESOTA
WISCONSIN
I O W A
ILLINOIS
INDIANA
OHIO
PENNSYLVANIA
NEW YORK
NEW JERSEY
VERMONT
NEW HAMPSHIRE
MAINE
MASS.
CONN.
RHODE I.
James Bay
Lake Superior
Lake Huron
Georgian Bay
L. Michigan
L. Ontario
Lake Erie
Gulf of St. Lawrence
R. St. Lawrence
Str. of Belle Isle
Cabot Str.
B. of Fundy
Northumberland Str.
Nelson
York Factory
Ft. Severn
Winisk
Attawapiskat
Moosonee
Ft. Albany
Thunder Bay
Kenora
L. of the Woods
Rainy L.
Sault Ste. Marie
Sudbury
North Bay
Timmins
Cochrane
Kirkland Lake
TORONTO
Hamilton
London
Kitchener
Ottawa
Kingston
MONTRÉAL
Québec
Trois-Rivières
Sherbrooke
Chicoutimi
Sept Îles
Baie-Comeau
Gaspé
Moncton
Fredericton
Saint John
Halifax
Dartmouth
Sydney
Charlottetown
St. John's
C. Race
Sable I. (Nova Scotia)
Minneapolis
St. Paul
Duluth
Milwaukee
Madison
CHICAGO
DETROIT
Toledo
Cleveland
Buffalo
Rochester
Syracuse
Albany
Boston
Providence
NEW YORK
Portland
Bangor
Projection: Bonne
West from Greenwich
m 2000 200 0 200 400 1000 1500 2000
ft 6000 600 0 600 1200 3000 4500 6000

A
B
C
4
5
6
7
8
9
10
Hudson Bay
Somerset Island
Boothia Peninsula
Prince of Wales Island
Franklin Str.
M'Clintock Channel
Viscount Melville Sound
Victoria Island
Banks Island
Prince Albert Pen.
Amundsen Gulf
Coronation Gulf
Wollaston Pen.
Queen Maud Gulf
King William I.
Chantrey Inlet
Chesterfield Inlet
Baker Lake
Rankin Inlet
Whale Cove
Arviat
N U N A V U T
Arctic Circle
Kent Pen.
Bathurst Inlet
Dolphin & Union Str.
Coppermine
Kugluktuk
Great Bear Lake
Great Slave L.
Yellowknife
Lake Athabasca
N O R T H W E S T T E R R I T O R I E S
YUKON TERRITORY
Mackenzie Mountains
Franklin Mts.
Ft. Good Hope
Norman Wells
Ft. Norman
Inuvik
Tuktoyaktuk
Aklavik
Old Crow
Ft. McPherson
Fort Providence
Hay River
Fort Resolution
Ft. Smith
Ft. Simpson
Ft. Liard
Ft. Nelson
Dawson
Klondike
Whitehorse
Watson Lake
Cassiar Mountains
Rocky Mountains
Churchill Pk. 3200
Coast Mts.
St. Elias Mts.
Mt. Logan 5959
Mt. Fairweather 4663
Wrangell Mts.
Mt. Sanford 4940
A L A S K A
Fairbanks
Anchorage
Mt Gerdine 3840
Valdez
Seward
Cordova
Yakutat
Juneau
Skagway
Sitka
Ketchikan
Pr. Rupert
Queen Charlotte Is.
Dixon Entrance
Hecate Str.
Caribou Mts. 1036
P A C I F I C O C E
3959

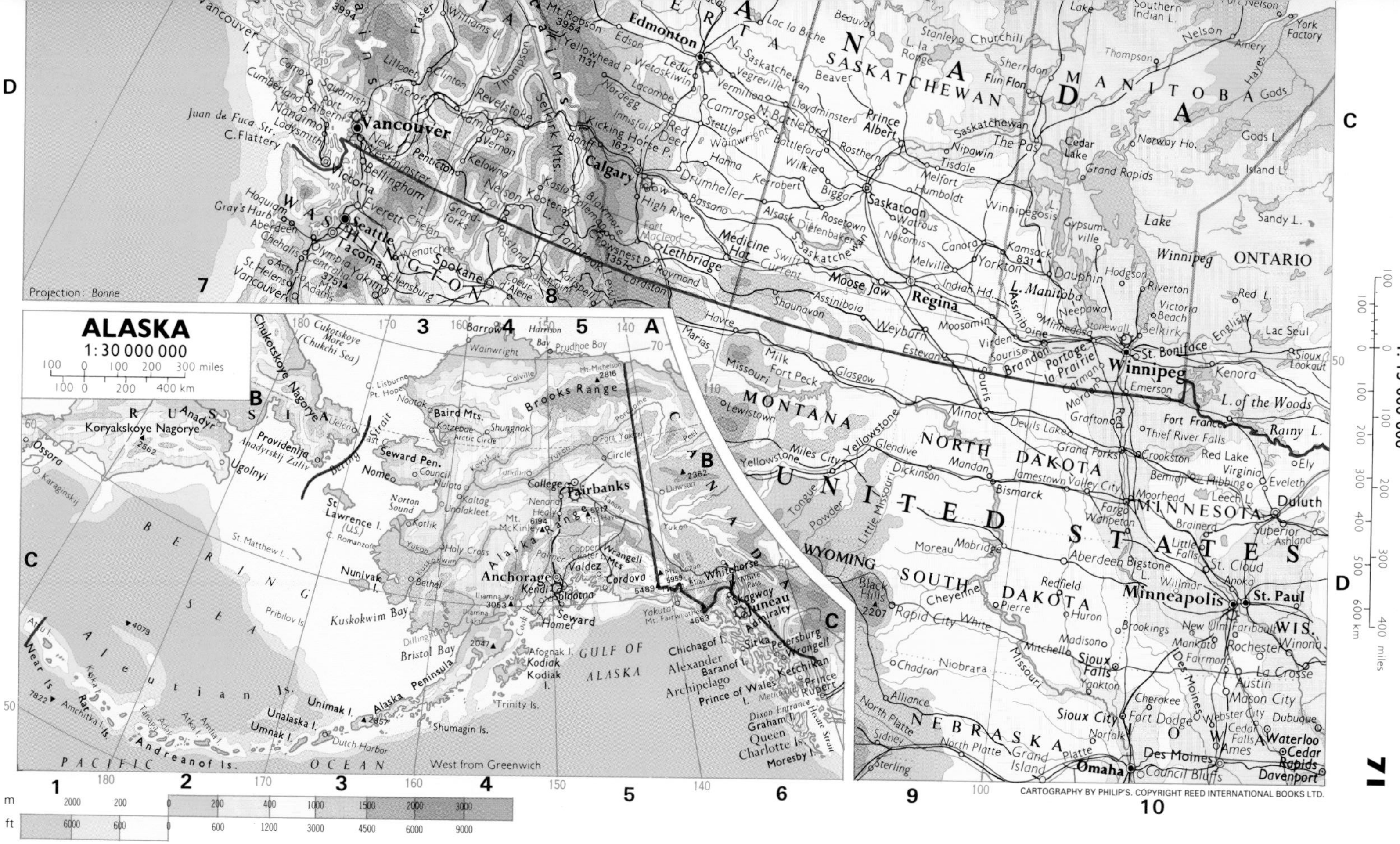

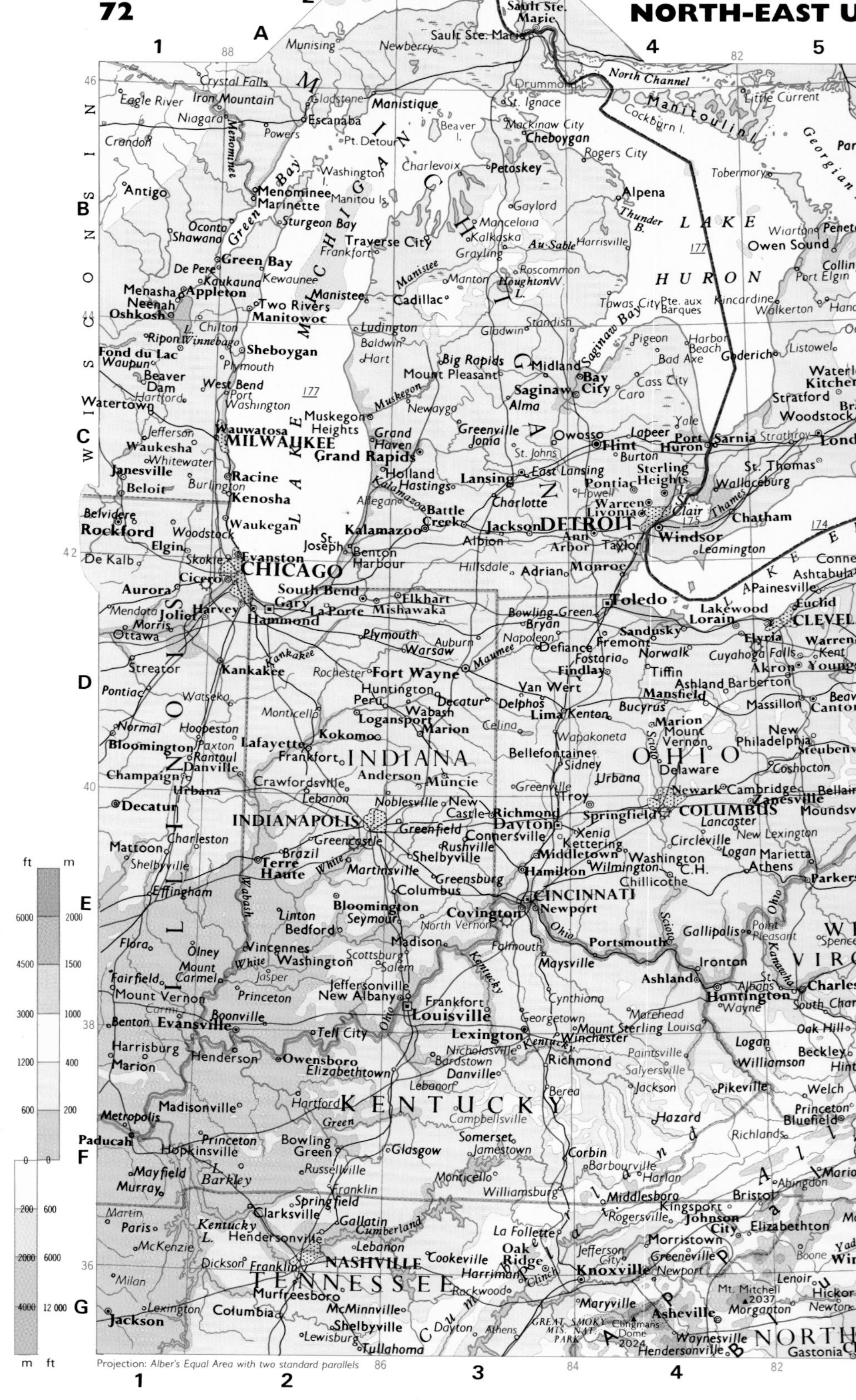

A
B
C
D
E
F
G
1
2
3
4
5
88
86
84
82
46
44
42
40
38
36
Whitefish Pt.
Sault Ste. Marie
Sault Ste. Marie
Munising
Newberry
North Channel
Manitoulin I.
Cockburn I.
Drummond I.
St. Ignace
Little Current
Georgian Bay
Parry
Crystal Falls
Eagle River
Iron Mountain
Gladstone
Manistique
Mackinaw City
Cheboygan
Niagara
Escanaba
Beaver I.
Crandon
Powers
Pt. Detour
Rogers City
Menominee
Tobermory
Washington I.
Charlevoix
Petoskey
Antigo
Menominee
Marinette
Manitou Is.
Alpena
Green Bay
Gaylord
Thunder B.
Oconto
Sturgeon Bay
Mancelona
LAKE HURON
Wiarton
Penetang
Shawano
Traverse City
Kalkaska
Au Sable
Harrisville
Owen Sound
Frankfort
Grayling
177
Collingwood
Green Bay
De Pere
Kewaunee
Manistee
Manton
Roscommon
Houghton L.
Port Elgin
Kaukauna
Menasha
Appleton
Neenah
Oshkosh
Two Rivers
Manitowoc
Manistee
Cadillac
Tawas City
Pte. aux Barques
Kincardine
Walkerton
Hanover
Chilton
L. Winnebago
Ludington
Gladwin
Standish
Saginaw Bay
Ripon
Sheboygan
Baldwin
Pigeon
Harbor Beach
Listowel
Fond du Lac
Waupun
Plymouth
Hart
Big Rapids
Midland
Bad Axe
Goderich
Waterloo
Kitchener
Beaver Dam
Mount Pleasant
Bay City
Cass City
West Bend
Port Washington
177
Muskegon
Newaygo
Saginaw
Caro
Stratford
Hartford
Watertown
Alma
Woodstock
Muskegon Heights
Yale
Jefferson
Wauwatosa
MILWAUKEE
Grand Haven
Greenville
Ionia
Owosso
Lapeer
Flint
Port Huron
Sarnia
London
Waukesha
Grand Rapids
St. Johns
Burton
Whitewater
St. Thomas
Janesville
Racine
Holland
Lansing
East Lansing
Sterling Heights
Beloit
Burlington
Hastings
Pontiac
Wallaceburg
Kenosha
Allegan
Charlotte
Howell
Belvidere
Battle Creek
Warren
Livonia
L. St. Clair
Thames
Chatham
Rockford
Woodstock
Waukegan
Kalamazoo
Jackson
DETROIT
175
174
Elgin
St. Joseph
Benton Harbour
Albion
Ann Arbor
Taylor
Windsor
De Kalb
Skokie
Evanston
Leamington
LAKE ERIE
Conneaut
CHICAGO
Hillsdale
Adrian
Monroe
Ashtabula
Aurora
Cicero
South Bend
Painesville
Elkhart
Toledo
Mendota
Joliet
Harvey
Gary
La Porte
Mishawaka
Bowling Green
Lakewood
Euclid
Morris
Hammond
Bryan
Lorain
CLEVELAND
Ottawa
Plymouth
Auburn
Napoleon
Sandusky
Elyria
Warren
Warsaw
Defiance
Fremont
Cuyahoga Falls
Kent
Kankakee
Maumee
Fostoria
Norwalk
Akron
Youngstown
Streator
Kankakee
Rochester
Fort Wayne
Findlay
Tiffin
Ashland
Barberton
Pontiac
Watseka
Huntington
Van Wert
Mansfield
Beaver
Peru
Decatur
Delphos
Massillon
Canton
Monticello
Wabash
Lima
Kenton
Bucyrus
Logansport
Marion
Celina
Marion
Normal
Hoopeston
Kokomo
Wapakoneta
Mount Vernon
New Philadelphia
Bloomington
Paxton
Lafayette
Scioto
Steubenville
Rantoul
Frankfort
INDIANA
Bellefontaine
OHIO
Danville
Sidney
Delaware
Coshocton
Champaign
Crawfordsville
Anderson
Urbana
Urbana
Muncie
Greenville
Newark
Cambridge
Bellaire
Decatur
Lebanon
Noblesville
New Castle
Troy
Zanesville
Richmond
Springfield
COLUMBUS
Moundsville
INDIANAPOLIS
Dayton
Lancaster
Charleston
Greenfield
Connersville
Xenia
Circleville
New Lexington
Greencastle
Rushville
Kettering
Logan
Marietta
Mattoon
Brazil
Shelbyville
Middletown
Washington C.H.
Shelbyville
Terre Haute
White
Martinsville
Greensburg
Hamilton
Wilmington
Athens
Parkersburg
Chillicothe
Effingham
Columbus
CINCINNATI
Wabash
Bloomington
Newport
Linton
Seymour
Covington
Bedford
North Vernon
Ohio
Gallipolis
Point Pleasant
WEST VIRGINIA
Flora
Madison
Falmouth
Portsmouth
Spencer
Olney
Vincennes
Scottsburg
Kentucky
Maysville
White
Washington
Salem
Ironton
Mount Carmel
Jasper
Ashland
Fairfield
Jeffersonville
Cynthiana
Kanawha
Charleston
Mount Vernon
Princeton
New Albany
Frankfort
Huntington
St. Albans
Carmi
Louisville
Georgetown
Wayne
South Charleston
Boonville
Morehead
Benton
Evansville
Tell City
Lexington
Mount Sterling
Louisa
Oak Hill
Harrisburg
Winchester
Logan
Beckley
Henderson
Owensboro
Nicholasville
Kentucky
Paintsville
Marion
Bardstown
Richmond
Williamson
Hinton
Elizabethtown
Danville
Salyersville
Lebanon
Berea
Jackson
Pikeville
Welch
Madisonville
Hartford
KENTUCKY
Campbellsville
Princeton
Metropolis
Hazard
Bluefield
Green
Paducah
Princeton
Bowling Green
Somerset
Richlands
Hopkinsville
Glasgow
Jamestown
Corbin
Mayfield
L. Barkley
Russellville
Barbourville
Marion
Murray
Monticello
Harlan
Abingdon
Franklin
Williamsburg
Middlesboro
Bristol
Springfield
Kingsport
Martin
Clarksville
Johnson City
Paris
Kentucky L.
Gallatin
Cumberland
Rogersville
Elizabethton
Hendersonville
La Follette
Morristown
McKenzie
Lebanon
Oak Ridge
Jefferson City
Greeneville
Boone
Dickson
NASHVILLE
Cookeville
Franklin
Harriman
Knoxville
Newport
TENNESSEE
Clinch
Milan
Murfreesboro
Rockwood
Mt. Mitchell 2037
Lenoir
Hickory
Lexington
Columbia
McMinnville
Maryville
Morganton
Newton
Jackson
Shelbyville
Dayton
Athens
GREAT SMOKY MTS. NAT. PARK
Clingmans Dome 2024
Asheville
Lewisburg
Tullahoma
Waynesville
Hendersonville
NORTH CAROLINA
Gastonia
Cumberland Plateau
Appalachian Mountains
Blue Ridge
MICHIGAN
LAKE MICHIGAN
WISCONSIN
ILLINOIS
ft
m
6000
2000
4500
1500
3000
1000
1200
400
600
200
0
0
200
600
2000
6000
4000
12 000
m
ft
Projection: Alber's Equal Area with two standard parallels

1 : 6 000 000

50   0   50   100 miles
0   50   100   150 km

West from Greenwich

CARTOGRAPHY BY PHILIP'S. COPYRIGHT REED INTERNATIONAL BOOKS LTD.

Continuation
Eastwards
On same scale

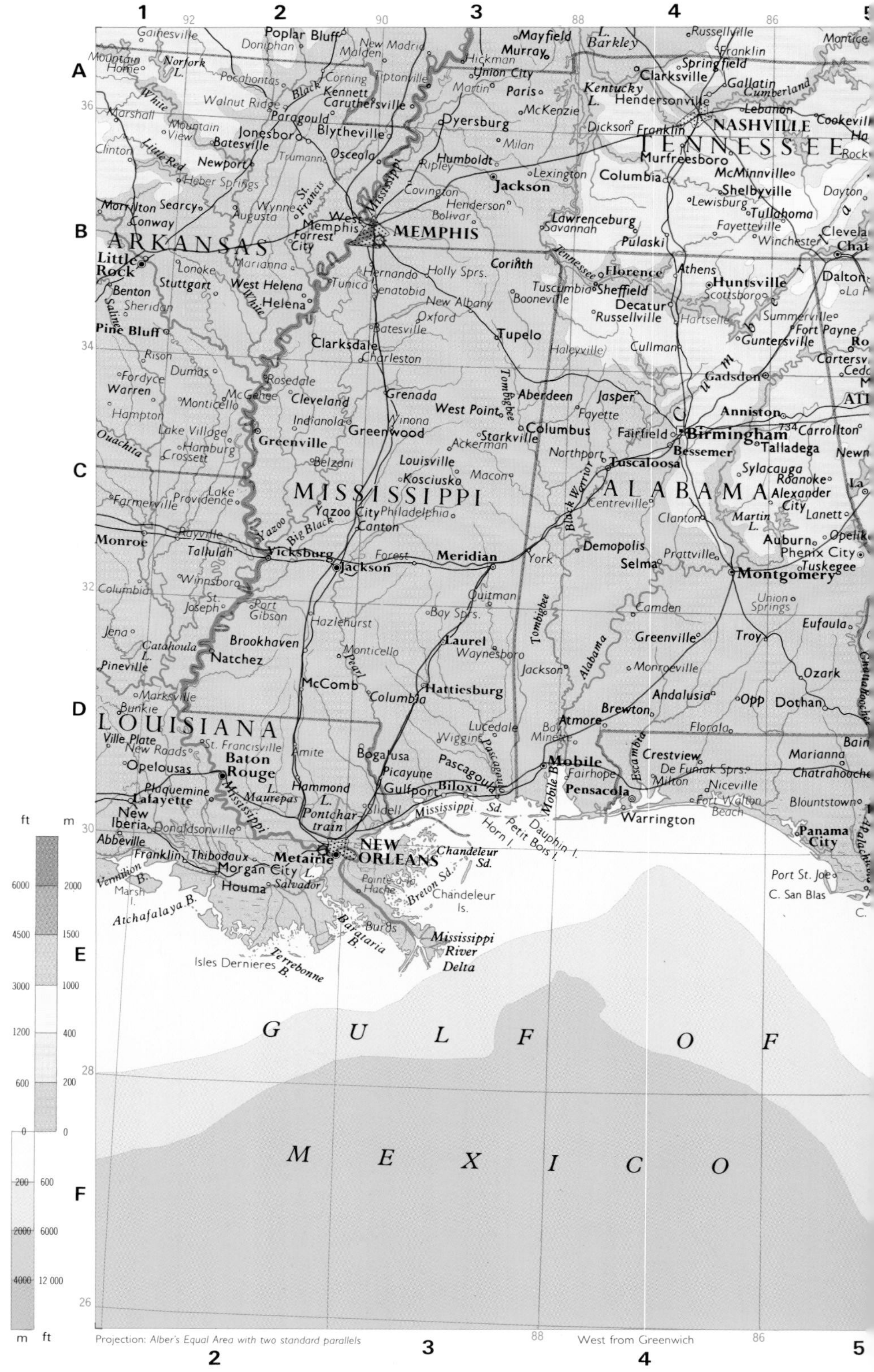

Projection: Alber's Equal Area with two standard parallels   West from Greenwich

1: 6 000 000

50   0   50   100   miles
50   0   50   100   150   km

A
Harlan · Middlesboro · Kingsport · Bristol · Abingdon · Marion · Galax · Martinsville · Eden · Danville · Roxboro · Roanoke · Winton · Elizabeth City · Currituck Sd.
Rogersville · Johnson City · Elizabethton · Mount Airy · Reidsville · Oxford · Henderson · Edenton · Albemarle Sd. · Manteo
Morristown · Greeneville · Newport · Yadkin · Greensboro · Burlington · Durham · Rocky Mount · Williamston · Roanoke I.
Knoxville · Asheville · Mt. Mitchell 2037 · Morganton · Newton · Hickory · Statesville · Salisbury · Lexington · High Point · Thomasville · Winston-Salem · Graham · Chapel Hill · Raleigh · Wilson · Greenville · Pamlico Sound

B
Maryville · Clingmans Dome 2024 · Waynesville · Hendersonville · Brevard · Shelby · Gastonia · Charlotte · Concord · Kannapolis · Albemarle · Asheboro · Sanford · Smithfield · Dunn · Goldsboro · Kinston · New Bern · Hatteras
NORTH CAROLINA · Washington · Neuse
Murphy · Brown Bald 458 · Spartanburg · Gaffney · Rock Hill · Monroe · Lancaster · Southern Pines · Fayetteville · Clinton · Jacksonville · Beaufort · Raleigh B. · C. Lookout
Greenville · Easley · Seneca · Union · Chester · Bennettsville · Lourinburg · Cape Fear · Onslow B.

C
Toccoa · Anderson · Laurens · Newberry · Hartsville · Dillon · Darlington · Mullins · Whiteville · Wilmington
Hartwell · Belton · Greenwood · Abbeville · Saluda · L. Murray · Columbia · Sumter · Florence · Marion · Conway · Southport
Gainesville · Elberton · Athens · Clark Hill L. · Manning · Lake City · Myrtle Beach · C. Fear
Lawrenceville · Covington · Orangeburg · L. Marion · Kingstree · Georgetown
GEORGIA · Augusta · Aiken · Bamberg · L. Maultrie · Summerville · Cooper
Sparta · Milledgeville · Waynesboro · Walterboro · North Charleston · Charleston · Mt. Pleasant
Macon · Warner Robins · Swainsboro · Millen · Ogeechee · Ridgeland · Hampton · Combahee · Beaufort

D
Cochran · Dublin · Statesboro · Vidalia · Parris I.
Eastman · Ohoopee · Oconee · Savannah · Hinesville · Ossabaw I.
Cordele · Hazlehurst · Fitzgerald · Altamaha · Baxley · Jesup · St. Catherines I.
Sylvester · Tifton · Douglas · Sapelo I.
Adel · Waycross · Brunswick
Okefenokee · Satilla · Cumberland I.

E
Quitman · Valdosta · Swamp · Folkston · Fernandina Beach
Monticello · Madison · Jasper · St. Johns · Jacksonville Beach
Live Oak · Lake City · JACKSONVILLE · A T L A N T I C
Perry · Starke · Green Cove Springs · St. Augustine
High Springs · Palatka · Bunnell
Cross City · Gainesville · Ormond Beach
Ocala · L. George · De Land · Daytona Beach · New Smyrna Beach · O C E A N
Crystal River · Inverness · Eustis · Sanford
Brooksville · Leesburg · Titusville · C. Canaveral

F
Dade City · Winter Park · Orlando · Cocoa · Merritt Island
Tarpon Springs · Kissimmee · Haines City · Melbourne · Indian River
Clearwater · Lakeland · Winter Haven · Bartow
Largo · TAMPA · Vero Beach
St. Petersburg · Tampa Bay · Sebring · Fort Pierce · Stuart · Grand Cays
Bradenton · Sarasota · Istokpoga · Okeechobee · Little Abaco I. · Gt. Guana Cay
Arcadia · L. Okeechobee · Pahokee · Settlement Pt. · Hope Town
Punta Gorda · La Belle · Belle Glade · West Palm Beach · Grand Bahama I. · Great Abaco I.
Charlotte Harb. · Fort Myers · Immokalee · Boca Raton · Delray Beach · Freeport · B A H A M A S

G
Cape Coral · Naples · Big Cypress Swamp · Everglades · Pompano Beach · Fort Lauderdale · Hollywood · Miami Beach
Carol City · MIAMI
Hialeah · Biscayne B.
EVERGLADES NAT. PARK · Homestead

SOUTH CAROLINA

FLORIDA

CARTOGRAPHY BY PHILIP'S. COPYRIGHT REED INTERNATIONAL BOOKS LTD.

Column numbers (top): 1 2 3 4 5

104 102 100 98

States: MONTANA, NORTH DAKOTA, SOUTH DAKOTA, WYOMING, NEBRASKA, COLORADO, KANSAS

North Dakota and vicinity:
Scobey, Plentywood, Crosby, Kenmare, Bowbells, Mohall, Bottineau, Rolla, Cavalier, Langdon, Cando, Grafton, Park River, Souris, Towner, Rugby, Williston, Stanley, Minot, Velva, New Town, L. Sakakawea, Watford City, Garrison, Harvey, Fessenden, McClusky, New Rockford, Northwood, Cooperstown, Hillsb, Sheyenne, Larimore, Gran Forks, Devils Lake, Lakota

Wolf Point, Missouri, Fairview, Sidney, Circle, Glendive, Terry, Wibaux, Beach, Dickinson, Manning, Stanton, Washburn, Center, Hebron, Mandan, Bismarck, Steele, Napoleon, Jamestown, Valley City, Lisbon, La Moure, Forma

Montana:
Fort Peck L., Yellowstone, Miles City, Powder, Tongue, Baker, Ekalaka, Broadus, Little Missouri, White Butte 1069, Bowman, Mott, Heart, Carson, Cannonball, Fort Yates, Selfridge, Linton, Ashley, Ellendale, Lehr

Hettinger, Lemmon, McIntosh, Grand, Bison, Timber Lake, Mobridge, Oahe, Selby, Mound City, Eureka, Leola, Britton, Sisse

South Dakota:
Moreau, Dupree, Eagle Butte, Gettysburg, Faulkton, Redfield, Clark, De Smet, Belle Fourche, Spearfish, Lead, Deadwood, Sturgis, Cheyenne, Onida, Highmore, Miller, Huron, Gillette, Sundance, Belle Fourche, Newcastle, Black Hills, Custer, Harney Pk. 2207, Rapid City, Philip, Oahe Dam, Fort Pierre, Pierre, Bad, Wessington Sprs., Woonsocket, Mad

Hot Springs, Edgemont, Kadoka, Murdo, White, Kennebec, Chamberlain, Mitchell, Salem, Alexandria, Badlands, White River, Little White, L. Francis Case, Armour, Par, Winner, Missouri, Lake Andes, Yankton, Martin, Pine Ridge, Chadron, Niobrara, Butte

Nebraska / Wyoming:
Douglas, Lusk, Harrison, Crawford, Rushville, Valentine, Bassett, Atkinson, O'Neill, Elkhorn, Plainvi, Neligh, N. Platte, Hemingford, Alliance, Sand Hills 1036, Mullen, North Loup, Ainsworth, Madison, W

Torrington, Wheatland, Laramie Mountains 3131, Scottsbluff, Gering, Bridgeport, Hyannis, Thedford, Taylor, Burwell, Albion, Greeley, Fullerton, Middle, Loup, Central, Laramie, Lodgepole Cr., Kimball, Sidney, Oshkosh, Stapleton, Broken Bow, Loup City, St. Paul, David C, Cheyenne, Ogallala, L. McConaughy, North Platte, Gothenburg, Cozad, Lexington, Grand Island, Aurora, York, Sew, Platte

Colorado / Kansas:
Fort Collins, Loveland, Greeley, Sterling, South Platte, Julesburg, Grant, Imperial, Curtis, Elwood, Kearney, Hastings, Gen, Frenchman Cr., Boulder, Longmont, Fort Morgan, Akron, Wray, Trenton, Benkelman, McCook, Beaver City, Holdrege, Red Cloud, Hebron, Fairbu, Lafayette, Brighton, Republican, Alma, Franklin, Golden, Denver, Aurora, Englewood, Lakewood, Byers, St. Francis, Atwood, Oberlin, Norton, Phillipsburg, Smith Center, Solomon, Mankato, Concordia, Repu, Belle, Castle Rock, Limon, Colby, N. Fork, Solomon, Stockton, Osborne, Minneapolis, Lincoln, Ju, Abilen, Hugo, Burlington, Goodland, Oakley, Hill City, S. Fork, Smoky Hills, Russell, Salina, COLORADO, Pikes Pk. 4300, Colorado Springs, Cheyenne Wells, Saline, Minneapolis, Fountain, Canon City, Sharon Springs, Smoky Hill, Hays, Ellsworth, Pueblo, Ordway, Eads, Leoti, Scott City, Dighton, La Crosse, Great Bend, Larned, Lyons, McPh, Canon City, Las Animas, Lamar, Tribune, KANSAS

Elevation scale (left):
ft / m
12 000 / 4000
9000 / 3000
6000 / 2000
4500 / 1500
3000 / 1000
1200 / 400
600 / 200
0 / 0
200 / 600
m / ft

Projection: Alber's Equal Area with two standard parallels

West from Greenwich

Column numbers (bottom): 2 3 4 5

102 100 98

1: 6 000 000

50   0   50   100   miles
50   0   50   100   150   km

CANADA

Lake of the Woods

Warroad   Rainy   Rainy Lake
Baudette   River
International Falls   Fort Frances   Atikokan   **Thunder Bay**   183   **A**

River Falls   Upper Red L.   Big Fork   Lac la Croix   Isle Royale   48

Lake Falls   Lower Red   Little Fork   Vermilion L.   Grand Marais   Copper Harbor

Bagley   Winnibigoshish   Virginia   **LAKE SUPERIOR**   Keweenaw Pt.   Keweenaw Pen.
Bemidji   L.   Hibbing   Eveleth   Hancock   Keweenaw B.   **B**
Mahnomen   Cass Lake   Leech L.   Grand Rapids   Apostle Is.   Houghton   Ishpeming   Marquette

Detroit Lakes   Park Rapids   Walker   Two Harbors   Ontonagon   L'Anse   604   Negaunee
Perham   **Duluth**   **MICHIGAN**
MINNESOTA   Aitkin   Cloquet   **Superior**   Washburn   Bessemer   Crystal Falls

Fergus Falls   Wadena   Staples   Brainerd   Mille Lacs L.   Moose Lake   Ashland   Hurley   **Ironwood**   Iron Mountain
Alexandria   Little Falls   Hayward   Park Falls   Eagle River   Niagara   Powers

Glenwood   Mora   Spooner   Phillips   Rhinelander   Crandon   Menominee   **C**
Morris   Milaca   Pine City   Grantsburg   Rice Lake   Ladysmith   Tomahawk   Antigo   Green Bay   Marinette
St. Cloud   Sauk Rapids   Cumberland   Cornell   Medford   Merrill   **Wausau**   Oconto   Sturgeon Bay
Paynesville   Mississippi   Cambridge   Chippewa Falls   **WISCONSIN**   Shawano   **Green Bay**

Willmar   Litchfield   Anoka   St. Croix   Menomonie   Eau Claire   Marshfield   Stevens Point   De Pere   Kaukauna   Kewaunee
Montevideo   **MINNEAPOLIS**   **St. Paul**   Stillwater   Hudson   Waupaca   **Appleton**   Two Rivers
Granite Falls   Hutchinson   **Bloomington**   Hastings   Red Wing   Menasha   Neenah   **Manitowoc**
Redwood Falls   Glencoe   Northfield   Lake City   Whitehall   Wisconsin Rapids   Wautoma   **Oshkosh**   L. Chilton   Sheboygan
Marshall   New Ulm   St. Peter   Faribault   Alma   Black River Falls   Ripon   Winnebago
Mankato   **Owatonna**   Winona   Sparta   Tomah   Montello   Fond du Lac   West Bend
Redstone   Waseca   **Rochester**   Onalaska   Mauston   Waupun   Beaver Dam   Port Washington
Windom   St. James   Preston   **La Crosse**   Virroqua   Reedsburg   Baraboo   Portage   Hartford   **MICHIGAN**
Fairmont   Albert Lea   Austin   Northwood   Decorah   Richland Center   Prairie du Chien   Wisconsin   **Madison**   Jefferson   Wauwatosa
Jackson   Estherville   Osage   Waukon   Dodgeville   **Waukesha**   **MILWAUKEE**   **D**
Sheldon   Spencer   Forest City   **Mason City**   Charles City   New Hampton   Lancaster   Darlington   Whitewater   **Racine**
Cherokee   Emmetsburg   Algona   Garner   Clarion   Hampton   Waverly   Oelwein   **Janesville**   Monroe   Beloit   Burlington   **Kenosha**
Storm Lake   Pocahontas   Fort Dodge   Iowa Falls   Cedar Falls   Independence   **Dubuque**   Freeport   **Rockford**   Belvidere   Woodstock   Waukegan
Sac City   Webster   Waterloo   Wapsipinicon   Maquoketa   Elgin   Skokie   Evanston
Ida Grove   Carroll   Boone   **Ames**   Marshalltown   **Cedar Rapids**   De Kalb   Dixon   Aurora   Cicero   **CHICAGO**
Denison   **IOWA**   Jefferson   Vinton   Marion   **Clinton**   Sterling   Harvey   **E**
Audubon   Perry   Newton   Grinnell   Marengo   Iowa City   **Davenport**   **Moline**   Mendota   **Joliet**
Harlan   W. Des Moines   **Des Moines**   Montezuma   Muscatine   Tipton   Princeton   Morris   Ottawa
Atlantic   Winterset   Indianola   Pella   L. Red Rock   Washington   Rock Island   Kewanee   Peru   Streator   **Kankakee**
Council Bluffs   Greenfield   Knoxville   Oskaloosa   Fairfield   Aledo   Galesburg   Chillicothe   Pontiac
Glenwood   Red Oak   Creston   Osceola   Albia   Ottumwa   Mt. Pleasant   Monmouth   **Peoria**   Pekin
Shenandoah   Corning   Bloomfield   Burlington   Canton   Normal   Paxton
Clarinda   Bedford   Centerville   Fort Madison   Macomb   **Bloomington**   Rantoul
Rockport   Grant City   Princeton   Unionville   Keokuk   Kahoka   Rushville   Lincoln   **Champaign**   **F**
Falls City   Bethany   Milan   Trenton   Edina   Beardstown   **ILLINOIS**   Decatur
Hiawatha   Savannah   Chillicothe   Brookfield   Palmyra   **Quincy**   **Springfield**   Mattoon   Shelbyville
Troy   Macon   **Hannibal**   Jacksonville   Taylorville   Pana   Effingham
St. Joseph   Excelsior Sprs.   Carrollton   Richmond   Moberly   Fayette   Mexico   Jerseyville   Carlinville   Litchfield   Vandalia
Leavenworth   Independence   Lexington   Marshall   Columbia   Fulton   Troy   **Alton**   Greenville   Flora
Kansas City   **Kansas City**   Boonville   Jefferson City   Hermann   St. Charles   Granite City   Centralia   Fairfield
Lawrence   Olathe   Warrensburg   Sedalia   **St. LOUIS**   St. Louis   **Belleville**   Mount Vernon
Ottawa   Paola   Harrisonville   **MISSOURI**   Union   Waterloo
Emporia   Garnett   Clinton   Butler   Lake of the Ozarks   Osage   Sullivan   De Soto   Ste. Genevieve   Pinckneyville   Benton   Du Quoin

Projection: Albers' Equal Area with two standard parallels

West from Greenwich

1: 6 000 000

50 0 50 100 miles
50 0 50 100 150 km
MISSOURI
Springfield
Joplin
Ozark Plateau
Cape Girardeau
Poplar Bluff
Sikeston
Cairo
Paducah
Carbondale
Murphysboro
Metropolis
Mayfield
TENNESSEE
MEMPHIS
Jackson
Dyersburg
Humboldt
ARKANSAS
Little Rock
Fayetteville
Springdale
Rogers
Boston Mts.
Ouachita Mts.
Ft. Smith
Hot Springs
Pine Bluff
Texarkana
Jonesboro
Batesville
Newport
Russellville
Conway
El Dorado
Camden
Tulsa
Muskogee
Okmulgee
MISSISSIPPI
Jackson
Vicksburg
Greenville
Greenwood
Meridian
Hattiesburg
Laurel
Tupelo
Columbus
Natchez
Biloxi
Gulfport
LOUISIANA
Shreveport
Bossier City
Monroe
Alexandria
Lafayette
Baton Rouge
Lake Charles
NEW ORLEANS
Metairie
Houma
Morgan City
Beaumont
Port Arthur
Orange
HOUSTON
Pasadena
Baytown
Galveston
Texas City
Tyler
Longview
Marshall
Mississippi River Delta
Chandeleur Sd.
Chandeleur Is.
Breton Sd.
Mississippi Sd.
Isles Dernieres
GULF OF MEXICO
Kingsville
Falfurrias
Hebbronville
Zapata
Falcon L.
Rio Grande City
Raymondville
Edinburg
McAllen
Harlingen
San Benito
Brownsville
Padre I.
Laguna Madre
MEXICO
Continuation Southwards on same scale

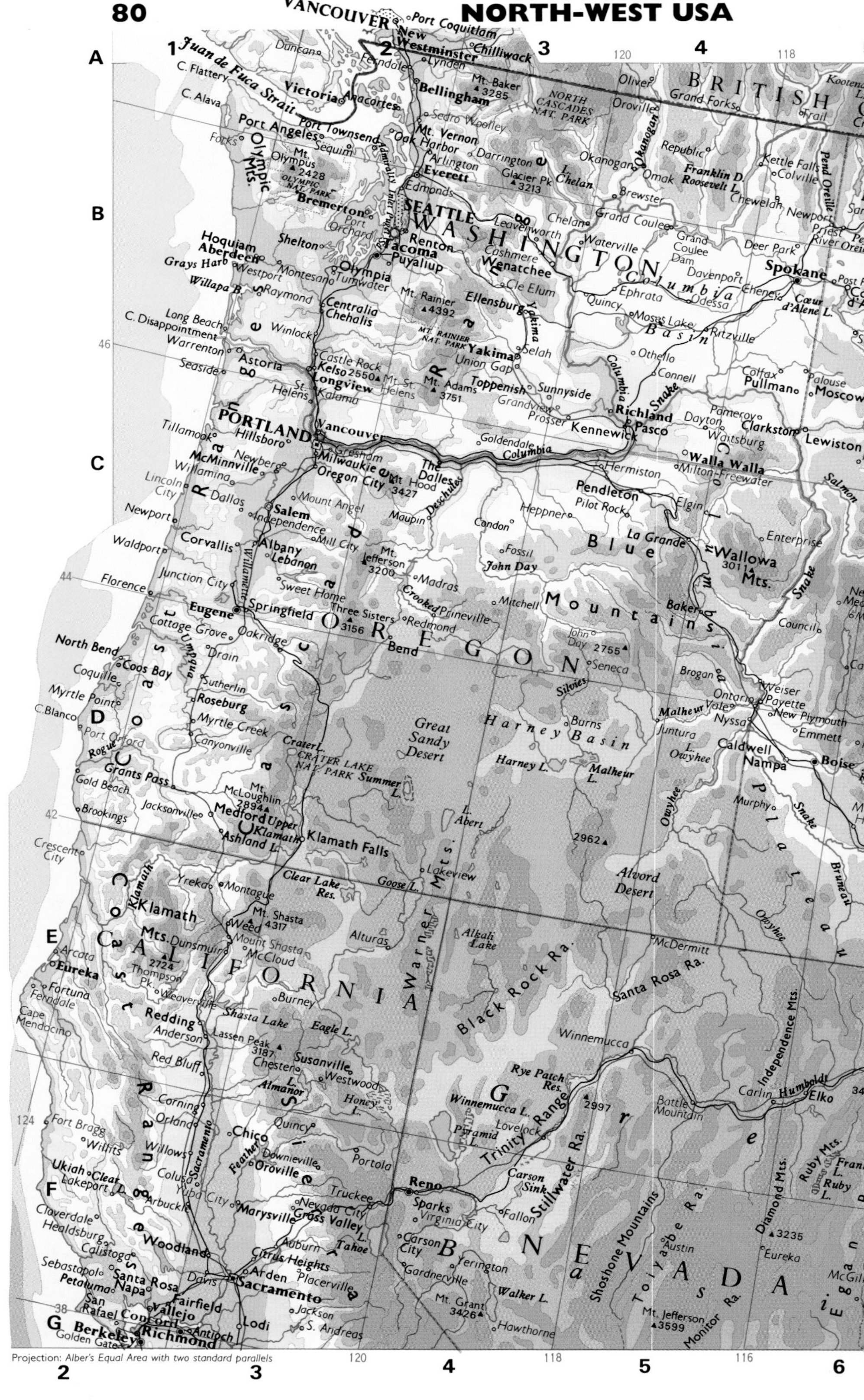
VANCOUVER
Port Coquitlam
New Westminster
Chilliwack
Juan de Fuca Strait
Victoria
Anacortes
Bellingham
Mt. Baker 3285
NORTH CASCADES NAT. PARK
BRITISH
Oliver
Oroville
Grand Forks
Trail
Port Angeles
Port Townsend
Mt. Vernon
Olympic Mts.
Mt. Olympus 2428
OLYMPIC NAT. PARK
Everett
Glacier Pk 3213
L. Chelan
Okanogan
Omak
Republic
Franklin D. Roosevelt L.
Kettle Falls
Colville
Bremerton
SEATTLE
WASHINGTON
Tacoma
Olympia
Hoquiam
Aberdeen
Grays Harb.
Willapa B.
Wenatchee
Ellensburg
Yakima
Spokane
Columbia Basin
Mt. Rainier 4392
MT. RAINIER NAT. PARK
Long Beach
C. Disappointment
Astoria
Kelso
Longview
Mt. St. Helens 2550
Mt. Adams 3751
Toppenish
Richland
Pasco
Kennewick
Pullman
Moscow
Clarkston
Lewiston
PORTLAND
Vancouver
Walla Walla
Milwaukie
Oregon City
Mt Hood 3427
The Dalles
Pendleton
Salem
Corvallis
Albany
Blue Mountains
Wallowa Mts. 3011
Mt. Jefferson 3200
Eugene
Springfield
OREGON
Three Sisters 3156
Bend
Coos Bay
Roseburg
Great Sandy Desert
Harney Basin
Grants Pass
Medford
Crater L.
CRATER LAKE NAT. PARK
Mt. McLoughlin 2894
Klamath Falls
Boise
Nampa
Klamath Mts.
Mt. Shasta 4317
CALIFORNIA
Eureka
Redding
Lassen Peak 3187
Black Rock Ra.
Winnemucca
Chico
Reno
Sacramento
Berkeley
Richmond
Elko
NEVADA
Mt. Jefferson 3599
Projection: Alber's Equal Area with two standard parallels

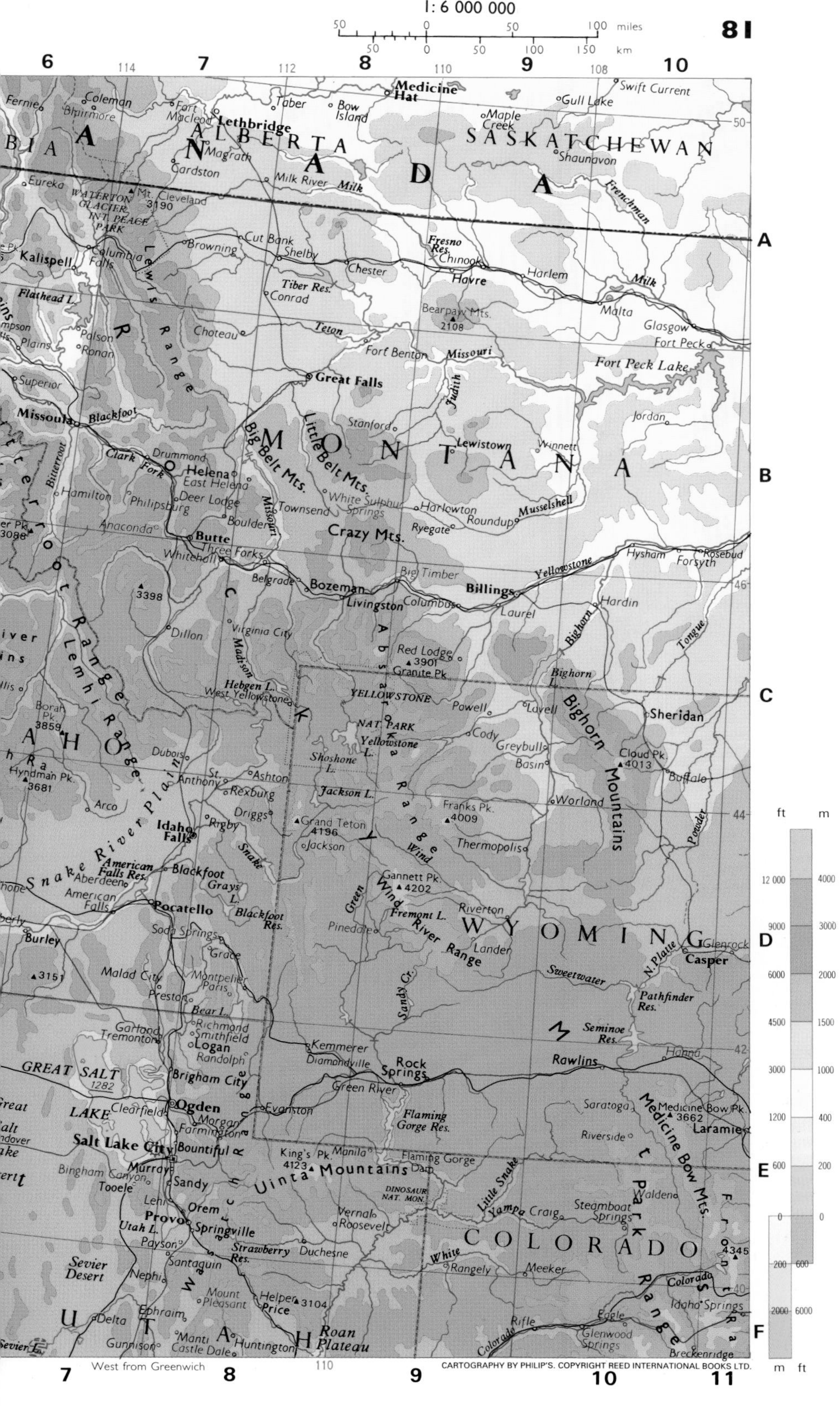

1: 6 000 000

50   0   50   100 miles
50 0 50 100 150 km

6 114 **7** 112 **8** 110 **9** 108 **10**

Medicine Hat
Swift Current
Coleman
Fernie
Blairmore
Fort Macleod
Taber
Bow Island
Maple Creek
Gull Lake

A L B E R T A
S A S K A T C H E W A N
C A N A D A

Magrath
Shaunavon
Lethbridge
Milk River
Milk
Frenchman

Eureka
WATERTON GLACIER INT. PEACE PARK
Mt. Cleveland 3190
Gardston
Browning
Cut Bank
Shelby
Fresno Res.
Chinook
Harlem
50
A

Kalispell
Columbia Falls
Conrad
Chester
Havre
Malta

Flathead L.
Tiber Res.
Bearpaw Mts. 2108
Glasgow
Fort Peck

Plains
Polson
Ronan
Choteau
Teton
Fort Benton
Missouri
Fort Peck Lake

Superior
Great Falls
Jordan

Missoula
Blackfoot
Stanford
Lewistown
Winnett

Clark Fork
Drummond
Helena
East Helena
Big Belt Mts.
Little Belt Mts.
White Sulphur Springs
Harlowton
Roundup
Musselshell
Rosebud
Forsyth
B

Hamilton
Philipsburg
Deer Lodge
Boulder
Townsend
Ryegate
Hysham

3088
Anaconda
Butte
Whitehall
Three Forks
Missouri
Crazy Mts.
Big Timber
Yellowstone
Hardin

M O N T A N A

3398
Belgrade
Bozeman
Livingston
Columbus
Laurel
Bighorn
Sheridan
46
C

Dillon
Virginia City
Madison
Red Lodge 3901
Granite Pk.
Powell
Lovell
Greybull
Basin
Worland
Cloud Pk. 4013
Buffalo

Borah Pk. 3859
Dubois
YELLOWSTONE NAT. PARK
Yellowstone L.
Shoshone L.
Cody
Bighorn Mountains

Hyndman Pk. 3681
Arco
St. Anthony
Ashton
Rexburg
Driggs
Rigby
Jackson L.
Franks Pk. 4009
Thermopolis
44

Idaho Falls
Grand Teton 4196
Jackson
Wind
Riverton

American Falls Res.
Blackfoot
Grays L.
Gannett Pk. 4202
Fremont L.
Lander
Riverside
D

Aberdeen
American Falls
Blackfoot Res.
Pinedale
Green
Wind River Range
W Y O M I N G
Glenrock
Casper
42

Burley
Soda Springs
Grace
Sweetwater
Pathfinder Res.

3151
Malad City
Montpelier
Paris
Preston
Seminoe Res.
Rawlins
Medicine Bow Pk. 3662
Laramie

Bear L.
Richmond
Smithfield
Logan
Kemmerer
Diamondville
Rock Springs
Saratoga
Medicine Bow Mts.

GREAT SALT 1282
Brigham City
Evanston
Green River
Flaming Gorge Res.
Riverside
E

LAKE
Clearfield
Ogden
Morgan
Flaming Gorge Dam
Walden

Salt Lake City
Bountiful
Farmington
King's Pk.
Manila
Mountains
DINOSAUR NAT. MON.
Craig
Steamboat Springs

Murray
Sandy
Uinta
4123
Vernal
Roosevelt
Yampa
C O L O R A D O

Tooele
Lehi
Orem
Strawberry
Duchesne
White
Rangely
Meeker
4345

Provo
Springville
Payson
Santaquin
Vernal
Colorado
Idaho Springs

Sevier Desert
Nephi
Mount Pleasant
Helper
Price 3104
Roan Plateau
Rifle
Eagle
Glenwood Springs
Breckenridge
F

U T A H
Delta
Ephraim
Manti
Castle Dale
Huntington
Colorado
Sevier

7 West from Greenwich **8** 110 **9** **10** **11**

ft   m

12 000   4000

9000   3000

6000   2000

4500   1500

3000   1000

1200   400

600   200

0   0

200   600

2000   6000

m   ft

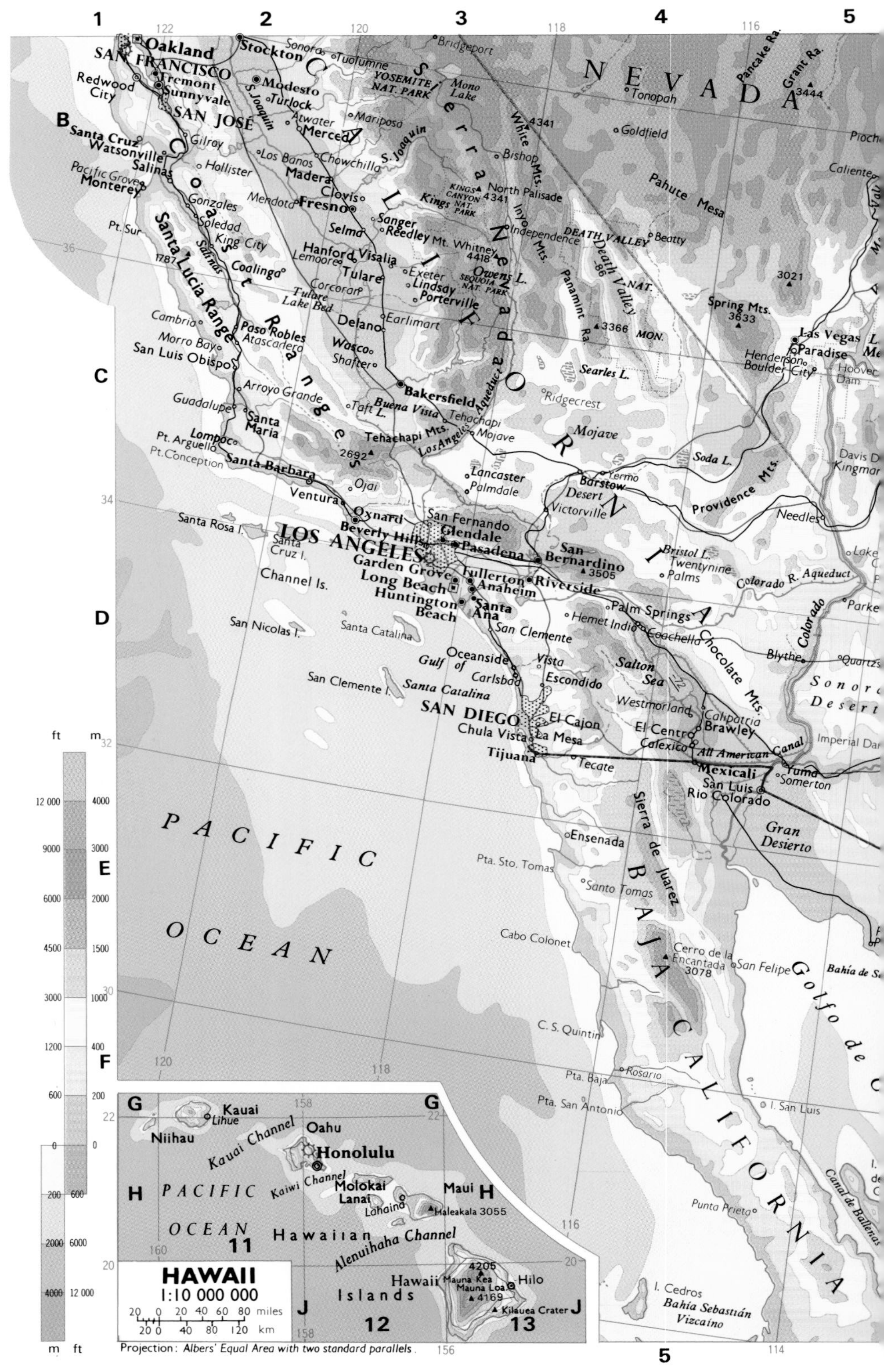

HAWAII
1:10 000 000

20 0   20 40 60 80 miles
20 0 20 40 60 80 120 km

Projection: Albers' Equal Area with two standard parallels.

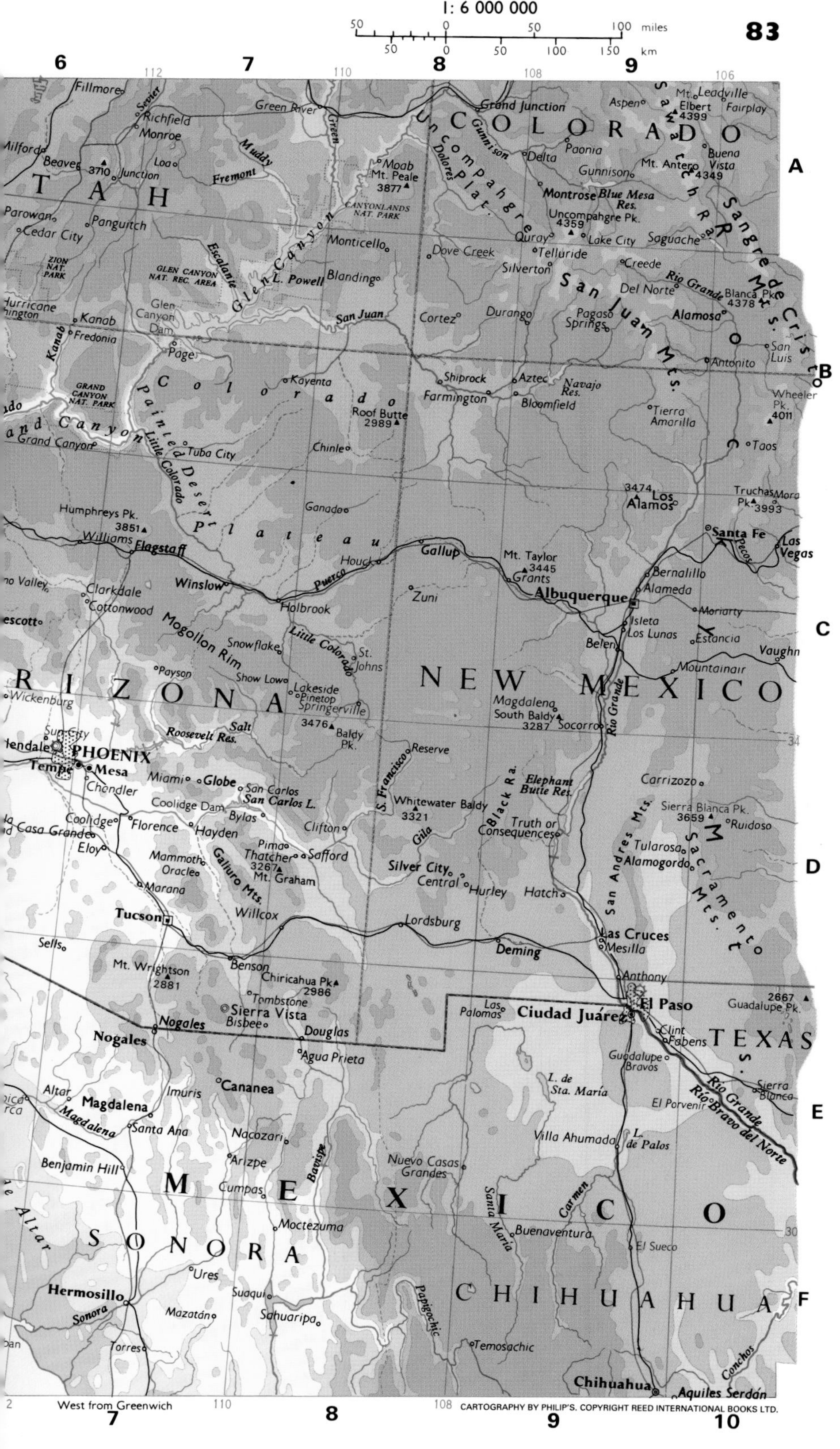

1: 6 000 000

50   0   50   100 miles
50   0   50   100   150 km

COLORADO

Fillmore
Sevier
Richfield
Monroe
Milford
Beaver
3710
Loa
Junction
Fremont

Green River
Green
Grand Junction
Gunnison
Aspen
Mt. Elbert
4399
Leadville
Fairplay

U T A H
Parowan
Cedar City
Panguitch
Delta
Paonia
Mt. Antero
4349
Buena Vista

Uncompahgre
Moab
Mt. Peale
3877
Dolores
Montrose
Blue Mesa
Res.
Gunnison
Uncompahgre Pk.
4359
Mt. Antero

ZION
NAT.
PARK
GLEN CANYON
NAT. REC. AREA
CANYONLANDS
NAT. PARK
Monticello
Dove Creek
Ouray
Lake City
Saguache

Hurricane
ington
Kanab
Fredonia
Glen
L. Powell
Blanding
Silverton
Telluride
Creede
Rio Grande
Del Norte
Blanca Pke.
4378

GRAND
CANYON
NAT. PARK
Page
Glen
Canyon
Dam
San Juan
Cortez
Durango
Pagosa
Springs
Alamosa

San Juan Mts.
San Luis
Antonito

ado
nd Canyon
Grand Canyon
Kayenta
Shiprock
Aztec
Navajo
Res.
Farmington
Bloomfield
Tierra
Amarilla
Wheeler
Pk.
4011

Tuba City
Little Colorado
Chinle
Roof Butte
2989
Taos

Humphreys Pk.
3851
Williams
Flagstaff
Painted Desert
Ganado
3474
Los
Alamos
Truchas Mora
Pk.
3993

no Valley
Clarkdale
Cottonwood
scott
Winslow
Holbrook
Houck
Puerco
Gallup
Mt. Taylor
3445
Grants
Santa Fe
Las
Vegas

A R I Z O N A
Mogollon Rim
Snowflake
Little Colorado
Zuni
Bernalillo
Alameda
Albuquerque
Moriarty
Estancia
Vaughn

Wickenburg
Payson
Show Low
Lakeside
Pinetop
Springerville
St.
Johns
Isleta
Los Lunas
Belen
34

Sun City
endale
PHOENIX
Tempe
Mesa
Roosevelt Res.
Salt
3476
Baldy
Pk.
Reserve
Magdalena
South Baldy
3287
Socorro
Mountainair
Carrizozo

Chandler
Miami
Globe
San Carlos
San Carlos L.
S. Francisco
Whitewater Baldy
3321
Elephant
Butte Res.
Sierra Blanca Pk.
3659
Ruidoso

Coolidge
Florence
Hayden
Clifton
Gila
Truth or
Consequences
Tularosa
Alamogordo

la Casa Grande
Eloy
Mammoth
Oracle
Pima
Thatcher
Mt. Graham
3267
Safford
Silver City
Central
Hurley
Hatch
NEW MEXICO

Marana
Galiuro Mts.
Willcox
Lordsburg
Las Cruces
Mesilla
Sacramento Mts.
San Andres Mts.

Tucson
Sells
Mt. Wrightson
2881
Benson
Chiricahua Pk.
2986
Deming
Anthony
2667
Guadalupe Pk.

Nogales
Sierra Vista
Bisbee
Tombstone
Las
Palomas
Ciudad Juárez
El Paso
Guadalupe Pk.

Nogales
Douglas
Agua Prieta
TEXAS
Clint
Fabens

Altar
Magdalena
Imuris
Cananea
Guadalupe
Bravos
Sierra
Blanca

ica
rca
Magdalena
Santa Ana
Nacozari
L. de
Sta. María
El Porvenir
Rio Grande
Rio Bravo del Norte

Benjamin Hill
Arizpe
Nuevo Casas
Grandes
Villa Ahumada
L.
de Palos

M E X I C O
Cumpas
Santa
María
Carmen
El Sueco
30

Moctezuma
CHIHUAHUA

SONORA
Ures

Hermosillo
Suaqui
Sahuaripa
Papagochic

Sonora
Mazatán
Temosachic

Torres
Chihuahua
Aquiles Serdán
Conchos

A
B
C
D
E
F

San Diego
Tijuana
Mexicali
Ensenada
Phoenix
Tucson
Deming
3658
Wichita Falls
Carlsbad
Abilene
Fort W.
Bro
S. Angelo
Te
Austi

Nogales
Bisbee
Ciudad
Agua Prieta
Juárez
El Paso
U N I T

Pta. Baja
30
3078
Cananea
Nacozari
Galeana
Sta. María
Villa Ahumada
Pecos
Rio
Grande
San Carlos
2896
Piedras Negras
Eagle Pass

Pta. Sta.
Eugenia
Tiburón
Ures
Hermosillo
Torres
Empalme
Madera
Conchos
Nueva Rosita
Monclova
Sabinas
Falcón Res.
Laredo
Nuevo Laredo

Sta. Rosalía
Guaymas
Chihuahua
Ciudad
Camargo
Delicias
Jiménez
M
Sabinas
Hidalgo
Reynosa

B. Ballenas
Muleje
Ciudad
Obregón
Huatabampo
El Fuerte
Los Mochis
Sinaloa
Hidalgo del
Parral
3160
E
S. Pedro
Gómez Palacio
Lerdo
Nazas
Matamoros
Saltillo
Monterrey

25
Pta. S. Juanico
Culiacán
Elota
Torreón
Concepción
del Oro
Catorce
4054
Montemorelos

C. San Lucas
2406
La Paz
Mazatlán
Rosario
Elota
Durango
Sombrerete
Matehuala
Ciudad
Victoria

C. San Lucas
Escuinapa
Acaponeta
Cd. García
Fresnillo
Zacatecas
Charcas
Tula

Is. Tres
Marías
Tuxpan
Tepic
R. Grande de
3353
San Luis
Potosí
Pánuco

20
C. Corrientes
Ameca
Zacoalco
Guadalajara
Santiago
León
Guanajuato
Irapuato
Celaya
Querétaro
Papantla
Pachuca
Is. de
Revillagigedo
(Mex.)
Colima Vol.
4339
Zamora
L. de Chapala
Colima
Morelia
MEXICO
Toluca
Cuernavaca
Iguala
Popocatepetl
5452
Puebla
Tlaxcala

Manzanillo
Balsas
3703
Popo
Mexcala
Chilpancingo
Chilapa
Ayutla
Oaxa
Acapulco
Ometepec
Verde Te

P A C I F I C

O C E A N

Projection: Bonne

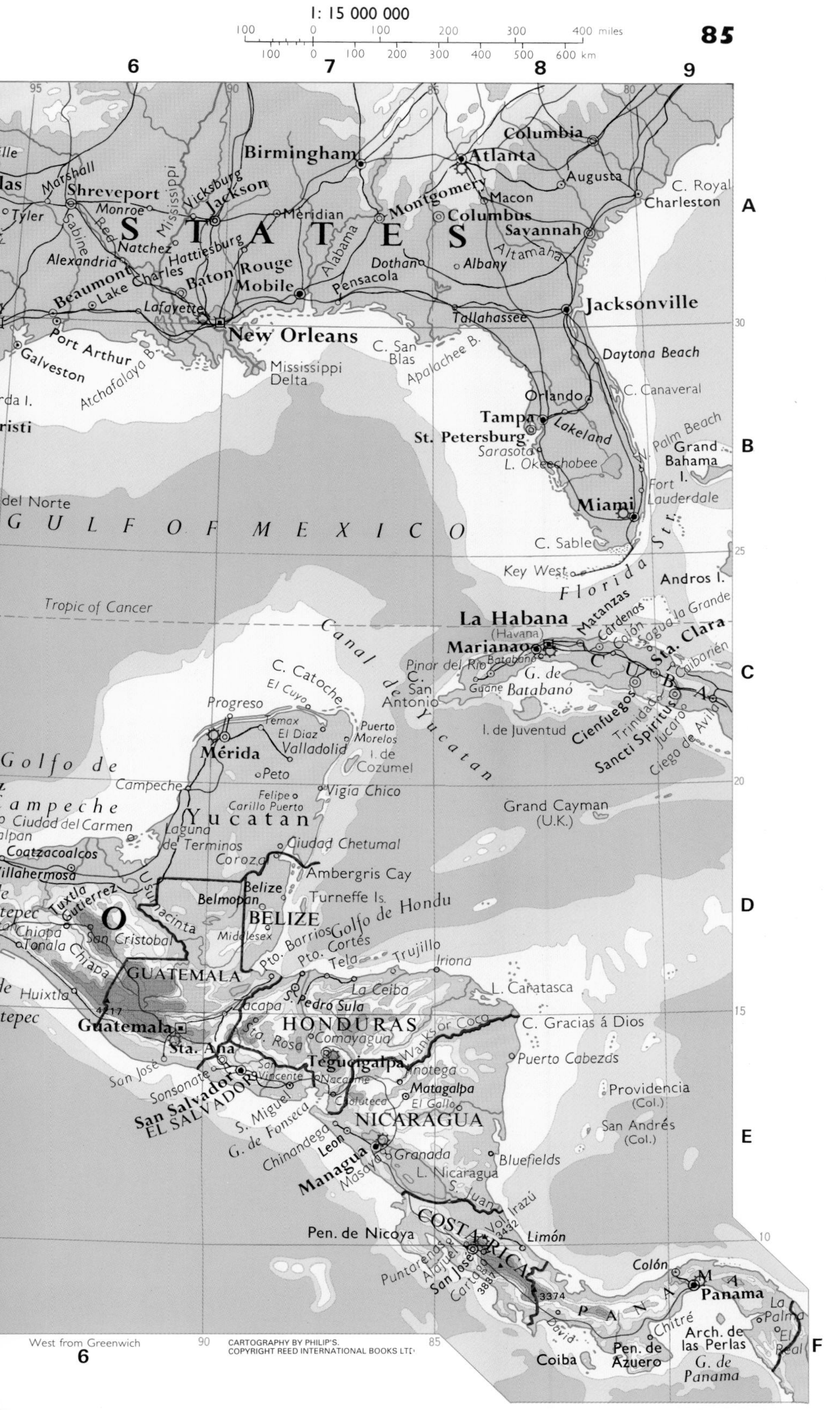

1: 15 000 000

100   0   100   200   300   400 miles

100   0   100   200   300   400   500   600 km

6   7   8   9

95   90   80

Birmingham   **Columbia**

Atlanta   Augusta   C. Royal
                                       Charleston   A

Shreveport   Vicksburg   Macon
Monroe   Jackson   Meridian   **Montgomery**   Savannah
Tyler   **Columbus**
Natchez   Hattiesburg   Alabama
Alexandria   Albany
Beaumont   Lake Charles   Baton Rouge   **Mobile**   Pensacola   Dothan
Lafayette   Tallahassee   **Jacksonville**   30
Port Arthur   Daytona Beach
Galveston   **New Orleans**   C. San   Apalachee B.
                            Blas
risti   Mississippi   C. Canaveral
del Norte   Delta   Orlando
                                    Tampa   Lakeland   W. Palm Beach
                            St. Petersburg   **Grand**   B
                            Sarasota   L. Okeechobee   **Bahama**
G U L F   O F   M E X I C O   **Miami**   Fort
                                            Lauderdale
                            C. Sable
                                            Key West   25
Tropic of Cancer   Florida Str.
                                            Andros I.
                    Canal   **La Habana**   Matanzas   Cárdenas   Sagua la Grande
                    C. Catoche   (Havana)   Colón   **Sta.**
                    El Cuyo   **Marianao**   C U B A   **Clara**   C
Progreso   C. San   Pinar del Rio   Batabanó   Caibarién
        Temax   Antonio   G. de   Guane   Batabanó
        El Diaz   Puerto   Batabanó   Sancti Spiritus
Mérida   Valladolid   Morelos   Cienfuegos   Trinidad   Ciego de Avila
        Peto   I. de   I. de Juventud   Jucaro
Campeche   Cozumel   Vigia Chico   Grand Cayman   20
Y u c a t a n   Felipe   (U.K.)
Ciudad del Carmen   Carillo Puerto
Laguna   Ciudad Chetumal
de Terminos   Corozal   Ambergris Cay
Coatzacoalcos   Usumacinta   **BELIZE**   Turneffe Is.   D
Villahermosa   Belmopan   Golfo de Hondu
        San Cristobal   Middlesex   Pto. Barrios   Pto. Cortés
O   **GUATEMALA**   Zacapa   Pedro Sula   Tela   Trujillo   Iriona   L. Caratasca
Chiapa   4217   Sta. Rosa   La Ceiba   15
Guatemala   **HONDURAS**   Comayagua   Wanks or Coco   C. Gracias á Dios
Sta. Ana   **Tegucigalpa**   Jinotega   Puerto Cabezas
San José   San Vicente   Jinocaré   Matagalpa
San Salvador   Choluteca   El Gallo   Providencia
EL SALVADOR   **NICARAGUA**   (Col.)   E
San Miguel   G. de Fonseca   León   Masaya   Granada   Bluefields   San Andrés
Chinandega   **Managua**   L. Nicaragua   (Col.)
Pen. de Nicoya   C O S T A   R I C A   Limón
Puntarenas   Alajuel   Colón   La
San José   Cartago   3374   Chitré   Palma   El
Coiba   Pen. de   G. de   Arch. de   Real
        Azuero   Panama   las Perlas   F

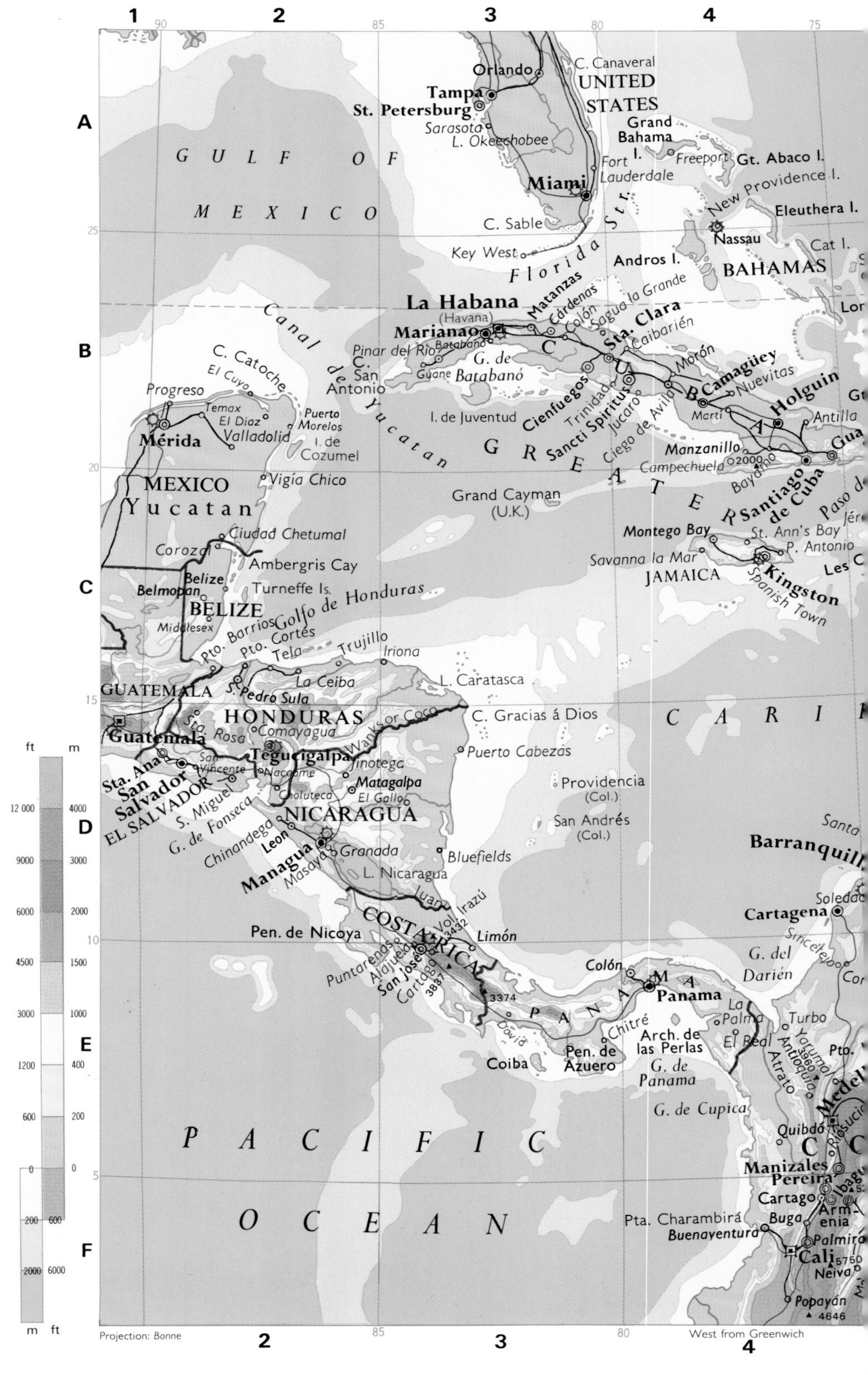

Orlando
C. Canaveral
Tampa
UNITED
St. Petersburg
STATES
Sarasota
Grand
Bahama
L. Okeechobee
I.
Freeport
Gt. Abaco I.
Fort
Lauderdale
New Providence I.
Miami
Eleuthera I.
C. Sable
Nassau
Cat I.
Key West
Andros I.
BAHAMAS
La Habana
Matanzas
(Havana)
Cárdenas
Colón
Sagua la Grande
Marianao
C
Caibarién
Sta. Clara
Pinar del Río
Batabanó
Morón
B Camagüey
C. San
G. de
Nuevitas
Antonio
Guane
Batabanó
Cienfuegos
Trinidad
Sancti Spíritus
Holguín
I. de Juventud
Júcaro
Ciego de Ávila
Martí
Antilla
Manzanillo
2000
Gua
Campechuela
Bay
Santiago
Mérida
Grand Cayman
(U.K.)
de Cuba
Montego Bay
St. Ann's Bay
P. Antonio
Savanna la Mar
JAMAICA
Kingston
Spanish Town

GULF OF MEXICO
FLORIDA
MEXICO
Yucatan
GREATER
CARI

1 : 15 000 000

100   0   100   200   300   400 miles

100   0 100 200 300 400 500 600 km

A T L A N T I C

O C E A N

Tropic of Cancer

guana

Caicos I. (U.K.)

Turks Is. (U.K.)

de Paix

Cap Haitien
Monte Cristi
Pto. Plata
Santiago
S. Francisco de Macoris
Valverde
Sanchez

PUERTO RICO (U.S.A.)
Arecibo
San Juan
St. Thomas (U.S.A.)
Charlotte Amalie
Virgin Is. (U.K.)
Sombrero (U.K.)
Anguilla (U.K.)
St. Martin (Fr. & Neth.)

Vega
2880
DOMINICAN
REP.
La Romana
1338
Caguas
St. Croix
(U.S.A.)
ST. KITTS-NEVIS
ANTIGUA &
BARBUDA

S. Pedro de Macoris
Santo Domingo
Ponce
Mayagüez
Guayama
Christiansted
Basseterre
Charlestown
Plymouth
Montserrat (U.K.)
St. John's
Guadeloupe (Fr.)

Hispaniola
Santo Domingo
Bani
Barahona
Duverge

Leeward
Islands
Pointe à Pitre

I L L E S

L E S S E R
DOMINICA
Roseau

A N   S E A

ANTILLES
Fort de France
Martinique (Fr.)

Windward
ST. VINCENT
& Kingstown
THE GRENADINES
Islands
Castries
ST. LUCIA
BARBADOS
Bridgetown

La Blanquilla
(Ven.)
GRENADA
St. George's

Venezuela
Golfo de
Aruba (Neth.)
Curaçao
Willemstad
Bonaire
NETH.
ANTILLES

Margarita
La Asunción
Carúpano
Tobago
Port of Spain
TRINIDAD & TOBAGO
San Fernando

Gallinas
de la
ra

Pto. Cabello
Maiquetia
La Tortuga
(Ven.)
Cumaná
G. de
Paria

Dabajuro
Coro
Cabimas
Maracaibo
Maracay
Caracas
Barcelona
2596
Cupito
Maturín

L. de
Maracaibo
Trujillo
Valera
San Felipe
Valencia
Barquisimeto
Calabozo
Las Mercedes
El Tigre
Tucupita

Cord. de Mérida
5007
San Cristóbal
Portuguesa
San Fernando
de Apure
Orinoco
Ciudad
Guayana
Ciudad Bolívar

G U Y A N A
Georgetown

Pamplona
ucaramanga
Arauca
Arauca
Apure
Caicara
El Callao
Tumeremo
Barico
New
Amsterdam
Wismari

Guanare
Pto. Páez
Meta
Pto. Carreño
2285
Pto. Ayacucho
Caura
2560
Roraima
2810
Cuyuni
Essequibo
1280
SURINAM

V E N E Z U E L A

O M B I A

tá

Sierra Pacaraima

Guaviare
Casiquiare

B R A Z I L

NORTH ATLANTIC OCEAN
Caribbean Sea
Tropic of Cancer
Equator
MEXICO
BELIZE
GUATEMALA
Guatemala
HONDURAS
Tegucigalpa
EL SALVADOR
San Salvador
NICARAGUA
Managua
COSTA RICA
San José
PANAMA
Panamá
Gulf of Panama
G. of Darién
CUBA
Havana
BAHAMAS
Turks & Caicos Is. (U.K.)
JAMAICA
Kingston
HAITI
Port-au-Prince
DOMINICAN REP.
PUERTO RICO (U.S.A.)
San Juan
Virgin Is. (U.K.)
ST. KITTS NEVIS
ANTIGUA & BARBUDA
GUADELOUPE (Fr.)
Basse-Terre
DOMINICA
MARTINIQUE (Fr.)
Fort-de-France
ST. LUCIA
Castries
BARBADOS
Bridgetown
ST. VINCENT
Kingstown
GRENADA
St. George's
TRINIDAD & TOBAGO
Port of Spain
Aruba
Curaçao
C. de la Aguja
Barranquilla
Cartagena
Maracaibo
Barquisimeto
Valencia
Caracas
VENEZUELA
Ciudad Guayana
Orinoco
San Cristóbal
Cúcuta
Bucaramanga
COLOMBIA
Bogotá
Medellín
Cali
Magdalena
GUYANA
Georgetown
Essequibo
SURINAM
Paramaribo
FRENCH GUIANA
Cayenne
C. Orange
ECUADOR
Quito
Guayaquil
G. of Guayaquil
Galapagos Is. (Ecuador)
PERU
Iquitos
Napo
Putumayo
Marañón
Ucayali
Chiclayo
Trujillo
Chimbote
Callao
LIMA
BRAZIL
RORAIMA
Branco
AMAPÁ
Marajó I.
Belém
Amazon
Santarém
Manaus
PARÁ
Xingu
Tapajós
AMAZONAS
Japurá
Juruá
Purus
Madeira
ACRE
RONDÔNIA
Pôrto Velho
Madre de Dios
TOCANTINS
Tocantins
Araguaia
MARANHÃO
São Luís
Teresina
PIAUÍ
Parnaíba
CEARÁ
Fortaleza
RIO G. DO NORTE
Natal
C. de São Roque
PARAÍBA
Campina Grande
PERNAMBUCO
Recife
ALAGOAS
Maceió
SERGIPE
Aracaju

1 : 35 000 000

200   0   200   400   600   800 miles
400   0   400   800   1200 km

PACIFIC

OCEAN

Tropic of Capricorn

San Félix
(Chile)

San Ambrosio
(Chile)

Arch. de Juan Fernández
(Chile)

Iquique

Antofagasta

San Miguel
de Tucumán

Salta

Sucre

PARAGUAY

Asunción

Pilcomayo

Paraguay

MATO GROSSO
DO SUL

MINAS GERAIS

Belo
Horizonte

Ribeirão
Prêto

Juiz
de Fora

Campinas

SÃO PAULO

SÃO
PAULO

Curitiba

PARANÁ

Paraná

SANTA CATARINA

Uruguay

RIO GRANDE
DO SUL

Pôrto Alegre

Pelotas

URUGUAY

Montevideo

ESPÍRITO
SANTO

Vitória

Campos

Niterói
RIO DE
JANEIRO

SOUTH

ATLANTIC

OCEAN

Resistencia

Corrientes

Santa Fe

Salado

Córdoba

San Juan

Mendoza

A
R
G
E
N
T
I
N
A

Rosario

Paraná

BUENOS AIRES

La Plata

Río de la Plata

Mar del Plata

Bahía
Blanca

Viedma

Colorado

Negro

Chubut

Comodoro Rivadavia

Gulf of San Jorge

C. Horn

Tierra del Fuego

Magellan's Str.

Punta Arenas

Gulf of Penas

Puerto Montt

Valdivia

Concepción

Talca

SANTIAGO

Valparaíso
Viña del Mar

C
H
I
L
E

San Felix

FALKLAND IS.
(U.K.)

West Falkland

Stanley

East Falkland

South Georgia
(U.K.)

West from Greenwich

■ LIMA   Capital Cities

Projection: Lambert's Azimuthal Equal Area

F   G   H

1   2   3   4   5   6   7

SOUTH AMERICA-NORTH-WEST

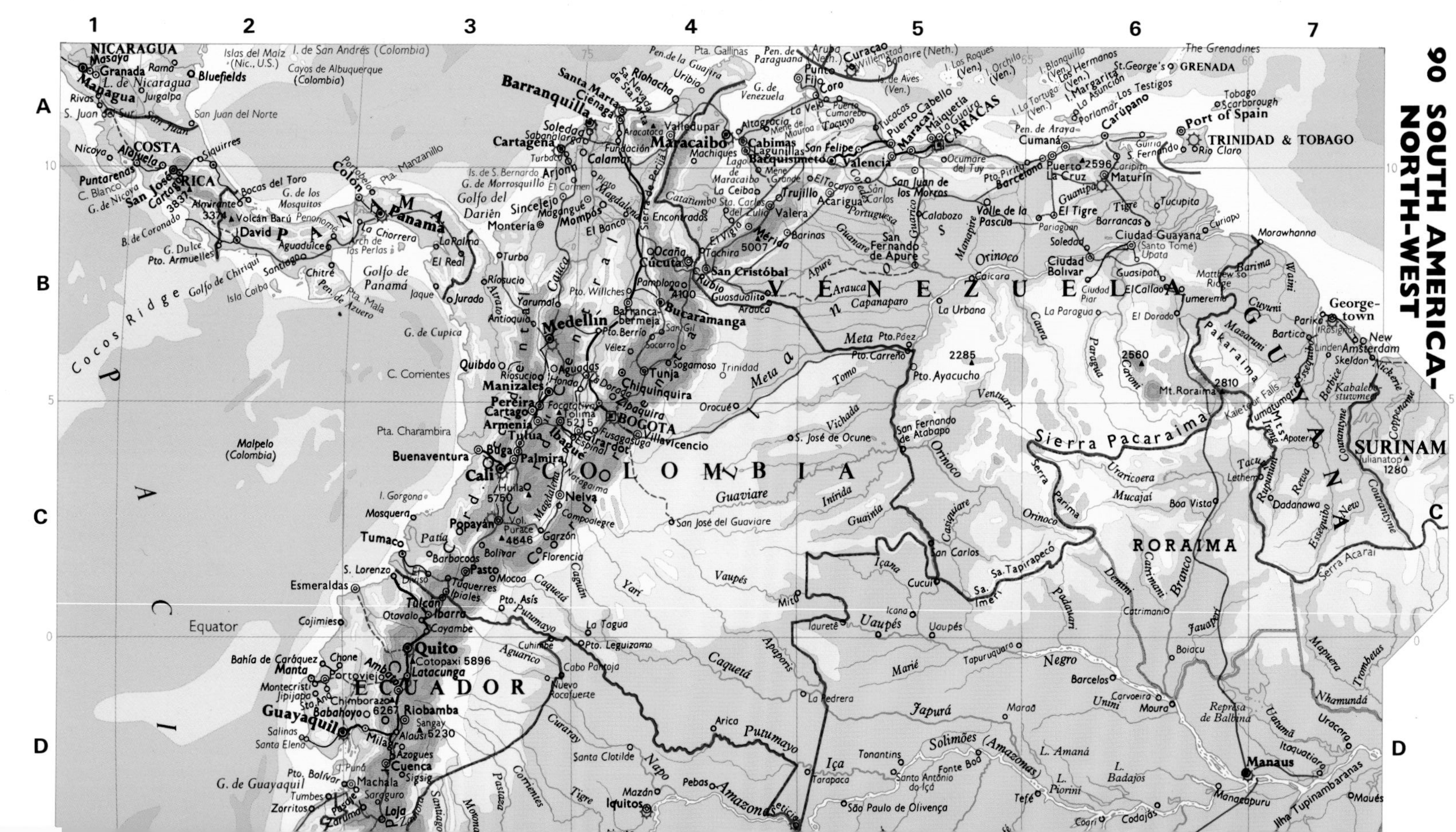

NICARAGUA
COSTA RICA
PANAMA
COLOMBIA
VENEZUELA
GUYANA
SURINAM
ECUADOR
RORAIMA
TRINIDAD & TOBAGO
GRENADA
Port of Spain
CARACAS
Maracaibo
Barranquilla
Cartagena
Medellín
BOGOTA
Cali
Quito
Guayaquil
Georgetown
Manaus
Iquitos
Managua
Colón
Panamá
Ciudad Bolívar
Ciudad Guayana
Sierra Pacaraima
Orinoco
Equator
Cocos Ridge

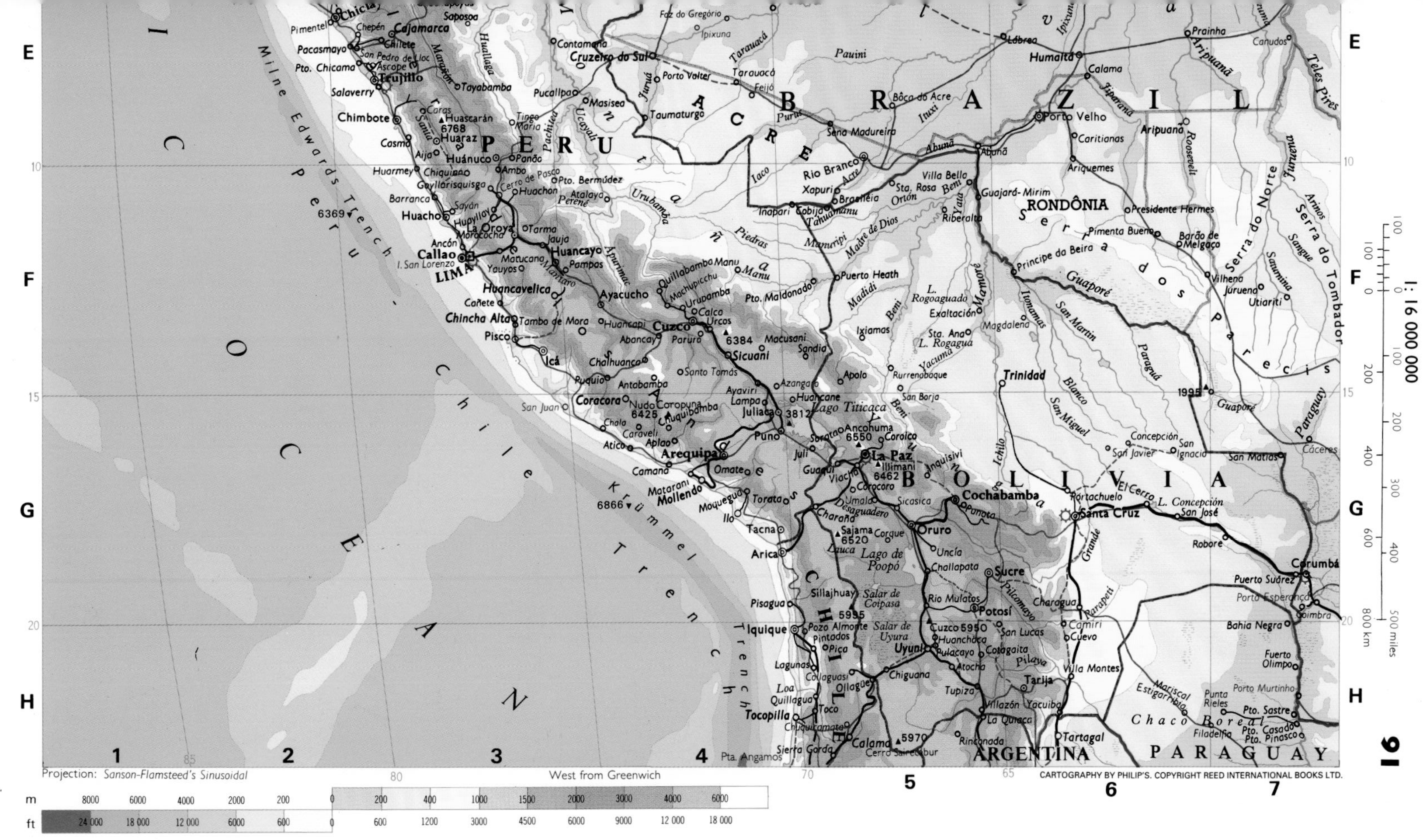
1: 16 000 000
PERU
BRAZIL
BOLIVIA
CHILE
ARGENTINA
PARAGUAY
ACRE
RONDÔNIA
PACIFIC OCEAN
Milne Edwards Trench
Peru - Chile Trench
Krümmel Trench
Serra dos Parecis
Serra do Norte
Serra do Tombador
Chaco Boreal
Lago Titicaca
Lago de Poopó
Salar de Coipasa
Salar de Uyura
LIMA
Callao
Cuzco
Arequipa
La Paz
Cochabamba
Sucre
Potosí
Oruro
Santa Cruz
Trinidad
Rio Branco
Porto Velho
Humaitá
Corumbá
Tacna
Arica
Iquique
Tocopilla
Calama
Trujillo
Chimbote
Huancayo
Ayacucho
Huancavelica
Pisco
Icá
Pucallpa
Cruzeiro do Sul
Projection: Sanson-Flamsteed's Sinusoidal
West from Greenwich

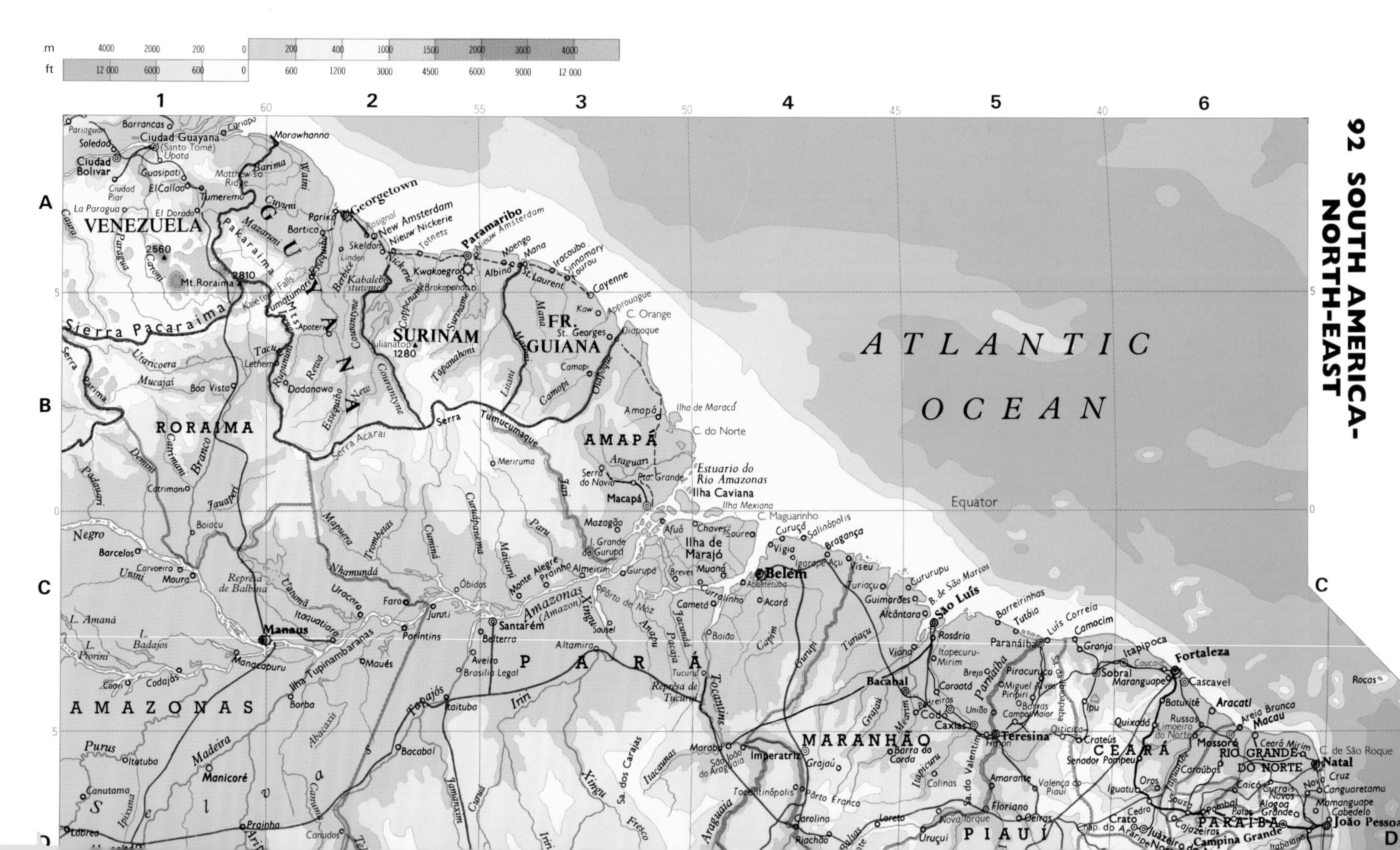
ATLANTIC OCEAN
Equator
VENEZUELA
GUYANA
SURINAM
FR. GUIANA
AMAPÁ
RORAIMA
AMAZONAS
PARÁ
MARANHÃO
PIAUÍ
CEARÁ
RIO GRANDE DO NORTE
PARAÍBA
Georgetown
Paramaribo
Cayenne
Macapá
Belém
São Luís
Fortaleza
Natal
João Pessoa
Teresina
Manaus
Santarém
Ciudad Bolívar
Ciudad Guayana
Ilha de Marajó
Estuario do Rio Amazonas
Ilha Caviana
Tocantins
Xingu
Amazonas
Mt. Roraima 2810
Sierra Pacaraima
Serra Acaraí
Tumucumaque
m
ft
4000
2000
200
0
400
1000
1500
3000
12 000
6000
600
1200
4500
9000

1 : 16 000 000

100 0 100 200 300 400 500 miles
100 0 200 400 600 800 km
B R A Z I L
BAHIA
TOCANTINS
MATO GROSSO
MATO GROSSO DO SUL
GOIÁS
MINAS GERAIS
ESPÍRITO SANTO
SÃO PAULO
PARANÁ
RONDÔNIA
SERGIPE
BOLIVIA
PARAGUAY
ARGENTINA
DIST. FED.
Brasília
Salvador
Belo Horizonte
Goiânia
Cuiabá
Campo Grande
Santa Cruz
Asunción
Curitiba
Santos
Niterói
RIO DE JANEIRO
Vitória
Aracaju
Uberlândia
Corumbá
Concepción
Resistencia
Corrientes
Posadas
Encarnación
Planalto do Mato Grosso
Serra do Roncador
Serra do Tombador
Serra Formosa
Serra dos Parecis
Serra do Espinhaço
Chaco Boreal
Chaco Central
Pilcomayo
Tropic of Capricorn
West from Greenwich
Projection: Sanson-Flamsteed's Sinusoidal

MATO GROSSO DO SUL
PARAGUAY
URUGUAY
RIO GRANDE DO SUL
SANTA CATARINA
SÃO PAULO
RIO DE JANEIRO
BUENOS AIRES
MONTEVIDEO
Asunción
Pôrto Alegre
Curitiba
Florianópolis
Santos
Campinas
Córdoba
Rosario
Santa Fe
Mendoza
SANTIAGO
Valparaíso
Viña del Mar
Antofagasta
San Miguel de Tucumán
Salta
Concepción
Río de la Plata
Peru — Chile Trench
Richard's Trench
Tropic of Capricorn
OCEAN

1 : 16 000 000

100   0   100   200   300   400   500 miles
100   0   200   400   600   800 km

CARTOGRAPHY BY PHILIP'S. COPYRIGHT REED INTERNATIONAL BOOKS LTD.

South Georgia
(Br.)

S O U T H   A T L

5830

FALKLAND ISLANDS
(ISLAS MALVINAS)
(Br.)
C. Dolphin
K. George   708   ▲ Stanley
West Falkland   700   Port Darwin
Weddell   Port Darwin
Jason Is.   East Falkland
C. Meredith   Falkland Sound

60 West from Greenwich 55

C. San
Diego I. de los Estados
(Staten I.)

Estrecho de Le Maire

Projection: Sanson-Flamsteed's Sinusoidal

m   ft
8000   24000
6000   18000
4000   12000
2000   6000
1000   3000
600   1800
200   600
0   0

6000   18 000
4000   12 000
3000   9000
2000   6000
1500   4500
1000   3000
600   1200
400   1200
200   600
0   0

1 : 35 000 000

200   0   200   400   600   800 miles

400   0   200   400   600   800   1200 km

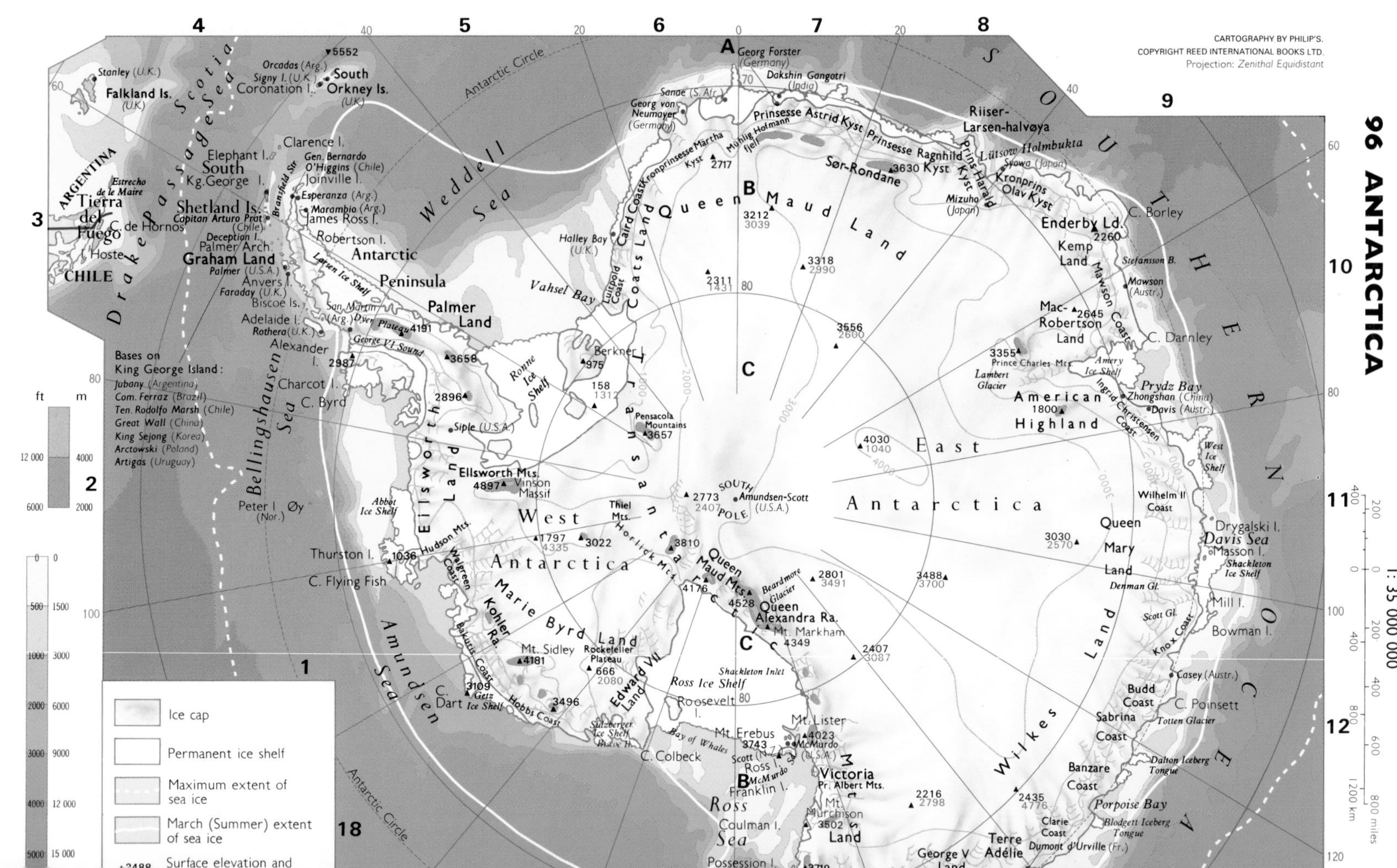

SOUTHERN OCEAN

Bases on King George Island:
Jubany (Argentina)
Com. Ferraz (Brazil)
Ten Rodolfo Marsh (Chile)
Great Wall (China)
King Sejong (Korea)
Arctowski (Poland)
Artigas (Uruguay)

Ice cap

Permanent ice shelf

Maximum extent of sea ice

March (Summer) extent of sea ice

Surface elevation and

m   ft
4000   12 000
2000   6000

0
500   1500
1000   3000
2000   6000
3000   9000
4000   12 000
    15 000

Index to Map Pages

The index contains the names of all principal places and features shown on the maps. Physical features composed of a proper name Erie) and a description (Lake) are positioned alphabetically by the proper ıame. The description is positioned after the proper name and is usually ıbbreviated:

Erie, L. **72** **C5**

Vhere a description forms part of a settlement or administrative name ıowever, it is always written in full and put in its true alphabetical ›osition:

Lake Charles **79** **D7**

ıames beginning St. are alphabetized under Saint, but Sankt, Sint, Sant, ›anta and San are all spelt in full and are alphabetized accordingly.

'he number in bold type which follows each name in the index refers to he number of the map page where that feature or place will be found. 'his is usually the largest scale at which the place or feature appears.

'he letter and figure which are in bold type immediately after the page ıumber give the grid square on the map page, within which the feature is ituated.

Rivers carry the symbol → after their names. A solid square ■ follows he name of a country while an open square □ refers to a first order ıdministrative area.

A

Coruña = La Coruña **18** **A1**
achen **14** **C4**
alborg = Ålborg **9** **G9**
alen **14** **D6**
arau **13** **C8**
are → **13** **C8**
arhus = Århus **9** **G10**
ba **55** **G6**
bādān **47** **E7**
bādeh **44** **D3**
badla **54** **B4**
baetetuba ... **92** **C4**
bakan **30** **D7**
bancay **91** **F4**
barqū **44** **D3**
bashiri **32** **F12**
bay **29** **E8**
baya, L. **53** **G6**
bbay = Nîl el Azraq → ... **53** **E5**
bbeville **12** **A4**
bbieglassie .. **63** **A4**
bbot Ice Shelf **96** **B2**
bbottabad ... **42** **B8**
bd al Kūrī ... **49** **E5**
béché **53** **F3**
beokuta **55** **G5**
bercorn = Mbala **57** **F6**
bercorn **63** **A5**
berdeen, *Australia* **63** **B5**
berdeen, *U.K.* **10** **C5**
berdeen, *S. Dak., U.S.A.* **76** **C5**
Aberdeen, *Wash., U.S.A.* **80** **B2**
Aberystwyth .. **11** **E4**
Abidjan **55** **G4**
Abilene **78** **C4**
Abitibi L. **69** **D3**
Abkhaz Republic □ = Abkhazia □ . **25** **E5**
Abkhazia □ ... **25** **E5**
Abminga **62** **A1**
Åbo = Turku .. **9** **F12**
Abohar **42** **D9**
Abomey **55** **G5**
Abong-Mbang . **56** **D2**
Abou-Deïa **53** **F2**
Abri **52** **D5**
Abrolhos, Banka **93** **F6**
Abrud **17** **E6**
Absaroka Range **81** **C9**
Abū al Khaşīb . **47** **E6**
Abū 'Alī **47** **F7**
Abu 'Arīsh **49** **D3**
Abu Dhabi = Abū Ẓāby ... **44** **E3**
Abû Dis **53** **E5**
Abu Hamed ... **53** **E5**
Abū Kamāl **46** **D5**
Abû Madd, Ra's **47** **F4**
Abu Matariq .. **53** **F4**
Abu Rudeis ... **47** **E3**
Abu Tig **52** **C5**
Abû Zabad **53** **F4**
Abū Ẓāby **44** **E3**
Abuja **55** **G6**
Abukuma-Gawa → ... **33** **G12**
Abunã **91** **E5**
Abunã → **91** **E5**
Abut Hd. **65** **E4**
Abwong **53** **G5**
Acaponeta **84** **C3**
Acapulco **84** **D5**
Acarigua **90** **B5**
Accra **55** **G4**
Aceh □ **36** **D1**
Achalpur **43** **J10**
Achill I. **11** **E1**
Achinsk **30** **D7**
Acireale **21** **F5**
Acklins I. **86** **B5**
Aconcagua, Cerro **94** **C3**
Aconquija, Mt. . **94** **B3**
Açores, Is. dos = Azores ... **50** **C1**
Acraman, L. ... **62** **B2**
Acre = 'Akko .. **46** **D3**
Acre □ **91** **E4**
Acre → **91** **E5**
Ad Dahnā **47** **F7**
Ad Dammām .. **47** **F7**
Ad Dawhah ... **44** **E2**
Ad Dilam **47** **G6**
Ad Dīwānīyah . **47** **E6**
Ada **79** **B5**
Adaja → **18** **B3**
Adam **44** **F4**
Adamaoua, Massif de l' . **53** **G1**
Adamawa Highlands = Adamaoua, Massif de l' . **53** **G1**
Adamello, Mte. **20** **A3**
Adaminaby ... **63** **C4**
Adam's Bridge **43** **Q11**
Adams Mt. **80** **B3**
Adana **46** **C3**
Adapazarı **46** **B2**
Adarama **53** **E5**
Adare, C. **96** **B15**
Adaut **39** **F4**
Adavale **63** **A3**
Adda → **20** **B2**
Addis Ababa = Addis Abeba **53** **G6**
Addis Abeba .. **53** **G6**
Addis Alem ... **53** **G6**
Adelaide **62** **B2**
Adelaide I. **96** **A3**
Adelaide Pen. . **70** **B10**
Adélie, Terre .. **96** **A14**
Adélie Land = Adélie, Terre **96** **A14**
Aden = Al 'Adan **49** **E4**
Aden, G. of ... **49** **E4**
Adi **39** **E4**
Adi Ugri **53** **F6**
Adige → **20** **B4**
Adilabad **43** **K11**
Adirondack Mts. **73** **C8**
Admer **54** **D6**
Admiralty I. ... **71** **C6**
Admiralty Is. .. **64** **K9**
Ado-Ekiti **55** **G6**
Adonara **39** **F2**
Adoni **43** **M10**
Adour → **12** **E3**
Adra **18** **D4**
Adrano **21** **F5**
Adrar **54** **C4**
Adré **53** **F3**
Adrī **52** **C1**
Adriatic Sea ... **20** **C5**
Adua **39** **E3**

Adwa 53 F6
Adzhar Republic □ = Ajaria □ 25 E5
Ægean Sea ... 23 E5
Aerhtai Shan .. 34 B4
Afghanistan ■ . 45 C6
Afgoi 49 G3
'Afif → 47 G5
Afognak I. ... 71 C4
Afuá 92 C3
Afyonkarahisar 46 C2
Agadès = Agadez 55 E6
Agadez 55 E6
Agadir 54 B3
Agapa 30 B6
Agartala 41 F8
Agats 39 F5
Agboville 55 G4
Agde 13 E5
Agen 12 D4
Agra 42 F10
Agri → 21 D6
Ağrı Dağı 46 C6
Ağrı Karakose . 46 C5
Agrigento 21 F4
Agrinion 23 E3
Água Clara 93 G3
Agua Prieta ... 84 A3
Aguadas 90 B3
Aguadilla 87 C6
Aguarico → .. 90 D3
Aguas Blancas 94 A3
Aguascalientes 84 C4
Aguilas 19 D5
Agulhas, C. ... 58 E4
Agung 37 F5
Agusan → ... 38 C3
Ahaggar 54 D6
Ahar 46 C6
Ahipara B. ... 64 A5
Ahiri 43 K12
Ahmadabad ... 43 H8
Ahmadnagar .. 43 K9
Ahmadpur .. 42 E7
Ahmedabad = Ahmadabad . 43 H8
Ahmednagar = Ahmadnagar 43 K9
Ahväz 47 E7
Ahvenanmaa = Åland 9 F11
Aḥwar 49 E4
Aigues-Mortes . 13 E6
Aihui 35 A7
Aija 91 E3
Aiken 75 C7
Aimere 39 F2
Aimorés 93 F5
Ain Banaiyan . 44 F2
Aïn Beïda 54 A6
Aïn Ben Tili .. 54 C3
Aïn-Sefra 54 B4
Ainabo 49 F4
Aïr 55 E6
Aisne → 13 B5
Aiud 17 E6
Aix-en-Provence 13 E6
Aix-la-Chapelle = Aachen ... 14 C4
Aix-les-Bains . 13 D6
Aiyion 23 E4
Aizawl 41 F9
Ajaccio 13 F8
Ajanta Ra. ... 43 J9
Ajari Rep. = Ajaria □ 25 E5
Ajaria □ 25 E5

Ajdâbiyah 52 B3
Ajka 16 E3
'Ajmān 44 E3
Ajmer 42 F9
Ajo, C. de 18 A4
Akaroa 65 E5
Akashi 32 B4
Akelamo 39 D3
Aketi 56 D4
Akharnaí 23 E4
Akhelóös → .. 23 E3
Akhisar 23 E6
Akhmîm 52 C5
Akimiski I. 69 C2
Akita 33 G12
Akjoujt 55 E2
'Akko 46 D3
Akkol 29 E8
Aklavik 70 B6
Akmolinsk = Aqmola 29 D8
Akobo → 53 G5
Akola 43 J10
Akordat 53 E6
Akpatok I. 68 B4
Akreïjit 55 E3
Akron 72 D5
Aksai Chin ... 42 B11
Aksaray 46 C3
Aksarka 28 C7
Akşehir 46 C2
Aksu 34 B3
Aksum 53 F6
Aktogay 29 E8
Aktsyabrski ... 17 B9
Aktyubinsk = Aqtöbe 29 D6
Aku 55 G6
Akure 55 G6
Akyab = Sittwe 41 G9
Al 'Adan 49 E4
Al Aḥsā 47 F7
Al Amādīyah .. 46 C5
Al Amārah 47 E6
Al 'Aqabah ... 47 E3
Al 'Aramah ... 47 F6
Al Ashkhara ... 45 F4
Al Badi' 47 G6
Al Başrah 47 E6
Al Bayḍā 52 B3
Al Bu'ayrāt al Ḥasūn 52 B2
Al Fallūjah ... 46 D5
Al Fāw 47 E7
Al Fujayrah .. 44 E4
Al Hābah 47 F6
Al Haddār ... 47 G6
Al Hāmad 47 E4
Al Hamar 47 G6
Al Hamrā' 47 F4
Al Harīq 47 G6
Al Hasakah ... 46 C5
Al Hawrah ... 49 E4
Al Hayy 47 D6
Al Ḥijāz 47 F4
Al Hillah, Iraq . 47 D6
Al Hillah, Si. Arabia ... 47 G6
Al Hindīyah ... 47 D6
Al Hoceïma ... 54 A4
Al Hudaydah .. 49 E3
Al Hufūf 47 F7
Al Hulwah ... 47 G6
Al Ittihad = Madīnat ash Sha'b ... 49 E3
Al Jāfūrah ... 47 F7
Al Jaghbūb ... 52 C3
Al Jahrah 47 E6

Al Jalāmīd 47 E4
Al Jawf, Libya . 52 D3
Al Jawf, Si. Arabia ... 47 E4
Al Jazirah, Iraq 46 D5
Al Jazirah, Libya 52 C3
Al Jubayl 47 F7
Al Jubaylah ... 47 F6
Al Junaynah .. 53 F3
Al Khābūra .. 44 F4
Al Khalīl 47 E3
Al Kharfah ... 47 G6
Al Kharj 47 F6
Al Khasab 44 E4
Al Kufrah 52 D3
Al Kūt 47 D6
Al Kuwayt ... 47 E7
Al Lādhiqīyah . 46 D3
Al Luhayyah .. 49 D3
Al Madīnah ... 47 F4
Al Majma'ah .. 47 F6
Al Manāmah .. 44 E2
Al Marj 52 B3
Al Mawṣil ... 46 C5
Al Midhnab .. 47 F6
Al Mish'āb 47 E7
Al Mubarraz ... 47 F7
Al Muharraq .. 44 E2
Al Mukallā ... 49 E4
Al Mukhā 49 E3
Al Musayyib . 47 D6
Al Muwayliḥ .. 47 F3
Al Qadīmah ... 47 G4
Al Qā'iyah ... 47 F5
Al Qāmishli ... 46 C5
Al Qaşabát ... 52 B1
Al Qaşim 47 F5
Al Qaţif 47 F7
Al Qaţrūn ... 52 D2
Al Qayşūmah . 47 E6
Al Quaisūmah . 47 E6
Al Quds = Jerusalem ... 47 E3
Al Qurayyāt ... 45 F4
Al Qurnah 47 E6
Al 'Ulā 47 F4
Al Uqaylah ash Sharqīgah . 52 B2
Al Uqayr 47 F7
Al 'Uthmānīyah 47 F7
Al 'Uwaynid .. 47 F6
Al 'Uwayqīlah . 47 E5
Al 'Uyūn 47 F5
Al Wakrah 44 E2
Al Wari'āh 47 F6
Al Yamāmah . 47 F6
Alabama □ ... 74 C4
Alabama → .. 74 D4
Alaçam Dağları 23 E7
Alagoa Grande 92 D6
Alagoas □ ... 93 D6
Alagoinhas ... 93 E6
Alajuela 86 D3
Alamosa 83 B10
Åland 9 F11
Alania = North Ossetia □ ... 25 E5
Alanya 46 C2
Alapayevsk ... 29 D7
Alaşehir 23 E7
Alaska □ 71 B4
Alaska, G. of .. 71 C5
Alaska Peninsula 71 C4
Alaska Range . 71 B4
Alataw Shankou 34 B3
Alatyr 24 C6
Alausi 90 D3
Alawoona 62 B3
Alba 20 B2

Alba-Iulia ..... 17 E
Albacete ...... 19 C
Albacutya, L. .. 62 C
Albania ■ ... 23 D
Albany, Australia .... 60 H
Albany, Ga., U.S.A. ...... 75 D
Albany, N.Y., U.S.A. ...... 73 C
Albany, Oreg., U.S.A. ...... 80 C
Albany → .... 69 C
Albardón ..... 94 C
Albemarle ... 75 B
Alberche → .. 18 C
Albert, L. .... 62 C
Albert L. ..... 57 D
Albert Nile → . 57 D
Albertville ... 13 D
Albi .... 12 E
Albina .... 92 A
Alborán ...... 18 E
Ålborg ...... 9 G
Alborz, Reshteh- ye Kūhhā-ye . 44 B
Albuquerque .. 83 C
Albury .... 63 C
Alcalá de Henares .... 18 B
Alcalá la Real . 18 D
Alcamo ...... 21 F
Alcaníz ...... 19 B
Alcântara .... 92 C
Alcántara, Embalse de . 18 C
Alcantarilla ... 19 D
Alcaraz, Sierra de .... 19 C
Alcaudete .... 18 D
Alcázar de San Juan .... 18 C
Alchevsk ..... 25 D
Alcira .... 19 C
Alcoy .... 19 C
Aldabra Is. ... 51 G
Aldan → 31 C1
Alderney .... 11 G
Aleg .... 55 E
Alegrete ..... 94 B
Aleisk .... 29 D
Aleksandriya = Oleksandriya 17 C
Aleksandrovskoye .... 29 C
Alemania .... 94 B
Alençon ..... 12 B
Aleppo = Ḩalab 46 C
Alès .... 13 D
Alessándria ... 20 B
Ålesund ..... 8 F
Aleutian Is. ... 71 C
Alexander Arch. 71 C
Alexander I. ... 96 A
Alexandra, Australia .... 63 C
Alexandra, N.Z. 65 F
Alexandria = El Iskandarîya .. 52 B
Alexandria, Canada .... 71 C
Alexandria, Romania .... 22 C
Alexandria, S. Africa .... 59 E
Alexandria, La., U.S.A. ...... 79 D
Alexandria, Va., U.S.A. ...... 73 E

lexandrina, L. 62 C2
lexandroúpolis 22 D5
lga 29 E6
lgarve 18 D1
lgeciras 18 D3
lgemesí 19 C5
lger 54 A5
lgeria ■ 54 C5
lghero 21 D2
lgiers = Alger 54 A5
lgoa B. 59 E5
lhucemas = Al Hoceïma 54 A4
lī al Gharbī 47 D6
lī Khēl 42 C6
liağa 23 E6
libo 53 G6
licante 19 C5
lice Springs 60 E5
ligarh 42 F11
līgūdarz 46 D7
lipur 42 E7
lipur Duar 41 D7
liwal North 59 E5
ljustrel 18 D1
lkmaar 14 B3
ll American Canal 82 D5
llahabad 40 E3
llanmyo 41 H10
llegheny → 73 D5
llegheny Plateau 73 F5
llentown 73 D8
lleppey 43 Q10
ller → 14 B5
llier → 13 C5
llora 63 A5
lma Ata = Almaty 29 E8
lmada 18 C1
lmadén 18 C3
lmansa 19 C5
lmanzor, Pico del Moro 18 B3
lmanzora → 19 D5
lmaty 29 E8
lmazán 19 B4
lmeirim 92 C3
lmelo 14 B4
lmendralejo 18 C2
lmería 19 D4
lmora 42 E11
lnwick 10 D6
lon 41 F10
lor 39 F2
lor Setar 36 C2
lps 14 E5
lsace 13 B7
lsask 71 C9
lsásua 19 A4
lta Gracia 94 C4
ltagracia 90 A4
ltai = Aerhtai Shan 34 B4
ltamira 92 C3
ltamura 21 D6
ltanbulag 35 A5
ltay 34 B3
ltea 19 C5
lto Araguaia 93 F3
lto Molocue 59 B7
lton 77 F9
lton Downs 62 A2
ltoona 73 D6
ltun Shan 34 C3
lùla 49 E5
lusi 39 F4
lvarado 85 D5
Alvear 94 B5
Alvie 62 C3
Alwar 42 F10
Alxa Zuoqi 35 C5
Am Dam 53 F3
Am-Timan 53 F3
Amâdi, *Sudan* 53 G5
Amadi, *Dem. Rep. of the Congo* 57 D5
Amadjuak 68 B3
Amadjuak L. 68 B3
Amagasaki 32 B4
Amakusa-Shotō 32 C2
Amaliás 23 F3
Amalner 43 J9
Amambay, Cordillera de 94 A5
Amangeldy 29 D7
Amapá 92 B3
Amapá □ 92 B3
Amarante 92 D5
Amargosa 93 E6
Amarillo 78 B3
Amaro, Mte. 20 C5
Amasra 46 B3
Amasya 46 B3
Amazon = Amazonas → 92 C3
Amazonas □ 90 D6
Amazonas → 92 C3
Ambala 42 D10
Ambalavao 59 J9
Ambam 56 D2
Ambanja 59 G9
Ambartsevo 29 D9
Ambato 90 D3
Ambatolampy 59 H9
Ambatondrazaka 59 H9
Amberg 15 D6
Ambergris Cay 85 D7
Amberley 65 E5
Ambikapur 40 F4
Ambilobé 59 G9
Ambo 91 F3
Amboise 12 C4
Ambon 39 E3
Ambositra 59 J9
Amboyna I. 36 C4
Ambriz 56 F2
Amby 63 A4
Amchitka I. 71 C1
Amderma 28 C7
Ameca 84 C4
Ameland 14 B3
American Highland 96 B10
American Samoa ■ 65 L13
Americus 75 C5
Amery 71 C10
Amery Ice Shelf 96 A10
Ames 77 D8
Amherst, *Burma* 41 J11
Amherst, *Canada* 69 D4
Amiata, Mte. 20 C3
Amiens 12 B5
Amirante Is. 26 K9
'Ammān 47 E3
Amorgós 23 F5
Amoy = Xiamen 35 D6
Ampanihy 59 J8
Ampenan 37 F5
Amper → 15 D6
Amravati 43 J10
Amreli 43 J7
Amritsar 42 D9
Amroha 42 E11
Amsterdam 14 B3
Amstetten 15 D8
Amudarya → 29 E6
Amundsen Gulf 70 A7
Amundsen Sea 96 B1
Amuntai 37 E5
Amur → 31 D12
Amurang 39 D2
Amuri Pass 65 E5
Amyderya = Amudarya → 29 E6
An Nafūd 47 E5
An Najaf 47 D6
An Nhon 36 B3
An Nu'ayrīyah 47 F7
Anabar → 30 B9
Anaconda 81 B7
Anadolu 46 C2
'Ānah 46 D5
Anaheim 82 D4
Anakapalle 40 J4
Analalava 59 G9
Anambas, Kepulauan 37 D3
Anambas Is. = Anambas, Kepulauan 37 D3
Anamur 46 C3
Anan 32 C4
Anantnag 42 C9
Ananyiv 17 E9
Anápolis 93 F4
Anār 44 D3
Anārak 44 C3
Anatolia = Anadolu 46 C2
Añatuya 94 B4
Anaye 53 E1
Anchorage 71 B5
Ancohuma, Nevada 91 G5
Ancón 91 F3
Ancona 20 C4
Ancud 95 E2
Ancud, G. de 95 E2
Andalgalá 94 B3
Andalucía □ 18 D3
Andalusia 74 D4
Andalusia □ = Andalucía □ 18 D3
Andaman Is. 27 H13
Andaman Sea 36 B1
Andara 58 B4
Anderson 72 D3
Anderson → 70 B7
Andes = Andes, Cord. de los 91 G4
Andes, Cord. de los 91 G4
Andhra Pradesh □ 43 L11
Andijon 29 E8
Andikíthira 23 G4
Andizhan = Andijon 29 E8
Andkhvoy 45 B6
Andoany 59 G9
Andorra ■ 19 A6
Andorra La Vella 19 A6
Andreanof Is. 71 C2
Andrewilla 62 A2
Ándria 20 D6
Andriba 59 H9
Andropov = Rybinsk 24 B4
Ándros 23 F5
Andros I. 86 B4
Andújar 18 C3
Andulo 56 G3
Anécho 55 G5
Aneto, Pico de 19 A6
Angamos, Punta 94 A2
Ang'angxi 35 B7
Angara → 30 D7
Angarsk 30 D8
Angaston 62 B2
Ånge 8 F11
Angeles 38 A2
Angellala 63 A4
Ångermanälven → 8 F11
Angers 12 C3
Anglesey 11 E4
Ango 57 D5
Angola ■ 58 A3
Angoulême 12 D4
Angoumois 12 D4
Angra dos Reis 94 A8
Angren 29 E8
Anguilla ■ 87 C7
Anhui □ 35 C6
Anhwei □ = Anhui □ 35 C6
Anjidiv I. 43 M9
Anjou 12 C3
Anjozorobe 59 H9
Anju 35 C7
Anka 55 F6
Ankang 35 C5
Ankara 46 C3
Ankazoabo 59 J8
Ankazobe 59 H9
Ankoro 57 F5
Ann Arbor 72 C4
Annaba 54 A6
Annan 11 D5
Annapolis 73 E7
Annecy 13 D7
Anning 34 D5
Anniston 74 C5
Annobón 51 G4
Annuello 62 B3
Anqing 35 C6
Ansbach 14 D6
Anshan 35 B7
Anshun 35 D5
Ansirabe 59 H9
Ansongo 55 E5
Ansudu 39 E5
Antabamba 91 F4
Antakya 46 C4
Antalaha 59 G10
Antalya 46 C2
Antalya Körfezi 46 C2
Antananarivo 59 H9
Antarctic Pen. 96 A4
Antarctica 96 C
Antequera 18 D3
Anti Atlas 54 C3
Antibes 13 E7
Anticosti, I. d' 69 D4
Antigua & Barbuda ■ 87 C7
Antilla 86 B4
Antioquia 90 B3
Antofagasta 94 A2
Antofagasta de la Sierra 94 B3
Antongila, Helodrano 59 H9
Antonina 94 B7
Antrim 11 D3
Antsalova 59 H8
Antsiranana 59 G9
Antsohihy 59 G9
Antwerp = Antwerpen 14 C3
Antwerpen 14 C3

Anupgarh 42 E8
Anvers =
Antwerpen .. 14 C3
Anvers I. 96 A3
Anxi 34 B4
Anxious B. 62 B1
Anyang 35 C6
Anzhero-
Sudzhensk .. 29 D9
Ánzio 20 D4
Aomori 33 F12
Aosta 20 B1
Aoudéras 55 E6
Aoulef el Arab . 54 C5
Apalachicola ─► 74 E5
Apaporis ─► .. 90 D5
Aparri 38 A2
Apeldoorn 14 B3
Apennines =
Appennini .. 20 B3
Apia 65 L13
Apiacás, Serra
dos 91 E7
Aplao 91 G4
Apo, Mt. 38 C3
Apollonia =
Marsá Susah 52 B3
Apolo 91 F5
Apoteri 90 C7
Appalachian
Mts. 73 F5
Appennini 20 B3
Appleton 72 B1
Approuague .. 92 B3
Aprília 20 D4
Apucarana 94 A6
Apure ─► 90 B5
Apurimac ─► . 91 F4
Aqabah = Al
'Aqabah 47 E3
'Aqabah, Khalīj
al 47 E3
Āqcheh 45 B6
Aqīq 53 E6
Aqmola 29 D8
Aqrah 46 C5
Aqtöbe 29 D6
Aquidauana ... 93 G2
Aquitain, Bassin 12 D3
Ar Rachidiya .. 54 B4
Ar Ramādī 46 D5
Ar Raqqah 46 D4
Ar Rass 47 F5
Ar Rifā'ī 47 E6
Ar Riyāḍ 47 F6
Ar Ruṭbah 46 D5
Ar Ruwayḍah . 47 G6
Ara 40 E5
'Arab, Bahr
el ─► 53 G4
Arab, Shatt
al ─► 47 E7
Arabian Desert
= Es Sahrā'
Esh Sharqîya 52 C5
Arabian Gulf =
Gulf, The .. 44 E2
Arabian Sea ... 26 H10
Araç 46 B3
Aracaju 93 E6
Aracataca 90 A4
Aracati 92 C6
Araçatuba ... 93 G3
Aracena 18 D2
Araçuaí 93 F5
Arad 16 E5
Arada 53 F3
Arafura Sea ... 39 F4
Aragón □ 19 B5

Aragón ─► ... 19 A5
Araguacema .. 92 D4
Araguaia ─► .. 92 D4
Araguari 93 F4
Araguari ─► .. 92 B4
Arak 54 C5
Arakan Coast .. 41 H9
Arakan Yoma . 41 H10
Araks = Aras,
Rūd-e ─► ... 46 B7
Aral 29 E7
Aral Sea 29 E6
Aral Tengizi =
Aral Sea ... 29 E6
Aralsk = Aral .. 29 E7
Aralskoye More
= Aral Sea .. 29 E6
Aran I. 10 D2
Aran Is. 11 E2
Aranda de
Duero 18 B4
Aranjuez 18 B4
Aranos 58 C3
Araouane 55 E4
Arapgir 46 C4
Arapiraca 93 D6
Arapongas 94 A6
Araranguá 94 B7
Araraquara .. 93 G4
Ararat 62 C3
Ararat, Mt. =
Ağrı Dağı .. 46 C6
Araripe,
Chapada do . 92 D6
Aras, Rūd-e ─► 46 B7
Arauca 90 B4
Arauca ─► 90 B5
Arauco 94 D2
Araxá 93 F4
Araya, Pen. de . 90 A6
Arbatax 21 E2
Arbīl 46 C6
Arbroath 10 C5
Arcachon 12 D3
Archangel =
Arkhangelsk . 28 C5
Arcila = Asilah 54 A3
Arckaringa ... 62 A1
Arckaringa
Cr. ─► 62 A2
Arcos de la
Frontera 18 D3
Arcot 43 N11
Arcoverde 92 D6
Arctic Bay 68 A2
Arctic Red River 70 B6
Arda ─► 22 D6
Ardabīl 46 C7
Ardahan 46 B5
Ardakān =
Sepīdān 44 D3
Ardenne 14 D3
Ardennes =
Ardenne 14 D3
Ardestān 44 C3
Ardlethan 63 B4
Ardmore 78 B5
Ardrossan 62 B2
Arecibo 87 C6
Areia Branca .. 92 C6
Arendal 9 G9
Arequipa 91 G4
Arero 53 H6
Arévalo 18 B3
Arezzo 20 C3
Argamakmur . 37 E2
Arganda 18 B4
Argentan 12 B3
Argentário, Mte. 20 C3

Argentina ■ .. 94 D3
Argentina Is. .. 96 A3
Argentino, L. .. 95 G2
Argeş ─► 22 B6
Arghandab ─► . 42 D4
Argo 53 E5
Argolikós
Kólpos 23 F4
Árgos 23 F4
Argostólion ... 23 E3
Argungu 55 F5
Århus 9 G10
Arica, Chile ... 91 G4
Arica, Colombia 90 D4
Aridh 47 F6
Arinos ─► 91 F7
Aripuanã 91 E6
Aripuanã ─► .. 90 E6
Ariquemes ... 91 E6
Arizona 94 D3
Arizona □ 83 C7
Arjona 90 A3
Arkalyk =
Arqalyk 29 D7
Arkansas □ ... 79 B7
Arkansas ─► .. 79 C8
Arkansas City . 78 A5
Arkhangelsk .. 28 C5
Arklow 11 E3
Arkticheskiy,
Mys 30 A7
Arlanzón ─► . 18 A3
Arlberg P. 14 E6
Arles 13 E6
Arlington, Va.,
U.S.A. 73 E7
Arlington,
Wash., U.S.A. 80 A2
Arlon 14 D3
Armagh 11 D3
Armavir 25 D5
Armenia 90 C3
Armenia ■ ... 25 E5
Armidale 63 B5
Armstrong ... 69 C2
Arnaud ─► ... 68 B3
Arnauti, C. ... 46 D3
Arnhem 14 C3
Arnhem, C. ... 60 C6
Arnhem Land . 60 C5
Arno ─► 20 C3
Arno Bay 62 B2
Arnsberg 14 C5
Aroab 58 D3
Arqalyk 29 D7
Arrabury 62 A3
Arrah = Ara .. 40 E5
Arran 10 D4
Arras 13 A5
Arrecife 54 C2
Arrée, Mts. d' . 12 B2
Arrowtown ... 65 F3
Árta 23 E3
Arthur ─► 62 D3
Arthur's Pass . 65 E4
Artigas 94 C5
Artois 12 A5
Artsyz 17 E9
Artvin 46 B5
Aru, Kepulauan 39 F4
Aru Is. = Aru,
Kepulauan . 39 F4
Arua 57 D6
Aruanã 93 E3
Aruba ■ 87 D6
Arumpo 62 B3
Arunachal
Pradesh □ .. 41 C10
Arusha 57 E7

Aruwimi ─► ... 56 D4
Arviat 70 B10
Arxan 35 B6
Arys 29 E7
Arzamas 24 B5
Arzew 54 A4
'As Saffānīyah . 47 E7
As Samāwah .. 47 E6
As
Sulaymānīyah,
Iraq 46 D6
As
Sulaymānīyah,
Si. Arabia ... 47 F6
As Summān .. 47 F6
As Sūq 47 G5
As Suwaydā' . 46 D4
As Suwayh ... 45 F4
As Suwayrah . 47 D6
Asahigawa ... 32 F12
Asansol 40 F6
Ascension I. ... 51 G2
Aschaffenburg . 14 D5
Aschersleben . 15 C6
Áscoli Piceno .. 20 C4
Ascope 91 E3
Aseb 49 E3
Asela 53 G6
Asenovgrad .. 22 C5
Ash Shām,
Bādiyat 47 D4
Ash Shāmīyah . 47 E6
Ash Shāriqah . 44 E3
Ash Shaṭrah .. 47 E6
Ash Shaykh, J. 46 D3
Ash Shu'aybah 47 F6
Ash Shu'bah .. 47 E6
Ashburton ... 65 E4
Ashcroft 71 C7
Asheville 75 B6
Ashford,
Australia ... 63 A5
Ashford, U.K. .. 11 F7
Ashgabat 29 F6
Ashikaga 32 A6
Ashizuri-Zaki . 32 C3
Ashkhabad =
Ashgabat ... 29 F6
Ashmyany ... 17 A7
Ashqelon 47 E3
Ashtabula ... 72 D5
Ashuanipi, L. .. 69 C4
Asia, Kepulauan 39 D4
Asifabad 43 K11
Asike 39 F6
Asilah 54 A3
Asinara 20 D2
Asinara, G. dell' 20 D2
Asino 29 D9
Asipovichy ... 17 B9
'Asīr □ 48 D3
Asir, Ras 49 E5
Asmara =
Asmera 53 E6
Asmera 53 E6
Aspiring, Mt. .. 65 F3
Assam □ 41 D9
Assen 14 B4
Assini 55 G4
Assiniboia ... 71 D9
Assiniboine ─► 71 D10
Assis 94 A6
Assisi 20 C5
Asti 20 B2
Astipálaia 23 F6
Astorga 18 A2
Astoria 80 B2
Astrakhan ... 25 D6
Astrakhan-Bazàr 25 F6

Asturias □ 18 A3
Asunción 94 B5
Aswân 52 D5
Aswân High
  Dam = Sadd
  el Aali 52 D5
Asyût 52 C5
At Ţafilah 47 E3
At Ţā'if 48 C3
Atacama,
  Desierto de . 94 A3
Atacama, Salar
  de 94 A3
Atakpamé 55 G5
Atalaya 91 F4
Atami 32 B6
Atapupu 39 F2
Atâr 54 D2
Atasu 29 E8
Atauro 39 F3
Atbara 53 E5
'Atbara → 53 E5
Atbasar 29 D7
Athabasca ... 71 C8
Athabasca → . 70 C8
Athabasca, L. .. 70 C8
Athens =
  Athínai 23 F4
Athens, Ala.,
  U.S.A. 74 B4
Athens, Ga.,
  U.S.A. 75 C6
Athínai 23 F4
Athlone 11 E3
Áthos 23 D5
Athy 11 E3
Ati 53 F2
Atico 91 G4
Atlanta 75 C5
Atlantic City .. 73 E8
Atlas Mts. =
  Haut Atlas .. 54 B3
Atrak =
  Atrek → 44 B3
Atrek → 44 B3
Attawapiskat → 69 C2
Attock 42 C8
Attopeu 36 B3
Attur 43 P11
Atuel → 94 D3
Atyraū 29 E6
Aubagne 13 E6
Aube → 13 B5
Auburn 74 C5
Auburn Ra. ... 63 A5
Aubusson 12 D5
Auch 12 E4
Auckland 64 B6
Aude → 13 E5
Augathella ... 63 A4
Augsburg 14 D6
Augusta, Italy . 21 F5
Augusta, Ga.,
  U.S.A. 75 C7
Augusta, Maine,
  U.S.A. 73 B11
Aunis 12 C3
Auponhia 39 E3
Aurangabad,
  Bihar, India . 40 E5
Aurangabad,
  Maharashtra,
  India 43 K9
Aurich 14 B4
Aurillac 12 D5
Aurora, Colo.,
  U.S.A. 76 F2
Aurora, Ill.,
  U.S.A. 72 D1

Aus 58 D3
Auschwitz =
  Oświęcim ... 16 C4
Austin, Minn.,
  U.S.A. 77 D8
Austin, Tex.,
  U.S.A. 78 D5
Austral Is. =
  Tubuai Is. ... 65 M16
Austral
  Seamount
  Chain 65 M16
Australia ■ ... 60 E6
Australian Alps 63 C4
Australian
  Capital
  Territory □ .. 63 C4
Austria ■ 15 E8
Autun 13 C6
Auvergne 13 D5
Auvergne, Mts.
  d' 13 D5
Auxerre 13 C5
Avallon 13 C5
Aveiro, Brazil .. 92 C2
Aveiro, Portugal 18 B1
Ãvej 46 D7
Avellaneda ... 94 C5
Avellino 21 D5
Aversa 21 D5
Avezzano 20 C4
Aviá Terai 94 B4
Aviemore 10 C5
Avignon 13 E6
Ávila 18 B3
Avilés 18 A3
Avoca → 62 C3
Avola 21 F5
Avranches 12 B3
'Awālī 44 E2
Awash 49 F3
Awatere → ... 65 D6
Awbārī 52 C1
Awjilah 52 C3
Axim 55 H4
Axiós → 23 D4
Ayabaca 90 D3
Ayabe 32 B4
Ayacucho,
  Argentina ... 94 D5
Ayacucho, Peru 91 F4
Ayaguz 29 E9
Ayamonte 18 D2
Ayaviri 91 F4
Āybak 45 B7
Aydın 23 F6
Ayers Rock ... 60 F5
Áyios Evstrátios 23 E5
Aylmer, L. 70 B8
Ayn Dār 47 F7
Ayn Zālah 46 C5
Ayr 10 D4
Aytos 22 C6
Ayu, Kepulauan 39 D4
Ayutla 84 D5
Ayvacık 23 E6
Ayvalık 23 E6
Aẕ Ẕahrān ... 47 F7
Az Zarqā 46 D4
Az-Zilfī 47 F6
Az Zubayr ... 47 E6
Az Zuwaytīnah 52 B3
Azamgarh ... 40 D4
Azärbayjan =
  Azerbaijan ■ 25 E6
Āzarbāyjān-e
  Gharbī □ ... 46 C6
Āzarbāyjān-e
  Sharqī □ 46 C6

Azare 55 F7
Azbine = Aïr .. 55 E6
Azerbaijan ■ .. 25 E6
Azerbaijchan =
  Azerbaijan ■ 25 E6
Azogues 90 D3
Azores 50 C1
Azov 25 D4
Azov, Sea of .. 25 D4
Azovskoye More
  = Azov, Sea
  of 25 D4
Azovy 28 C7
Azúa 87 C5
Azuaga 18 C3
Azuero, Pen. de 86 E3
Azul 94 D5

B

Ba Don 36 A3
Ba Ria 36 B3
Bab el Mandeb 49 E3
Baba Burnu ... 23 E6
Babadag 22 B7
Babadayhan .. 29 F7
Babaeski 22 D6
Babahoyo 90 D3
Babana 55 F5
Babar 39 F3
Babo 39 E4
Bābol 44 B3
Bābol Sar 44 B3
Baboua 56 C2
Babruysk 17 B9
Babura 55 F6
Babuyan Chan. 38 A2
Babylon 47 D6
Bacabal 92 C5
Bacan,
  Kepulauan .. 39 E3
Bacan, Pulau . 39 E3
Bacarra 38 A2
Bacău 17 E8
Bachelina 29 D7
Back → 70 B9
Backstairs
  Passage 62 C2
Bacolod 38 B2
Bad Ischl 15 E7
Bad Kissingen . 14 C6
Bad Lands ... 76 D3
Badagara 43 P9
Badajoz 18 C2
Badalona 19 B7
Badalzai 42 E4
Badampahar .. 40 F6
Badanah 47 E5
Badarinath ... 42 D11
Badas 36 D4
Badas,
  Kepulauan .. 37 D3
Baddo → 42 E4
Bade 39 F5
Baden 15 D9
Baden-Baden . 14 D5
Baden-
  Württemberg □
  .... 14 D5
Badgastein ... 15 E7
Bādghīsāt □ .. 42 B3
Badin 43 G6
Baduen 49 F4
Baena 18 D3
Baeza 18 D4
Bafatá 55 F2

Baffin B. 68 A4
Baffin I. 68 B3
Bafia 56 D2
Bafing → 55 F2
Bafoulabé 55 F2
Bäfq 44 D3
Bafra 46 B3
Bäft 44 D4
Bafwasende .. 57 D5
Bagamoyo ... 57 F7
Baganga 38 C3
Bagansiapiapi . 37 D2
Bagdarin 30 D9
Bagé 94 C6
Baghdād 46 D6
Bagheria 21 E4
Baghlān 42 A6
Baghlān □ ... 45 C7
Baguio 38 A2
Bahamas ■ ... 86 A4
Baharampur .. 40 E7
Bahawalpur .. 42 E7
Bahía =
  Salvador ... 93 E6
Bahía □ 93 E5
Bahía Blanca .. 94 D4
Bahía de
  Caráquez ... 90 D2
Bahía Laura .. 95 F3
Bahía Negra .. 91 H7
Bahr Aouk → . 56 C3
Bahr
  Salamat → . 53 G2
Bahraich 40 D3
Bahrain ■ 44 E2
Baia Mare ... 17 E6
Baïbokoum ... 53 G2
Baidoa 49 G3
Baie Comeau . 69 D4
Ba'ījī 46 D5
Baikal, L. =
  Baykal, Oz. .. 30 D8
Baile Atha Cliath
  = Dublin ... 11 E3
Băileşti 22 B4
Bailundo 58 A3
Bā'ir 47 E4
Baird Mts. ... 71 B3
Bairnsdale ... 63 C4
Baitadi 40 C3
Baiyin 35 C5
Baja 16 E4
Baja, Pta. 84 B1
Baja California . 84 A1
Bajimba, Mt. .. 63 A5
Bakala 56 C4
Bakchar 29 D9
Bakel 55 F2
Baker, L. 70 B10
Baker I. 64 J13
Baker Lake .. 70 B10
Baker Mt. ... 80 A3
Baker's Dozen
  Is. 69 C3
Bakersfield ... 82 C3
Bäkhtarān ... 46 D6
Bakı 25 E6
Bakony Forest =
  Bakony
  Hegyseg 16 E3
Bakony Hegyseg 16 E3
Bakouma 56 C4
Baku = Bakı .. 25 E6
Bakutis Coast . 96 B1
Baky = Bakı .. 25 E6
Balabac I. ... 36 C5
Balabac Str. ... 36 C5
Balabalangan,
  Kepulauan .. 37 E5

Balaghat Ra. 43 K10
Balaguer 19 B6
Balaklava, *Australia* 62 B2
Balaklava, *Ukraine* 25 E3
Balakovo 24 C6
Balashov 24 C5
Balasore = Baleshwar 40 G6
Balaton 16 E3
Balbina, Reprêsa de 90 D7
Balchik 22 C7
Balclutha 65 G3
Baleares, Is. 19 C7
Balearic Is. = Baleares, Is. 19 C7
Baler 38 A2
Baleshwar 40 G6
Bali, *Cameroon* 55 G7
Bali, *Indonesia* 37 F5
Bali □ 37 F5
Balikeşir 23 E6
Balikpapan 37 E5
Balimbing 38 C1
Balipara 41 D9
Baliza 93 F3
Balkan Mts. = Stara Planina 22 C4
Balkh 45 B6
Balkhash = Balqash 29 E8
Balkhash, Ozero = Balqash Köl 29 E8
Balla 41 E8
Ballarat 62 C3
Ballater 10 C5
Ballina, *Australia* 63 A5
Ballina, *Ireland* 11 D2
Ballinasloe 11 E2
Ballymena 11 D3
Balmaceda 95 F2
Balmoral 62 C3
Balonne → 63 A4
Balqash 29 E8
Balqash Köl 29 E8
Balrampur 40 D4
Balranald 62 B3
Balsas → 84 D4
Balta 17 D9
Bălţi 17 E8
Baltic Sea 9 G11
Baltimore 73 E7
Baluchistan □ 42 F4
Balya 23 E6
Bam 44 D4
Bama 53 F1
Bamako 55 F3
Bamba 55 E4
Bambari 56 C4
Bamberg 14 D6
Bambili 57 D5
Bamenda 55 G7
Bāmīān □ 42 B5
Bampūr 45 E5
Ban Don = Surat Thani 36 C1
Ban Mê Thuôt = Buon Me Thuot 36 B3
Banaba 64 K11
Banalia 57 D5
Banam 36 B3
Banamba 55 F3
Bananal, I. do 93 E3
Banaras = Varanasi 40 E4
Band-e Torkestān 45 C6
Banda, Kepulauan 39 E3
Banda Aceh 36 C1
Banda Banda, Mt. 63 B5
Banda Elat 39 F4
Banda Is. = Banda, Kepulauan 39 E3
Banda Sea 39 F3
Bandanaira 39 E3
Bandar = Machilipatnam 40 J3
Bandār 'Abbās 44 E4
Bandar-e Anzalī 46 C7
Bandar-e Bushehr = Būshehr 44 D2
Bandar-e Chārak 44 E3
Bandar-e Deylam 47 E7
Bandar-e Khomeyni 47 E7
Bandar-e Lengeh 44 E3
Bandar-e Ma'shur 47 E7
Bandar-e Nakhīlū 44 E3
Bandar-e Rīg 44 D2
Bandar-e Torkeman 44 B3
Bandar Maharani = Muar 37 D2
Bandar Penggaram = Batu Pahat 37 D2
Bandar Seri Begawan 36 D5
Bandawe 59 A6
Bandeira, Pico da 93 G5
Bandera 94 B4
Bandiagara 55 F4
Bandırma 23 D7
Bandon 11 F2
Bandundu 56 E3
Bandung 37 F3
Banff, *Canada* 71 C8
Banff, *U.K.* 10 C5
Banfora 55 F4
Bang Saphan 36 B1
Bangalore 43 N10
Bangassou 56 D4
Banggai, Kepulauan 39 E2
Banggi, P. 36 C5
Banghāzī 52 B3
Bangka, P., *Sulawesi, Indonesia* 39 D3
Bangka, P., *Sumatera, Indonesia* 37 E3
Bangka, Selat 37 E3
Bangkinang 37 D2
Bangko 37 E2
Bangkok 36 B2
Bangladesh ■ 41 E7
Bangong Co 42 B11
Bangor, *Down, U.K.* 11 D4
Bangor, *Gwynedd, U.K.* 11 E4
Bangor, *U.S.A.* 73 B11
Bangued 38 A2
Bangui 56 D3
Bangweulu, L. 57 G6
Bani 87 C5
Banī Walīd 52 B1
Banīnah 52 B3
Bāniyās 46 D3
Banja Luka 20 B6
Banjarmasin 37 E4
Banjul 55 F1
Bankipore 40 E5
Banks I. 70 A7
Banks Pen. 65 E5
Banks Str. 62 D4
Bankura 40 F6
Banningville = Bandundu 56 E3
Bannu 42 C7
Banská Bystrica 16 D4
Banswara 43 H9
Bantry 11 F2
Banu 42 B6
Banyak, Kepulauan 37 D1
Banyo 55 G7
Banzare Coast 96 A13
Banzyville = Mobayi 56 D4
Baoding 35 C6
Baoji 35 C5
Baoshan 34 D4
Baotou 35 B6
Bapatla 40 K3
Ba'qūbah 46 D6
Bar, *Montenegro, Yug.* 22 C2
Bar, *Ukraine* 17 D8
Bar-le-Duc 13 B6
Barabai 37 E5
Barabinsk 29 D8
Baracaldo 19 A4
Baracoa 86 B5
Barahona 87 C5
Barail Range 41 E9
Barakhola 41 E9
Barakpur 41 F7
Barakula 63 A5
Baramula 42 B9
Baran 43 G10
Baranavichy 17 B8
Baranof I. 71 C6
Barão de Melgaço 91 F6
Barapasi 39 E5
Barat Daya, Kepulauan 39 F3
Barbacena 93 G5
Barbacoas 90 C3
Barbados ■ 87 D8
Barbastro 19 A6
Barberton 59 D6
Barcellona Pozzo di Gotto 21 E5
Barcelona, *Spain* 19 B7
Barcelona, *Venezuela* 90 A6
Barcelos 90 D6
Bardai 52 D2
Barddhaman 40 F6
Bardejov 16 D5
Bardera 49 G3
Bardi, Ra's 47 F4
Bardīyah 52 B4
Bareilly 42 E11
Barentu 53 E6
Barfleur, Pte. de 12 B3
Barga 34 C3
Bargal 49 E5
Barhi 40 E5
Bari 20 D6
Bari Doab 42 D8
Barīm 49 E3
Barinas 90 B4
Baring, C. 70 B8
Bârîs 52 D5
Barisal 41 F8
Barisan, Bukit 37 E2
Barito → 37 E4
Barkly Tableland 60 D6
Barlee, L. 60 F2
Barletta 20 D6
Barmedman 63 B4
Barmer 42 G7
Barmera 62 B3
Barnato 63 B4
Barnaul 29 D9
Barnsley 11 E6
Barnstaple 11 F4
Baro 55 G6
Baroda = Vadodara 43 H8
Barpeta 41 D8
Barquísimeto 90 A5
Barra, *Brazil* 93 E5
Barra, *U.K.* 10 C3
Barra do Corda 92 D4
Barra do Piraí 93 G5
Barra Falsa, Pta. da 59 C7
Barraba 63 B5
Barrackpur = Barakpur 41 F7
Barraigh = Barra 10 C3
Barranca, *Lima, Peru* 91 F3
Barranca, *Loreto, Peru* 90 D3
Barrancabermeja 90 B4
Barrancas 90 B6
Barrancos 18 C2
Barranqueras 94 B5
Barranquilla 90 A4
Barras 92 C5
Barreiras 93 E5
Barreirinhas 92 C5
Barreiro 18 C1
Barreiros 92 D6
Barretos 93 G4
Barrier Ra. 62 B3
Barrington Tops 63 B5
Barringun 63 A4
Barrow 71 A4
Barrow-in-Furness 11 D5
Barry 11 F5
Barsi 43 K9
Barsoi 40 E6
Barstow 82 C4
Bartica 90 B7
Bartin 46 B3
Bartle Frere 61 D8
Bartlesville 79 A6
Barysaw 17 A9
Bāsa'idū 44 E3
Basankusa 56 D3
Basarabeasca 17 E9
Basel 13 C7
Bashi Channel 35 D7
Bashkir Republic = Bashkortostan □ 29 D6
Bashkortostan □ 29 D6
Basilan 38 C2
Basilan Str. 38 C2
Basildon 11 F7
Basim = Washim 43 J10

Basingstoke ...	11	F6
Basle = Basel .	13	C7
Basoka	56	D4
Basongo	56	E4
Basque Provinces = País Vasco □	19	A4
Basra = Al Başrah	47	E6
Bass Str.	61	H8
Bassano	71	C8
Bassano del Grappa ...	20	B3
Bassas da India	59	C7
Bassein	41	J10
Basseterre	87	C7
Bassikounou ..	55	E3
Bastak	44	E3
Bastar	40	H3
Basti	40	D4
Bastia	13	E8
Bastogne	14	C3
Bata	56	D1
Bataan	38	B2
Batabanó	86	B3
Batabanó, G. de	86	B3
Batac	38	A2
Batagoy	31	C11
Batamay	31	C10
Batang	34	C4
Batangafo	56	C3
Batangas	38	B2
Batanta	39	E4
Bateman's B. .	63	C5
Batemans Bay .	63	C5
Bath	11	F5
Bathurst, Australia	63	B4
Bathurst, Canada	69	D4
Bathurst, C. ..	70	A7
Bathurst Harb. .	62	D4
Bathurst Inlet ..	70	B9
Batinah	44	F4
Batlow	63	C4
Batman	46	C3
Batna	54	A6
Baton Rouge ..	79	D8
Batouri	56	D2
Battambang ...	36	B2
Battipáglia	21	D5
Battle Creek ..	72	C3
Battle Harbour .	69	C5
Battleford	71	C9
Batu	49	F2
Batu, Kepulauan	37	E1
Batu Is. = Batu, Kepulauan ..	37	E1
Batu Pahat	37	D2
Batuata	39	F2
Batumi	25	E5
Baturaja	37	E2
Baturité	92	C6
Bau	37	D4
Baubau	39	F2
Bauchi	55	F6
Bauer, C.	62	B1
Baukau	39	F3
Bauru	93	G4
Baús	93	F3
Bautzen	15	C8
Bavaria = Bayern □ ...	15	D6
Bawdwin	41	F11
Bawean	37	F4
Bawku	55	F4
Bawlake	41	H11
Bay, L. de	38	B2
Bay City	72	C4
Bay View	64	C7
Bayamo	86	B4
Bayan Har Shan	34	C4
Bayan Hot = Alxa Zuoqi ..	35	C5
Bayanaūyl	29	D8
Bayanhongor ..	35	B5
Bayázeh	44	C3
Baybay	38	B2
Bayburt	46	B5
Bayern □	15	D6
Bayeux	12	B3
Bayındır	23	E6
Baykal, Oz.	30	D8
Baykit	30	C7
Baykonur = Bayqongyr .	29	E7
Bayombong ...	38	A2
Bayonne	12	E3
Bayovar	91	E2
Bayqongyr	29	E7
Bayram-Ali = Bayramaly ..	29	F7
Bayramaly ...	29	F7
Bayramiç	23	E6
Bayreuth	15	D6
Bayrūt	46	D3
Baytown	79	E6
Baza	19	D4
Bazaruto, I. do .	59	C7
Beachport	62	C2
Beagle, Canal .	95	G3
Beardmore Glacier	96	C14
Béarn	12	E3
Beauce, Plaine de la	12	B4
Beaudesert ...	63	A5
Beaufort	36	C5
Beaufort Sea ..	66	B6
Beaufort West .	58	E4
Beaumont	79	D6
Beaune	13	C6
Beauvais	12	B5
Beauval	71	C9
Beaver	71	B5
Beaver →	71	C9
Beawar	42	F9
Bečej	22	B3
Béchar	54	B4
Bedford	11	E6
Beenleigh	63	A5
Be'er Sheva ..	47	E3
Beersheba = Be'er Sheva .	47	E3
Befale	56	D4
Bega	63	C4
Behbehān	47	E7
Behshahr	44	B3
Bei Jiang → ..	35	D6
Bei'an	35	B7
Beibei	35	D5
Beihai	35	D5
Beijing	35	C6
Beilpajah	63	B3
Beinn na Faoghla = Benbecula ..	10	C3
Beira	59	B6
Beirut = Bayrūt .	46	D3
Beitbridge	59	C6
Beja, Portugal .	18	C2
Béja, Tunisia .	54	A6
Bejaia	54	A6
Béjar	18	B3
Bejestān	44	C4
Békéscsaba ...	16	E5
Bela, India ...	40	E4
Bela, Pakistan .	42	F5
Bela Crkva	22	B3
Bela Vista	94	A5
Belarus ■	24	C2
Belau = Palau ■	38	C4
Belawan	37	D1
Belaya Tserkov = Bila Tserkva	17	D10
Belcher Is.	69	C3
Belém	92	C4
Belén	94	A5
Belet Uen	49	G4
Belev	24	C4
Belfast	11	D4
Belfort	13	C7
Belgaum	43	M9
Belgium ■	14	C3
Belgorod	24	C4
Belgorod-Dnestrovskiy = Bilhorod-Dnistrovskyy	25	D3
Belgrade = Beograd ...	22	B3
Beli Drim → ..	22	C3
Belinga	56	D2
Belinyu	37	E3
Beliton Is. = Belitung ...	37	E3
Belitung	37	E3
Belize ■	85	D7
Belize City ...	85	D7
Belkovskiy, Ostrov......	30	B11
Bell Bay	62	D4
Bell Peninsula .	68	B2
Bell Ville	94	C4
Bella Unión ..	94	C5
Bella Vista ...	94	B5
Bellary	43	M10
Bellata	63	A4
Belle-Ile	12	C2
Belle Isle	69	C5
Belle Isle, Str. of	69	C5
Belleville, Canada	69	D3
Belleville, U.S.A.	77	F10
Bellin = Kangirsuk ...	68	C4
Bellingen	63	B5
Bellingham ...	80	A2
Bellingshausen Sea	96	A2
Bellinzona ...	13	C8
Belluno	20	A4
Belmont	63	B5
Belmonte	93	F6
Belmopan	85	D7
Belo Horizonte .	93	F5
Belo-Tsiribihina	59	H8
Beloit	77	D10
Belokorovichi .	17	C9
Belomorsk	28	C4
Belonia	41	F8
Belorussia ■ = Belarus ■ ...	24	C2
Belovo	29	D9
Beloye, Ozero .	24	A4
Beloye More ..	28	C4
Belozersk	24	A4
Beltana	62	B2
Belterra	92	C3
Beltsy = Bălți .	17	E8
Belukha	29	E9
Beluran	36	C5
Belyy, Ostrov .	28	B8
Belyy Yar	29	D9
Bembéréke ...	55	F5
Bemidji	77	B7
Ben Gardane ..	52	B1
Ben Lomond, N.S.W., Australia	63	B5
Ben Lomond, Tas., Australia	62	D4
Ben Nevis	10	C4
Bena	55	F6
Bena Dibele ...	56	E4
Benagerie	62	B3
Benalla	63	C4
Benambra, Mt.	63	C4
Benares = Varanasi	40	E4
Benavente ...	18	A3
Benbecula ...	10	C3
Benbonyathe ..	62	B2
Bend	80	C3
Bender Beila .	49	F5
Bendery = Tighina	17	E9
Bendigo	63	C3
Benevento	20	D5
Bengal, Bay of .	41	J7
Bengbu	35	C6
Benghazi = Banghāzī ...	52	B3
Bengkalis	37	D2
Bengkulu	37	E2
Bengkulu □ ...	37	E2
Benguela	58	A2
Beni	57	D5
Beni →	91	F5
Beni Abbès ...	54	B4
Beni Mazâr ...	52	C5
Beni Mellal ...	54	B3
Beni Ounif	54	B4
Beni Suef	52	C5
Benidorm	19	C5
Benin ■	55	G5
Benin, Bight of	55	H5
Benin City	55	G6
Benjamin Constant	90	D4
Benoni	59	D5
Bent	44	E4
Benteng	39	F2
Benton Harbor	72	C2
Benue →	55	G6
Benxi	35	B7
Beo	38	D3
Beograd	22	B3
Beppu	32	C2
Berati	23	D2
Berau, Teluk ..	39	E4
Berber	53	E5
Berbera	49	E4
Berbérati	56	D3
Berbice → ...	90	B7
Berdichev = Berdychiv ...	17	D9
Berdsk	29	D9
Berdyansk	25	D4
Berdychiv	17	D9
Berebere	39	D3
Bereda	49	E5
Berehove	17	D6
Berekum	55	G4
Berestechko ..	17	C7
Bereza	17	B7
Berezhany	17	D7
Berezina = Byarezina →	17	B10
Berezniki	28	D6
Berezovo	28	C7
Berga	19	A6
Bergama	23	E6
Bérgamo	20	B2
Bergen	8	F9
Bergerac	12	D4

Berhala, Selat .	37	E2
Berhampore =		
Baharampur .	40	E7
Berhampur =		
Brahamapur .	40	H5
Bering Sea	71	C1
Bering Strait ..	71	B3
Berja	19	D4
Berkeley	80	G2
Berkner I.	96	B4
Berlin	15	B7
Bermejo →,		
Formosa,		
Argentina ...	94	B5
Bermejo →,		
San Juan,		
Argentina ...	94	C3
Bermuda ■ ...	67	F13
Bern	13	C7
Bernardo de		
Irigoyen	94	B6
Bernburg	15	C6
Berne = Bern .	13	C7
Bernina, Piz ..	13	C8
Beroroha	59	J9
Beroun	16	D2
Berrechid	54	B3
Berri	62	B3
Berry, Australia	63	B5
Berry, France ..	12	C5
Bershad	17	D9
Bertoua	56	D2
Berwick-upon-		
Tweed	10	D6
Besalampy	59	H8
Besançon	13	C7
Besar	37	E5
Besni	46	C4
Bessarabiya ...	17	E9
Bessarabka =		
Basarabeasca	17	E9
Bessemer	74	C4
Betanzos	18	A1
Bétaré Oya	56	C2
Bethanien	58	D3
Bethel	71	B3
Bethlehem,		
S. Africa	59	D5
Bethlehem,		
U.S.A.	73	D8
Béthune	13	A5
Bethungra	63	B4
Betioky	59	J8
Betroka	59	J9
Betsiamites ..	69	D4
Bettiah	40	D5
Betul	43	J10
Betung	37	D4
Beverley	11	E6
Beverly Hills ..	82	C3
Beyla	55	G3
Beyneu	29	E6
Beypazarı	46	B2
Beyşehir Gölü .	46	C2
Bezhitsa	24	C3
Béziers	13	E5
Bezwada =		
Vijayawada .	40	J3
Bhachau	43	H7
Bhadrakh	40	G6
Bhadravati	43	N9
Bhagalpur	40	E6
Bhakra Dam ..	42	D10
Bhamo	41	E11
Bhandara	43	J11
Bhanrer Ra. ...	43	H11
Bharat =		
India ■	43	J10
Bharatpur	42	F10
Bhatpara	41	F7
Bhaunagar =		
Bhavnagar ..	43	J8
Bhavnagar	43	J8
Bhawanipatna .	40	H3
Bhilsa = Vidisha	43	H10
Bhilwara	43	G9
Bhima →	43	L10
Bhimavaram ..	40	J3
Bhind	42	F11
Bhiwandi	43	K8
Bhiwani	42	E10
Bhola	41	F8
Bhopal	43	H10
Bhubaneshwar	40	G5
Bhuj	43	H6
Bhumiphol Dam		
= Phumiphon,		
Khuan	36	A1
Bhusaval	43	J9
Bhutan ■	41	D8
Biafra, B. of =		
Bonny, Bight		
of	56	D1
Biak	39	E5
Biała Podlaska .	17	B6
Białogard	16	A2
Białystok	17	B6
Biaro	39	D3
Biarritz	12	E3
Bibala	58	A2
Biberach	14	D5
Bibiani	55	G4
Bida	55	G6
Bidar	43	L10
Biddeford	73	C10
Bidon 5 = Poste		
Maurice		
Cortier	54	D5
Bié, Planalto de	58	A3
Biel	13	C7
Bielefeld	14	B5
Biella	20	B2
Bielsk Podlaski	17	B6
Bielsko-Biała ..	16	D4
Bien Hoa	36	B3
Bienne = Biel .	13	C7
Bienville, L. ...	69	C3
Big Horn Mts. =		
Bighorn Mts.	81	C10
Big Spring	78	C3
Big Trout L. ...	69	C2
Biğa	23	D6
Bigadiç	23	E7
Biggar	71	C9
Biggenden	63	A5
Bighorn → ...	81	B10
Bighorn Mts. ..	81	C10
Bihać	20	B5
Bihar	40	E5
Bihar □	40	E5
Bihor, Munții ..	17	E6
Bijagós,		
Arquipélago		
dos	55	F1
Bijapur,		
Karnataka,		
India	43	L9
Bijapur, Mad. P.,		
India	40	H3
Bījār	46	D6
Bijeljina	20	B7
Bijnor	42	E11
Bikaner	42	E8
Bikini Atoll ...	64	H11
Bila Tserkva ..	17	D10
Bilara	42	F8
Bilaspur	40	F4
Bilauk Taungdan	36	B1
Bilbao	19	A4
Bilbo = Bilbao .	19	A4
Bilecik	46	B2
Bilhorod-		
Dnistrovskyy	25	D3
Bilir	31	C11
Billings	81	C9
Billiton Is. =		
Belitung	37	E3
Bilma	53	E1
Biloxi	79	D9
Biltine	53	F3
Bima	39	F1
Bimbo	56	D3
Bina-Etawah ..	43	G11
Binalbagan ...	38	B2
Binalong	63	B4
Bīnālūd, Kūh-e	44	B4
Binatang	37	D4
Binda	63	A4
Bindle	63	A4
Bindura	59	B6
Bingara, N.S.W.,		
Australia ...	63	A5
Bingara,		
Queens.,		
Australia ...	63	A3
Bingham		
Canyon	81	E7
Binghamton ...	73	C8
Bingöl	46	C5
Binh Dinh = An		
Nhon	36	B3
Binh Son	36	A3
Binjai	37	D1
Binnaway	63	B4
Binongko	39	F2
Bintan	37	D2
Bintulu	37	D4
Bintuni	39	E4
Binzert = Bizerte	54	A6
Bioko	56	D1
Bir	43	K9
Bir Autrun	53	E4
Bir Mogrein ...	54	C2
Bîr Ungât	52	D5
Bira	39	E4
Birao	53	F3
Birchip	62	C3
Birecik	46	C4
Bireuen	36	C1
Bîrlad	17	E8
Bîrlad →	17	F8
Birmingham,		
U.K.	11	E6
Birmingham,		
U.S.A.	74	C4
Birmitrapur ...	40	F5
Birni Nkonni ..	55	F6
Birnin Kebbi ..	55	F5
Birr	11	E3
Birrie →	63	A4
Birsk	29	D6
Birur	43	N9
Bisa	39	E3
Biscay, B. of ..	12	D2
Biscoe Bay ...	96	B17
Biscoe Is.	96	A3
Bishkek	29	E8
Biskra	54	B6
Bislig	38	C3
Bismarck	76	B4
Bismarck Arch.	64	K9
Bissagos =		
Bijagós,		
Arquipélago		
dos	55	F1
Bissau	55	F1
Bistrița	17	E7
Bistriţa →	17	E8
Bitam	56	D2
Bitkine	53	F1
Bitlis	46	C5
Bitola	22	D3
Bitolj = Bitola .	22	D3
Bitter L. =		
Buheirat-		
Murrat-el-		
Kubra	52	B3
Bitterfontein ..	58	E2
Bitterroot Range	81	B6
Biu	53	F1
Biwa-Ko	32	B4
Biysk	29	D9
Bizerte	54	A6
Bjelovar	20	B6
Black Forest =		
Schwarzwald	14	D5
Black Hills	76	D3
Black Sea	25	E6
Black Volta →	55	G4
Blackball	65	E4
Blackburn	11	E5
Blackpool	11	E5
Blackwater → .	11	E3
Blagodarnoye =		
Blagodarnyy	25	D5
Blagodarnyy ..	25	D5
Blagoevgrad ..	22	C4
Blagoveshchensk		
....	31	D10
Blairmore	71	D7
Blanc, Mont ..	13	D7
Blanca, B.	95	D4
Blanca Peak ..	83	B10
Blanche, C. ...	62	B1
Blanche, L. ...	62	A2
Blanes	19	B7
Blantyre	59	B6
Blayney	63	B4
Blednaya, Gora	28	B8
Blenheim	65	D5
Blida	54	A5
Bligh Sound ..	65	F2
Blitta	55	G5
Blodgett Iceberg		
Tongue	96	A11
Bloemfontein ..	59	D5
Bloemhof	59	D5
Blois	12	C4
Bloomington,		
Ill., U.S.A. ...	77	E10
Bloomington,		
Ind., U.S.A. ..	72	E2
Blue Mts., Oreg.,		
U.S.A.	80	C4
Blue Mts., Pa.,		
U.S.A.	73	D7
Blue Nile = Nîl		
el Azraq → .	53	E5
Blue Ridge Mts.	75	A9
Bluefields	86	D3
Bluff	65	G2
Blumenau	94	B3
Bo	55	G2
Bo Duc	36	B3
Bo Hai	35	C6
Boa Vista	90	C6
Boatman	63	A4
Bobadah	63	B4
Bobbili	40	H4
Bobo-Dioulasso	55	F4
Bóbr →	16	B2
Bobraomby,		
Tanjon' i ...	59	G9
Bobruysk =		
Babruysk ...	17	B9
Bôca do Acre .	91	E5

Boca Raton ... 75 F7
Bocaiúva 93 F5
Bocanda 55 G4
Bocaranga 56 C3
Bochnia 16 D5
Bochum 14 C4
Boda 56 D3
Bodaybo 30 D9
Boden 8 E12
Bodensee 13 C8
Bodhan 43 K10
Bodø 8 E10
Bodrog → ... 16 D5
Bodrum 23 F6
Boende 56 E4
Boffa 55 F2
Bogalusa 79 D9
Bogan Gate ... 63 B4
Boggabilla ... 63 A5
Boggabri 63 B5
Bogo 38 B2
Bogong, Mt. .. 63 C4
Bogotá 90 C4
Bogotol 29 D9
Bogra 41 E7
Bogué 55 E2
Bohemian
  Forest =
  Böhmerwald 15 D7
Bohena Cr. → 63 B4
Böhmerwald .. 15 D7
Bohol 38 C2
Bohol Sea 38 C2
Bohotleh 49 F4
Boise 80 D5
Boise City 78 A2
Bojador C. 54 C2
Bojana → ... 22 D2
Bojnūrd 44 B4
Boké 55 F2
Bokhara → .. 63 A4
Bokoro 53 F2
Bokote 56 E4
Bokungu 56 E4
Bol 53 F1
Bolama 55 F1
Bolan Pass ... 42 E5
Bolbec 12 B4
Bole 34 B3
Bolekhiv 17 D6
Bolekhov =
  Bolekhiv ... 17 D6
Bolesławiec ... 16 C2
Bolgrad =
  Bolhrad 17 F9
Bolhrad 17 F9
Bolinao C. 38 A1
Bolívar,
  Argentina .. 94 D4
Bolívar,
  Colombia .. 90 C3
Bolivia ■ 91 G6
Bollon 63 A4
Bolobo 56 E3
Bologna 20 B3
Bologoye 24 B3
Bolomba 56 D3
Bolong 38 C2
Bolsena, L. di . 20 C3
Bolshereche .. 29 D8
Bolshevik,
  Ostrov 30 B8
Bolshoi Kavkas
  = Caucasus
  Mountains .. 25 E5
Bolshoy Atlym 28 C7
Bolshoy
  Begichev,
  Ostrov 30 B9

Bolshoy
  Lyakhovskiy,
  Ostrov 31 B12
Bolton 11 E5
Bolu 46 B2
Bolvadin 46 C2
Bolzano 20 A3
Bom Despacho 93 F4
Bom Jesus da
  Lapa 93 E5
Boma 56 F2
Bomaderry ... 63 B5
Bombala 63 C4
Bombay 43 K8
Bomboma 56 D3
Bomili 57 D5
Bomongo 56 D3
Bomu → 56 D4
Bon, C. 52 A1
Bonaire 87 D6
Bonang 63 C4
Bonavista 69 D5
Bondo 56 D4
Bondoukou ... 55 G4
Bone, Teluk .. 39 E2
Bonerate 39 F2
Bonerate,
  Kepulauan .. 39 F2
Bong Son =
  Hoai Nhon .. 36 B3
Bongandanga . 56 D4
Bongor 53 F2
Bonifacio 13 F8
Bonn 14 C4
Bonney, L. ... 62 C3
Bonoi 39 E5
Bontang 37 D5
Bonthain 39 F1
Bonthe 55 G2
Bontoc 38 A2
Boolaboolka L. 62 B3
Booligal 63 B3
Boonah 63 A5
Boorindal 63 B4
Boorowa 63 B4
Boothia, Gulf of 68 A2
Boothia Pen. .. 70 A10
Booué 56 E2
Bor,
  Serbia, Yug. . 22 B4
Bôr, Sudan ... 53 G5
Borama 49 F3
Borås 9 G10
Borāzjān 44 D2
Borba 90 D7
Borda, C. 62 C2
Bordeaux 12 D3
Bordertown ... 62 C3
Bordj Fly Ste.
  Marie 54 C4
Bordj-in-Eker .. 54 D6
Bordj Omar
  Driss 54 C6
Bordj-Tarat ... 54 C6
Borger 78 B3
Borisoglebsk .. 24 C5
Borisov =
  Barysaw 17 A9
Borja 90 D3
Borkou 53 E2
Borkum 14 B4
Borley, C. 96 A9
Borneo 37 D4
Bornholm 9 G11
Boromo 55 F4
Borongan 38 B3
Borovichi 24 B3
Borşa 17 E7

Borūjerd 46 D7
Boryslav 17 D6
Bosa 21 D2
Bosanska
  Gradiška 20 B6
Bosaso 49 E4
Boshan 35 C6
Boshrūyeh ... 44 C4
Bosna → ... 20 B7
Bosna i
  Hercegovina
  = Bosnia-
  Herzegovina ■ 20 B6
Bosnia-
  Herzegovina ■ 20 B6
Bosnik 39 E5
Bosobolo 56 D3
Bosporus =
  Karadeniz
  Boğazı 22 D7
Bossangoa 56 C3
Bossembélé ... 53 G2
Bosso 53 F1
Bosten Hu ... 34 B3
Boston, U.K. .. 11 E6
Boston, U.S.A. . 73 C10
Botany B. 63 B5
Bothnia, G. of . 8 F12
Bothwell 62 D4
Botletle → ... 58 C4
Botoşani 17 E8
Botswana ■ ... 58 C4
Botucatu 94 A7
Bou Djébéha .. 55 E4
Bou Izakarn .. 54 C3
Bouaké 55 G3
Bouar 56 C3
Bouârfa 54 B4
Bouca 56 C3
Bougie = Bejaia 54 A6
Bougouni 55 F3
Boulder 76 E2
Boulder Dam =
  Hoover Dam 82 B5
Boulogne-sur-
  Mer 12 A4
Boultoum 55 F7
Bouna 55 G4
Boundiali 55 G3
Bourbonnais .. 13 C5
Bourem 55 E4
Bourg-en-Bresse 13 C6
Bourg-St.-
  Maurice 13 D7
Bourges 12 C5
Bourgogne ... 13 C6
Bourke 63 B4
Bournemouth . 11 F6
Bousso 53 F2
Boutilimit 55 E2
Bowen Mts. ... 63 C4
Bowman I. 96 A12
Bowmans 62 B2
Bowral 63 B5
Bowraville ... 63 B5
Boyne → 11 E3
Boyni Qara ... 45 B6
Boz Dağları .. 23 E7
Bozburun 23 F7
Bozcaada 23 E6
Bozdoğan 23 F7
Bozeman 81 C8
Bozen =
  Bolzano 20 A3
Bozoum 56 C3
Bra 20 B1
Brač 20 C6
Bracciano, L. di 20 C4
Brach 52 C1

Bräcke 8 F11
Brad 17 E6
Bradenton ... 75 F6
Bradford 11 E6
Braemar 62 B2
Braga 18 B1
Bragança, Brazil 92 C4
Bragança,
  Portugal 18 B2
Brahamapur .. 40 H5
Brahmanbaria . 41 F8
Brahmani → .. 40 G6
Brahmaputra → 41 F7
Braidwood 63 C4
Brăila 17 F8
Branco → 90 D6
Brandenburg =
  Neubrandenburg
  .... 15 B7
Brandenburg .. 15 B7
Brandenburg □ 15 B7
Brandon 71 D10
Brandvlei 58 E4
Braniewo 16 A4
Bransfield Str. . 96 A4
Brantford 69 D2
Branxholme .. 62 C3
Brasiléia 91 F5
Brasília 93 F4
Braşov 17 F7
Brassey,
  Banjaran 36 D5
Bratislava 16 D3
Bratsk 30 D8
Braunau 15 D7
Braunschweig . 14 B6
Brava 49 G3
Bravo del Norte,
  R. → =
  Grande,
  Rio → 79 F5
Brawley 82 D5
Bray 11 E3
Bray, Pays de . 12 B4
Brazil ■ 93 E4
Brazos → 79 E6
Brazzaville ... 56 E3
Brčko 20 B7
Breaksea Sd. .. 65 F2
Bream B. 64 A6
Bream Hd. 64 A6
Brecon 11 F5
Breda 14 C3
Bredasdorp ... 58 E4
Bredbo 63 C4
Bregenz 14 E5
Brejo 92 C5
Bremen 14 B5
Bremerhaven .. 14 B5
Bremerton ... 80 B2
Brenner P. 15 E6
Bréscia 20 B3
Breslau =
  Wrocław 16 C3
Bressanone ... 20 A3
Brest, Belarus . 17 B6
Brest, France .. 12 B1
Brest-Litovsk =
  Brest 17 B6
Bretagne 12 B2
Brett, C. 64 A6
Brewarrina ... 63 A4
Brezhnev =
  Naberezhnyye
  Chelny 29 D6
Bria 56 C4
Briançon 13 D7
Bribie I. 63 A5
Bridgeport 73 D9

Bridgetown ... 87 D8
Bridgewater ... 69 D4
Bridgewater, C. 62 C3
Bridlington .. 11 D6
Bridport 62 D4
Brig 13 C7
Brigham City .. 81 E7
Bright 63 C4
Brighton,
  Australia 62 C2
Brighton, U.K. . 11 F6
Bríndisi 21 D6
Brinkworth 62 B2
Brisbane 63 A5
Brisbane → . 63 A5
Bristol, U.K. ... 11 F5
Bristol, U.S.A. . 75 A6
Bristol B. 71 C3
Bristol Channel 11 F4
Britstown 58 E4
Brittany =
  Bretagne 12 B2
Brive-la-
  Gaillarde 12 D4
Brixen =
  Bressanone . 20 A3
Brlik 29 E8
Brno 16 D3
Brocken 14 C6
Brodeur Pen. .. 68 A2
Brodnica 16 B4
Brody 17 C7
Broken Hill =
  Kabwe 59 A5
Broken Hill 62 B3
Bronte Park 62 D4
Brooks Ra. .. 71 B5
Brooloo 63 A5
Broome 60 D3
Broughton
  Island 68 B4
Brown, Pt. ... 62 B1
Brownsville ... 78
Brownwood ... 78 D4
Bruay-en-Artois 13 A5
Bruce, Mt. 60 E2
Bruck an der
  Mur 15 E8
Bruges =
  Brugge 14 C2
Brugge 14 C2
Brumado 93 E5
Brunei = Bandar
  Seri Begawan 36 D5
Brunei ■ 36 D4
Brunner, L. 65 E4
Brunswick =
  Braunschweig 14 B6
Brunswick 75 D7
Brunswick, Pen.
  de 95 G2
Brusque 94 B7
Brussel 14 C3
Brussels =
  Brussel 14 C3
Bruthen 63 C4
Bruxelles =
  Brussel 14 C3
Bryan 79 D5
Bryan, Mt. ... 62 B2
Bryansk 24 C3
Bu Craa 54 C2
Buapinang .. 39 E2
Buayan 38 C3
Bucak 46 C2
Bucaramanga . 90 B4
Buchach 17 D7
Buchanan 55 G2
Buchans 69 D5

Bucharest =
  Bucureşti ... 22 B6
Buckie 10 C5
Buckleboo ... 62 B2
Bucureşti 22 B6
Budalin 41 F10
Budapest 16 E4
Budd Coast ... 96 A12
Bude 11 F4
Budennovsk .. 25 E5
Budgewoi 63 B5
Budjala 56 D3
Buenaventura . 90 C3
Buenos Aires .. 94 C5
Buenos Aires, L. 95 F2
Buffalo 73 C6
Bug → =
  Buh → 25 D3
Bug → 16 B5
Buga 90 C3
Bugel, Tanjung 37 F4
Bugsuk 36 C5
Bugun Shara .. 35 B5
Buguruslan ... 29 D6
Buh → 25 D3
Buheirat-Murrat-
  el-Kubra 52 B5
Buir Nur 35 B6
Bujumbura ... 57 E5
Bukama 57 F5
Bukavu 57 E5
Bukene 57 E6
Bukhara =
  Bukhoro 29 F7
Bukhoro 29 F7
Bukittinggi ... 37 E2
Bukoba 57 E6
Bula 39 E4
Bulahdelah ... 63 B5
Bulan 38 B2
Bulandshahr .. 42 E10
Bulawayo 59 C5
Buldan 23 E7
Bulgan 35 B5
Bulgaria ■ 22 C5
Bulgroo 63 A3
Bulgunnia 62 B1
Bulhar 49 E3
Buli, Teluk 39 D3
Buliluyan, C. .. 36 C5
Bulli 63 B5
Bulloo → 63 A3
Bulloo Downs . 62 A3
Bulloo L. 62 A3
Bulls 64 D6
Bulo Burti 49 G4
Bulsar = Valsad 43 J8
Bulukumba ... 39 F2
Bulun 30 B10
Bumba 56 D4
Bumhpa Bum . 41 D11
Buna 57 D7
Bunbah, Khalīj . 52 B3
Bunbury 60 G2
Buncrana 11 D3
Bundaberg ... 63
Bundi 43 G9
Bundoran 11 D2
Bungo-Suidō .. 32 C3
Bunia 57 D6
Bunji 42 B9
Buntok 37 E4
Bunyu 37 D5
Buol 39 D2
Buon Me Thuot 36 B3
Buorkhaya, Mys 31 B11
Buqayq 47 F7
Bur Acaba 49 G3
Bûr Safâga ... 52 C5

Bûr Sa'îd 52 B5
Bûr Sûdân 53 E6
Burao 49 F4
Buraydah 47 F6
Buraymī, Al
  Wāhāt al 44 E3
Burcher 63 B4
Burdur 46 C2
Burdwan =
  Barddhaman 40 F6
Burgas 22 C6
Burgersdorp .. 59 E5
Burgos 18 A4
Burgundy =
  Bourgogne .. 13 C6
Burhaniye 23 E6
Burhanpur 43 J10
Burias 38 B2
Buriram 36 A2
Burji 53 G6
Burkina Faso ■ 55 F4
Burlington,
  Iowa, U.S.A. . 77 E9
Burlington, N.C.,
  U.S.A. 75 A8
Burlington, Vt.,
  U.S.A. 73 B9
Burlyu-Tyube . 29 E8
Burma ■ 41 G11
Burnie 62 D4
Burnley 11 E5
Burnside → .. 70 B9
Burqān 47 E6
Burqin 34 B3
Burra 62 B2
Burren Junction 63 B4
Burrendong
  Dam 63 B4
Burrinjuck Res. 63 C4
Burruyacú 94 B4
Bursa 23 D7
Burtundy 62 B3
Buru 39 E3
Burundi ■ 57 E6
Burutu 55 G6
Bury St.
  Edmunds ... 11 E7
Buşayyah 47 E6
Būshehr 44 D2
Būshehr □ 44 D2
Bushire =
  Būshehr 44 D2
Businga 56 D4
Busra ash Shām 46 D4
Busto Arsízio . 20 B2
Busu-Djanoa .. 56 D4
Busuanga 38 B1
Buta 57 D4
Butare 57 E5
Butaritari 64 J12
Butembo 57 D5
Butha Qi 35 B7
Buton 39 E2
Butte 81 B7
Butterworth .. 36 C2
Butuan 38 C3
Butung = Buton 39 E2
Buturlinovka .. 24 C5
Buxtehude ... 14 B5
Buy 24 B5
Büyük
  Menderes → 23 F6
Büyükçekmece 22 D7
Buzău 17 F8
Buzău → 17 F8
Buzen 32 C2
Buzi → 59 B6
Buzuluk 29 D6
Byarezina → .. 17 B10

Bydgoszcz 16 B3
Byelarus =
  Belarus ■ .. 24 C2
Byelorussia =
  Belarus ■ ... 24 C2
Bykhaw 17 B10
Bykhov =
  Bykhaw 17 B10
Bylot I. 68 A3
Byrd, C. 96 A3
Byrock 63 B4
Byron Bay 63 A5
Byrranga, Gory 30 B8
Byrranga Mts. =
  Byrranga,
  Gory 30 B8
Bytom 16 C4
Bytów 16 A3

C

Ca Mau = Quan
  Long 36 C3
Caála 58 A3
Cabanatuan .. 38 C2
Cabedelo 92 D7
Cabimas 90 A4
Cabinda 56 F2
Cabinda □ 56 F2
Cabinet Mts. .. 81 B6
Cabo Blanco . 95 F3
Cabo Frio 93 G5
Cabo Pantoja .. 90 D3
Cabonga,
  Réservoir ... 69 D3
Caboolture 63 A5
Cabora Bassa
  Dam =
  Cahora Bassa
  Dam 59 B6
Cabot Str. 69 D5
Cabra 18 D3
Cabrera 19 C7
Cabriel → 19 C5
Čačak 22 C3
Cáceres, Brazil . 91 G7
Cáceres, Spain 18 C2
Cachimbo, Serra
  do 93 D2
Cachoeira 93 E6
Cachoeira de
  Itapemirim .. 93 G5
Cachoeira do
  Sul 94 C6
Cacólo 56 G3
Caconda 58 A3
Cacongo 56 F2
Cadibarrawirracanna,
  L. 62 A2
Cadiz, Phil. ... 38 B2
Cádiz, Spain . 18 D2
Cádiz, G. de ... 18 D2
Cadney Park .. 62 A1
Caen 12 B3
Caeté 93 F5
Caetité 93 E5
Cagayan → .. 38 A2
Cagayan de Oro 38 C2
Cágliari 21 E2
Cágliari, G. di . 21 E2
Caguas 87 C6
Cahora Bassa
  Dam 59 B6
Cahors 12 D4
Cahuapanas .. 91 E3
Cahul 17 F9

Caia 59 B7
Caibarién 86 B4
Caicara 90 B5
Caicó 92 D6
Caicos Is. 87 B5
Caird Coast 96 B5
Cairns 61 D8
Cairo = El Qâhira 52 B5
Cairo 79 A9
Caiundo 58 B3
Caiza 91 H5
Cajamarca 91 E3
Cajàzeiras 92 D6
Calabar 55 H6
Calábria □ 21 E6
Calafate 95 G2
Calahorra 19 A5
Calais 12 A4
Calama, *Brazil* 91 E6
Calama, *Chile* 94 A3
Calamar, *Bolívar, Colombia* 90 A4
Calamar, *Vaupés, Colombia* 90 C4
Calamian Group 38 B1
Calamocha 19 B5
Calang 36 D1
Calapan 38 B2
Călăraşi 22 B6
Calatayud 19 B5
Calauag 38 B2
Calavite, C. 38 B2
Calbayog 38 B2
Calca 91 F4
Calcutta 41 F7
Caldas da Rainha 18 C1
Caldera 94 B2
Caldwell 80 D5
Caledon 58 E3
Caledon → 59 E5
Calgary 71 C8
Cali 90 C3
Calicut 43 P9
California □ 82 B3
California, G. de 84 B2
Calingasta 94 C3
Callabonna, L. 62 A3
Callao 91 F3
Caloundra 63 A5
Caltagirone 21 F5
Caltanissetta 21 F5
Calulo 56 G2
Calunda 58 A4
Calvi 13 E8
Calviá 19 C7
Calvinia 58 E3
Camabatela 56 F3
Camacupa 58 A3
Camagüey 86 B4
Camaná 91 G4
Camargo 91 H5
Camargue 13 E6
Camarones 95 E3
Cambay = Khambhat 43 H8
Cambay, G. of = Khambat, G. of 43 J8
Cambodia ■ 36 B3
Cambrai 13 A5
Cambrian Mts. 11 E5
Cambridge, *N.Z.* 64 B6
Cambridge, *U.K.* 11 E7
Cambridge, *U.S.A.* 73 C10
Cambridge Bay = Ikaluktutiak 70 B9
Cambridge G. 60 C4
Cambundi-Catembo 56 G3
Camden, *Ark., U.S.A.* 79 C7
Camden, *N.J., U.S.A.* 73 E8
Cameroon ■ 56 C2
Cameroun, Mt. 56 D1
Cametá 92 C4
Caminha 18 B1
Camira Creek 63 A5
Camissombo 56 F4
Camocim 92 C5
Camopi → 92 B3
Campana, I. 95 F1
Campánia □ 21 D5
Campbell Town 62 D4
Campbellton 69 D4
Campbelltown 63 B5
Campbeltown 10 D4
Campeche 85 D6
Campeche, B. de 85 D6
Camperdown 62 C3
Campina Grande 92 D6
Campinas 94 A7
Campo 56 D1
Campo Belo 93 G4
Campo Formoso 93 E5
Campo Grande 93 G3
Campo Maíor 92 C5
Campo Mourão 93 G3
Campoalegre 90 C3
Campobasso 20 D5
Campos 93 G5
Campos Belos 93 E4
Campuya → 90 D4
Camrose 71 C8
Çan 23 D6
Can Tho 36 B3
Canada ■ 70 C8
Cañada de Gómez 94 C4
Çanakkale 23 D6
Çanakkale Boğazı 23 D6
Cananea 84 A2
Canarias, Is. 54 C1
Canary Is. = Canarias, Is. 54 C1
Canavieiras 93 F6
Canbelego 63 B4
Canberra 63 C4
Candala 49 E4
Candelo 63 C4
Candia = Iráklion 23 G5
Canea = Khaniá 23 G5
Canelones 94 C5
Cañete, *Chile* 94 D2
Cañete, *Peru* 91 F3
Cangas de Narcea 18 A2
Canguaretama 92 D6
Canguçu 94 C6
Canicattì 21 F4
Canigou, Mt. 12 E5
Canipaan 36 C5
Çankırı 46 B3
Cann River 63 C4
Cannanore 43 P9
Cannes 13 E7
Canoas 94 B6
Canora 71 C9
Canowindra 63 B4
Cantabria □ 18 A4
Cantabrian Mts. = Cantábrica, Cordillera 18 A3
Cantábrica, Cordillera 18 A3
Cantal, Plomb du 13 D5
Canterbury 11 F7
Canterbury □ 65 E4
Canterbury Bight 65 F4
Canterbury Plains 65 E4
Canton = Guangzhou 35 D6
Canton 72 D5
Canudos 91 E7
Canutama 91 E6
Cap-Haïtien 87 C5
Cap St.-Jacques = Vung Tau 36 B3
Capaia 56 F4
Capanaparo → 90 B5
Cape Barren I. 62 D4
Cape Breton I. 69 D4
Cape Coast 55 G4
Cape Dorset 68 B3
Cape Dyer 68 B4
Cape Girardeau 79 A9
Cape Jervis 62 C2
Cape Town 58 E3
Cape Verde Is. ■ 50 E1
Cape York Peninsula 61 C7
Capela 93 E6
Capim → 92 C4
Capraia 20 C2
Capri 21 D5
Caprivi Strip 58 B4
Captain's Flat 63 C4
Caquetá → 90 D5
Caracal 22 B5
Caracas 90 A5
Caracol 93 D5
Caradoc 62 B3
Carajás, Serra dos 92 D3
Carangola 93 G5
Caransebeş 17 F6
Caratasca, L. 86 C3
Caratinga 93 F5
Caraúbas 92 D6
Caravaca 19 C5
Caravelas 93 F6
Caraveli 91 G4
Carballo 18 A1
Carbonara, C. 21 E2
Carbondale 79 A9
Carbonear 69 D5
Carbonia 21 E2
Carcassonne 12 E5
Carcross 70 B6
Cardamon Hills 43 Q10
Cárdenas 86 B3
Cardiff 11 F5
Cardigan B. 11 E4
Cardston 71 D8
Carei 17 E6
Careysburg 55 G2
Carhué 94 D4
Caria 23 F7
Cariacica 93 G5
Caribbean Sea 86 D5
Cariboo Mts. 71 C7
Carinda 63 B4
Carinhanha 93 E5
Carinthia □ = Kärnten □ 15 E7
Caripito 90 A6
Caritianas 91 E6
Carlisle 11 D5
Carlow 11 E3
Carlsbad 78 C1
Carmacks 70 B6
Carman 71 D10
Carmarthen 11 F4
Carmaux 12 D5
Carmelo 94 C5
Carmen 90 B3
Carmen de Patagones 95 E4
Carmona 18 D3
Carnac 12 C2
Carnarvon, *Australia* 60 E1
Carnarvon, *S. Africa* 58 E4
Carnegie, L. 60 F3
Carnic Alps = Karnische Alpen 20 A4
Carniche Alpi = Karnische Alpen 20 A4
Carnot 56 D3
Carnot, C. 62 B2
Carolina 92 D4
Caroline I. 65 K15
Caroline Is. 64 J10
Caroni → 90 B6
Caroníe = Nébrodi, Monti 21 F5
Caroona 63 B5
Carpathians 16 D5
Carpaţii Meridionali 17 F7
Carpentaria, G. of 60 C6
Carpentras 13 D6
Carpi 20 B3
Carpolac = Morea 62 C3
Carrara 20 B3
Carrauntoohill 11 E2
Carrick-on-Suir 11 E3
Carrieton 62 B2
Carrizal Bajo 94 B2
Çarşamba 46 B4
Carson City 80 F4
Cartagena, *Colombia* 90 A3
Cartagena, *Spain* 19 D5
Cartago, *Colombia* 90 C3
Cartago, *Costa Rica* 86 E3
Carterton 65 D6
Carthage 79 A6
Cartwright 68 C5
Caruaru 92 D6
Carúpano 90 A6
Carvoeiro 90 D6
Carvoeiro, C. 18 C1
Casablanca 54 B3
Cascade Ra. 80 B3
Cascais 18 C1
Cascavel 94 A6
Cáscina 20 C3
Caserta 20 D5
Casiguran 38 A2
Casilda 94 C4
Casino 63 A5
Casiquiare → 90 C5
Casma 91 E3
Caspe 19 B5
Casper 81 D10

Caspian Sea .. 29 E6
Cassinga 58 B3
Castellammare
di Stábia 21 D5
Castellón de la
Plana 19 C5
Castelo Branco 18 C2
Castelsarrasin . 12 D4
Castelvetrano . 21 F4
Casterton 62 C3
Castilla La
Mancha □ .. 18 C4
Castilla y
Leon □ 18 A3
Castlebar 11 E2
Castleblaney .. 11 D3
Castlemaine ... 63 C3
Castlereagh → 63 B4
Castres 12 E5
Castries 87 D7
Castro 95 E2
Castro Alves . 93 E6
Castuera 18 C3
Cat I. 86 B4
Catacáos 91 E2
Catalão 93 F4
Çatalca 22 D7
Catalonia =
Cataluña □ .. 19 B6
Cataluña □ .. 19 B6
Catamarca .. 94 B3
Catanduanes .. 38 B2
Catanduva .. 93 G4
Catánia 21 F5
Catanzaro 21 E6
Catarman 38 B2
Cateel 38 C3
Catoche, C. ... 85 C7
Catrimani 90 C6
Catskill Mts. .. 73 C8
Cauca → 90 B4
Caucaia 92 C6
Caucasus
Mountains .. 25 E5
Caúngula 56 F3
Cauquenes ... 94 D2
Caura → 90 B6
Cauvery → .. 43 P11
Caux, Pays de . 12 B4
Cavan 11 D3
Cavendish ... 62 C3
Caviana, I. ... 92 B3
Cavite 38 B2
Cawndilla L. ... 62 B3
Cawnpore =
Kanpur 40 D3
Caxias 92 C5
Caxias do Sul . 94 B6
Caxito 56 F2
Cayambe 90 C3
Cayenne 92 A3
Cayman Is. ■ . 67 H11
Cazombo 58 A4
Ceadâr-Lunga . 17 E9
Ceanannus Mor 11 E3
Ceará =
Fortaleza 92 C6
Ceará □ 92 D6
Ceará Mirim . 92 D6
Cebollar 94 B3
Cebu 38 B2
Cecil Plains .. 63 A5
Cedar L. 71 C10
Cedar Rapids .. 77 E9
Cedro 92 D6
Ceduna 62 B1
Cefalù 21 E5
Cegléd 16 E4
Celaya 84 C4

Celebes =
Sulawesi □ . 39 E2
Celebes Sea ... 39 D2
Celje 20 A5
Celle 14 B6
Celtic Sea 11 F2
Central,
Cordillera ... 90 C3
Central African
Rep. ■ 56 C4
Central Makran
Range 42 F4
Cephalonia =
Kefalliniá ... 23 E3
Ceram = Seram 39 E3
Ceram Sea =
Seram Sea .. 39 E3
Ceres, Argentina 94 B4
Ceres, S. Africa 58 E3
Cerignola 20 D5
Cerigo = Kíthira 23 F4
Çerkeş 46 B3
Çerkeşköy 22 D6
Cervera 19 B6
Cesena 20 B4
Česka Republika
= Czech
Rep. ■ 16 D2
České
Budějovice .. 16 D2
Ceskomoravská
Vrchovina ... 16 D2
Çeşme 23 E6
Cessnock 63 B5
Cetinje 22 C2
Cetraro 21 E5
Ceuta 18 E3
Cévennes 13 D5
Ceyhan 46 C3
Ceylon = Sri
Lanka ■ 43 R12
Chachapoyas .. 91 E3
Chachran 42 E7
Chad ■ 53 E2
Chad, L. =
Tchad, L. ... 53 F1
Chadileuvú → 94 D3
Chadyr-Lunga =
Ceadâr-Lunga 17 E9
Chagai Hills .. 42 E3
Chagos Arch. .. 27 K11
Chāh Bahār .. 45 E5
Chāh Gay Hills 45 D6
Chahar Burjak . 42 D3
Chaibasa 40 F5
Chakhānsūr .. 42 D3
Chakradharpur 40 F5
Chakwal 42 C8
Chala 91 G4
Chalcis =
Khalkís 23 E4
Chalhuanca ... 91 F4
Chalisgaon ... 43 J9
Chalky Inlet .. 65 G2
Challapata 91 G5
Chalon-sur-
Saône 13 C6
Châlons-en-
Champagne . 13 B6
Chaman 42 D5
Chamba, India . 42 C10
Chamba,
Tanzania 59 A7
Chambal → .. 42 F11
Chambéry ... 13 D6
Chamical 94 C3
Chamonix-Mont
Blanc 13 D7
Champagne .. 13 B6

Champaign ... 72 D1
Champlain, L. . 73 B9
Chañaral 94 B2
Chandigarh .. 42 D10
Chandler 62 A1
Chandmani ... 34 B4
Chandpur 41 F8
Chandrapur ... 43 K11
Chang Jiang → 35 C7
Changanacheri 43 Q10
Changane → . 59 C6
Changchiak'ou
= Zhangjiakou 35 B6
Ch'angchou =
Changzhou .. 35 C6
Changchun .. 35 B7
Changde 35 D6
Changhai =
Shanghai .. 35 C7
Changjiang ... 35 E5
Changsha ... 35 D6
Changting ... 35 D6
Changzhi 35 C6
Changzhou ... 35 C6
Channapatna .. 43 N10
Channel Is. 11 G5
Chantada 18 A2
Chanthaburi .. 36 B2
Chantrey Inlet . 70 B10
Chanute 79 A6
Chao Phraya → 36 B2
Chao'an 35 D6
Chaoyang ... 35 D6
Chapala, L. de . 84 C4
Chapayevsk .. 24 C6
Chapra =
Chhapra 40 E5
Châr 54 D2
Chara 31 D9
Charadai 94 B5
Charagua 91 G6
Charaña 91 G5
Chardara 29 E7
Chardzhou =
Chärjew 29 F7
Charente → .. 12 D3
Chari → 53 F1
Chärikär 42 B6
Chärjew 29 F7
Charleroi 14 C3
Charles, C. ... 73 F8
Charleston, S.C.,
U.S.A. 75 C8
Charleston,
W. Va., U.S.A. 72 E5
Charlesville ... 56 F4
Charleville 63 A4
Charleville-
Mézières 13 B6
Charlotte 75 B7
Charlotte Amalie 87 C7
Charlottesville . 73 E6
Charlottetown . 69 D4
Charlton 62 C3
Charolles 13 C6
Charouine 52 C5
Charters Towers 61 E8
Chartres 12 B4
Chascomús ... 94 D5
Châteaubriant . 12 C3
Châteaulin 12 B1
Châteauroux .. 12 C4
Châtellerault .. 12 C4
Chatham, N.B.,
Canada 69 D4
Chatham, Ont.,
Canada 69 D2
Chatham, U.K. . 11 F7
Chatrapur 40 H5

Chattahoochee →
.... 74 D
Chattanooga .. 74 B
Chauk 41 G1
Chaukan La ... 41 D1
Chaumont ... 13 B
Chaves, Brazil . 92 C
Chaves, Portugal 18 B
Chavuma ..... 58 A
Cheb .... 16 C
Cheboksary ... 24 B
Chech, Erg ... 54 D
Chechenia □ .. 25 E
Checheno-
Ingush
Republic =
Chechenia □ 25 E
Chechnya =
Chechenia □ 25 E
Cheduba I. .... 41 H
Cheepie ...... 63 A
Chegga ...... 54 C
Chegutu ..... 59 B
Chehalis ..... 80 B
Cheju Do .... 35 C
Chekiang =
Zhejiang □ .. 35 D
Cheleken .... 29 F
Chelforó ...... 95 D
Chelkar =
Shalqar .... 29 E
Chelkar Tengiz,
Solonchak .. 29 E
Chełm .... 17 C
Chełmno ..... 16 B
Chelmsford ... 11 F
Cheltenham .. 11 F
Chelyabinsk .. 29 D
Chemnitz .... 15 C
Chen Xian ... 35 D
Chenab → ... 42 D
Chencha .... 53 G
Chenchiang =
Zhenjiang ... 35 C
Chengde .... 35 B
Chengdu .... 35 C
Chengjiang ... 34 D
Ch'engtu =
Chengdu .... 35 C
Chennai =
Madras 43 N1
Cheo Reo ... 36 B
Cheom Ksan . 36 B
Chepén ...... 91 E
Chepes ...... 94 C
Cher → ...... 12 C
Cherbourg ... 12 B
Cherchell .... 54 A
Cherdyn ..... 28 C
Cherepanovo . 29 D
Cherepovets .. 24 B
Chergui, Chott
ech .... 54 B
Cherikov =
Cherykaw ... 17 B10
Cherkasy .... 24 D
Cherlak ..... 29 D
Chernaya ... 30 B
Chernigov =
Chernihiv ... 24 C
Chernihiv .... 24 C
Chernivtsi ... 17 D
Chernobyl =
Chornobyl .. 17 C10
Chernovtsy =
Chernivtsi ... 17 D
Chernyakhovsk 28 D
Cherquenco .. 94 D
Cherrapunji .. 41 E

Cherven 17 B9
Chervonohrad . 17 C7
Cherykaw 17 B10
Chesapeake .. 73 F7
Chesapeake B. . 73 E7
Cheshskaya
  Guba 28 C5
Chester, *U.K.* .. 11 E5
Chester, *U.S.A.* 73 E8
Chesterfield ... 11 E6
Chesterfield, Is. 64 L10
Chesterfield Inlet 70 B10
Chesterton Ra. 63 A4
Cheviot Hills .. 10 D5
Chew Bahir ... 53 H6
Cheyenne 76 E2
Cheyenne →. 76 C4
Chhapra 40 E5
Chhatarpur ... 43 G11
Chhindwara ... 43 H11
Chhlong 36 B3
Chi →. 36 A2
Chiamussu =
  Jiamusi 35 B8
Chiange 58 B2
Chiapa →. .. 85 D6
Chiávari 20 B2
Chiavenna 20 A2
Chiba 32 B7
Chibemba 58 B2
Chibia 58 B2
Chibougamau . 69 D3
Chibuk 53 F1
Chicacole =
  Srikakulam .. 40 H4
Chicago 72 D2
Chichagof I. ... 71 C6
Chichibu 32 A6
Ch'ich'ihaerh =
  Qiqihar 35 B7
Chickasha 78 B5
Chiclana de la
  Frontera 18 D2
Chiclayo 91 E3
Chico 80 F3
Chico →,
  Chubut,
  Argentina ... 95 E3
Chico →,
  Santa Cruz,
  Argentina ... 95 F3
Chicoutimi 69 D3
Chidambaram . 43 P11
Chidley, C. 68 B4
Chiemsee 15 E7
Chiengi 57 F5
Chiese →. 20 B3
Chieti 20 C5
Chiguana 91 H5
Chihli, G. of =
  Bo Hai 35 C6
Chihuahua 84 B3
Chiili 29 E7
Chik Bollapur .. 43 N10
Chikmagalur .. 43 N9
Chilapa 84 D5
Chilas 42 B9
Chilaw 43 R11
Childers 63 A5
Chile ■ 94 D2
Chilete 91 E3
Chililabombwe 59 A5
Chilin = Jilin .. 35 B7
Chilka L. 40 H5
Chillán 94 D2
Chiloé, I. de ... 95 E2
Chilpancingo .. 84 D5
Chiluage 56 F4
Chilwa, L. 59 B7

Chimbay 29 E6
Chimborazo ... 90 D3
Chimbote 91 E3
Chimkent =
  Shymkent ... 29 E7
Chimoio 59 B6
Chin □ 41 F9
China ■ 35 C5
Chinan = Jinan 35 C6
Chinandega ... 85 E7
Chincha Alta .. 91 F3
Chinchilla 63 A5
Chinchou =
  Jinzhou 35 B7
Chinde 59 B7
Chindwin →. .. 41 G10
Chingola 59 A5
Ch'ingtao =
  Qingdao 35 C7
Chinguetti 54 D2
Chinhoyi 59 B6
Chiniot 42 D8
Chinju 35 C7
Chinnampo ... 35 C7
Chinon 12 C4
Chinsali 57 G6
Chióggia 20 B4
Chíos = Khíos . 23 E6
Chipata 59 A6
Chiquián 91 F3
Chiquinquira .. 90 B4
Chirchiq 29 E7
Chirmiri 40 F4
Chiromo 59 B7
Chisamba 59 A5
Chisapani Garhi 40 D5
Chişinău 17 E9
Chistopol 24 B7
Chita 30 D9
Chitado 58 B2
Chitembo 58 A3
Chitral 42 B7
Chitré 86 E3
Chittagong ... 41 F8
Chittagong □ .. 41 E8
Chittaurgarh .. 43 G9
Chittoor 43 N11
Chiusi 20 C3
Chivasso 20 B1
Chivilcoy 94 B4
Chkalov =
  Orenburg ... 29 D6
Choele Choel .. 95 D3
Chojnice 16 B3
Cholet 12 C3
Choluteca 85 E7
Choma 59 B5
Chomutov 16 C1
Chon Buri 36 B2
Chone 90 D3
Chŏngjin 35 B7
Chŏngju 35 C7
Chongqing ... 35 D5
Chŏnju 35 C7
Chonos, Arch.
  de los 95 F2
Chop 17 D6
Chornobyl ... 17 C10
Chortkiv 17 D7
Chorzów 16 C4
Chos-Malal ... 94 D2
Chōshi 32 B7
Choszczno ... 16 B2
Chotila 43 H7
Choybalsan ... 35 B6
Christchurch .. 65 E5
Christiana 59 D5
Christmas I. =
  Kiritimati ... 65 J15

Chu = Shu 29 E8
Ch'uanchou =
  Quanzhou ... 35 D6
Chubut →. 95 E3
Chudskoye, Oz. 24 B2
Chūgoku-Sanchi 32 B3
Chula Vista .. 82 D4
Chulucanas ... 90 E2
Chulym →. ... 29 D9
Chumbicha ... 94 B3
Chumphon ... 36 B1
Chuna →. 30 D7
Chunchŏn 35 C7
Chungking =
  Chongqing .. 35 D5
Chunya 57 F6
Chuquibamba . 91 G4
Chuquicamata . 94 A3
Chur 13 C8
Churachandpur 41 E9
Churchill →. .. 70 C10
Churchill →,
  Man., Canada 70 C10
Churchill →,
  Nfld., Canada 69 C4
Churchill, C. ... 70 C10
Churchill Falls . 69 C4
Churchill L. ... 71 C9
Churu 42 E9
Chushal 42 C11
Chusovoy 28 D6
Chuvash
  Republic □ =
  Chuvashia □ . 24 B6
Chuvashia □ .. 24 B6
Cicero 72 D2
Ciechanów ... 16 B5
Ciego de Avila . 86 B4
Ciénaga 90 A4
Cienfuegos ... 86 B3
Cieszyn 16 D4
Cieza 19 C5
Cijara, Pantano
  de 18 C3
Cilician Gates P. 46 C3
Cill Chainnigh =
  Kilkenny ... 11 E3
Cimişlia 17 E9
Cimone, Mte. .. 20 B3
Cîmpina 17 F7
Cîmpulung 17 F7
Cinca →. 19 B6
Cincar 20 C6
Cincinnati ... 72 E3
Çine 23 F7
Cinto, Mte. .. 13 E8
Circle 71 B5
Cirebon 37 F3
Citlaltépetl ... 84 D5
Città di Castello 20 C4
Ciudad Bolívar 90 B6
Ciudad
  Chetumal ... 85 D7
Ciudad del
  Carmen 85 D6
Ciudad Delicias
  = Delicias ... 84 B3
Ciudad Guayana 90 B6
Ciudad Juárez . 84 A3
Ciudad Madero 84 C5
Ciudad Mante . 84 C5
Ciudad Obregón 84 B3
Ciudad Real .. 18 C4
Ciudad Rodrigo 18 B2
Ciudad Trujillo
  = Santo
  Domingo ... 87 C6
Ciudad Victoria 84 C5
Civitanova
  Marche 20 C4

Civitavécchia .. 20 C3
Cizre 46 C5
Clanwilliam ... 58 E3
Clare 62 B2
Clarence →,
  Australia ... 63 A5
Clarence →,
  N.Z. 65 E5
Clarence, I. 95 G2
Clarence I. 96 A4
Clarie Coast .. 96 A13
Clarke I. 62 D4
Clarksdale 79 B8
Clarksville 74 A4
Claveria 38 A2
Clear, C. 11 F2
Clearwater 75 F6
Clearwater Mts. 81 B6
Clermont-
  Ferrand 13 D5
Cleveland,
  Australia 63 A5
Cleveland,
  U.S.A. 72 D5
Clifden 65 G2
Clifton 63 A5
Clifton Hills .. 62 A2
Clinton, *Canada* 71 C7
Clinton, *N.Z.* .. 65 G3
Clinton, *U.S.A.* 77 E9
Clinton Colden
  L. 70 B9
Clones 11 D3
Clonmel 11 E3
Clovis 78 B2
Cluj-Napoca ... 17 E6
Clunes 62 C3
Clutha →. ... 65 G3
Clyde 65 F3
Clyde →. ... 10 D4
Clyde, Firth of . 10 D4
Clyde River .. 68 A4
Coari 90 D6
Coast Mts. ... 70 C7
Coast Ranges . 80 F2
Coats I. 68 B2
Coats Land ... 96 B5
Coatzacoalcos . 85 D6
Cobalt 69 D3
Cobar 63 B4
Cóbh 11 F2
Cobham 62 B3
Cobija 91 F5
Cobourg 69 D3
Cobram 63 C4
Cóbué 59 A6
Coburg 15 C6
Cocanada =
  Kakinada ... 40 J4
Cochabamba .. 91 G5
Cochin 43 Q10
Cochin China =
  Nam-Phan .. 36 B3
Cochrane 69 D2
Cochrane, L. .. 95 F2
Cockburn 62 B3
Cockburn, Canal 95 G2
Coco →. 86 D3
Cocobeach ... 56 D1
Cod, C. 73 C10
Codajás 90 D6
Codó 92 C5
Cœur d'Alene . 80 B5
Coffeyville ... 79 A6
Coffin B. 62 B2
Coffin Bay
  Peninsula .. 62 B2
Coffs Harbour . 63 B5
Cognac 12 D3

Cohuna

Cohuna	63	C3	Communism Pk.			Cook Is.	65	L14	Corowa	63	C4
Coiba, I.	86	E3	=			Cook Strait	65	D6	Corpus Christi	78	F5
Coig →	95	G3	Kommunizma,			Cooktown	61	D8	Corque	91	G5
Coihaique	95	F2	Pik	29	F8	Coolabah	63	B4	Corrib, L.	11	E2
Coimbatore	43	P10	Como	20	B2	Cooladdi	63	A4	Corrientes	94	B5
Coimbra, *Brazil*	91	G7	Como, L. di	20	B2	Coolah	63	B4	Corrientes →	90	D4
Coimbra,			Comodoro			Coolamon	63	B4	Corrientes, C.,		
Portugal	18	B1	Rivadavia	95	F3	Coolangatta	63	A5	*Colombia*	90	B3
Coín	18	D3	Comorin, C.	43	Q10	Cooma	63	C4	Corrientes, C.,		
Cojimies	90	C3	Comoro Is. =			Coonabarabran	63	B4	*Mexico*	84	C3
Colac	62	C3	Comoros ■	51	H8	Coonamble	63	B4	Corse	13	E8
Colatina	93	F5	Comoros ■	51	H8	Coondapoor	43	N9	Corse, C.	13	E8
Colbeck, C.	96	B17	Comox	71	D7	Coongie	62	A3	Corsica = Corse	13	E8
Colbinabbin	63	C3	Compiègne	13	B5	Coongoola	63	A4	Corsicana	79	C5
Colchester	11	F7	Compton Downs	63	B4	Cooninie, L.	62	A2	Corte	13	E8
Colebrook	62	D4	Comrat	17	E9	Cooper Cr. →,			Çorum	46	B3
Coleman	71	D8	Conakry	55	G2	*N. Terr.,*			Corumbá	91	G7
Coleraine,			Conara Junction	62	D4	*Australia*	60	C5	Corumbá de		
Australia	62	C3	Concarneau	12	C2	Cooper Cr. →,			Goiás	93	F4
Coleraine, *U.K.*	11	D3	Conceição da			*S. Austral.,*			Corunna = La		
Coleridge, L.	65	E4	Barra	93	F6	*Australia*	62	A2	Coruña	18	A1
Colesberg	59	E5	Concepción,			Cooroy	63	A5	Corvallis	80	C2
Colhué Huapi, L.	95	F3	*Bolivia*	91	G6	Cootamundra	63	B4	Cosenza	21	E6
Colima	84	D4	Concepción,			Cooyar	63	A5	Costa Blanca	19	C5
Colinas	92	D5	*Chile*	94	D2	Copenhagen =			Costa Brava	19	B7
Coll	10	C3	Concepción,			København	9	G10	Costa del Sol	18	D3
Collaguasi	91	H5	*Paraguay*	94	A5	Copiapó	94	B2	Costa Dorada	19	B6
Collarenebri	63	A4	Concepción, L.	91	G6	Copiapó →	94	B2	Costa Rica ■	86	E3
Collingwood	64	D5	Concepción del			Copley	62	B2	Cotabato	38	C2
Colmar	13	B7	Oro	84	C4	Copper Center	71	B5	Cotagaita	91	H5
Colo →	63	B5	Concepción del			Copper Cliff	69	D2	Côte d'Azur	13	E7
Cologne = Köln	14	C4	Uruguay	94	C5	Coppermine =			Côte-d'Ivoire ■		
Colomb-Béchar			Conchos →	84	B3	Kugluktuk	70	B8	= Ivory		
= Béchar	54	B4	Concord, *N.C.,*			Coppermine →	70	B8	Coast ■	55	G3
Colômbia	93	G4	*U.S.A.*	75	B7	Coquimbo	94	C2	Cotentin	12	B3
Colombia ■	90	C4	Concord, *N.H.,*			Corabia	22	C5	Cotonou	55	G5
Colombo	43	R11	*U.S.A.*	73	C10	Coracora	91	G4	Cotopaxi	90	D3
Colón, *Cuba*	86	B3	Concordia,			Coral Harbour =			Cotswold Hills	11	F5
Colón, *Panama*	85	F9	*Argentina*	94	C5	Salliq	68	B2	Cottbus	15	C8
Colonia	94	C5	Concórdia, *Brazil*	90	D5	Coral Sea	64	L10	Couedic, C. du	62	C2
Colonia Dora	94	B4	Condamine	63	A5	Corato	21	D6	Coulman I.	96	B15
Colonsay	10	C3	Condeúba	93	E5	Corby	11	E6	Council	71	B3
Colorado □	83	A10	Condobolin	63	B4	Corcaigh = Cork	11	F2	Council Bluffs	77	E7
Colorado →,			Conegliano	20	B4	Corcubión	18	A1	Courantyne →	90	B7
Argentina	95	D4	Confuso →	94	B5	Córdoba,			Courtrai =		
Colorado →,			Congo ■	56	E3	*Argentina*	94	C4	Kortrijk	14	C2
N. Amer.	82	E5	Congo →	56	F2	Córdoba, *Spain*	18	D3	Coventry	11	E6
Colorado			Congo, Dem.			Córdoba, Sierra			Covilhã	18	B2
Plateau	83	B7	Rep. of the ■	56	E4	de	94	C4	Covington	72	E3
Colorado			Conjeeveram =			Cordon	38	A2	Cowal, L.	63	B4
Springs	76	F2	Kanchipuram	43	N11	Cordova	71	B5	Cowangie	62	C3
Columbia, *Mo.,*			Conlea	63	B3	Corfu = Kérkira	23	E2	Cowarie	62	A2
U.S.A.	77	F8	Conn, L.	11	D2	Coria	18	C2	Cowell	62	B2
Columbia, *S.C.,*			Connacht □	11	E2	Corigliano			Cowra	63	B4
U.S.A.	75	B7	Connecticut □	73	D9	Cálabro	21	E6	Coxim	93	F3
Columbia,			Connecticut →	73	D9	Corinna	62	D4	Cox's Bazar	41	G8
Tenn., U.S.A.	74	B4	Connemara	11	E2	Corinth =			Cozumel, I. de	85	C7
Columbia →	80	B1	Conoble	63	B3	Kórinthos	23	F4	Craboon	63	B4
Columbia,			Cononaco →	90	D3	Corinth, G. of =			Cracow =		
District of □	73	E7	Conran, C.	63	C4	Korinthiakós			Kraków	16	C4
Columbia Basin	80	B4	Conselheiro			Kólpos	23	E4	Cracow	63	A5
Columbretes, Is.	19	C6	Lafaiete	93	G5	Corinto	93	F5	Cradock	59	E5
Columbus, *Ga.,*			Constance =			Cork	11	F2	Craigavon	11	D3
U.S.A.	74	C5	Konstanz	14	E5	Çorlu	22	D6	Crailsheim	14	D6
Columbus,			Constance, L. =			Corner Brook	69	D5	Craiova	22	B4
Miss., U.S.A.	74	C3	Bodensee	13	C8	Corneşti	17	E9	Cranbrook,		
Columbus, *Ohio,*			Constanţa	22	B7	Cornwall	69	D3	*Australia*	62	D4
U.S.A.	72	E4	Constantine	54	A6	Corny Pt.	62	B2	Cranbrook,		
Colville →	71	A4	Constitución	94	D2	Coro	90	A5	*Canada*	71	D8
Colville, C.	64	B6	Contai	40	G6	Coroatá	92	C5	Crateús	92	D5
Colwyn Bay	11	E5	Contamana	91	E4	Corocoro	91	G5	Crato	92	D6
Comácchio	20	B4	Contas →	93	E6	Coroico	91	G5	Crawley	11	F6
Comallo	95	E2	Conway, L.	62	A2	Coromandel	64	B6	Crazy Mts.	81	B8
Comilla	41	F8	Coober Pedy	62	A1	Corona	62	B3	Crema	20	B2
Comino, C.	21	D2	Cooch Behar =			Coronation Gulf	70	B8	Cremona	20	B3
Committee B.	68	B2	Koch Bihar =	41	D7	Coronation I.	96	A4	Cres	20	B5
Commonwealth			Cook, B.	95	H2	Coronel	94	D2	Cressy	62	C3
B.	96	A14	Cook, Mt.	65	E4	Coronel Dorrego	94	D4	Crete = Kríti	23	G5
Commoron			Cook Inlet	71	C4	Coronel Suárez	94	D4	Créteil	12	B5
Cr. →	63	A5									

Creus, C. de ... 19 A7
Creuse → 12 C4
Crewe 11 E5
Criciúma 94 B7
Crimean Pen. =
 Krymskyy
 Pivostriv 25 D3
Crişul Alb → . 16 E5
Crişul Negru → 16 E5
Crna Gora =
 Montenegro □ 22 C2
Crna Gora ... 22 C3
Crna Reka → . 22 D3
Croatia ■ 20 B6
Crocker,
 Banjaran 36 C5
Croker, C. 60 C5
Cromer 11 E7
Cromwell 65 F3
Cronulla 63 B5
Crookwell 63 B4
Cross Sound .. 71 C6
Crotone 21 E6
Crows Nest .. 63 A5
Crowsnest Pass 71 D8
Cruz Alta 94 B6
Cruz del Eje .. 94 C4
Cruzeiro 93 G5
Cruzeiro do Sul 91 E4
Crystal Brook .. 62 B2
Csongrád 16 E5
Cuamba 59 A7
Cuando → ... 58 B4
Cuarto → 94 C4
Cuba ■ 86 B4
Cubango → .. 58 B4
Cuchi 58 A3
Cúcuta 90 B4
Cuddalore ... 43 P11
Cuddapah 43 M11
Cudgewa 63 C4
Cuenca, Ecuador 90 D3
Cuenca, Spain . 19 B4
Cuenca,
 Serranía de . 19 C5
Cuernavaca ... 84 D5
Cuevas del
 Almanzora .. 19 D5
Cuevo 91 H6
Cuiabá 93 F2
Cuiabá → 93 F2
Cuima 58 A3
Cuito → 58 B4
Cukai 36 D2
Culcairn 63 C4
Culgoa → 63 A4
Culiacán 84 C3
Culion 38 B2
Cullarin Ra. ... 63 B4
Cullera 19 C5
Culuene → ... 93 E3
Culverden 65 E5
Cumaná 90 A6
Cumberland,
 Canada 71 D7
Cumberland,
 U.S.A. 73 E6
Cumberland
 Pen. 68 B4
Cumberland
 Plateau 72 F3
Cumberland Sd. 68 B4
Cumborah 63 A4
Cumbum 43 M11
Cummins 62 B2
Cumnock 63 B4
Cunene → ... 58 B2
Cúneo 20 B1
Cunnamulla .. 63 A4

Cupica, G. de .. 90 B3
Curaçao 87 D6
Curaray → ... 90 D4
Curiapo 90 B6
Curicó 94 C2
Curitiba 94 B7
Currabubula .. 63 B5
Currais Novos . 92 D6
Curralinho 92 C4
Curraweena .. 63 B4
Currie 62 C3
Curtea de Argeş 17 F7
Curtis Group .. 62 C4
Curuápanema →
 .... 92 C2
Curuçá 92 C4
Curup 37 E2
Cururupu 92 C5
Curuzú Cuatiá . 94 B5
Cuttaburra → . 63 A3
Cuttack 40 G5
Cuvier I. 64 B6
Cuxhaven 14 B5
Cuyo 38 B2
Cuzco, Bolivia . 91 H5
Cuzco, Peru .. 91 F4
Cwmbran 11 F5
Cyclades =
 Kikládhes ... 23 F5
Cygnet 62 D4
Cyprus ■ 46 D3
Cyrenaica 52 C3
Cyrene =
 Shaḥḥāt 52 B3
Czech Rep. ■ .. 16 D2
Częstochowa .. 16 C4

D

Da Hinggan Ling 35 B7
Da Lat 36 B3
Da Nang 36 A3
Da Qaidam ... 34 C4
Da Yunhe → .. 35 C7
Daba Shan 35 C5
Dabakala 55 G4
Dabo 37 E2
Dabola 55 F2
Daboya 55 G4
Dacca = Dhaka 41 F8
Dacca =
 Dhaka □ 41 E8
Dachau 15 D6
Dadanawa 90 C7
Dadra and
 Nagar
 Haveli □ 43 J8
Dadu 42 F5
Daet 38 B2
Dagana 55 E1
Dagestan □ ... 25 E6
Daghestan
 Republic =
 Dagestan □ . 25 E6
Dagö = Hiiumaa 24 B1
Dagupan 38 A2
Dahlak Kebir .. 49 D3
Dahod 43 H9
Dahomey =
 Benin ■ 55 G5
Dahra 55 E1
Daiō-Misaki .. 32 B5
Dairût 52 C5
Dakar 55 F1
Dakhla 54 D1

Dakhla, El
 Wâhât el- ... 52 C4
Dakhovskaya .. 25 E5
Đakovica 22 C3
Dalaman → .. 23 F7
Dalandzadgad . 35 B5
Dālbandīn 42 E4
Dalby 63 A5
Dalhousie 69 D4
Dali 34 D5
Dalian 35 C7
Daliang Shan .. 34 D5
Dallarnil 63 A5
Dallas 79 C5
Dalmacija 20 C6
Dalmatia =
 Dalmacija ... 20 C6
Daloa 55 G3
Dalton 74 B5
Dalton Iceberg
 Tongue 96 A13
Daly Waters ... 60 D5
Daman 43 J8
Damanhûr 52 B5
Damar 39 F3
Damaraland ... 58 C3
Damascus =
 Dimashq 46 D4
Damāvand 44 C3
Damāvand,
 Qolleh-ye ... 44 C3
Damba 56 F3
Dāmghān 44 B3
Damiel 18 C4
Damietta =
 Dumyât 52 B5
Dammam = Ad
 Dammām ... 47 F7
Damoh 43 H11
Dampier 60 E2
Dampier, Selat 39 E4
Danbury 73 D9
Dandeldhura .. 40 C3
Dandeli 43 M9
Dandenong ... 63 C4
Dandong 35 B7
Danger Is. =
 Pukapuka ... 65 L14
Danger Pt. 58 E3
Dangora 55 F6
Danilov 24 B5
Dankhar Gompa 42 C11
Dannemora ... 9 F11
Dannevirke ... 64 D7
Dante 49 E5
Danube =
 Dunărea → . 17 F9
Danville 75 A8
Danzig =
 Gdańsk 16 A4
Dao 38 B2
Daoud = Aïn
 Beïda 54 A6
Dar el Beida =
 Casablanca .. 54 B3
Dar es Salaam . 57 F7
Dārāb 44 D3
Daraj 54 B7
Darband 42 B8
Darbhanga ... 40 D5
Dardanelles =
 Çanakkale
 Boğazı 23 D6
Dârfûr 53 F3
Dargai 42 B7
Dargan Ata ... 29 E7
Dargaville 64 A5
Darıca 22 D7
Darién, G. del . 90 B3

Darjeeling =
 Darjiling 40 D7
Darjiling 40 D7
Darling → 62 B3
Darling Downs . 63 A5
Darling Ra. 60 G2
Darlington ... 11 D6
Darłowo 16 A3
Darmstadt ... 14 D5
Darnah 52 B3
Darnley, C. 96 A10
Darnley B. 70 B7
Dart, C. 96 B18
Dartmoor 11 F5
Dartmouth ... 69 D4
Dartmouth, L. . 63 A4
Darvaza 29 E6
Darvel, Teluk .. 38 D1
Darwha 43 J10
Darwin 60 C5
Daryoi Amu =
 Amudarya → 29 E6
Dās 44 E3
Dashhowuz ... 29 E6
Dasht → 42 G2
Dasht-e Kavīr .. 44 C3
Dasht-e Mārgow 42 D3
Datça 23 F6
Datia 43 G11
Datong 35 B6
Datu, Tanjung . 37 D3
Datu Piang ... 38 C2
Daugava → ... 24 B1
Daugavpils ... 24 B2
Daulpur 42 F10
Dauphin 71 C9
Dauphiné 13 D6
Davangere ... 43 M9
Davao 38 C3
Davao, G. of .. 38 C3
Dāvar Panāh .. 45 E5
Davenport ... 77 E9
David 86 E3
David Gorodok
 = Davyd
 Haradok ... 17 B8
Davis Sea 96 A11
Davis Str. 68 B5
Davos 13 C8
Davyd Haradok 17 B8
Dawson 70 B6
Dawson, I. 95 G2
Dax 12 E3
Daxian 35 C5
Daxue Shan .. 34 C5
Daylesford ... 62 C3
Dayr az Zawr .. 46 D5
Dayton 72 E3
Daytona Beach 75 E7
Dead Sea 47 E3
Deakin 60 G4
Deal I. 62 C4
Deán Funes .. 94 C4
Death Valley .. 82 B4
Deba Habe 55 F7
Debar 22 D3
Dębica 16 C5
Debre Markos . 53 F6
Debre Tabor .. 53 F6
Debrecen 16 E5
Decatur, Ala.,
 U.S.A. 74 B4
Decatur, Ill.,
 U.S.A. 77 F10
Deccan 43 L11
Děčín 16 C2
Dedéagach =
 Alexandroúpolis
 .... 22 D5

Dédougou 55 F4
Dee → 10 C5
Deepwater 63 A5
Degeh Bur .. 49 F3
Deggendorf ... 15 D7
Deh Bīd 44 D3
Dehi Titan .. 42 C3
Dehibat 54 B7
Dehkareqan .. 46 C6
Dehra Dun 42 D11
Dej 17 E6
Dekese 56 E4
Delano 82 C3
Delaware □ ... 73 E8
Delaware → .. 73 E8
Delegate 63 C4
Delgado, C. ... 57 G8
Delgo 53 D5
Delhi 42 E10
Delice → 46 C3
Delicias 84 B3
Delmenhorst . 14 B5
Delmiro Gouveia 93 D6
Deloraine 62 D4
Delungra 63 A5
Delvinë 23 E3
Demanda, Sierra
de la 18 A4
Demavand =
Damāvand .. 44 C3
Demba 56 F4
Dembecha 53 F6
Dembidolo ... 53 G5
Demini → ... 90 D6
Demirci 23 E7
Demirköy 22 D6
Dempo 37 E2
Den Haag = 's-
Gravenhage . 14 B3
Den Helder .. 14 B3
Denau 29 F7
Dendang 37 E3
Denia 19 C6
Denial B. 62 B1
Deniliquin ... 63 C3
Denman Glacier 96 A11
Denmark ■ ... 9 G9
Denmark Str. .. 66 C17
Denpasar 37 F5
Denton 78 C5
D'Entrecasteaux
Is. 61 B9
Denver 76 F2
Deoghar 40 E6
Deolali 43 K8
Deoria 40 D4
Deosai Mts. .. 42 B9
Dêqên 34 D4
Dera Ghazi Khan 42 D7
Dera Ismail
Khan 42 D7
Derbent 25 E6
Derby, Australia 60 D3
Derby, U.K. ... 11 E6
Derg, L. 11 E2
Dergaon 41 D9
Derry =
Londonderry 11 D3
Derudub 53 E6
Des Moines .. 77 E8
Des Moines → 77 E9
Desaguadero → 91 G5
Dese 49 E2
Desna → 17 C10
Desolación, I. .. 95 G2
Despeñaperros,
Paso 18 C4
Dessau 15 C7
Dessye = Dese 49 E2

D'Estrees B. ... 62 C2
Detmold 14 C5
Detroit 72 C4
Deutsche Bucht 14 A5
Deva 17 F6
Devakottai 43 Q11
Deventer 14 B4
Devonport,
Australia 62 D4
Devonport, N.Z. 64 B6
Dewas 43 H10
Deyhūk 44 C4
Deyyer 44 E2
Dezfūl 47 D7
Dezhneva, Mys 31 C16
Dhafra 44 F3
Dhahira 44 F4
Dhahran = Az
Zahrān 47 F7
Dhaka 41 F8
Dhaka □ 41 E8
Dhamar 49 E3
Dhamtari 40 G3
Dhanbad 40 F6
Dhangarhi 40 C3
Dhankuta 40 D6
Dhar 43 H9
Dharmapuri ... 43 N11
Dharwad 43 M9
Dhaulagiri 40 C4
Dhenkanal ... 40 G5
Dhíkti Óros ... 23 G5
Dhírfis 23 E4
Dhodhekánisos 23 F6
Dhrol 43 H7
Dhubaibah ... 44 F3
Dhuburi 41 D7
Dhule 43 J9
Dhut → 49 E5
Diafarabé 55 F4
Diamantina ... 93 F5
Diamantina → 62 A2
Diamantino ... 93 E2
Diamond
Harbour 40 F7
Diapaga 55 F5
Dibā 44 E4
Dibaya 56 F4
Dibaya-Lubue . 56 E3
Dibbi 49 G3
Dibrugarh 41 D10
Dickson 28 B9
Didiéni 55 F3
Diébougou 55 F4
Diefenbaker L. . 71 C9
Dieppe 12 B4
Digby 69 D4
Digges Is. 68 B3
Dighinala 41 F9
Digne-les-Bains 13 D7
Digos 38 C3
Digul → 39 F5
Dihang → 41 D10
Dijlah, Nahr → 47 E6
Dijon 13 C6
Dikimdya 31 D10
Dikson =
Dickson 28 B9
Dikwa 53 F1
Dili 39 F3
Dilling 53 F4
Dillingham 71 C4
Dilolo 56 G4
Dilston 62 D4
Dimashq 46 D4
Dimbokro 55 G4
Dimboola 62 C3
Dîmbovita → . 22 B6
Dimitrovgrad,
Bulgaria 22 C5

Dimitrovgrad,
Russia 24 C6
Dimitrovo =
Pernik 22 C4
Dinagat 38 B3
Dinajpur 41 E7
Dinan 12 B2
Dinant 14 C3
Dinar 46 C2
Dīnār, Kūh-e .. 44 D2
Dinara Planina . 20 B6
Dinard 12 B2
Dinaric Alps =
Dinara Planina 20 B6
Dindigul 43 P11
Dingle 11 E1
Dinguiraye 55 F2
Dingwall 10 C4
Dinosaur
National
Monument .. 81 E9
Diourbel 55 F1
Dipolog 38 C2
Dir 42 B7
Diré 55 E4
Dire Dawa 49 F3
Dirico 58 B4
Dirranbandi ... 63 A4
Disa 43 G8
Disappointment,
L. 60 E3
Disaster B. 63 C4
Discovery B. .. 62 C3
Disteghil Sar .. 42 A9
Distrito
Federal □ ... 93 F4
Diu 43 J7
Divinópolis ... 93 G5
Divnoye 25 D5
Dīwāl Kol 42 B5
Diyarbakır ... 46 C5
Diz Chah 44 C3
Djado 52 D1
Djakarta =
Jakarta 37 F3
Djambala 56 E2
Djanet 54 D6
Djawa = Jawa . 37 F3
Djelfa 54 B5
Djema 57 C5
Djenné 55 F4
Djerba, I. de .. 52 B1
Djerid, Chott .. 54 B6
Djibo 55 F4
Djibouti 49 E3
Djibouti ■ 49 E3
Djolu 56 D4
Djougou 55 G5
Djoum 56 D2
Djourab 53 E2
Djugu 57 D6
Dmitriya
Lapteva, Proliv 31 B12
Dnepr → =
Dnipro → .. 25 D3
Dneprodzerzhinsk
=
Dniprodzerzhynsk
.... 25 D3
Dnepropetrovsk
=
Dnipropetrovsk
.... 25 D4
Dnestr → =
Dnister → .. 17 E10
Dnestrovski =
Belgorod ... 24 C4
Dnieper =
Dnipro → .. 25 D3

Dniester =
Dnister → .. 17 E10
Dnipro → ... 25 D3
Dniprodzerzhynsk
.... 25 D3
Dnipropetrovsk 25 D4
Dnister → ... 17 E10
Dnistrovskyy
Lyman 17 E10
Dnyapro =
Dnipro → .. 25 D3
Doba 53 G2
Doberai, Jazirah 39 E4
Doblas 94 D4
Dobo 39 F4
Doboj 20 B7
Dobreta-Turnu-
Severin 22 B4
Dobrich 22 C6
Dobruja 22 B7
Dobrush 17 B10
Dodecanese =
Dhodhekánisos
.... 23 F6
Dodge City 78 A3
Dodoma 57 F7
Dogi 42 C3
Doha = Ad
Dawhah 44 E2
Dohazari 41 F9
Doi 39 D3
Dois Irmãos, Sa. 93 D5
Dolbeau 69 D3
Dole 13 C6
Dolomites =
Dolomiti 20 A3
Dolomiti 20 A3
Dolores 94 D5
Dolphin, C. ... 95 G5
Dolphin and
Union Str. .. 70 B8
Dombarovskiy . 29 D6
Dominica ■ .. 87 C7
Dominican
Rep. ■ 87 C5
Domo 49 F4
Domodóssola .. 20 A2
Domville, Mt. .. 63 A5
Don →, Russia 25 D4
Don →, U.K. .. 10 C5
Don Benito ... 18 C3
Donald 62 C3
Donau =
Dunărea → . 17 F9
Donauwörth .. 14 D6
Doncaster 11 E6
Dondo, Angola 56 F2
Dondo, Mozam. 59 B6
Dondo, Teluk .. 39 D2
Donegal 11 D2
Donets → 25 D5
Donetsk 25 D4
Donggala 39 E1
Dongola 53 E5
Dongou 56 D3
Dongting Hu .. 35 D6
Dongxing 35 D5
Donington, C. . 62 B2
Donnelly's
Crossing 64 A5
Donostia = San
Sebastián .. 19 A5
Dora Báltea → 20 B2
Dorchester, C. . 68 B3
Dordogne → .. 12 D3
Dordrecht 14 C3
Dori 55 F4
Dornbirn 14 E5
Dorohoi 17 E8

öröö Nuur 34 B4
orrigo 63 B5
ortmund 14 C4
oruma 57 D5
os Bahías, C. 95 E3
os Hermanas 18 D3
osso 55 F5
othan 74 D5
ouai 13 A5
ouala 56 D1
ouarnenez 12 B1
ouble Island Pt. 63 A5
oubs → 13 C6
oubtful Sd. 65 F2
oubtless B. 64 A5
ouentza 55 F4
ouglas, *U.K.* 11 D4
ouglas, *U.S.A.* 83 E8
oumé 56 D2
ourados 94 A6
ouro → 18 B1
over, *Australia* 62 D4
over, *U.K.* 11 F7
over, Str. of 11 F7
ovrefjell 8 F9
owlat Yār 45 C6
owlatābād 44 D4
owshī 45 C7
raa, Oued → 54 C2
răgăşani 22 B5
ragichyn 17 B7
ragoman, Prokhod 22 C4
raguignan 13 E7
rake 63 A5
akensberg 59 E5
áma 22 D5
rammen 9 G10
rau = Drava → 20 B7
ava → 20 B7
resden 15 C7
reux 12 B4
rina → 20 B7
ini → 22 C2
rochia 17 D8
rogheda 11 E3
rogichin = Dragichyn 17 B7
rogobych = Drohobych 17 D6
ohobych 17 D6
oichead Atha = Drogheda 11 E3
romedary, C. 63 C5
umheller 71 C8
ummond Pt. 62 B2
ut → 17 B10
rygalski I. 96 A11
schang 55 G7
ubā 47 F3
ubai = Dubayy 44 E3
ubăsari 17 E9
ubăsari Vdkhr. 17 E9
ubawnt → 70 B9
ubawnt, L. 70 B9
ubayy 44 E3
ubbo 63 B4
ublin, *Ireland* 11 E3
ublin, *U.S.A.* 75 C6
ubno 17 C7
ubossary = Dubăsari 17 E9
ubossary Vdkhr. = Dubăsari Vdkhr. 17 E9
ubovka 24 D5
Dubréka 55 G2
Dubrovitsa = Dubrovytsya 17 C8
Dubrovnik 20 C7
Dubrovytsya 17 C8
Dudhi 40 E4
Dudinka 30 C6
Duero = Douro → 18 B1
Dugi Otok 20 B5
Duisburg 14 C4
Dukelský Průsmyk 16 D5
Dukhān 44 E2
Duki 42 D6
Duku 55 F7
Dulce → 94 C4
Dulit, Banjaran 37 D4
Duluth 77 B8
Dum Duma 41 D10
Dum Hadjer 53 F2
Dumaguete 38 C2
Dumai 37 D2
Dumaran 38 B1
Dumfries 11 D5
Dumyât 52 B5
Dún Dealgan = Dundalk 11 D3
Dun Laoghaire 11 E3
Duna = Dunărea → 17 F9
Dunaj = Dunărea → 17 F9
Dunakeszi 16 E4
Dunărea → 17 F9
Dunaújváros 16 E4
Dunav = Dunărea → 17 F9
Dunback 65 F4
Dunbar 10 D5
Duncan 78 B5
Dundalk 11 D3
Dundee, *S. Africa* 59 D6
Dundee, *U.K.* 10 C5
Dundoo 63 A3
Dunedin 65 F4
Dunfermline 10 C5
Dungarvan 11 E3
Dungog 63 B5
Dungu 57 D5
Dunhuang 34 B4
Dunkerque 12 A5
Dunkirk = Dunkerque 12 A5
Dunkwa 55 G4
Dúnleary = Dun Laoghaire 11 E3
Dunolly 62 C3
Dunqul 52 D5
Dunstan Mts. 65 F3
Durance → 13 E6
Durango, *Mexico* 84 C4
Durango, *Spain* 19 A4
Durazno 94 C5
Durazzo = Durrësi 22 D2
Durban 59 D6
Düren 14 C4
Durg 40 G3
Durgapur 40 F6
Durham, *U.K.* 11 D6
Durham, *U.S.A.* 75 B8
Durham Downs 63 A4
Durmitor 22 C2
Durrësi 22 D2
Dursunbey 23 E7
D'Urville, Tanjung 39 E5
D'Urville I. 65 D5
Dusa Mareb 49 F4
Dushak 29 F7
Dushanbe 29 F7
Dusky Sd. 65 F2
Düsseldorf 14 C4
Dutch Harbor 71 C3
Duwādimi 47 F6
Duyun 35 D5
Düzce 46 B2
Duzdab = Zāhedān 45 D5
Dvina, Severnaya → 28 C5
Dvinsk = Daugavpils 24 B2
Dwarka 43 H6
Dyatlovo = Dzyatlava 17 B7
Dyer, C. 68 B4
Dyer Plateau 96 B3
Dyersburg 79 A9
Dymer 17 C10
Dynevor Downs 63 A3
Dzamin Üüd 35 B6
Dzerzhinsk 24 B5
Dzhambul = Zhambyl 29 E8
Dzhankoy 25 D3
Dzhardzhan 30 C10
Dzhezkazgan = Zhezqazghan 29 E7
Dzhizak = Jizzakh 29 E7
Działdowa 16 B5
Dzierzoniów 16 C3
Dzungaria = Junggar Pendi 34 B3
Dzungarian Gate = Alataw Shankou 34 B3
Dzuumod 35 B5
Dzyarzhynsk 17 B8
Dzyatlava 17 B7

E

Earnslaw, Mt. 65 F3
East Bengal 41 E7
East Beskids = Vychodné Beskydy 17 D5
East C. 64 B8
East China Sea 35 C7
East Falkland 95 G5
East Kilbride 10 D4
East London 59 E5
East Main = Eastmain 69 C3
East Orange 73 D8
East St. Louis 77 F9
East Toorale 63 B4
Eastbourne, *N.Z.* 65 D6
Eastbourne, *U.K.* 11 F7
Eastern Ghats 43 N11
Eastmain 69 C3
Eastmain → 69 C3
Eau Claire 77 C9
Eberswalde-Finow 15 B7
Ebolowa 56 D2
Ebro → 19 B6
Eceabat 23 D6
Ech Cheliff 54 A5
Echo Bay 70 B8
Echuca 63 C3
Ecija 18 D3
Ecuador ■ 90 D3
Ed Dâmer 53 E5
Ed Debba 53 E5
Ed Dueim 53 F5
Edd 49 E3
Eddystone Pt. 62 D4
Édea 56 D2
Eden 63 C4
Eder → 14 C5
Édhessa 23 D4
Edievale 65 F3
Edinburg 78 F4
Edinburgh 10 D5
Ediniţa 17 D8
Edirne 22 D6
Edithburgh 62 C2
Edmonton 71 C8
Edmundston 69 D4
Edremit 23 E6
Edremit Körfezi 23 E6
Edson 71 C8
Edward → 62 C3
Edward, L. 57 E5
Edward VII Land 96 C17
Edwards Plateau 78 D3
Égadi, Ísole 21 F4
Eger = Cheb 16 C1
Eger 16 E5
Egersund 9 G9
Egmont, C. 64 C5
Egmont, Mt. 64 C6
Eğridir 46 C2
Eğridir Gölü 46 C2
Egypt ■ 52 C5
Eibar 19 A4
Eidsvold 63 A5
Eifel 14 C4
Eigg 10 C3
Eil 49 F4
Eildon, L. 63 C4
Eindhoven 14 C3
Eire = Ireland ■ 11 E3
Eirunepé 91 E5
Eisenach 14 C6
Eisenerz 15 E8
Eivissa = Ibiza 19 C6
Eketahuna 64 D6
Ekibastuz 29 D8
El Aaiún 54 C2
El Alamein 52 B4
El Aricha 54 B4
El 'Arîsh 52 B5
El Asnam = Ech Cheliff 54 A5
El Bawiti 52 C4
El Bayadh 54 B5
El Callao 90 B6
El Centro 82 D5
El Cerro 91 G6
El Cuy 95 D3
El Cuyo 85 C7
El Dere 49 G4
El Diviso 90 C3
El Djouf 55 D3
El Dorado, *Ark., U.S.A.* 79 C7
El Dorado, *Kans., U.S.A.* 78 A5
El Dorado, *Venezuela* 90 B6
El Escorial 18 B3
El Faiyûm 52 C5
El Fâsher 53 F4
El Ferrol 18 A1
El Fuerte 84 B3
El Gal 49 E5

El Geneina

El Geneina = Al
Junaynah ... 53 F3
El Geteina 53 F5
El Gîza 52 C5
El Iskandarîya . 52 B4
El Jadida 54 B3
El Jebelein 53 F5
El Kab 53 E5
El Kala 54 A6
El Kamlin 53 E5
El Kef 54 A6
El Khandaq ... 53 E5
El Khârga 52 C5
El Khartûm ... 53 E5
El Khartûm
Bahrî 53 E5
El Laqâwa 53 F4
El Mafâza 53 F5
El Mahalla el
Kubra 52 B5
El Mansûra ... 52 B5
El Minyâ 52 C5
El Obeid 53 F5
El Odaiya 53 F4
El Oued 54 B6
El Paso 83 E9
El Prat de
Llobregat ... 19 B7
El Puerto de
Santa María . 18 D2
El Qâhira 52 B5
El Qantara 52 B5
El Qasr 52 C4
El Reno 78 B5
El Salvador ■ . 85 E7
El Shallal 52 D5
El Suweis 52 C5
El Tigre 90 B6
El Tocuyo 90 B5
El Turbio 95 G2
El Uqsur 52 C5
El Vigía 90 B4
El Wak 57 D8
El Wuz 53 E5
Elat 47 E3
Elâzığ 46 C4
Elba 20 C3
Elbasani 22 D3
Elbe ➜ 14 B5
Elbert, Mt. 83 A9
Elbeuf 12 B4
Elbidtan 46 C4
Elbing = Elbląg 16 A4
Elbląg 16 A4
Elbrus 25 E5
Elburz Mts. =
Alborz,
Reshteh-ye
Kühhä-ye ... 44 B3
Elche 19 C5
Elda 19 C5
Elde ➜ 15 B6
Eldoret 57 D7
Elektrostal 24 B4
Elephant I. 96 A4
Eleuthera 86 A4
Elgin, U.K. 10 C5
Elgin, U.S.A. .. 72 C1
Elgon, Mt. 57 D6
Eliase 39 F4
Elisabethville =
Lubumbashi . 59 A5
Elista 25 D5
Elizabeth,
Australia 62 B2
Elizabeth, U.S.A. 73 D8
Elizabeth City . 75 A9
Elizabethton ... 75 A6
Ełk 16 B6

Elkhart 72 D3
Elkhovo 22 C6
Elko 80 E6
Ellery, Mt. ... 63 C4
Ellesmere, L. .. 65 G5
Ellice Is. =
Tuvalu ■ ... 64 K12
Elliston 62 B1
Ellore = Eluru . 40 J3
Ellsworth Land 96 B2
Ellsworth Mts. . 96 B2
Elmore 63 C3
Elmshorn 14 B5
Eltham 64 C6
Eluru 40 J3
Elvas 18 C2
Elx = Elche .. 19 C5
Ely 11 E7
Emämrüd 44 B3
Emba = Embi . 29 E6
Emba ➜ =
Embi ➜ 29 E6
Embarcación .. 94 A4
Embi 29 E6
Embi ➜ 29 E6
Embrun 13 D7
Embu 57 E7
Emden 14 B4
Emerson 71 D10
Emet 23 E7
Emi Koussi ... 53 E2
Emine, Nos .. 22 C6
Emmen 14 B4
Empalme 84 B2
Empangeni ... 59 D6
Empedrado ... 94 B5
Empty Quarter
= Rub' al
Khali 48 D4
Ems ➜ 14 B4
En Nahud 53 F4
Enaratoli 39 E5
Enare =
Inarijärvi 8 E13
Encanto, C. ... 38 A2
Encarnación .. 94 B5
Encounter B. .. 62 C2
Ende 39 F2
Enderby Land . 96 A9
Enewetak Atoll 64 H11
Enez 23 D6
Engadin 13 C9
Engaño, C. 38 A2
Engels 24 C6
Enggano 37 F2
Engkilili 37 D4
England □ ... 11 E6
Englewood ... 76 F2
English Bazar =
Ingraj Bazar . 40 E7
English Channel 11 F5
Enid 78 A5
Enna 21 F5
Ennedi 53 E3
Enngonia 63 A4
Ennis 11 E2
Enniskillen ... 11 D3
Enns ➜ 15 D8
Enschede 14 B4
Ensenada 84 A1
Entebbe 57 D6
Entroncamento 18 C1
Enugu 55 G6
Enugu Ezike .. 55 G6
Eólie, Ís. 21 E5
Épernay 13 B5
Ephesus 23 F6
Épinal 13 B7
Epukiro 58 C3

Equatorial
Guinea ■ ... 56 D1
Er Rahad 53 F5
Er Rif 54 A4
Er Roseires .. 53 F5
Erâwadî Myit =
Irrawaddy ➜ 41 K10
Erbil = Arbîl .. 46 C6
Ercıyaş Dağı .. 46 C3
Érd 16 E4
Erdek 23 D6
Erebus, Mt. ... 96 B15
Erechim 94 B6
Ereğli, Konya,
Turkey 46 C3
Ereğli,
Zonguldak,
Turkey 46 B2
Eresma ➜ ... 18 B3
Erewadi
Myitwanya .. 41 K10
Erfurt 15 C6
Ergani 46 C4
Érice 21 E4
Erie 73 C5
Erie, L. 72 C5
Erigavo 49 E4
Erímanthos ... 23 F3
Erimo-misaki .. 32 F12
Eritrea ■ 49 E2
Erlangen 15 D6
Ermenak 46 C3
Ermoúpolis =
Síros 23 F5
Ernakulam =
Cochin 43 Q10
Erne, Lower L. . 11 D3
Erode 43 P10
Eromanga ... 63 A3
Erramala Hills . 43 M11
Ertis ➜ =
Irtysh ➜ ... 28 C7
Erzgebirge ... 15 C7
Erzincan 46 C4
Erzurum 46 C5
Es Sahrâ' Esh
Sharqîya ... 52 C5
Es Sînâ' 52 C5
Esbjerg 9 G9
Esch-sur-Alzette 13 B6
Escuinapa 84 C3
Eşfahän 44 C2
Esh Sham =
Dimashq 46 D4
Esil ➜ =
Ishim ➜ ... 29 D8
Eskilstuna 9 G11
Eskimo Pt. =
Arviat 70 B10
Eskişehir 46 C2
Esla ➜ 18 B2
Eslämäbäd-e
Gharb 46 D6
Eşme 23 E7
Esmeraldas ... 90 C3
Esperance 60 G3
Esperanza 94 C4
Espichel, C. .. 18 C1
Espinal 90 C4
Espinazo, Sierra
del =
Espinhaço,
Serra do ... 93 F5
Espinhaço, Serra
do 93 F5
Espírito Santo □ 93 G5
Esquel 95 E2
Esquina 94 C5
Essaouira 54 B3

Essen .... 14 ●
Essequibo ➜ . 90 ●
Esslingen ..... 14 ●
Estados, I. de
Los .... 95 C
Estância ...... 93 ●
Estevan ...... 71 ●
Estonia ■ ..... 24 ●
Estrêla, Serra da 18 ●
Estremoz ..... 18 ●
Estrondo, Serra
do .... 92 ●
Esztergom .... 16 ●
Etadunna .... 62 ▲
Étampes ..... 12 ●
Etawah ...... 42 F
Ethiopia ■ 49
Etna .... 21 ●
Etosha Pan ... 58 ●
Euboea =
Évvoia ...... 23 ●
Eucumbene, L. 63 ●
Eufaula ...... 74 ●
Eugene ...... 80 ●
Eugowra ..... 63 ●
Eulo .... 63 ▲
Euphrates =
Furât, Nahr
al ➜ .... 47 ●
Eureka .... 80 ●
Euroa .... 63 ●
Europa, I. ..... 59 ◄
Europa, Picos de 18 ◄
Europa, Pta. de 18 ●
Europa Pt. =
Europa, Pta.
de .... 18 ●
Evans Head ... 63 ▲
Evanston .... 72 ●
Evansville .... 72 ●
Everard, L. .... 62 ●
Everest, Mt. ... 40 ●
Everett ...... 80 ●
Everglades
National Park 75 ●
Evinayong .... 56 ●
Évora .... 18 ●
Évreux ...... 12 ●
Évros ➜ ..... 22 ●
Evry .... 12 ●
Évvoia .... 23 ●
Ewo .... 56 ●
Exaltación ... 91 ●
Exeter .... 11 ●
Exmoor ...... 11 ●
Exmouth ..... 11 ●
Extremadura □ 18 ●
Eyasi, L. ...... 57 ●
Eyre (North), L. 62 ▲
Eyre (South), L. 62 ▲
Eyre, L. ...... 60 ●
Eyre Cr. ➜ ... 62 ▲
Eyre Mts. ..... 65 ●
Eyre Pen. ..... 62 ●
Ezine .... 23 ●

F

F.Y.R.O.M. =
Macedonia ■ 22 ●
Fabriano ..... 20 ●
Facatativá .... 90 ●
Fachi .... 55 ●
Fada .... 53 ●
Fada-n-Gourma 55 ●
Faddeyevskiy,
Ostrov ...... 31 B

ăḡilī 47 F7
aenza 20 B3
æroe Is. =
　Føroyar 6 C4
ăḡăras 17 F7
agnano, L. ... 95 G3
ahraj 45 D4
ahüd 44 F4
air Isle 10 B6
airbanks 71 B5
airfield, *Ala.*,
　U.S.A. 74 C4
airfield, *Calif.*,
　U.S.A. 80 F2
airlie 65 F4
airweather, Mt. 71 C6
aisalabad 42 D8
aizabad 40 D4
akfak 39 E4
alaise 12 B3
alam 41 F9
alconara
　Maríttima ... 20 C4
alcone, C. 20 D2
aleshty =
　Fălești 17 E8
ălești 17 E8
alkland Is. □ . 95 G5
alkland Sd. .. 95 G5
all River 73 D10
almouth 11 F4
alse B. 58 E3
ălticeni 17 E8
alun 9 F11
amagusta 46 D3
andriana 59 J9
ano 20 C4
ao = Al Fāw . 47 E7
aradje 57 D5
arafangana .. 59 J9
arăh 42 C3
arăh □ 42 C3
aranah 55 F2
arasăn, Jazá'ir 49 D3
arasan Is. =
　Farasān,
　Jazá'ir 49 D3
areham 11 F6
arewell, C. .. 64 D5
arewell C. =
　Farvel, Kap . 68 C6
arghona 29 E8
argo 76 B6
arim 55 F1
arīmān 45 C4
arina 62 B2
aro, *Brazil* ... 92 C2
aro, *Portugal* . 18 D2
arrāshband .. 44 D3
arrell Flat 62 B2
arrukhabad-
　cum-
　Fatehgarh .. 42 F11
ărs □ 44 D3
ársala 23 E4
artak, Rás .. 47 E3
arvel, Kap ... 68 C6
āryăb □ 45 B6
asă 44 D3
asano 21 D6
astiv 17 C9
astov = Fastiv 17 C9
atagar, Tanjung 39 E4
atehgarh 42 F11
atehpur, *Raj.*,
　India 42 F9
atehpur, *Ut. P.*,
　India 40 E3
avara 21 F4

Favignana ... 21 F4
Faya-Largeau .. 53 E2
Fayd 47 F5
Fayetteville,
　Ark., U.S.A. . 79 A6
Fayetteville,
　N.C., U.S.A. . 75 B8
Fazilka 42 D9
Fdérik 54 D2
Feather → ... 80 F3
Featherston ... 65 D6
Fécamp 12 B4
Fehmarn 15 A6
Feilding 64 D6
Feira de Santana 93 E6
Feldkirch 14 E5
Felipe Carrillo
　Puerto 85 D7
Felixstowe 11 F7
Fengjie 35 C5
Fenyang 35 C6
Feodosiya 25 D4
Ferdows 44 C4
Ferfer 49 F4
Fergana =
　Farghona .. 29 E8
Fermo 20 C4
Fernando de
　Noronha 92 C7
Fernando Póo =
　Bioko 56 D1
Ferozepore =
　Firozpur ... 42 D9
Ferrara 20 B3
Ferreñafe 91 E3
Ferret, C. 12 D3
Ferrol = El
　Ferrol 18 A1
Fès 54 B4
Feshi 56 F3
Feteşti 22 B6
Fetlar 10 A6
Feuilles → ... 68 C3
Fezzan 52 C2
Fianarantsoa .. 59 J9
Fianga 53 G2
Ficksburg 59 D5
Fieri 23 D2
Figeac 12 D5
Figueira da Foz 18 B1
Figueras 19 A7
Figuig 54 B4
Fiji ■ 64 L12
Filiatrá 23 F3
Filyos → 46 B3
Fíngöe 59 A6
Finike 46 C2
Finisterre, C. .. 18 A1
Finke → 62 A2
Finland ■ 8 F13
Finland, G. of . 9 G13
Finlay → 70 C7
Finley 63 C4
Finniss, C. 62 B1
Fiora → 20 C3
Firat = Furăt,
　Nahr al → .. 47 E6
Firenze 20 C3
Firozabad 42 F11
Firozpur 42 D9
Firūzābād ... 44 D3
Firūzkūh 44 C3
Fish → 58 D3
Fishguard 11 E4
Fitri, L. 53 F2
Fitz Roy 95 F3
Fiume = Rijeka 20 B5
Fizi 57 E5
Flagstaff 83 C7

Flaming Gorge
　Reservoir ... 81 E9
Flamingo, Teluk 39 F5
Flandre 14 C2
Flathead L. 81 B6
Flattery, C. 80 A1
Flensburg 14 A5
Flers 12 B3
Flesko, Tanjung 39 D2
Flin Flon 71 C9
Flinders → ... 61 D7
Flinders I. 62 C4
Flinders Ras. .. 62 B2
Flint 72 C4
Flint I. 65 L15
Flinton 63 A4
Florence =
　Firenze 20 C3
Florence, *Ala.*,
　U.S.A. ... 74 B4
Florence, *S.C.*,
　U.S.A. ... 75 B8
Florence, L. ... 62 A2
Flores 39 F2
Flores Sea = . 39 F2
Floreşti 17 E9
Floriano 92 D5
Florianópolis .. 94 B7
Florida 94 C5
Florida □ ... 75 F6
Florida, Straits
　of 86 B3
Flórina 23 D3
Florø 8 F9
Fluk 39 E3
Flushing =
　Vlissingen .. 14 C2
Fly → 61 B7
Flying Fish, C. . 96 B1
Foça 23 E6
Focşani 17 F8
Fóggia 20 D5
Föhr 14 A5
Foix 12 E4
Foligno 20 C4
Folkestone ... 11 F7
Fond du Lac .. 77 D10
Fondi 20 D4
Fonsagrada ... 18 A2
Fonseca, G. de 85 E7
Fontainebleau . 13 B5
Fonte Boa ... 90 D5
Fontenay-le-
　Comte 12 C3
Foochow =
　Fuzhou 35 D6
Forbes 63 B4
Ford's Bridge . 63 A4
Forécariah ... 55 G2
Forestier Pen. . 62 D4
Forfar 10 C5
Forlì 20 B4
Formentera ... 19 C6
Formentor, C. de 19 C7
Former
　Yugoslav
　Republic of
　Macedonia =
　Macedonia ■ 22 D3
Fórmia 20 D4
Formosa =
　Taiwan ■ ... 35 D7
Formosa 94 B5
Formosa, Serra 93 E3
Formosa Bay .. 57 E8
Føroyar =
　Føroyar 6 C4
Føroyar 6 C4
Forrest 62 C3

Forsayth 61 D7
Forst 15 C8
Forster 63 B5
Fort Albany ... 69 C2
Fort Collins ... 76 E2
Fort-de-France . 87 D7
Fort de Possel =
　Possel 56 C3
Fort Dodge ... 77 D7
Fort Franklin . 70 B7
Fort Good-Hope 70 B7
Fort Hertz =
　Putao 41 D11
Fort Lauderdale 75 F7
Fort Liard 70 B7
Fort Macleod . 71 D8
Fort MacMahon 54 C5
Fort McPherson 70 B6
Fort Miribel .. 54 C5
Fort Myers ... 75 F7
Fort Norman .. 70 B7
Fort Peck L. .. 81 B10
Fort Pierce ... 75 F7
Fort Portal 57 D6
Fort Providence 70 B8
Fort Resolution 70 B8
Fort Rosebery =
　Mansa 57 G5
Fort Rupert =
　Waskaganish 69 C3
Fort Sandeman 42 D6
Fort Scott 79 A6
Fort Severn ... 69 C2
Fort Shevchenko 29 E6
Fort Simpson . 70 B7
Fort Smith,
　Canada 70 B8
Fort Smith,
　U.S.A. 79 B6
Fort Trinquet =
　Bir Mogrein . 54 C2
Fort Walton
　Beach 74 D4
Fort Wayne ... 72 D3
Fort William .. 10 C4
Fort Worth ... 78 C5
Fort Yukon 71 B5
Fortaleza 92 C6
Forūr 44 E3
Foshan 35 D6
Fossano 20 B1
Fougamou ... 56 E2
Fougères 12 B3
Foula 10 A5
Foumban 55 G7
Foúrnoi 23 F6
Fouta Djalon .. 55 F2
Foveaux Str. .. 65 G3
Foxe Basin ... 68 B3
Foxe Chan. ... 68 B2
Foxe Pen. ... 68 B3
Foxton 64 D6
Foz do Gregório 91 E4
Foz do Iguaçu . 94 B6
Franca 93 G4
Francavilla
　Fontana 21 D6
France ■ 13 C5
Frances 62 C3
Franceville ... 56 E2
Franche-Comté 13 C6
Francistown ... 59 C5
Frankfurt,
　Brandenburg,
　Germany ... 15 B8
Frankfurt,
　Hessen,
　Germany ... 14 C5
Fränkische Alb 15 D6

Franklin B.

Franklin B. 70 B7
Franklin I. 96 B15
Franklin Mts. .. 70 B7
Franklin Str. ... 70 A10
Frankston 63 C4
Frantsa Iosifa,
 Zemlya 28 A6
Franz 69 D2
Franz Josef
 Land =
 Frantsa Iosifa,
 Zemlya 28 A6
Fraser → 71 D7
Fraser I. 63 A5
Fraserburgh ... 10 C5
Fray Bentos ... 94 C5
Fredericksburg 73 E7
Fredericton ... 69 D4
Fredrikstad 9 G10
Freeport,
 Bahamas ... 86 A4
Freeport, U.S.A. 77 D10
Freetown 55 G2
Fregenal de la
 Sierra 18 C2
Freibourg =
 Fribourg 13 C7
Freiburg 14 E4
Freire 95 D2
Freising 15 D6
Freistadt 15 D8
Fréjus 13 E7
Fremont 82 B2
French
 Guiana ■ ... 92 B3
French
 Polynesia ■ . 65 M16
Fresco → 92 D3
Freshfield, C. .. 96 A14
Fresnillo 84 C4
Fresno 82 B3
Freycinet Pen. . 62 D4
Fria, C. 58 B2
Frías 94 B3
Fribourg 13 C7
Friedrichshafen 14 E5
Friendly Is. =
 Tonga ■ 65 L13
Frobisher B. ... 68 B4
Frobisher Bay =
 Iqaluit 68 B4
Frome, L. 62 B2
Frome Downs . 62 B2
Front Range ... 81 E11
Frosinone 20 D4
Frunze =
 Bishkek 29 E8
Frutal 93 F4
Frýdek-Místek . 16 D4
Fuchou =
 Fuzhou 35 D6
Fuengirola 18 D3
Fuentes de
 Oñoro 18 B2
Fuerte → 84 B3
Fuerte Olimpo . 91 H7
Fuerteventura . 54 C2
Fuhai 34 B3
Fuji-San 32 B6
Fujian □ 35 D6
Fujinomiya ... 32 B6
Fujisawa 32 B6
Fukien =
 Fujian □ 35 D6
Fukuchiyama .. 32 B4
Fukui 32 A5
Fukuoka 32 C2
Fukushima 33 G12
Fukuyama 32 B3

Fulda 14 C5
Fulda → 14 C5
Fullerton 82 D4
Funabashi 32 B7
Funchal 54 B1
Fundación 90 A4
Fundão 18 B2
Fundy, B. of ... 69 D4
Funtua 55 F6
Furät, Nahr
 al → 47 E6
Furneaux Group 62 D4
Fürstenwalde .. 15 B8
Fürth 14 D6
Fury and Hecla
 Str. 68 B2
Fusagasuga ... 90 C4
Fushun 35 B7
Futuna 64 L12
Fuxin 35 B7
Fuyuan 35 B8
Fuzhou 35 D6
Fyn 9 G10

G

Gabela 56 G2
Gabès 54 B7
Gabès, G. de .. 52 B1
Gabon ■ 56 E2
Gaborone 59 C5
Gabrovo 22 C5
Gachsārān 44 D2
Gadag 43 M9
Gadarwara ... 43 H11
Gadhada 43 J7
Gadsden 74 B4
Gadwal 43 L10
Gafsa 54 B6
Gagnoa 55 G3
Gagnon 69 C4
Gaillimh =
 Galway 11 E2
Gainesville, Fla.,
 U.S.A. 75 E6
Gainesville, Ga.,
 U.S.A. 75 B6
Gainesville,
 Tex., U.S.A. .. 78 C5
Gairdner, L. ... 62 B2
Galangue 58 A3
Galashiels 10 D5
Galaţi 17 F9
Galatina 21 D7
Galcaio 49 F4
Galdhøpiggen . 8 F9
Galela 39 D3
Galesburg 77 E9
Galich 24 B5
Galicia □ 18 A2
Galilee, Sea of
 = Yam
 Kinneret 46 D3
Gallabat 53 F6
Gállego → .. 19 B5
Gallegos → .. 95 G3
Gallinas, Pta. .. 90 A4
Gallipoli =
 Gelibolu 23 D6
Gallípoli 21 D6
Gällivare 8 E12
Galloway, Mull
 of 11 D4
Galong 63 B4
Galveston 79 E6
Gálvez 94 C4

Galway 11 E2
Galway B. 11 E2
Gambaga 55 F4
Gambela 53 G5
Gambia ■ 55 F1
Gambia → ... 55 F1
Gambier Is. ... 62 C2
Gamboma 56 E3
Gan Jiang → . 35 D6
Ganāveh 44 D2
Gäncä 25 E6
Gand = Gent .. 14 C2
Ganda 58 A2
Gandak → ... 40 E5
Gandava 42 E5
Gander 69 D5
Gandhi Sagar . 43 G9
Gandi 55 F6
Gandía 19 C5
Ganedidalem =
 Gani 39 E3
Ganga → 41 F8
Ganganagar .. 42 E8
Gangara 55 F6
Gangaw 41 F10
Gangdisê Shan 40 B3
Ganges =
 Ganga → .. 41 F8
Gangtok 41 D7
Gani 39 E3
Gansu □ 34 C5
Ganta 55 G3
Gantheaume, C. 62 C2
Gantsevichi =
 Hantsavichy . 17 B8
Ganyem 39 E6
Ganzhou 35 D6
Gaoua 55 F4
Gaoual 55 F2
Gaoxiong 35 D7
Gap 13 D7
Gar 34 C2
Garabogazköl
 Aylagy 29 E6
Garanhuns 92 D6
Garawe 55 H3
Gard 49 F4
Garda, L. di ... 20 B3
Garden City ... 78 A3
Garden Grove . 82 D4
Gardēz 42 C6
Gargano, Mte. . 20 D5
Garigliano → . 20 D5
Garland 81 E7
Garm 29 F8
Garmisch-
 Partenkirchen 14 E6
Garmsār 44 C3
Garoe 49 F4
Garonne → .. 12 D3
Garoua 53 G1
Garrison Res. =
 Sakakawea, L. 76 B4
Garry, L. 70 B9
Garsen 57 E8
Garvie Mts. ... 65 F3
Garwa =
 Garoua 53 G1
Gary 72 D2
Garzê 34 C5
Garzón 90 C3
Gasan Kuli =
 Hasan Kuli .. 29 F6
Gascogne 12 E4
Gascogne, G. de 12 D2
Gascony =
 Gascogne ... 12 E4
Gashaka 55 G7
Gaspé 69 D4

Gaspé, C. de .. 69 D4
Gaspé, Pén. de 69 D4
Gasteiz = Vitoria 19 A4
Gastonia 75 B5
Gastre 95 E2
Gata, C. de 19 D4
Gata, Sierra de 18 B2
Gateshead 11 D6
Gauhati 41 D8
Gavāter 45 E5
Gávdhos 23 G5
Gävle 8 F11
Gawilgarh Hills 43 J10
Gawler 62 B2
Gaxun Nur 34 B5
Gaya, India ... 40 E5
Gaya, Niger ... 55 F5
Gayndah 63 A5
Gaysin =
 Haysyn 17 D9
Gayvoron =
 Hayvoron ... 17 D9
Gaza 47 E3
Gaziantep 46 C4
Gazli 29 E6
Gdańsk 16 A4
Gdańska, Zatoka 16 A4
Gdov 24 B2
Gdynia 16 A4
Gebe 39 D3
Gebeit Mine ... 52 D3
Gebze 22 D2
Gedaref 53 F5
Gede, Tanjung 37 F3
Gediz → 23 E6
Gedser 9 H11
Geelong 63 C3
Geesthacht ... 14 B6
Geidam 53 F1
Geili 53 E5
Geita 57 E6
Gejiu 34 D5
Gela 21 F5
Geladi 49 F4
Gelehun 55 G2
Gelibolu 23 D6
Gelsenkirchen . 14 C4
Gemas 37 D2
Gemena 56 D3
Gemerek 46 C6
Gemlik 23 D7
General Acha . 94 D3
General Alvear,
 Buenos Aires,
 Argentina ... 94 D4
General Alvear,
 Mendoza,
 Argentina ... 94 D3
General Artigas 94 B4
General
 Belgrano 94 D4
General Guido . 94 D4
General Juan
 Madariaga .. 94 D5
General La
 Madrid 94 D4
General
 MacArthur .. 38 B6
General Martín
 Miguel de
 Güemes 94 A4
General Paz ... 94 B4
General Pico .. 94 D3
General Pinedo 94 B4
General Santos 38 C5
General Villegas 94 D3
Geneva =
 Genève 13 C7

Geneva, L. = Léman, L. 13 C7
Genève 13 C7
Genil → 18 D3
Gennargentu, Mti. del 21 D2
Genoa = Génova 20 B2
Genoa 63 C4
Génova 20 B2
Génova, G. di . 20 C2
Gent 14 C2
Georga, Zemlya 28 A5
George 58 E4
George → 68 C4
George, L., *N.S.W., Australia* 63 C4
George, L., *S. Austral., Australia* 62 C3
George, L., *Uganda* 57 D6
George River = Kangiqsualujjuaq 68 C4
George Sound . 65 F2
George Town . 36 C2
George V Land 96 A14
George VI Sound 96 B3
Georgetown, *Gambia* 55 F2
Georgetown, *Guyana* 90 B7
Georgia □ 75 C6
Georgia ■ 25 E5
Georgian B. ... 69 D2
Georgiu-Dezh = Liski 24 C4
Georgiyevsk .. 25 E5
Gera 15 C7
Geral de Goiás, Serra 93 E4
Geraldton 60 F1
Gerede 46 B3
Gereshk 42 D4
Gerlogubi 49 F4
Germany ■ ... 14 C6
Germiston 59 D5
Gerona 19 B7
Geser 39 E4
Getafe 18 B4
Gettysburg 73 E7
Getz Ice Shelf . 96 B18
Ghaghara → . 40 E5
Ghana ■ 55 G4
Ghanzi 58 C4
Ghardaïa 54 B5
Gharyān 52 B1
Ghat 54 D7
Ghawdex = Gozo 21 F5
Ghayl 47 G6
Ghazal, Bahr el →, *Chad* . 53 F2
Ghazâl, Bahr el →, *Sudan* 57 C6
Ghazaouet 54 A4
Ghaziabad 42 E10
Ghazipur 40 E4
Ghaznī 42 C6
Ghaznī □ 42 C6
Ghèlinsor 49 F4
Ghent = Gent . 14 C2
Ghizao 42 C4
Ghowr □ 42 C4
Ghugus 43 K11
Ghūrīān 42 B2
Gia Lai = Pleiku 36 B3
Gian 38 C3
Giarabub = Al Jaghbūb 52 C3
Giarre 21 F5
Gibraltar ■ ... 18 D3
Gibraltar, Str. of 18 E3
Gibson Desert . 60 E4
Gidole 53 G6
Giessen 14 C5
Gifu 32 B5
Giglio 20 C3
Gijón 18 A3
Gila → 82 D5
Gīlān □ 46 C7
Gilbert Is. 64 J12
Gilgandra 63 B4
Gilgit 42 B9
Gilles, L. 62 B2
Gilmore 63 C4
Gimbi 53 G6
Gin Gin 63 A5
Ginir 49 F3
Giohar 49 G4
Gióna, Óros ... 23 E4
Girardot 90 C4
Giresun 46 B4
Girga 52 C5
Giridih 40 E6
Girilambone .. 63 B4
Girne = Kyrenia 46 D3
Girona = Gerona 19 B7
Gironde → ... 12 D3
Girvan 10 D4
Gisborne 64 C8
Gisenyi 57 E5
Gitega 57 E5
Giuba → 49 G3
Giurgiu 22 C5
Giza = El Gîza . 52 C5
Giżycko 16 A5
Gjirokastra 23 D3
Gjoa Haven ... 70 B10
Glace Bay 69 D5
Gladstone, *Queens., Australia* 61 E9
Gladstone, *S. Austral., Australia* 62 B2
Glåma = Glomma → . 9 G10
Glasgow 10 D4
Glazov 28 D6
Gleiwitz = Gliwice 16 C4
Glen Canyon National Recreation Area 83 B7
Glen Innes 63 A5
Glendale 82 C3
Glenelg 62 B2
Glenelg → ... 62 C3
Glenmorgan .. 63 A4
Glenorchy 62 D4
Glenreagh 63 B5
Glenrothes 10 C5
Glens Falls 73 C9
Gliwice 16 C4
Głogów 16 C3
Glomma → .. 9 G10
Glorieuses, Is. . 59 G9
Gloucester, *Australia* 63 B5
Gloucester, *U.K.* 11 F5
Glusk 17 B9
Gmünd 15 D8
Gmunden 15 E7
Gniezno 16 B3
Go Cong 36 B3
Goa 43 M8
Goa □ 43 M8
Goalen Hd. ... 63 C5
Goalpara 41 D8
Goba, *Ethiopia* 49 F2
Goba, *Mozam.* . 59 D6
Gobabis 58 C3
Gobi 35 B6
Gochas 58 C3
Godavari → .. 40 J4
Godavari Point 40 J4
Godhra 43 H8
Gods → 71 C10
Gods L. 71 C10
Godthåb 68 B5
Godwin Austen = K2 .... 42 B10
Goeie Hoop, Kaap die = Good Hope, C. of 58 E3
Gogra = Ghaghara → 40 E5
Goiânia 93 F4
Goiás 93 F3
Goiás □ 93 E4
Goio-Ere 94 A6
Gojra 42 D8
Gökçeada 23 D5
Gokteik 41 F11
Gold Coast 63 A5
Golden Gate .. 80 G2
Goldsboro 75 B9
Goleniów 16 B2
Golfo Aranci .. 20 D2
Golspie 10 C5
Goma 57 E5
Gomel = Homyel 17 B10
Gomera 54 C1
Gómez Palacio 84 B4
Gomogomo ... 39 F4
Gomoh 40 F6
Gompa = Ganta 55 G3
Gonābād 44 C4
Gonaïves 87 C5
Gonbab-e Kāvūs 44 B3
Gonda 40 D3
Gonder 53 F6
Gönen 23 D6
Gonghe 34 C5
Gongolgon ... 63 B4
Goniri 53 F1
Good Hope, C. of 58 E3
Goodooga 63 A4
Goolgowi 63 B4
Goombalie 63 A4
Goondiwindi .. 63 A5
Gooray 63 A5
Gop 43 H6
Göppingen 14 D5
Gorakhpur 40 D4
Goražde 20 C7
Gordon → ... 62 D4
Gore, *Australia* 63 A5
Goré, *Chad* ... 53 G2
Gore, *Ethiopia* . 53 G6
Gore, *N.Z.* 65 G3
Gorgān 44 B3
Gorgona, I. ... 90 C3
Gorízia 20 B4
Gorki = Nizhniy Novgorod ... 24 B5
Gorkiy = Nizhniy Novgorod ... 24 B5
Gorkovskoye Vdkhr. 24 B5
Görlitz 15 C8
Gorlovka = Horlivka 25 D4
Gorna Dzhumayo = Blagoevgrad 22 C4
Gorna Oryakhovitsa 22 C5
Gorno-Altay □ . 29 D9
Gorno-Altaysk . 29 D9
Gorno Slinkino = Gornopravdinsk 29 C8
Gornopravdinsk 29 C8
Gorodenka = Horodenka .. 17 D7
Gorodok = Horodok 17 D6
Gorokhov = Horokhiv 17 C7
Gorontalo 39 D2
Gorzów Wielkopolski 16 B2
Gosford 63 B5
Goslar 14 C6
Gospič 20 B5
Göta kanal 9 G11
Göteborg 9 G10
Gotha 14 C6
Gothenburg = Göteborg ... 9 G10
Gotland 9 G11
Göttingen 14 C5
Gottwaldov = Zlin 16 D3
Gouda 14 B3
Gouin, Rés. ... 69 D3
Goulburn 63 B4
Gounou-Gaya . 53 G2
Gouri 53 E2
Gourma Rharous 55 E4
Gourock Ra. ... 63 C4
Governador Valadares ... 93 F5
Gowd-e Zirreh . 42 E3
Goya 94 B5
Goyder Lagoon 62 A2
Goyllarisquisga 91 F3
Goz Beîda 53 F3
Gozo 21 F5
Graaff-Reinet .. 58 E4
Gračac 20 B5
Gracias a Dios, C. 86 D3
Grado 18 A2
Gradule 63 A4
Grafton 63 A5
Graham Bell, Os. 28 A7
Graham Land . 96 A3
Grahamstown . 59 E5
Grajaú 92 D4
Grajaú → 92 C5
Grampian Highlands = Grampian Mts. 10 C4
Grampian Mts. 10 C4
Gran Canaria .. 54 C1
Gran Chaco ... 94 B4
Gran Paradiso . 20 B1
Gran Sasso d'Italia 20 C4
Granada, *Nic.* . 85 E7
Granada, *Spain* 18 D4

Granby

Granby 69 D3
Grand Bahama 86 A4
Grand Bassam 55 G4
Grand Canyon . 83 B6
Grand Cayman 86 C3
Grand Coulee
Dam 80 B4
Grand Forks,
Canada 71 D8
Grand Forks,
U.S.A. 76 B6
Grand Island . . 76 E5
Grand Lahou . . 55 G3
Grand Rapids,
Canada 71 C10
Grand Rapids,
U.S.A. 72 C3
Grand St.-
Bernard, Col
du 13 D7
Grand Teton . . 81 D8
Grande →,
Argentina . . . 94 A3
Grande →,
Bolivia 91 G6
Grande →,
Bahia, Brazil . 93 E5
Grande →,
Minas Gerais,
Brazil 93 G3
Grande, B. 95 G3
Grande, Rio → 79 F5
Grande Baleine,
R. de la → . . 69 C3
Grande de
Santiago → 84 C3
Granite City . . . 77 F9
Granity 65 D4
Granja 92 C5
Granollers 19 B7
Grantham 11 E6
Granville 12 B3
Gras, L. de 70 B8
Grasse 13 E7
Grassmere 62 B3
Graulhet 12 E4
's-Gravenhage . 14 B3
Gravesend 63 A5
Graz 15 E8
Great Abaco I. . 86 A4
Great Australian
Bight 60 G4
Great Barrier I. 64 B6
Great Barrier
Reef 61 D8
Great Basin . . . 80 F5
Great Bear → . 70 B7
Great Bear L. . . 70 B7
Great Belt =
Store Bælt . . 9 G10
Great Dividing
Ra. 61 E8
Great Falls . . . 81 B8
Great Inagua I. 86 B5
Great Indian
Desert = Thar
Desert 42 F7
Great Karoo . . . 58 E4
Great Lake . . . 62 D4
Great Ouse → 11 E7
Great Ruaha → 57 F7
Great Saint
Bernard P. =
Grand St.-
Bernard, Col
du 13 D7
Great Salt L. . . 81 E7
Great Salt Lake
Desert 81 E7

Great Sandy
Desert 60 E3
Great Sangi =
Sangihe, P. . . 39 D3
Great Slave L. . 70 B8
Great Smoky
Mts. Nat. Pk. 75 B6
Great Victoria
Desert 60 F4
Great Wall 35 C5
Great Yarmouth 11 E7
Greater Antilles 86 C5
Greater Sunda
Is. 37 F4
Gredos, Sierra
de 18 B3
Greece ■ 23 E4
Greeley 76 E2
Green → 83 A8
Green Bay 72 B2
Green C. 63 C5
Greenland ■ . . 66 C9
Greenock 10 D4
Greensboro . . . 75 A8
Greenville,
Liberia 55 G3
Greenville, Ala.,
U.S.A. 74 D4
Greenville,
Miss., U.S.A. . 79 C8
Greenville, N.C.,
U.S.A. 75 B9
Greenville, S.C.,
U.S.A. 75 B6
Greenwood,
Miss., U.S.A. . 79 C8
Greenwood,
S.C., U.S.A. . 75 B6
Gregory, L. . . . 62 A2
Greifswald . . . 15 A7
Greiz 15 C7
Gremikha 28 C4
Grenada ■ . . . 87 D7
Grenfell 63 B4
Grenoble 13 D6
Grey → 65 E4
Grey Ra. 63 A3
Greymouth . . . 65 E4
Greytown, N.Z. 65 D6
Greytown,
S. Africa . . . 59 D6
Griffin 75 C5
Griffith 63 B4
Grimari 56 C4
Grimaylov =
Hrymayliv . . . 17 D8
Grimsby 11 E6
Gris-Nez, C. . . . 12 A4
Grodno =
Hrodna 17 B6
Grodzyanka =
Hrodzyanka . . 17 B9
Grójec 16 C5
Groningen 14 B4
Grootfontein . . 58 B3
Gross Glockner 15 E7
Grosser Arber . 15 D7
Grosseto 20 C3
Groznyy 25 E6
Grudziądz 16 B4
Gryazi 24 C4
Gryazovets . . . 28 D5
Gua 40 F5
Guadalajara,
Mexico 84 C4
Guadalajara,
Spain 18 B4
Guadalcanal . . 64 K11
Guadalete → . 18 D2
Guadalquivir → 18 D2

Guadalupe =
Guadeloupe ■ 87 C7
Guadalupe,
Sierra de . . . 18 C3
Guadarrama,
Sierra de . . . 18 B4
Guadeloupe ■ . 87 C7
Guadiana → . . 18 D2
Guadix 18 D4
Guafo, Boca del 95 E2
Guaíra 94 A6
Guaitecas, Is. . . 95 E2
Guajará-Mirim . 91 F5
Guajira, Pen. de
la 90 A4
Gualeguay 94 C5
Gualeguaychú . 94 C5
Guam ■ 64 H9
Guamúchil . . . 84 B3
Guan Xian . . . 34 C5
Guanahani =
San Salvador 86 B5
Guanajuato . . . 84 C4
Guandacol . . . 94 B3
Guane 86 B3
Guangdong □ . 35 D6
Guanghua . . . 35 C6
Guangxi
Zhuangzu
Zizhiqu □ . . 35 D5
Guangzhou . . . 35 D6
Guanipa → . . . 90 B6
Guantánamo . . 86 B4
Guaporé → . 91 F5
Guaqui 91 G5
Guarapuava . . . 94 B6
Guarda 18 B2
Guardafui, C. =
Asir, Ras . . . 49 E5
Guasdualito . . . 90 B4
Guasipati 90 B6
Guatemala . . . 85 E6
Guatemala ■ . . 85 D6
Guatire 90 A5
Guaviare □ . . . 90 C4
Guaviare → . . 90 C5
Guaxupé 93 G4
Guayama 87 C6
Guayaquil 90 D3
Guayaquil, G. de 90 D2
Guaymas 84 B2
Guddu Barrage 42 E6
Gudivada 40 J3
Gudur 43 M11
Guecho 19 A4
Guékédou 55 G2
Guelma 54 A6
Guelph 69 D2
Guéréda 53 F3
Guéret 12 C4
Guernica 19 A4
Guernsey 11 G5
Guidónia-
Montecélio . . 20 C4
Guiglo 55 G3
Guildford 11 F6
Guilin 35 D6
Guimarães,
Brazil 92 C5
Guimarães,
Portugal 18 B1
Guimaras 38 B2
Guinea ■ 55 F2
Guinea, Gulf of 51 F3
Guinea-Bissau ■ 55 F1
Guingamp 12 B2
Guiping 35 D6
Güiria 90 A6
Guiuan 38 B3
Guiyang 35 D5

Guizhou □ 35 D5
Gujarat □ 43 H1
Gujranwala . . . 42 C5
Gujrat 42 C5
Gulbarga 43 L10
Gulf, The 44 E2
Gulgong 63 B4
Güllük 23 F6
Gulshad 29 E8
Gulu 57 D6
Gum Lake 62 B3
Gummi 55 F6
Gümüşhane . . . 46 B4
Gumzai 39 F4
Guna 43 G10
Gundagai 63 C4
Gungu 56 F3
Gunnedah 63 B5
Gunningbar
Cr. → 63 B4
Guntakal 43 M10
Guntur 40 J11
Gunungapi . . . 39 F3
Gunungsitoli . . 37 D1
Gunza 56 G2
Gupis 42 A8
Gürchān 46 D7
Gurdaspur . . . 42 C9
Gurgaon 42 E10
Gurkha 40 C5
Gurley 63 A4
Gurupá 92 C3
Gurupá, I.
Grande de . . 92 C3
Gurupi → . . . 92 C4
Guryev =
Atyraū 29 E6
Gusau 55 F6
Güstrow 15 B7
Gütersloh 14 C5
Guthrie 78 B5
Guyana ■ 90 B7
Guyane
française ■ =
French
Guiana ■ . . . 92 B3
Guyenne 12 D4
Guyra 63 B5
Gwa 41 J10
Gwaai 59 B5
Gwabegar . . . 63 B4
Gwādar 42 G3
Gwalior 42 F11
Gwanda 59 C5
Gweru 59 B5
Gwydir → . . . 63 A4
Gyandzha =
Gäncä 25 E6
Gyaring Hu . . . 34 C4
Gydanskiy P-ov. 28 B4
Gympie 63 A5
Gyöngyös . . . 16 E4
Györ 16 E3
Gypsumville . . 71 C10
Gyula 16 E5
Gyumri 25 E5
Gyzylarbat . . . 29 F6

H

Ha 'Arava → . 47 E3
Haarlem 14 B3
Haast → 65 E3
Habaswein . . . 57 D7
Hachinohe . . . 33 F12
Hadarba, Ras . . 52 D5

Hadd, R'as al .. 45 F4
Hadejia 55 F7
Haden 63 A5
Hadera 46 D3
Hadhramaut =
  Hadramawt . 49 D4
Hadramawt ... 49 D4
Haeju 35 C7
Haerhpin =
  Harbin 35 B7
Hafar al Bāţin . 47 E6
Hafizabad 42 C8
Haflong 41 E9
Haft Gel 47 E7
Hafun, Ras ... 49 E5
Hagen 14 C4
Hagerstown ... 73 E7
Hagi 32 B2
Hagondange-
  Briey 13 B7
Hague, C. de la 12 B3
Hague, The = 's-
  Gravenhage . 14 B3
Haguenau 13 B7
Hai'an 35 C7
Haifa = Hefa .. 46 D3
Haikou 35 D6
Ḩā'il 47 F5
Hailar 35 B6
Haileybury 69 D3
Hailun 35 B7
Hainan □ 35 E5
Haiphong 35 D5
Haiti ■ 87 C5
Haiya Junction 53 E6
Hajar Bangar .. 53 F3
Hajdúböszörmény
  .... 16 E5
Hajnówka 17 B6
Hakken-Zan .. 32 B4
Hakodate 32 F12
Hala 42 G6
Ḩalab 46 C4
Ḩalabjah 46 D6
Halaib 52 D6
Halberstadt .. 15 C6
Halcombe 64 D6
Halcon, Mt. .. 38 B2
Halden 9 G10
Haldia 40 F7
Haldwani 42 E11
Halifax, Canada 69 D4
Halifax, U.K. .. 11 E6
Halīl → 44 E4
Hall Beach =
  Sanirajak ... 68 B2
Halle 15 C6
Hallett 62 B2
Halmahera 39 D3
Halmstad 9 G10
Halq el Oued .. 52 A1
Hälsingborg =
  Helsingborg . 9 G10
Halul 44 E3
Hamada 32 B3
Hamadān 46 D7
Hamadān □ ... 46 D7
Hamāh 46 D4
Hamamatsu .. 32 B5
Hamar 8 F10
Hamburg 14 B5
Hameln 14 B5
Hamersley Ra. . 60 E2
Hamhung 35 C7
Hami 34 B4
Hamilton,
  Australia 62 C3
Hamilton,
  Canada 69 D3

Hamilton, N.Z. . 64 B6
Hamilton, U.K. .. 10 D4
Hamley Bridge 62 B2
Hamlin =
  Hameln 14 B5
Hamm 14 C4
Hammerfest .. 8 D12
Hammond 72 D2
Hampden 65 F4
Hampton 73 F7
Hamrat esh
  Sheykh 53 F4
Han Pijesak .. 20 B7
Hanamaki ... 33 G12
Hanau 14 C5
Hancock 77 C7
Handa 49 E5
Handan 35 C6
Handeni 57 F7
Hangayn Nuruu 34 B4
Hangchou =
  Hangzhou ... 35 C7
Hangu 35 C6
Hangzhou ... 35 C7
Hangzhou Wan 35 C7
Ḩanīsh 49 E3
Hanle 42 C11
Hanmer Springs 65 E5
Hanna 71 C8
Hannibal 77 F9
Hannover 14 B5
Hanoi 35 D5
Hanover =
  Hannover ... 14 B5
Hanover, I. ... 95 G2
Hansi 42 E9
Hanson, L. ... 62 B2
Hantsavichy .. 17 B8
Hanzhong ... 35 C5
Haora 40 F7
Haparanda ... 8 E12
Happy Valley-
  Goose Bay .. 69 C4
Hapur 42 E10
Ḩaql 47 E3
Har 39 F4
Har Hu 34 C4
Har Us Nuur . 34 B4
Ḩaraḍ 47 F7
Haraisan Plateau
  = Ḩuraysān . 47 G6
Harardera 49 G4
Harare 59 B6
Harazé 53 F2
Harbin 35 B7
Harbour Grace 69 D5
Hardangerfjorden
  .... 8 F9
Hardap Dam .. 58 C3
Hardwar =
  Haridwar .. 42 E11
Hardy, Pen. ... 95 H3
Harer 49 F3
Hargeisa 49 F3
Hari → 37 E2
Haridwar 42 E11
Haringhata → 41 G7
Harīrūd 45 C5
Harīrūd → ... 42 A2
Harlingen ... 78 F5
Harlow 11 F7
Harney Basin . 80 D4
Härnösand .. 8 F11
Ḩarrat al Kishb 47 G5
Harrat al
  'Uwairidh .. 47 F4
Harris 10 C3
Harris L. 62 B2
Harrisburg ... 73 D7

Harrison, C. ... 68 C5
Harrison Bay .. 71 A4
Harrogate 11 D6
Hart, L. 62 B2
Hartford 73 D9
Hartlepool ... 11 D6
Harvey 72 D2
Harwich 11 F7
Haryana □ ... 42 E10
Haryn → 17 B8
Harz 14 C6
Hasa 47 F7
Hasan Kuli .. 29 F6
Hassi Inifel ... 54 C5
Hassi Messaoud 54 B6
Hastings, N.Z. .. 64 C7
Hastings, U.K. .. 11 F7
Hastings, U.S.A. 76 E5
Hastings Ra. .. 63 B5
Hatay = Antalya 46 C2
Hatfield P.O. .. 62 B3
Hatgal 34 A5
Hathras 42 F11
Hatia 41 F8
Hattah 62 B3
Hatteras, C. .. 75 B10
Hattiesburg .. 79 D9
Hatvan 16 E4
Hau Bon = Cheo
  Reo 36 B3
Haugesund ... 9 G9
Hauraki G. ... 64 B6
Haut Atlas ... 54 B3
Hautah, Waḩāt
  al 47 G6
Hauts Plateaux 54 B4
Havana = La
  Habana 86 B3
Havant 11 F6
Havel → 15 B7
Havelock 65 D5
Haverfordwest . 11 F4
Havlíčkův Brod 16 D2
Havre 81 A9
Havza 46 B3
Hawaii □ 82 J12
Hawaiian Is. .. 82 H12
Hawea, L. 65 F3
Hawera 64 C6
Hawick 10 D5
Hawke B. 64 C7
Hawker 62 B2
Hawkwood ... 63 A5
Hay 63 B3
Hay River 70 B8
Haya 39 E3
Hayes → 71 C10
Hayrabolu ... 22 D6
Haysyn 17 D9
Hayvoron ... 17 D9
Hazaribag 40 F5
Healesville ... 63 C4
Hearst 69 D2
Hebei □ 35 C6
Hebel 63 A4
Hebron = Al
  Khalīl 47 E3
Hebron 68 C4
Hechi 35 D5
Hechuan 35 C5
Heerlen 13 A6
Hefa 46 D3
Hefei 35 C6
Hegang 35 B8
Heidelberg ... 14 D5
Heilbron 59 D5
Heilbronn 14 D5
Heilongjiang □ 35 B7

Heilunkiang =
  Heilongjiang □
  .... 35 B7
Heinze Is. 41 K11
Hejaz = Al Ḩijāz 47 F4
Hekımhan ... 46 C4
Hekou 34 D5
Helena, Ark.,
  U.S.A. 79 B8
Helena, Mont.,
  U.S.A. 81 B7
Helensville 64 B6
Helgoland ... 14 A4
Heligoland =
  Helgoland ... 14 A4
Heligoland B. =
  Deutsche
  Bucht 14 A5
Hellín 19 C5
Helmand □ .. 42 D3
Helmand → . 42 D2
Helmand,
  Hamun 45 D5
Helmsdale 10 B5
Helsingborg .. 9 G10
Helsingfors =
  Helsinki 9 F13
Helsinki 9 F13
Helwân = 52 C5
Hemel
  Hempstead .. 11 F6
Henan □ 35 C6
Henares → .. 18 B4
Henderson ... 75 A8
Hendon 63 A5
Hengyang 35 D6
Henrietta Maria,
  C. 69 C2
Hentiyn Nuruu 35 B5
Henty 63 C4
Henzada 41 J10
Herāt 42 B3
Herāt □ 42 B3
Hercegnovi .. 22 C2
Hereford 11 E5
Herford 14 B5
Hermidale 63 B4
Hermitage ... 65 E4
Hermite, I. ... 95 H3
Hermon, Mt. =
  Ash Shaykh,
  J. 46 D3
Hermosillo ... 84 B2
Hernád → ... 16 E5
Hernandarias . 94 B6
Heroica Nogales
  = Nogales .. 84 A2
Heron Bay ... 69 D2
Herrick 62 D4
's-
Hertogenbosch
  .... 14 C3
Hesse =
  Hessen □ .. 14 C5
Hessen □ ... 14 C5
Hewett, C. 68 A4
Hexham 11 D5
Heyfield 63 C4
Heywood 62 C3
Hibbing 77 B8
Hibbs B. 62 D4
Hickory 75 B7
Hicks, Pt. 63 C4
Hida-Sammyaku 32 A5
Hidalgo del
  Parral 84 B3
Higashiōsaka . 32 B4
High Atlas =
  Haut Atlas .. 54 B3

High Point

High Point 75 B8
High River 71 C8
High Tatra =
Tatry 16 D4
High Wycombe 11 F6
Hiiumaa 24 B1
Ḥijārah, Ṣaḥrā'
al 47 E6
Ḥijāz □ 48 C2
Hijo = Tagum . 38 C3
Hikone 32 B5
Hikurangi 64 A6
Hikurangi, Mt. . 64 C7
Hildesheim ... 14 B5
Hillston 63 B4
Hilo 82 J13
Hilversum 14 B3
Himachal
Pradesh □ . 42 D10
Himalaya 40 C5
Himatnagar ... 43 H8
Himeji 32 B4
Himi 32 A5
Ḥimş 46 D4
Hindmarsh, L. . 62 C3
Hindu Kush ... 42 B7
Hindubagh 42 D5
Hindupur 43 N10
Hinganghat ... 43 J11
Hingoli 43 K10
Hinna = Imi .. 49 F3
Hinojosa del
Duque 18 C3
Hirakud Dam .. 40 G4
Hiratsuka 32 B6
Hirosaki 33 F12
Hiroshima 32 B3
Hisar 42 E9
Hispaniola ... 87 C5
Hita 32 C2
Hitachi 32 A7
Hjälmaren 9 G11
Hlyboka 17 D7
Ho 55 G5
Ho Chi Minh
City = Phanh
Bho Ho Chi
Minh 36 B3
Hoai Nhon 36 B3
Hoare B. 68 B4
Hobart 62 D4
Hobbs Coast . 96 B18
Hodgson 71 C10
Hódmezövásárhely
.... 16 E5
Hodna, Chott el 54 A5
Hodonín 16 D3
Hoek van
Holland 14 B3
Hof 15 C6
Hōfu 32 B2
Hogan Group . 62 C4
Hoggar =
Ahaggar ... 54 D6
Hoh Xil Shan . 34 C3
Hohe Rhön ... 14 C5
Hohhot 35 B6
Hoi An 36 A3
Hokianga
Harbour ... 64 A5
Hokitika 65 E4
Hokkaidō □ ... 32 F12
Holbrook 63 C4
Holguín 86 B4
Hollandia =
Jayapura ... 39 E6
Holman Island . 70 A8
Holy Cross ... 71 B4
Holyhead 11 E4

Homalin 41 E10
Hombori 55 E4
Home B. 68 B4
Homer 71 C4
Homs = Ḥimş . 46 D4
Homyel 17 B10
Hon Chong ... 36 B2
Honan =
Henan □ 35 C6
Honda 90 B4
Hondeklipbaai . 58 E3
Honduras ■ ... 85 E7
Honduras, G. de 85 D7
Honfleur 12 B4
Hong Kong ... 35 D6
Hongjiang 35 D5
Hongshui He → 35 D5
Hongze Hu ... 35 C6
Honiara 64 K10
Honolulu 82 H12
Honshū 32 G11
Hood, Mt. 80 C3
Hooghly → =
Hughli → .. 40 G7
Hook of Holland
= Hoek van
Holland 14 B3
Hoorn 14 B3
Hoover Dam .. 82 B5
Hope, L. 62 A2
Hope, Pt. 71 B3
Hopedale 68 C4
Hopei =
Hebei □ 35 C6
Hopetoun 62 C3
Hopetown 58 D4
Hoquiam 80 B2
Horlick Mts. ... 96 C1
Horlivka 25 D4
Hormoz 44 E3
Hormoz, Jaz. ye 44 E4
Hormozgān □ . 44 E3
Hormuz, Str. of 44 E4
Horn 15 D8
Horn, Cape =
Hornos, C. de 95 H3
Hornavan 8 E11
Hornos, C. de . 95 H3
Hornsby 63 B5
Horodenka ... 17 D7
Horodok,
Khmelnytskyy,
Ukraine 17 D8
Horodok, Lviv,
Ukraine 17 D6
Horokhiv 17 C7
Horqin Youyi
Qianqi 35 B7
Horqueta 94 A5
Horsham 62 C3
Horton → 70 B7
Hose, Gunung-
Gunung 37 D4
Hoshangabad . 43 H10
Hoshiarpur ... 42 D9
Hospet 43 M10
Hospitalet de
Llobregat .. 19 B7
Hoste, I. 95 H3
Hot Springs .. 79 B7
Hotan 34 C2
Houhora Heads 64 A5
Houlton 73 A12
Houma 79 E8
Houston 79 E6
Hovd 34 B4
Hövsgöl Nuur . 34 A5
Howard 63 A5
Howe, C. 63 C5

Howitt, L. 62 A2
Howrah = Haora 40 F7
Höxter 14 C5
Hoy 10 B5
Høyanger 8 F9
Hoyerswerda .. 15 C8
Hpungan Pass . 41 D11
Hradec Králové 16 C2
Hrodna 17 B6
Hrodzyanka ... 17 B9
Hron → 16 E4
Hrvatska =
Croatia ■ .. 20 B6
Hrymayliv ... 17 D8
Hsenwi 41 F11
Hsiamen =
Xiamen 35 D6
Hsian = Xi'an . 35 C5
Hsinhailien =
Lianyungang 35 C6
Hsisha Chuntao 36 A4
Hsüchou =
Xuzhou = ... 35 C6
Hua Hin 36 B1
Huacho 91 F3
Huachón 91 F3
Huai He → ... 35 C6
Huainan 35 C6
Huallaga → .. 90 E3
Huambo 58 A3
Huancabamba . 91 E3
Huancane 91 G5
Huancapi 91 F4
Huancavelica .. 91 F3
Huancayo 91 F3
Huang Hai =
Yellow Sea .. 35 C7
Huang He → .. 35 C6
Huangliu 35 E5
Huangshi 35 C6
Huánuco 91 E3
Huaraz 91 E3
Huarmey 91 F3
Huascarán ... 91 E3
Huasco 94 B2
Huatabampo .. 84 B3
Huayllay 91 F3
Hubei □ 35 C6
Hubli-Dharwad
= Dharwad . 43 M9
Huddersfield .. 11 E6
Hudiksvall ... 8 F11
Hudson → ... 73 D8
Hudson Bay ... 68 B2
Hudson Mts. .. 96 B2
Hudson Str. .. 68 B4
Hue 36 A3
Huelva 18 D2
Huesca 19 A5
Hughenden ... 61 E7
Hughli → 40 G7
Huila, Nevado
del 90 C3
Huinca Renancó 94 C4
Huize 34 D5
Hukawng Valley 41 D11
Hulan 35 B7
Ḥulayfā' 47 F5
Huld 35 B5
Hull = Kingston
upon Hull .. 11 E6
Hull 69 D3
Hulun Nur ... 35 B6
Humahuaca ... 94 A3
Humaitá, Brazil 91 E6
Humaitá,
Paraguay .. 94 B5
Humber → ... 11 E6
Humboldt 71 C9

Humboldt → . 80 F4
Hume, L. 63 C4
Humenné 16 D5
Hūn 52 C2
Hunan □ 35 D6
Hunedoara ... 17 F6
Hungary ■ ... 16 E4
Hungerford ... 63 A3
Hŭngnam 35 C7
Hunsrück 14 D4
Hunter I. 62 D3
Hunter Ra. ... 63 B5
Hunterville ... 64 C6
Huntington ... 72 E4
Huntington
Beach 82 D3
Huntly, N.Z. ... 64 B6
Huntly, U.K. .. 10 C5
Huntsville ... 74 B4
Huonville 62 D4
Hupeh =
Hubei □ 35 C6
Huraysān ... 47 G6
Huron, L. 72 B4
Hurunui → ... 65 E5
Huşi 17 E9
Hutchinson ... 78
Hutton, Mt. ... 63 A4
Hvar 20 C6
Hwang Ho =
Huang He → . 35 C6
Hwange 59 B5
Hyargas Nuur . 34 B4
Hyderabad,
India 43 L11
Hyderabad,
Pakistan 42 G6
Hyères 13 E7
Hyères, Is. d' .. 13 E7

I

I-n-Gall 55 E6
Iaco → 91 E5
Ialomița → ... 22 B6
Iaşi 17 E8
Iba 38 A2
Ibadan 55 G5
Ibagué 90 C3
Ibar → 22 C3
Ibarra 90 C3
Ibi 55 G6
Ibiá 93 F4
Ibicuy 94 C5
Ibioapaba, Sa.
da 92 C5
Ibiza 19 C6
Ibonma 39 E4
Ibotirama 93 E5
Ibu 39 D3
Ica 91 F3
Içá → 90 D5
Içana 90 C5
Içel = Mersin . 46 C3
Iceland ■ 8 B4
Ich'ang =
Yichang 35 C6
Ichchapuram .. 40 H5
Ichihara 32 B7
Ichikawa 32 B6
Ichilo → 91 G6
Ichinomiya ... 32 B5
Idaho □ 81 C6
Idaho Falls ... 81 D7
Idar-Oberstein . 14 D4
Idd el Ghanam 53 F3

Iddan 49 F4	Imperatriz 92 D4	International	Ise 32 B5
Idehan 52 C1	Impéria 20 C2	Falls 77 A8	Ise-Wan 32 B5
Idehan Marzūq 52 D1	Imperial Dam . 82 D5	Intiyaco 94 B4	Isère → 13 D6
Idelès 54 D6	Impfondo 56 D3	Inukjuak 68 C3	Isérnia 20 D5
Idfû 52 D5	Imphal 41 E9	Inútil, B. 95 G2	Ishikari-Wan .. 32 F12
Ídhi Óros 23 G5	Imroz =	Inuvik 70 B6	Ishim → 29 D8
Ídhra 23 F4	Gökçeada ... 23 D5	Invercargill 65 G3	Ishinomaki ... 33 G12
Idi 36 C1	Imuruan B. ... 38 B1	Inverell 63 A5	Ishkuman 42 A8
Idiofa 56 E3	In Belbel 54 C5	Invergordon .. 10 C4	Isil Kul 29 D8
Idlip 46 D4	In Salah 54 C5	Inverness 10 C4	Isiolo 57 D7
Ierápetra 23 G5	Ina 32 B5	Inverurie 10 C5	Isiro 57 D5
Iesi 20 C4	Inangahua	Investigator	İskenderun ... 46 C4
Ifanadiana ... 59 J9	Junction 65 D4	Group 62 B1	Iskŭr → 22 C5
Ife 55 G5	Inanwatan ... 39 E4	Investigator Str. 62 C2	Islamabad 42 C8
Ifni 54 C2	Iñapari 91 F5	Inya 29 D9	Island L. 71 C10
Iforas, Adrar des 54	Inarijärvi 8 E13	Inza 24 C6	Island Lagoon . 62 B2
Igarapava ... 93 G4	Inca 19 C7	Ioánnina 23 E3	Islay 10 D3
Igarapé Açu ... 92 C4	Ince-Burnu ... 46 B3	Ionian Is. =	Isle → 12 D3
Igarka 28 C9	Inchon 35 C7	Iónioi Nísoi . 23 E3	Isle of Wight □ 11 F6
Igbetti 55 G5	Incirliova 23 F6	Ionian Sea ... 21 F6	Ismail = Izmayil 17 F9
Iglésias 21 E2	Incomáti → . 59 D6	Iónioi Nísoi ... 23 E3	Ismâ'ilîya 47 E3
Igli 54 B4	Indalsälven → 8 F11	Íos 23 F5	Isna 52 C5
Igloolik 68 B2	Indaw 41 E11	Iowa □ 77 D8	Ísparta 46 C2
Igluligaarjuk ... 68 B1	Independence,	Iowa City 77 E9	İspica 21 F5
Igneada Burnu 22 D7	Kans., U.S.A. 79 A6	Ipameri 93 F4	Israel ■ 46 E3
Igoumenítsa .. 23 E3	Independence,	Ipatinga 93 F5	Issoire 13 D5
Iguaçu → ... 94 B6	Mo., U.S.A. . 77 F7	Ipiales 90 C3	Issyk-Kul, Ozero
Iguaçu, Cat. del 94 B6	India ■ 43 J10	Ipin = Yibin .. 35 D5	= Ysyk-Köl,
Iguaçu Falls =	Indian → 75 F7	Ipixuna 91 E4	Ozero 29 E8
Iguaçu, Cat.	Indian Harbour 68 C5	Ipoh 36 D2	İstanbul 22 D7
del 94 B6	Indian Head .. 71 C9	Ippy 56 C4	Istiaía 23 E4
Iguala 84 D5	Indiana □ 72 D3	Ipsala 22 D6	Istra 20 B4
Igualada 19 B6	Indianapolis ... 72 E2	Ipswich,	İstranca Dağları 22 D6
Iguassu =	Indiga 28 C5	Australia 63 A5	Istres 13 E6
Iguaçu → . 94 B6	Indigirka → .. 31 B12	Ipswich, U.K. .. 11 E7	Istria = Istra .. 20 B4
Iguatu 92 D6	Indonesia ■ ... 37 E4	Ipu 92 C5	Itabaiana 92 D6
Iguéla 56 E1	Indore 43 H9	Iqaluit 68 B4	Itaberaba 93 E5
Ihosy 59 J9	Indravati → .. 40 H3	Iquique 91 H4	Itabira 93 F5
Iida 32 B5	Indre → 12 C4	Iquitos 90 D4	Itabuna 93 E6
Iisalmi 8 F13	Indus → 43 G5	Iracoubo 92 A3	Itaipú, Reprêsa
Iizuka 32 C2	Inebolu 46 B3	Iráklion 23 G5	de 94 B6
Ijebu-Ode 55 G5	Ingende 56 E3	Iran ■ 44 C3	Itaituba 92 C2
IJsselmeer 14 B3	Inglewood,	Iran, Gunung-	Itajaí 94 B7
Ikaluktutiak .. 70 B9	Queens.,	Gunung 37 D4	Italy ■ 20 C4
Ikaría 23 F6	Australia 63 A5	Iran Ra. = Iran,	Itapecuru-Mirim 92 C5
Ikela 56 E4	Inglewood, Vic.,	Gunung-	Itaperuna 93 G5
Iki 32 C1	Australia 62 C3	Gunung 37 D4	Itapicuru →,
Ilagan 38 A2	Inglewood, N.Z. 64 C6	Īrānshahr 45 E5	Bahia, Brazil . 93 E6
Ilâm 46 D6	Ingolstadt 15 D6	Irapuato 84 C4	Itapicuru →,
Ilawa 16 B4	Ingraj Bazar ... 40 E7	Iraq ■ 46 D5	Maranhão,
Île-de-France .. 12 B5	Ingrid	Irbid 46 D3	Brazil 92 C5
Ilebo 56 E4	Christensen	Irebu 56 E3	Itapipoca 92 C6
Ilhéus 93 E6	Coast 96 A10	Ireland ■ 11 E3	Itaquatiara ... 90 D7
Ili → 29 E8	Ingulec =	Irian Jaya □ ... 39 E5	Itaquí 94 B5
Ilich 29 E7	Inhulec 25 D3	Iringa 57 F7	Itatuba 91 E6
Iligan 38 C2	Inhambane ... 59 C7	Iriri → 92 C3	Ithaca = Itháki . 23 E3
Illampu =	Inhaminga 59 B7	Irish Sea 11 E4	Itháki 23 E3
Ancohuma,	Inharrime 59 C7	Irkineyeva ... 30 D7	Ito 32 B6
Nevada 91 G5	Inhulec 25 D3	Irkutsk 30 D8	Itonamas → . 91 F6
Illana B. 38 C2	Ining = Yining . 34 B3	Iron Baron 62 B2	Ituaçu 93 E5
Illapel 94 C2	Inírida → 90 C5	Iron Gate =	Ituiutaba 93 F4
Iller → 14 D5	Injune 63 A4	Portile de Fier 22 B4	Itumbiara 93 F4
Illimani 91 G5	Inle L. 41 G11	Iron Knob 62 B2	Iturbe 94 A3
Illium = Troy . 23 E6	Inn → 15 D7	Ironwood 77 B9	Itzehoe 14 B5
Ilmen, Ozero .. 24 B3	Innamincka ... 62 A3	Irpin 17 C10	Ivanava 17 B7
Ilo 91 G4	Inner Hebrides 10 C3	Irrara Cr. → .. 63 A4	Ivanhoe 63 B3
Iloilo 38 B2	Inner Mongolia	Irrawaddy □ .. 41 J10	Ivano-Frankivsk 17 D7
Ilorin 55 G5	= Nei	Irrawaddy → . 41 K10	Ivano-Frankovsk
Ilwaki 39 F3	Monggol	Irtysh → 28 C7	= Ivano-
Imabari 32 B3	Zizhiqu □ ... 35 B6	Irumu 57 D5	Frankivsk ... 17 D7
Imandra, Ozero 28 C4	Innisfail 71 C8	Irún 19 A5	Ivanovo =
Imari 32 C1	Innsbruck 15 E6	Irunea =	Ivanava 17 B7
Imeni 26	Inongo 56 E3	Pamplona ... 19 A5	Ivanovo 24 B5
Bakinskikh	Inoucdjouac =	Irvine 10 D4	Ivatsevichy ... 17 B7
Komissarov =	Inukjuak 68 C3	Irymple 62 B3	Ivory Coast ■ . 55 G3
Neftçala 46 C7	Inowrocław ... 16 B4	Isabella 38 C2	Ivrea 20 B1
Imeri, Serra .. 90 C5	Inquisivi 91 G5	Isangi 56 D4	Ivujivik 68 B3
Imi 49 F3	Insein 41 J11	Isar → 15 D7	Iwahig 36 C5
Imola 20 B3	Interlaken 13 C7	Ischia 21 D4	Iwaki 33 G12

Iwakuni

Iwakuni	32	B3
Iwata	33	H11
Iwate-San	33	G12
Iwo	55	G5
Ixiamas	91	F5
Izhevsk	28	D6
Izmayil	17	F9
İzmir	23	E6
İzmit	25	E2
İznik Gölü	23	D7
Izumi-sano	32	B4
Izumo	32	B3
Izyaslav	17	C8

J

Jabalpur	43	H11
Jablah	46	D4
Jablanica	22	D3
Jablonec	16	C2
Jaboatão	92	D6
Jaca	19	A5
Jacareí	94	A7
Jacarèzinho	94	A7
Jackson, Australia	63	A4
Jackson, Mich., U.S.A.	72	C3
Jackson, Miss., U.S.A.	79	C8
Jackson, Tenn., U.S.A.	74	B3
Jackson B.	65	E3
Jacksons	65	E4
Jacksonville, Fla., U.S.A.	75	D7
Jacksonville, Ill., U.S.A.	77	F9
Jacksonville, N.C., U.S.A.	75	B9
Jacmel	87	C5
Jacobabad	42	E6
Jacobina	93	E5
Jacundá →	92	C3
Jadotville = Likasi	57	G5
Jādū	52	B1
Jaén, Peru	91	E3
Jaén, Spain	18	D4
Jaffa = Tel Aviv-Yafo	46	D3
Jaffa, C.	62	C2
Jaffna	43	Q12
Jagadhri	42	D10
Jagdalpur	40	H3
Jagraon	42	D9
Jagtial	43	K11
Jaguariaíva	94	A7
Jaguaribe →	92	C6
Jahrom	44	D3
Jailolo	39	D3
Jailolo, Selat	39	D3
Jaipur	42	F9
Jakarta	37	F3
Jalalabad	42	B7
Jalapa Enríquez	84	D5
Jalas, Jabal al	47	F4
Jalgaon, Maharashtra, India	43	J10
Jalgaon, Maharashtra, India	43	J9
Jalna	43	K9
Jalón →	19	B5
Jalpaiguri	41	D7

Jalq	45	E5
Jaluit I.	64	J11
Jamaica ■	86	C4
Jamalpur, Bangla.	41	E7
Jamalpur, India	40	E6
Jamanxim →	92	C2
Jambe	39	E4
Jambi	37	E2
Jambi □	37	E2
James →	76	D6
James B.	69	C2
James Ross I.	96	A4
Jamestown, Australia	62	B2
Jamestown, N. Dak., U.S.A.	76	B5
Jamestown, N.Y., U.S.A.	73	C6
Jamkhandi	43	L9
Jammu	42	C9
Jammu & Kashmir □	42	B10
Jamnagar	43	H7
Jamrud	42	C7
Jamshedpur	40	F6
Jand	42	C8
Jandaq	44	C3
Jandowae	63	A5
Janesville	77	D10
Januária	93	F5
Jaora	43	H9
Japan ■	33	G11
Japan, Sea of	33	G11
Japen = Yapen	39	E5
Japurá →	90	D5
Jaque	90	B3
Jarama →	18	B4
Jargalant = Hovd	34	B4
Jarosław	17	C6
Jarso	53	G6
Jarvis I.	65	K15
Jarwa	40	D4
Jäsk	44	E4
Jasło	16	D5
Jasper	74	C4
Jászberény	16	E4
Jataí	93	F3
Játiva	19	C5
Jaú	93	G4
Jauja	91	F3
Jaunpur	40	E4
Java = Jawa	37	F3
Java Sea	37	E3
Javhlant = Ulyasutay	34	B4
Jawa	37	F3
Jaya, Puncak	39	E5
Jayanti	41	D7
Jayapura	39	E6
Jayawijaya, Pegunungan	39	E5
Jaynagar	40	D6
Jean Marie River	70	B7
Jebba	55	G5
Jebel, Bahr el →	53	G5
Jedburgh	10	D5
Jedda = Jiddah	47	G4
Jędrzejów	16	C5
Jefferson City	77	F8
Jega	55	F5
Jelenia Góra	16	C2
Jelgava	24	B1
Jemaja	37	D3
Jembongan	36	C5
Jena	15	C6

Jeparit	62	C3
Jequié	93	E5
Jequitinhonha	93	F5
Jequitinhonha →	93	F6
Jerada	54	B4
Jerantut	37	D2
Jérémie	86	C5
Jerez de la Frontera	18	D2
Jerez de los Caballeros	18	C2
Jerilderie	63	C4
Jersey	11	G5
Jersey City	73	D8
Jerusalem	47	E3
Jervis B.	63	C5
Jesselton = Kota Kinabalu	36	C5
Jessore	41	F7
Jeypore	40	H4
Jhal Jhao	42	F4
Jhalawar	43	G10
Jhang Maghiana	42	D8
Jhansi	43	G11
Jharsaguda	40	G5
Jhelum	42	C8
Jhelum →	42	D8
Jhunjhunu	42	E9
Jiamusi	35	B8
Ji'an	35	D6
Jianchuan	34	D4
Jiangling	35	C6
Jiangmen	35	D6
Jiangsu □	35	C6
Jiangxi □	35	D6
Jian'ou	35	D6
Jianshui	34	D5
Jiao Xian	35	C7
Jiaozuo	35	C6
Jiaxing	35	C7
Jiayi	35	D7
Jibuti = Djibouti ■	49	E3
Jiddah	47	G4
Jido	41	C10
Jihlava	16	D2
Jihlava →	16	D3
Jijel	54	A6
Jijiga	49	F3
Jilin	35	B7
Jilong	35	D7
Jima	53	G6
Jiménez	84	B4
Jinan	35	C6
Jindabyne	63	C4
Jindrichuv Hradeç	16	D2
Jingdezhen	35	D6
Jinggu	34	D5
Jingxi	35	D5
Jinhua	35	D6
Jining, Nei Mongol Zizhiqu, China	35	B6
Jining, Shandong, China	35	C6
Jinja	57	D6
Jinnah Barrage	42	C7
Jinotega	85	E7
Jinshi	35	D6
Jinzhou	35	B7
Jiparaná →	91	E6
Jipijapa	90	D2
Jisr ash Shughūr	46	D4
Jiu →	22	C4
Jiujiang	35	D6

Jiuquan	34	C4
Jixi	35	B8
Jizzakh	29	E7
Joaçaba	94	B6
João Pessoa	92	D7
Joaquín V. González	94	B4
Jodhpur	42	F8
Jofane	59	C6
Jogjakarta = Yogyakarta	37	F4
Johannesburg	59	D5
Johnson City	75	A6
Johnston Falls = Mambilima Falls	57	G5
Johnstown	73	D6
Johor Baharu	37	D2
Joinvile	94	B7
Joinville I.	96	A4
Joliet	72	D1
Joliette	69	D3
Jolo	38	C2
Jome	39	E3
Jonesboro	79	B8
Jönköping	9	G10
Jonquière	69	D3
Joplin	79	A6
Jordan ■	47	E4
Jorhat	41	D10
Jorong	37	E4
Jos	55	G6
Jowzjān □	45	B6
Juan de Fuca Str.	80	A1
Juan de Nova	59	H8
Juan Fernández, Arch. de	89	G3
Juárez	94	D5
Juàzeiro	93	D5
Juàzeiro do Norte	92	D6
Jubbulpore = Jabalpur	43	H11
Juby, C.	54	C2
Júcar →	19	C5
Juchitán	85	D5
Jugoslavia = Yugoslavia ■	22	B3
Juiz de Fora	93	G5
Juli	91	G5
Juliaca	91	G4
Jullundur	42	D9
Jumilla	19	C5
Jumla	40	C4
Jumna = Yamuna →	40	E3
Junagadh	43	J7
Jundiaí	94	A7
Juneau	71	C6
Junee	63	B4
Jungfrau	13	C7
Junggar Pendi	34	B3
Junín	94	C4
Junín de los Andes	95	D2
Jūniyah	46	D3
Jur, Nahr el →	53	G4
Jura = Jura, Mts. du	13	C7
Jura = Schwäbische Alb	14	D5
Jura	10	D4
Jura, Mts. du	13	C7
Jurado	90	B3
Juruá →	90	D5
Juruena →	91	E7
Juruti	92	C2

Justo Daract .. 94 C3
Jutland =
  Jylland 9 G9
Juventud, I. de
  la 86 B3
Juwain 42 D2
Jylland 9 G9
Jyväskylä 8 F13

K

K2 .... 42 B10
Kaapkruis ... 58 C2
Kaapstad =
  Cape Town .. 58 E3
Kabaena 39 F2
Kabala 55 G2
Kabale 57 E6
Kabalo 57 F5
Kabambare ... 57 E5
Kabanjahe 37 D1
Kabara 55 E4
Kabardino-
  Balkar
  Republic =
  Kabardino
  Balkaria □ .. 25 E5
Kabardino
  Balkaria □ .. 25 E5
Kabare 39 E4
Kabarega Falls 57 D6
Kabasalan 38 C2
Kabba 55 G6
Kabīr, Zab al → 46 C5
Kabīr Kūh 47 D6
Kabkabīyah ... 53 F3
Kabompo → .. 58 A4
Kabongo 57 F5
Kabūd Gonbad 44 B4
Kābul 42 B6
Kābul □ 42 B6
Kabul → 42 C8
Kaburuang ... 39 D3
Kabwe 59 A5
Kachchh, Gulf of 43 H6
Kachchh, Rann
  of 43 G6
Kachin □ 41 D11
Kachiry 29 D8
Kaçkar 46 B5
Kadan Kyun ... 36 B1
Kadina 62 B2
Kadirli 46 C4
Kadiyevka =
  Stakhanov .. 25 D4
Kadoma 59 B5
Kâdugli 53 F4
Kaduna 55 F6
Kaédi 55 E2
Kaelé 53 F1
Kaesŏng 35 C7
Kāf 47 E4
Kafakumba ... 56 F4
Kafan = Kapan 25 F6
Kafanchan ... 55 G6
Kaffrine 55 F1
Kafia Kingi ... 53 G3
Kafirévs, Ákra . 23 E5
Kafue → 59 B5
Kafulwe 57 F5
Kaga Bandoro . 56 C3
Kagan 29 F7
Kağizman 46 B5
Kagoshima ... 33 D2
Kagoshima-Wan 33 D2
Kagul = Cahul . 17 F9

Kahama 57 E6
Kahayan → .. 37 E4
Kahemba 56 F3
Kahnūj 44 E4
Kahoolawe ... 82 H12
Kahramanmaraş 46 C4
Kai, Kepulauan 39 F4
Kai Besar 39 F4
Kai Is. = Kai,
  Kepulauan .. 39 F4
Kai Kecil 39 F4
Kaiama 55 G5
Kaiapoi 65 E5
Kaieteur Falls . 90 B7
Kaifeng 35 C6
Kaikohe 64 A5
Kaikoura 65 E5
Kaikoura Ra. .. 65 D5
Kaimana 39 E4
Kaimanawa Mts. 64 C6
Kaingaroa
  Forest 64 C7
Kainji Res. 55 F5
Kaipara Harbour 64 B6
Kaironi 39 E4
Kairouan 54 A7
Kaiserslautern . 14 D4
Kaitaia 64 A5
Kaitangata 65 G3
Kajaani 8 F13
Kajabbi 61 D6
Kajana =
  Kajaani 8 F13
Kajo Kaji 53 H5
Kaka 53 F5
Kakamas 58 D4
Kakamega 57 D6
Kakanui Mts. .. 65 F4
Kakhovka 25 D3
Kakhovske
  Vdskh. 25 D3
Kakinada 40 J4
Kalaallit Nunaat
  =
  Greenland ■ 66 C9
Kalabagh 42 C7
Kalabahi 39 F2
Kalabo 58 A4
Kalach 24 C5
Kaladan → ... 41 G9
Kalahari 58 C4
Kalakan 31 D9
Kalámai 23 F4
Kalamata =
  Kalámai 23 F4
Kalamazoo ... 72 C3
Kalan 46 C4
Kalao 39 F2
Kalaotoa 39 F2
Kalat 42 E5
Kalce 20 B5
Kale 23 F7
Kalegauk Kyun 41 K11
Kalemie 57 F5
Kalewa 41 F10
Kalgan =
  Zhangjiakou . 35 B6
Kalgoorlie-
  Boulder 60 G3
Kaliakra, Nos . 22 C7
Kalianda 37 F3
Kalibo 38 B2
Kalima 57 E5
Kalimantan ... 37 E4
Kalimantan
  Barat □ 37 D4
Kalimantan
  Selatan □ ... 37 E5

Kalimantan
  Tengah □ ... 37 E4
Kalimantan
  Timur □ 37 D5
Kálimnos 23 F6
Kalinin = Tver . 24 B4
Kaliningrad,
  Kaliningd.,
  Russia 24 C1
Kaliningrad,
  Moskva,
  Russia 24 B4
Kalinkavichy .. 17 B9
Kalinkovichi =
  Kalinkavichy . 17 B9
Kalispell 81 A6
Kalisz 16 C4
Kaliua 57 F6
Kalkrand 58 C3
Kalmar 9 G11
Kalmyk Republic
  = Kalmykia □ 25 D6
Kalmykia □ ... 25 D6
Kalocsa 16 E4
Kalomo 59 B5
Kaluga 24 C4
Kalush 17 D7
Kalutara 43 R11
Kama → 29 D6
Kamaishi 33 G12
Kamaran 49 D3
Kamchatka, P.-
  ov. 31 D13
Kamchatka Pen.
  = Kamchatka,
  P.-ov. 31 D13
Kamchiya → .. 22 C6
Kamen 29 D9
Kamenjak, Rt. . 20 B4
Kamenka
  Bugskaya =
  Kamyanka-
  Buzka 17 C7
Kamensk
  Uralskiy 29 D7
Kamin-
  Kashyrskyy .. 17 C7
Kamina 57 F5
Kamloops 71 C7
Kampala 57 D6
Kampar → ... 37 D2
Kampen 14 B3
Kampot 36 B2
Kampuchea =
  Cambodia ■ 36 B3
Kampung → .. 39 F5
Kampungbaru =
  Tolitoli 39 D2
Kamrau, Teluk . 39 E4
Kamsack 71 C9
Kamyanets-
  Podilskyy ... 17 D8
Kamyanka-Buzka 17 C7
Kamyshin 24 C6
Kanaaupscow . 69 C3
Kananga 56 F4
Kanash 24 B6
Kanastraíon,
  Ákra =
  Palioúrion,
  Ákra 23 E4
Kanazawa 32 A5
Kanchanaburi . 36 B1
Kanchenjunga . 40 D7
Kanchipuram . 43 N11
Kanda Kanda . 56 F4
Kandahar =
  Qandahār .. 42 D4
Kandalaksha .. 28 C4

Kandalu 42 E3
Kandangan ... 37 E5
Kandi 55 F5
Kandla 43 H7
Kandos 63 B4
Kandy 43 R12
Kangaroo I. ... 62 C2
Kangāvar 46 D7
Kangean,
  Kepulauan .. 37 F5
Kangean Is. =
  Kangean,
  Kepulauan .. 37 F5
Kangiqsualujjuaq
  .... 68 C4
Kangiqsujuaq . 68 B3
Kangirsuk 68 C4
Kangnŭng 35 C7
Kango 56 D2
Kangto 41 D9
Kaniapiskau → 68 C4
Kaniapiskau L. . 69 C4
Kanin,
  Poluostrov .. 28 C5
Kanin Nos, Mys 28 C5
Kanin Pen. =
  Kanin,
  Poluostrov .. 28 C5
Kaniva 62 C3
Kankakee 72 D2
Kankan 55 F3
Kankendy =
  Xankändi ... 25 F6
Kanker 40 G3
Kannapolis ... 75 B7
Kannauj 42 F11
Kannod 43 H10
Kano 55 F6
Kanowit 37 D4
Kanoya 33 D2
Kanpetlet 41 G9
Kanpur 40 D3
Kansas □ 76 F5
Kansas City,
  Kans., U.S.A. 77 F7
Kansas City,
  Mo., U.S.A. . 77 F7
Kansk 30 D7
Kansu =
  Gansu □ 34 C5
Kantang 36 C1
Kanuma 32 A6
Kanye 59 C5
Kaohsiung =
  Gaoxiong ... 35 D7
Kaokoveld 58 B2
Kaolack 55 F1
Kapan 25 F6
Kapanga 56 F4
Kapchagai =
  Qapshaghay . 29 E8
Kapfenberg ... 15 E8
Kapiri Mposhi . 59 A5
Kāpīsā □ 45 C7
Kapit 37 D4
Kapoeta 53 H5
Kaposvár 16 E3
Kapuas → ... 37 E3
Kapuas Hulu,
  Pegunungan 37 D4
Kapuas Hulu Ra.
  = Kapuas
  Hulu,
  Pegunungan 37 D4
Kapunda 62 B2
Kapuni 64 C6
Kaputar 63 B5
Kara 28 C7

Kara Bogaz Gol, Zaliv

Kara Bogaz Gol,
Zaliv =
Garabogazköl
Aylagy 29 E6
Kara Kalpak
Republic □ =
Karakalpakstan □
.... 29 E6
Kara Kum 29 F6
Kara Sea 28 B8
Karabiğa 23 D6
Karabük 46 B3
Karaburun ... 23 E6
Karabutak =
Qarabutaq .. 29 E7
Karacabey ... 23 D7
Karacasu 23 F7
Karachi 43 G5
Karad 43 L9
Karadeniz
Boğazı 22 D7
Karaganda =
Qaraghandy . 29 E8
Karagayly 29 E8
Karaikal 43 P11
Karaikkudi 43 P11
Karaj 44 C2
Karakalpakstan □
.... 29 E6
Karakas 29 E9
Karakelong ... 38 D3
Karakitang 39 D3
Karaklis =
Vanadzor ... 25 E5
Karakoram Pass 42 B10
Karakoram Ra. 42 B10
Karalon 30 D9
Karaman 46 C3
Karamay 34 B3
Karambu 37 E5
Karamea Bight 65 D4
Karasburg ... 58 D3
Karasino 28 C9
Karasuk 29 D8
Karatau =
Qarataū 29 E8
Karatau, Khrebet 29 E7
Karawanken .. 20 A5
Karazhal 29 E8
Karbalā 47 D6
Karcag 16 E5
Kardhítsa 23 E3
Karelia □ 28 C4
Karelian
Republic □ =
Karelia □ ... 28 C4
Kargānrūd 46 C7
Kargasok 29 D9
Kargat 29 D9
Kargil 42 B10
Kariba, L. 59 B5
Kariba Dam .. 59 B5
Kariba Gorge .. 59 B5
Karibib 58 C3
Karimata,
Kepulauan .. 37 E3
Karimata, Selat 37 E3
Karimata Is. =
Karimata,
Kepulauan .. 37 E3
Karimnagar ... 43 K11
Karimunjawa,
Kepulauan .. 37 F4
Karin 49 E4
Karkaralinsk =
Qarqaraly ... 29 E8
Karkinitska
Zatoka 25 D3

Karkinitskiy Zaliv
= Karkinitska
Zatoka 25 D3
Karl-Marx-Stadt
= Chemnitz . 15 C7
Karlovac 20 B5
Karlovo 22 C5
Karlovy Vary .. 16 C1
Karlsbad =
Karlovy Vary 16 C1
Karlskrona 9 G11
Karlsruhe 14 D5
Karlstad 9 G10
Karnal 42 E10
Karnali ➤ 40 C3
Karnaphuli Res. 41 F9
Karnataka □ .. 43 N10
Karnische Alpen 20 A4
Kärnten □ 15 E7
Karonga 57 F6
Karoonda 62 C2
Karora 53 E6
Kárpathos 23 G6
Kars 46 B5
Karsakpay 29 E7
Karshi = Qarshi 29 F7
Karsun 24 C6
Karufa 39 E4
Karungu 57 E6
Karviná 16 D4
Karwar 43 M9
Kasai ➤ 56 E3
Kasama 57 G6
Kasanga 57 F6
Kasangulu ... 56 E3
Kasaragod ... 43 N9
Kasba L. 70 B9
Kasempa 59 A5
Kasenga 57 G5
Kāshān 44 C2
Kashi 34 C2
Kashk-e Kohneh 42 B3
Kāshmar 44 C4
Kashun Noerh =
Gaxun Nur .. 34 B5
Kasimov 24 C5
Kasiruta 39 E3
Kasongo 57 E5
Kasongo Lunda 56 F3
Kásos 23 G6
Kassalā 53 E6
Kassel 14 C5
Kassue 39 F5
Kastamonu ... 46 B3
Kasulu 57 E6
Kasur 42 D9
Katako Kombe . 56 E4
Katamatite .. 63 C4
Katanga =
Shaba □ ... 57 F4
Katangi 43 J11
Kateríni 23 D4
Katha 41 E11
Kathiawar 43 H7
Katihar 40 E6
Katima Mulilo . 58 B4
Katingan =
Mendawai ➤ 37 E4
Katiola 55 G3
Katmandu 40 D5
Katoomba 63 B5
Katowice 16 C4
Katsina 55 F6
Kattegat 9 G10
Kauai 82 G11
Kaunas 24 C1
Kaura Namoda 55 F6
Kaválla 22 D5
Kaw 92 B3

Kawagoe 32 B6
Kawaguchi ... 32 B6
Kawambwa .. 57 F5
Kawardha 40 G3
Kawasaki 32 B6
Kawerau 64 C7
Kawhia Harbour 64 C6
Kawio,
Kepulauan .. 38 D3
Kawnro 41 F12
Kawthoolei =
Kawthule □ . 41 H11
Kawthule □ ... 41 H11
Kaya 55 F4
Kayah □ 41 H11
Kayan ➤ 37 D5
Kayeli 39 E3
Kayes 55 F2
Kayoa 39 D3
Kayrunnera ... 62 B3
Kayseri 46 C3
Kayuagung ... 37 E2
Kazachye 31 B11
Kazakstan ■ .. 29 E7
Kazan 24 B6
Kazanlŭk 22 C5
Kazatin =
Kozyatyn ... 17 D9
Kāzerūn 44 D2
Kazumba 56 F4
Kazym ➤ 28 C7
Ké-Macina ... 55 F3
Kéa 23 F5
Kebnekaise .. 8 E11
Kebri Dehar . 49 F3
Kecskemét ... 16 E4
Kediri 37 F4
Kédougou ... 55 F2
Keetmanshoop 58 D3
Kefallinía 23 E3
Kefamenanu . 39 F2
Keffi 55 G6
Keighley 11 E6
Keith 62 C3
Keith Arm 70 B7
Kekri 42 G9
Kël 30 C10
Kelang 37 D2
Kelibia 52 A1
Kellé 56 E2
Kells =
Ceanannus
Mor 11 E3
Kélo 53 G2
Kelowna 71 D8
Kelso 65 F3
Keluang 37 D2
Kem 28 C4
Kema 39 D3
Kemah 46 C4
Kemerovo ... 29 D9
Kemi 8 E12
Kemi älv =
Kemijoki ➤ . 8 E12
Kemijoki ➤ .. 8 E12
Kemp Land .. 96 A9
Kempsey 63 B5
Kempten 14 E6
Kendal 37 F4
Kendall 63 B5
Kendari 39 E2
Kendawangan . 37 E4
Kende 55 F5
Kendrapara ... 40 G6
Kenema 55 G2
Keng Tawng . 41 G12
Keng Tung .. 41 G12
Kenge 56 E3
Kenhardt 58 D4

Kenitra 54 B3
Kennedy
Taungdeik .. 41 F9
Kennewick ... 80 B4
Kenogami ➤ . 69 C2
Kenosha 72 C2
Kent Group .. 62 C4
Kent Pen. 70 B9
Kentau 29 E7
Kentucky □ .. 72 F3
Kentville 69 D4
Kenya ■ 57 D7
Kenya, Mt. .. 57 E7
Kepi 39 F5
Kerala □ 43 P10
Kerang 62 C3
Kerch 25 D4
Kerchoual ... 55 E5
Keren 53 E6
Kericho 57 E7
Kerinci 37 E2
Kerki 29 F7
Kérkira 23 E2
Kermadec Is. .. 64 M13
Kermadec
Trench 65 N13
Kermān 44 D4
Kermān □ ... 44 D4
Kermānshāh =
Bākhtarān .. 46 D6
Kerme Körfezi . 23 F6
Kerrobert 71 C9
Kerulen ➤ ... 35 B6
Kerzaz 54 C4
Keşan 22 D6
Kestenga 28 C4
Ket ➤ 29 D9
Keta 55 G5
Ketapang 37 E4
Ketchikan ... 71 C6
Ketrzyn 16 A5
Keweenaw B. . 69 D2
Key West 86 B3
Khabarovo ... 28 C7
Khabarovsk .. 31 E11
Khābūr ➤ ... 46 D5
Khairpur 42 F6
Khakassia □ . 30 D6
Khakhea 58 C4
Khalkhāl 46 C7
Khalkís 23 E4
Khalmer-Sede =
Tazovskiy ... 28 C8
Khalmer Yu ... 28 C7
Khalturin 24 B6
Khalūf 48 C6
Khambat, G. of 43 J8
Khambhat ... 43 H8
Khamir 49 D3
Khānābād ... 45 B7
Khānaqīn ... 46 D6
Khandwa 43 J10
Khanewal ... 42 D7
Khaniá 23 G5
Khaníon, Kólpos 23 G4
Khankendy =
Xankändi ... 25 F6
Khanty-
Mansiysk ... 29 C7
Khapcheranga . 30 E9
Kharagpur 40 F6
Kharan Kalat . 42 E4
Kharānaq 44 C3
Kharda 43 K9
Khârga, El
Wâhât el ... 52 C5
Khargon 43 J9
Khārk, Jazireh . 47 E7
Kharkiv 24 D4

Kharkov =
Kharkiv 24 D4
Kharovsk 24 B5
Kharsānīya 47 F7
Kharta 22 D7
Khartoum = El
Khartûm 53 E5
Khâsh 42 E2
Khashm el Girba 53 F6
Khaskovo 22 D5
Khatanga 30 B8
Khatanga → .. 30 B8
Khaybar, Harrat 47 F5
Khed Brahma . 43 G8
Khemmarat ... 36 A3
Khenchela 54 A6
Khenifra 54 B3
Kherson 25 D3
Kheta → 30 B8
Khilok 30 D9
Khíos 23 E6
Khiuma =
Hiiumaa 24 B1
Khiva 29 E7
Khīyāv 46 C6
Khmelnik 17 D8
Khmelnitskiy =
Khmelnytskyy 17 D8
Khmelnytskyy . 17 D8
Khmer Rep. =
Cambodia ■ 36 B3
Khodoriv 17 D7
Khodzent =
Khudzhand .. 29 E7
Khojak P. 42 D5
Kholm, Afghan. 45 B6
Kholm, Russia . 24 B3
Khomeyn 44 C2
Khon Kaen ... 36 A2
Khoper → 29 E5
Khóra Sfakíon . 23 G5
Khorat =
Nakhon
Ratchasima . 36 B2
Khorramābād . 46 D7
Khorrāmshahr . 47 E7
Khotyn 17 D8
Khouribga 54 B3
Khowai 41 E8
Khoyniki 17 C9
Khu Khan 36 B2
Khudzhand ... 29 E7
Khūgiānī 42 D4
Khulna 41 F7
Khulna □ 41 F7
Khūr 44 C4
Khurayş 47 F7
Khūrīyā Mūrīyā,
Jazā 'ir 48 D6
Khush 42 C3
Khushab 42 C8
Khust 17 D6
Khuzdar 42 F5
Khvor 44 C3
Khvormūj 44 D2
Khvoy 46 C6
Khyber Pass .. 42 B7
Kiama 63 B5
Kiamba 38 C2
Kiangsi =
Jiangxi □ ... 35 D6
Kiangsu =
Jiangsu □ ... 35 C6
Kibangou 56 E2
Kibombo 57 E5
Kibondo 57 E6
Kibwesa 57 F5
Kibwezi 57 E7
Kicking Horse
Pass 71 C8

Kidal 55 E5
Kidnappers, C. . 64 C7
Kiel 14 A6
Kiel Canal =
Nord-Ostsee-
Kanal → ... 14 A5
Kielce 16 C5
Kieler Bucht ... 14 A6
Kiev = Kyyiv .. 17 C10
Kiffa 55 E2
Kifrī 46 D6
Kigali 57 E6
Kigoma-Ujiji .. 57 E5
Kihee 62 A3
Kii-Suidō 32 C4
Kikinda 22 B3
Kikládhes 23 F5
Kikwit 56 E3
Kilcoy 63 A5
Kilimanjaro ... 57 E7
Kilindini 57 E7
Kilis 46 C4
Kiliya 17 F9
Kilkenny 11 E3
Kilkís 23 D4
Killarney,
Australia 63 A5
Killarney, Ireland 11 E2
Killeen 78 D5
Killíni 23 F4
Kilmarnock ... 10 D4
Kilmore 63 C3
Kilosa 57 F7
Kilrush 11 E2
Kilwa Kivinje .. 57 F7
Kimaam 39 F5
Kimba 62 B2
Kimberley 58 D4
Kimberley
Plateau 60 D4
Kimry 24 B4
Kinabalu,
Gunong 36 C5
Kindia 55 G2
Kindu 57 E5
Kineshma 24 B5
King George B. . 95 G4
King George I. .. 96 A4
King George Is. 69 C2
King I. = Kadan
Kyun 36 B1
King I. 62 C3
King William I. . 70 B10
King William's
Town 59 E5
Kingaroy 63 A5
Kingoonya 62 B2
Kings Canyon
National Park 82 B3
King's Lynn ... 11 E7
Kingscote 62 C2
Kingsport 75 A6
Kingston,
Canada 69 D3
Kingston,
Jamaica 86 C4
Kingston, N.Z. . 65 F3
Kingston South
East 62 C2
Kingston upon
Hull 11 E6
Kingstown 87 D7
Kingsville 78 F5
Kınık 23 E6
Kinkala 56 E2
Kinleith 64 C6
Kinsale 11 F2
Kinshasa 56 E3
Kinston 75 B9

Kintampo 55 G4
Kintap 37 E5
Kiparissía 23 F3
Kiparissiakós
Kólpos 23 F3
Kipembawe ... 57 F6
Kipili 57 F6
Kipushi 59 A5
Kirghizia ■ =
Kyrgyzstan ■ 29 E8
Kirghizstan =
Kyrgyzstan ■ 29 E8
Kiri 56 E3
Kiribati ■ 64 K12
Kırıkkale 46 C3
Kirillov 24 B4
Kirin = Jilin .. 35 B7
Kiritimati 65 J15
Kirkcaldy 10 C5
Kirkcudbright .. 11 D4
Kirkee 43 K8
Kirkenes 8 E14
Kirkland Lake .. 69 D2
Kırklareli 22 D6
Kirkūk 46 D6
Kirkwall 10 B5
Kirov 28 D5
Kirovabad =
Gäncä 25 E6
Kirovakan =
Vanadzor ... 25 E5
Kirovograd =
Kirovohrad .. 25 D3
Kirovohrad 25 D3
Kirovsk =
Babadayhan . 29 F7
Kirovsk 28 C4
Kirsanov 24 C5
Kırşehir 46 C3
Kīrteh 45 C5
Kirthar Range . 42 F5
Kiruna 8 E12
Kirundu 57 E5
Kiryū 32 A6
Kisangani 57 D5
Kisar 39 F3
Kiselevsk 29 D9
Kishanganj ... 40 D7
Kishangarh ... 42 F7
Kishinev =
Chișinău ... 17 E9
Kishiwada 32 B4
Kishtwar 42 C9
Kisii 57 E6
Kisiju 57 F7
Kiska I. 71 C1
Kiskörös 16 E4
Kiskunfélegyháza
.... 16 E4
Kiskunhalas .. 16 E4
Kislovodsk ... 25 E5
Kiso-Sammyaku 32 B5
Kissidougou .. 55 G2
Kisumu 57 E6
Kita 55 F3
Kitab 29 F7
Kitakami-
Gawa → ... 33 G12
Kitakyūshū .. 32 C2
Kitale 57 D7
Kitchener 69 D2
Kitega = Gitega 57 E5
Kitgum 57 D6
Kíthira 23 F4
Kíthnos 23 F5
Kittakittaooloo,
L. 62 A2
Kitui 57 E7
Kitwe 59 A5

Kivertsi 17 C7
Kivu, L. 57 E5
Kiyev = Kyyiv . 17 C10
Kiyevskoye
Vdkhr. =
Kyyivske
Vdskh. 17 C10
Kızıl Irmak → . 25 E4
Kizlyar 25 E6
Kizyl-Arvat =
Gyzylarbat . 29 F6
Kladno 16 C2
Klagenfurt 15 E8
Klaipeda 24 B1
Klamath Falls . 80 D3
Klamath Mts. .. 80 E2
Klarälven → . 9 G10
Klatovy 16 D1
Klawer 58 E3
Klerksdorp ... 59 D5
Kletsk = Klyetsk 17 B8
Klin 28 D4
Kłodzko 16 C3
Klondike 70 B6
Klouto 55 G5
Kluane L. 70 B6
Kluczbork 16 C4
Klyetsk 17 B8
Knossós 23 G5
Knox Coast .. 96 A12
Knoxville 75 B6
Koartac =
Quaqtaq 68 B4
Koba, Aru,
Indonesia ... 39 F4
Koba, Bangka,
Indonesia ... 37 E3
Kobarid 20 A4
Kobdo = Hovd 34 B4
Kōbe 32 B4
København ... 9 G10
Koblenz 14 C4
Kobroor,
Kepulauan . 39 F4
Kobryn 17 B7
Kocaeli = İzmit 25 E2
Kočani 22 D4
Koch Bihar ... 41 D7
Kōchi 32 C3
Kochiu = Gejiu 34 D5
Kodiak 71 C4
Kodiak I. 71 C4
Koes 58 D3
Kofiau 39 E3
Koforidua 55 G4
Kōfu 32 B6
Kogan 63 A5
Koh-i-Bābā ... 42 B5
Kohat 42 C7
Kohima 41 E10
Kohkīlūyeh va
Būyer
Aḥmadi □ .. 44 D2
Kohler Ra. 96 B1
Kokand =
Qŭqon 29 E8
Kokas 39 E4
Kokchetav =
Kökshetaū .. 29 D7
Koko Kyunzu . 41 K9
Kokomo 72 D2
Kokonau 39 E5
Kökshetaū ... 29 D7
Koksoak → .. 68 C4
Kokstad 59 E5
Kola, Indonesia 39 F4
Kola, Russia .. 28 C4
Kola Pen. =
Kolskiy
Poluostrov .. 28 C4

Kolaka

Kolaka 39 E2
Kolar 43 N11
Kolar Gold
  Fields 43 N11
Kolayat 42 F8
Kolchugino =
  Leninsk-
  Kuznetskiy .. 29 D9
Kolda 55 F2
Kole 56 E4
Kolepom = Yos
  Sudarso,
  Pulau 39 F5
Kolguyev,
  Ostrov 28 C5
Kolhapur 43 L9
Kolín 16 C2
Köln 14 C4
Koło 16 B4
Kołobrzeg 16 A2
Kolokani 55 F3
Kolomna 24 B4
Kolomyya 17 D7
Kolonodale ... 39 E2
Kolosib 41 E9
Kolpashevo ... 29 D9
Kolpino 24 B3
Kolskiy
  Poluostrov .. 28 C4
Kolwezi 57 G5
Kolyma → ... 31 C13
Komárno 16 E4
Komatsu 32 A5
Komi □ 28 C6
Kommunarsk =
  Alchevsk ... 25 D4
Kommunizma,
  Pik 29 F8
Komodo 39 F1
Komono 56 E2
Komoran, Pulau 39 F5
Komotini 22 D5
Kompong Cham 36 B3
Kompong
  Chhnang 36 B2
Kompong Som 36 B2
Komrat =
  Comrat 17 E9
Komsomolets,
  Ostrov 30 A7
Konarhá □ 42 B7
Konch 42 G11
Kondoa 57 E7
Konduga 53 F1
Köneürgench .. 29 E6
Kong 55 G4
Kong, Koh ... 36 B2
Konglu 41 D11
Kongolo 57 F5
Kongor 53 G5
Königsberg =
  Kaliningrad . 24 C1
Konin 16 B4
Konjic 20 C6
Konosha 28 C5
Konotop 24 C3
Konqi He → .. 34 B4
Końskie 16 C5
Konstanz 14 E5
Kontagora ... 55 F6
Kontum 36 B3
Konya 46 C3
Konya Ovası . 46 C3
Konza 57 E7
Kooloonong .. 62 B3
Koondrook ... 63 C3
Koonibba 62 B1
Koorawatha .. 63 B4
Kootenay L. ... 71 D8

Kopaonik 22 C3
Koper 20 B4
Kopeysk 29 D7
Kopi 62 B2
Koprivnica ... 20 A6
Kopychyntsi .. 17 D7
Korab 22 D3
Korça 23 D3
Korce = Korça . 23 D3
Korčula 20 C6
Kordestan 46 D5
Kordestän □ .. 46 D6
Kordofân 53 F4
Korea, North ■ 35 C7
Korea, South ■ 35 C7
Korea Bay ... 35 C7
Korea Strait ... 35 C7
Korets 17 C8
Korhogo 55 G3
Korim 39 E5
Korinthiakós
  Kólpos 23 E4
Kórinthos 23 F4
Kōriyama 33 G12
Korneshty =
  Corneşti 17 E9
Koro, Ivory C. . 55 G3
Koro, Mali ... 55 F4
Korogwe 57 F7
Koroit 62 C3
Koror 38 C4
Körös → ... 16 E5
Korosten 17 C9
Korostyshev .. 17 C9
Korti 53 E5
Kortrijk 14 C2
Kos 23 F6
Kościan 16 B3
Kosciuszko, Mt. 63 C4
Kosha 52 D5
K'oshih = Kashi 34 C2
Košice 16 D5
Kosovo □ 22 C3
Kosovska-
  Mitrovica ... 22 C3
Kôstî 53 F5
Kostopil 17 C8
Kostroma 24 B5
Kostrzyn 16 B2
Koszalin 16 A3
Kota 43 G9
Kota Baharu .. 36 C2
Kota Belud ... 36 C5
Kota Kinabalu . 36 C5
Kota Tinggi .. 37 D2
Kotaagung ... 37 F2
Kotabaru 37 E5
Kotabumi 37 E2
Kotamobagu .. 39 D2
Kotawaringin .. 37 E4
Kotelnich 24 B6
Kotelnyy, Ostrov 31 B11
Kotka 9 F13
Kotlas 28 C5
Kotli 42 C8
Kotor 22 C2
Kotovsk 17 E9
Kotri 42 G6
Kottayam 43 Q10
Kotturu 43 M10
Kotuy → 30 B8
Kotzebue 71 B3
Kouango 56 D4
Koudougou ... 55 F4
Kouilou → .. 56 E2
Kouki 56 C3
Koula Moutou . 56 E2
Koulen 36 B2
Koulikoro ... 55 F3

Koumra 53 G2
Kounradskiy .. 29 E8
Kouroussa ... 55 F3
Kousseri 53 F1
Koutiala 55 F3
Kovel 17 C7
Kovrov 24 B5
Kowloon 35 D6
Köyceğiz 23 F7
Koyuk 71 B3
Koyukuk → .. 71 B4
Kozan 46 C3
Kozáni 23 D3
Kozhikode =
  Calicut 43 P9
Kozyatyn 17 D9
Kpalimé 55 G5
Kra, Isthmus of
  = Kra, Kho
  Khot 36 B1
Kra, Kho Khot . 36 B1
Kragujevac ... 22 B3
Krajina 20 B6
Krakatau =
  Rakata, Pulau 37 F3
Kraków 16 C4
Kraljevo 22 C3
Kramatorsk .. 25 D4
Kranj 20 A5
Krašnik 16 C6
Krasnoarmeysk 29 D5
Krasnodar ... 25 D4
Krasnoperekopsk
  .... 25 D3
Krasnoselkupsk 28 C9
Krasnoturinsk . 28 D7
Krasnoufimsk . 29 D6
Krasnouralsk .. 29 D7
Krasnovodsk =
  Krasnowodsk 29 E6
Krasnowodsk .. 29 E6
Krasnoyarsk .. 30 D7
Krasnyy Luch . 25 D4
Krasnyy Yar ... 25 D6
Kratie 36 B3
Krau 39 E6
Krefeld 14 C4
Kremen 20 B5
Kremenchug =
  Kremenchuk . 24 D3
Kremenchuk .. 24 D3
Kremenchuksk
  Vdskh. 24 D3
Kremenets 17 C7
Krems 15 D8
Kribi 56 D1
Krichev =
  Krychaw 17 B10
Krishna → ... 40 K3
Krishnanagar .. 41 F7
Kristiansand .. 9 G9
Kristiansund .. 8 F9
Kríti 23 G5
Krivoy Rog =
  Kryvyy Rih .. 25 D3
Krk 20 B5
Kronprins Olav
  Kyst 96 A9
Kronshtadt 24 B2
Kroonstad ... 59 D5
Kropotkin,
  Irkutsk, Russia 30 D9
Kropotkin,
  Krasnodar,
  Russia 25 D5
Krosno 16 D5
Krotoszyn 16 C3
Krugersdorp .. 59 D5

Krung Thep =
  Bangkok 36 B2
Krupki 17 A9
Kruševac 22 C3
Krychaw 17 B10
Krymskiy
  Poluostrov =
  Krymskyy
  Pivostriv 25 D3
Krymskyy
  Pivostriv 25 D3
Kryvyy Rih 25 D3
Ksar el Boukhari 54 A5
Ksar el Kebir . 54 B3
Ksar es Souk =
  Ar Rachidiya . 54 B4
Kuala 37 D3
Kuala Kubu
  Baharu 37 D2
Kuala Lipis ... 37 D2
Kuala Lumpur . 37 D2
Kuala
  Terengganu . 36 C2
Kualajelai 37 E4
Kualakapuas . 37 E4
Kualakurun ... 37 E4
Kualapembuang 37 E4
Kualasimpang . 37 D1
Kuandang 39 D2
Kuangchou =
  Guangzhou . 35 D6
Kuantan 37 D2
Kuba = Quba . 25 E6
Kuban → 25 D4
Kucing 37 D4
Kuda 43 H7
Kudat 36 C5
Kudymkar 28 D6
Kueiyang =
  Guiyang 35 D5
Kufra Oasis = Al
  Kufrah 52 D3
Kufstein 15 E7
Kugluktuk 70 B8
Kūh-e 'Alijūq . 44 D2
Kūh-e-Hazārām 44 D4
Kūh-e Sorkh .. 44 C4
Kūh-e Taftān . 45 D5
Kūhak 42 F3
Kūhhā-ye-
  Bashākerd . 45 E4
Kūhpāyeh 44 C3
Kuito 58 A3
Kujū-San 32 C2
Kukawa 53 F1
Kukësi 22 C3
Kula 23 E7
Kulasekarappattinam
  .... 43 Q11
Kuldja = Yining 34 B3
Kūlob 29 F7
Kulsary 29 E6
Kulunda 29 D8
Kulwin 62 C3
Kulyab = Kūlob 29 F7
Kum Tekei ... 29 E8
Kuma → 25 E6
Kumagaya ... 32 A6
Kumai 37 E4
Kumamba,
  Kepulauan .. 39 E5
Kumamoto ... 32 C2
Kumanovo ... 22 C3
Kumara 65 E4
Kumasi 55 G4
Kumayri =
  Gyumri 25 E5
Kumba 56 D1
Kumbakonam . 43 P11

Kumbarilla 63 A5
Kumo 55 F7
Kumon Bum .. 41 D11
Kunama 63 C4
Kungala 63 A5
Kungrad =
Qŭnghirot .. 29 E6
Kungur 29 D6
Kunlong 41 F12
Kunlun Shan .. 34 C3
Kunming 34 D5
Kunsan 35 C7
Kunya-Urgench
=
Köneürgench 29 E6
Kuopio 8 F13
Kupa → 20 B6
Kupyansk 28 E4
Kuqa 34 B3
Kür → 25 E6
Kura = Kür → 25 E6
Kurashiki 32 B3
Kurayoshi 32 B3
Kŭrdzhali 22 D5
Kure 32 B3
Kurgaldzhinskiy 29 D8
Kurgan 29 D7
Kuria Maria Is.
= Khūrīyā
Mūrīyā, Jazā
'ir 48 D6
Kurigram 41 E7
Kuril Is. =
Kurilskiye
Ostrova 31 E12
Kurilskiye
Ostrova 31 E12
Kurmuk 53 F5
Kurnool 43 L11
Kurow 65 F4
Kurrajong 63 B5
Kurri Kurri 63 B5
Kursk 24 C4
Kuruktag 34 B3
Kuruman 58 D4
Kurume 32 C2
Kus Gölü 23 D6
Kuşadası 23 F6
Kushiro 32 F12
Kushtia 41 F7
Kuskokwim → 71 B3
Kuskokwim B. . 71 C3
Kustanay =
Qostanay ... 29 D7
Kütahya 46 C2
Kutaisi 25 E5
Kutaraja =
Banda Aceh . 36 C1
Kutch, Gulf of =
Kachchh, Gulf
of 43 H6
Kutch, Rann of
= Kachchh,
Rann of 43 G6
Kutno 16 B4
Kutu 56 E3
Kutum 53 F3
Kuujjuaq 68 C4
Kuwait = Al
Kuwayt 47 E7
Kuwait ■ 47 E6
Kuwana 32 B5
Kuybyshev =
Samara 24 C7
Kuybyshev 29 D8
Kuybyshevskoye
Vdkhr. 24 B6
Kŭysanjaq 46 C6
Kuyumba 30 C7

Kuzey Anadolu
Dağları 46 B3
Kuznetsk 24 C6
Kvarner 20 B5
Kvarnerič 20 B5
Kwakoegron .. 92 A2
Kwamouth 56 E3
Kwando → ... 58 B4
Kwangju 35 C7
Kwangsi-Chuang
= Guangxi
Zhuangzu
Zizhiqu □ ... 35 D5
Kwangtung =
Guangdong □ 35 D6
Kwatisore 39 E4
Kweichow =
Guizhou □ ... 35 D5
Kwekwe 59 B5
Kwidzyn 16 B4
Kwoka 39 E4
Kyabé 53 G2
Kyabra Cr. → . 63 A3
Kyabram 63 C4
Kyancutta 62 B2
Kyangin 41 H10
Kyaukpadaung 41 G10
Kyaukpyu 41 H9
Kyaukse 41 G11
Kyle Dam 59 C6
Kyneton 63 C3
Kyō-ga-Saki .. 32 B4
Kyoga, L. 57 D6
Kyogle 63 A5
Kyongpyaw ... 41 J10
Kyōto 32 B4
Kyrenia 46 D3
Kyrgyzstan ■ .. 29 E8
Kystatyam 30 C10
Kytal Ktakh .. 31 C10
Kyunhla 41 F10
Kyūshū 32 C2
Kyūshū-Sanchi 32 C2
Kyustendil ... 22 C4
Kyusyur 30 B10
Kywong 63 B4
Kyyiv 17 C10
Kyyivske Vdskh. 17 C10
Kyzyl Kum ... 29 E7
Kyzyl-Kyya 29 E8
Kzyl-Orda =
Qyzylorda ... 29 E7

L

La Albufera ... 19 C5
La Alcarria 19 B4
La Asunción .. 90 A6
La Banda 94 B4
La Calera 94 C2
La Carlota 94 C4
La Ceiba 85 D7
La Chaux de
Fonds 13 C7
La Cocha 94 B3
La Coruña 18 A1
La Crosse 77 D9
La Dorada 90 B4
La Estrada 18 A1
La Grange 74 C5
La Guaira 90 A5
La Güera 54 D1
La Habana 86 B3
La Línea de la
Concepción .. 18 D3
La Mancha 19 C4

La Palma,
Canary Is. ... 54 C1
La Palma,
Panama 86 E4
La Palma del
Condado 18 D2
La Paragua ... 90 B6
La Paz,
Entre Ríos,
Argentina ... 94 C5
La Paz, San Luis,
Argentina ... 94 C3
La Paz, Bolivia . 91 G5
La Paz, Mexico . 84 C2
La Pedrera ... 90 D5
La Plata 94 D5
La Quiaca 94 A3
La Rioja 94 B3
La Rioja □ 19 A4
La Robla 18 A3
La Roche-sur-
Yon 12 C3
La Rochelle ... 12 C3
La Roda 19 C4
La Romana ... 87 C6
La Serena 94 B2
La Seyne-sur-
Mer 13 E6
La Spézia 20 B2
La Tortuga ... 87 D6
La Tuque 69 D3
La Unión 95 E2
La Urbana 90 B5
La Vega 87 C5
Labe = Elbe → 14 B5
Labé 55 F2
Labis 37 D2
Laboulaye 94 C4
Labrador, Coast
of □ 69 C4
Lábrea 91 E6
Labuan, Pulau . 36 C5
Labuha 39 E3
Labuhanbajo .. 39 F2
Labuk, Telok . 36 C5
Labyrinth, L. .. 62 B2
Labytnangi 28 C7
Lac La Biche .. 71 C8
Lac la Martre .. 70 B8
Lacanau 12 D3
Laccadive Is. =
Lakshadweep
Is. 26 H11
Lacepede B. ... 62 C2
Lachine 69 D3
Lachlan → ... 63 B3
Lackawanna .. 73 C6
Lacombe 71 C8
Ladakh Ra. ... 42 B10
Lādīz 45 D5
Ladoga, L. =
Ladozhskoye
Ozero 28 C4
Ladozhskoye
Ozero 28 C4
Ladysmith,
Canada 71 D7
Ladysmith,
S. Africa ... 59 D5
Lae 61 B8
Lafayette 79 D7
Lafia 55 G6
Laghmān □ ... 45 C7
Laghouat 54 B5
Lagonoy Gulf . 38 B2
Lagos, Nigeria . 55 G5
Lagos, Portugal 18 D1
Laguna 94 B7
Lagunas, Chile 91 H5

Lagunas, Peru . 90 E3
Lahad Datu ... 38 C1
Lahat 37 E2
Lahewa 37 D1
Lāhījān 46 C7
Lahn → 14 C4
Lahore 42 D9
Lahti 8 F13
Lahtis = Lahti . 8 F13
Laï 53 G2
Laibin 35 D5
Laidley 63 A5
Laila = Laylá . 47 G6
Lairg 10 B4
Lajere 55 F7
Lajes 94 B6
Lake Cargelligo 63 B4
Lake Charles .. 79 D7
Lake City 75 D6
Lake Harbour . 68 B4
Lake Worth ... 75 F7
Lakeland 75 E7
Lakes Entrance 63 C4
Lakewood 72 D5
Lakonikós
Kólpos 23 F4
Lakor 39 F3
Lakota 55 G3
Lakshadweep Is. 26 H11
Lala Ghat 41 E9
Lalibela 53 F6
Lalín 18 A1
Lalitapur =
Patan 40 D5
Lamaing 41 K11
Lamas 91 E3
Lambaréné ... 56 E2
Lambert Glacier 96 B10
Lame 55 F6
Lamego 18 B2
Lameroo 62 C3
Lamía 23 E4
Lamon Bay ... 38 B2
Lampa 91 G4
Lampedusa ... 21 G4
Lampione 21 G4
Lampung □ ... 37 F2
Lamu 57 E8
Lanai I. 82 H12
Lanak La 42 B11
Lanak'o
Shank'ou =
Lanak La 42 B11
Lanao, L. 38 C2
Lancaster, U.K. 11 D5
Lancaster,
U.S.A. 73 D7
Lancaster Sd. . 68 A2
Lanchow =
Lanzhou ... 35 C5
Lanciano 20 C5
Landeck 14 E6
Landes 12 D3
Landi Kotal ... 42 B7
Land's End ... 11 F4
Landshut 15 D7
La'nga Co 40 B3
Langkawi, P. .. 36 C1
Langkon 36 C5
Langres 13 C6
Langres, Plateau
de 13 C6
Langsa 36 D1
Languedoc ... 13 E5
Langzhong ... 35 C5
Lannion 12 B2
Lansdowne ... 63 B5
Lansing 72 C3
Lanusei 21 E2

Lanzarote 54 C2
Lanzhou 35 C5
Laoag 38 A2
Laoang 38 B3
Laon 13 B5
Laos ■ 36 A3
Lapa 94 B7
Laparan 38 C1
Lapland =
　Lappland ... 8 E12
Lappland 8 E12
Lapseki 23 D6
Laptev Sea .. 30 B10
L'Áquila 20 C4
Lär 44 E3
Larache 54 A3
Laramie 76 E2
Larantuka 39 F2
Larap 38 B2
Larat 39 F4
Laredo 78 F4
Lariang 39 E1
Lárisa 23 E4
Larnaca 46 D3
Larne 11 D4
Larrimah 60 D5
Larsen Ice Shelf 96 A3
Larvik 9 G9
Laryak 29 C8
Las Anod 49 F4
Las Cruces ... 83 D9
Las Flores 94 D5
Las Khoreh ... 49 E4
Las Lajas 94 D2
Las Lomitas ... 94 A4
Las Palmas ... 54 C1
Las Pipinas ... 94 D5
Las Plumas ... 95 E3
Las Rosas 94 C4
Las Varillas ... 94 C4
Las Vegas 82 B5
Lashio 41 F11
Lassen Pk. ... 80 E3
Lastoursville .. 56 E2
Lastovo 20 C6
Latacunga 90 D3
Latakia = Al
　Lãdhiqīyah .. 46 D3
Latina 20 D4
Latium =
　Lazio □ 20 C4
Latrobe 62 D4
Latvia ■ 24 B1
Lauchhammer . 15 C7
Launceston .. 62 D4
Laurel 79 D9
Lauria 21 D5
Laurium 69 D2
Lausanne 13 C7
Laut 36 D3
Laut Kecil,
　Kepulauan .. 37 E5
Laval 12 B3
Lávrion 23 F5
Lawas 36 D5
Lawele 39 F2
Lawng Pit 41 E11
Lawrence, N.Z. 65 F3
Lawrence,
　U.S.A. 77 F7
Lawton 78 B4
Laylá 47 G6
Lazio □ 20 C4
Le Creusot 13 C6
Le Havre 12 B4
Le Mans 12 C4
Le Mont-St.-
　Michel 12 B3
Le Moule 87 C7

Le Puy-en-Velay 13 D5
Le Touquet-
　Paris-Plage .. 12 A4
Le Tréport 12 A4
Le Verdon-sur-
　Mer 12 D3
Leamington Spa
　= Royal
　Leamington
　Spa 11 E6
Leandro Norte
　Alem 94 B5
Leavenworth .. 77 F7
Lebak 38 C2
Lebanon ■ 46 D3
Lębork 16 A3
Lebrija 18 D2
Lebu 94 D2
Lecce 23 D2
Lecco 20 B2
Lech ─► 14 D6
Łęczyca 16 B4
Leduc 71 C8
Leeds 11 E6
Leer 14 B4
Leeton 63 B4
Leeuwarden .. 14 B3
Leeuwin, C. ... 60 G2
Leeward Is. ... 87 C7
Leganés 18 B4
Legazpi 38 B2
Leghorn =
　Livorno 20 C3
Legionowo ... 16 B5
Legnago 20 B3
Legnica 16 C3
Legume 63 A5
Leh 42 B10
Leicester 11 E6
Leiden 14 B3
Leie ─► 14 C2
Leine ─► 14 B5
Leinster □ 11 E3
Leipzig 15 C7
Leiria 18 C1
Leitrim 11 D2
Leizhou Bandao 35 D6
Leksula 39 E3
Lékva Ori 23 G5
Leleque 95 E2
Léman, L. 13 C7
Lemhi Ra. 81 C7
Lena ─► 30 B10
Leninabad =
　Khudzhand .. 29 E7
Leninakan =
　Gyumri 25 E5
Leningrad =
　Sankt-
　Peterburg ... 24 B3
Leninogorsk =
　Ridder 29 D9
Leninsk 25 D6
Leninsk-
　Kuznetskiy .. 29 D9
Lenmalu 39 E4
Lens 13 A5
Lentini 21 F5
Leoben 15 E8
Leodhas =
　Lewis 10 B3
León, Mexico .. 84 C4
León, Nic. 85 E7
León, Spain .. 18 A3
León, Montañas
　de 18 A2
Leongatha 63 C4
Léopold II, Lac
　= Mai-
　Ndombe, L. . 56 E3

Léopoldville =
　Kinshasa 56 E3
Leova 17 E9
Lepel = Lyepyel 24 C2
Lepikha 31 C10
Léré 53 G1
Lérida 19 B6
Lerwick 10 A6
Les Cayes 86 C5
Les Sables-
　d'Olonne ... 12 C3
Lesbos =
　Lésvos 23 E6
Leskovac 22 C3
Lesotho ■ 59 D5
Lesser Antilles . 87 D7
Lesser Sunda Is. 39 F2
Lésvos 23 E6
Leszno 16 C3
Lethbridge 71 D8
Leti, Kepulauan 39 F3
Leti Is. = Leti,
　Kepulauan .. 39 F3
Leticia 90 D4
Letpadan 41 J10
Letpan 41 H10
Letterkenny ... 11 D3
Leuser, G. 37 D1
Leuven 14 C3
Levádhia 23 E4
Levice 16 D4
Levin 64 D6
Lévis 69 D3
Levkás 23 E3
Levkôsia =
　Nicosia 46 D3
Levskigrad =
　Karlovo 22 C5
Lewis 10 B3
Lewisporte 69 D5
Lewiston, Idaho,
　U.S.A. 80 B5
Lewiston,
　Maine, U.S.A. 73 B10
Lexington, Ky.,
　U.S.A. 72 E3
Lexington, N.C.,
　U.S.A. 75 B7
Leyte 38 B2
Lezha 22 D2
Lhasa 34 D4
Lhazê 34 D3
Lhokkruet 36 D1
Lhokseumawe . 36 C1
Lhuntsi Dzong . 41 D8
Lianga 38 C3
Lianyungang .. 35 C6
Liaoning □ ... 35 B7
Liaoyuan 35 B7
Liard ─► 70 B7
Libau = Liepāja 24 B1
Libenge 56 D3
Liberal 78 A3
Liberec 16 C2
Liberia ■ 55 G3
Lîbîya, Sahrâ' . 52 C4
Libobo, Tanjung 39 E3
Libonda 58 A4
Libourne 12 D3
Libreville 56 D1
Libya ■ 52 C2
Libyan Desert =
　Lîbîya, Sahrâ' 52 C4
Licantén 94 D2
Licata 21 F4
Lichinga 59 A7
Lichtenburg ... 59 D5
Lida 17 B7
Liechtenstein ■ 14 E5

Liège .... 14 C
Liegnitz =
　Legnica .... 16 C
Lienyünchiangshih
　=
　Lianyungang 35 C
Lienz .... 15 E
Liepāja .... 24 B
Liffey ─► .... 11 E
Lifford .... 11 D
Lightning Ridge 63 A
Liguria □ .... 20 B
Ligurian Sea . 20 C
Lijiang .... 34 D
Likasi .... 57 G
Lille .... 13 A
Lillehammer .. 8 F1
Lilongwe ..... 59 A
Liloy .... 38 C
Lim ─► ...... 20 C
Lima, Indonesia 39 E
Lima, Peru ... 91 F
Lima, U.S.A. .. 72 D
Lima ─► ..... 18 B
Limassol ..... 46 D
Limay Mahuida 94 D
Limbang ...... 36 D
Limbe .... 56 D
Limbri .... 63 B
Limburg ..... 14 C
Limeira ...... 94 A
Limerick ..... 11 E
Limfjorden ... 9 G
Limia =
　Lima ─► .... 18 B
Límnos ...... 23 E
Limoeiro do
　Norte ...... 92 D
Limoges ..... 12 D
Limón .... 86 E
Limousin ..... 12 D
Limoux ...... 12 E
Limpopo ─► .. 59 D
Limuru .... 57 E
Linares, Chile . 94 D
Linares, Mexico 84 C
Linares, Spain . 18 C
Linchuan ..... 35 D
Lincoln,
　Argentina ... 94 C
Lincoln, N.Z. .. 65 E
Lincoln, U.K. .. 11 E
Lincoln, U.S.A. 77 E
Linden .... 90 B
Líndhos ...... 23 F
Lindi .... 57 F
Lingayen ..... 38 A
Lingayen G. ... 38 A
Lingen .... 14 B
Lingga .... 37 E
Lingga,
　Kepulauan .. 37 E
Lingga Arch. =
　Lingga,
　Kepulauan .. 37 E
Linguéré ..... 55 E
Lingyun ...... 35 D
Linhai .... 35 D
Linhares ..... 93 F
Linköping 9 G1
Linosa, I. .... 21 G
Lins .... 94 A
Linville ...... 63 A
Linxia .... 34 C
Linz .... 15 D
Lion, G. du .. 13 E
Lions, G. of =
　Lion, G. du .. 13 E
Lipa .... 38 B

ípari 21 E5
ípari, Is. =
  Eólie, Ís. 21 E5
ipcani 17 D8
ipetsk 24 C4
ipkany =
  Lipcani 17 D8
ipovets 17 D9
ippe → 14 C4
iptrap C. 63 C4
ira 57 D6
iria 19 C5
isala 56 D4
isboa 18 C1
isbon = Lisboa 18 C1
isburn 11 D3
isburne, C. .. 71 B3
ishui 35 D6
isichansk =
  Lysychansk . 25 D4
isieux 12 B4
iski 24 C4
ismore 63 A5
ister, Mt. .. 96 B15
iston 63 A5
istowel 11 E2
itang 38 C1
itani → 46 D3
ithgow 63 B5
ithinon, Ákra . 23 G5
itoměřice ... 16 C2
ittle Barrier I. . 64 B6
ittle Laut Is. =
  Laut Kecil,
  Kepulauan . 37 E5
ittle
  Missouri → . 76 B3
ittle River 65 E5
ittle Rock 79 B7
iukang
  Tenggaja ... 39 F1
iuwa Plain ... 58 A4
iuzhou 35 D5
iverpool,
  Australia 63 B5
iverpool,
  Canada 69 D4
iverpool, U.K. 11 E5
iverpool Plains 63 B5
iverpool Ra. . 63 B5
ivingstone ... 59 B5
ivingstonia ... 57 G6
ivny 24 C4
ivorno 20 C3
ivramento .. 94 C5
iwale 57 F7
jubljana 20 A5
jungan → ... 8 F11
jusnan → ... 8 F11
lancanelo,
  Salina 94 D3
lanelli 11 F4
lanes 18 A3
lano Estacado 78 C2
lanos 90 C4
leida = Lérida 19 B6
lobregat → . 19 B7
loret de Mar . 19 B7
luchmayor ... 19 C7
lullaillaco,
  Volcán 94 A3
oa → 94 A2
obatse 59 D5
obería 94 D5
obito 58 A2
ocarno 13 C8
och Garman =
  Wexford 11 E3

Loches 12 C4
Lock 62 B2
Lodhran 42 E7
Lodi, *Italy* 20 B2
Lodi, *U.S.A.* ... 80 F3
Lodja 56 E4
Lodwar 57 D7
Łódź 16 C4
Lofoten 8 E10
Logan 81 E8
Logan, Mt. ... 70 B5
Logone → ... 53 F2
Logroño 19 A4
Lohardaga ... 40 F5
Loi-kaw 41 H11
Loir → 12 C3
Loire → 12 C2
Loja, *Ecuador* . 90 D3
Loja, *Spain* ... 18 D3
Loji 39 E3
Lokandu 57 E5
Lokitaung 57 D7
Lokoja 55 G6
Lokolama 56 E3
Loliondo 57 E7
Lom 22 C4
Lomami → ... 56 D4
Lombárdia □ .. 20 B2
Lombardy =
  Lombárdia □ 20 B2
Lomblen 39 F2
Lombok 37 F5
Lomé 55 G5
Lomela 56 E4
Lomela → ... 56 E4
Lomié 56 D2
Lomond, L. ... 10 C4
Lompobatang . 39 F1
Łomża 16 B6
Loncoche ... 95 D2
Londa 43 M9
London 11 F6
Londonderry .. 11 D3
Londonderry, C. 60 C4
Londonderry, I. 95 H2
Londrina 94 A6
Long Beach .. 82 D3
Long I.,
  Bahamas ... 86 B4
Long I., *U.S.A.* . 73 D9
Long Xuyen .. 36 B3
Longford,
  Australia 62 D4
Longford,
  Ireland 11 E3
Longiram 37 E5
Longlac 69 D2
Longnawan ... 37 D4
Longreach 61 E7
Longview, *Tex.,*
  U.S.A. 79 C6
Longview,
  Wash., U.S.A. 80 B2
Lons-le-Saunier 13 C6
Lop Nor = Lop
  Nur 34 B4
Lop Nur 34 B4
Lopez, C. 56 E1
Lora → 42 D4
Lora, Hamun-i- 42 E4
Lora Cr. → ... 62 A2
Lora del Río ... 18 D3
Lorain 72 D4
Loralai 42 D6
Lorca 19 D5
Lorestān □ 46 D6
Loreto 92 D4
Lorient 12 C2
Lorne 62 C3

Lorraine 13 B7
Los Alamos ... 83 C9
Los Andes 94 C2
Los Angeles,
  Chile 94 D2
Los Angeles,
  U.S.A. 82 C3
Los Blancos .. 94 A4
Los Hermanos . 90 A6
Los Mochis .. 84 B3
Los Roques .. 90 A5
Los Testigos . 90 A6
Los Vilos 94 C2
Lošinj 20 B5
Lot → 12 D4
Lota 94 D2
Loubomo 56 E2
Louga 55 E1
Louis Trichardt 59 C5
Louis XIV, Pte. . 69 C3
Louisiade Arch. 61 C9
Louisiana □ ... 79 D8
Louisville 72 E3
Loulé 18 D1
Lourdes 12 E3
Louth, *Australia* 63 B4
Louth, *U.K.* ... 11 E6
Louvain =
  Leuven 14 C3
Lovech 22 C5
Low Tatra =
  Nízké Tatry .. 16 D4
Lowell 73 C10
Lower California
  = Baja
  California ... 84 A1
Lower Hutt 65 D6
Lower Saxony =
  Niedersachsen □
  .... 14 B5
Lower Tunguska
  = Tunguska,
  Nizhnyaya → 30 C6
Lowestoft 11 E7
Łowicz 16 B4
Lowyar □ 45 C7
Loxton 62 B3
Loyalty Is. =
  Loyauté, Is. . 64 M11
Loyang =
  Luoyang 35 C6
Loyauté, Is. ... 64 M11
Loyev = Loyew 17 C10
Loyew 17 C10
Luachimo 56 F4
Luacono 56 G4
Lualaba → ... 57 D5
Luanda 56 F2
Luangwa 59 B6
Luangwa → ... 59 A6
Luanshya 59 A5
Luapula → ... 57 F5
Luarca 18 A2
Luashi 56 G4
Luau 56 G4
Lubalo 56 F3
Lubang Is. 38 B2
Lubbock 78 C3
Lübeck 15 B6
Lubefu 56 E4
Lubero = Luofu 57 E5
Lubin 16 C3
Lublin 17 C6
Lubuagan ... 38 A2
Lubuk Antu ... 37 D4
Lubuklinggau . 37 E2
Lubuksikaping . 37 D2
Lubumbashi .. 59 A5
Lubutu 57 E5

Lucca 20 C3
Lucena, *Phil.* .. 38 B2
Lucena, *Spain* . 18 D3
Lučenec 16 D4
Lucerne =
  Luzern 13 C8
Lucira 58 A2
Luckenwalde . 15 B7
Lucknow 40 D3
Lüda = Dalian . 35 C7
Lüderitz 58 D3
Ludhiana 42 D9
Ludwigsburg .. 14 D5
Ludwigshafen . 14 D5
Luebo 56 F4
Lufira → 57 F5
Lufkin 79 D6
Luga 24 B2
Lugano 13 C8
Lugansk =
  Luhansk 25 D4
Lugh Ganana .. 49 G3
Lugo, *Italy* 20 B3
Lugo, *Spain* ... 18 A2
Lugoj 17 F5
Lugovoy 29 E8
Luhansk 25 D4
Luiana 58 B4
Luimneach =
  Limerick 11 E2
Luís Correia ... 92 C5
Luitpold Coast . 96 B5
Luiza 56 F4
Luján 94 C5
Lukanga Swamp 59 A5
Lukenie → ... 56 E3
Lukolela 56 E3
Łuków 17 C6
Lule älv → ... 8 E12
Luleå 8 E12
Lüleburgaz ... 22 D6
Lulonga → ... 56 D3
Lulua → 56 E4
Luluabourg =
  Kananga 56 F4
Lumai 58 A4
Lumbala
  N'guimbo ... 58 A4
Lumsden 65 F3
Lumut, Tg. 37 E3
Lundazi 59 A6
Lundu 37 D3
Lüneburg 14 B6
Lüneburg Heath
  = Lüneburger
  Heide 14 B6
Lüneburger
  Heide 14 B6
Lunéville 13 B7
Lunglei 41 F9
Luni 42 G8
Luni → 43 G7
Luninets =
  Luninyets ... 17 B8
Luninyets ... 17 B8
Luofu 57 E5
Luoyang 35 C6
Luozi 56 E2
Luremo 56 F3
Lurgan 11 D3
Lusaka 59 B5
Lusambo 56 E4
Lushnja 23 D2
Lushoto 57 E7
Luta = Dalian . 35 C7
Luton 11 F6
Lutong 36 D4
Lutsk 17 C7

Lützow
  Holmbukta .. 96 A8
Luwuk 39 E2
Luxembourg .. 13 B7
Luxembourg ■ 14 D4
Luxor = El
  Uqsur 52 C5
Luza 24 A6
Luzern 13 C8
Luzhou 35 D5
Luziânia 93 F4
Luzon 38 A2
Lviv 17 D7
Lvov = Lviv .. 17 D7
Lyakhavichy .. 17 B8
Lyakhovskiye,
  Ostrova 31 B12
Lyallpur =
  Faisalabad .. 42 D8
Lydenburg ... 59 D6
Lydia 23 E7
Lyell 65 D5
Lyepyel 24 C2
Łyna → 16 A5
Lynchburg 73 F6
Lynd Ra. 63 A4
Lyndhurst 62 B2
Lynn Lake 71 C9
Lyon 13 D6
Lyonnais 13 D6
Lyons = Lyon . 13 D6
Lys = Leie → . 14 C2
Lysychansk ... 25 D4
Lyttelton 65 E5
Lyubertsy 24 B4
Lyuboml 17 C7

M

Ma'alah 47 F6
Ma'ān 47 E3
Ma'anshan ... 35 C6
Ma'arrat an
  Nu'mān 46 D4
Maas → 14 C3
Maastricht 13 A6
Mabrouk 55 E4
Macaé 93 G5
McAllen 78 F4
Macao =
  Macau ■ ... 35 D6
Macapá 92 B3
Macau 92 D6
Macau ■ 35 D6
M'Clintock Chan. 70 A9
McComb 79 D8
Macdonnell Ras. 60 E5
McDouall Peak 62 A1
Macdougall L. . 70 B10
Macedonia =
  Makedhonía □ 23 D4
Macedonia ■ .. 22 D3
Maceió 93 D6
Macenta 55 G3
Macerata 20 C4
Macfarlane, L. . 62 B2
Macgillycuddy's
  Reeks 11 F2
McGregor Ra. . 62 A3
Mach 42 E5
Machado =
  Jiparaná → . 91 E6
Machakos 57 E7
Machala 90 D3
Machilipatnam 40 J3
Machiques 90 A4

Machupicchu .. 91 F4
Macintyre → . 63 A5
Mackay 61 E8
Mackay, L. 60 E4
Mackenzie → . 70 B6
Mackenzie City
  = Linden ... 90 B7
Mackenzie Mts. 70 B6
McKinley, Mt. . 71 B4
McKinney 79 C5
Macksville 63 B5
Maclean 63 A5
Maclear 59 E5
Macleay → ... 63 B5
McMurdo Sd. . 96 B15
Mâcon, France 13 C6
Macon, U.S.A. . 75 C6
Macondo 58 A4
McPherson Ra. 63 A5
Macquarie
  Harbour ... 62 D4
MacRobertson
  Land 96 B10
Madagali 53 F1
Madagascar ■ . 59 J9
Mada'in Sālih . 47 F4
Madama 52 D1
Madang 61 B8
Madaoua 55 F6
Madaripur 41 F8
Madauk 41 J11
Madaya 41 F11
Maddalena ... 20 D2
Madeira 54 B1
Madeira → ... 90 D7
Madha 43 L9
Madhya
  Pradesh □ .. 43 H10
Madikeri 43 N9
Madimba 56 E3
Madīnat ash
  Sha'b 49 E3
Madingou 56 E2
Madison 77 D10
Madiun 37 F4
Madras = Tamil
  Nadu □ 43 P10
Madras 43 N12
Madre, Laguna 78 F5
Madre, Sierra . 38 A2
Madre de
  Dios → 91 F5
Madre de Dios,
  I. 95 G1
Madre
  Occidental,
  Sierra 84 B3
Madrid 18 B4
Madurai 43 Q11
Madurantakam 43 N11
Mae Sot 36 A1
Maebashi 32 A6
Maestrazgo,
  Mts. del 19 B5
Maevatanana .. 59 H9
Mafeking =
  Mafikeng ... 59 D5
Maffra 63 C4
Mafia I. 57 F7
Mafikeng 59 D5
Mafra, Brazil .. 94 B7
Mafra, Portugal 18 C1
Magadan 31 D13
Magadi 57 E7
Magallanes,
  Estrecho de . 95 G2
Magangué 90 B4
Magburaka ... 55 G2
Magdalena,
  Argentina ... 94 D5

Magdalena,
  Bolivia 91 F6
Magdalena,
  Malaysia 36 D5
Magdalena → . 90 A4
Magdeburg ... 15 B6
Magelang 37 F4
Magellan's Str.
  = Magallanes,
  Estrecho de . 95 G2
Maggiore, L. .. 20 B2
Magnetic Pole
  (South) =
  South
  Magnetic Pole 96 A13
Magnitogorsk . 29 D6
Magosa =
  Famagusta .. 46 D3
Maguarinho, C. 92 C4
Mağusa =
  Famagusta .. 46 D3
Magwe 41 G10
Mahābād 46 C6
Mahabo 59 J8
Mahagi 57 D6
Mahajanga ... 59 H9
Mahakam → .. 37 E5
Mahalapye ... 59 C5
Maḥallāt 44 C2
Mahanadi → . 40 G6
Mahanoro 59 H9
Maharashtra □ 43 J9
Mahbubnagar . 43 L10
Mahdia 52 A1
Mahenge 57 F7
Maheno 65 F4
Mahesana 43 H8
Mahia Pen. ... 64 C7
Mahilyow 17 B10
Mahón 19 C8
Mai-Ndombe, L. 56 E3
Maicurú → ... 92 C3
Maidstone 11 F7
Maiduguri 53 F1
Maijdi 41 F8
Maikala Ra. ... 40 G3
Main → 14 C5
Maine 12 C3
Maingkwan ... 41 D11
Mainit, L. 38 C3
Mainland,
  Orkney, U.K. 10 B5
Mainland, Shet.,
  U.K. 10 A6
Maintirano ... 59 H8
Mainz 14 C5
Maipú 94 D5
Maiquetía 90 A5
Mairabari 41 D9
Maitland,
  N.S.W.,
  Australia 63 B5
Maitland,
  S. Austral.,
  Australia 62 B2
Maizuru 32 B4
Majene 39 E1
Maji 53 G6
Majorca =
  Mallorca 19 C7
Maka 55 F2
Makale 39 E1
Makari 56 B2
Makarikari =
  Makgadikgadi
  Salt Pans .. 59 C5
Makasar =
  Ujung
  Pandang ... 39 F1

Makasar, Selat 39 E
Makasar, Str. of
  = Makasar,
  Selat .... 39 E
Makat .... 29 E
Makedhonía □ 23 D
Makedonija =
  Macedonia ■ 22 D
Makeni ...... 55 G
Makeyevka =
  Makiyivka .. 25 D
Makgadikgadi
  Salt Pans ... 59 C
Makhachkala . 25 E
Makian ...... 39 D
Makindu ..... 57 E
Makinsk ..... 29 D
Makiyivka ... 25 D
Makkah ...... 47 G
Makó .... 16 E
Makokou .... 56 D
Makoua ..... 56 E
Makrai 43 H1
Makran ...... 45 E
Makran Coast
  Range ..... 42 G
Maksimkin Yar 29 D
Mākū .... 46 C
Makumbi .... 56 F
Makurazaki .. 33 D
Makurdi ..... 55 G
Malabang .... 38 C
Malabar Coast . 43 P
Malabo = Rey
  Malabo .... 56 D
Malacca, Str. of 36 D
Maladzyechna . 17 A
Málaga ...... 18 D
Malakâl ..... 53 G
Malakand .... 42 B
Malang ...... 37 F
Malanje ..... 56 F
Mälaren 9 G1
Malargüe .... 94 D
Malaryta .... 17 C
Malatya ..... 46 C
Malawi ■ .... 59 A
Malawi, L. ... 59 A
Malaybalay ... 38 C
Malāyer ..... 46 D
Malaysia ■ ... 36 D
Malazgirt .... 46 C
Malbooma .... 62 B
Malbork ..... 16 A
Malden I. 65 K1
Maldives ■ ... 26 J1
Maldonado ... 94 C
Malé Karpaty .. 16 D
Maléa, Ákra .. 23 F
Malegaon .... 43 J
Malema ...... 59 A
Malha .... 53 E
Mali ■ ...... 55 E
Mali → 41 E1
Malik .... 39 E
Malili .... 39 E
Malin Hd. .... 10 D
Malindi ..... 57 E
Malines =
  Mechelen ... 14 C
Malino ...... 39 D
Malita ...... 38 C
Malkara ..... 22 D
Mallacoota ... 63 C
Mallacoota Inlet 63 C
Mallaig ...... 10 C
Mallawi ..... 52 C
Mallorca ..... 19 C
Mallow ...... 11 C

Malmö	9	G10
Malolos	38	B2
Malpelo	90	C2
Malta ■	21	G5
Maltahöhe	58	C3
Maluku	39	E3
Maluku □	39	E3
Maluku Sea =		
Molucca Sea	39	E2
Malvan	43	L8
Malvinas, Is. =		
Falkland Is. □	95	G5
Malyn	17	C9
Malyy		
Lyakhovskiy,		
Ostrov	31	B12
Mamahatun	46	C5
Mamanguape	92	D6
Mamasa	39	E1
Mamberamo →	39	E5
Mambilima Falls	57	G5
Mamburao	38	B2
Mamfe	55	G6
Mamoré →	91	F5
Mamou	55	F2
Mamuju	39	E1
Man	55	G3
Man, I. of	11	D4
Man Na	41	F11
Mana	92	A3
Manaar, G. of =		
Mannar, G. of	43	Q11
Manacapuru	90	D6
Manacor	19	C7
Manado	39	D2
Managua	85	E7
Manakara	59	J9
Manama = Al		
Manāmah	44	E2
Mananara	59	H9
Mananjary	59	J9
Manaos =		
Manaus	90	D7
Manapouri	65	F2
Manapouri, L.	65	F2
Manas	34	B3
Manas →	41	D8
Manasir	44	E2
Manaung	41	H9
Manaus	90	D7
Manay	38	C3
Manchester,		
U.K.	11	E5
Manchester,		
U.S.A.	73	C10
Mand →	44	D3
Manda	57	G6
Mandal	9	G9
Mandalay	41	F11
Mandale =		
Mandalay	41	F11
Mandalī	46	D6
Mandar, Teluk	39	E1
Mandaue	38	B2
Mandi	42	D10
Mandimba	59	A7
Mandioli	39	E3
Mandla	40	F3
Mandritsara	59	H9
Mandsaur	43	G9
Mandvi	43	H6
Mandya	43	N10
Manfalût	52	C5
Manfred	63	B3
Manfredónia	20	D5
Mangalia	22	C7
Mangaung	43	N9
Mangaweka	64	C6
Manggar	37	E3
Manggawitu	39	E4
Mangkalihat,		
Tanjung	39	D1
Mangla Dam	42	C8
Mangnai	34	C4
Mango	55	F5
Mangoche	59	A7
Mangole	39	E3
Mangonui	64	A5
Mangueigne	53	F3
Mangueira, L. da	94	C6
Mangyshlak		
Poluostrov	29	E6
Manhuaçu	93	G5
Manica	59	B6
Manicoré	91	E6
Manicouagan →		
	69	D4
Manīfah	47	F7
Manihiki	65	L14
Manila	38	B2
Manila B.	38	B2
Manilla	63	B5
Manipur □	41	E9
Manipur →	41	F10
Manisa	23	E6
Manitoba □	71	C10
Manitoba, L.	71	C10
Manitowoc	72	B2
Manizales	90	B3
Manja	59	J8
Manjacaze	59	C6
Manjhand	42	G6
Manjil	46	C7
Manjra →	43	K10
Mankono	55	G3
Manly	63	B5
Manmad	43	J9
Manna	37	E2
Mannahill	62	B3
Mannar	43	Q11
Mannar, G. of	43	Q11
Mannar I.	43	Q11
Mannheim	14	D5
Mannum	62	B2
Mano	55	G2
Manokwari	39	E4
Manombo	59	J8
Manono	57	F5
Manosque	13	E6
Manresa	19	B6
Mansa	57	G5
Mansel I.	68	B2
Mansfield,		
Australia	63	C4
Mansfield, U.K.	11	E6
Mansfield,		
U.S.A.	72	D4
Manta	90	D2
Mantalingajan,		
Mt.	36	C5
Mantes-la-Jolie	12	B4
Manthani	43	K11
Mantiqueira,		
Serra da	93	G5
Mántova	20	B3
Mantua =		
Mántova	20	B3
Manu	91	F4
Manuae	65	L15
Manuel		
Alves →	93	E4
Manui	39	E2
Manyara, L.	57	E7
Manych-Gudilo,		
Ozero	25	D5
Manyoni	57	F6
Manzai	42	C7
Manzanares	18	C4
Manzanillo,		
Cuba	86	B4
Manzanillo,		
Mexico	84	D4
Manzhouli	35	B6
Mao	53	F2
Maoke,		
Pegunungan	39	E5
Maoming	35	D6
Mapam Yumco	40	B3
Mapia,		
Kepulauan	39	D4
Mapuera →	90	D7
Maputo	59	D6
Maqnā	47	E3
Maquela do		
Zombo	56	F3
Maquinchao	95	E3
Mar, Serra do	94	B7
Mar Chiquita, L.	94	C4
Mar del Plata	94	D5
Mar Menor	19	D5
Maraã	90	D5
Marabá	92	D4
Maracá, I. de	92	B3
Maracaibo	90	A4
Maracaibo, L. de	90	B4
Maracay	90	A5
Marādah	52	C2
Maradi	55	F6
Marāgheh	46	C6
Marāh	47	F6
Marajó, I. de	92	C4
Maralal	57	D7
Marama	62	C3
Marampa	55	G2
Marand	46	C6
Maranguape	92	C6
Maranhão =		
São Luís	92	C5
Maranhão □	92	D4
Maranoa →	63	A4
Marañón →	90	D4
Marão	59	C6
Maraş =		
Kahramanmaraş		
	46	C4
Maratua	39	D1
Marbella	18	D3
Marburg	14	C5
Marche	12	C4
Marchena	18	D3
Mardan	42	B8
Mardin	46	C5
Marek = Stanke		
Dimitrov	22	C4
Marek	39	E2
Margarita, I. de	90	A6
Margate	11	F7
Margelan =		
Marghilon	29	E8
Marghilon	29	E8
Mari El □	24	B6
Mari Republic □		
= Mari El □	24	B6
Maria I.	62	D4
Maria van		
Diemen, C.	64	A5
Mariana Trench	64	H9
Marianao	86	B3
Ma'rib	49	D4
Maribor	20	A5
Marîdî	53	H4
Marie Byrd Land	96	B18
Marie-Galante	87	C7
Mariecourt =		
Kangiqsujuaq	68	B3
Mariental	58	C3
Mariinsk	29	D9
Marília	93	G3
Marín	18	A1
Marinduque	38	B2
Maringá	94	A6
Marion	79	A9
Mariscal		
Estigarribia	91	H6
Maritime Alps =		
Maritimes,		
Alpes	13	D7
Maritimes, Alpes	13	D7
Maritsa =		
Évros →	22	D6
Mariupol	25	D4
Marīvān	46	D6
Markazī □	44	C2
Markham, Mt.	96	C15
Marks	24	C6
Marla	62	A1
Marmagao	43	M8
Marmara	23	D6
Marmara, Sea of		
= Marmara		
Denizi	22	D7
Marmara Denizi	22	D7
Marmaris	23	F7
Marmolada,		
Mte.	20	A3
Marne →	12	B5
Maroantsetra	59	H9
Marondera	59	B6
Maroni →	92	A3
Maroochydore	63	A5
Maroona	62	C3
Maroua	53	F1
Marovoay	59	H9
Marquesas Is. =		
Marquises, Is.	65	K17
Marquette	69	D2
Marquises, Is.	65	K17
Marrakech	54	B3
Marrawah	62	D3
Marree	62	A2
Marromeu	59	B7
Marrowie Cr. →	63	B4
Marrupa	59	A7
Marsá Matrûh	52	B4
Marsá Susah	52	B3
Marsabit	57	D7
Marsala	21	F4
Marsden	63	B4
Marseille	13	E6
Marseilles =		
Marseille	13	E6
Marshall, Liberia	55	G2
Marshall, U.S.A.	79	C6
Marshall Is. ■	64	J12
Marshalltown	77	D8
Martaban	41	J11
Martaban, G. of	41	J11
Martapura,		
Kalimantan,		
Indonesia	37	E4
Martapura,		
Sumatera,		
Indonesia	37	E2
Marte	53	F1
Martigny	13	C7
Martigues	13	E6
Martin	16	D4
Martina Franca	21	D6
Martinborough	65	D6
Martinique ■	87	D7
Martinique		
Passage	87	C7
Martinsville	75	A8
Marton	64	D6
Martos	18	D4
Marudi	37	D4

Ma'ruf 42 D5
Marugame 32 B3
Marulan 63 B5
Marwar 42 G8
Mary 29 F7
Maryborough =
  Port Laoise .. 11 E3
Maryborough,
  Queens.,
  Australia 63 A5
Maryborough,
  Vic., Australia 62 C3
Maryland □ ... 73 E7
Maryvale 63 A5
Marzūq 52 C1
Masaka 57 E6
Masalembo,
  Kepulauan .. 37 F4
Masalima,
  Kepulauan .. 37 F5
Masamba 39 E2
Masan 35 C7
Masandam, Ras 44 E4
Masasi 57 G7
Masaya 85 E7
Masbate 38 B2
Mascara 54 A5
Masela 39 F3
Maseru 59 D5
Mashābih 47 F4
Mashhad 44 B4
Mashike 32 F12
Mashkel,
  Hamun-i- .. 42 E3
Mashki Chāh .. 42 E3
Masi Manimba 56 E3
Masindi 57 D6
Masisea 91 E4
Masjed
  Soleyman ... 47 E7
Mask, L. 11 E2
Masohi 39 E3
Mason City ... 77 D8
Masqat 45 F4
Massa 20 B3
Massachusetts □
  .... 73 C9
Massaguet ... 53 F2
Massakory ... 53 F2
Massangena .. 59 C6
Massawa =
  Mitsiwa 53 E6
Massena 73 B8
Massénya 53 F2
Massif Central . 13 D5
Massinga 59 C7
Masson I. 96 A11
Mastanli =
  Momchilgrad 22 D5
Masterton ... 65 D6
Mastuj 42 A8
Mastung 42 E5
Masty 17 B7
Masuda 32 B2
Masvingo 59 C6
Mataboor 39 E5
Matad 35 B6
Matadi 56 F2
Matagalpa 85 E7
Matagami, L. .. 69 D3
Matak, P. 37 D3
Matakana ... 63 B4
Matam 55 E2
Matamoros,
  Coahuila,
  Mexico 84 B4
Matamoros,
  Tamaulipas,
  Mexico 84 B5

Ma'ṭan as Sarra 52 D3
Matane 69 D4
Matanzas 86 B3
Matapan, C. =
  Taínaron, Ákra 23 F4
Mataram 37 F5
Matarani 91 G4
Mataró 19 B7
Mataura 65 G3
Matehuala 84 C4
Matera 21 D6
Mathura 42 F10
Mati 38 C3
Matiri Ra. 65 D5
Matmata 54 B6
Mato Grosso □ 93 E3
Mato Grosso,
  Planalto do .. 93 F3
Mato Grosso do
  Sul □ 93 F3
Matochkin Shar 28 B6
Matosinhos ... 18 B1
Matrah 45 F4
Matsue 32 B3
Matsumoto ... 32 A6
Matsusaka ... 32 B5
Matsuyama ... 32 C3
Mattagami → . 69 C2
Mattancheri ... 43 Q10
Matterhorn ... 13 D7
Matthew's Ridge 90 B6
Matucana 91 F3
Matun 42 C6
Maturín 90 B6
Mau Ranipur .. 43 G11
Maubeuge 13 A5
Maude 63 B3
Maudin Sun ... 41 K10
Maúés 90 D7
Mauganj 40 E3
Maui 82 H12
Maulamyaing =
  Moulmein ... 41 J11
Maumere 39 F2
Maun 58 B4
Maungmagan
  Kyunzu 41 K11
Mauritania ■ .. 55 D2
Mauritius ■ ... 51 H9
Mavinga 58 B4
Mawk Mai ... 41 G11
Mawlaik 41 F10
Mawson Coast 96 A10
Maxixe 59 C7
Mayaguana ... 87 B5
Mayagüez ... 87 C6
Maydena 62 D4
Mayenne → . 12 C3
Maykop 25 E5
Mayo 70 B6
Mayo L. 70 B6
Mayon Volcano 38 B2
Mayor I. 64 B7
Mayu 39 D3
Mazabuka 59 B5
Mazagán = El
  Jadida 54 B3
Mazagão 92 C3
Mazán 90 D4
Māzandarān □ 44 B3
Mazar-e Sharīf . 45 B6
Mazara del Vallo 21 F4
Mazarredo ... 95 F3
Mazarrón 19 D5
Mazaruni → . 90 B7
Mazatlán 84 C3
Māzhān 44 C4
Mazīnān 44 B4
Mazoe → 59 B6

Mazurian Lakes
  = Mazurski,
  Pojezierze ... 16 B5
Mazurski,
  Pojezierze ... 16 B5
Mazyr 17 C9
Mbabane 59 D6
Mbaïki 56 D3
Mbala 57 F6
Mbale 57 D6
Mbalmayo 56 D2
Mbamba Bay .. 57 G6
Mbandaka 56 D3
Mbanza Congo 56 F2
Mbanza Ngungu 56 F2
Mbarara 57 E6
Mbeya 57 F6
Mbini □ 56 D2
Mbour 55 F1
Mbout 55 E2
Mbuji-Mayi ... 56 F4
Mbulu 57 E7
Mchinji 59 A6
Mead, L. 82 B5
Mearim → .. 92 C5
Meaux 13 B5
Mecca =
  Makkah 47 G4
Mechelen 14 C3
Mecheria 54 B4
Mecklenburg .. 15 B6
Mecklenburger
  Bucht 15 A6
Meconta 59 A7
Medan 37 D1
Medanosa, Pta. 95 F3
Medéa 54 A5
Medellín 90 B3
Mederdra 55 E1
Medford 80 D2
Medgidia 22 B7
Mediaş 17 E7
Medicine Bow
  Ra. 81 E10
Medicine Hat .. 71 C8
Medina = Al
  Madīnah 47 F4
Medina del
  Campo 18 B3
Medina-Sidonia 18 D3
Medinipur 40 F6
Mediterranean
  Sea 50 C5
Médoc 12 D3
Medveditsa → 24 D5
Medvezhyegorsk 28 C4
Meekatharra .. 60 F2
Meerut 42 E10
Mega 53 H6
Mégara 23 F4
Meghalaya □ . 41 E8
Mei Xian 35 D6
Meiganga 56 C2
Meiktila 41 G10
Meissen 15 C7
Mejillones ... 94 A2
Mékambo 56 D2
Mekdela 53 F6
Mekhtar 42 D6
Meknès 54 B3
Mekong → ... 36 C3
Mekongga 39 E2
Mekvari =
  Kür → 25 E6
Melagiri Hills .. 43 N10
Melaka 37 D2
Melalap 36 C5
Melanesia 64 K10
Melbourne,
  Australia 63 C3

Melbourne,
  U.S.A. ...... 75 E
Mélèzes → .. 68 C
Melfi ...... 53 F
Melfort ...... 71 C
Melilla ...... 19 E
Melitopol ..... 25 C
Melk ...... 15 D
Melo ...... 94 C
Melolo ...... 39 F
Melrose .... 63 B
Melun ..... 13 B
Melut ...... 53 F
Melville ..... 71 C
Melville I. .... 60 C
Melville Pen. .. 68 B
Memba ...... 59 G
Memboro ..... 39 F
Memel =
  Klaipėda .... 24 B
Memmingen .. 14 E
Mempawah ... 37 D
Memphis, Tenn.,
  U.S.A. ...... 74 B
Memphis, Tex.,
  U.S.A. ...... 78 B
Ménaka ..... 55 E
Menan = Chao
  Phraya → . 36 B
Menate .... 37 E
Mendawai → . 37 E
Mende ...... 13 D
Mendocino, C. . 80 E
Mendoza .... 94 C
Mene Grande . 90 B
Menemen ... 23 E
Menggala ... 37 E
Mengzi .... 34 D
Menindee .... 62 B
Menindee L. .. 62 B
Meningie .... 62 C
Menominee ... 72 B
Menongue .... 58 A
Menorca .... 19 C
Mentawai,
  Kepulauan .. 37 E
Menton ..... 13 E
Meppel .... 14 B
Merabéllou,
  Kólpos .... 23 G
Meran =
  Merano .... 20 A
Merano .... 20 A
Merauke .... 39 F
Merbein .... 62 B
Merca ...... 49 G
Merced ...... 82 G
Mercedes,
  Buenos Aires,
  Argentina ... 94 C
Mercedes,
  Corrientes,
  Argentina ... 94 B
Mercedes,
  San Luis,
  Argentina ... 94 C
Mercedes,
  Uruguay .... 94 C
Merceditas ... 94 B
Mercer ...... 64 E
Mercy C. .... 68 B
Meredith, C. ... 95 G
Merga =
  Nukheila .... 53 E
Mergui Arch. =
  Myeik Kyunzu 36 E
Mérida, Mexico 85 C
Mérida, Spain . 18 C

Mérida, Venezuela ... 90 B4
Mérida, Cord. de 87 E5
Meridian 74 C3
Meriruma 92 B3
Merowe 53 E5
Merriwa 63 B5
Merriwagga .. 63 B4
Merrygoen 63 B4
Mersa Fatma . 49 E3
Merseburg ... 15 C6
Mersin 46 C3
Mersing 37 D2
Merthyr Tydfil . 11 F5
Mértola 18 D2
Meru 57 D7
Mesa 83 D7
Meshed = Mashhad ... 44 B4
Meshra er Req 53 G4
Mesolóngion .. 23 E3
Mesopotamia = Al Jazirah .. 46 D5
Messina, *Italy* . 21 E5
Messina, *S. Africa* 59 C6
Messina, Str. di 21 E5
Messíni 23 F4
Messiniakós Kólpos 23 F4
Mesta → 22 D5
Meta → 90 B5
Metairie 79 E8
Metán 94 B4
Metangula 59 A6
Metema 53 F6
Methven 65 E4
Metil 59 B7
Metlakatla 71 C6
Mettur Dam .. 43 P10
Metz 13 B7
Meulaboh 37 D1
Meureudu 36 C1
Meuse → 13 A6
Mexiana, I. ... 92 C4
Mexicali 84 A1
México 84 D5
México □ 84 D5
Mexico ■ 84 C4
Mexico, G. of . 85 B7
Meymaneh ... 42 B4
Mezen 28 C5
Mezen → 28 C5
Mézene 13 D6
Mezökövesd .. 16 E5
Mezötúr 16 E5
Mhow 43 H9
Miami 75 G7
Miami Beach . 75 G7
Miändowäb ... 46 C6
Miandrivazo .. 59 H9
Miäneh 46 C6
Mianwali 42 C7
Miaoli 35 D7
Miarinarivo ... 59 H9
Miass 29 D7
Michalovce ... 17 D5
Michigan □ ... 72 C3
Michigan, L. .. 72 C2
Michipicoten .. 69 D2
Michurin 22 C6
Michurinsk ... 24 C5
Micronesia, Federated States of ■ .. 64 J10
Middelburg ... 58 E5
Middlesbrough 11 D6
Midi, Canal du → 12 E4

Midland 78 D3
Midyat 46 C5
Midzör 22 C4
Międzychód ... 16 B2
Międzyrzec Podlaski 17 C6
Mielec 16 C5
Miercurea Ciuc 17 E7
Mieres 18 A3
Miguel Alves .. 92 C5
Mihara 32 B3
Mikhaylovgrad 22 C4
Míkonos 23 F5
Mikura-Jima . 32 C6
Milagro 90 D3
Milan = Milano 20 B2
Milang 62 B2
Milano 20 B2
Milâs 23 F6
Milazzo 21 E5
Mildura 62 B3
Miles 63 A5
Miletus 23 F6
Milford Haven . 11 F4
Milford Sd. ... 65 F2
Milh, Bahr al .. 47 D5
Miliana 54 C5
Mill I. 96 A12
Millau 13 D5
Millicent 62 C3
Millinocket ... 73 B11
Millmerran ... 63 A5
Milne Inlet ... 68 A2
Mílos 23 F5
Milparinka P.O. 62 A3
Milton 65 G3
Milton Keynes . 11 E6
Miltou 53 F2
Milwaukee ... 72 C2
Min Chiang → 35 D6
Min Jiang → .. 35 D6
Mina Pirquitas . 94 A3
Mīnā Su'ud ... 47 E7
Mīnā'al Ahmadī 47 E7
Mīnāb 44 E4
Minamata 32 C2
Minas 94 C5
Minas Gerais □ 93 F4
Minbu 41 G10
Mindanao 38 C2
Mindanao Sea = Bohol Sea .. 38 C2
Mindanao Trench 38 B3
Minden 14 B5
Mindiptana ... 39 F6
Mindoro 38 B2
Mindoro Str. .. 38 B2
Mindouli 56 E2
Mingäçevir Su Anbarı 25 E6
Mingan 69 C4
Mingechaurskoye Vdkhr. = Mingäçevir Su Anbarı 25 E6
Mingin 41 F10
Mingt'iehkaitafan = Mintaka Pass 42 A9
Minho = Miño → 18 B1
Minho 18 B1
Minna 55 G6
Minneapolis .. 77 C8
Minnedosa ... 71 C10
Minnesota □ .. 77 B7
Minnipa 62 B2
Miño → 18 B1

Minorca = Menorca 19 C7
Minore 63 B4
Minot 76 A4
Minsk 24 C2
Mińsk Mazowiecki . 16 B5
Mintaka Pass .. 42 A9
Minto 71 B5
Minutang 41 C11
Minvoul 56 D2
Mir 53 F1
Mira 20 B4
Miraj 43 L9
Miram Shah .. 42 C7
Miranda 93 G2
Miranda de Ebro 19 A4
Miranda do Douro 18 B2
Miri 36 D4
Mirim, L. 94 C6
Mirpur Khas .. 42 G6
Mirzapur 40 E4
Mirzapur-cum-Vindhyachal = Mirzapur 40 E4
Mish'āb, Ra'as al 47 E7
Mishan 35 B8
Miskin 44 F4
Miskolc 16 D5
Misool 39 E4
Misrātah 52 B2
Misriç 46 C5
Missinaibi → . 69 C2
Mississippi □ . 79 C9
Mississippi → . 79 E9
Mississippi River Delta 79 E9
Missoula 81 B6
Missouri □ ... 77 F8
Missouri → .. 77 F9
Mistassini L. .. 69 C3
Misurata = Misrātah 52 B2
Mitchell, *Australia* 63 A4
Mitchell, *U.S.A.* 76 D5
Mitchell → ... 61 D7
Mitilíni 23 E6
Mito 32 A7
Mitrovica = Titova-Mitrovica .. 22 C3
Mitsinjo 59 H9
Mitsiwa 53 E6
Mittagong ... 63 B5
Mitú 90 C4
Mitumba, Chaîne des .. 57 F5
Mitumba Mts. = Mitumba, Chaîne des .. 57 F5
Mitwaba 57 F5
Mitzic 56 D2
Miyake-Jima . 32 B6
Miyako 33 G12
Miyakonojō .. 32 D2
Miyazaki 32 D2
Miyet, Bahr el = Dead Sea ... 47 E3
Mizal 47 G6
Mizdah 52 B1
Mizoram □ ... 41 F9
Mjøsa 8 F10
Mladá Boleslav 16 C2
Mława 16 B5
Mljet 20 C6
Mmabatho ... 59 D5

Moa 39 F3
Moabi 56 E2
Moalie Park ... 62 A3
Moba 57 F5
Mobaye 56 D4
Mobayi 56 D4
Mobile 74 D3
Mobutu Sese Seko, L. = Albert L. 57 D6
Moçambique .. 59 H8
Moçâmedes = Namibe 58 B2
Mochudi 59 C5
Mocimboa da Praia 57 G8
Mocoa 90 C3
Mocuba 59 B7
Modane 13 D7
Módena 20 B3
Modesto 82 B2
Módica 21 F5
Moe 63 C4
Moengo 92 A3
Mogadishu = Muqdisho .. 49 G4
Mogador = Essaouira ... 54 B3
Mogami → ... 33 G12
Mogaung 41 E11
Mogi das Cruzes 94 A7
Mogi-Mirim .. 94 A7
Mogilev = Mahilyow ... 17 B10
Mogilev-Podolskiy = Mohyliv-Podilskyy ... 17 D8
Mogoi 39 E4
Mogok 41 F11
Mohács 16 F4
Mohammadābād 44 B4
Mohoro 57 F7
Mohyliv-Podilskyy ... 17 D8
Mointy 29 E8
Moisie 69 C4
Moisie → 69 C4
Moïssala 53 G2
Mojave Desert . 82 C4
Mokai 64 C6
Mokokchung .. 41 D10
Mokra Gora .. 22 C3
Molchanovo .. 29 D9
Moldavia ■ = Moldova ■ .. 17 E9
Molde 8 F9
Moldova ■ ... 17 E9
Moldoveana .. 17 F7
Molepolole ... 59 C5
Molfetta 20 D6
Moline 77 E9
Moliro 57 F6
Mollendo 91 G4
Molodechno = Maladzyechna 17 A8
Molokai 82 H12
Molong 63 B4
Molopo → ... 58 D4
Molotov = Perm 29 D6
Moloundou ... 56 D3
Molu 39 F4
Molucca Sea . 39 E2
Moluccas = Maluku 39 E3
Moma 59 B7
Mombasa 57 E7
Momchilgrad . 22 D5

Mompós 90 B4
Mon → 41 G10
Mona, Canal de
la 87 C6
Monaco ■ 13 E7
Monahans 78 D2
Monastir =
Bitola 22 D3
Monastir 52 A1
Moncayo, Sierra
del 19 B5
Mönchengladbach
.... 14 C4
Monchique ... 18 D1
Monclova 84 B4
Mondego → .. 18 B1
Mondeodo 39 E2
Mondovì 20 B1
Monforte de
Lemos 18 A2
Mong Hsu .. 41 G12
Mong Kung .. 41 G11
Mong Nai 41 G11
Mong Pawk ... 41 F12
Mong Ton ... 41 G12
Mong Wa ... 41 G13
Mong Yai ... 41 F12
Mongalla 53 G5
Monghyr =
Munger 40 E6
Mongibello =
Etna 21 F5
Mongo 53 F2
Mongolia ■ .. 35 B5
Mongororo ... 53 F3
Mongu 58 B4
Monkoto 56 E4
Monópoli 21 D6
Monqoumba .. 56 D3
Monroe, La.,
U.S.A. 79 C7
Monroe, N.C.,
U.S.A. 75 B7
Monrovia 55 G2
Mons 14 C2
Monse 39 E2
Mont-de-Marsan 12 E3
Mont-St.-Michel,
Le = Le Mont-
St.-Michel ... 12 B3
Montalbán 19 B5
Montana □ ... 81 B9
Montargis 13 C5
Montauban ... 12 D4
Montbéliard .. 13 C7
Montceau-les-
Mines 13 C6
Monte Alegre . 92 C3
Monte Azul .. 93 F5
Monte-Carlo .. 20 C1
Monte Caseros 94 C5
Monte Comán . 94 C3
Monte Santu, C.
di 21 D2
Montecristi ... 90 D2
Montecristo .. 20 C3
Montego Bay . 86 C4
Montélimar .. 13 D6
Montemorelos . 84 B5
Montenegro □ 22 C2
Montepuez .. 59 A7
Monterey 82 B2
Montería 90 B3
Monterrey 84 B4
Montes Claros . 93 F5
Montesilvano
Marina 20 C5
Montevideo .. 94 C5
Montgomery =
Sahiwal 42 D8

Montgomery .. 74 C4
Montijo 18 C2
Montilla 18 D3
Montluçon ... 13 C5
Montmorillon . 12 C4
Montoro 18 C3
Montpellier .. 13 E5
Montréal 69 D3
Montreux 13 C7
Montrose, U.K. 10 C5
Montrose,
U.S.A. 83 A9
Montserrat ■ .. 87 C7
Monveda 56 D4
Monywa 41 F10
Monza 20 B2
Monze 59 B5
Monze, C. ... 43 G5
Monzón 19 B6
Moolawatana . 62 A2
Moomin Cr. → 63 A4
Moonie 63 A5
Moonie → ... 63 A4
Moonta 62 B2
Mooroopna .. 63 C4
Moose Jaw ... 71 C9
Moosomin ... 71 C9
Moosonee ... 69 C2
Mopeia Velha . 59 B7
Mopti 55 F4
Moquegua .. 91 G4
Mora 8 F10
Moradabad .. 42 E11
Morafenobe . 59 H8
Moramanga . 59 H9
Moratuwa ... 43 R11
Morava →,
Serbia, Yug. . 22 B3
Morava →,
Slovak Rep. . 16 D3
Moravian Hts. =
Ceskomoravská
Vrchovina ... 16 D2
Morawhanna . 90 B7
Moray Firth ... 10 C5
Morden 71 D10
Mordovian
Republic □ =
Mordvinia □ . 24 C5
Mordvinia □ .. 24 C5
Morea 62 C3
Moree 63 A4
Morelia 84 D4
Morella 19 B5
Morena, Sierra 18 C3
Moreton I. ... 63 A5
Morgan 62 B2
Morgan City .. 79 E8
Morioka 33 G12
Morlaix 12 B2
Mornington .. 63 C4
Mornington, I. . 95 F1
Moro G. 38 C2
Morocco ■ .. 54 B3
Morococha .. 91 F3
Morogoro ... 57 F7
Morombe 59 J8
Morón 86 B4
Mörön → ... 35 B6
Morón de la
Frontera 18 D3
Morondava .. 59 J8
Morotai 39 D3
Moroto 57 D6
Morphou 46 D3
Morrinhos .. 93 F4
Morrinsville .. 64 B6
Morristown ... 75 A6
Morrumbene .. 59 C7

Morshansk 24 C5
Morteros 94 C4
Mortes, R.
das → 93 E3
Mortlake 62 C3
Morundah 63 B4
Moruya 63 C5
Morvan 13 C6
Morven 63 A4
Morwell 63 C4
Moscos Is. 41 L11
Moscow =
Moskva 24 B4
Moscow 80 B5
Mosel → 13 A7
Moselle =
Mosel → ... 13 A7
Mosgiel 65 F4
Moshi 57 E7
Moskva 24 B4
Moskva → ... 24 B4
Moson-
magyaróvar . 16 E3
Mosquera .. 90 C3
Moss Vale ... 63 B5
Mossaka 56 E3
Mossburn ... 65 F3
Mosselbaai ... 58 E4
Mossendjo ... 56 E2
Mossgiel 63 B3
Mossoró 92 D6
Mossuril 59 G8
Most 16 C1
Mostaganem .. 54 A5
Mostar 20 C6
Mostardas .. 94 C6
Mostiska =
Mostyska ... 17 D6
Mosty = Masty 17 B7
Mostyska ... 17 D6
Mosul = Al
Mawşil 46 C5
Motihari 40 D5
Motril 18 D4
Motueka 65 D5
Motueka → .. 65 D5
Mouanda 56 E2
Moúdhros ... 23 E5
Moudjeria ... 55 E2
Mouila 56 E2
Moulamein .. 63 C3
Moulins 13 C5
Moulmein ... 41 J11
Moundou ... 53 G2
Mount Barker . 62 C2
Mount Darwin . 59 B6
Mount Eba ... 62 B2
Mount Gambier 62 C3
Mount Hope,
N.S.W.,
Australia 63 B4
Mount Hope,
S. Austral.,
Australia 62 B2
Mount Howitt . 62 A3
Mount Isa ... 61 E6
Mount Lofty Ra. 62 B2
Mount McKinley
National Park 71 B4
Mount Margaret 63 A3
Mount
Maunganui .. 64 B7
Mount Olympus
= Uludağ .. 23 D7
Mount Perry .. 63 A5
Mount Vernon . 73 D9
Mountain View 82 B1
Moura, Brazil .. 90 D6
Moura, Portugal 18 C2

Mourdi,
Dépression du 53 E3
Mourdiah 55 F3
Moussoro 53 F2
Moutohara ... 64 C7
Moutong 39 D2
Moyale 57 D7
Moyamba ... 55 G2
Moyen Atlas .. 54 B3
Moyo 37 F5
Moyyero → . 30 C8
Mozambique =
Moçambique 59 H8
Mozambique ■ 59 B7
Mozambique
Chan. 59 H8
Mozdok 25 E5
Mozyr = Mazyr 17 C9
Mpanda 57 F6
Mpika 59 A6
Mpwapwa ... 57 F7
Msaken 52 A1
Msoro 59 A6
Mu Us Shamo . 35 C5
Muaná 92 C4
Muar 37 D2
Muarabungo .. 37 E2
Muaraenim .. 37 E2
Muarajuloi ... 37 E4
Muarakaman .. 37 E5
Muaratebo ... 37 E2
Muaratembesi . 37 E2
Muaratewe .. 37 E4
Mubarraz = Al
Mubarraz ... 47 F7
Mubende 57 D6
Mubi 53 F1
Muckadilla ... 63 A4
Muconda ... 56 G4
Mucuri 93 F6
Mudanjiang .. 35 B7
Mudanya 23 D7
Mudgee 63 B4
Mufulira 59 A5
Muğla 23 F7
Mugu 40 C4
Muhammad Qol 52 D6
Mühlhausen .. 14 C6
Mühlig Hofmann
fjell 96 B7
Mukacheve .. 17 D6
Mukachevo =
Mukacheve .. 17 D6
Mukah 37 D4
Mukden =
Shenyang .. 35 B7
Mukomuko .. 37 E2
Muktsar 42 D9
Mukur 42 C5
Mula 19 C5
Mulchén 94 D2
Mulde → ... 15 C7
Mulgathing .. 62 B1
Mulgrave 69 D4
Mulhacén ... 18 D4
Mulhouse ... 13 C7
Mull 10 C4
Mullengudgery 63 B4
Muller,
Pegunungan 37 D4
Mullingar ... 11 E3
Mullumbimby . 63 A5
Multan 42 D7
Mulwala 63 C4
Mumbaï =
Bombay 43 K8
Mumbwa 59 A5
Muna 39 F2
München 15 D6

Munchen-
   Gladbach =
   Mönchengladbach
   .... 14 C4
Muncie 72 D3
Mundala 39 E6
Münden 14 C5
Mundo Novo .. 93 E5
Mungallala 63 A4
Mungallala
   Cr. → 63 A4
Mungbere 57 D5
Munger 40 E6
Mungindi 63 A4
Munhango 58 A3
Munich =
   München ... 15 D6
Muñoz Gamero,
   Pen. 95 G2
Münster 14 C4
Munster □ 11 E2
Muntok 37 E3
Mupa 58 B3
Muqdisho 49 G4
Murallón,
   Cuerro 95 F2
Murang'a 57 E7
Murashi 24 B6
Muratlı 22 D6
Murchison → . 60 F1
Murchison, Mt. 96 B15
Murchison Falls
   = Kabarega
   Falls 57 D6
Murcia 19 C5
Murcia □ 19 D5
Mureş → 16 E5
Mureşul =
   Mureş → ... 16 E5
Murfreesboro . 74 B4
Murgab =
   Murghob ... 29 F8
Murghob 29 F8
Murgon 63 A5
Müritz-see 15 B7
Murmansk 28 C4
Murom 24 B5
Muroran 32 F12
Muroto-Misaki . 32 C4
Murray → 62 C2
Murray Bridge . 62 C2
Murree 42 C8
Murrumbidgee →
   .... 62 B3
Murrumburrah 63 B4
Murrurundi ... 63 B5
Murtoa 62 C3
Murwara 40 F3
Murwillumbah . 63 A5
Mürzzuschlag . 15 E8
Muş 46 C5
Mûsa, G. 47 E3
Musa Khel 42 D6
Müsá Qal'eh .. 42 C4
Musaffargarh .. 42 D7
Musala, Bulgaria 22 C4
Musala,
   Indonesia .. 37 D1
Musay'id 44 E2
Muscat =
   Masqat 45 F4
Muscat & Oman
   = Oman ■ .. 48 C6
Muscatine 77 E9
Musgrave Ras. . 60 F5
Mushie 56 E3
Musi → 37 E2
Muskogee 79 B6
Musmar 53 E6

Musoma 57 E6
Mussoorie ... 42 D11
Mustafakemalpaşa
   .... 23 D7
Mustang 40 C4
Musters, L. ... 95 F3
Muswellbrook . 63 B5
Mût, Egypt ... 52 C4
Mut, Turkey .. 46 C3
Mutare 59 B6
Muting 39 F6
Mutoray 30 C8
Muxima 56 F2
Muynak 29 E6
Muzaffarabad . 42 B8
Muzaffarnagar . 42 E10
Muzaffarpur .. 40 D5
Muzhi 28 C7
Muztag 34 C3
Mvuma 59 B6
Mwanza,
   Tanzania ... 57 E6
Mwanza,
   Dem. Rep. of the Congo
   .... 57 F5
Mweka 56 E4
Mwenezi 59 C6
Mwenga 57 E5
Mweru, L. ... 57 F5
Mwinilunga .. 58 A4
My Tho 36 B3
Myanaung 41 H10
Myanmar =
   Burma ■ ... 41 G11
Myaungmya .. 41 J10
Mycenæ 23 F4
Myeik Kyunzu . 36 B1
Myingyan 41 G10
Myitkyina 41 E11
Mykolayiv ... 25 D3
Mymensingh .. 41 E8
Mysia 23 E6
Mysore =
   Karnataka □ . 43 N10
Mysore 43 N10
Myszków 16 C4
Mytishchi 24 B4

N

Na Hearadh =
   Harris 10 C3
Naab → 15 D7
Naberezhnyye
   Chelny 29 D6
Nabeul 52 A1
Nabire 39 E5
Nablus =
   Nābulus ... 46 D3
Nābulus 46 D3
Nachingwea .. 57 G7
Nackara 62 B2
Nacogdoches . 79 D6
Nacozari 84 A3
Nadiad 43 H8
Nadūshan 44 C3
Nadvirna 17 D7
Nadvornaya =
   Nadvirna ... 17 D7
Nadym 28 C8
Nadym → 28 C8
Nafada 55 F7
Nafūd ad Dahy 47 G6
Nafud Desert =
   An Nafūd .. 47 E5
Naga 38 B2

Nagaland □ ... 41 E10
Nagano 32 A6
Nagaoka 33 G11
Nagappattinam 43 P11
Nagar Parkar . 43 G7
Nagasaki 32 C1
Nagaur 42 F8
Nagercoil 43 Q10
Nagīneh 44 C4
Nagoya 32 B5
Nagpur 43 J11
Nagykanizsa .. 16 E3
Nagykörös 16 E4
Nahanni Butte . 70 B7
Nahāvand 46 D7
Nā'ifah 48 D5
Nain, Canada .. 68 C4
Nā'īn, Iran ... 44 C3
Nairn 10 C5
Nairobi 57 E7
Naivasha 57 E7
Najafābād 44 C2
Najd 47 F5
Najibabad 42 E11
Nakamura ... 32 C3
Nakfa 53 E6
Nakhichevan =
   Naxçıvan ... 25 F6
Nakhichevan
   Republic □ =
   Naxçıvan □ . 25 F6
Nakhodka 31 E11
Nakhon Phanom 36 A2
Nakhon
   Ratchasima . 36 B2
Nakhon Sawan 36 A2
Nakhon Si
   Thammarat . 36 C2
Nakina 69 C2
Nakuru 57 E7
Nal → 42 G4
Nalchik 25 E5
Nalgonda 43 L11
Nallamalai Hills 43 M11
Nālūt 52 B1
Nam Co 34 C4
Nam-Phan ... 36 B3
Namacurra ... 59 B7
Namak,
   Daryācheh-ye 44 C3
Namak, Kavir-e 44 C4
Namaland 58 C3
Namangan ... 29 E8
Namapa 59 A7
Namber 39 E4
Nambour 63 A5
Nambucca
   Heads 63 B5
Nameh 37 D5
Namib Desert =
   Namibwoestyn
   .... 58 C2
Namibe 58 B2
Namibia ■ ... 58 C3
Namibwoestyn 58 C2
Namlea 39 E3
Namoi → 63 B4
Nampa 80 D5
Nampula 59 B7
Namrole 39 E3
Namse Shankou 40 C4
Namtu 41 F11
Namur 14 C3
Namutoni 58 B3
Namwala 59 B5
Nanaimo 71 D7
Nanango 63 A5
Nanao 32 A5
Nanchang ... 35 D6

Nanching =
   Nanjing 35 C6
Nanchong 35 C5
Nancy 13 B7
Nanda Devi .. 42 D11
Nanded 43 K10
Nandewar Ra. . 63 B5
Nandurbar ... 43 J9
Nandyal 43 M11
Nanga-Eboko . 56 D2
Nanga Parbat . 42 B9
Nangapinoh .. 37 E4
Nangarhár □ . 42 B7
Nangatayap .. 37 E4
Nanjing 35 C6
Nanking =
   Nanjing 35 C6
Nanning 35 D5
Nanping 35 D6
Nansei-Shotō =
   Ryūkyū-rettō 35 D7
Nantes 12 C3
Nanuque 93 F5
Nanusa,
   Kepulauan .. 38 D3
Nanyang 35 C6
Nanyuki 57 D7
Nao, C. de la .. 19 C6
Naoetsu 32 A6
Napa 80 F2
Napier 64 C7
Naples = Nápoli 21 D5
Naples 75 F7
Napo → 90 D4
Nápoli 21 D5
Nappa Merrie . 62 A3
Nara, Japan .. 32 B4
Nara, Mali ... 55 E3
Naracoorte ... 62 C3
Naradhan 63 B4
Narasapur ... 40 J3
Narathiwat ... 36 C2
Narayanganj .. 41 F8
Narayanpet ... 43 L10
Narbonne 13 E5
Nardò 23 D2
Narew → 16 B5
Narin 42 A6
Narmada → .. 43 J8
Narooma 63 C5
Narrabri 63 B4
Narran → 63 A4
Narrandera .. 63 B4
Narromine ... 63 B4
Narsimhapur .. 43 H11
Narva 24 B2
Narvik 8 E11
Naryan-Mar ... 28 C6
Naryilco 62 A3
Narym 29 D9
Narymskoye .. 29 E9
Naryn 29 E8
Nasarawa 55 G6
Naseby 65 F4
Naser, Buheirat
   en 52 D5
Nashville 74 A4
Nasik 43 K8
Nasirabad ... 42 F9
Nassau 86 A4
Nassau, B. ... 95 H3
Nasser, L. =
   Naser,
   Buheirat en . 52 D5
Nat Kyizin ... 41 K11
Nata 59 C5
Natagaima ... 90 C3
Natal, Brazil ... 92 D6
Natal, Indonesia 37 D1

Naţanz

Naţanz 44 C2
Natashquan . . . 69 C4
Natashquan → 69 C4
Natchez 79 D8
Nathalia 63 C4
Nathdwara . . . 43 G8
Natitingou . . . 55 F5
Natron, L. 57 E7
Natuna Besar,
  Kepulauan . . 37 D3
Natuna Is. =
  Natuna Besar,
  Kepulauan . . 37 D3
Natuna Selatan,
  Kepulauan . . 37 D3
Naturaliste, C. . 62 D4
Naumburg 15 C6
Nauru ■ 64 K11
Naushahra =
  Nowshera . . . 42 B8
Nauta 90 D4
Nautanwa . . . 40 D4
Navahrudak . . . 17 B7
Navalmoral de
  la Mata 18 C3
Navarino, I. . . . 95 H3
Navarra □ 19 A5
Năvodari 22 B7
Navoi = Nawoiy 29 E7
Navojoa 84 B3
Návpaktos . . . 23 E3
Návplion 23 F4
Navsari 43 J8
Nawabshah . . . 42 F6
Nawakot 40 D5
Nawalgarh 42 F9
Nawāsif, Harrat 47 G5
Nawoiy 29 E7
Naxçıvan 25 F6
Naxçıvan □ . . . 25 F6
Náxos 23 F5
Năy Band 44 E3
Nazas → 84 B4
Nazilli 23 F7
Nazir Hat 41 F8
Ncheu 59 A6
Ndalatando . . . 56 F2
Ndélé 56 C4
Ndendé 56 E2
Ndjamena 53 F1
Ndjolé 56 E2
Ndola 59 A5
Neagh, Lough . 11 D3
Near Is. 71 C1
Neath 11 F5
Nebine Cr. → . 63 A4
Nebitdag 29 F6
Nebraska □ . . . 76 E5
Nébrodi, Monti 21 F5
Neckar → 14 D5
Necochea 94 D5
Neemuch =
  Nimach 43 G9
Neepawa 71 C10
Nefta 54 B6
Neftçala 46 C7
Negapatam =
  Nagappattinam
  . . . . 43 P11
Negele 49 F2
Negombo 43 R11
Negotin 22 B4
Negra Pt. 38 A2
Negrais, C. =
  Maudin Sun . 41 K10
Negro →,
  Argentina . . . 95 E4
Negro →, Brazil 90 D6

Negro →,
  Uruguay 94 C5
Negros 38 C2
Nehbandān . . . 45 D5
Nei Monggol
  Zizhiqu □ . . 35 B6
Neijiang 35 D5
Neiva 90 C3
Nejd = Najd . . 47 F5
Nekemte 53 G6
Nellore 43 M11
Nelson, Canada 71 D8
Nelson, N.Z. . . 65 D5
Nelson → 71 C10
Nelson, C. 62 C3
Nelson, Estrecho 95 G2
Nelspruit 59 D6
Néma 55 E3
Neman → 24 B1
Nemunas =
  Neman → . . 24 B1
Nemuro 32 F13
Nemuro-Kaikyō 32 F13
Nenagh 11 E2
Nenana 71 B5
Nenjiang 35 B7
Nepal ■ 40 D5
Nepalganj 40 C3
Neretva → . . . 20 C6
Ness, L. 10 C4
Nesterov 17 C6
Nesvizh =
  Nyasvizh . . . 17 B8
Netherlands ■ . 14 B3
Netherlands
  Antilles ■ . . . 87 D6
Nettilling L. . . . 68 B3
Neubrandenburg
  . . . . 15 B7
Neuchâtel 13 C7
Neuchâtel, Lac
  de 13 C7
Neumünster . . 14 A5
Neunkirchen . . 14 D4
Neuquén 94 D3
Neuruppin 15 B7
Neustrelitz . . . 15 B7
Neva → 24 B3
Nevada □ 80 F5
Nevada, Sierra,
  Spain 18 D4
Nevada, Sierra,
  U.S.A. 80 F3
Nevers 13 C5
Nevertire 63 B4
Nevinnomyssk 25 E5
Nevis 87 C7
Nevşehir 46 C3
New Amsterdam 90 B7
New Angledool 63 A4
New Bedford . 73 D10
New Bern 75 B9
New Brighton . 65 E5
New Britain,
  Papua N. G. . 64 K10
New Britain,
  U.S.A. 73 D9
New
  Brunswick □ . 69 D4
New
  Caledonia ■ . 64 M11
New Delhi □ . . 42 E10
New England
  Ra. 63 B5
New Glasgow . 69 D4
New Guinea . . 64
New
  Hampshire □ . 73 C10
New Haven . . . 73 D9

New Hebrides =
  Vanuatu ■ . . 64 L11
New Ireland . . 64 K10
New Jersey □ . 73 E9
New London . . 73 D9
New Mexico □ . 83 C9
New Norfolk . . 62 D4
New Orleans . . 79 E8
New Plymouth . 64 C6
New Providence 86 A4
New Siberian Is.
  =
  Novosibirskiye
  Ostrova 31 B12
New South
  Wales □ 63 B4
New
  Westminster . 71 D7
New York □ . . . 73 C8
New York City . 73 D9
New Zealand ■ 64 D7
Newala 57 G7
Newark 73 D8
Newburgh 73 D8
Newbury 11 F6
Newcastle,
  Australia 63 B5
Newcastle,
  S. Africa 59 D5
Newcastle-upon-
  Tyne 11 D6
Newfoundland □
  . . . . 69 C5
Newman 60 E2
Newport,
  I. of W., U.K. 11 F6
Newport, Newp.,
  U.K. 11 F5
Newport, U.S.A. 73 D10
Newport News 73 F7
Newquay 11 F4
Newry 11 D3
Newton Boyd . 63 A5
Neya 24 B5
Neyrīz 44 D3
Neyshābūr 44 B4
Nezhin = Nizhyn 24 C3
Ngabang 37 D3
Ngabordamlu,
  Tanjung 39 F4
Ngami
  Depression . . 58 C4
Nganglong
  Kangri 40 A3
Ngaoundéré . . 56 C2
Ngapara 65 F4
Ngoring Hu . . 34 C4
Ngudu 57 E6
Nguigmi 53 F1
Nguru 55 F7
Nha Trang 36 B3
Nhill 62 C3
Niafounké 55 E4
Niagara Falls,
  Canada 69 D3
Niagara Falls,
  U.S.A. 73 C6
Niah 37 D4
Niamey 55 F5
Niangara 57 D5
Nias 37 D1
Nicaragua ■ . . 85 E7
Nicaragua, L. de 85 E7
Nicastro 21 E6
Nice 13 E7
Nichinan 33 D2
Nicobar Is. 27 J13
Nicosia 46 D3
Nicoya, Pen. de 85 F7

Niedersachsen □
  . . . . 14 B5
Niemen =
  Neman → . . 24 B1
Nienburg 14 B5
Nieuw
  Amsterdam . 92 A2
Nieuw Nickerie 92 A2
Niğde 46 C3
Niger ■ 55 E6
Niger → 55 G6
Nigeria ■ 55 G6
Nightcaps 65 F3
Nii-Jima 32 B6
Niigata 33 G11
Niihama 32 C3
Niihau 82
Nijmegen 14 C3
Nikiniki 39 F2
Nikki 55 G5
Nikolayev =
  Mykolayiv . . . 25 D3
Nikolayevsk . . 24 C6
Nikopol 25 D3
Nīkshahr 45 E5
Nikšić 22 C2
Nîl, Nahr en → 52 B5
Nîl el Abyad → 53 E5
Nîl el Azraq → 53 E5
Nile = Nîl, Nahr
  en → 52 B5
Nimach 43 G9
Nîmes 13 E6
Nimfaíon, Ákra
  = Pínnes,
  Ákra 23 D5
Nimmitabel . . . 63 C4
Nīmrūz □ 45 D5
Nimule 57 D6
Nīnawá 46 C5
Nindigully 63 A4
Nineveh =
  Nīnawá 46 C5
Ningbo 35 D7
Ningde 35 D6
Ningpo =
  Ningbo 35 D7
Ningsia Hui A.R.
  = Ningxia
  Huizu
  Zizhiqu □ . . . 35 C5
Ningxia Huizu
  Zizhiqu □ . . 35 C5
Niobrara → . . 76 D5
Nioro du Sahel 55 E3
Niort 12 C3
Nipawin 71 C9
Nipigon, L. . . . 69 D2
Niquelândia . . 93 E4
Nirmal 43 K11
Nirmali 40 D6
Niš 22 C3
Nişāb, Si. Arabia 47 E6
Nişāb, Yemen . 49 E4
Nishinomiya . . 32 B4
Nistru =
  Dnister → . . 17 E10
Niţa' 47 F7
Niterói 93 G5
Nitra 16 D4
Nitra → 16 E4
Niue 65 L14
Niut 37 D4
Nivernais 13 C5
Nizamabad . . . 43 K11
Nizamghat . . . 41 C10
Nizhne-Vartovsk 29 C8
Nizhneyansk . . 31 B11
Nizhniy
  Novgorod . . . 24 B5

Nizhniy Tagil . . 29 D6
Nizhyn 24 C3
Nizip 46 C4
Nízké Tatry . . 16 D4
Njombe 57 F6
Nkambe 55 G7
Nkawkaw 55 G4
Nkhata Bay . . 57 G6
Nkhota Kota . . 59 A6
Nkongsamba . . 56 D1
Nmai → 41 E11
Noakhali =
Maijdi 41 F8
Noatak 71 B3
Nobeoka 32 C2
Nocera Inferiore 21 D5
Nockatunga . . 62 A3
Nogales, Mexico 84 A2
Nogales, U.S.A. 83 E7
Nõgata 32 C2
Noginsk 30 C7
Noire, Mts. . . . 12 B2
Noirmoutier, I.
de 12 C2
Nok Kundi 42 E3
Nokhtuysk . . . 30 C9
Nokomis 71 C9
Nola 56 D3
Nome 71 B3
Nong Khai 36 A2
Noondoo 63 A4
Nóqui 56 F2
Noranda 69 D3
Nord-Ostsee-
Kanal → . . . 14 A5
Nordegg 71 C8
Norderney 14 B4
Norderstedt . . . 14 B5
Nordfriesische
Inseln 14 A5
Nordhausen . . . 14 C6
Nordkapp . . . 8 D13
Nordrhein-
Westfalen □ . 14 C4
Nordvik 30 B9
Norfolk 73 F7
Norfolk I. 64 M11
Norilsk 30 C6
Norley 63 A3
Norman 78 B5
Norman Wells . 70 B7
Normandie . . . 12 B4
Normandy =
Normandie . . 12 B4
Normanton . . . 61 D7
Norquinco . . . 95 E2
Norrköping . . 9 G11
Norrland 8 F11
Norseman 60 G3
North Battleford 71 C9
North Bay . . . 69 D3
North Bend . . . 80 D1
North C. 64 A5
North Cape =
Nordkapp . . . 8 D13
North
Carolina □ . . 75 B7
North Channel,
Canada 69 D2
North Channel,
U.K. 11 D4
North Dakota □ 76 B4
North Frisian Is.
=
Nordfriesische
Inseln . . . 14 A5
North I. 64 B5
North Korea ■ . 35 C7

North
Lakhimpur . . 41 D10
North Minch . . 10 B4
North Ossetia □ 25 E5
North Pagai, I. =
Pagai Utara . 37 E2
North Platte . . . 76 E4
North Platte → 76 E4
North Rhine
Westphalia □
= Nordrhein-
Westfalen □ . 14 C4
North
Saskatchewan →
. . . . 71 C8
North Sea 10 D8
North Sporades
= Voríai
Sporádhes . . 23 E4
North Taranaki
Bight 64 C6
North
Thompson → 71 C7
North Uist 10 C3
North West C. . 60 E1
North West
Frontier □ . . 42 B8
North West
Highlands . . . 10 C4
North West
River 69 C4
North West
Territories □ . 70 B7
Northampton . . 11 E6
Northern Circars 40 J4
Northern
Ireland □ . . . 11 D3
Northern
Marianas ■ . 64 H9
Northern
Territory □ . . 60 D5
Northland □ . . 64 A5
Northumberland,
C. 62 C3
Northumberland
Str. 69 D4
Norton Sd. . . . 71 B3
Norway ■ 8 F10
Norway House 71 C10
Norwegian Sea 6 B5
Norwich 11 E7
Nosok 28 B9
Noşratābād . . . 45 D4
Nossob → . . . 58 D4
Nosy Bé 59 G9
Nosy Boraha . . 59 H9
Nosy Mitsio . . 59 G9
Nosy Varika . . 59 J9
Noteć → 16 B2
Noto-Hanto . . 33 G11
Notre Dame B. 69 D5
Notre Dame de
Koartac =
Quaqtaq . . . 68 B4
Notre Dame
d'Ivugivic =
Ivujivik . . . 68 B3
Nottaway → . . 69 C3
Nottingham . . 11 E6
Nouâdhibou . . 54 D1
Nouâdhibou,
Ras 54 D1
Nouakchott . . 55 E1
Nouméa 64 M11
Noupoort 58 E4
Nouveau
Comptoir =
Wemindji . . . 69 C3

Nouvelle-
Calédonie =
New
Caledonia ■ . 64 M11
Nova Casa Nova 93 D5
Nova Cruz 92 D6
Nova Friburgo . 93 G5
Nova Gaia =
Cambundi-
Catembo 56 G3
Nova Iguaçu . . 93 G5
Nova Iorque . . 92 D5
Nova Lima 93 F5
Nova Mambone 59 C7
Nova Scotia □ . 69 D4
Nova Sofala . . 59 C6
Nova Venécia . 93 F5
Nova Zagora . . 22 C5
Novara 20 B2
Novaya Ladoga 24 A3
Novaya Lyalya 29 D7
Novaya Zemlya 28 B6
Nové Zámky . . 16 D4
Novgorod 24 B3
Novgorod-
Severskiy =
Novhorod-
Siverskyy . . . 24 C3
Novhorod-
Siverskyy . . . 24 C3
Novi Lígure . . 20 B2
Novi Pazar . . . 22 C3
Novi Sad 22 B2
Novo Mesto . . 20 B5
Novo Remanso 93 D5
Novoataysk . . 29 D9
Novocherkassk 25 D5
Novogrudok =
Navahrudak . 17 B7
Novohrad-
Volynskyy . . . 17 C8
Novokazalinsk =
Zhangaqazaly 29 E7
Novokuybyshevsk
. . . . 24 C6
Novokuznetsk . 29 D9
Novomoskovsk 24 C4
Novorossiysk . . 25 E4
Novorybnoye . . 30 B8
Novoselytsya . . 17 D8
Novoshakhtinsk 25 D4
Novosibirsk . . . 29 D9
Novosibirskiye
Ostrova . . . 31 B12
Novotroitsk . . . 29 D6
Novouzensk . . 24 C6
Novovolynsk . . 17 C7
Novska 20 B6
Novyy Port . . . 28 C8
Now Shahr . . . 44 B2
Nowa Sól 16 C2
Nowgong 41 D9
Nowra 63 B5
Nowshera 42 B8
Nowy Sącz . . . 16 D5
Nowy Targ . . . 16 D5
Nowy Tomyśl . 16 B3
Noyon 13 B5
Nsanje 59 B7
Nsawam 55 G4
Nsukka 55 G6
Nubian Desert =
Nûbîya, Es
Sahrâ En . . 52 D5
Nûbîya, Es
Sahrâ En . . 52 D5
Nuboai 39 E5
Nueltin L. 70 B10
Nueva Imperial 94 D2

Nueva Rosita . . 84 B4
Nuéve de Julio 94 D4
Nuevitas 86 B4
Nuevo, G. 95 E4
Nuevo Laredo . 84 B5
Nugget Pt. . . . 65 G3
Nuhaka 64 C7
Nukey Bluff . . 62 B2
Nukheila 53 E4
Nukus 29 E6
Nulato 71 B4
Nullarbor Plain 60 G4
Numalla, L. . . . 63 A3
Numan 53 G1
Numazu 32 B6
Numfoor 39 E4
Numurkah 63 C4
Nunavut □ . . . 66 C10
Nuneaton 11 E6
Nunivak I. 71 B3
Nunkun 42 C10
Núoro 21 D2
Nuremberg =
Nürnberg . . . 15 D6
Nuriootpa 62 B2
Nürnberg 15 D6
Nurran, L. =
Terewah, L. . 63 A4
Nusa Tenggara
Barat □ . . . 37 F5
Nusa Tenggara
Timur □ . . . 39 F2
Nushki 42 E5
Nutak 68 C4
Nuuk =
Godthåb 68 B5
Nuwakot 40 C4
Nuweveldberge 58 E4
Nuyts Arch. . . 62 B1
Nyah West . . . 62 C3
Nyahanga 57 E6
Nyahururu . . . 57 D7
Nyainqentanglha
Shan 34 C4
Nyâlâ 53 F3
Nyasa, L. =
Malawi, L. . . 59 A6
Nyasvizh 17 B8
Nyda 28 C8
Nyeri 57 E7
Nyíregyháza . . 17 E5
Nylstroom . . . 59 C5
Nymagee 63 B4
Nyngan 63 B4
Nyoman =
Neman → . . 24 B1
Nysa 16 C3
Nysa → 16 B2
Nyurbe 30 C9
Nzega 57 E6
N'Zérékoré . . . 55 G3
Nzeto 56 F2

O

Ō-Shima 32 B6
Oahe, L. 76 C4
Oahu 82 H12
Oak Ridge . . . 75 A5
Oakbank 62 B3
Oakey 63 A5
Oakland 82 B1
Oamaru 65 F4
Oates Land . . . 96 A15
Oaxaca 84 D5
Ob → 28 C7

Oba 69 D2
Oban 10 C4
Obbia 49 F4
Oberhausen . . . 14 C4
Oberon 63 B4
Obi, Kepulauan 39 E3
Obi Is. = Obi,
  Kepulauan . . 39 E3
Óbidos 92 C2
Obihiro 32 F12
Obilatu 39 E3
Obo 57 C5
Obozerskaya =
  Obozerskiy . . 28 C5
Obozerskiy . . . 28 C5
Obskaya Guba . 28 C8
Obuasi 55 G4
Ocala 75 E6
Ocaña 18 C4
Occidental,
  Cordillera . . 90 C3
Ocean I. =
  Banaba 64 K11
Oceanside 82 D4
Ocniţa 17 D8
Ocumare del
  Tuy 90 A5
Odate 33 F12
Odawara 32 B6
Oddur 49 G3
Ödemiş 23 E7
Odense 9 G10
Oder → 15 B8
Odesa 25 D3
Odessa = Odesa 25 D3
Odessa 78 D2
Odienné 55 G3
Odintsovo 24 B4
Odorheiu
  Secuiesc 17 E7
Odra = Oder → 15 B8
Odra → 16 B2
Oeiras 92 D5
Ofanto → 20 D6
Offa 55 G5
Offenbach 14 C5
Offenburg 14 D4
Oga-Hantō 33 G11
Ōgaki 32 B5
Ogbomosho . . . 55 G5
Ogden 81 E8
Ogdensburg . . 73 B8
Oglio → 20 B3
Ogooué → . . . 56 E1
Ogowe =
  Ogooué → . 56 E1
Ohai 65 F2
Ohakune 64 C6
Ohanet 54 C6
Ohau, L. 65 F3
Ohio □ 72 D4
Ohio → 72 F1
Ohre → 16 C2
Ohrid 22 D3
Ohridsko Jezero 23 D3
Oise → 12 B5
Ōita 32 C2
Oiticica 92 D5
Ojos del Salado,
  Cerro 94 B3
Oka → 28 D5
Okaba 39 F5
Okahandja 58 C3
Okahukura . . . 64 C6
Okandja 56 E2
Okanogan → . 80 A4
Okara 42 D8
Okarito 65 E4
Okaukuejo 58 B3

Okavango
  Swamps . . . 58 B4
Okaya 32 A6
Okayama 32 B3
Okazaki 32 B5
Okeechobee, L. 75 F7
Okefenokee
  Swamp 75 D6
Okhotsk, Sea of 31 D12
Oki-Shotō 32 A3
Okiep 58 D3
Okinawa-Jima . 35 D7
Oklahoma □ . . 78 B5
Oklahoma City 78 B5
Okmulgee 79 B6
Oknitsa =
  Ocniţa 17 D8
Okrika 55 H6
Oktabrsk =
  Oktyabrsk . . . 29 E6
Oktyabrsk 29 E6
Oktyabrskiy =
  Aktsyabrski . 17 B9
Oktyabrskoy
  Revolyutsii,
  Os. 30 B7
Oktyabrskoye . 28 C7
Okuru 65 E3
Okushiri-Tō . . 32 F11
Öland 9 G11
Olary 62 B3
Olavarría 94 D4
Oława 16 C3
Ólbia 20 D2
Old Crow 70 B6
Oldenburg . . . 14 B5
Oldham 11 E5
Olekma → . . . 31 C10
Olekminsk . . . 31 C10
Oleksandriya . . 17 C8
Olenek 30 C9
Olenek → 30 B10
Oléron, I. d' . . 12 D3
Oleśnica 16 C3
Olevsk 17 C8
Olhão 18 D2
Olifants → . . . 59 C6
Ólimbos, Óros . 23 D4
Olinda 92 D7
Oliveira 93 G5
Olivenza 18 C2
Ollagüe 91 H5
Olomouc 16 D3
Olongapo 38 B2
Olot 19 A7
Olsztyn 16 B5
Olt → 22 C5
Olteniţa 22 B6
Oltu 46 B5
Olympia, Greece 23 F3
Olympia, U.S.A. 80 B2
Olympic Mts. . . 80 B2
Olympus, Mt. =
  Ólimbos, Óros 23 D4
Om → 29 D8
Omagh 11 D3
Omaha 77 E7
Oman ■ 48 C6
Oman, G. of . . . 45 E4
Omaruru 58 C3
Omate 91 G4
Ombai, Selat . . 39 F2
Omboué 56 E1
Ombrone → . . 20 C3
Omdurmân . . . 53 E5
Ometepec 84 D5
Ōmiya 32 B6
Omo → 53 G6
Omsk 29 D8

Omul, Vf. 17 F7
Ōmura 32 C1
Omuramba
  Omatako → . 58 B4
Ōmuta 32 C2
Onang 39 E1
Oncócua 58 B2
Onda 19 C5
Ondangua 58 B3
Ondo 55 G5
Öndörhaan . . . 35 B6
Onega 28 C4
Onega → 8 F15
Onega, G. of =
  Onezhskaya
  Guba 28 C4
Onega, L. =
  Onezhskoye
  Ozero 28 C4
Onehunga 64 B6
Oneşti 17 E8
Onezhskaya
  Guba 28 C4
Onezhskoye
  Ozero 28 C4
Ongarue 64 C6
Onilahy → . . . 59 J8
Onitsha 55 G6
Onoda 32 B2
Ontario □ 69 D2
Ontario, L. 73 C7
Oodnadatta . . . 62 A2
Oostende 14 C2
Ootacamund . . 43 P10
Opala 56 E4
Opava 16 D3
Opole 16 C3
Oporto = Porto 18 B1
Opotiki 64 C7
Opua 64 A6
Opunake 64 C5
Oradea 17 E5
Orai 42 G11
Oral =
  Zhayyq → . 29 E6
Oral 24 C7
Oran, Algeria . 54 A4
Oran, Argentina 94 A4
Orange =
  Oranje → . 58 D3
Orange,
  Australia 63 B4
Orange, France 13 D6
Orange, U.S.A. 79 D7
Orange, C. 92 B3
Orangeburg . . . 75 C7
Oranienburg . . 15 B7
Oranje → 58 D3
Oranjemund . . 58 D3
Oras 38 B3
Oraşul Stalin =
  Braşov 17 F7
Orbetello 20 C3
Orbost 63 C4
Orchila, I. 90 A5
Ordos = Mu Us
  Shamo 35 C5
Ordu 46 B4
Ordzhonikidze =
  Vladikavkaz . 25 E5
Ore Mts. =
  Erzgebirge . . 15 C7
Örebro 9 G11
Oregon □ 80 C3
Orekhovo-
  Zuyevo . . . 24 B4
Orel 24 C4
Ören 23 F6
Orenburg 29 D6

Orense 18 A2
Orepuki 65 G2
Øresund 9 G10
Orgaz 18 C4
Orgeyev =
  Orhei 17 E9
Orgün 45 C7
Orhaneli 23 E7
Orhangazi 23 D7
Orhei 17 E9
Orhon Gol → . 35 A5
Orient 62 A3
Oriental,
  Cordillera . . 90 B4
Orihuela 19 C5
Orinoco → . . . 90 B6
Orissa □ 40 G5
Oristano 21 E2
Oristano, G. di . 21 E2
Orizaba 84 D5
Orkney Is. 10 B5
Orlando 75 E7
Orléanais 12 C5
Orléans 12 C4
Ormara 42 G4
Ormoc 38 B2
Ormond 64 C7
Örnsköldsvik . . 8 F11
Orocué 90 C4
Orol Dengizi =
  Aral Sea 29 E6
Oroquieta 38 C2
Orós 92 D6
Orosháza 16 E5
Orroroo 62 B2
Orsha 24 C3
Orsk 29 D6
Orşova 22 B4
Ortaca 23 F7
Ortegal, C. . . . 18 A2
Orthez 12 E3
Ortigueira 18 A2
Ortles 20 A3
Ortón → 91 F5
Orümīyeh 46 C6
Orümīyeh,
  Daryācheh-ye 46 C6
Oruro 91 G5
Oruzgān □ . . . 42 C5
Orvieto 20 C4
Oryakhovo . . . 22 C4
Ōsaka 32 B4
Ösel =
  Saaremaa . . 24 B1
Osh 29 E8
Oshawa 69 D3
Oshkosh 76 E3
Oshmyany =
  Ashmyany . . 17 A7
Oshogbo 55 G5
Oshwe 56 E3
Osijek 20 B7
Osipenko =
  Berdyansk . 25 D4
Osipovichi =
  Asipovichy . 17 B9
Oskarshamn . . 9 G11
Öskemen 29 E9
Oslo 9 G10
Oslob 38 C2
Oslofjorden . . . 9 G10
Osmanabad . . 43 K10
Osmaniye 46 C4
Osnabrück . . . 14 B5
Osorio 94 B6
Osorno 95 E2
Ossa, Mt. 62 D4
Óssa, Oros . . . 23 E4
Ostend =
  Oostende . . 14 C2

Oster 17 C10
Österdalälven . 8 F10
Östersund 8 F10
Ostfriesische
Inseln 14 B4
Ostrava 16 D4
Ostróda 16 B4
Ostroh 17 C8
Ostrołęka 16 B5
Ostrów
Mazowiecka . 16 B5
Ostrów
Wielkopolski 16 C3
Ostrowiec-
Świętokrzyski 16 C5
Ostuni 21 D6
Ōsumi-Kaikyō . 33 G2
Osuna 18 D3
Oswego 73 C7
Oświęcim 16 C4
Otago □ 65 F3
Otago Harbour 65 F4
Ōtake 32 B3
Otaki 64 D6
Otaru 32 F12
Otaru-Wan =
Ishikari-Wan . 32 F12
Otavalo 90 C3
Otavi 58 B3
Otira Gorge ... 65 E4
Otjiwarongo .. 58 C3
Otorohanga .. 64 C6
Otranto 23 D2
Otranto, C. d' .. 23 D2
Otranto, Str. of 23 D2
Ōtsu 32 B4
Ottawa 69 D3
Ottawa Is. ... 68 C2
Ottumwa 77 E8
Oturkpo 55 G6
Otway, B. ... 95 G2
Otway, C. 62 C3
Otwock 16 B5
Ouachita Mts. . 79 B6
Ouadâne 54 D2
Ouadda 56 C4
Ouagadougou . 55 F4
Ouahran = Oran 54 A4
Ouallene 54 D5
Ouanda Djallé . 56 C4
Ouango 56 D4
Ouargla 54 B6
Ouarzazate ... 54 B3
Oubangi → .. 56 E3
Oudtshoorn .. 58 E4
Ouessant, I. d' . 12 B1
Ouesso 56 D3
Ouezzane 54 B3
Ouidah 55 G5
Oujda 54 B4
Oujeft 55 D2
Ouled Djellal .. 54 B6
Oulu 8 E13
Oulujärvi 8 F13
Oulujoki → ... 8 E13
Oum Chalouba 53 E3
Ounianga-Kébir 53 E3
Ounianga Sérir 53 E3
Ourense =
Orense 18 A2
Ouricuri 92 D5
Ouro Prêto 93 G5
Ouse 62 D4
Outer Hebrides 10 C3
Outjo 58 C3
Ouyen 62 C3
Ovalle 94 C2
Ovamboland .. 58 B3
Oviedo 18 A3

Ovruch 17 C9
Owaka 65 G3
Owambo =
Ovamboland 58 B3
Owase 32 B5
Owbeh 42 B3
Owen Sound . 69 D2
Owen Stanley
Ra. 61 B8
Owendo 56 D1
Owo 55 G6
Owyhee → ... 80 D5
Oxford, N.Z. .. 65 E5
Oxford, U.K. .. 11 F6
Oxley 63 B3
Oxnard 82 C3
Oxus =
Amudarya → 29 E6
Oya 37 D4
Oyama 32 A6
Oyem 56 D2
Oyo 55 G5
Ozamiz 38 C2
Ozark Plateau . 79 A8
Ózd 16 D5

P

Pa-an 41 J11
Paarl 58 E3
Pab Hills 42 F5
Pabianice 16 C4
Pabna 41 E7
Pacaja → ... 92 C3
Pacaraima,
Sierra 90 C6
Pacasmayo .. 91 E3
Pachpadra ... 42 G8
Pachuca 84 C5
Padaido,
Kepulauan .. 39 E5
Padang 37 E2
Padangpanjang 37 E2
Padangsidempuan
.... 37 D1
Paderborn 14 C5
Padloping Island 68 B4
Pádova 20 B3
Padua = Pádova 20 B3
Paducah 72 F1
Paeroa 64 B6
Pafúri 59 C6
Pag 20 B5
Pagadian 38 C2
Pagai Selatan, P. 37 E2
Pagai Utara .. 37 E2
Pagalu =
Annobón ... 51 G4
Pagastikós
Kólpos ... 23 E4
Pagatan 37 E5
Pahiatua 64 D6
Painan 37 E2
Paint Hills =
Wemindji .. 69 C3
Painted Desert . 83 C7
País Vasco □ .. 19 A4
Paisley 10 D4
Paita 90 E2
Pajares, Puerto
de 18 A3
Pakaraima Mts. 90 B6
Pakistan ■ ... 42 E7
Pakokku 41 G10
Pakse 36 A3
Paktīā □ 42 C6

Pala 53 G2
Palagruža 20 C6
Palam 43 K10
Palampur 42 C10
Palana 62 C4
Palanan 38 A2
Palanan Pt. ... 38 A2
Palangkaraya . 37 E4
Palani Hills .. 43 P10
Palanpur 43 G8
Palanro 39 E1
Palapye 59 C5
Palau ■ 38 C4
Palawan 36 C5
Palayankottai . 43 Q10
Paleleh 39 D2
Palembang ... 37 E2
Palencia 18 A3
Palermo 21 E4
Palestine 79 D6
Paletwa 41 G9
Palghat 43 P10
Pali 42 G8
Palioúrion, Ákra 23 E4
Palitana 43 J7
Palk Bay 43 Q11
Palk Strait ... 43 Q11
Pallanza =
Verbánia ... 20 B2
Palm Springs .. 82 D4
Palma 57 G8
Palma → 93 E4
Palma, B. de .. 19 C7
Palma de
Mallorca 19 C7
Palmares 92 D6
Palmas, C. 55 H3
Pálmas, G. di .. 21 E2
Palmeira dos
Índios 93 D6
Palmeirinhas,
Pta. das .. 56 F2
Palmer 71 B5
Palmer Arch. .. 96 A3
Palmer Land .. 96 B3
Palmerston ... 65 F4
Palmerston
North 64 D6
Palmi 21 E5
Palmira 90 C3
Palmyra =
Tudmur 46 D4
Palopo 39 E2
Palos, C. de .. 19 D5
Palu, Indonesia 39 E1
Palu, Turkey .. 46 C5
Paluan 38 B2
Pama 55 F5
Pamiers 12 E4
Pamirs 29 F8
Pamlico Sd. ... 75 B10
Pampa 78 B3
Pampa de las
Salinas 94 C3
Pampanua ... 39 E2
Pampas,
Argentina ... 94 D4
Pampas, Peru . 91 F4
Pamplona,
Colombia ... 90 B4
Pamplona,
Spain ... 19 A5
Panaji 43 M8
Panamá 85 F9
Panama ■ ... 86 E4
Panamá, G. de 86 E4
Panama City .. 74 D5
Panão 91 E3
Panay 38 B2

Panay, G. 38 B2
Pančevo 22 B3
Pandan 38 B2
Pandharpur .. 43 L9
Pando 94 C5
Pando, L. =
Hope, L. ... 62 A2
Panevežys ... 24 B1
Panfilov 29 E8
Pang-Long ... 41 F12
Pang-Yang ... 41 F12
Pangani 57 F7
Pangfou =
Bengbu 35 C6
Pangkajene .. 39 E1
Pangkalanbrandan
.... 37 D1
Pangkalanbuun 37 E4
Pangkalansusu 37 D1
Pangkalpinang 37 E3
Pangkoh 37 E4
Pangnirtung .. 68 B4
Pangutaran
Group 38 C2
Panjgur 42 F4
Panjim = Panaji 43 M8
Panjinad
Barrage .. 42 E7
Panorama ... 94 A6
Pantar 39 F2
Pante Macassar 39 F2
Pantelleria ... 21 F3
Pánuco 84 C5
Panyam 55 G6
Paoting =
Baoding 35 C6
Paot'ou =
Baotou 35 B6
Paoua 56 C3
Pápa 16 E3
Papakura 64 B6
Papantla 84 C5
Papar 36 C5
Papua New
Guinea ■ ... 61 B8
Papudo 94 C2
Papun 41 H11
Pará = Belém . 92 C4
Pará □ 92 C3
Paracatu 93 F4
Paracel Is. =
Hsisha
Chuntao 36 A4
Parachilna ... 62 B2
Parachinar ... 42 C7
Paradip 40 G6
Parado → ... 39 F1
Paragua → .. 90 B6
Paraguaçu → . 93 E6
Paraguaná, Pen.
de 90 A4
Paraguarí ... 94 B5
Paraguay ■ .. 94 A5
Paraguay → .. 94 B5
Paraíba = João
Pessoa ... 92 D7
Paraíba □ 92 D6
Paraíba do
Sul → 93 G5
Parakou 55 G5
Paramaribo .. 92 A2
Paraná,
Argentina ... 94 C4
Paranã, Brazil . 93 E4
Paraná □ 94 A6
Paraná → ... 94 C5
Paranaguá .. 94 B7
Paranaíba → . 93 G3

Paranapanema → 94 A6
Paranapiacaba, Serra do 94 A7
Parang, *Jolo, Phil.* 38 C2
Parang, *Mindanao, Phil.* 38 C2
Paratinga 93 E5
Paratoo 62 B2
Parattah 62 D4
Parbhani 43 K10
Parchim 15 B6
Pardo →, *Bahia, Brazil* 93 F6
Pardo →, *Mato Grosso, Brazil* 93 G3
Pardo →, *São Paulo, Brazil* 93 G4
Pardubice 16 C2
Parecis, Serra dos 91 F7
Parepare 39 E1
Párga 23 E3
Pariaguán 90 B6
Pariaman 37 E2
Parigi 39 E2
Parika 90 B7
Parima, Serra 90 C6
Parinari 90 D4
Parîngul Mare 17 F6
Parintins 92 C2
Pariparit Kyun 41 K9
Paris, *France* 12 B5
Paris, *U.S.A.* 79 C6
Park Range 81 F10
Parkersburg 72 E5
Parkes 63 B4
Parla 18 B4
Parma 20 B3
Parnaguá 93 E5
Parnaíba, *Piauí, Brazil* 92 C5
Parnaíba, *São Paulo, Brazil* 93 F3
Parnaíba → 92 C5
Parnassós 23 E4
Parnu 24 B1
Paroo → 63 B3
Páros 23 F5
Parral 94 D2
Parramatta 63 B5
Parry Sound 69 D3
Partinico 21 E4
Paru → 92 C3
Paruro 91 F4
Parvān □ 42 B6
Parvatipuram 40 H4
Pasadena, *Calif., U.S.A.* 82 C3
Pasadena, *Tex., U.S.A.* 79 E6
Pasaje 90 D3
Pascagoula 79 D9
Paşcani 17 E8
Pasco 80 B4
Pasco, Cerro de 91 F3
Pashmakli = Smolyan 22 D5
Pašman 20 C5
Pasni 42 G3
Paso de Indios 95 E3
Passau 15 D7
Passero, C. 21 F5
Passo Fundo 94 B6
Passos 93 G4
Pastaza → 90 D3
Pasto 90 C3
Patagonia 95 F3
Patan, *India* 43 H8
Patan, *Nepal* 40 D5
Patani 39 D3
Patchewollock 62 C3
Patea 64 C6
Pategi 55 G6
Paternò 21 F5
Paterson 73 D8
Pathankot 42 C9
Patiala 42 D10
Patkai Bum 41 D10
Pátmos 23 F6
Patna 40 E5
Patos, L. dos 94 C6
Patos de Minas 93 F4
Patquía 94 C3
Pátrai 23 E3
Pátraikós Kólpos 23 E3
Patras = Pátrai 23 E3
Patrocínio 93 F4
Pattani 36 C2
Patuakhali 41 F8
Pau 12 E3
Pauini → 90 D6
Pauk 41 G10
Paulis = Isiro 57 D5
Paulistana 92 D5
Paulo Afonso 93 D6
Pavia 20 B2
Pavlodar 29 D8
Pavlograd = Pavlohrad 25 D4
Pavlohrad 25 D4
Pavlovo 24 B5
Pavlovsk 24 C5
Pawtucket 73 D10
Paxoí 23 E3
Payakumbuh 37 E2
Payne Bay = Kangirsuk 68 C4
Paysandú 94 C5
Paz, B. la 84 C2
Pazar 46 B5
Pazardzhik 22 C5
Peace → 70 C8
Peak Hill 63 B4
Peake 62 C2
Peake Cr. → 62 A2
Pebane 59 B7
Pebas 90 D4
Peć 22 C3
Pechenga 28 C4
Pechenizhyn 17 D7
Pechora → 28 C6
Pechorskaya Guba 28 C6
Pecos → 78 E3
Pécs 16 E4
Pedder, L. 62 D4
Pedirka 62 A2
Pedra Azul 93 F5
Pedreiras 92 C5
Pedro Afonso 93 D4
Pedro Juan Caballero 94 A5
Peebinga 62 B3
Peel →, *Australia* 63 B5
Peel →, *Canada* 70 B6
Peera Peera Poolanna L. 62 A2
Pegasus Bay 65 E5
Pegu 41 J11
Pegu Yoma 41 H10
Pehuajó 94 D4
Peine 14 B6
Peip'ing = Beijing 35 C6
Peipus, L. = Chudskoye, Oz. 24 B2
Peixe 93 E4
Pekalongan 37 F3
Pekanbaru 37 D2
Pekin 77 E10
Peking = Beijing 35 C6
Pelagie, Is. 21 G4
Pelaihari 37 E4
Peleaga, Vf. 17 F6
Peleng 39 E2
Pelješac 20 C6
Pelly → 70 B6
Pelly Bay 68 B2
Pelly L. 70 B9
Peloponnese = Pelopónnisos □ 23 F4
Pelopónnisos □ 23 F4
Peloro, C. 21 E5
Pelorus Sd. 65 D5
Pelotas 94 C6
Pelvoux, Massif du 13 D7
Pematangsiantar 37 D1
Pemba I. 57 F7
Pembroke, *Canada* 69 D3
Pembroke, *U.K.* 11 F4
Penang = Pinang 36 C2
Penápolis 94 A6
Peñarroya-Pueblonuevo 18 C3
Peñas, C. de 18 A3
Penas, G. de 95 F2
Pench'i = Benxi 35 B7
Pend Oreille L. 80 A5
Pendembu 55 G2
Pendleton 80 C4
Penedo 93 E6
Penguin 62 D4
Peniche 18 C1
Penida 37 F5
Peninsular Malaysia □ 37 D2
Penmarch, Pte. de 12 C1
Pennines 11 D5
Pennsylvania □ 73 D7
Penola 62 C3
Penong 60 G5
Penrith 63 B5
Pensacola 74 D4
Pensacola Mts. 96 C4
Penshurst 62 C3
Penticton 71 D8
Pentland Firth 10 B5
Penza 24 C6
Penzance 11 F4
Peoria 77 E10
Perabumulih 37 E2
Perche, Collines du 12 B4
Perdido, Mte. 19 A6
Perdu, Mt. = Perdido, Mte. 19 A6
Pereira 90 C3
Perekerten 62 B3
Pereyaslav-Khmelnytskyy 24 C3
Pergamino 94 C4
Péribonca → 69 D3
Perico 94 A3
Périgueux 12 D4
Perijá, Sierra de 90 B
Perlas, Arch. de las 86 E
Perm 29 D
Pernambuco = Recife 92 D
Pernatty Lagoon 62 B
Pernik 22 C
Perpendicular Pt. 63 B
Perpignan 13 E
Persepolis 44 D
Pershotravensk 17 C
Persian Gulf = Gulf, The 44 E
Perth, *Australia* 60 G
Perth, *U.K.* 10 C
Perth Amboy 73 D
Peru ■ 90 C
Perúgia 20 C
Pervomaysk 25 D
Pervouralsk 29 D
Pésaro 20 C
Pescara 20 C
Peshawar 42 B
Peshkopi 22 D
Pesqueira 92 D
Petah Tiqwa 46 D
Petauke 59 A
Peter I.s Øy 96 A
Peterborough, *Australia* 62 B
Peterborough, *Canada* 69 D
Peterborough, *U.K.* 11 E
Peterhead 10 C
Petersburg, *Alaska, U.S.A.* 71 C
Petersburg, *Va., U.S.A.* 73 F
Petitsikapau, L. 69 C
Petlad 43 H
Peto 85 C
Petone 65 D
Petrich 22 D
Petrikov = Pyetrikaw 17 B
Petrograd = Sankt-Peterburg 24 B
Petrolândia 93 D
Petrolina 93 D
Petropavl 29 D
Petropavlovsk = Petropavl 29 D
Petropavlovsk-Kamchatskiy 31 D1
Petrópolis 93 G
Petroşani 17 F
Petrovaradin 22 B
Petrovsk 24 C
Petrozavodsk 28 C
Peureulak 36 D
Pforzheim 14 D
Phagwara 42 D
Phalodi 42 F
Phan Rang 36 B
Phangan, Ko 36 C
Phangnga 36 C
Phanh Bho Ho Chi Minh 36 B
Phatthalung 36 C
Phetchabun 36 A
Philadelphia 73 E
Philippines ■ 38 B
Philippopolis = Plovdiv 22 C
Phillip I. 63 C

Phillott 63 A4
Phitsanulok . . . 36 A2
Phnom Dangrek 36 B2
Phnom Penh . . 36 B2
Phoenix 83 D6
Phra Nakhon Si
Ayutthaya . . . 36 B2
Phuket 36 C1
Phumiphon,
Khuan 36 A1
Piacenza 20 B2
Pialba 63 A5
Pian Cr. → . . . 63 B4
Pianosa 20 C3
Piatra Neamţ . . 17 E8
Piauí □ 92 D5
Piave → 20 B4
Pibor Post 53 G5
Pica 91 H5
Picardie 13 B5
Picardy =
Picardie 13 B5
Pichilemu 94 C2
Pico Truncado . 95 F3
Picton, Australia 63 B5
Picton, N.Z. . . 65 D6
Pictou 69 D4
Picún Leufú . . 95 D3
Piedmont =
Piemonte □ . 20 B1
Piedras, R. de
las → 91 F5
Piedras Negras 84 B4
Piemonte □ . . . 20 B1
Piet Retief 59 D6
Pietermaritzburg 59 D6
Pietersburg . . . 59 C5
Pietrosul,
Romania 17 E7
Pietrosul,
Romania 17 E7
Pigüe 94 D4
Piketberg 58 E3
Piła 16 B3
Pilar, Brazil . . . 93 D6
Pilar, Paraguay 94 B5
Pilas Group . . . 38 C2
Pilcomayo → . 94 B5
Pilibhit 42 E11
Pilica → 16 C5
Pílos 23 F3
Pilsen = Plzeň . 16 D1
Pimba 62 B2
Pimenta Bueno 91 F6
Pimentel 91 E3
Pinang 36 C2
Pinar del Río . . 86 B3
Pınarhisar 22 D6
Pińczów 16 C5
Pindiga 55 G7
Pindos Óros . . 23 E3
Pindus Mts. =
Pindos Óros . 23 E3
Pine Bluff 79 B7
Pine Point 70 B8
Pinega → 28 C5
Pinerolo 20 B1
Pinetown 59 D6
Ping → 36 A2
Pingdong 35 D7
Pingliang 35 C5
Pingwu 35 C5
Pingxiang 35 D5
Pinhel 18 B2
Pini 37 D1
Piniós → 23 E4
Pinnaroo 62 C3
Pínnes, Ákra . . 23 D5
Pinrang 39 E1

Pinsk 17 B8
Pintados 91 H5
Pinyug 24 A6
Piombino 20 C3
Pioner, Os. . . . 30 B7
Piorini, L. 90 D6
Piotrków
Trybunalski . 16 C4
Pip 45 E5
Piquiri → . . . 94 A6
Piracicaba . . . 94 A7
Piracuruca . . . 92 C5
Piræus =
Piraiévs . . . 23 F4
Piraiévs 23 F4
Pirané 94 B5
Pirapora 93 F5
Pírgos 23 F3
Pirin Planina . . 22 D4
Piripiri 92 C5
Pirmasens . . . 14 D4
Pirot 22 C4
Piru 39 E3
Pisa 20 C3
Pisagua 91 G4
Pisciotta 21 D5
Pisco 91 F3
Písek 16 D2
Pishan 34 C2
Pising 39 F2
Pistóia 20 C3
Pisuerga → . . 18 B3
Pitarpunga, L. . 62 B3
Pitcairn I. 65 M17
Piteå 8 E12
Piteşti 22 B5
Pithapuram . . . 40 J4
Pittsburg 79 A6
Pittsburgh 73 D5
Pittsworth 63 A5
Piura 90 E2
Placentia 69 D5
Placentia B. . . 69 D5
Plainview 78 B3
Pláka, Ákra . . 23 G6
Plakhino 28 C9
Plasencia 18 B2
Plata, Río de la 94 C5
Platani → . . . 21 F4
Plato . . . .➤. . . 90 B4
Platte → 77 F7
Plauen 15 C7
Pleiku 36 B3
Plenty, B. of . . 64 B7
Pleven 22 C5
Plevlja 22 C2
Płock 16 B4
Plöckenstein . 15 D7
Ploieşti 22 B6
Plovdiv 22 C5
Plumtree 59 C5
Plymouth 11 F4
Plzeň 16 D1
Po → 20 B4
Po Hai = Bo Hai 35 C6
Pobedy Pik . . . 29 E8
Pocatello 81 D7
Poços de Caldas 93 G4
Podgorica . . . 22 C2
Podilska
Vysochyna . . 17 D8
Podkamennaya
Tunguska → 30 C7
Podolsk 24 B4
Podor 55 E1
Pofadder 58 D3
Poh 39 E2
Pohnpei 64 J10

Poinsett, C. . . . 96 A12
Pointe-à-Pitre . 87 C7
Pointe Noire . . 56 E2
Poitiers 12 C4
Poitou 12 C3
Pokaran 42 F7
Pokataroo . . . 63 A4
Pokrovsk =
Engels 24 C6
Pola = Pula . . 20 B4
Polan 45 E5
Poland ■ 16 B5
Polatsk 24 B2
Polcura 94 D2
Polesye = Pripet
Marshes . . . 17 B9
Poli 56 C2
Police 16 B2
Polillo Is. 38 B2
Políyiros 23 D4
Pollachi 43 P10
Polnovat 28 C7
Polonne 17 C8
Polonnoye =
Polonne . . . 17 C8
Poltava 24 D3
Polunochnoye . 28 C7
Polynesia 65 L15
Polynésie
française =
French
Polynesia ■ . 65 M16
Pombal, Brazil . 92 D6
Pombal,
Portugal . . . 18 C1
Pomézia 20 D4
Pomorski,
Pojezierze . . 16 B3
Ponape =
Pohnpei . . . 64 J10
Ponca City . . . 78 A5
Ponce 87 C6
Pond Inlet . . . 68 A3
Pondicherry . . 43 P11
Ponferrada . . . 18 A2
Ponnani 43 P9
Ponnyadaung . 41 F10
Ponoy → 28 C5
Ponta Grossa . 94 B6
Ponta Pora . . . 94 A5
Pontarlier 13 C7
Pontchartrain L. 79 D8
Ponte Nova . . 93 G5
Pontevedra . . . 18 A1
Pontiac 72 C4
Pontianak 37 E3
Pontine Is. =
Ponziane,
Ísole 21 D4
Pontine Mts. =
Kuzey
Anadolu
Dağları 46 B3
Pontivy 12 B2
Pontoise 12 B5
Ponziane, Ísole 21 D4
Poochera 62 B1
Poole 11 F6
Poona = Pune . 43 K8
Pooncarie 62 B3
Poopelloe L. . . 63 B3
Poopó, L. de . . 91 G5
Popayán 90 C3
Popigay 30 B9
Popilta, L. 62 B3
Popio L. 62 B3
Poplar Bluff . . 79 A8
Popocatépetl,
Volcán 84 D5

Popokabaka . . 56 F3
Poprád 16 D5
Porbandar . . . 43 J6
Porcupine → . 71 B5
Pordenone . . . 20 B4
Pori 8 F12
Porkkala 9 G12
Porlamar 90 A6
Poroshiri-Dake . 32 F12
Porpoise B. . . 96 A13
Porretta, Passo
di 20 B3
Port Adelaide . 62 B2
Port Alberni . . 71 D7
Port Alfred . . . 59 E5
Port Angeles . . 80 A2
Port Antonio . . 86 C4
Port Arthur,
Australia 62 D4
Port Arthur,
U.S.A. 79 E7
Port-au-Prince . 87 C5
Port Augusta . . 62 B2
Port Augusta
West 62 B2
Port Bergé
Vaovao 59 H9
Port Bou 19 A7
Port Broughton 62 B2
Port-Cartier . . 69 C4
Port Chalmers . 65 F4
Port Darwin . . 95 G5
Port Davey . . . 62 D4
Port Dickson . . 37 D2
Port Elizabeth . 59 E5
Port Fairy 62 C3
Port-Gentil . . . 56 E1
Port Harcourt . 55 H6
Port Harrison =
Inukjuak . . . 68 C3
Port
Hawkesbury . 69 D4
Port Hedland . . 60 E2
Port Huron . . . 72 C4
Port Kembla . . 63 B5
Port Kenny . . . 62 B1
Port Lairge =
Waterford . . 11 E3
Port Laoise . . . 11 E3
Port Lincoln . . 62 B2
Port Loko 55 G2
Port MacDonnell 62 C3
Port Macquarie . 63 B5
Port Moresby . 61 B8
Port Nelson . . 71 C10
Port Nolloth . . 58 D3
Port Nouveau-
Québec =
Kangiqsualujjuaq
. . . . 68 C4
Port of Spain . 87 D7
Port Pegasus . 65 G2
Port Phillip B. . 63 C3
Port Pirie 62 B2
Port Safaga =
Bûr Safâga . 52 C5
Port Said = Bûr
Sa'îd 52 B5
Port Shepstone 59 E6
Port Stanley =
Stanley 95 G5
Port Sudan =
Bûr Sûdân . . 53 E6
Port Talbot . . . 11 F5
Port-Vendres . 13 E5
Port Wakefield . 62 B2
Port Weld 36 D2
Porta Orientalis 22 B4

Portachuelo	91	G6
Portadown	11	D3
Portage La Prairie	71	D10
Portalegre	18	C2
Portile de Fier	22	B4
Portimão	18	D1
Portland, N.S.W., Australia	63	B4
Portland, Vic., Australia	62	C3
Portland, Maine, U.S.A.	73	C10
Portland, Oreg., U.S.A.	80	C2
Portland B.	62	C3
Portland Prom.	68	C3
Porto	18	B1
Pôrto Alegre	94	C6
Porto Amboim = Gunza	56	G2
Pôrto de Móz	92	C3
Porto Empédocle	21	F4
Pôrto Esperança	91	G7
Pôrto Franco	92	D4
Porto Mendes	94	A6
Pôrto Murtinho	91	H7
Pôrto Nacional	93	E4
Porto Novo	55	G5
Porto Santo	54	B1
Pôrto Seguro	93	F6
Porto Tórres	20	D2
Pôrto União	94	B6
Pôrto Válter	91	E4
Porto-Vecchio	13	F8
Pôrto Velho	91	E6
Portoferráio	20	C3
Portoscuso	21	E2
Portovíejo	90	D2
Portree	10	C3
Portsmouth, U.K.	11	F6
Portsmouth, U.S.A.	73	F7
Porttipahtan tekojärvi	8	E13
Portugal ■	18	C1
Porvenir	95	G2
Posadas	94	B5
Poshan = Boshan	35	C6
Poso	39	E2
Posse	93	E4
Possel	56	C3
Possession I.	96	B15
Poste Maurice Cortier	54	D5
Postojna	20	B5
Potchefstroom	59	D5
Potenza	21	D5
Poteriteri, L.	65	G2
Potgietersrus	59	C5
Poti	25	E5
Potiskum	55	F7
Potomac →	73	E7
Potosí	91	G5
Pototan	38	B2
Potrerillos	94	B3
Potsdam	15	B7
Poughkeepsie	73	D9
Pouso Alegre	93	E2
Považská Bystrica	16	D4
Povenets	28	C4
Poverty B.	64	C8
Póvoa de Varzim	18	B1
Powder →	76	B2
Powell L.	83	B7
Poyang Hu	35	D6
Požarevac	22	B3
Poznań	16	B3
Pozo Almonte	91	H5
Pozoblanco	18	C3
Pozzuoli	21	D5
Prachuap Khiri Khan	36	B1
Prado	93	F6
Prague = Praha	16	C2
Praha	16	C2
Prainha, Amazonas, Brazil	91	E6
Prainha, Pará, Brazil	92	C3
Prairies	71	C9
Prapat	37	D1
Prata	93	F4
Prato	20	C3
Pravia	18	A2
Praya	37	F5
Preparis North Channel	41	K9
Preparis South Channel	41	K9
Přerov	16	D3
Preservation Inlet	65	G2
Presidencia Roque Saenz Peña	94	B4
Presidente Epitácio	93	G3
Presidente Hermes	91	F6
Presidente Prudente	93	G3
Prešov	16	D5
Prespa, L. = Prespansko Jezero	23	D3
Prespansko Jezero	23	D3
Presque Isle	73	A11
Preston	11	E5
Pretoria	59	D5
Préveza	23	E3
Příbram	16	D2
Prichard	74	D3
Prieska	58	D4
Prievidza	16	D4
Prilep	22	D3
Priluki = Pryluky	24	C3
Prime Seal I.	62	D4
Prince Albert	71	C9
Prince Albert Mts.	96	B15
Prince Albert Pen.	70	A8
Prince Albert Sd.	70	A8
Prince Charles I.	68	B3
Prince Charles Mts.	96	B10
Prince Edward I. □	69	D4
Prince of Wales I., Canada	70	A10
Prince of Wales I., U.S.A.	71	C6
Principe da Beira	91	F6
Prins Harald Kyst	96	B8
Prinsesse Astrid Kyst	96	B7
Prinsesse Ragnhild Kyst	96	B8
Pripet → = Prypyat →	17	C10
Pripet Marshes	17	B9
Pripyat Marshes = Pripet Marshes	17	B9
Pripyats = Prypyat →	17	C10
Priština	22	C3
Privas	13	D6
Privolzhskaya Vozvyshennost	24	C6
Prizren	22	C3
Proddatur	43	M11
Progreso	85	C7
Prokopyevsk	29	D9
Prokuplje	22	C3
Prome = Pyè	41	H10
Propriá	93	E6
Prostějov	16	D3
Proston	63	A5
Provence	13	E6
Providence	73	D10
Providencia, I. de	86	D3
Provins	13	B5
Provo	81	E8
Prozna →	16	B3
Pruszków	16	B5
Prut →	17	F9
Pruzhany	17	B7
Prydz B.	96	A10
Pryluky	24	C3
Prypyat →	17	C10
Przemyśl	17	D6
Przhevalsk	29	E8
Psará	23	E5
Pskov	24	B2
Ptich = Ptsich →	17	B9
Ptsich →	17	B9
Puán	94	D4
Pucallpa	91	E4
Pudukkottai	43	P11
Puebla	84	D5
Pueblo	76	F2
Pueblo Hundido	94	B2
Puelches	94	D3
Puente Alto	94	C2
Puente-Genil	18	D3
Puerto Aisén	95	F2
Puerto Ayacucho	90	B5
Puerto Barrios	85	D7
Puerto Bermejo	94	B5
Puerto Bermúdez	91	F4
Puerto Bolívar	90	D3
Puerto Cabello	90	A5
Puerto Cabezas	86	D3
Puerto Carreño	90	B5
Puerto Chicama	91	E3
Puerto Coig	95	G3
Puerto Cortés	85	D7
Puerto Cumarebo	90	A5
Puerto del Rosario	54	C2
Puerto Deseado	95	F3
Puerto Heath	91	F5
Puerto La Cruz	90	A6
Puerto Leguízamo	90	D4
Puerto Lobos	95	E3
Puerto Madryn	95	E3
Puerto Maldonado	91	F5
Puerto Montt	95	E2
Puerto Morelos	85	C7
Puerto Natales	95	G2
Puerto Páez	90	B5
Puerto Pinasco	94	A5
Puerto Pirámides	95	E4
Puerto Plata	87	C5
Puerto Princesa	38	C1
Puerto Quellón	95	E2
Puerto Rico ■	87	C6
Puerto Sastre	91	H7
Puerto Suárez	91	G7
Puerto Wilches	90	B4
Puertollano	18	C3
Pueyrredón, L.	95	F2
Pugachev	24	C6
Puget Sound	80	B2
Puigcerdá	19	A6
Pukaki L.	65	F4
Pukapuka	65	L14
Pukekohe	64	B6
Pula	20	B4
Puławy	16	C5
Pullman	80	B5
Pulog	38	A2
Pułtusk	16	B5
Puna	91	G5
Puná, I.	90	D2
Punakha	41	D7
Punata	91	G5
Punch	42	C9
Pune	43	K8
Punjab □, India	42	D9
Punjab □, Pakistan	42	D8
Puno	91	G4
Punta Alta	94	D4
Punta Arenas	95	G2
Punta de Díaz	94	B2
Puntabie	62	B1
Puntarenas	86	E3
Punto Fijo	90	A4
Puquio	91	F4
Pur →	28	C8
Purace, Vol.	90	C3
Puralia = Puruliya	40	F6
Puri	40	H5
Purnia	40	E6
Purukcahu	37	E4
Puruliya	40	F6
Purus →	90	D6
Pusan	35	C7
Pushkino	24	C6
Putao	41	D11
Putaruru	64	C6
Puthein Myit →	41	K10
Putignano	21	D6
Puting, Tanjung	37	E4
Putorana, Gory	30	C7
Puttalam	43	Q11
Puttgarden	15	A6
Putumayo →	90	D5
Putussibau	37	D4
Puy-de-Dôme	13	D5
Pweto	57	F5
Pwllheli	11	E4
Pyapon	41	J10
Pyasina →	30	B6
Pyatigorsk	25	E5
Pyè	41	H10
Pyetrikaw	17	B9
Pyinmana	41	H11
P'yŏngyang	35	C7
Pyrénées	19	A6
Pyu	41	H11

Q

Qādib 49 E5
Qā'emshahr ... 44 B3
Qahremānshahr
 = Bākhtarān . 46 D6
Qaidam Pendi . 34 C4
Qalāt 45 C6
Qal'at al Akhḍar 47 E4
Qal'eh Shaharak 42 B4
Qal'eh-ye Now 45 C5
Qamar, Ghubbat
 al 49 D5
Qamruddin
 Karez 42 D6
Qandahār 42 D4
Qandahār □ ... 42 D4
Qapshaghay .. 29 E8
Qâra 52 C4
Qarabutaq ... 29 E7
Qarachuk 46 C5
Qaraghandy .. 29 E8
Qārah 47 E5
Qarataū 29 E8
Qarqan 34 C3
Qarqan He → . 34 C3
Qarqaraly 29 E8
Qarshi 29 F7
Qaşr-e Qand .. 45 E5
Qasr Farāfra . 52 C4
Qatar ■ 44 E2
Qattâra,
 Munkhafed el 52 C4
Qattâra
 Depression =
 Qattâra,
 Munkhafed el 52 C4
Qāyen 44 C4
Qazaqstan =
 Kazakhstan ■ . 29 E7
Qazvin 46 C7
Qena 52 C5
Qeshm 44 E4
Qila Safed ... 42 E2
Qila Saifullāh .. 42 D6
Qilian Shan ... 34 C4
Qingdao 35 C7
Qinghai □ 34 C4
Qinghai Hu ... 34 C5
Qinhuangdao . 35 C6
Qinzhou 35 D5
Qiqihar 35 B7
Qitai 34 B3
Qom 44 C2
Qomsheh 44 C2
Qondūz 45 B7
Qondūz □ 45 B7
Qostanay 29 D7
Qu Xian,
 Sichuan,
 China 35 C5
Qu Xian,
 Zhejiang,
 China 35 D6
Quambatook .. 62 C3
Quambone 63 B4
Quan Long ... 36 C3
Quandialla ... 63 B4
Quang Ngai ... 36 A3
Quanzhou 35 D6
Quaqtaq 68 B4
Quaraí 94 C5
Quartu
 Sant'Elena .. 21 E2
Quatsino 71 C7
Quba 25 E6
Qūchān 44 B4
Queanbeyan .. 63 C4
Québec 69 D3

Québec □ 69 D3
Queen
 Alexandra Ra. 96 C15
Queen Charlotte
 Is. 70 C6
Queen Charlotte
 Str. 71 C7
Queen Elizabeth
 Is. 66 B9
Queen Mary
 Land 96 B11
Queen Maud G. 70 B9
Queen Maud
 Land 96 B7
Queen Maud
 Mts. 96 C16
Queenscliff ... 63 C3
Queensland □ . 61 E7
Queenstown,
 Australia 62 D4
Queenstown,
 N.Z. 65 F3
Queenstown,
 S. Africa 59 E5
Queimadas ... 93 E6
Quela 56 F3
Quelimane ... 59 B7
Quelpart =
 Cheju Do .. 35 C7
Quequén 94 D5
Querétaro 84 C4
Quetta 42 D5
Quezon City ... 38 B2
Qui Nhon 36 B3
Quibaxe 56 F2
Quibdo 90 B3
Quiberon 12 C2
Quilán, C. 95 E2
Quilengues ... 58 A2
Quillabamba .. 91 F4
Quillagua 91 H5
Quillota 94 C2
Quilon 43 Q10
Quilpie 63 A3
Quimilí 94 B4
Quimper 12 B1
Quimperlé 12 C2
Quincy 77 F9
Quines 94 C3
Quinga 59 H8
Quintanar de la
 Orden 18 C4
Quintero 94 C2
Quinyambie .. 62 B3
Quipungo 58 A2
Quirindi 63 B5
Quissanga ... 59 G8
Quitilipi 94 B4
Quito 90 D3
Quixadá 92 C6
Qünghirot 29 E6
Quondong ... 62 B3
Quorn 62 B2
Qūqon 29 E8
Qûs 52 C5
Quseir 52 C5
Qyzylorda 29 E7

R

Raahe 8 F12
Raba 39 F1
Rába → 16 E3
Rabat, Malta . 21 G5
Rabat, Morocco 54 B3
Rabaul 64 K10

Rābigh 47 G4
Race, C. 69 D5
Rach Gia 36 B3
Racibórz 16 C4
Racine 72 C2
Rădăuţi 17 E7
Radekhiv 17 C7
Radekhov =
 Radekhiv ... 17 C7
Radhwa, Jabal 47 F4
Radom 16 C5
Radomsko 16 C4
Radomyshl ... 17 C9
Radstock, C. .. 62 B1
Rae 70 B8
Rae Bareli ... 40 D3
Rae Isthmus . 68 B2
Raetihi 64 C6
Rafaela 94 C4
Rafai 56 D4
Rafhā 47 E5
Rafsanjān ... 44 D4
Ragachow ... 17 B10
Ragama 43 R11
Raglan 64 B6
Ragusa 21 F5
Raha 39 E2
Rahad al Bardī 53 F3
Rahaeng = Tak 36 A1
Rahimyar Khan 42 E7
Raichur 43 L10
Raigarh 40 G4
Railton 62 D4
Rainier, Mt. .. 80 B3
Raipur 40 G3
Ra'is 47 G4
Raj Nandgaon . 40 G3
Raja, Ujung .. 37 D1
Raja Ampat,
 Kepulauan .. 39 E3
Rajahmundry .. 40 J3
Rajang → 37 D4
Rajapalaiyam .. 43 Q10
Rajasthan □ .. 42 F8
Rajasthan Canal 42 F8
Rajgarh 43 G10
Rajkot 43 H7
Rajpipla 43 J8
Rajshahi 41 E7
Rakaia 65 E5
Rakaia → 65 E5
Rakan, Ra's .. 44 E2
Rakaposhi ... 42 A9
Rakata, Pulau . 37 F3
Rakhiv 17 D7
Raleigh 75 B8
Ram Hd. 63 C4
Ramanathapuram
 .... 43 Q11
Ramechhap ... 40 D6
Ramelau 39 F3
Ramgarh, Bihar,
 India 40 F5
Ramgarh, Raj.,
 India 42 F7
Rāmhormoz .. 47 E7
Ramnad =
 Ramanathapuram
 .... 43 Q11
Rampur 42 E11
Rampur Hat .. 40 E6
Ramree I. =
 Ramree Kyun 41 H9
Ramree Kyun . 41 H9
Ramtek 43 J11
Ranaghat 41 F7
Ranau 36 C5
Rancagua 94 C2
Ranchi 40 F5

Randers 9 G10
Rangaunu B. .. 64 A5
Rangia 41 D8
Rangiora 65 E5
Rangitaiki → . 64 B7
Rangitata → . 65 E4
Rangon → ... 41 J11
Rangoon 41 J11
Rangpur 41 E7
Ranibennur .. 43 M9
Raniganj 40 F6
Raniwara 43 G8
Rankin Inlet ... 70 B10
Rankins Springs 63 B4
Ranong 36 C1
Ransiki 39 E4
Rantau 37 E5
Rantauprapat .. 37 D1
Rantemario ... 39 E1
Rapa 65 M16
Rapallo 20 B2
Rāpch 45 E4
Rapid City ... 76 C3
Rarotonga ... 65 M14
Ra's al Khaymah 44 E4
Ra's al-Unuf .. 52 B2
Ras Bânâs ... 52 D6
Ras Dashen .. 57 B7
Râs Timirist .. 55 E1
Rasa, Punta .. 95 E4
Rashad 53 F5
Rashīd 52 B5
Rasht 46 C7
Rat Islands .. 71 C1
Ratangarh ... 42 E9
Rathenow 15 B7
Ratibor =
 Racibórz 16 C4
Ratlam 43 H9
Ratnagiri 43 L8
Raukumara Ra. 64 C7
Raurkela 40 F5
Rava-Ruska .. 17 C6
Rava Russkaya
 = Rava-Ruska 17 C6
Rāvar 44 D4
Ravenna 20 B4
Ravensburg ... 14 E5
Ravi → 42 D7
Rawalpindi ... 42 C8
Rawāndūz ... 46 C6
Rawene 64 A5
Rawlins 81 E10
Rawson 95 E3
Ray, C. 69 D5
Rayadurg 43 M10
Rayagada 40 H4
Raymond 71 D8
Raz, Pte. du .. 12 B1
Razdel'naya =
 Rozdilna ... 17 E10
Razelm, Lacul . 22 B7
Razgrad 22 C6
Ré, I. de 12 C3
Reading, U.K. . 11 F6
Reading, U.S.A. 73 D8
Realicó 94 D4
Rebi 39 F4
Rebiana 52 D3
Rebun-Tō ... 32 E12
Rechytsa 17 B10
Recife 92 D7
Reconquista .. 94 B5
Recreo 94 B3
Red →, La.,
 U.S.A. 79 D8
Red →, N. Dak.,
 U.S.A. 76 A6
Red Cliffs 62 B3

Red Deer 71 C8
Red Sea 48 C2
Red Tower Pass = Turnu Roşu, P. 17 F7
Redcar 11 D6
Redcliffe 63 A5
Redding 80 E2
Redditch 11 E6
Redon 12 C2
Redondela 18 A1
Redwood City . 82 B1
Ree, L. 11 E3
Reefton 65 E4
Regensburg . . . 15 D7
Réggio di Calábria 21 E5
Réggio nell'Emília . . 20 B3
Reghin 17 E7
Regina 71 C9
Rehoboth 58 C3
Rehovot 46 E3
Rei-Bouba 53 G1
Reichenbach . . 15 C7
Reidsville 75 A8
Reigate 11 F6
Reims 13 B6
Reina Adelaida, Arch. 95 G2
Reindeer L. . . . 71 C9
Reinga, C. 64 A5
Reinosa 18 A3
Reliance 70 B9
Remarkable, Mt. 62 B2
Remeshk 45 E4
Rendsburg 14 A5
Rengat 37 E2
Reni 17 F9
Renk 53 F5
Renmark 62 B3
Rennes 12 B3
Reno 80 F4
Reno ➝ 20 B4
Rentería 19 A5
Republican ➝ 76 F6
Repulse Bay . . 68 B2
Requena, *Peru* . 90 E4
Requena, *Spain* 19 C5
Resadiye = Datça 23 F6
Resht = Rasht . 46 C7
Resistencia . . . 94 B5
Reşiţa 17 F5
Resolution I., *Canada* 68 B4
Resolution I., *N.Z.* 65 F2
Réthímnon 23 G5
Réunion ■ 51 J9
Reus 19 B6
Reutlingen 14 D5
Reval = Tallinn 24 B1
Revelstoke 71 C8
Rewa 40 E3
Rewari 42 E10
Rey Malabo . . . 56 D1
Reykjavík 8 B2
Reynosa 84 B5
Rhein ➝ 14 C4
Rhein-Main-Donau-Kanal ➝ . . . 15 D6
Rheine 14 B4
Rheinland-Pfalz □ 14 C4
Rhin = Rhein ➝ . . . 14 C4
Rhine = Rhein ➝ . . . 14 C4
Rhineland-Palatinate □ = Rheinland-Pfalz □ 14 C4
Rhode Island □ 73 D10
Rhodes = Ródhos 23 F7
Rhodope Mts. = Rhodopi Planina 22 D5
Rhodopi Planina 22 D5
Rhön = Hohe Rhön 14 C5
Rhondda 11 F5
Rhône ➝ 13 E6
Rhum 10 C3
Riachão 92 D4
Riasi 42 C9
Riau □ 37 E2
Riau, Kepulauan 37 D2
Riau Arch. = Riau, Kepulauan . . 37 D2
Ribadeo 18 A2
Ribeirão Prêto . 93 G4
Riberalta 91 F5
Rîbniţa 17 E9
Riccarton 65 E5
Richland 80 B4
Richmond, *Australia* 63 B5
Richmond, *N.Z.* 65 D5
Richmond, *Calif., U.S.A.* 80 G2
Richmond, *Va., U.S.A.* 73 F7
Richmond Ra. . 63 A5
Ridder 29 D9
Ried 15 D7
Riesa 15 C7
Rieti 20 C4
Rig Rig 53 F1
Rīga 24 B1
Riga, G. of 24 B1
Rīgas Jūras Līcis = Riga, G. of 24 B1
Rīgestān □ 42 D4
Rigolet 68 C5
Riiser-Larsen-halvøya 96 A8
Rijeka 20 B5
Rimah, Wadi ar ➝ 47 F5
Rímini 20 B4
Rîmnicu Sărat . 17 F8
Rîmnicu Vîlcea 17 F7
Rimouski 69 D4
Rinca 39 F1
Rinconada 94 A3
Rinjani 37 F5
Rio Branco, *Brazil* 91 E5
Río Branco, *Uruguay* 94 C6
Río Cuarto 94 C4
Rio de Janeiro . 93 G5
Rio de Janeiro □ . . . 93 G5
Rio do Sul 94 B7
Río Gallegos . . 95 G3
Río Grande, *Argentina* . . . 95 G3
Rio Grande, *Brazil* 94 C6
Rio Grande ➝ 78
Rio Grande do Norte □ 92 D6
Rio Grande do Sul □ 94 B6
Rio Largo 93 D6
Río Mulatos . . . 91 G5
Río Muni = Mbini □ 56 D2
Rio Negro 94 B7
Rio Verde 93 F3
Ríobamba 90 D3
Ríohacha 90 A4
Ríosucio, *Caldas, Colombia* . . . 90 B3
Ríosucio, *Choco, Colombia* . . . 90 B3
Rishiri-Tō 32 E12
Riva del Garda 20 B3
Rivadavia 94 B2
Rivera 94 C5
Riversdale 58 E4
Riverside 82 D4
Riverton, *Australia* 62 B2
Riverton, *Canada* 71 C10
Riverton, *N.Z.* . 65 G2
Riviera di Levante 20 B2
Riviera di Ponente 20 B2
Rivière-du-Loup 69 D4
Rivne 17 C8
Rívoli 20 B1
Rivoli B. 62 C3
Riyadh = Ar Riyāḑ 47 F6
Rize 46 B5
Rizzuto, C. 21 E6
Roanne 13 C6
Roanoke 73 F6
Robbins I. 62 D4
Robertson 58 E3
Robertson I. . . . 96 A4
Robertsport . . . 55 G2
Robertstown . . 62 B2
Robinvale 62 B3
Roboré 91 G7
Robson, Mt. . . . 71 C8
Roca, C. da . . . 18 C1
Rocas, I. 92 C7
Rocha 94 C6
Rochefort 12 D3
Rochester, *Minn., U.S.A.* 77 C8
Rochester, *N.Y., U.S.A.* 73 C7
Rock Hill 75 B7
Rock Island . . . 77 E9
Rock Springs . . 81 E9
Rockefeller Plateau 96 C18
Rockford 77 D10
Rockhampton . 61 E9
Rocky Mount . . 75 B9
Rocky Mts. 70 C7
Rod 42 E3
Rodez 13 D5
Ródhos 23 F7
Rodney, C. 64 B6
Roes Welcome Sd. 68 B2
Rogachev = Ragachow . . 17 B10
Rogagua, L. . . . 91 F5
Rogatyn 17 D7
Rogoaguado, L. 91 F5
Rohri 42 F6
Rohtak 42 E10
Roi Et 36 A2
Rojas 94 C4
Rojo, C. 84 C5
Rokan ➝ . . . . . 37 D
Rolândia . . . . . . 94 A
Roma, *Australia* 63 A
Roma, *Italy* . . . 20 D
Roman . . . . 17 E
Romang . . . . . . 39 F
Romania ■ . . . 22 B
Romanovka = Basarabeasca 17 E
Romans-sur-Isère . . . . 13 D
Romblon . . . . . 38 B
Rome = Roma 20 D
Rome . . . . 74 B
Romorantin-Lanthenay . . 12 C
Roncador, Serra do . . . . 93 E
Ronda . . . . 18 D
Rondônia □ . . . 91 F
Rondonópolis . 93 F
Ronge, L. la . . . 71 C
Ronne Ice Shelf 96 B
Roodepoort . . . 59 D
Roorkee 42 E1
Roosevelt ➝ . 91 E
Roosevelt I. . . . 96 B1
Roquetas de Mar . . . . 19 D
Roraima □ . . . . 90 C
Roraima, Mt. . . 90 B
Rosa . . . . 57 F
Rosa, Monte . . 13 D
Rosario, *Argentina* . . . 94 C
Rosário, *Brazil* . 92 C
Rosario, *Mexico* 84 C
Rosario, *Paraguay* . . . 94 A
Rosario de la Frontera . . . . 94 B
Rosário do Sul 94 C
Rosas, G. de . . 19 A
Roscommon . . 11 E
Roseau, *Domin.* 87 C
Roseau, *U.S.A.* 77 A
Rosebery . . . . . 62 D
Roseburg . . . . . 80 D
Rosenheim . . . 15 E
Rosetown . . . . . 71 C
Rosetta = Rashîd . . . . . 52 B
Roseville . . . . . 80 F
Rosewood . . . . 63 A
Rosignano Maríttimo . . . 20 C
Rosignol . . . . . . 90 B
Roşiori-de-Vede 22 B
Roslavl . . . . 24 C
Roslyn . . . . 63 B
Ross, *Australia* 62 D
Ross, *N.Z.* . . . . 65 E
Ross I. 96 B1
Ross Ice Shelf . 96 C1
Ross Sea 96 B1
Rossano Cálabro 21 E
Rossland . . . . . 71 D
Rosslare . . . . . . 11 E
Rosso . . . . 55 E
Rossosh . . . . . . 24 C
Rosthern . . . . . 71 C
Rostock . . . . . . 15 A
Rostov, *Don, Russia* . . . . . . 25 D
Rostov, *Yarosl., Russia* . . . . . . 24 B
Roswell . . . . . . 78 C
Rotherham . . . . 11 E
Roto . . . . 63 B

Rotondo Mte. . 13 E8
Rotorua 64 C7
Rotorua, L. 64 C7
Rotterdam 14 C3
Rottweil 14 D5
Rotuma 64 L12
Roubaix 13 A5
Rouen 12 B4
Round Mt. 63 B5
Roussillon 13 E5
Rouyn 69 D3
Rovaniemi 8 E13
Rovereto 20 B3
Rovigo 20 B3
Rovinj 20 B4
Rovno = Rivne 17 C8
Rovuma → . . . 57 G8
Rowena 63 A4
Roxas 38 B2
Roxburgh 65 F3
Royal Leamington Spa 11 E6
Royan 12 D3
Rozdilna 17 E10
Rozhyshche . . . 17 C7
Rtishchevo 24 C5
Ruahine Ra. . . . 64 C7
Ruapehu 64 C6
Ruapuke I. 65 G3
Rub' al Khali . . 48 D4
Rubio 90 B4
Rubtsovsk 29 D9
Rudall 62 B2
Rudolf, Ostrov . 28 A6
Rufa'a 53 F5
Rufiji → 57 F7
Rufino 94 C4
Rufisque 55 F1
Rugby 11 E6
Rügen 15 A7
Ruhr → 14 C4
Rukwa L. 57 F6
Rum = Rhum . 10 C3
Rumāḩ 47 F6
Rumania = Romania ■ . . 22 B5
Rumbêk 53 G4
Rumia 16 A4
Rumoi 32 F12
Runanga 65 E4
Runaway, C. . . 64 B7
Rungwa 57 F6
Ruoqiang 34 C3
Rupa 41 D9
Rupat 37 D2
Rupert → 69 C3
Rupert House = Waskaganish 69 C3
Rurrenabaque . 91 F5
Rusape 59 B6
Ruschuk = Ruse 22 C5
Ruse 22 C5
Rushworth 63 C4
Russas 92 C6
Russellkonda . . 40 H5
Russkaya Polyana 29 D8
Rustavi 25 E6
Rustenburg . . . 59 D5
Ruteng 39 F2
Rutshuru 57 E5
Ruwenzori 57 D5
Ružomberok . . 16 D4
Rwanda ■ 57 E6
Ryazan 24 C4
Ryazhsk 24 C5
Rybache = Rybachye . . . 29 E9
Rybachye 29 E9
Rybinsk 24 B4
Rybinskoye Vdkhr. 24 B4
Rybnitsa = Rîbniţa 17 E9
Rylstone 63 B4
Rypin 16 B4
Ryūkyū Is. = Ryūkyū-rettō 35 D7
Ryūkyū-rettō . . 35 D7
Rzeszów 16 C5
Rzhev 24 B3

S

Sa Dec 36 B3
Sa'ādatābād . . 44 D3
Saale → 15 C6
Saalfeld 15 C6
Saar → 13 B7
Saarbrücken . . 14 D4
Saaremaa 24 B1
Šabac 22 B2
Sabadell 19 B7
Sabah □ 36 C5
Şabāḩ, Wadi → 47 G7
Sabalān, Kūhhā-ye 46 C6
Sábanalarga . . 90 A4
Sabang 36 C1
Sabará 93 F5
Saberania 39 E5
Sabhah 52 C1
Sabinas 84 B4
Sabinas Hidalgo 84 B4
Sablayan 38 B2
Sable, C., *Canada* 69 D4
Sable, C., *U.S.A.* 86 A3
Sable I. 69 D5
Sabrina Coast . 96 A12
Sabulubek 37 E1
Sabzevār 44 B4
Sabzvārān 44 D4
Săcele 17 F7
Sachsen □ 15 C7
Sachsen-Anhalt □ 15 C7
Sacramento . . . 80 F3
Sacramento → 80 F3
Sacramento Mts. 83 D10
Sadani 57 F7
Sadd el Aali . . . 52 D5
Sado 33 G11
Sadon 41 E11
Safi 54 B3
Safīd Kūh 42 B3
Saga, *Indonesia* 39 E4
Saga, *Japan* . . 32 C2
Sagala 55 F3
Sagar 43 M9
Sagil 34 A4
Saginaw 72 C4
Şagīr, Zāb aş → 46 D5
Saglouc = Salluit 68 B3
Sagua la Grande 86 B3
Saguenay → . 69 D3
Sagunto 19 C5
Sahagún 18 A3
Sahand, Kūh-e 46 C6
Sahara 54 D6
Saharan Atlas = Saharien, Atlas 54 B5
Saharanpur . . . 42 E10
Saharien, Atlas 54 B5
Sahiwal 42 D8
Sa'id Bundas . . 53 G3
Saïda 54 B5
Sa'īdābād 44 D3
Sa'īdīyeh 46 C7
Saidpur 41 E7
Saidu 42 B8
Saigon = Phanh Bho Ho Chi Minh 36 B3
Saijō 32 C3
Saikhoa Ghat . . 41 D10
Saiki 32 C2
Sailolof 39 E4
St. Andrews . . . 10 C5
St. Arnaud 62 C3
St-Augustin-Saguenay . . . 69 C5
St. Augustine . 75 E7
St. Austell 11 F4
St. Boniface . . . 71 D10
St.-Brieuc 12 B2
St. Catharines . 69 D3
St.-Chamond . . 13 D6
St. Christopher-Nevis ■ = St. Kitts & Nevis 87 C7
St. Cloud 77 C7
St. Croix 87 C7
St.-Denis 12 B5
St.-Dizier 13 B6
St. Elias, Mt. . . 70 B5
St.-Étienne 13 D6
St.-Flour 13 D5
St. Francis, C. . 58 E4
St. Gallen = Sankt Gallen 13 C8
St.-Gaudens . . . 12 E4
St. George 63 A4
St.-Georges, *Fr. Guiana* . . 92 B3
St. George's, *Grenada* 87 D7
St. George's Channel 11 F3
St. Georges Hd. 63 C5
St. Gotthard P. = San Gottardo, P. del 13 C8
St. Helena ■ . . 51 H3
St. Helena B. . . 58 E3
St. Helens 62 D4
St. Helier 11 G5
St-Hyacinthe . . 69 D3
St. John 69 D4
St. John's, *Antigua* 87 C7
St. John's, *Canada* 69 D5
St. Johns → . . 75 D7
St. Joseph 77 F7
St. Joseph, L. . 69 C1
St. Kilda, *N.Z.* . 65 F4
St. Kilda, *U.K.* . 10 C2
St. Kitts & Nevis 87 C7
St.-Laurent 92 A3
St. Lawrence → 69 D4
St. Lawrence, Gulf of 69 D4
St. Lawrence I. 71 B2
St. Leonard . . . 69 D4
St.-Lô 12 B3
St-Louis 55 E1
St. Louis 77 F9
St. Lucia ■ 87 D7
St. Lucia, L. . . . 59 D6
St. Maarten . . . 87 C7
St.-Malo 12 B2
St-Marc 87 C5
St. Mary Pk. . . . 62 B2
St. Marys 62 D4
St.-Mathieu, Pte. 12 B1
St. Matthews, I. = Zadetkyi Kyun 36 C1
St.-Nazaire 12 C2
St.-Omer 12 A5
St. Paul 77 C8
St. Peter Port . . 11 G5
St. Petersburg = Sankt-Peterburg . . . 24 B3
St. Petersburg . 75 F6
St.-Pierre et Miquelon □ . 69 D5
St.-Quentin . . . 13 B5
St. Thomas I. . . 87 C7
St.-Tropez 13 E7
St. Vincent, G. . 62 C2
St. Vincent & the Grenadines ■ 87 D7
Saintes 12 D3
Saintonge 12 D3
Saipan 64 H9
Sairang 41 F9
Sairecábur, Cerro 94 A3
Sajama 91 G5
Sajó 16 D5
Sakai 32 B4
Sakākah 47 E5
Sakakawea, L. . 76 B4
Sakarya = Adapazarı . . . 46 B2
Sakarya → . . . 25 E3
Sakata 33 G11
Sakhalin 31 D12
Sakon Nakhon . 36 A2
Sala 9 G11
Sala Consilina . 21 D5
Saladillo 94 D5
Salado →, *Buenos Aires, Argentina* . . . 94 D5
Salado →, *La Pampa, Argentina* . . . 94 D3
Salado →, *Santa Fe, Argentina* . . . 94 C4
Salaga 55 G4
Salālah 49 D5
Salamanca, *Chile* 94 C2
Salamanca, *Spain* 18 B3
Salamís 23 F4
Salar de Atacama 94 A3
Salar de Uyuni 91 H5
Salaverry 91 E3
Salawati 39 E4
Salayar 39 F2
Saldanha 58 E3
Sale, *Australia* . 63 C4
Salé, *Morocco* . 54 B3
Salekhard 28 C7
Salem, *India* . . 43 P11
Salem, *U.S.A.* . 80 C2
Salerno 21 D5
Salgótarján . . . 16 D4
Salihli 23 E7
Salihorsk 17 B8
Salima 59 A6

Salina, *Italy* ...	21	E5
Salina, *U.S.A.* ..	76	F6
Salina Cruz ...	85	D5
Salinas, *Brazil* .	93	F5
Salinas, *Ecuador*	90	D2
Salinas, *U.S.A.*	82	B2
Salinas Grandes	94	C3
Salinópolis	92	C4
Salisbury, *Australia*	62	B2
Salisbury, *U.K.*	11	F6
Salisbury, *U.S.A.*	75	B7
Salliq	68	B2
Salluit	68	B3
Salmäs	46	C6
Salmon → ...	80	C5
Salmon River Mts.	81	C6
Salon-de-Provence ...	13	E6
Salonica = Thessaloníki .	23	D4
Salonta	16	E5
Salsk	25	D5
Salso →	21	F4
Salt Creek	62	C2
Salt Lake City .	81	E8
Salta	94	A3
Saltillo	84	B4
Salto	94	C5
Salto →	20	C4
Salton Sea	82	D5
Saltpond	55	G4
Salûm	52	B4
Salûm, Khâlig el	52	B4
Salur	40	H4
Salvador	93	E6
Salwa	44	E2
Salween → ...	41	J11
Salyan	25	F6
Salzach → ...	15	D7
Salzburg	15	E7
Salzgitter	14	B6
Salzwedel	15	B6
Sama	28	C7
Sama de Langreo	18	A3
Samales Group	38	C2
Samangán □ ..	45	B7
Samar	38	B3
Samara	24	C7
Samarinda	37	E5
Samarkand = Samarqand .	29	F7
Samarqand ...	29	F7
Sāmarrā	46	D5
Sambalpur	40	G5
Sambar, Tanjung	37	E4
Sambas	37	D3
Sambava	59	G10
Sambhal	42	E11
Sambhar	42	F9
Sambiase	21	E6
Sambir	17	D6
Same	57	E7
Samokov	22	C4
Sámos	23	F6
Samothráki, *Évros, Greece*	23	D5
Samothráki, *Kérkira, Greece*	23	E2
Sampacho	94	C4
Sampit	37	E4
Sampit, Teluk .	37	E4
Samra	47	F5
Samsun	46	B4
Samui, Ko	36	C2
Samut Prakan .	36	B2
Samut Songkhram →	36	B2
San	55	F4
San →	16	C5
San Agustin, C.	38	C3
San Andrés, I. de	86	D3
San Andrés Tuxtla	85	D5
San Angelo ...	78	D3
San Antonio, *Chile*	94	C2
San Antonio, *Spain*	19	C6
San Antonio, *U.S.A.*	78	E4
San Antonio, C., *Argentina* ...	94	D5
San Antonio, C., *Cuba*	85	C8
San Antonio Oeste	95	E4
San Benedetto del Tronto ..	20	C4
San Bernardino	82	C4
San Bernardino Str.	38	B2
San Bernardo .	94	C2
San Bernardo, I. de	90	B3
San Borja	91	F5
San Carlos, *Argentina* ...	94	C3
San Carlos, *Chile*	94	D2
San Carlos, *Phil.*	38	B2
San Carlos, *Amazonas, Venezuela* ...	90	C5
San Carlos, *Cojedes, Venezuela* ...	90	B5
San Carlos de Bariloche ...	95	E2
San Carlos del Zulia	90	B4
San Cristóbal, *Argentina* ...	94	C4
San Cristóbal, *Mexico*	85	D6
San Cristóbal, *Venezuela* ...	90	B4
San Diego	82	D4
San Diego, C. .	95	G3
San Felipe, *Chile*	94	C2
San Felipe, *Venezuela* ...	90	A5
San Felíu de Guíxols	19	B7
San Fernando, *Chile*	94	C2
San Fernando, *La Union, Phil.*	38	A2
San Fernando, *Pampanga, Phil.*	38	A2
San Fernando, *Spain*	18	D2
San Fernando, *Trin. & Tob.* .	87	D7
San Fernando, *U.S.A.*	82	C3
San Fernando de Apure ..	90	B5
San Fernando de Atabapo .	90	C5
San Francisco, *Argentina* ...	94	C4
San Francisco, *U.S.A.*	82	B1
San Francisco de Macorís ..	87	C5
San Francisco del Monte de Oro	94	C3
San Gil	90	B4
San Gottardo, P. del	13	C8
San Ignacio, *Bolivia*	91	G6
San Ignacio, *Paraguay* ...	94	B5
San Ildefonso, C.	38	A2
San Javier, *Argentina* ...	94	C5
San Javier, *Bolivia*	91	G6
San Joaquin →	82	A2
San Jorge, B. de	84	A2
San Jorge, G. .	95	F3
San Jorge, G. de	19	B6
San José, *Bolivia*	91	G6
San José, *Costa Rica* ..	86	E3
San José, *Guatemala* ..	85	E6
San Jose, *Phil.*	38	A2
San Jose, *U.S.A.*	82	B2
San Jose de Buenovista ..	38	B2
San José de Jáchal	94	C3
San José de Mayo	94	C5
San José de Ocune	90	C4
San José del Guaviare	90	C4
San Juan, *Argentina* ...	94	C3
San Juan, *Phil.*	38	C3
San Juan, *Puerto Rico* .	87	C6
San Juan → ..	86	D3
San Juan, C. ..	56	D1
San Juan de los Morros	90	B5
San Juan Mts. .	83	B9
San Julián	95	F3
San Justo	94	C4
San Leandro ..	82	B1
San Lorenzo ..	90	C3
San Lorenzo, I.	91	F3
San Lorenzo, Mt.	95	F2
San Lucas	91	H5
San Lucas, C. .	84	C2
San Luis	94	C3
San Luis Obispo	82	C2
San Luis Potosí	84	C4
San Marino ...	20	C4
San Marino ■ .	20	C4
San Martín, L. .	95	F2
San Matías ...	91	G7
San Matías, G.	95	E4
San Miguel ..	85	E7
San Miguel →	91	F6
San Miguel de Tucumán ...	94	B3
San Narciso ...	38	A2
San Nicolás de los Arroyas .	94	C4
San-Pédro	55	H3
San Pedro de las Colonias .	84	B4
San Pedro de Lloc	91	E
San Pedro de Macorís	87	C
San Pedro del Paraná	94	B
San Pedro Sula	85	D
San Pieto	21	E
San Rafael, *Argentina* ...	94	C
San Rafael, *U.S.A.*	80	G
San Ramón de la Nueva Orán	94	A
San Remo	20	C
San Roque, *Argentina* ...	94	B
San Roque, *Spain*	18	D
San Rosendo ..	94	D
San Salvador, *Bahamas* ...	86	B
San Salvador, *El Salv.*	85	E
San Salvador de Jujuy	94	A
San Sebastián, *Argentina* ...	95	G
San Sebastián, *Spain*	19	A
San Severo ...	20	D
San Valentin, Mte.	95	F
San Vicente de la Barquera .	18	A
Sana'	49	D
Sana →	20	B
Sanaga → ...	56	D
Sanana	39	E
Sanandaj	46	D
Sanco Pt.	38	C
Sancti-Spíritus .	86	B
Sancy, Puy de .	13	D
Sandakan	36	C
Sandanski	22	D
Sanday	10	B
Sandgate	63	A
Sandía	91	F
Sandıklı	46	C
Sandoa	56	F
Sandomierz ...	16	C
Sandoway	41	H1
Sandusky	72	D
Sandwip Chan. .	41	F
Sandy C.	62	D
Sandy L.	71	C1
Sanford, *Fla., U.S.A.*	75	E
Sanford, *N.C., U.S.A.*	75	B
Sanford, Mt. ..	71	B
Sanga →	56	E
Sangamner ...	43	K
Sangar	31	C1
Sangasangadalam	37	E
Sangeang	39	F
Sangerhausen .	15	C
Sanggau	37	D
Sangihe, P. ...	39	D
Sangkapura ...	37	F
Sangli	43	L
Sangmélina ..	56	D
Sangre de Cristo Mts.	78	A
Sanirajak	68	B
Sankt Gallen ..	13	C
Sankt Moritz ..	13	C
Sankt-Peterburg	24	B

Sankt Pölten .. **15 D8**
Sankuru → .. **56 E4**
Sanliurfa **46 C4**
Sanlúcar de
  Barrameda .. **18 D2**
Sannicandro
  Gargánico .. **20 D5**
Sanok **17 D6**
Sanshui **35 D6**
Santa Ana,
  Bolivia **91 F5**
Santa Ana,
  Ecuador **90 D2**
Santa Ana,
  El Salv. **85 E7**
Santa Ana,
  U.S.A. **82 D4**
Santa Barbara . **82 C3**
Santa Catalina I. **82 D3**
Santa
  Catarina □ .. **94 B7**
Santa Clara ... **86 B4**
Santa Clotilde . **90 D4**
Santa Coloma
  de Gramanet **19 B7**
Santa Cruz,
  Argentina ... **95 G3**
Santa Cruz,
  Bolivia **91 G6**
Santa Cruz, *Phil.* **38 B2**
Santa Cruz,
  U.S.A. **82 B1**
Santa Cruz → . **95 G3**
Santa Cruz de
  Tenerife **54 C1**
Santa Cruz do
  Sul **94 B6**
Santa Cruz I. .. **64 L11**
Santa Elena ... **90 D2**
Santa Eugenia,
  Pta. **84 B1**
Santa Fe,
  Argentina ... **94 C4**
Santa Fe, *U.S.A.* **83 C10**
Santa Filomena **93 D4**
Santa Inés, I. .. **95 G2**
Santa Isabel =
  Rey Malabo . **56 D1**
Santa Isabel,
  Argentina ... **94 D3**
Santa Isabel,
  Brazil **93 E3**
Santa Lucia
  Range **82 C2**
Santa Maria,
  Brazil **94 B6**
Santa Maria,
  U.S.A. **82 C2**
Santa María → **84 A3**
Santa Maria da
  Vitória **93 E5**
Santa Maria di
  Leuca, C. ... **23 E2**
Santa Marta ... **90 A4**
Santa Marta,
  Sierra Nevada
  de **90 A4**
Santa Maura =
  Levkás **23 E3**
Santa Rosa,
  La Pampa,
  Argentina ... **94 D4**
Santa Rosa,
  San Luis,
  Argentina ... **94 .C3**
Santa Rosa,
  Bolivia **91 F5**
Santa Rosa,
  Brazil **94 B6**

Santa Rosa,
  U.S.A. **80 F2**
Santa Rosa de
  Copán **85 E7**
Santa Vitória do
  Palmar **94 C6**
Santai **35 C5**
Santana, Coxilha
  de **94 C5**
Santana do
  Livramento .. **94 C5**
Santander **18 A4**
Sant'Antíoco .. **21 E2**
Santarém, *Brazil* **92 C3**
Santarém,
  Portugal **18 C1**
Santiago, *Brazil* **94 B6**
Santiago, *Chile* **94 C2**
Santiago → .. **90 D3**
Santiago de
  Compostela . **18 A1**
Santiago de
  Cuba **86 C4**
Santiago de los
  Cabelleros .. **87 C5**
Santiago del
  Estero **94 B4**
Santo Amaro .. **93 E6**
Santo Ângelo . **94 B6**
Santo Antonio . **93 F2**
Santo Corazón **91 G7**
Santo Domingo **87 C6**
Santo Tomás .. **91 F4**
Santo Tomé .. **94 B5**
Santo Tomé de
  Guayana =
  Ciudad
  Guayana **90 B6**
Santoña **18 A4**
Santoríni =
  Thíra **23 F5**
Santos **94 A7**
Santos Dumont **94 A8**
Sanza Pombo . **56 F3**
São Anastácio . **94 A6**
São Bernado de
  Campo **93 G4**
São Borja **94 B5**
São Carlos **94 A7**
São Cristóvão . **93 E6**
São Domingos **93 E4**
São Francisco . **93 F5**
São
  Francisco → **93 E6**
São Francisco
  do Sul **94 B7**
São Gabriel ... **94 C6**
São João da
  Madeira **18 B1**
São João del
  Rei **93 G5**
São João do
  Araguaia **92 D4**
São João do
  Piauí **92 D5**
São José do Rio
  Prêto **94 A7**
São Leopoldo . **94 B6**
São Lourenço . **93 G4**
São
  Lourenço → **93 F2**
São Luís **92 C5**
São Marcos → **93 F4**
São Marcos, B.
  de **92 C5**
São Mateus ... **93 F6**
São Paulo **94 A7**
São Paulo □ .. **94 A7**
São Roque, C.
  de **92 D6**

São Sebastião, I.
  de **94 A7**
São Tomé &
  Principe ■ .. **51 F4**
São Vicente, C.
  de **18 D1**
Saône → **13 D6**
Saonek **39 E4**
Saparua **39 E3**
Sapele **55 G6**
Saposoa **91 E3**
Sapporo **32 F12**
Sapulpa **79 B5**
Saqqez **46 C6**
Sar-e Pol **45 B6**
Sar-e Pol □ ... **45 B6**
Sar Planina ... **22 C3**
Saráb **46 C6**
Sarada → **40 D3**
Saragossa =
  Zaragoza ... **19 B5**
Saraguro **90 D3**
Sarajevo **20 C7**
Saran, G. **37 E4**
Sarandí del Yi . **94 C5**
Sarangani B. .. **38 C3**
Sarangani Is. .. **38 C3**
Sarangarh **40 G4**
Saransk **24 C6**
Sarapul **29 D6**
Sarasota **75 F6**
Saratov **24 C6**
Saravane **36 A3**
Sarawak □ **37 D4**
Saray **22 D6**
Sarayköy **23 F7**
Sarbáz **45 E5**
Sarbisheh **45 C4**
Sarda → =
  Sarada → ... **40 D3**
Sardalas **54 C7**
Sardarshahr ... **42 E9**
Sardegna □ ... **21 D2**
Sardinia =
  Sardegna □ . **21 D2**
Sardis **23 E7**
Sargodha **42 C8**
Sarh **53 G2**
Sári **44 B3**
Sarigöl **23 E7**
Sarikamiş **46 B5**
Sarikei **37 D4**
Sark **11 G5**
Şarköy **23 D6**
Sarlat-la-Canéda **12 D4**
Sarmi **39 E5**
Sarmiento **95 F3**
Sarnia **69 D2**
Sarny **24 C2**
Sarolangun ... **37 E2**
Saronikós
  Kólpos **23 F4**
Sarre = Saar → **13 B7**
Sarreguemines **13 B7**
Sarro **55 F3**
Sarthe → **12 C3**
Sartynya **28 C7**
Sarvestän **44 D3**
Sary-Tash **29 F8**
Saryshagan ... **29 E8**
Sasabeneh **49 F3**
Sasaram **40 E5**
Sasebo **32 C1**
Saser **42 B10**
Saskatchewan □ **71 C9**
Saskatchewan →
  .... **71 C9**
Saskatoon **71 C9**
Saskylakh **30 B9**

Sasovo **24 C5**
Sassandra **55 H3**
Sassandra → . **55 H3**
Sássari **21 D2**
Sassnitz **15 A7**
Sassuolo **20 B3**
Sasyk, Ozero .. **17 F9**
Sata-Misaki ... **33 D2**
Satadougou ... **55 F2**
Satara **43 L8**
Satmala Hills .. **43 J9**
Satna **40 E3**
Sátoraljaújhely **16 D5**
Satpura Ra. ... **43 J10**
Satu Mare **17 E6**
Satui **37 E5**
Saturnina → .. **91 F7**
Saudi Arabia ■ **47 F6**
Sauerland **14 C4**
Sault Ste. Marie,
  Canada **69 D2**
Sault Ste. Marie,
  U.S.A. **72 A3**
Saumlaki **39 F4**
Saumur **12 C3**
Saunders C. ... **65 F4**
Sauri **55 F6**
Saurimo **56 F4**
Sava → **22 B3**
Savage I. =
  Niue **65 L14**
Savalou **55 G5**
Savanna la Mar **86 C4**
Savannah **75 C7**
Savannah → .. **75 C7**
Savannakhet .. **36 A2**
Savanur **43 M9**
Savé **55 G5**
Save → **59 C6**
Säveh **46 D7**
Savelugu **55 G4**
Savoie □ **13 D7**
Savona **20 B2**
Sawahlunto ... **37 E2**
Sawai **39 E3**
Sawai
  Madhopur .. **42 F10**
Sawara **32 B7**
Sawatch Mts. . **83 A9**
Sawmills **59 B5**
Sawu **39 F2**
Sawu Sea ... **39 F2**
Saxony, Lower
  =
  Niedersachsen □
  .... **14 B5**
Say **55 F5**
Sayán **91 F3**
Sayan,
  Zapadnyy ... **30 D7**
Saydá **46 D3**
Sayghän **45 C6**
Sayhut **49 D5**
Saynshand ... **35 B6**
Sazanit **23 D2**
Sázava → **16 D2**
Sazin **42 B8**
Scandicci **20 C3**
Scandinavia ... **8 F10**
Scarborough .. **11 D6**
Scebeli,
  Wabi → **49 G3**
Schaffhausen . **13 C8**
Schefferville .. **69 C4**
Schelde → ... **14 C3**
Schenectady .. **73 C9**
Schiermonnikoog
  .... **14 B4**
Schio **20 B3**

Schleswig

Schleswig 14 A5
Schleswig-
Holstein ☐ .. 14 A5
Schouten I. ... 62 D4
Schouten Is. =
Supiori 39 E5
Schwäbische
Alb 14 D5
Schwaner,
Pegunungan 37 E4
Schwarzwald .. 14 D5
Schwedt 15 B8
Schweinfurt ... 14 C6
Schwenningen
= Villingen-
Schwenningen 14 D5
Schwerin 15 B6
Schwyz 13 C8
Sciacca 21 F4
Scilla 21 E5
Scilly, Isles of . 11 G3
Scone 63 B5
Scotland ☐ ... 10 C4
Scott Glacier .. 96 A12
Scott Inlet 68 A3
Scottsbluff 76 E3
Scottsdale 62 D4
Scranton 73 D8
Scunthorpe ... 11 E6
Scusciuban ... 49 E5
Scutari =
Üsküdar 25 E2
Seaspray 63 C4
Seattle 80 B2
Sebastopol =
Sevastopol . 25 E3
Sebha =
Sabhah 52 C1
Şebinkarahisar 46 B4
Sebta = Ceuta . 18 E3
Sebuku 37 E5
Sebuku, Teluk . 37 D5
Secretary I. ... 65 F2
Secunderabad . 43 L11
Sedalia 77 F8
Sedan, Australia 62 B2
Sedan, France . 13 B6
Seddon 65 D6
Seddonville ... 65 D5
Sedhiou 55 F1
Sedova, Pik ... 28 B6
Seeheim 58 D3
Seferihisar 23 E6
Segamat 37 D2
Segesta 21 F4
Seget 39 E4
Ségou 55 F3
Segovia =
Coco → 86 D3
Segovia 18 B3
Segre → 19 B6
Séguéla 55 G3
Segura → 19 C5
Sehitwa 58 C4
Sehore 43 H10
Seine → 12 B4
Seistan 45 D5
Seistan,
Daryācheh-ye 45 D5
Sekayu 37 E2
Sekondi-
Takoradi 55 H4
Selaru 39 F4
Selçuk 23 F6
Sele → 21 D5
Selenga =
Selenge
Mörön → .. 35 A5
Selenge
Mörön → .. 35 A5

Seletan, Tg. ... 37 E4
Sélibabi 55 E2
Selîma, El
Wâhât el 52 D4
Selkirk 71 C10
Selkirk Mts. ... 71 C8
Selma 75 B8
Selpele 39 E4
Selu 39 F4
Selva 94 B4
Selvas 91 E5
Semani → ... 23 D2
Semarang 37 F4
Semey 29 D9
Semiozernoye . 29 D7
Semipalatinsk =
Semey 29 D9
Semirara Is. ... 38 B2
Semisopochnoi
I. 71 C1
Semitau 37 D4
Semiyarka 29 D8
Semiyarskoye =
Semiyarka .. 29 D8
Semmering P. . 15 E8
Semnān 44 C3
Semnān ☐ 44 C3
Semporna 38 D1
Semuda 37 E4
Sena Madureira 91 E5
Senador
Pompeu 92 D6
Senaja 36 C5
Senanga 58 B4
Sendai,
Kagoshima,
Japan 32 D2
Sendai, Miyagi,
Japan 33 G12
Senegal ■ 55 F2
Senegal → 55 E1
Senge Khambab
= Indus → . 43 G5
Sengkang 39 E2
Senhor-do-
Bonfim 93 E5
Senigállia 20 C4
Senj 20 B5
Senja 8 E11
Senlis 13 B5
Senmonorom . 36 B3
Sennār 53 F5
Senneterre ... 69 D3
Sens 13 B5
Senta 22 B3
Sentani 39 E6
Seo de Urgel .. 19 A6
Seoul = Sŏul .. 35 C7
Sepīdān 44 D3
Sept-Îles 69 C4
Sequoia
National Park 82 B3
Seram 39 E3
Seram Laut,
Kepulauan . 39 E4
Seram Sea 39 E3
Serasan 37 D3
Serbia ☐ 22 C3
Serdobsk 24 C5
Seremban 37 D2
Serenje 59 A6
Sereth =
Siret → 17 F9
Sergino 28 C7
Sergipe ☐ 93 E6
Sergiyev Posad 24 B4
Seria 36 D4
Serian 37 D4
Seribu,
Kepulauan .. 37 F3

Sérifos 23 F5
Sermata 39 F3
Serny Zavod .. 29 F6
Serov 28 D7
Serowe 59 C5
Serpukhov 24 C4
Sérrai 22 D4
Serrezuela 94 C3
Serrinha 93 E6
Sertânia 92 D6
Serua 39 F4
Serui 39 E5
Serule 59 C5
Sesepe 39 E3
Sesfontein 58 B2
Sesheke 58 B4
Sète 13 E5
Sete Lagôas .. 93 F5
Sétif 54 A6
Seto 32 B5
Settat 54 B3
Setté-Cama ... 56 E1
Setúbal 18 C1
Setúbal, B. de . 18 C1
Seulimeum ... 36 C1
Sevan, Ozero =
Sevana Lich . 25 E6
Sevana Lich .. 25 E6
Sevastopol 25 E3
Severn → ,
Canada 69 C2
Severn → , U.K. 11 F5
Severnaya
Zemlya 30 B7
Severnyye Uvaly 24 B6
Severo-
Yeniseyskiy . 30 C7
Severodvinsk .. 28 C4
Sevilla 18 D2
Seville = Sevilla 18 D2
Sevlievo 22 C5
Seward 71 B5
Seward Pen. .. 71 B3
Sewer 39 F4
Seychelles ■ .. 26 K9
Seymour 63 C4
Sfax 52 B1
Sfîntu Gheorghe 17 F7
Shaanxi ☐ ... 35 C5
Shaba ☐ 57 F4
Shabunda 57 E5
Shache 34 C2
Shackleton Ice
Shelf 96 A11
Shackleton Inlet 96 C15
Shadrinsk 29 D7
Shāhābād 44 B4
Shahdād 44 D4
Shahdād,
Namakzār-e . 44 D4
Shahdadkot ... 42 F5
Shahgarh 42 F6
Shaḥḥāt 52 B3
Shahjahanpur . 42 F11
Shahr Kord ... 44 C2
Shahrig 42 D5
Shaikhabad ... 42 B6
Shajapur 43 H10
Shakhty 25 D5
Shakhunya ... 24 B6
Shaki 55 G5
Shala, L. 53 G6
Shalqar 29 E6
Sham, J. ash .. 44 F4
Shamil 44 E4
Shammar, Jabal 47 F5
Shamo = Gobi 35 B6
Shamo, L. 53 G6
Shamva 59 B6

Shan ☐ 41 G1
Shandong ☐ .. 35 C
Shanghai ..... 35 C
Shangqiu ..... 35 C
Shangrao ..... 35 D
Shangshui .... 35 C
Shannon ..... 64 D
Shannon → .. 11 E
Shansi =
Shanxi ☐ ... 35 C
Shantou ..... 35 D
Shantung =
Shandong ☐ 35 C
Shanxi ☐ .... 35 C
Shaoguan .... 35 D
Shaowu ...... 35 D
Shaoxing ..... 35 C
Shaoyang .... 35 D
Shaqra',
Si. Arabia ... 47 F
Shaqrā', Yemen 49 E
Sharjah = Ash
Shāriqah ... 44 E
Sharon .... 72 D
Sharya .... 24 B
Shashi,
Botswana ... 59 C
Shashi, China . 35 C
Shasta, Mt. .. 80 E
Shatt al'Arab → 47 E
Shaunavon ... 71 D
Shawan ...... 34 B
Shawinigan .. 69 D
Shcherbakov =
Rybinsk ..... 24 B
Shchuchinsk .. 29 D
Shebele =
Scebeli,
Wabi → .... 49 G
Sheboygan ... 72 C
Sheffield ..... 11 E
Shekhupura .. 42 D
Shelburne .... 69 D
Shelby .... 75 B
Shelbyville ... 74 B
Shellharbour .. 63 B
Shenandoah → 73 E
Shendam ..... 55 G
Shendî .... 53 E
Shensi =
Shaanxi ☐ .. 35 C
Shenyang .... 35 B
Sheopur Kalan 42 G1
Shepetivka ... 17 C
Shepetovka =
Shepetivka .. 17 C
Shepparton .. 63 C
Sherbro I. .... 55 G
Sherbrooke ... 69 D
Sheridan 81 C1
Sherman ..... 79 C
Sherridon .... 71 C
Shetland Is. ... 10 A
Shibām .... 49 D
Shigaib ...... 53 E
Shihchiachuangi
=
Shijiazhuang 35 C
Shijiazhuang .. 35 C
Shikarpur .... 42 F
Shikoku ...... 32 C
Shikoku ☐ ... 33 H1
Shikoku-Sanchi 32 C
Shilabo ...... 49 F
Shiliguri ..... 40 D
Shillong ..... 41 E
Shilong ...... 35 D
Shimada ..... 32 B
Shimizu ...... 32 B

himoga 43 N9
himonoseki 32 C2
hinano → 32 A6
hīndand 42 C3
hingū 32 C4
hinyanga 57 E6
hipehenski Prokhod 22 C5
hipki La 42 D11
hīr Kūh 44 D3
hirane-San 32 A6
hīrāz 44 D3
hire → 59 B7
hiretoko-Misaki 32 F13
hiriya-Zaki 32 F12
hīrvān 44 B4
hirwa, L. = Chilwa, L. 59 B7
hivpuri 43 G10
hizuoka 32 B6
hklov = Shklow 17 A10
hklow 17 A10
hkoder = Shkodra 22 C2
hkodra 22 C2
hkumbini → 23 D2
hmidta, O. 30 A7
holapur = Solapur 43 L9
hoshone Mts. 80 F5
hoshong 59 C5
hreveport 79 C7
hrewsbury 11 E5
hrirampur 40 F7
hu 29 E8
huangyashan 35 B8
hule 34 C2
humagin Is. 71 C4
hungnak 71 B4
hūr → 44 D3
hurugwi 59 B5
hūsf 45 D5
hūshtar 47 D7
hwebo 41 F10
hwegu 41 E11
hweli → 41 F11
hymkent 29 E7
hyok 42 B11
hyok → 42 B9
Kiang = Xi Jiang → 35 D6
-ngan = Xi'an 35 C5
Racha 36 B2
ah 47 G6
ahan Range 42 F4
aksriindrapura 37 D2
alkot 42 C9
antan, P. 37 D3
äreh 45 D5
argao 38 C3
asi 38 C2
au 39 D3
'auliai 24 B1
benik 20 C5
berut 37 E1
bi 42 E5
bil 39 E6
biti 56 E2
biu 17 F7
bolga 37 D1
bsagar 41 D10
bu 37 D4
buco 38 C2
buguey B. 38 C2
but 56 C3
butu 38 D1
butu Passage 38 D1
buyan 38 B2
Sibuyan Sea 38 B2
Sichuan □ 34 C5
Sicilia 21 F5
Sicily = Sicilia 21 F5
Sicuani 91 F4
Siddipet 43 K11
Sidéradougou 55 F4
Sîdi Barrâni 52 B4
Sidi-bel-Abbès 54 A4
Sidley, Mt. 96 B18
Sidon = Saydā 46 D3
Sidra, G. of = Surt, Khalīj 52 B2
Siedlce 17 B6
Sieg → 14 C4
Siegen 14 C5
Siem Reap 36 B2
Siena 20 C3
Sieradz 16 C4
Sierra Colorada 95 E3
Sierra Gorda 94 A3
Sierra Leone ■ 55 G2
Sífnos 23 F5
Sighetu-Marmatiei 17 E6
Sighişoara 17 E7
Sigli 36 C1
Sigsig 90 D3
Sigüenza 19 B4
Siguiri 55 F3
Sihanoukville = Kompong Som 36 B2
Siirt 46 C5
Sikar 42 F9
Sikasso 55 F3
Sikhote Alin, Khrebet 31 E11
Sikhote Alin Ra. = Sikhote Alin, Khrebet 31 E11
Síkinos 23 F5
Sikkim □ 40 D7
Sil → 18 A2
Silchar 41 E9
Silesia = Śląsk 16 C3
Silgarhi Doti 40 C3
Silghat 41 D9
Silifke 46 C3
Siliguri = Shiliguri 40 D7
Siling Co 34 C3
Silistra 22 B6
Silivri 22 D7
Sillajhuay, Cordillera 91 G5
Silva Porto = Kuito 58 A3
Simanggang 37 D4
Simav 23 E7
Simbirsk 24 C6
Simeria 17 F6
Simeulue 37 D1
Simferopol 25 E3
Sími 23 F6
Simikot 40 C3
Simla 42 D10
Simplon P. 13 C8
Simpson Desert 60 F6
Simunjan 37 D4
Sinabang 37 D1
Sinadogo 49 F4
Sinai = Es Sînâ' 52 C5
Sinai, Mt. = Mûsa, G. 47 E3
Sinaloa de Levya 84 B3
Sīnāwan 54 B7
Sincelejo 90 B3
Sincorá, Serra do 93 E5
Sind □ 42 F6
Sind Sagar Doab 42 D7
Sindangan 38 C2
Sines 18 D1
Sines, C. de 18 D1
Singa 53 F5
Singapore ■ 37 D2
Singaraja 37 F5
Singida 57 E6
Singitikós Kólpos 23 D5
Singkaling Hkamti 41 E10
Singkawang 37 D3
Singleton 63 B5
Singora = Songkhla 36 C2
Sinjai 39 F2
Sinjār 46 C5
Sinkat 53 E6
Sinkiang Uighur = Xinjiang Uygur Zizhiqu □ 34 B3
Sinni → 21 D6
Sinnuris 52 C5
Sinop 46 B3
Sintang 37 D4
Sintra 18 C1
Sinŭiju 35 B7
Siocon 38 C2
Siófok 16 E4
Sioma 58 B4
Sion 13 C7
Sioux City 77 D6
Sioux Falls 76 D6
Sioux Lookout 71 C10
Siping 35 B7
Sipura 37 E1
Siquijor 38 C2
Siracusa 21 F5
Sirajganj 41 E7
Sirdaryo = Syrdarya → 29 E7
Siret → 17 F9
Sirohi 43 G8
Sironj 43 G10
Síros 23 F5
Sirsa 42 E9
Sisak 20 B6
Sisaket 36 A2
Sisophon 36 B2
Sīstān va Balūchestān □ 45 E5
Sitapur 40 D3
Sitges 19 B6
Sitía 23 G6
Sitka 71 C6
Sittang Myit → 41 J11
Sittwe 41 G9
Siuri 40 F6
Sīvand 44 D3
Sivas 46 C4
Siverek 46 C4
Sivrihisar 46 C2
Sîwa 52 C4
Siwalik Range 40 D4
Siwan 40 D5
Sjælland 9 G10
Sjumen = Šumen 22 C6
Skadarsko Jezero 22 C2
Skagerrak 9 G9
Skagway 71 C6
Skala-Podilska 17 D8
Skala Podolskaya = Skala-Podilska 17 D8
Skalat 17 D7
Skardu 42 B9
Skarzysko-Kamienna 16 C5
Skeena → 70 C6
Skegness 11 E7
Skeldon 90 B7
Skellefte älv → 8 F12
Skellefteå 8 F12
Skíathos 23 E4
Skien 9 G9
Skierniewice 16 C5
Skikda 54 A6
Skipton 62 C3
Skíros 23 E5
Skole 17 D6
Skópelos 23 E4
Skopje 22 C3
Skvyra 17 D9
Skye 10 C3
Skyros = Skíros 23 E5
Slamet 37 F3
Śląsk 16 C3
Slatina 22 B5
Slave → 70 B8
Slavgorod 29 D8
Slavonski Brod 20 B7
Slavuta 17 C8
Slavyansk = Slovyansk 25 D4
Slawharad 17 B10
Sleaford B. 62 B2
Sleeper Is. 68 C2
Sligeach = Sligo 11 D2
Sligo 11 D2
Sliven 22 C6
Slobodskoy 24 B7
Slobozia 22 B6
Slonim 17 B7
Slough 11 F6
Slovak Rep. ■ 16 D5
Slovakia = Slovak Rep. ■ 16 D5
Slovakian Ore Mts. = Slovenské Rudohorie 16 D4
Slovenia ■ 20 B5
Slovenija = Slovenia ■ 20 B5
Slovenská Republika = Slovak Rep. ■ 16 D5
Slovenské Rudohorie 16 D4
Slovyansk 25 D4
Sluch → 17 C8
Słupsk 16 A3
Slutsk 17 B8
Smara 54 B3
Smarhon 17 A8
Smederevo 22 B3
Smith Arm 70 B7
Smithton 62 D4
Smithtown 63 B5
Smoky Bay 62 B1
Smolensk 24 C3
Smolikas, Óros 23 D3
Smolyan 22 D5
Smorgon = Smarhon 17 A8
Smyrna = İzmir 23 E6
Snake → 80 B4
Snake I. 63 C4
Snake River Plain 81 D7

Sneek

Sneek 14 B3
Snĕžka 16 C2
Snøhetta 8 F9
Snowdon 11 E4
Snowdrift 70 B8
Snowtown 62 B2
Snowy –▸ 63 C4
Snowy Mts. ... 63 C4
Snyatyn 17 D7
Snyder 78 C3
Soalala 59 H9
Sobat, Nahr –▸ 53 G5
Sobral 92 C5
Soc Trang 36 C3
Soch'e =
  Shache 34 C2
Sochi 25 E4
Société, Is. de la 65 L15
Society Is. =
  Société, Is. de
  la 65 L15
Socompa,
  Portezuelo de 94 A3
Socorro 90 B4
Socotra 49 E5
Soda Plains ... 42 B11
Söderhamn ... 8 F11
Sodiri 53 F4
Sodo 53 G6
Sofia = Sofiya . 22 C4
Sofia –▸ 59 H9
Sofiya 22 C4
Sogamoso 90 B4
Sognefjorden . 8 F9
Sohâg 52 C5
Soissons 13 B5
Sokal 17 C7
Söke 23 F6
Sokhumi 25 E5
Sokodé 55 G5
Sokol 24 B5
Sokółka 17 B6
Sokolo 55 F3
Sokolów
  Podlaski 17 B6
Sokoto 55 F6
Solano 38 A2
Solapur 43 L9
Soledad 90 B6
Soligalich 24 B5
Soligorsk =
  Salihorsk ... 17 B8
Solikamsk 28 D6
Solimões =
  Amazonas –▸ 92 C3
Solingen 14 C4
Sóller 19 C7
Sologne 12 C4
Solok 37 E2
Solomon Is. ■ . 64 K10
Solomon Sea . 61 B9
Solon 35 B7
Solor 39 F2
Solothurn 13 C7
Šolta 20 C6
Solţānābād ... 44 B4
Solunska Glava 22 D3
Solwezi 59 A5
Soma 23 E6
Somali Rep. ■ . 49 F4
Somalia =
  Somali Rep. ■ 49 F4
Sombor 22 B2
Sombrerete ... 84 C4
Sombrero 87 C7
Somerset East . 59 E5
Somerset I. ... 70 A10
Someş –▸ 17 E6
Sommariva ... 63 A4

Somme –▸ ... 12 A4
Somosierra,
  Puerto de ... 18 B4
Somport, Puerto
  de 12 E3
Søndre
  Strømfjord .. 68 B5
Sóndrio 20 A2
Sonepur 40 G4
Song Cau 36 B3
Songea 57 G7
Songhua
  Jiang –▸ ... 35 B8
Songkhla 36 C2
Songpan 34 C5
Sonipat 42 E10
Sonmiani 42 G5
Sono –▸ 93 D4
Sonora –▸ 84 B2
Sonsonate 85 E7
Soochow =
  Suzhou 35 C7
Sopi 39 D3
Sopot 16 A4
Sopron 16 E3
Sør-Rondane . 96 B8
Sorata 91 G5
Sorel 69 D3
Sorgono 21 D2
Soria 19 B4
Sorkh, Kuh-e .. 44 C4
Soroca 17 D9
Sorocaba 94 A7
Soroki = Soroca 17 D9
Sorong 39 E4
Soroti 57 D6
Sørøya 8 D12
Sorrento 63 C3
Sorsogon 38 B2
Sosnowiec 16 C4
Souanké 56 D2
Soúdhas, Kólpos 23 G5
Sŏul 35 C7
Sound, The =
  Øresund 9 G10
Sources, Mt. aux 59 D5
Soure 92 C4
Souris 71 D9
Souris –▸ 71 D10
Sousa 92 D6
Sousel 92 C3
Sousse 52 A1
South Africa ■ 58 E4
South
  Australia □ .. 62 B2
South Bend ... 72 D2
South
  Carolina □ .. 75 C7
South China Sea 36 C4
South Dakota □ 76 C4
South East C. . 62 D4
South Horr ... 57 D7
South I. 65 E3
South
  Invercargill .. 65 G3
South Korea ■ . 35 C7
South Magnetic
  Pole 96 A13
South
  Nahanni –▸ . 70 B7
South Natuna Is.
  = Natuna
  Selatan,
  Kepulauan .. 37 D3
South Orkney Is. 96 A4
South Pagai, I.
  = Pagai
  Selatan, P. .. 37 E2
South Platte –▸ 76 E4

South Pole .... 96 C
South
  Ronaldsay .. 10 B5
South
  Saskatchewan –▸
  .... 71 C9
South Shetland
  Is. 96 A4
South Shields . 11 D6
South Taranaki
  Bight 64 C6
South Uist 10 C3
South West C. . 62 D4
Southampton . 11 F6
Southampton I. 68 B2
Southbridge .. 65 E5
Southend-on-
  Sea 11 F7
Southern Alps . 65 E4
Southern Indian
  L. 71 C10
Southern Ocean 96 A9
Southern
  Uplands 10 D5
Southport 63 A5
Southwest C. . 65 G2
Soutpansberg . 59 C5
Sovetsk,
  Kaliningd.,
  Russia 24 B1
Sovetsk, Kirov,
  Russia 24 B6
Sōya-Misaki .. 32 E12
Soyo 56 F2
Sozh –▸ 17 C10
Spain ■ 18 C4
Spalding 62 B2
Spanish Town . 86 C4
Sparta = Spárti 23 F4
Spartanburg .. 75 B7
Spárti 23 F4
Spartivento, C.,
  Calabria, Italy 21 F6
Spartivento, C.,
  Sard., Italy .. 21 E2
Spátha, Ákra .. 23 G4
Spence Bay ... 70 B10
Spencer, C. ... 62 C2
Spencer G. ... 62 B2
Spenser Mts. .. 65 E5
Spey –▸ 10 C5
Speyer 14 D5
Split 20 C6
Spokane 80 B5
Spoleto 20 C4
Sporyy Navolok,
  Mys 28 B7
Spratly I. 36 C4
Spree –▸ 15 B7
Springbok 58 D3
Springfield, N.Z. 65 E4
Springfield, Ill.,
  U.S.A. 77 F10
Springfield,
  Mass., U.S.A. 73 C9
Springfield, Mo.,
  U.S.A. 79 A7
Springfield,
  Ohio, U.S.A. . 72 E4
Springfield,
  Oreg., U.S.A. 80 C2
Springfontein . 59 E5
Springhill 69 D4
Springhurst .. 63 C4
Springs 59 D5
Squamish 71 D7
Srbija =
  Serbia □ 22 C3
Sre Umbell ... 36 B2

Srebrnica ..... 20 ▮
Sredinny Ra. =
  Sredinnyy
  Khrebet ..... 31 D
Sredinnyy
  Khrebet ..... 31 D
Srednevilyuysk 31 C
Śrem .... 16 ▮
Sremska
  Mitrovica ... 22 ▮
Sri Lanka ■ ... 43 R
Srikakulam .... 40 ▮
Srinagar ...... 42 ▮
Stade .... 14 ▮
Stadlandet .... 8 ▮
Stafford ...... 11 ▮
Stakhanov ... 25 ▮
Stalingrad =
  Volgograd .. 25 ▮
Staliniri =
  Tskhinvali ... 25 ▮
Stalino =
  Donetsk .... 25 ▮
Stalinogorsk =
  Novomoskovsk
  .... 24 ▮
Stalowa Wola . 17 ▮
Stamford ..... 73 ▮
Stanislav =
  Ivano-
  Frankivsk ... 17 ▮
Stanke Dimitrov 22 ▮
Stanley,
  Australia .... 62 ▮
Stanley, Canada 71 ▮
Stanley, Falk. Is. 95 ▮
Stanovoy
  Khrebet ..... 31 D
Stanovoy Ra. =
  Stanovoy
  Khrebet ..... 31 D
Stanthorpe ... 63 ▮
Stara Planina . 22 ▮
Stara Zagora .. 22 ▮
Starachowice . 16 ▮
Staraya Russa . 24 ▮
Starbuck I. .... 65 K
Stargard
  Szczeciński . 16 ▮
Staritsa ...... 24 ▮
Starogard
  Gdański .... 16 ▮
Starokonstantinov
  =
  Starokonstyantyniv
  .... 17 ▮
Starokonstyantyniv
  .... 17 ▮
Staryy
  Chartoriysk .. 17 ▮
Staryy Oskol .. 24 ▮
State College .. 73 ▮
Staten, I. =
  Estados, I. de
  Los .... 95 ▮
Statesville .... 75 ▮
Stavanger .... 9 ▮
Staveley ...... 65 ▮
Stavropol .... 25 ▮
Stawell ...... 62 ▮
Steenkool =
  Bintuni ..... 39 ▮
Stefanie L. =
  Chew Bahir . 53 ▮
Stefansson Bay 96 ▮
Steiermark □ .. 15 ▮
Steinkjer ..... 8 F▮
Stellenbosch .. 58 ▮
Stendal .... 15 ▮

Steornabhaigh
= Stornoway 10 B3
Stepanakert =
Xankändi .. 25 F6
Stephens Creek 62 B3
Stepnoi = Elista 25 D5
Stepnyak 29 D8
Sterlitamak ... 29 D6
Stettin =
Szczecin 16 B2
Stettiner Haff .. 15 B8
Stettler 71 C8
Steubenville .. 72 D5
Stevenage 11 F6
Stewart 70 B6
Stewart, I. 95 G2
Stewart I. 65 G2
Steyr 15 D8
Stillwater, N.Z. 65 E4
Stillwater,
U.S.A. 78 A5
Štip 22 D4
Stirling 10 C5
Stockerau 15 D9
Stockholm 9 G11
Stockport 11 E5
Stockton 82 B2
Stockton-on-
Tees 11 D6
Stoke on Trent 11 E5
Stokes Pt. 62 D3
Stolac 20 C6
Stolbovoy,
Ostrov 30 B11
Stolbtsy =
Stowbtsy ... 17 B8
Stolin 17 C8
Stonehaven ... 10 C5
Stonewall 71 C10
Stony Tunguska
=
Podkamennaya
Tunguska ➝ 30 C7
Stora Lulevatten 8 E11
Storavan 8 E11
Store Bælt 9 G10
Store Creek ... 63 B4
Storm B. 62 D4
Stormberge ... 59 E5
Stornoway ... 10 B3
Storozhinets =
Storozhynets 17 D7
Storozhynets .. 17 D7
Storsjön 8 F10
Storuman 8 E11
Stowbtsy 17 B8
Strahan 62 D4
Stralsund 15 A7
Strand 58 E3
Stranraer 11 D4
Strasbourg ... 13 B7
Stratford,
Canada 69 D2
Stratford, N.Z. . 64 C6
Strathalbyn ... 62 C2
Straubing 15 D7
Streaky B. 62 B1
Streaky Bay ... 62 B1
Strelka 30 D7
Strezhevoy 29 C8
Strimón ➝ ... 23 D4
Strimonikós
Kólpos 23 D5
Strómboli 21 E5
Stronsay 10 B5
Stroud Road .. 63 B5
Strumica 22 D4
Stryy 17 D6
Strzelecki Cr. ➝ 62 A2

Stuart Ra. 62 A1
Stung Treng .. 36 B3
Stutterheim ... 59 E5
Stuttgart 14 D5
Styria =
Steiermark □ 15 E8
Suakin 53 E6
Subansiri ➝ .. 41 D9
Subi 37 D3
Subotica 16 E4
Suceava 17 E8
Suchou =
Suzhou 35 C7
Süchow =
Xuzhou 35 C6
Sucre 91 G5
Sudair 47 F6
Sudan ■ 53 E4
Sudbury 69 D2
Sûdd 53 G4
Sudeten Mts. =
Sudety 16 C3
Sudety 16 C3
Sudirman,
Pegunungan 39 E5
Sueca 19 C5
Suez = El
Suweis 52 C5
Suez, G. of =
Suweis, Khalîg
el 52 C5
Sugluk = Salluit 68 B3
Suhār 44 E4
Suhbaatar 35 A5
Suhl 14 C6
Suihua 35 B7
Sukadana,
Kalimantan,
Indonesia ... 37 E3
Sukadana,
Sumatera,
Indonesia ... 37 F3
Sukaraja 37 E4
Sukarnapura =
Jayapura ... 39 E6
Sukhona ➝ .. 28 C5
Sukhumi =
Sokhumi 25 E5
Sukkur 42 F6
Sukkur Barrage 42 F6
Sula, Kepulauan 39 E3
Sulaiman Range 42 D6
Sulawesi □ ... 39 E2
Sulawesi Sea =
Celebes Sea . 39 D2
Sulima 53 G2
Sulina 17 F9
Sulitjelma 8 E11
Sullana 90 D2
Sultanpur 40 D4
Sulu Arch. 38 C2
Sulu Sea 38 C2
Suluq 52 B3
Sulzberger Ice
Shelf 96 B17
Sumalata 39 D2
Sumatera □ ... 37 D2
Sumatra =
Sumatera □ . 37 D2
Sumba 39 F1
Sumba, Selat .. 39 F1
Sumbawa 37 F5
Sumbawa Besar 37 F5
Sumbe 56 G2
Šumen 22 C6
Sumgait =
Sumqayıt ... 25 E6
Summerside .. 69 D4
Sumperk 16 D3

Sumqayıt 25 E6
Sumter 75 C7
Sumy 24 C3
Sunbury 63 C3
Sunda, Selat .. 37 F3
Sunda Str. =
Sunda, Selat 37 F3
Sundarbans,
The 41 G7
Sundargarh ... 40 F5
Sunderland ... 11 D6
Sundsvall 8 F11
Sungaigerong . 37 E2
Sungailiat 37 E3
Sungaipakning 37 D2
Sungaipenuh .. 37 E2
Sungaitiram ... 37 E5
Sungari =
Songhua
Jiang ➝ ... 35 B8
Sungguminasa 39 F1
Sunghua Chiang
= Songhua
Jiang ➝ ... 35 B8
Sungurlu 46 B3
Sunnyvale 82 B1
Suntar 30 C9
Supaul 40 D6
Superior 77 B8
Superior, L. ... 69 D2
Suphan Dağı .. 46 C5
Supiori 39 E5
Sūr, Lebanon .. 46 D3
Sūr, Oman 45 F4
Sura ➝ 24 B6
Surabaja =
Surabaya ... 37 F4
Surabaya 37 F4
Surakarta 37 F4
Surat, Australia 63 A4
Surat, India ... 43 J8
Surat Thani .. 36 C1
Suratgarh 42 E8
Surgut 29 C8
Suriapet 43 L11
Surigao 38 C3
Surinam ■ ... 92 B2
Suriname ■ =
Surinam ■ . 92 B2
Suriname ➝ .. 92 A2
Surt 52 B2
Surt, Khalīj ... 52 B2
Suruga-Wan .. 32 B6
Süsangerd 47 E7
Susanville 80 E3
Susquehanna ➝
.... 73 E7
Susques 94 A3
Susunu 39 E4
Susurluk 23 E7
Sutherland Falls 65 F2
Sutlej ➝ 42 E7
Suva 64 L12
Suva Planina .. 22 C4
Suvorov Is. =
Suwarrow Is. 65 L14
Suwałki 17 A6
Suwarrow Is. .. 65 L14
Suweis, Khalîg
el 52 C5
Suzdal 24 B5
Suzhou 35 C7
Suzu-Misaki ... 32 A5
Svealand □ ... 9 G10
Sverdlovsk =
Yekaterinburg 29 D7
Svetlogorsk =
Svyetlahorsk 17 B9
Svetozarevo ... 22 B3

Svishtov 22 C5
Svislach 17 B7
Svyetlahorsk . 17 B9
Swabian Alps =
Schwäbische
Alb 14 D5
Swakopmund . 58 C2
Swan Hill 62 C3
Swansea,
Australia 63 B5
Swansea, U.K. . 11 F5
Swatow =
Shantou 35 D6
Swaziland ■ .. 59 D6
Sweden ■ 9 G10
Sweetwater ... 78 C3
Swellendam .. 58 E4
Świdnica 16 C3
Świdnik 17 C6
Świebodzin ... 16 B2
Świecie 16 B4
Swift Current .. 71 C9
Swindon 11 F6
Swinemünde =
Świnoujście . 16 B2
Świnoujście ... 16 B2
Switzerland ■ . 13 C8
Sydney,
Australia 63 B5
Sydney, Canada 69 D4
Sydra, G. of =
Surt, Khalīj .. 52 B2
Syktyvkar 28 C6
Sylhet 41 E8
Sylt 14 A5
Sym 29 C9
Syracuse 73 C7
Syrdarya ➝ .. 29 E7
Syria ■ 46 D4
Syrian Desert =
Ash Shām,
Bādiyat 47 D4
Syzran 24 C6
Szczecin 16 B2
Szczecinek ... 16 B3
Szczytno 16 B5
Szechwan =
Sichuan □ .. 34 C5
Szeged 16 E5
Székesfehérvár 16 E4
Szekszárd 16 E4
Szentes 16 E5
Szolnok 16 E5
Szombathely .. 16 E3

T

Tabacal 94 A4
Tabaco 38 B2
Tābah 47 F5
Tabarka 54 A6
Ţabas,
Khorāsān, Iran 44 C4
Ţabas,
Khorāsān, Iran 45 C5
Tabatinga, Serra
da 93 E5
Tablas 38 B2
Table B. =
Tafelbaai ... 58 E3
Table Mt. 58 E3
Tábor 16 D2
Tabora 57 F6
Tabou 55 H3
Tabrīz 46 C6
Tabūk 47 E4

Tacheng 34 B3
Tacloban 38 B2
Tacna 91 G4
Tacoma 80 B2
Tacuarembó 94 C5
Tademaït, Plateau du 54 C5
Tadjoura 49 E3
Tadmor 65 D5
Tadoussac 69 D4
Tadzhikistan = Tajikistan ■ 29 F8
Taegu 35 C7
Taejŏn 35 C7
Tafalla 19 A5
Tafelbaai 58 E3
Tafermaar 39 F4
Taft 38 B3
Taga Dzong 41 D7
Taganrog 25 D4
Tagbilaran 38 C2
Tagish 70 B6
Tagish L. 70 B6
Tagliamento → 20 B4
Taguatinga 93 E5
Tagum 38 C3
Tagus = Tejo → 18 C1
Tahakopa 65 G3
Tahan, Gunong 36 D2
Tahat 54 D6
Tāherī 44 E3
Tahiti 65 L16
Tahoe, L. 80 F3
Tahoua 55 F6
Tahta 52 C5
Tahulandang 39 D3
Tahuna 39 D3
Taï 55 G3
Tai Hu 35 C7
Taibei 35 D7
T'aichung = Taizhong 35 D7
Taidong 35 D7
Taieri → 65 G4
Taihape 64 C6
Tailem Bend 62 C2
Taimyr Peninsula = Taymyr, Poluostrov 30 B7
Tain 10 C4
Tainan 35 D7
Taínaron, Ákra 23 F4
T'aipei = Taibei 35 D7
Taiping 36 D2
Taitao, Pen. de 95 F1
Taiwan ■ 35 D7
Taïyetos Óros 23 F4
Taiyuan 35 C6
Taizhong 35 D7
Ta'izz 49 E3
Tajikistan ■ 29 F8
Tajo = Tejo → 18 C1
Tājūrā 52 B1
Tak 36 A1
Takada 32 A6
Takaka 65 D5
Takamatsu 32 B4
Takaoka 32 A5
Takapuna 64 B6
Takasaki 32 A6
Takatsuki 32 B4
Takaungu 57 E7
Takayama 32 A5
Takefu 32 B5
Takengon 36 D1
Takeo 36 B2
Tākestān 46 D7
Takhār □ 45 B7
Takum 55 G6
Talara 90 D2
Talas 29 E8
Talaud, Kepulauan 38 D3
Talaud Is. = Talaud, Kepulauan 38 D3
Talavera de la Reina 18 C3
Talayan 38 C2
Talbragar → 63 B4
Talca 94 D2
Talcahuano 94 D2
Talcher 40 G5
Taldy Kurgan = Taldyqorghan 29 E8
Taldyqorghan 29 E8
Ţalesh, Kūhhā-ye 46 C7
Tali Post 53 G5
Talibon 38 B2
Taliwang 37 F5
Tall 'Afar 46 C5
Talladega 74 C4
Tallahassee 75 D5
Tallangatta 63 C4
Tallarook 63 C4
Tallinn 24 B1
Talodi 53 F5
Taltal 94 B2
Talwood 63 A4
Talyawalka Cr. → 62 B3
Tamale 55 G4
Tamanrasset 54 D6
Tamarang 63 B5
Tamaské 55 F6
Tambacounda 55 F2
Tambelan, Kepulauan 37 D3
Tambo de Mora 91 F3
Tambora 37 F5
Tambov 24 C5
Tamburâ 53 G4
Tâmchekket 55 E2
Tamega → 18 B1
Tamenglong 41 E9
Tamgak, Mts. 55 E6
Tamil Nadu □ 43 P10
Tammerfors = Tampere 8 F12
Tamo Abu, Pegunungan 37 D5
Tampa 75 F6
Tampere 8 F12
Tampico 84 C5
Tamrida = Qādib 49 E5
Tamsagbulag 35 B6
Tamu 41 E10
Tamworth 63 B5
Tana →, *Kenya* 57 E8
Tana →, *Norway* 8 D13
Tana, L. 53 F6
Tanahbala 37 E1
Tanahgrogot 37 E5
Tanahjampea 39 F2
Tanahmasa 37 E1
Tanahmerah 39 F6
Tanami Desert 60 D5
Tanana 71 B4
Tanana → 71 B4
Tananarive = Antananarivo 59 H9
Tánaro → 20 B2
Tandag 38 C3
Tandil 94 D5
Tandil, Sa. del 94 D5
Tando Adam 42 G6
Tandou L. 62 B3
Tane-ga-Shima 33 D2
Taneatua 64 C7
Tanen Tong Dan 41 J12
Tanezrouft 54 D5
Tanga 57 F7
Tanganyika, L. 57 F5
Tanger = Tangier 54 A3
Tanggula Shan 34 C4
Tangier 54 A3
Tangshan 35 C6
Tanimbar, Kepulauan 39 F4
Tanimbar Is. = Tanimbar, Kepulauan 39 F4
Tanjay 38 C2
Tanjore = Thanjavur 43 P11
Tanjung 37 E5
Tanjungbalai 37 D1
Tanjungbatu 37 D5
Tanjungkarang Telukbetung 37 F3
Tanjungpandan 37 E3
Tanjungpinang 37 D2
Tanjungredeb 37 D5
Tanjungselor 37 D5
Tanout 55 F6
Tanta 52 B5
Tantung = Dandong 35 B7
Tanunda 62 B2
Tanzania ■ 57 F6
Taolanaro 59 K9
Taoudenni 54 D4
Taourirt 54 B4
Tapa Shan = Daba Shan 35 C5
Tapah 37 D2
Tapajós → 92 C3
Tapaktuan 37 D1
Tapanui 65 F3
Tapauá → 91 E6
Tapeta 55 G3
Tapi → 43 J8
Tapirapecó, Serra 90 C6
Tapuaenuku, Mt. 65 D5
Tapul Group 38 C2
Taquari → 91 G7
Tara, *Australia* 63 A5
Tara, *Russia* 29 D8
Tara →, *Montenegro, Yug.* 22 C2
Tara →, *Russia* 29 D8
Tarabagatay, Khrebet 29 E9
Tarābulus, *Lebanon* 46 D3
Tarābulus, *Libya* 52 B1
Tarakan 37 D5
Taralga 63 B4
Taranaki □ 64 C6
Tarancón 19 B4
Taranga Hill 43 H8
Táranto 21 D6
Táranto, G. di 21 D6
Tarapacá 90 D5
Tararua Ra. 64 D6
Tarashcha 17 D10
Tarauacá 91 E4
Tarauacá → 91 E5
Tarawera 64 C7
Tarawera L. 64 C7
Tarazona 19 B5
Tarbela Dam 42 B8
Tarbes 12 E4
Tarcoola 62 B1
Tarcoon 63 B4
Taree 63 B5
Tarfaya 54 C2
Tarifa 18 D3
Tarija 94 A4
Tariku → 39 E5
Tarim Basin = Tarim Pendi 34 C3
Tarim He → 34 C3
Tarim Pendi 34 C3
Taritatu → 39 E5
Tarkhankut, Mys 25 D3
Tarko Sale 28 C8
Tarkwa 55 G4
Tarlac 38 A2
Tarma 91 F3
Tarn → 12 D4
Tarnobrzeg 16 C5
Tarnów 16 C5
Tarnowskie Góry 16 C4
Taroom 63 A4
Taroudannt 54 B3
Tarragona 19 B6
Tarrasa 19 B7
Tarso Emissi 52 D2
Tarsus 46 C3
Tartagal 94 A4
Tartu 24 B2
Tarţūs 46 D3
Tarutung 37 D1
Tasāwah 52 C1
Taschereau 69 D3
Tash-Kömür 29 E8
Tash-Kumyr = Tash-Kömür 29 E8
Tashauz = Dashhowuz 29 E6
Tashi Chho Dzong = Thimphu 41 D7
Tashkent = Toshkent 29 E7
Tashtagol 29 D9
Tasman B. 65 D5
Tasman Mts. 65 D5
Tasman Pen. 62 D4
Tasmania □ 62 D4
Tatabánya 16 E4
Tatar Republic □ = Tatarstan □ 29 D6
Tatarbunary 17 F9
Tatarsk 29 D8
Tatarstan □ 29 D6
Tateyama 32 B6
Tathra 63 C4
Tatra = Tatry 16 D4
Tatry 16 D4
Tatta 43 G5
Tatuī 94 A7
Tat'ung = Datong 35 B6
Tatvan 46 C5
Taubaté 94 A7
Tauern 15 E7
Taumarunui 64 C6
Taumaturgo 91 E4
Taungdwingyi 41 G10
Taunggyi 41 G11
Taungup 41 H10
Taungup Pass 41 H10
Taungup Taunggya 41 H9
Taunton 11 F5

Taunus 14 C5
Taupo 64 C7
Taupo, L. 64 C6
Tauranga 64 B7
Tauranga Harb. 64 B7
Taurianova ... 21 E6
Taurus Mts. =
  Toros Dağları 46 C3
Tavda 29 D7
Tavda → 29 D7
Taveta 57 E7
Tavira 18 D2
Tavoy 36 B1
Tawau 36 D5
Tawitawi 38 C2
Tay → 10 C5
Tayabamba .. 91 E3
Taylakova ... 29 D8
Taylakovy =
  Taylakova ... 29 D8
Taymä 47 F4
Taymyr, Oz. ... 30 B8
Taymyr,
  Poluostrov .. 30 B7
Taytay 38 B1
Taz → 28 C8
Taza 54 B4
Tazovskiy 28 C8
Tbilisi 25 E5
Tchad = Chad ■ 53 E2
Tchad, L. 53 F1
Tch'eng-tou =
  Chengdu 35 C5
Tchibanga ... 56 E2
Tch'ong-k'ing =
  Chongqing .. 35 D5
Tczew 16 A4
Te Anau, L. .. 65 F2
Te Aroha 64 B6
Te Awamutu .. 64 C6
Te Kuiti 64 C6
Te Puke 64 B7
Te Waewae B. . 65 G2
Tebakang 37 D4
Tébessa 54 A6
Tebicuary → . 94 B5
Tebingtinggi .. 37 D1
Tecuci 22 B6
Tedzhen =
  Tejen 29 F7
Tefé 90 D6
Tegal 37 F3
Tegina 55 F6
Tegucigalpa ... 85 E7
Tehachapi 82 C3
Tehrān 44 C2
Tehuantepec . 85 D5
Tehuantepec, G.
  de 85 D5
Tehuantepec,
  Istmo de 85 D6
Tejen 29 F7
Tejo → 18 C1
Tekapo, L. 65 E4
Tekeli 29 E8
Tekirdağ 22 D6
Tekkali 40 H5
Tel Aviv-Yafo . 46 D3
Tela 85 D7
Telanaipura =
  Jambi 37 E2
Telavi 25 E6
Telekhany =
  Tsyelyakhany 17 B7
Teles Pires → . 91 E7
Telford 11 E5
Télimélé 55 F2
Tellicherry 43 P9
Telsen 95 E3

Teluk Anson .. 37 D2
Teluk Betung =
  Tanjungkarang
  Telukbetung . 37 F3
Teluk Intan =
  Teluk Anson . 37 D2
Telukbutun ... 37 D3
Telukdalem ... 37 D1
Tema 55 G4
Temax 85 C7
Temerloh 37 D2
Temir 29 E6
Temirtau,
  Kazakstan ... 29 D8
Temirtau, Russia 29 D9
Temma 62 D3
Temora 63 B4
Tempe 83 D7
Temple 78 D5
Temuco 94 D2
Temuka 65 F4
Tenali 40 J3
Tenasserim ... 36 B1
Tenda, Col di .. 20 B1
Tendaho 49 E3
Tenerife 54 C1
Teng Xian 35 C6
Tengah □ 39 E2
Tengah
  Kepulauan .. 37 F5
Tengchong 34 D4
Tenggara □ ... 39 E2
Tenggarong ... 37 E5
Tengiz, Ozero . 29 D7
Tenkasi 43 Q10
Tenke 57 G5
Tenkodogo ... 55 F4
Tennessee □ .. 74 B4
Tennessee → . 72 F1
Tenom 36 C5
Tenryū-
  Gawa → ... 32 B5
Tenterfield ... 63 A5
Teófilo Otoni .. 93 F5
Tepa 39 F3
Tepic 84 C4
Teplice 16 C1
Ter → 19 A7
Téra 55 F5
Téramo 20 C4
Terang 62 C3
Terebovlya ... 17 D7
Terek → 25 E6
Teresina 92 D5
Terewah, L. ... 63 A4
Terhazza 54 D3
Teridgerie
  Cr. → 63 B4
Termez =
  Termiz 29 F7
Términi Imerese 21 F4
Termiz 29 F7
Térmoli 20 C5
Ternate 39 D3
Terni 20 C4
Ternopil 17 D7
Ternopol =
  Ternopil 17 D7
Terowie, N.S.W.,
  Australia 63 B4
Terowie,
  S. Austral.,
  Australia ... 62 B2
Terracina 20 D4
Terralba 21 E2
Terranova =
  Ólbia 20 D2
Terrassa =
  Tarrasa 19 B7

Terre Haute ... 72 E2
Terschelling ... 14 B3
Teruel 19 B5
Teryaweyna L. . 62 B3
Teshio-Gawa → 32 F12
Tesiyn Gol → . 34 A4
Teslin 70 B6
Tessalit 54 D5
Tessaoua 55 F6
Tetas, Pta. 94 A2
Tete 59 B6
Teterev → ... 17 C10
Teteven 22 C5
Tetiyev 17 D9
Tétouan 54 A3
Tetovo 22 C3
Teuco → 94 B4
Teun 39 F3
Teutoburger
  Wald 14 B5
Tévere → 20 D4
Tewantin 63 A5
Texarkana 79 C6
Texas □ 63 A5
Texas □ 78 D4
Texas City 79 E6
Texel 14 B3
Teyvareh 45 C6
Tezpur 41 D9
Thabana
  Ntlenyana ... 59 D5
Thabazimbi ... 59 C5
Thailand ■ ... 36 A2
Thailand, G. of 36 B2
Thakhek 36 A2
Thal 42 C7
Thala La 41 C11
Thallon 63 A4
Thames 64 B6
Thames → ... 11 F7
Thane 43 K8
Thanh Pho Ho
  Chi Minh =
  Phanh Bho Ho
  Chi Minh ... 36 B3
Thanjavur 43 P11
Thar Desert .. 42 F7
Tharad 43 G7
Thargomindah 63 A3
Tharrawaddy .. 41 J10
Thásos 23 D5
Thaton 41 J11
Thaungdut 41 E10
Thayetmyo ... 41 H10
Thazi 41 G11
The Alberga → 62 A2
The Coorong .. 62 C2
The Frome → . 62 A2
The Grampians 62 C3
The Great Divide
  = Great
  Dividing Ra. . 61 E8
The Hague = 's-
  Gravenhage . 14 B3
The
  Hamilton → 62 A2
The
  Macumba → 62 A2
The Neales → . 62 A2
The Pas 71 C9
The Rock 63 C4
The Salt L. 62 B3
The
  Stevenson → 62 A2
The
  Warburton → 62 A2
Thebes = Thívai 23 E4
Theebine 63 A5

Thermaïkós
  Kólpos 23 D4
Thermopylae P. 23 E4
Thessaloníki .. 23 D4
Thessaloniki,
  Gulf of =
  Thermaïkós
  Kólpos 23 D4
Thetford 11 E7
Thetford Mines 69 D3
Thevenard 62 B1
Thiel Mts. 96 C2
Thiers 13 D5
Thies 55 F1
Thika 57 E7
Thimphu 41 D7
Thionville 13 B7
Thíra 23 F5
Thistle I. 62 C2
Thívai 23 E4
Thomas, L. 62 A2
Thomasville,
  Ga., U.S.A. .. 75 D6
Thomasville,
  N.C., U.S.A. . 75 B7
Thompson ... 71 C10
Thomson's Falls
  = Nyahururu 57 D7
Thrace 22 D6
Three Hummock
  I. 62 D3
Three Points, C. 55 H4
Thun 13 C7
Thunder Bay .. 69 D2
Thung Song .. 36 C1
Thunkar 41 D8
Thüringer Wald 14 C6
Thurles 11 E3
Thurloo Downs 63 A3
Thurso 10 B5
Thurston I. ... 96 B2
Thylungra 63 A3
Tia 63 B5
Tian Shan 34 B3
Tianjin 35 C6
Tianshui 35 C5
Tiaret 54 A5
Tiassalé 55 G4
Tibati 53 G1
Tiber =
  Tévere → .. 20 D4
Tiberias, L. =
  Yam Kinneret 46 D3
Tibesti 52 D2
Tibet =
  Xizang □ ... 34 C3
Tibooburra ... 62 A3
Tiburón 84 B2
Tîchît 55 E3
Ticino → 20 B2
Tiddim 41 F9
Tidjikja 55 E2
Tidore 39 D3
Tiel 55 F1
Tierra de
  Campos 18 A3
Tierra del
  Fuego, I. Gr.
  de 95 G3
Tiétar → 18 C2
Tieyon 62 A1
Tiflis = Tbilisi . 25 E5
Tifu 39 E3
Tighina 17 E9
Tignish 69 D4
Tigre → 90 D4
Tigris = Dijlah,
  Nahr → 47 E6
Tigyaing 41 F11

Tîh, Gebel el .. 52 C5
Tijuana 84 A1
Tikamgarh ... 43 G11
Tikhoretsk 25 D5
Tikrīt 46 D5
Tiksi 30 B10
Tilamuta 39 D2
Tilburg 14 C3
Tillabéri 55 F5
Tílos 23 F6
Tilpa 63 B3
Tilsit = Sovetsk 24 B1
Timaru 65 F4
Timbedgha ... 55 E3
Timboon 62 C3
Timbuktu =
  Tombouctou 55 E4
Timimoun 54 C5
Timişoara 16 F5
Timmins 69 D2
Timok → 22 B4
Timon 92 D5
Timor 39 F2
Tinaca Pt. 38 C3
Tindouf 54 C3
Tingo Maria ... 91 E3
Tinjoub 54 C3
Tinnevelly =
  Tirunelveli .. 43 Q10
Tinogasta 94 B3
Tínos 23 F5
Tintinara 62 C3
Tioman, Pulau . 37 D2
Tipongpani ... 41 D10
Tipperary 11 E2
Tirān 44 C2
Tirana 22 D2
Tiranë = Tirana 22 D2
Tiraspol 17 E9
Tire 23 E6
Tirebolu 46 B4
Tiree 10 C3
Tîrgoviște 22 B5
Tîrgu-Jiu 17 F6
Tîrgu Mureş .. 17 E7
Tirich Mir 42 A7
Tîrnăveni 17 E7
Tírnavos 23 E4
Tirodi 43 J11
Tirol □ 14 E6
Tirso → 21 E2
Tiruchchirappalli 43 P11
Tirunelveli 43 Q10
Tirupati 43 N11
Tiruppur 43 P10
Tiruvannamalai 43 N11
Tisa → 22 B3
Tisdale 71 C9
Tisza = Tisa → 22 B3
Tit-Ary 30 B10
Titicaca, L. 91 G5
Titograd =
  Podgorica .. 22 C2
Titov Veles 22 D3
Titova-Mitrovica
  = Kosovska-
  Mitrovica ... 22 C3
Titovo Užice .. 22 C2
Titule 57 D5
Tivaouane 55 F1
Tívoli 20 D4
Tiwī 45 F4
Tizi-Ouzou ... 54 A5
Tiznit 54 C3
Tjirebon =
  Cirebon 37 F3
Tlaxcala 84 D5
Tlaxiaco 84 D5
Tlemcen 54 B4

Tmassah 52 C2
Toamasina 59 H9
Toay 94 D4
Toba 32 B5
Toba Kakar ... 42 D6
Tobago 87 D7
Tobelo 39 D3
Tobermory 10 C3
Toboali 37 E3
Tobol → 29 D7
Toboli 39 E2
Tobolsk 29 D7
Tobruk =
  Tubruq 52 B3
Tobyl =
  Tobol → ... 29 D7
Tocantinópolis 92 D4
Tocantins □ .. 93 E4
Tocantins → .. 92 C4
Tochigi 32 A6
Tocopilla 94 A2
Tocumwal 63 C4
Tocuyo → 90 A5
Todeli 39 E2
Todenyang ... 57 D7
Todos os
  Santos, B. de 93 E6
Togba 55 E2
Togian,
  Kepulauan . 39 E2
Togliatti 24 C6
Togo ■ 55 G5
Toinya 53 G4
Tojikiston =
  Tajikistan ■ . 29 F8
Tojo 39 E2
Tokala 39 E2
Tōkamachi ... 32 A6
Tokanui 65 G3
Tokar 53 E6
Tokarahi 65 F4
Tokat 46 B4
Tokelau Is. 65 K13
Tokmak 29 E8
Tokushima ... 32 B4
Tokuyama 32 B2
Tōkyō 32 B6
Tolaga Bay ... 64 C8
Tolbukhin =
  Dobrich 22 C6
Toledo, Spain . 18 C3
Toledo, U.S.A. . 72 D4
Toledo, Montes
  de 18 C3
Tolga 54 B6
Toliara 59 J8
Tolima 90 C3
Tolitoli 39 D2
Tolo 56 E3
Tolo, Teluk .. 39 E2
Toluca 84 D5
Tomakomai ... 32 F12
Tomar 18 C1
Tomaszów
  Mazowiecki . 16 C4
Tombé 53 G5
Tombouctou .. 55 E4
Tombua 58 B2
Tomelloso 18 C4
Tomingley ... 63 B4
Tomini 39 D2
Tomini, Teluk . 39 E2
Tomorit 23 D3
Tomsk 29 D9
Tonantins ... 90 D5
Tonawanda ... 73 C6
Tondano 39 D2
Tonekābon ... 44 B2
Tong Xian 35 C6

Tonga ■ 65 L13
Tonga Trench . 65 L13
Tongareva 65 K15
Tongchuan ... 35 C5
Tonghua 35 B7
Tongjiang 35 B8
Tongking, G. of
  = Tonkin, G.
  of 35 D5
Tongoy 94 C2
Tongren 35 D5
Tongsa Dzong . 41 D8
Tongue → ... 76 B2
Tonk 42 F9
Tonkin, G. of . 35 D5
Tonlé Sap 36 B2
Toompine 63 A3
Toora 63 C4
Toowoomba .. 63 A5
Topeka 77 F7
Topki 29 D9
Topol'čany ... 16 D4
Topolobampo . 84 B3
Torata 91 G4
Torbalı 23 E6
Torbat-e
  Heydārīyeh .. 44 C4
Torbat-e Jām .. 45 C5
Torbay 11 F5
Tordesillas ... 18 B3
Torgau 15 C7
Torino 20 B1
Torit 53 H5
Tormes → 18 B2
Torne älv → .. 8 E12
Torneå = Tornio 8 E12
Torneträsk ... 8 E11
Tornio 8 E12
Tornquist 94 D4
Toro, Cerro del 94 B3
Toroníios
  Kólpos 23 D4
Toronto,
  Australia 63 B5
Toronto, Canada 69 D3
Toropets 24 B3
Tororo 57 D6
Toros Dağları .. 46 C3
Tôrre de
  Moncorvo ... 18 B2
Torre del Greco 21 D5
Torrejón de
  Ardoz 18 B4
Torrelavega ... 18 A3
Torremolinos . 18 D3
Torrens, L. ... 62 B2
Torrente 19 C5
Torreón 84 B4
Torres 84 B2
Torres Vedras . 18 C1
Torrevieja 19 D5
Tortosa 19 B6
Tortosa, C. de . 19 B6
Torūd 44 C3
Toruń 16 B4
Tosa-Wan 32 C3
Toscana □ ... 20 C3
Toshkent 29 E7
Tostado 94 B4
Tosya 46 B3
Toteng 58 C4
Totma 24 A5
Totten Glacier . 96 A12
Tottenham ... 63 B4
Tottori 32 B4
Touba 55 G3
Toubkal, Djebel 54 B3
Tougan 55 F4
Touggourt 54 B6

Tougué 55 F2
Toul 13 B6
Toulepleu 55 G3
Toulon 13 E6
Toulouse 12 E4
Toummo 52 D1
Toungoo 41 H11
Touraine 12 C4
Tourane = Da
  Nang 36 A3
Tourcoing 13 A5
Touriñán, C. .. 18 A1
Tournai 14 C2
Tournon 13 D6
Tours 12 C4
Towamba 63 C4
Towang 41 D8
Townsville ... 61 D8
Toyama 32 A5
Toyohashi ... 32 B5
Toyonaka 32 B4
Toyooka 32 B4
Toyota 32 B5
Tozeur 54 B6
Trá Li = Tralee 11 E2
Trabzon 46 B4
Trafalgar, C. .. 18 D2
Trail 71 D8
Tralee 11 E2
Trancas 94 B3
Trang 36 C1
Trangan 39 F4
Trangie 63 B4
Trani 20 D6
Transantarctic
  Mts. 96 C3
Transilvania ... 17 F7
Transilvanian
  Alps =
  Carpaţii
  Meridionali .. 17 F7
Transylvania =
  Transilvania . 17 F7
Trápani 21 E4
Traralgon 63 C4
Trasimeno, L. . 20 C4
Traun 15 D8
Travemünde . 15 B6
Travers, Mt. .. 65 E5
Travnik 20 B6
Trébbia → ... 20 B2
Třebíč 16 D2
Trebinje 20 C7
Treinta y Tres . 94 C6
Trelew 95 E3
Tremp 19 A6
Trenčín 16 D4
Trenque
  Lauquen 94 D4
Trent → 11 E6
Trento 20 A3
Trenton 73 D8
Trepassey 69 D5
Tres Arroyos . 94 D4
Três Corações . 93 G4
Três Lagoas . 93 G3
Tres Montes, C. 95 F1
Tres Puentes . 94 B2
Tres Puntas, C. 95 F3
Três Rios 93 G5
Treviso 20 B4
Triabunna 62 D4
Trichinopoly =
  Tiruchchirappalli
  .... 43 P11
Trichur 43 P10
Trida 63 B4
Trier 14 D4
Trieste 20 B4

Triglav 20 A4
Tríkkala 23 E3
Trikora, Puncak 39 E5
Trinidad,
  Colombia . . . 90 B4
Trinidad, Cuba 86 B3
Trinidad,
  Uruguay 94 C5
Trinidad, U.S.A. 78 A1
Trinidad, I. 95 D4
Trinidad &
  Tobago ■ . . . 87 D7
Trinity ➤ 79 E6
Trinity B. 69 D5
Trinity Range . . 80 E4
Trinkitat 53 E6
Tripoli =
  Tarābulus,
  Lebanon 46 D3
Tripoli =
  Tarābulus,
  Libya 52 B1
Trípolis 23 F4
Tripura □ 41 F8
Trivandrum . . 43 Q10
Trnava 16 D3
Troglav 20 C6
Trois-Rivières . 69 D3
Troitsko
  Pechorsk . . . 28 C6
Trollhättan 9 G10
Tronador 95 E2
Trondheim 8 F10
Trondheimsfjorden
  . . . . 8 F10
Trout L. 70 B7
Trouville-sur-
  Mer 12 B4
Troy, Turkey . . 23 E6
Troy, Ala.,
  U.S.A. 74 D5
Troy, N.Y.,
  U.S.A. 73 C9
Troyes 13 B6
Trucial States =
  United Arab
  Emirates ■ . . 44 F3
Trujillo,
  Honduras . . . 85 D7
Trujillo, Peru . . 91 E3
Trujillo, Spain . 18 C3
Trujillo,
  Venezuela . . 90 B4
Truk 64 J10
Trundle 63 B4
Truro, Canada . 69 D4
Truro, U.K. . . . 11 F4
Truskavets 17 D6
Trutnov 16 C2
Tsaratanana . . 59 H9
Tsarevo =
  Michurin . . . 22 C6
Tsau 58 C4
Tselinograd =
  Aqmola 29 D8
Tsetserleg 34 B5
Tshabong 58 D4
Tshane 58 C4
Tshela 56 E2
Tshikapa 56 F4
Tshofa 57 F5
Tshwane 58 C4
Tsihombe 59 K9
Tsimlyansk Res.
  =
  Tsimlyanskoye
  Vdkhr. 25 D5
Tsimlyanskoye
  Vdkhr. 25 D5

Tsinan = Jinan 35 C6
Tsinghai =
  Qinghai □ . . 34 C4
Tsingtao =
  Qingdao 35 C7
Tskhinvali 25 E5
Tsna ➤ 24 C5
Tsu 32 B5
Tsuchiura 32 A7
Tsugaru-Kaikyō 32 F12
Tsumeb 58 B3
Tsumis 58 C3
Tsuruga 32 B5
Tsurugi-San . . . 32 C4
Tsuruoka 33 G11
Tsyelyakhany . 17 B7
Tual 39 F4
Tuamotu Arch.
  = Tuamotu Is. 65 L16
Tuamotu Is. . . . 65 L16
Tuamotu Ridge 65 M17
Tuao 38 A2
Tuapse 25 E4
Tuatapere 65 G2
Tubarão 94 B7
Tubau 37 D4
Tübingen 14 D5
Tubruq 52 B3
Tubuai Is. 65 M16
Tucacas 90 A5
Tucson 83 D7
Tucumcari 78 B2
Tucupita 90 B6
Tucuruí 92 C4
Tucuruí, Reprêsa
  de 92 C4
Tudela 19 A5
Tudmur 46 D4
Tuen 63 A4
Tuguegarao . . . 38 A2
Tukangbesi,
  Kepulauan . 39 F2
Tükrah 52 B3
Tuktoyaktuk . . 70 B6
Tukuyu 57 F6
Tula, Mexico . . 84 C5
Tula, Russia . . 24 C4
Tulak 45 C5
Tulancingo 84 C5
Tulare 82 B3
Tulcán 90 C3
Tulcea 17 F9
Tulchyn 17 D9
Tuli, Indonesia 39 E2
Tuli, Zimbabwe 59 C5
Tullamore,
  Australia . . . 63 B4
Tullamore,
  Ireland 11 E3
Tulle 12 D4
Tullibigeal 63 B4
Tulmaythah . . . 52 B3
Tulsa 79 A6
Tulua 90 C3
Tulungagung . . 37 F4
Tum 39 E4
Tumaco 90 C3
Tumatumari . . . 90 B7
Tumba, L. 56 E3
Tumbarumba . . 63 C4
Túmbes 90 D2
Tumby Bay . . . 62 B2
Tumeremo 90 B6
Tumkur 43 N10
Tump 42 F3
Tumpat 36 C2
Tumu 55 F4
Tumucumaque,
  Serra 92 B3

Tumut 63 C4
Tuncurry 63 B5
Tunduru 57 G7
Tundzha ➤ . . . 22 D6
Tunga Pass . . . 41 C10
Tungabhadra ➤
  . . . . 43 M11
Tungaru 53 F5
Tunguska,
  Nizhnyaya ➤ 30 C6
Tunis 54 A7
Tunisia ■ 54 B6
Tunja 90 B4
Tunuyán ➤ . . . 94 C3
Tunxi 35 D6
Tupelo 74 B3
Tupinambaranas 90 D7
Tupiza 94 A3
Tupungato,
  Cerro 94 C3
Túquerres 90 C3
Tura 30 C8
Turabah 47 E5
Tūrān 44 C4
Turayf 47 E4
Turda 17 E6
Turek 16 B4
Turfan = Turpan 34 B3
Turfan
  Depression =
  Turpan Hami 34 B3
Tŭrgovishte . . . 22 C6
Turgutlu 23 E6
Turhal 46 B4
Turia ➤ 19 C5
Turiaçu 92 C4
Turiaçu ➤ 92 C4
Turin = Torino 20 B1
Turkana, L. . . . 57 D7
Turkestan =
  Türkistan . . . 29 E7
Turkey ■ 46 C3
Türkistan 29 E7
Turkmenistan ■ 29 F6
Turks & Caicos
  Is. ■ 87 B5
Turku 9 F12
Turnagain, C. . . 64 D7
Turneffe Is. . . . 85 D7
Turnhout 14 C3
Tŭrnovo =
  Veliko
  Tŭrnovo 22 C5
Turnu Măgurele 22 C5
Turnu Roşu, P. 17 F7
Turpan 34 B3
Turpan Hami . . 34 B3
Turukhansk . . . 30 C6
Tuscaloosa . . . 74 C4
Tuscany =
  Toscana □ . . 20 C3
Tuticorin 43 Q11
Tutóia 92 C5
Tutong 36 D4
Tutrakan 22 B6
Tuttlingen 14 E5
Tutuala 39 F3
Tutuila 65 L13
Tuvalu ■ 64 K12
Tuxpan 84 C5
Tuxtla Gutiérrez 85 D6
Tuy 18 A1
Tuz Gölü 46 C3
Ţūz Khurmātū . 46 D6
Tuzla 20 B7
Tver 24 B4
Tweed Heads . 63 A5
Twillingate . . . 69 D5
Twin Falls 81 D6

Twofold B. 63 C4
Tyachiv 17 D6
Tychy 16 C4
Tyler 79 C6
Tyre = Sūr 46 D3
Tyrol = Tirol □ 14 E6
Tyrrell ➤ 62 C3
Tyrrell, L. 62 C3
Tyrrhenian Sea 21 E4
Tyumen 29 D7
Tzaneen 59 C6
Tzukong =
  Zigong 35 D5

U

U.S.A. = United
  States of
  America ■ . . 67 F10
Uarsciek 49 G4
Uato-Udo 39 F3
Uatumã ➤ . . . 90 D7
Uaupés 90 D5
Uaupés ➤ 90 C5
Ubá 93 G5
Ubaitaba 93 E6
Ubangi =
  Oubangi ➤ . 56 E3
Ubauro 42 E6
Ube 32 C2
Ubeda 18 C4
Uberaba 93 F4
Uberlândia 93 F4
Ubon
  Ratchathani . 36 A2
Ubort ➤ 17 B9
Ubundu 57 E5
Ucayali ➤ 90 D4
Uchiura-Wan . . 32 F12
Udaipur 43 G8
Udaipur Garhi . 40 D6
Udgir 43 K10
Udhampur 42 C9
Udi 55 G6
Údine 20 A4
Udmurtia □ . . . 28 D6
Udon Thani . . . 36 A2
Udupi 43 N9
Ueda 32 A6
Uele ➤ 57 D4
Uelzen 14 B6
Ufa 29 D6
Ugab ➤ 58 C2
Ugalla ➤ 57 F6
Uganda ■ 57 D6
Ugljane 20 B5
Ugolyak 30 C10
Uibhist a Deas
  = South Uist 10 C3
Uibhist a Tuath
  = North Uist 10 C3
Uíge 56 F2
Uinta Mts. 81 E8
Uitenhage 59 E5
Ujjain 43 H9
Ujung Pandang 39 F1
Ukerewe I. 57 E6
Ukhrul 41 E10
Ukhta 28 C6
Ukraine ■ 25 D3
Ulaanbaatar . . 35 B5
Ulaangom 34 A4
Ulan Bator =
  Ulaanbaatar . 35 B5
Ulan Ude 30 D8
Ulcinj 22 D2

Ulhasnagar ...	43	K8
Ulladulla	63	C5
Ullapool	10	C4
Ulm	14	D5
Ulmarra	63	A5
Ulonguè	59	A6
Ulster □	11	D3
Ulubat Gölü ...	23	D7
Uludağ	23	D7
Ulungur He →	34	B3
Uluru = Ayers Rock	60	F5
Ulutau	29	E7
Ulverstone	62	D4
Ulyanovsk = Simbirsk ...	24	C6
Ulyasutay	34	B4
Umala	91	G5
Uman	17	D10
Umaria	40	F3
Umarkot	43	G6
Umba	28	C4
Umbrella Mts. .	65	F3
Ume älv → ..	8	F12
Umeå	8	F12
Umera	39	E3
Umm al Qaywayn ...	44	E3
Umm Bel	53	F4
Umm Lajj	47	F4
Umm Ruwaba .	53	F5
Umnak I.	71	C3
Umniati → ...	59	B5
Umtata	59	E5
Umuarama ...	93	G3
Una →	20	B6
Unalaska	71	C3
Uncía	91	G5
Underbool	62	C3
Ungarie	63	B4
Ungarra	62	B2
Ungava B.	68	C4
Ungava Pen. ..	68	B3
Ungeny = Ungheni	17	E8
Ungheni	17	E8
União da Vitória	94	B6
Unimak I.	71	C3
United Arab Emirates ■ ..	44	F3
United Kingdom ■ .	11	E5
United States of America ..	67	F10
Unnao	40	D3
Unst	10	A6
Ünye	46	B4
Upata	90	B6
Upemba, L. ...	57	F5
Upington	58	D4
Upper Hutt	65	D6
Upper Volta = Burkina Faso ■	55	F4
Uppsala	9	G11
Ur	47	E6
Uracara	90	D7
Ural = Zhayyq → .	29	E6
Ural	63	B4
Ural Mts. = Uralskie Gory	28	D6
Uralla	63	B5
Uralsk = Oral .	24	C7
Uralskie Gory .	28	D6
Uranquinty ...	63	C4
Urawa	32	B6
Uray	29	C7
Urbana	72	D1
Urbino	20	C4
Urbión, Picos de	19	A4
Urcos	91	F4
Urda	25	D6
Urdzhar	29	E9
Ures	84	B2
Urfa = Sanliurfa	46	C4
Urganch	29	E7
Urgench = Urganch	29	E7
Uribia	90	A4
Urla	23	E6
Urmia = Orūmīyeh ...	46	C6
Urmia, L. = Orūmīyeh, Daryācheh-ye	46	C6
Uroševac	22	C3
Uruana	93	F4
Urubamba	91	F4
Urubamba → .	91	F4
Uruçuí	92	D5
Uruguai → ...	94	B6
Uruguaiana ...	94	B5
Uruguay ■ ...	94	C5
Uruguay → ...	94	C5
Urumchi = Ürümqi	34	B3
Ürümqi	34	B3
Usakos	58	C3
Usedom	15	B8
Ush-Tobe	29	E8
Ushant = Ouessant, I. d'	12	B1
Ushuaia	95	G3
Üsküdar	25	E2
Usman	24	C4
Usoke	57	F6
Uspallata, P. de	94	C3
Uspenskiy	29	E8
Ussuriysk	31	E11
Ust-Aldan = Batamay	31	C10
Ust Ilimpeya = Yukti	30	C8
Ust Ishim	29	D8
Ust-Kamenogorsk = Öskemen .	29	E9
Ust-Karenga ..	31	D9
Ust Kuyga	31	B11
Ust Muya	30	D9
Ust Olenek	30	B10
Ust Port	28	C9
Ust Tsilma	28	C6
Ust Urt = Ustyurt, Plateau	29	E6
Ust Vorkuta ...	28	C7
Ústí nad Labem	16	C2
Ustica	21	E4
Ustinov = Izhevsk	28	D6
Ustye	30	D7
Ustyurt, Plateau	29	E6
Usu	34	B3
Usuki	32	C2
Usumacinta →	85	D6
Usumbura = Bujumbura ..	57	E5
Uta	39	E5
Utah □	81	F8
Utete	57	F7
Utiariti	91	F7
Utica	73	C8
Utrecht	14	B3
Utrera	18	D3
Utsunomiya ...	32	A6
Uttar Pradesh □	42	F11
Uttaradit	36	A2
Uummannarsuaq = Farvel, Kap	68	C6
Uusikaupunki .	8	F12
Uvat	29	D7
Uvinza	57	F6
Uvira	57	E5
Uvs Nuur	34	A4
Uwajima	32	C3
Uyuni	91	H5
Uzbekistan ■ ..	29	E7
Uzerche	12	D4
Uzh →	17	C10
Uzhgorod = Uzhhorod ...	17	D6
Uzhhorod	17	D6
Uzunköprü	22	D6

V

Vaal →	58	D4
Vaasa	8	F12
Vác	16	E4
Vach → = Vakh → ...	29	C8
Vadodara	43	H8
Vadsø	8	D13
Vaduz	13	C8
Váh →	16	E4
Vahsel B.	96	B5
Vaigach	28	B6
Vakh →	29	C8
Val d'Or	69	D3
Valahia	22	B5
Valandovo	22	D4
Valcheta	95	E3
Valdayskaya Vozvyshennost	24	B3
Valdepeñas ...	18	C4
Valdés, Pen. ...	95	E4
Valdez	71	B5
Valdivia	95	D2
Valdosta	75	D6
Valença	93	E6
Valença do Piauí	92	D5
Valence	13	D6
Valencia, *Spain*	19	C5
Valencia, *Venezuela* ...	90	A5
Valencia □	19	C5
Valencia, G. de	19	C6
Valencia de Alcántara ...	18	C2
Valencia I.	11	F1
Valenciennes ..	13	A5
Valentim, Sa. do	92	D5
Valera	90	B4
Valjevo	22	B2
Vall de Uxó ...	19	C5
Valladolid, *Mexico*	85	C7
Valladolid, *Spain*	18	B3
Valle de la Pascua	90	B5
Valledupar	90	A4
Vallejo	80	F2
Vallenar	94	B2
Valletta	21	G5
Valls	19	B6
Valognes	12	B3
Valona = Vlóra	23	D2
Valozhyn	17	A8
Valparaíso	94	C2
Vals, Tanjung .	39	F5
Valsad	43	J8
Valverde del Camino	18	D2
Van	46	C5
Van, L. = Van Gölü	46	C5
Van Gölü	46	C5
Van Rees, Pegunungan	39	E5
Vanadzor	25	E5
Vancouver, *Canada*	71	D7
Vancouver, *U.S.A.*	80	C2
Vancouver I. ..	71	D7
Vänern	9	G10
Vanga	57	E7
Vangaindrano .	59	J9
Vännäs	8	F11
Vannes	12	C2
Vanrhynsdorp .	58	E3
Vanua Levu ..	64	L12
Vanuatu ■	64	L11
Vapnyarka	17	D9
Varanasi	40	E4
Varangerfjorden	8	D13
Varaždin	20	A6
Varberg	9	G10
Vardak □	45	C7
Vardar = Axiós → ...	23	D4
Varese	20	B2
Varna	22	C6
Varzaneh	44	C3
Vasa Barris →	93	E6
Vascongadas = País Vasco □	19	A4
Vasht = Khāsh	42	E2
Vasilevichi	17	B9
Vasilkov = Vasylkiv	17	C10
Vaslui	17	E8
Västerås	9	G11
Västervik	9	G11
Vasto	20	C5
Vasylkiv	17	C10
Vatican City ■ .	20	D4
Vatomandry ...	59	H9
Vatra-Dornei ..	17	E7
Vättern	9	G10
Vaupés = Uaupés → ..	90	C5
Vawkavysk	17	B7
Vaygach, Ostrov	28	C6
Vedea →	22	C5
Vega →	8	E10
Vegreville	71	C8
Vejer de la Frontera	18	D3
Velebit Planina	20	B5
Vélez	90	B4
Vélez Málaga .	18	D3
Vélez Rubio ...	19	D4
Velhas →	93	F5
Velika Kapela .	20	B5
Velikaya → ...	24	B2
Veliki Ustyug .	24	A6
Velikiye Luki ..	24	B3
Veliko Tŭrnovo	22	C5
Velikonda Range	43	M11
Velletri	20	D4
Vellore	43	N11
Venado Tuerto	94	C4
Vendée □	12	C3
Vendôme	12	C4
Venézia	20	B4
Venézia, G. di .	20	B4

Venezuela ■ . . 90 B5
Venezuela, G. de 90 A4
Vengurla 43 M8
Venice =
  Venézia 20 B4
Venkatapuram . 40 H3
Ventotene 21 D4
Ventoux, Mt. . . 13 D6
Ventspils 24 B1
Ventuarí ➜ . . . 90 C5
Ventura 82 C3
Venus B. 63 C4
Vera, Argentina 94 B4
Vera, Spain . . . 19 D5
Veracruz 84 D5
Veraval 43 J7
Verbánia 20 B2
Vercelli 20 B2
Verde ➜ 95 E3
Verden 14 B5
Verdun 13 B6
Vereeniging . . 59 D5
Verga, C. 55 F2
Verín 18 B2
Verkhnevilyuysk 30 C10
Verkhniy
  Baskunchak . 25 D6
Verkhoyansk . . 31 C11
Verkhoyansk Ra.
  =
  Verkhoyanskiy
  Khrebet 31 C10
Verkhoyanskiy
  Khrebet 31 C10
Vermilion 71 C8
Vermont □ 73 C9
Vernon, Canada 71 C8
Vernon, U.S.A. 78 B4
Véroia 23 D4
Verona 20 B3
Versailles 12 B5
Vert, C. 55 F1
Verviers 14 C3
Veselovskoye
  Vdkhr. 25 D5
Vesoul 13 C7
Vesterålen 8 E11
Vestfjorden . . . 8 E10
Vesuvio 21 D5
Vesuvius, Mt. =
  Vesuvio 21 D5
Veszprém 16 E3
Vetlugu ➜ . . . 28 D5
Vettore, Mte. . . 20 C4
Veys 47 E7
Vezhen 22 C5
Viacha 91 G5
Viamão 94 C6
Viana 92 C5
Viana do
  Alentejo 18 C2
Viana do Castelo 18 B1
Vianópolis . . . 93 F4
Viaréggio 20 C3
Vibo Valéntia . . 21 E6
Vicenza 20 B3
Vich 19 B7
Vichy 13 C5
Vicksburg 79 C8
Viçosa 93 D6
Victor 43 J7
Victor Harbor . . 62 C2
Victoria, Canada 71 D7
Victoria, Chile . 94 D2
Victoria, Guinea 55 F2
Victoria,
  Malaysia 36 C5
Victoria □ 62 C3

Victoria, L.,
  Africa 57 E6
Victoria, L.,
  Australia . . . 62 B3
Victoria Beach . 71 C10
Victoria de
  Durango =
  Durango 84 C4
Victoria Falls . . 59 B5
Victoria I. 70 A8
Victoria Ld. . . 96 B14
Victoria
  Taungdeik . . 41 G9
Victoria West . . 58 E4
Victorica 94 D3
Vicuña 94 C2
Vidin 22 C4
Vidisha 43 H10
Viedma 95 E4
Viedma, L. 95 F2
Vienna = Wien 15 D9
Vienne 13 D6
Vienne ➜ 12 C4
Vientiane 36 A2
Vierzon 12 C5
Vietnam ■ 36 A3
Vigan 38 A2
Vigévano 20 B2
Vigia 92 C4
Vigo 18 A1
Vijayawada . . . 40 J3
Vikeke 39 F3
Vikna 8 F10
Vila da Maganja 59 B7
Vila de João
  Belo = Xai-Xai 59 D6
Vila do Bispo . . 18 D1
Vila Franca de
  Xira 18 C1
Vila Machado . 59 B6
Vila Nova de
  Gaia 18 B1
Vila Real 18 B2
Vila Real de
  Santo António 18 D2
Vila Velha 93 G5
Vilaine ➜ 12 C2
Vilanculos . . . 59 C7
Vileyka 17 A8
Vilhelmina 8 F11
Vilhena 91 F6
Vilkitskogo,
  Proliv 30 B8
Vilkovo =
  Vylkove 17 F9
Villa Ahumada 84 A3
Villa Ángela . . 94 B4
Villa Bella 91 F5
Villa Bens =
  Tarfaya 54 C2
Villa Colón 94 C3
Villa de María . 94 B4
Villa Dolores . . 94 C3
Villa Hayes . . . 94 B5
Villa María 94 C4
Villa Mazán . . 94 B3
Villa Montes . . 94 A4
Villa Ocampo . . 94 B5
Villacarrillo . . . 18 C4
Villach 15 E7
Villagarcía de
  Arosa 18 A1
Villaguay 94 C5
Villahermosa . . 85 D6
Villajoyosa . . . 19 C5
Villalba 18 A2
Villanueva de la
  Serena 18 C3

Villanueva y
  Geltrú 19 B6
Villarreal 19 C5
Villarrica, Chile 95 D2
Villarrica,
  Paraguay . . . 94 B5
Villarrobledo . . 19 C4
Villavicencio . . 90 C4
Villaviciosa . . . 18 A3
Villazón 94 A3
Villena 19 C5
Villeneuve-
  d'Ascq 13 A5
Villeneuve-sur-
  Lot 12 D4
Villingen-
  Schwenningen 14 D5
Vilnius 24 C2
Vilyuy ➜ 31 C10
Vilyuysk 31 C10
Viña del Mar . . 94 C2
Vinaroz 19 B6
Vindhya Ra. . . 43 H10
Vineland 73 E8
Vinkovci 20 B7
Vinnitsa =
  Vinnytsya . . . 17 D9
Vinnytsya 17 D9
Virac 38 B2
Viramgam 43 H8
Viranşehir . . 46 C4
Virden 71 D9
Vire 12 B3
Vírgenes, C. . . . 95 G3
Virgin Is.
  (British) ■ . 87 C7
Virginia □ 73 F6
Virginia Beach . 73 F8
Virovitica 20 B6
Virudunagar . . 43 Q10
Vis 20 C6
Visalia 82 B3
Visayan Sea . . . 38 B2
Visby 9 G11
Višegrad 20 C7
Viseu, Brazil . . 92 C4
Viseu, Portugal 18 B2
Vishakhapatnam 40 J4
Viso, Mte. 20 B1
Vistula =
  Wisła ➜ . . . 16 A4
Vitebsk =
  Vitsyebsk . . . 24 B3
Viterbo 20 C4
Viti Levu 64 L12
Vitigudino 18 B2
Vitória, Brazil . . 93 G5
Vitoria, Spain . 19 A4
Vitória da
  Conquista . . 93 E5
Vitsyebsk 24 B3
Vittória 21 F5
Vittório Véneto 20 B4
Vivero 18 A2
Vize 22 D6
Vizianagaram . 40 H4
Vjosa ➜ 23 D2
Vladikavkaz . . . 25 E5
Vladimir 24 B5
Vladimir
  Volynskiy =
  Volodymyr-
  Volynskyy . . . 17 C7
Vladivostok . . . 31 E11
Vlissingen 14 C2
Vlóra 23 D2
Vltava ➜ 16 C2
Vogelsberg . . . 14 C5

Voghera 20 B2
Vohibinany . . . 59 H9
Vohimarina . . . 59 G10
Vohimena,
  Tanjon' i 59 K9
Vohipeno 59 J9
Voi 57 E7
Voiron 13 D6
Vojvodina □ . . 22 B2
Volga ➜ 25 D6
Volga Hts. =
  Privolzhskaya
  Vozvyshennost
  . . . . 24 C6
Volgodonsk . . . 25 D5
Volgograd 25 D5
Volgogradskoye
  Vdkhr. 24 C6
Volkhov ➜ . . . 24 A3
Volkovysk =
  Vawkavysk . . 17 B7
Volochanka . . . 30 B7
Volodymyr-
  Volynskyy . . . 17 C7
Vologda 24 B4
Vólos 23 E4
Volovets 17 D6
Volozhin =
  Valozhyn . . . 17 A8
Volsk 24 C6
Volta ➜ 55 G5
Volta, L. 55 G5
Volta Redonda 93 G5
Volterra 20 C3
Volturno ➜ . . . 20 D4
Volzhskiy 25 D5
Voríai
  Sporádhes . . 23 E4
Vorkuta 28 C7
Voronezh 24 C4
Voroshilovgrad
  = Luhansk . . 25 D4
Voroshilovsk =
  Alchevsk 25 D4
Vosges 13 B7
Vostok I. 65 L15
Vouga ➜ 18 B1
Voznesensk . . . 25 D3
Voznesenye . . . 28 C4
Vrangelya,
  Ostrov 31 B15
Vranje 22 C3
Vratsa 22 C4
Vrbas ➜ 20 B6
Vrede 59 D5
Vredenburg . . . 58 E3
Vršac 22 B3
Vryburg 58 D4
Vryheid 59 D6
Vukovar 20 B7
Vulcan 17 F6
Vulcaneşti 17 F9
Vulcano 21 E5
Vulkaneshty =
  Vulcaneşti . . . 17 F9
Vung Tau 36 B3
Vyatka = Kirov 28 D5
Vyatskiye
  Polyany 24 B7
Vyazma 24 B3
Vyborg 28 C3
Vychegda ➜ . . 28 C5
Vychodné
  Beskydy 17 D5
Vylkove 17 F9
Vynohradiv . . . 17 D6
Vyshniy
  Volochek . . . 24 B3
Vyškov 16 D3

W

Wa 55 F4
Waal → 14 C3
Wabash → ... 72 F1
Waco 78 D5
Wad Banda .. 53 F4
Wad Hamid ... 53 E5
Wâd Medanî .. 53 F5
Waddington, Mt. 71 C7
Waddy Pt. 63
Wadi Halfa .. 52 D5
Wafrah 47 E6
Wager B. 68 B2
Wager Bay ... 68 B1
Wagga Wagga 63 C4
Waghete 39 E5
Wah 42 C8
Wahai 39 E3
Waiau → ... 65 E5
Waibeem 39 E4
Waigeo 39 E4
Waihi 64 B6
Waihou → ... 64 B6
Waikabubak .. 39 F1
Waikari 65 E5
Waikato → ... 64 B6
Waikerie 62 B2
Waikokopu ... 64 C7
Waikouaiti ... 65 F4
Waimakariri → 65 E5
Waimate 65 F4
Wainganga → 43 K11
Waingapu ... 39 F2
Wainwright,
  Canada ... 71 C8
Wainwright,
  U.S.A. 71 A3
Waiouru 64 C6
Waipara 65 E5
Waipawa 64 C7
Waipiro 64 C8
Waipu 64 A6
Waipukurau .. 64 D7
Wairakei 64 C7
Wairarapa, L. . 65 D6
Wairoa 64 C7
Waitaki → ... 65 F4
Waitara 64 C6
Waiuku 64 B6
Wajima 32 A5
Wajir 57 D8
Wakasa-Wan . 32 B4
Wakatipu, L. . 65 F3
Wakayama ... 32 B4
Wakefield 65 D5
Wakema 41 J10
Wakkanai 32 E12
Wakool 63 C3
Wakool → ... 62 C3
Wakre 39 E4
Wałbrzych ... 16 C3
Walcha 63 B5
Wałcz 16 B3
Wales □ 11 E4
Walgett 63 A4
Walgreen Coast 96 B1
Walhalla 63 C4
Walla Walla .. 80 B4
Wallachia =
  Valahia 22 B5
Wallal 63 A4
Wallaroo 62 B2
Wallerawang . 63 B5
Wallis & Futuna,
  Is. 64 L13
Wallowa Mts. . 80 C5
Wallsend 63 B5
Wallumbilla ... 63 A4

Walvisbaai 58 C2
Wamba 57 D5
Wamena 39 E5
Wamulan 39 E3
Wana 42 C6
Wanaaring ... 63 A3
Wanaka 65 F3
Wanaka L. ... 65 F3
Wanapiri 39 E5
Wanbi 62 B3
Wandoan 63 A4
Wangal 39 F4
Wanganella .. 63 C3
Wanganui 64 C6
Wangaratta .. 63 C4
Wangary 62 B2
Wangerooge . 14 B4
Wangiwangi . 39 F2
Wanxian 35 C5
Warangal 43 L11
Waratah 62 D4
Waratah B. ... 63 C4
Warburton ... 63 C4
Ward 65 D6
Ward → 63 A4
Wardha 43 J11
Wardha → ... 43 K11
Warialda 63 A5
Wariap 39 E4
Warkopi 39 E4
Warmbad,
  Namibia 58 D3
Warmbad,
  S. Africa ... 59 C5
Warner Mts. .. 80 E3
Warracknabeal 62 C3
Warragul 63 C4
Warrego → .. 63 B4
Warren 63 B4
Warrenton ... 58 D4
Warrenville ... 63 A4
Warri 55 G6
Warrina 62 A2
Warrington, U.K. 11 E5
Warrington,
  U.S.A. 74 D4
Warrnambool . 62 C3
Warsa 39 E5
Warsaw =
  Warszawa ... 16 B5
Warszawa ... 16 B5
Warta → 16 B2
Warthe =
  Warta → ... 16 B2
Waru 39 E4
Warwick 63 A5
Wasatch Ra. .. 81 E8
Wash, The ... 11 E7
Washim 43 J10
Washington .. 73 E7
Washington □ . 80 B3
Washington, Mt. 73 B10
Wasian 39 E4
Wasior 39 E4
Waskaganish .. 69 C3
Wasserkuppe .. 14 C5
Watangpone .. 39 E2
Waterbury 73 D9
Waterford 11 E3
Waterloo,
  S. Leone ... 55 G2
Waterloo, U.S.A. 72 D8
Waterton-Glacier
  International
  Peace Park .. 81 A6
Watertown ... 73 C8
Waterville ... 73 B11
Watford 11 F6
Watling I. = San
  Salvador 86 B5

Watrous 71 C9
Watsa 57 D5
Watson Lake .. 70 B7
Watsonville ... 82 B2
Wattiwarriganna
  Cr. → 62 A2
Watuata =
  Batuata ... 39 F2
Watubela,
  Kepulauan . 39 E4
Watubela Is. =
  Watubela,
  Kepulauan . 39 E4
Wauchope ... 63 B5
Waukegan 72 C2
Waukesha ... 72 C1
Wausau 77 C10
Wauwatosa .. 72 C2
Waverley 64 C6
Wâw 53 G4
Wâw al Kabîr .. 52 C2
Waxahachie .. 79 C5
Wayabula Rau . 39 D3
Wayatinah ... 62 D4
Waycross 75 D6
Wazirabad 42 C9
We 36 C1
Weda 39 D3
Weda, Teluk .. 39 D3
Weddell I. 95 G4
Weddell Sea .. 96 A4
Wedderburn .. 62 C3
Wee Waa 63 B4
Weemelah 63 A4
Weiden 15 D7
Weifang 35 C6
Weimar 15 C6
Weipa 61 C7
Weir → 63 A4
Wejherowo .. 16 A4
Welbourn Hill . 62 A1
Welkom 59 D5
Wellesley Is. .. 60 D6
Wellington,
  Australia 63 B4
Wellington, N.Z. 65 D6
Wellington, I. .. 95 F1
Wellington, L. . 63 C4
Wels 15 D8
Welshpool ... 11 E5
Wemindji 69 C3
Wenatchee ... 80 B3
Wenchi 55 G4
Wenchow =
  Wenzhou ... 35 D7
Wendesi 39 E4
Wensu 34 B3
Wentworth ... 62 B3
Wenut 39 E4
Wenzhou 35 D7
Werda 58 D4
Werder 49 F4
Weri → 39 E4
Werra → 14 C5
Werribee 63 C3
Werrimull 62 B3
Werris Creek .. 63 B5
Wersar 39 E4
Weser → 14 B5
Wesiri 39 F3
West Bengal □ 40 F7
West Beskids =
  Západné
  Beskydy ... 16 D4
West Falkland . 95 G4
West Fjord =
  Vestfjorden . 8 E10
West Ice Shelf . 96 A11
West Nicholson 59 C5

West Palm
  Beach 75 F7
West Pt. 62 C2
West Virginia □ 72 E5
West Wyalong . 63 B4
Westall Pt. 62 B1
Westbury 62 D4
Westerland ... 14 A5
Western
  Australia □ .. 60 F3
Western Dvina
  =
  Daugava → . 24 B1
Western Ghats 43 N9
Western
  Sahara ■ ... 54 D2
Western
  Samoa ■ ... 65 L13
Westerwald ... 14 C4
Westland Bight 65 E4
Weston 36 C5
Weston-super-
  Mare 11 F5
Westport,
  Ireland 11 E2
Westport, N.Z. . 65 D4
Westray 10 B5
Wetar 39 F3
Wetaskiwin ... 71 C8
Wetzlar 14 C5
Wewak 61
Wexford 11 E3
Weyburn 71 D9
Weymouth ... 11 F5
Whakatane ... 64 B7
Whale → 68 C4
Whale Cove ... 70 B10
Whales, B. of .. 96 B16
Whangamomona
  .... 64 C6
Whangarei ... 64 A6
Whangarei Harb. 64 A6
Wheeling 72 D5
White →, Ark.,
  U.S.A. 79 C8
White →, Ind.,
  U.S.A. 72 E2
White Cliffs ... 62 B3
White I. 64 B7
White Nile = Nîl
  el Abyad → . 53 E5
White Russia =
  Belarus ■ ... 24 C2
White Sea =
  Beloye More . 28 C4
Whitecliffs ... 65 E4
Whitehaven ... 11 D5
Whitehorse ... 70 B6
Whitemark ... 62 D4
Whitfield 63 C4
Whitianga 64 B6
Whitney, Mt. .. 82 B3
Whittlesea ... 63 C4
Wholdaia L. ... 70 B9
Whyalla 62 B2
Whyjonta 62 A3
Wichita 78 A5
Wichita Falls .. 78 C4
Wick 10 B5
Wickham, C. .. 62 C3
Wicklow Mts. . 11 E3
Wieluń 16 C4
Wien 15 D9
Wiener Neustadt 15 E9
Wiesbaden ... 14 C5
Wilcannia 62 B3
Wildspitze ... 14 E6
Wilhelm, Mt. .. 61 B8
Wilhelm II Coast 96 A11

Wilhelmshaven 14 B5
Wilkes-Barre . . 73 D8
Wilkie 71 C9
Willandra
  Billabong
  Creek → . . 63 B4
Willemstad . . 87 D6
William Creek . 62 A2
Williams Lake . 71 C7
Williamsburg . . 73 F7
Williamsport . . 73 D7
Williamstown . 63 C3
Williston 76 A3
Willowmore . . 58 E4
Willunga 62 C2
Wilmington,
  Australia 62 B2
Wilmington,
  Del., U.S.A. . 73 E8
Wilmington,
  N.C., U.S.A. . 75 B9
Wilpena Cr. → 62 B2
Wilson 75 B9
Wilson → 62 A3
Wilsons
  Promontory . 63 C4
Wimmera → . . 62 C3
Winchester . . 11 F6
Wind River
  Range 81 D9
Windau =
  Ventspils . . . 24 B1
Windhoek 58 C3
Windsor,
  Australia 63 B5
Windsor, N.S.,
  Canada . . . 69 D4
Windsor, Ont.,
  Canada . . . 69 D2
Windward Is. . . 87
Wingen 63 B5
Wingham 63 B5
Winisk → . . . 69 C2
Winneba 55 G4
Winnipeg 71 D10
Winnipeg, L. . 71 C10
Winnipegosis L. 71 C9
Winona 77 C9
Winston-Salem 75 A7
Winterthur 13 C8
Winton,
  Australia 61 E7
Winton, N.Z. . . 65 G3
Wirrulla 62 B1
Wisconsin □ . . 77 C10
Wisła → 16 A4
Wismar 15 B6
Witbank 59 D5
Wittenberg . . . 15 C7
Wittenberge . . . 15 B6
Wkra → 16 B5
Włocławek . . . 16 B4
Włodawa 17 C6
Wodonga 63 C4
Wokam 39 F4
Wolfsberg 15 E8
Wolfsburg 15 B6
Wolin 16 B2
Wollaston, Is. . 95 H3
Wollaston Pen. 70 B8
Wollongong . . . 63 B5
Wolseley 62 C3
Wolverhampton 11 E5
Wondai 63 A5
Wongalarroo L. 63 B3
Wŏnsan 35 C7
Wonthaggi 63 C4
Woocalla 62 B2
Woodburn 63 A5
Woodenbong . 63 A5

Woodend 63 C3
Woodland 80 F3
Woodroffe, Mt. 60 F5
Woods, L. of the 71 D10
Woodstock . . . 69 D4
Woodville 64 D6
Woolamai, C. . . 63 C4
Woolgoolga . . . 63 B5
Woombye 63 A5
Woomera 62 B2
Worcester,
  S. Africa 58 E3
Worcester, U.K. 11 E5
Worcester,
  U.S.A. 73 C10
Workington . . . 11 D5
Worms 14 D5
Worthing 11 F6
Wosi 39 E3
Wou-han =
  Wuhan 35 C6
Wour 52 D2
Wousi = Wuxi . 35 C7
Wowoni 39 E2
Woy Woy 63 B5
Wrangel I. =
  Vrangelya,
  Ostrov 31 B15
Wrangell 71 C6
Wrangell Mts. . 71 B5
Wrath, C. 10 B4
Wrexham 11 E5
Wright 38 B3
Wrigley 70 B7
Wrocław 16 C3
Września 16 B3
Wu Jiang → . . 35 D5
Wuhan 35 C6
Wuhsi = Wuxi . 35 C7
Wuhu 35 C6
Wukari 55 G6
Wuliaru 39 F4
Wulumuchi =
  Ürümqi 34 B3
Wum 55 G7
Wuntho 41 F10
Wuppertal 14 C4
Würzburg 14 D5
Wutongqiao . . 34 D5
Wuwei 34 C5
Wuxi 35 C7
Wuyi Shan . . . 35 D6
Wuzhi Shan . . . 35 E5
Wuzhong 35 C5
Wuzhou 35 D6
Wyandotte 72 C4
Wyandra 63 A4
Wyangala Res. 63 B4
Wyara, L. 63 A3
Wycheproof . . . 62 C3
Wynbring 62 B1
Wyndham,
  Australia 60 D4
Wyndham, N.Z. 65 G3
Wynnum 63 A5
Wynyard 62 D4
Wyoming □ . . 81 D10
Wyong 63 B5

X

Xai-Xai 59 D6
Xainza 34 C3
Xangongo 58 B3
Xankändi 25 F6
Xánthi 22 D5
Xapuri 91 F5

Xi Jiang → . . 35 D6
Xiaguan 34 D5
Xiamen 35 D6
Xi'an 35 C5
Xiang Jiang → 35 D6
Xiangfan 35 C6
Xiangtan 35 D6
Xiao Hinggan
  Ling 35 B7
Xiapu 35 D6
Xichang 34 D5
Xigazê 34 D3
Xinavane 59 D6
Xing'an 35 D6
Xingren 35 D5
Xingtai 35 C6
Xingu → 92 C3
Xining 34 C5
Xinjiang Uygur
  Zizhiqu □ . . 34 B3
Xinjin 35 C7
Xinxiang 35 C6
Xinyang 35 C6
Xinzhu 35 D7
Xique-Xique . . 93 E5
Xisha Qundao =
  Hsisha
  Chuntao 36 A4
Xixabangma
  Feng 40 C5
Xizang □ 34 C3
Xuanhua 35 B6
Xuchang 35 C6
Xuzhou 35 C6

Y

Ya'an 34 D5
Yaapeet 62 C3
Yabelo 53 H6
Yablonovy Ra. =
  Yablonovyy
  Khrebet 30 D9
Yablonovyy
  Khrebet 30 D9
Yacuiba 94 A4
Yadgir 43 L10
Yagoua 56 B3
Yahuma 56 D4
Yakima 80 B3
Yakutat 71 C6
Yakutsk 31 C10
Yala 36 C2
Yalinga 56 C4
Yalong Jiang → 34 D5
Yalova 22 D7
Yalta 25 E3
Yalutorovsk . . 29 D7
Yam Ha Melah
  = Dead Sea . 47 E3
Yam Kinneret . 46 D3
Yamagata 33 G12
Yamaguchi . . . 32 B2
Yamal,
  Poluostrov . . 28 B8
Yamal Pen. =
  Yamal,
  Poluostrov . . 28 B8
Yamantau, Gora 29 D6
Yamba, N.S.W.,
  Australia 63 A5
Yamba,
  S. Austral.,
  Australia . . . 62 B3
Yâmbiô 53 H4
Yambol 22 C6

Yamdena 39 F4
Yamethin 41 G11
Yamma-Yamma,
  L. 62 A3
Yamoussoukro 55 G3
Yampil 17 D9
Yampol =
  Yampil 17 D9
Yamuna → . . . 40 E3
Yamzho Yumco 34 D4
Yana → 31 B11
Yanac 62 C3
Yanbu 'al Baḥr 47 F4
Yancannia . . . 62 B3
Yanco Cr. → . . 63 C4
Yandoon 41 J10
Yangambi 56 D4
Yangch'ü =
  Taiyuan 35 C6
Yangchun 35 D6
Yangjiang 35 D6
Yangon =
  Rangoon 41 J11
Yangquan 35 C6
Yanji 35 B7
Yanna 63 A4
Yanqi 34 B3
Yantabulla . . . 63 A4
Yantai 35 C7
Yanykurgan . . 29 E7
Yao 53 F2
Yaoundé 56 D2
Yapen 39 E5
Yapen, Selat . . 39 E5
Yaqui → 84 B2
Yar-Sale 28 C8
Yaraka 61 E7
Yaransk 24 B6
Yardea P.O. . . 62 B2
Yaremcha 17 D7
Yarensk 28 C5
Yarí → 90 D4
Yarkand =
  Shache 34 C2
Yarkhun → . . . 42 A8
Yaroslavl 24 B4
Yarram 63 C4
Yarraman 63 A5
Yarranvale . . . 63 A4
Yarras 63 B5
Yartsevo 30 C7
Yaselda 17 B8
Yasinya 17 D7
Yass 63 B4
Yatağan 23 F7
Yathkyed L. . . 70 B10
Yatsushiro . . . 32 C2
Yauyos 91 F3
Yavari → 90 D4
Yavatmal 43 J11
Yavoriv 17 D6
Yavorov =
  Yavoriv 17 D6
Yawatahama . 32 C3
Yazd 44 D3
Yazd □ 44 C3
Yazdān 45 C5
Yazoo → 79 C8
Ye Xian 35 C6
Yebyu 41 K12
Yecla 19 C5
Yedintsy =
  Edinița 17 D8
Yeelanna 62 B2
Yegros 94 B5
Yei 53 H5
Yekaterinburg . 29 D7
Yekaterinodar =
  Krasnodar . . 25 D4

Yelarbon 63 A5
Yelets 24 C4
Yelizavetgrad =
  Kirovohrad . . 25 D3
Yell 10 A6
Yellow Sea . . . 35 C7
Yellowhead Pass 71 C8
Yellowknife . . . 70 B8
Yellowknife → 70 B8
Yellowstone → 76 B3
Yellowstone
  National Park 81 C8
Yelsk 17 C9
Yemen ■ 49 E3
Yenangyaung . 41 G10
Yenbo = Yanbu
  'al Baḥr 47 F4
Yenda 63 B4
Yenice 23 E6
Yenisey → . . . 28 B9
Yeniseysk 30 D7
Yeniseyskiy
  Zaliv 28 B9
Yenyuka 31 D10
Yeola 43 J9
Yeovil 11 F5
Yerbent 29 F6
Yerevan 25 E5
Yermak 29 D8
Yershov 24 C6
Yerushalayim =
  Jerusalem . . 47 E3
Yessey 30 C8
Yeu, I. d' 12 C2
Yevpatoriya . . . 25 D3
Yeysk 25 D4
Yezd = Yazd . . 44 D3
Yiannitsa 23 D4
Yibin 35 D5
Yichang 35 C6
Yichun 35 B7
Yilan 35 D7
Yinchuan 35 C5
Yingkou 35 B7
Yingtan 35 D6
Yining 34 B3
Yinmabin 41 F10
Yishan 35 D5
Yíthion 23 F4
Yiyang 35 D6
Yog Pt. 38 B2
Yogyakarta . . . 37 F4
Yokadouma . . . 56 D2
Yokkaichi 32 B5
Yoko 53 G1
Yokohama . . . 32 B6
Yokosuka 32 B6
Yola 53 G1
Yonago 32 B3
Yongji 35 C6
Yonibana 55 G2
Yonkers 73 D9
Yonne → 13 B5
York, U.K. 11 E6
York, U.S.A. . . . 73 E7
York, C. 61 C7
Yorke Pen. 62 B2
Yorkton 71 C9
Yos Sudarso,
  Pulau 39 F5
Yosemite
  National Park 82 B3
Yoshkar Ola . . . 24 B6
Youghal 11 F3
Young 63 B4
Younghusband,
  L. 62 B2
Younghusband
  Pen. 62 C2

Youngstown . . 72 D5
Yozgat 46 C3
Ysyk-Köl, Ozero 29 E8
Yu Jiang → . . 35 D6
Yu Shan 35 D7
Yuan Jiang → 35 D6
Yuanling 35 D6
Yuanyang 34 D5
Yuba City 80 F3
Yūbari 32 F12
Yucatán □ 85 C7
Yucatán, Canal
  de 85 C7
Yucatán,
  Península de 85 D7
Yucatan Str. =
  Yucatán,
  Canal de 85 C7
Yuci 35 C6
Yugoslavia ■ . . 22 B3
Yukon → 71 B3
Yukon
  Territory □ . . 70 B6
Yukti 30 C8
Yuma 82 D5
Yumen 34 C4
Yun Xian 35 C6
Yungas 91 G5
Yunnan □ 34 D5
Yunta 62 B2
Yurgao 29 D9
Yuribei 28 B8
Yurimaguas . . 91 E3
Yuryung Kaya . 30 B9
Yushu 34 C4
Yuzhno-
  Sakhalinsk . . 31 E12
Yvetot 12 B4

Z

Zabid 49 E3
Zábol 45 D5
Zābol □ 45 D6
Zābolī 45 E5
Zabrze 16 C4
Zacapa 85 E7
Zacatecas 84 C4
Zacoalco 84 C4
Zadar 20 B5
Zadetkyi Kyun . 36 C1
Zafra 18 C2
Żagań 16 C2
Zagazig 52 B5
Zagorsk =
  Sergiyev
  Posad 24 B4
Zagreb 20 B6
Zāgros, Kūhhā-
  ye 44 C2
Zagros Mts. =
  Zāgros,
  Kūhhā-ye . . . 44 C2
Zāhedān 45 D5
Zahlah 46 D3
Zaïre =
  Congo → . . 56 F2
Zaïre = Congo,
  Dem. Rep. of
  the ■ 56 E4
Zaječar 22 C4
Zakhodnaya
  Dzvina =
  Daugava → . 24 B1
Zākhū 46 C5
Zákinthos 23 F3

Zakopane 16 D4
Zalaegerszeg . . 16 E3
Zalău 17 E6
Zaleshchiki =
  Zalishchyky . 17 D7
Zalew Wiślany . 16 A4
Zalingei 53 F3
Zalishchyky . . . 17 D7
Zambeze → . . 59 B7
Zambezi =
  Zambeze → 59 B7
Zambezi 58 A4
Zambia ■ 59 B5
Zamboanga . . . 38 C2
Zamora, Mexico 84 D4
Zamora, Spain . 18 B3
Zamość 17 C6
Zanaga 56 E2
Zanesville 72 E4
Zanjān 46 C7
Zanjān □ 46 C7
Zante =
  Zákinthos . . . 23 F3
Zanzibar 57 F7
Zaouiet El-Kala
  = Bordj Omar
  Driss 54 C6
Zaouiet Reggane 54 C5
Zap Suyu =
  Kabīr, Zab
  al → 46 C5
Zapadnaya
  Dvina 28 D4
Zapadnaya
  Dvina → =
  Daugava → . 24 B1
Západné
  Beskydy 16 D4
Zaporizhzhya . 25 D4
Zaporozhye =
  Zaporizhzhya 25 D4
Zara 46 C4
Zaragoza 19 B5
Zarand 44 D4
Zaranj 42 D2
Zaria 55 F6
Zaruma 90 D3
Żary 16 C2
Zarzis 52 B1
Zaskar Mts. . . . 42 C10
Zavāreh 44 C3
Zawiercie 16 C4
Zāyandeh → . . 44 C3
Zaysan 29 E9
Zaysan, Oz. . . . 29 E9
Zbarazh 17 D7
Zdolbuniv 17 C8
Zduńska Wola . 16 C4
Zeebrugge 14 C2
Zeehan 62 D4
Zeerust 59 D5
Zeila 49 E3
Zeitz 15 C7
Zelenograd . . . 24 B4
Zémio 57 C5
Zemun 22 B3
Zenica 20 B6
Žepče 20 B7
Zêzere → 18 C1
Zgorzelec 16 C2
Zhabinka 17 B7
Zhailma 29 D7
Zhambyl 29 E8
Zhangaqazaly . 29 E7
Zhanghua 35 D7
Zhangjiakou . . 35 B6
Zhangye 34 C5
Zhangzhou . . . 35 D6
Zhanjiang 35 D6

Zhanyi . . . . 34 D
Zhaotong . . . . 34 D
Zhashkiv 17 D1
Zhayyq → . . . 29 E
Zhdanov =
  Mariupol . . . . 25 D
Zhejiang □ . . . 35 D
Zhengzhou . . . 35 C
Zhenjiang . . . . 35 C
Zhenyuan . . . . 35 D
Zhezqazghan . . 29 E
Zhigansk 30 C1
Zhijiang . . . . . 35 D
Zhilinda . . . . . . 30 B
Zhitomir =
  Zhytomyr . . . 17 C
Zhlobin 17 B1
Zhmerinka =
  Zhmerynka . . 17 D
Zhmerynka . . . 17 D
Zhodino =
  Zhodzina . . . 17 A
Zhodzina . . . . 17 A
Zhongdian . . . 34 D
Zhumadian . . . 35 C
Zhuzhou . . . . . 35 D
Zhytomyr . . . . 17 C
Zibo . . . . 35 C
Zielona Góra . . 16 C
Zigey . . . . 53 F
Zigong . . . . . . 35 D
Zigui . . . . 35 C
Ziguinchor . . . 55 F
Zile . . . . 46 B.
Žilina . . . . 16 D
Zillah . . . . 52 C.
Zimbabwe ■ . . 59 B
Zimnicea . . . . . 22 C
Zinder . . . . 55 F
Zion National
  Park . . . . 83 B
Zipaquirá . . . . 90 C
Ziway, L. . . . . . 53 G
Zlatograd . . . . 22 D
Zlatoust . . . . . 29 D
Zlín . . . . 16 D.
Žlitan . . . . 52 B
Zmeinogorsk . . 29 D
Znojmo . . . . . . 16 D.
Zolochev =
  Zolochiv . . . . 17 D
Zolochiv . . . . . 17 D
Zomba . . . . . . 59 B
Zongo . . . . 56 D
Zonguldak . . . 46 B.
Zorritos . . . . . . 90 D.
Zouar . . . . 52 D.
Zouérate . . . . . 54 D.
Zrenjanin . . . . 22 B.
Zuetina = Az
  Zuwaytīnah . 52 B3
Zufar . . . . 48 D
Zug . . . . 13 C
Zugspitze . . . . 14 E
Zula . . . . 53 E
Zumbo . . . . . . 59 B
Zungeru . . . . . 55 G
Zunyi . . . . 35 D
Zürich . . . . 13 C
Zuwārah . . . . . 52 B
Zvishavane . . . 59 C
Zvolen . . . . . . 16 D
Zwettl . . . . 15 D
Zwickau . . . . . 15 C
Zwolle . . . . 14 B
Żyrardów . . . . 16 B
Zyryan . . . . . . 29 E
Zyryanovsk =
  Zyryan . . . . . 29 E
Żywiec . . . . . . 16 D